HISTORY OF KERALA

HISTORY OF KERALA

WRITTEN IN THE FORM OF NOTES ON VISSCHER'S LETTERS FROM MALABAR

K. P. PADMANABHA MENON

EDITED BY
T. K. KRISHNA MENON

IN FOUR VOLUMES
VOLUME TWO

GYAN

Published by

Gyan Publishing House
5, Ansari Road
Daryaganj, New Delhi-110002
Phone: 011-47034999, 9811692060
E-mail: books@gyanbooks.com

Distribution Network
gyanbooks.com
India, USA, Canada, UK, Australia, France

ISBN : 978-81-212-3526-6 (Set)
ISBN : 978-81-212-4664-4 (HB)
First Published, 1929

2nd Impression 2020

Printed at: Gyan Press, Delhi.

History of Kerala Vol. II
Author: K. P. Padmanabha Menon

DEDICATION

TO

MRS. K. P. PADMANABHA MENON.

CONTENTS

CONTENTS

NOTES

LIST OF ILLUSTRATIONS

FOREWORD

BY THE EDITOR

What I have to say about this work and its author I have said in my preface to its first volume. Its repetition here will be profitless. I shall be doing a better service to the book if I were to quote a few extracts from the opinions expressed about it by competent authorities. Their reproduction will serve another purpose which the sequel will disclose.

* * * *

Professor L. D. Barnett.—In reading the book I have been struck by the wide reading, sobriety of judgment, and desire for truth shown by the author. * * It is a valuable repertory of information on a most interesting theme. * * I can see how much labour has gone to its making.

Professor A. V. Williams Jackson.—You have done valued service by editing the work of your friend, the late Mr. K. P. Paḍmanābha Mēnōn. This book does honour alike to his memory and credit to you as its editor. I am glad to have such a work of reference in my library and I feel a special interest in the subject because of my long study of India.

Professor Hermann Jacobi.—The work of the author has, indeed, been a labour of love carried on through all his life; and the result has been a singularly complete information on everything relating to Kērala and its history. And you deserve high praise for carrying the manuscript successfully through the press.

Professor J. Jolly.—I have found a great deal to interest and to attract me in it. In the modest form of a collection of learned Notes on Visscher's *Letters from Malabar*, this work gives an excellent account of the early history of all the places of note in Malabar and throws important light on the character of the several European Colonisations in Malabar. Many curious incidents and anecdotes are related which make this volume very lively reading in spite of its learned character.

Professor A. B. Keith.—The volume appears to contain much valuable matter throwing light on many sides of the history, polity, customs, organisation, life and material condition of the Kērala country. There is clear evidence of the author's competence and judgment in such discussions as those of the advent of the Brahmans, and the National Assemblies of the Malabar. His industry is sufficiently established by the large amount of really interesting information which he has accumulated and made accessible.

Professor Sten Kenow.—I have had great pleasure in going through it. It is written in a vivid and good style and contains very much of considerable interest. It would be a good thing if the work could be completed in the same way.

Professor E. I. Rapson.—The work is evidently full of important and interesting information and I am very glad to possess it. It will be most useful for reference.

Professor M. Winternitz.—I found it full of most interesting information on the history, geography, the natural history, the social and economic conditions of Malabar. I have read with the greatest interest the scholarly and instructive notices on the origin of Malabar, on the advent of the Brahmans into Malabar, on national assemblies of the Malabars, on customs observed at deaths and coronations. As an old seat of Brahminical learning and culture, the Kērala country is of great importance for the history of India. Hence the book, so well edited by you, will be studied with profit not only by your countrymen, but also by Indologists in general both in India and in the West.

Dr. Sudhindra Bose.—It is a distinguished contribution to our Indian local history. There is nothing else which even remotely resembles this historical masterpiece that has come to my knowledge in recent years. It will, I am sure, be treasured by every serious student of Indian civilization.

M. R. Ry. Ullur S. Parameswara Ayyar Avl., M A., B L.— Kērala indeed has never had a historian so gifted, so painstaking and so impartial as Mr. Paḍmanābha Mēnōn, and this great work, furnishing valuable information on a variety of topics, is undoubtedly the *magnum opus* of that illustrious author. It has always struck me that Visscher's *Letters from Malabar*, so accurate and comprehensive, is worthy of being made the basement for a large historical edifice, and I am glad that my lamented friend thought likewise and gave it such perfect practical shape. Mr. Paḍmanābha Mēnōn has laid the whole of Kērala under a deep debt of obligation by this book, which only a scholar of his encyclopædic knowledge and indefatigable energy could have commenced and completed. * * It is absolutely necessary that the remaining two volumes of the book should also be out as early as practicable, and I trust that patriotic Kērala will not fail to accelerate their appearance.

The London Times.—Mr. Paḍmanābha Mēnōn was an accomplished scholar, as his *History of Cochin* attests, and no praise can be too high for the unceasing toil and care with which he studied and sifted all available material. There was need for this intensive study of a country which has received little investigation from European scholars in comparison with other parts of India, and which, notwithstanding its many charms, remains unknown to the ordinary tourist in India. * * While Chaplain of Cochin (1717—1723), Jacobus Canter Visscher wrote descriptive letters to his friends, and happily they were edited and published. Mr. Paḍmanābha Mēnōn takes these letters for his text, and a mere passing reference gives scope for a voluminous note. Visscher does not mention the ancient name by which the Malabaris prefer to speak of their country, but his editor happens to refer to it in a foot-note, and this gives scope for a dozen learned pages on Kērala and allusions thereto in ancient literature. The mention of a place name leads to a note which, as in the case of Cranganūr, may run to thirty pages or more. The eight Visscher letters given in the first volume occupy only forty-three pages; the notes run to 540. The foundation is too slight for such massive treatment.

Journal of the Royal Asiatic Society.—It was a good idea of the late Mr. Paḍmanābha Mēnōn to re-edit the English translation of the letters with an extensive and exhaustive commentary. To this work he gave the somewhat puzzling title of history of Kērala, because such a commentary cannot by any means furnish us with a consecutive history of that interesting part of India, the Malabar. None the less, the first volume of the work, containing letters 1 to 8 is a real storehouse of useful information concerning that country.

The Indian Historical Quarterly.—The book under review was rightly intended to be published as Notes on Visscher's *Letters from Malabar*. Rev. J. C. Visscher addressed these letters to his friends at home during 1717—1723, in the form of memoirs, full of observations upon the manners and customs of the people, their laws, rites and ceremonies, the description of their kingdoms and other allied subjects. An annotated edition of these precious memoirs like the one in hand was badly needed. None can claim to be more competent than the late Mr. Paḍmanābha Mēnōn to fulfil this immensely useful task. His notes speak eloquently of his wide range of information and study and no less of his power to reduce the varied material into some sort of historical method and coherence. But the result obtained is substantially an annual or a gazetteer rather than a book of history. Even as such, it cannot fail to be attractive to a serious historian of India who can set to work only when publications of this kind have sufficiently helped him to clear up this ground. * * There is no denying the fact that these (quotations that abound in the work) enable the reader to portray to himself various shifting scenes of historical events with a racial, socio-economic and political back-ground which went to make the people of Kēraḷa or Malabar what they became. The corrected bequest from the author stands as a lasting memorial to his fame as a compilation of all invaluable information from traditional and authentic sources.

The Hindustan Review.—This volume which has now been published under the editorship of Mr. T. K. Kṛṣhṇa Mēnōn is a fascinating account of a little known period of South Indian History. A number of contemporary portraits add to its attraction, and the format is all that can be desired. It is a useful addition to Indian historical literature.

The Benarese Hindu University Magazine.—Malabar, or Kēraḷa to call it by its traditional name, is one of those unexplored lands of legend and romance which the student of history has yet to penetrate with any effectiveness. A particularly warm welcome will therefore be extended to this *History of Kerala*, written in the form of Notes on Visscher's *Letters from Malabar* by the late Mr. K. P. Paḍmanābha Mēnōn and edited by a well-known writer and scholar of Cochin, Mr. T. K. Kṛṣhṇa Mēnōn. Technically, this is no History of Kēraḷa, despite the name, but it is not difficult to realise the great historical value of the material collected in this ponderous volume of more than five hundred pages. Mr. Kṛshṇa Mēnōn has done his work as editor very well indeed—he has discharged worthily the task entrusted to him as the dying wish of another scholar.

The Servant of India.—His *History of Cochin* in two volumes written in Malayālam, which has been pronounced by a competent critic to be 'unique in the annals of literature' is, according to the editor of this work, merely a collection of bouquets he prepared from the superfluous flowers he gathered for this rare garland of Notes on Canter Visscher. * * But to attempt to give in the form of elaborate, and in some places discursive, notes on the topics raised in Visscher's *Letters*, information about the ancient history of the whole of Malabar is a very difficult task, though the present attempt has in our opinion been attended with a considerable amount of success. The arrangement of the matter has, however, to be necessarily disjointed, being a collection of notes of varying length and importance on different subjects, the value of some of which we cannot easily over-estimate. The more elaborate notes certainly deserve careful perusal. * * The accounts in the Notes of particular localities like Anjengo, the famed Muziris, Quilon, etc., are all samples of the author's patient and assiduous scholarship. * * The Editor is to be congratulated on his careful work which has contributed largely to the attractiveness of the book; he has done his best with the material left in its peculiar form by the author and we look forward eagerly to the succeeding volumes.

* * * *

More than one have taken objection to the name of the book. But no one has suggested a title more appropriate than the one it now bears. Do they want me to call it only "Notes on Visscher's Letters from Malabar"? Well, that title looks so tame that even an ordinary bookseller who vends his wares in front of schools will fight shy of it. Or, am I to designate it as "Notes that will have an important bearing on the ancient history of Kērala, prepared by the late Mr. K. P. Paḍmanābha Mēnōn who took the words on which the notes are strung from Visscher's Letters from Malabar and so on and so forth"? My critics themselves will turn round in disgust and tell me that it is no name, but an alphabetical procession marching across, perhaps, a historical landscape. To confess a truth, I found it difficult to find a name more suitable than the one I have given to this. To quote Mr. A. G. Gardiner: "Every one who lives by the pen knows the difficulty of the task. The thousand words come easily (sometimes); but the five words summary of the thousand, that is to blaze at the top like a beacon light, is a gem that has to be sought in travail, almost in tears."

None the less I welcome the criticism and am grateful to the distinguished scholars and editors for their appreciation of this great work and of my humble services in connection with its publication. The generous terms of their recognition are all the more timely as they enable me to brush aside with that mental attitude, in which alone they deserve to be treated, the remarks about this work of the reviewer in the columns of the *Modern Review*. He first came out in the *Hindu* with a disquisition on the Syrian Christians of Malabar which any college student could write and stated that that subject Mr. Mēnōn had only touched upon "in an unsatisfactory manner in a number of places." He was then politely told that it had received the author's best attention in the valuable Notes he had written in connection with Letters XVI and XVII. Then the indictment was altered in the *Modern Review* and the prosecution was conducted with more vehemence. It will be sheer waste of time and stationery to attempt to transcribe in detail the *dicta* pronounced by this critic. Suffice it to say that, according to this censor, these notes were meant " to explain the obscure parts in Visschers Letters"; "they are generally 'scrappy' and 'jumbled together by the editor', and 'they could have been compressed and a few left out'." 'As it is',—this is the sentence with which he crowns his amusing edifice,—'the book is almost an exhibition of futile scholarship.' It is some consolation to note that he did not apply to this what was said by a qualified critic of another book that "it is thin and slipshod and its merits are not sufficient to justify its publication". I do not consider that his adverse remarks deserve notice; and, if at all I condescend to make any reply, it is out of respect to the periodical in which they appeared. One can easily see that the primary aim of the late Mr. Paḍmanābha Mēnōn was not to annotate the Letters so as to make their meaning clear. Again, the Notes are arranged by the author himself in a logical and consistent order which the editor found no need to disturb. This also will be obvious to any discerning reader. Then our critic advises me to condense some notes and to delete some others. That is a blank shot; for there is no definite direction or clear specification. Even otherwise, I would have declined to follow this mentor; for, if an editor were to omit such portions of a book as contain matter with which one reader or another may be familiar, there would be little or nothing left for publication. Further, there was another person, nearer home, who, with equal vehemence, maintained that I had no right to alter a word in this work. Outside the ambit of these personal predilictions, I thought there was ample room for me to move about according to the solemn direction of the author's last testament. I have done my best to make the work up-to-date and useful to historians and research scholars of the world. If they detect any defect I would request them to realise that the lack of a decent reference library and the pressure of other duties have been no small impediments in my way.

In matters like this, 'one could hardly expect at home", as Disraeli expresses in despair 'the judicial impartiality of a foreign land'. I am tempted to quote the rest also of this part of his General Preface to his works as a fit answer to the aforesaid criticism. But I desist, as my purpose is not to retaliate. Moreover, if the critic fears that, by agreeing with other people, he is likely to be overlooked, or if he hopes by detraction to descend to posterity, let him please himself. Why should I stand in his way ? This work will not suffer by such attacks. It is a solid work and many are the years that have gone to its making. It exhibits a happy combination of proficiency in facts, of familiarity with the classic works of those who have written on the various subjects elaborated in the Notes and of 'a mastery of detail controlled and ordered by the sobriety of true historical scholarship'.

It now remains for me to express my obligations to the Government of Cochin for the loan of a few blocks to illustrate this volume, and to Mr. M. Achyuṭa Mēnōn, B. A., B. L., for the preparation of the Index and the assistance he rendered to me in revising the proofs. I desire to thank also the Superintendent, Mr. C. P. Nārāyaṇa Mēnōn, B. A., F. L. and the Head Examiner, Mr. N. M. Paramēśwara Ayyar, of the Government Press for the courteous help which has always been mine at their hands.

Kumārālayam,
Eṛṇākuḷam;
7th November 1929.

T. K. KṚṢHṆA MĒNŌN.

NOTES ON

Visscher's

LETTERS FROM MALABAR.

LETTER IX.

1. **System of Succession to the Malabar Thrones.** The following observations made by Barbosa regarding the system of succession to the Malabar thrones are interesting:—

"In this wise, the lineage of the Kings of this country, and the true stock, is in the women: that is to say, if a woman gives birth to 3 or 4 sons and 2 or 3 daughters, the first is King, and so on, all the other brothers inherit from one another, and when all these have died, the son of the eldest sister who is niece of the King inherits, and so also his other heirs after him, and when these have deceased, the children of the next sister. And the Kingdom always goes in this way to brothers, nephews, sons of sisters and if, by good or evil fortune, these women happen not to give birth to male children, they do not consider them as capable of inheriting the kingdom; and these ladies, in such a case, all unite in council and institute some relation of theirs as King, if they have one, and if there is none, they name any other person for this office. And, on this account, the Kings of Malabar are old men when they succeed to reign, and the nieces or sisters from whom has to proceed the lineage of the Kings are held in great honour, guarded and served, and they possess revenues for their maintenance"[1].

1. P. 107.

lose their family name. They are bound to obey the first, who is styled the *Molpad* or head[1].

The first of these kingdoms is Travancore in the south, which stretches along the sea coast from Cape Comorin to Porcad. Attingal, Signati, Perittalli, Ellida Suruvan, Marta, Kully Quilon, Tirkenapolie and Panapolie are comprehended in this kingdom[2].

Attingal[3] is the name of the maternal house of the Rajah of Travancore, who rules over the country lying between Tengepatnam and Paroor, three leagues south of the fortress of Quilon. Madura, which used to be comprehended in his territory, has been lately severed from it. In all Malabar there is no queen mother who possesses so much influence in public affairs as here. These Travancore Rajahs would willingly have entered into alliance with the East India Company, only they would never consent to pledge themselves to part with all their pepper to them alone; knowing that they could obtain a higher price for the article elsewhere: The Danes at Eddawa and the English at Anjengo at the present day buy it at the rate of 15 or 16 ducats per candy, while the East India Company give only 12 ducats.

Signati[4] is the name of the second family, descended from a younger sister of Travancore. Its territory extends from Paroor (where the East India Company have a station, established for the despatch of letters, and also as an outpost to watch over the soldiers at Quilon, lest they should attempt to desert to the English at Anjengo) to Coomaragam Polittooi.

This kingdom is sub-divided into three portions, the first belonging to the Rajah, who therefore bears the name of Signati; the second to the Poele Barriatte[6]; the third to the Goeryp of Travancore. This division originated with three co-heiresses[5], sisters of the house of Signati. The present Rajah of Signati is overbearing and haughty. The East India Company with difficulty keep on good terms with him, and his share in the pepper contract is performed with no good will. The fort of Quilon is situated within his territories and serves in some measure as a check upon his insolence. The country is for the most part high and rocky, and though in one direction watered by streams, it is too elevated for the cultivation of rice or paddy, but it is well-wooded, and large quantities of areca nuts are dried there and forwarded

1. Note 3, p. 5
2. Note 4, pp 5—25
3. Note 5, pp. 25—32
4. Note 6, pp. 32—58
5. Note 7, pp. 58—59
6. A Note on Poele Barriatte, p. 59.

to the Coast. It is also famous for its palm wine or Quilon arrack, which supplies this neighbourhood abundantly.

The Rajah of Peritalli[1], sprung from the third sister of Attingal, governs the district between Quilon and the mountains. Kully Quilon is at the present time united to his country by adoption. It possesses no sea-coast.

Ellidaseruwan[2], situated between Madura and Travancore, belongs lo the progeny of a younger sister of Travancore.

Marta or Carnagapole[3], lying between the river of Quilon or Arooveekuray and the village of Alappan along the shore, is subject to the Rajah of Kully Quilon, its borders encroaching with irregular outline on his kingdom and on that of Signati.

Kully Quilon[4] stretches along the Coast: a portion lying inland between Quilon and Porcad. It contains a good bazaar or market place, where all kinds of wares are sold. The East India Company have a factory in the interior. At the mouth of the river there is a preventive station.

Tercunapalli Rajah[5] is a powerful monarch of great authority, a small portion of his territory boarders on Kully Quilon and Porcad, and it stretches inland to Bittimeni[6].

Panapoli[7] lies in the interior, behind Kully Quilon, and its family having died out, it has devolved by adoption on the Rajah of that place. This forms the extremity of the kingdom of Travancore, between which and that of Cochin is another kingdom, independent of them both.

This is called Tekkenkoor[8], and lies beyond the lake called the Broad River. The Rajah possesses a beautiful territory, superior to any other I have yet seen in Malabar. The level part is low, and planted with rice; in the vicinity of the mountains the land is elevated, and produces pepper, cardamom, and wax in great abundance. This country is also very populous, and possesses good roads and a fresh and pleasant climate. The Bishop Mar Gabriel resides in it, his church and dwelling being situated on a hill, along the foot of which runs a river. The Rajah lives on the other side of the river in the plain, having a neat palace, according to the native fashion. He is very courteous, and as soon as he heard from the Bishop of my arrival, he came with all

1. Note 8, pp. 59—60
2. Note 9, pp. 60—62
3 Note 10, pp. 62—63
4. Note 11, pp. 63—68
5. Note 12, p. 68
Note 13, pp. 68—82—A Note on Rapolim or Edapilli
6. Note 14, pp. 82—83
7. Note 15, pp. 83—84
Note 16 pp. 84—85—A Note on Pantalam.
8. Note 17, p. 85
Note 18, pp. 85—91—A Note on Poonjar

haste from his country house at five miles distance to visit me, and presented me with two golden bracelets.

The second great royal house of Malabar is that of Cochin[1], which is to us the most noticeable, both because the capital of the East India Company, Cochin, is situated in it, and also because the Company has made a very close alliance with it, styling itself the protector of the kingdom of Cochin[2]. As a mark of this, the Rajah wears in his crown the arms of the Company.[3] The hereditary princes of Cochin consisted formerly of five families[4], which have been reduced by death to three, those of Paliat[5], Montata Viese, and Shalour; these were continually quarrelling for the supreme authority, till the Portuguese mixed in the business, when the dispute burst into an open war. Montata Viese withdrew into the North, and brought all the princes of that part over to his side; whilst Paliat and Shalour were aided by those of the South. At length the Rajah of Paliat, the last of his mother's family, died, when the Portuguese worked upon the queen mother to adopt a stranger of the family of Bettette and Aivoer, good friends of theirs. This family became so powerful by the help of the Portuguese, that when the Rajah of the house of Shalour died, the crown fell into the hands of four bold princes, adopted sons of the house of Bettette, who compelled the princes of Shalour to take to flight, and join those of the house of Montata Viese. Their united forces could however find no means of recovering the kingdom and succession; partly on account of the power of the Portuguese, and partly because the Nairs and land owners were favourable to the princes of Bettette. At length they repaired to their great enemy, the Zamorin, who took advantage of the opportunity to conclude a secret treaty both with them and with the Rajahs of Northern Cochin, in which it was agreed that the house of Montata Viese should be re-instated in possession of the crown; under promise that the latter should make compensation to the Zamorin for all the expenses he might incur during the war, and should leave in his hands, till this stipulation should be fulfilled, all the lands and strong places they might together conquer. Upon this, the Zamorin was immediately received by the lords of Narduveltenaad, Monadenaade, Billeastenaade, and Monnea Suta Pamboory, as Protector of their lawful sovereign. Affairs were in this state when Malabar was conquered by the East India Company; who having deposed the Rajah of the house of Bettette, their enemy

1. Note 19. pp. 91—92
2. Note 20, pp. 92—95
3. Note 21. p. 96
4. Note 22, pp. 96—100
5. Note 23, p. 100

restored that of Montata Viese to their lawful inheritance of the kingdom of Cochin. Meanwhile a dispute arose between the Zamorin and the Rajah of Cochin, the latter demanding the restoration of all the lands belonging to his kingdom of which the former was in possession ; whilst the Zamorin maintained that by the conditions of the treaty he was not bound to comply until he had been repaid for all the expenses of the war. This dispute lasted till a war broke out between the East India Company and the Zamorin, in which the Rajah of Cochin also became involved; when with the aid of the Company's arms, Cranganur being conquered, he recovered a great portion of the lands which the Zamorin had seized from him. Some other places in the Cochin territory still remained under the power of the Zamorin, but these in succeeding wars have from time to time been wrested from him. This is the foundation of the reciprocal claims of the Zamorin and the Cochin Rajah on each other, which have continually kindled wars between them.

These events show the dangers of adopting a son among the princes of a strange family; for this is often the cause of desperate wars, the weaker party seeking and finding assistance from the stronger. It is also to be apprehended, if a powerful prince of another family is adopted into that of Cochin, that the Rajah of that country will become too powerful for the East India Company, and that thus the title of Protector, which it now bears, would be an empty one ; and more than this, if that Rajah should ever become superior in power to the Zamorin, instead of being, as he now is, inferior, he might lose his respect for our arms, and even go to war with us.

The territories of the Rajah of Cochin are of considerable extent; to him appertain the island of Cochin, and a great portion of the higher country, but it is all so much broken up and divided that it is impossible to determine accurately the boundaries of his kingdom. To him have devolved :—

Moutan[1], bounded by Porcad on the south, and on the north by the free lordship of Paliat; to it belong also some districts on the other side of the great river. Mouton has fallen into the possession of the family of Cochin through adoption.

Coeronaad [2], a territory of great extent which has devolved upon Cochin, extending along the mountain chain to the district of the seven [3] Caimals, and terminating on the river bank opposite to Cochin, called in the country by the name of Antjecaimals. Two market days are held there weekly, when the Canarese and

1. Note 24, p. 100
2 Note 25, p. 101
3. Note 26, pp. 101—102
Note 27, pp. 102—104—A Note on other Kaimals.

Jews purchase provisions for themselves and for the inhabitants both within and without the city, consisting of butter, rice, fruit, salt, etc.

Vypeen, an island just opposite the city, bounded on one side by the sea, on the other by the river, where most of the Topasses live and have their principal church. This island affords a pleasant prospect to the city, being well planted with cocoanut trees; it runs up as far as Aicotte, and is about 4 leagues in length. The deaconry has some property on this island, and another portion belongs to the Rajah; but the greater part is the possession of the Paliat, who is considered the lord of the island.

Cranganoor[1], a small kingdom belonging to the Rajah of that name. Here the East India Company possesses a small fort, which in the time of the Portuguese was a town; in former days the Zamorin's palace was here, but he has been gradually expelled from the place. The Rajah of this place is poor, and therefore of small consideration.

Iyroor[2], the royal family of Cranganoor which possesses in the south Pooden and Jatecoil, and in the east Marianki, and other lands belonging to Cochin.

Besides these, Cochin has four tributary Rajahs[3], who are considered the pillars of the kingdom. These princes are independent, but are bound to respect the Rajah as their chief who settles the disputes of the kingdom, and whom they must aid against the common enemy. They may, however, have private wars amongst themselves, and even against the Rajah. Their names are Porcad and Berkenkoer in the south of Cochin, and Paroor and Mangatti in the north.

Porcad is subject to a spiritual prince[4]. It was formerly governed by twelve Brahmins, one of whom in the end raised himself to the throne, in the following manner. The eleven eldest Brahmins were in the habit of making a butt of the youngest, whom they treated as half-witted. Their victim not knowing how to defend himself, acted like a second Brutus, resolving in his own mind to have his revenge in due time. At length, it happened that 2,000 Nairs, having on some dissatisfaction deserted from the Zamorin, went about offering their services, and were everywhere refused. But, they came to Porcad, and offered themselves to the twelve Brahmins, as chance would have it, the eleven older ones were all together at the time, and sent them in jest to the youngest, who was bathing, telling the soldiers he was their chief.

1. Note 28, pp. 104—106
2. Note 29, pp. 106—109
3. Note 30, p. 109
4. Note 31, pp. 109—122

The Nairs did as they were bid, and going to the youngest Brahmin, informed him that the others had sent them to him as their chief. He, understanding their mockery, seized the opportunity for his own advantage, to revenge himself for their insults. He informed the soliders that he was the chief, and that he would take them into his service on condition that they should obey him before all others, and perform all his commands; he then promised them rich rewards if they would put the eleven other Brahmins to death. The soldiers consenting joyfully, he led them straight to the pagoda, where the other Brahmins were collected. He then commanded them to perform their business, and the words were scarcely said when it was done. His eleven companions being dead, he took the key of the pagoda, opened it, took out the treasure box, paid the soldiers liberally, and made himself monarch. In this dignity he and his heirs have maintained themselves to the present day. His deed was one which may well be likened to that of Brutus, with whom I have already compared him. The country of Porcad is very productive of rice and all the necessaries of life, so that this Rajah is one of the wealthiest in Malabar; he has not however many Nairs, in the place of whom he is served by Chegos. The Company's factory in this place has fallen into decay, being as it were swallowed up by the sea; a new one should be erected there, but, as the Rajah wishes that it should be on the model of the old one, whilst the Commandant desires to have a good factory, adapted both for a dwelling and for a pepper-magazine, the work has been up to this time suspended. The Raja begins now, however, to lower his tone, as they withold the pepper grants from him, and threaten to remove the factory to Chanamungalom [1] to which place the pepper can easily be conveyed over the great river from Tekkenkoor and Berkenkoor. Porcad lies between Tekkenkur, Berkenkur and Kully Quilon.

Berkenkoor[2] lies nearer to Cochin than Porcad, abutting on one side on the great river and on the other mountains; it is the second royalty of the kingdom, and produces pepper, cardamom and wax.

In the north of Cochin and in the interior, lie Paroor[3] and Mangatti[4]; they are close together, Paroor being nearer the coast in the direction of Cranganoor. Paroor is a powerful, ecclesiastical Rajah. His country is fruitful in rice, cattle and other articles of food. The present Rajah is prudent and crafty, and

1. Note 32, p. 122
2. Note 33, pp. 122—123
3. Note 34, p. 124

lives in friendship with the Commandant Hertenberg; though, during the late war, the former Commandant mistrusted him, fearing that he had a secret understanding with the Zamorin; this however has never been proved.

Mangatti[1] is the fourth and last royalty of the kingdom of Cochin, extending from Paroor to the mountains. In this country is the renowned river of Mangatti, where the Portuguese had formerly a celebrated bathing place, called *Fiera d' Alva*,[2] respecting which they held some superstition; higher up there is a no less celebrated spot, to which several native Christians resort on a certain day, to be cleansed and sprinkled with the water. Some of the Romanists assert that this river was derived from the Jordan, others that it cured all sicknesses, and even that it cleansed linen without being washed; nonsense which is not worth contradicting. It is indeed true that the water of this river is purer and more wholesome than any other hereabouts, and that those who drink it do not often get the Cochin disorder; the ships of the East India Company, and the principal personages here, are furnished with it. In the hot season many people go to this river for the sake of bathing, and erect booths along the shores, or on the sandy spots which are met with here and there. On one of these spots stands a heathen pagoda, made only of *olas*, in which they celebrate their religious services during the fine season; as the rainy season approaches, when the water rise, this temple is removed. From this it would seem that the heathens also have some superstition regarding this river. In this kingdom are two families, those of Bettette and Kartatavyd,[3] one of the latter house being the present Rajah, though that of Bettette is otherwise the most powerful.

Having thus described the two first royal houses, we will give a cursory glance on the two remaining: those of the Zamorin[4] and of Colastri, both situated in the north.

The former is a very powerful monarch whose influence has been much exalted by his arms, though at the present day his splendour has been considerably diminished in consequence of the wars waged upon him by the East India Company. He has a numerous and brave army, in which respect he is superior to all the other princes, who consequently are much in dread of him; but he is quite a fiction to say that he is master of Malabar.

1. Note 35, pp. 124—126
2. Note 36, pp. 126—127

(Ahlwhye or Alwaye is fourteen miles from Cochin, and is still a favourite resort among Europeans for bathing during the hot months. The houses are picturesquely situated on the banks of the river.—H. D.)

3. Note 37, p. 127
Note 38, pp. 127—128—A Note on Talapilly Nad
4. Note 39, pp. 128—174

Under him are—Onneterie, comprising the country behind Cranganoor as far as the river of Chetwa, which was formerly subject to the Zamorin and a portion of his kingdom, and here was situated his fort of Paponette; but in the war of 1716 [1] he was driven from the whole of this country, which fell into the hands of the Company who possess here enough fields of rice, to feed almost the whole garrison.

There is a new fort built in the corner of the country at the mouth of the river Chetwa, called Fort William, intended as a defence against the enterprises of this Raja.

Palingery Nairs[2], situated on the opposite bank of the Chetwa river and stretching in the north close to the river Ponany.

Repœcoil [3] in the south, bordered by the country of Parepacoil and extending in the north as far as Calicut. Here the maternal house of the Zamorin reside, and the Raja has his residence and court at Ponany[4], where the Company also have a station and maintain an accountant to keep a watch over the merchantile proceedings of the Zamorin, and to give intelligence of what passes to the Commandant.

Tameras Gerye[5], which is situated south of Calicut, and is bounded on the north by the territory of Geringal Namboori. This is the seat of the Zamorin's provinces towards the sea shore.

Geringal Namboori is a spiritual lord, whose lands extend from Balenoor in the kingdom of Colastri in the north, to the river Cottesal[6]. The most famous pirates inhabit his territories who make prey of vessels engaged in the inland navigation between Calicut and Cananoor, and even advance beyond Calicut to the borders of Cochin. They are called *Kotta Marrekarre*[7].

The fourth and last royal family of Malabar, named Colastri[8], was compelled by force of arms to conclude an alliance with the East India Company, when they deprived the Portuguese by craft of Cannanoor[9], since which time they have remained good friends, though they would never engage in the pepper contracts. The best cardamom is found in this kingdom; this, which is round in form and more delicate in taste than the other species,

1. See Note 39, The Zamorin, pp. 128—174
2. Note 40, pp. 174—180
3 Note 41, p. 181
Note 42, pp. 181—185. A Note on Walluvanad.
4. Note 43, p. 185
Note 44, p. 185
6. Note 45, pp. 185—186
7. Note 46, pp. 186—187
8. Note 47, pp. 187—230
9. Note 48, pp. 230—231

is the only kind which the East India Company buy for exportation to Europe and elsewhere. The royal family consists of four branches, of which the present representatives, both male and female, are so numerous that they live in great poverty for the most part, though it is true that the State is well managed and that it possesses a good army: knowing this, the Zamorin seldom ventures to invade this kingdom, and the Raja of Maisjoer, who is lord of an extensive territory, has encroached but little or not at all upon it. This kingdom is bounded in the south by the kingdom of the Zamorin, and in the north it extends to Canara.

In this territory the following Rajas are comprehended :—

Balenoor[1], stretching along the coast from the river Cottesal in the south to the river of Oermapatam in the north; it contains several nests of robbers, as Tritrambiere, Bergaree, Moetingal, Tjombaas and Niagillie. Towards the east it extends as far as the territories of the powerful free Prince Perreveacocil.

Perreveacocil[2] borders to the south on the country of the Zamorin, and to the south-east on that of Maisjoer; here is found the best cardamom, and in the greatest quantities.

Dermapatam, Cananoor, Welliapatam[3] and Marravy[4] are situated along the shore, bordering on Balenoor. This is the peculiar possession and inheritance of the family of Colastri.

Tallachery Mocta Nairo to the east of Dermapatam, circumscribes the territory of Colastri at the back, and in the north reaches Tjoenette Verre Caimal, in which district is also situated the English fort Tellicherry. To this succeeds Tjoenette Verre Caimal, which to the north again, is bounded by Allerte Serte Caimal, the latter stretches inland to Maisjoer, but northward towards the sea is bounded by Allerte Addayodde. This last district concludes the kingdom of Malabar, bordering on the territory of Canara. I have thus placed before you a small picture of the principal territories of Malabar, in the order in which they join each other, some indeed I have not mentioned[5], either because they are so small. or because they are situated in the mountains, where we are not well acquainted with the topography. But if you wish to know all the petty principalities and provinces, which lie there, I will take some opportunity to send you a list of the Nayars, whom all the lords of Malabar both small and great retain in their service: when I will also mention the names of these princes and lords.

1. Note 49, pp. 231—233
2. Note 50, pp. 233—238
3. Note 51, p. 238
4. Note 52, p. 238
5. Note 53, pp. 238—241. A Note on Kurumbarnad.
   Note 54, pp. 241—246. A Note on Nayar Militia.

LETTER X.

Laws of the Malabars—Strange manner of laying seizure on the property of another—Their trials by ordeal, sometimes thrusting the fingers into boiling oil, sometimes the hand into a basket containing a Cobra capella, sometimes swimming through a river inhabited by crocodiles—strange occurrence—Their prisons—The rights they possess over slaves—Sales and purchases.

As you have acquired fame by your knowledge of jurisprudence, you may like to hear something about the native laws here.

Their legal suits are tried according to old customs *viva voce.* No lengthy proceedings are required to obtain the decision of the causes which are always concluded within a few days by the fiat of the Rajah, who in obscure cases consults with his Brahmins[1].

For laying the property of another in arrest, the warrant of a magistrate is not required; any private individual may do it; so that a man of low caste has in his power to harass and annoy a Brahmin or a Caimal, through his lands and properties. The Rajas possess the same power over each other. However, although license is not required for the performance of this embargo, the Rajah's authority is necessary to settle the affair; both parties must appear before him, and after duly weighing the merits of the case; and receiving a sum of money [2], he gives judgment. When Rajahs thus arrest each other's property, it is a fruitful ground for wars and dissensions: mediators are sometimes called in to arrange the matter.

The token of this embargo or arrest, is the leaf of a cashew nut or other tree which is tied on the article thus arrested, or if it be land, it is stuck up on a stick, the party exercising this privilege announcing, "this is the *Rama*, or arrest of the Rajah." [3] After this no one may gather the fruits off the lands or remove the token: such act would be considered crimes of lese majesty. The East India Company exercise the same right, and on such occasions they plant their flag on the spot: but this is only done by order of the Commandant or the proper authorities. In the lands subject to the Company, the Commandant may remove any *rama* placed by a native. The residents in the small out-lying stations are obliged to suffer the ramas of the Malabars, and are allowed to exercise the same privilege on their side.

1. Note 1, pp. 247—252.
2. Note 2, p. 252.
3. Note 3, pp. 252—255.

The Resident of Porcad told me an entertaining anecdote on this subject. He had once caused a rafter to be brought to the station for the repair of the factory, when it was close to the building, a Nair came and fastened a *rama* to it, upon which the coolies who were carrying it, ran away, and it was illegal for them to touch it any longer. The Resident being informed of what had occurred immediately planted the Company's rama on the spot, so that the parties who were so ready with their arrest, were themselves arrested, and compelled to stand without stirring a foot in the heat of the sun, until such time as the first *rama* was removed by order of the Rajah, then the Resident released them.

In a similar manner, when the Rajah owes money to a Brahmin who can adduce satisfactory proof of the debt, the creditor can demand the money of the Rajah, three distinct times, and if the Rajah still delays payment, the Brahmin brings a *rama* from a pagoda, when the Rajah may neither eat, sleep or bathe till the dispute is settled and the *rama* removed. Such cases however do not often happen, for the people know that monarchs have long arms.

Dubious cases in which no proof can be obtained, must be decided by solemn oaths, which are ordinary in common affairs, but extraordinary where the cause is still difficult and important. When a dispute arises between two parties about a loan or debt of which there is no proof, the debtor and creditor go together to the pagoda, and having each given four fanams or one shilling to the priest, they are led to a wooden post, upon which the creditor lays a sum of money equal to that to which he lays claim. This is a solemn attestation before their gods of the lawfulness of the debt, which the other party is then bound to pay[1]. As however, this mode of swearing may be false, it is firmly believed among them that a person who has perjured himself in this way will meet with a great misfortune within three months.

The extraordinary oaths which are taken in important causes are very perilous, and resemble the trials by ordeal used formerly in Europe in the superstitious ages[2]. When a man is charged with a heavy crime, which cannot be proved or which he will not confess, a *tisal* or pan containing cocoanut oil is brought and heated in the presence of the Rajah and his courtiers and Brahmins, the accused is then asked whether he will confess the deed, and, if he refuses, he raises his eyes to heaven imploring the protection of the gods in the defence of his righteous cause, and then plunging his thumb and two first fingers into the boiling oil he

1. Note 4, pp. 255—256
2. Note 5, pp 256—272

pulls out a ring placed at the bottom of the pan. This being done, a *pandyt* or physician comes and binds up the three fingers with Pisang leaves, which must be left on them for three days; if at the end of this time the flesh where the skin has been burnt off is white, he is pronounced innocent, but if black, he is punished as a perjured man.

There is another ordeal, by snakes or Cobra capellas. When a man will not confess a crime, they take a mantle and wrap up in it one of these reptiles, which are not only poisonous, but are also reckoned sacred by them; after calling on the gods, the accused must thrust his hand into the mantle and lift up the snake. If he be bitten, he is considered guilty. Another ordeal takes place in a river or tank in which crocodiles are found. The *Cayman's* (alligator's) pagoda on the river Cranganur close to Paliporte is especially famous for this process. A small heathen temple stands on the bank of this river, in which two crocodiles have for a long time been supported, their daily food being thrown into the water, so that they are induced by the bait to remain there. To undergo this ordeal, the accused is compelled, after a solemn profession of innocence in the presence of the Brahmins and nobles, and of a great concourse of people, to swim across this river and back: or if he cannot do this he must be dragged through, holding on with his hands to a boat. If the crocodile pulls him under, it is a sign of his guilt; if otherwise, he is released as innocent.

The people of Malabar tell a strange story to confirm this ordeal. There were two brothers who inherited equally from their father; one of them secretly stole and concealed a large sum of money, and on being accused of the fraud by his brother, denied it, upon which he was compelled to take the oath by ordeal in the river. The fraudulent party, thinking to deceive the gods, having hidden the gold in his turban, handed it over to someone else, and then swore that he had not got his brother's inheritance—thinking that as the stolen property was in another person's hand with the turban, it could not be reckoned as his; after this, he sprang into the river, swam uninjured across it and back and was therefore pronounced innocent. But, a wonderful occurrence took place afterwards, for, as the perjured man, fearing nothing further, took back his turban, and stood by the river to wash his feet, a crocodile leaped up the bank, seized him by the legs, dragged him into the river, and devoured him. The spectators, aghast at such an occurrence, took up the turban which he had let drop, examined it more closely, and discovered the gold concealed in it; by which they perceived the cunning of the swearer, and the justice of their gods. I leave the truth or falsehood of this tale for what it is worth; one thing is certain, that these ordeals are not to be depended on, but that the ceremonies used, the danger, and their own superstition combine to cause criminals rather to confess, than to submit to these perilous ordeals.

The prisons of Malabar are of a peculiar construction, and are generally situated in the square of the royal courts. They are not heavy edifices of stone, nor furnished with iron gratings and strong bars, but are mere quadrangular enclosures, the size of a man in length, breadth, and height, made of wooden gratings nailed together. Above them is a small loft where the Nairs,who guard the prisoners pass the night and usually take a nap. Such prisons as these would in Europe be more fit to keep fowls than human beings. The prisoners often escape from them as did some Canarese lately, who had robbed their idol's temple. The Rajah confines in these prisons not only great criminals, but those who are condemned to pay him a fine for some misdemeanour; these seldom escape, as they would not wish to be banished from their country for the sake of a little money.

Among legal matters may be included the rights masters possess regarding the sale of their slaves[1]. The Pulleahs are born slaves. Every Zemindar, prince or wealthy Nayar, has a certain number of them whose children are also born in slavery. But as these poor creatures form a peculiar and numerous caste, they have certain privileges [2] granted them, which secure their maintenance, so that none may perish from want. Their masters are not bound to give them daily nourishment[3], but in the Malabar country they have the right of building and planting[4], for which labours they receive settled wages [5] paid either in fanams or in measures of rice ; and the estates on which they work may belong either to their own master or to somebody else ; for if their own master be not in want of out-of-door labour they may seek it elsewhere, always taking care under risk of punishment to appear before him at his summons.

When the paddy is cut they receive the tenth part in payment, and a sort of black paddy which springs fourteen days afterwards called *Neerab* is also their perquisite. Their masters have power to put them to death, without being called to account[6]

1. Note 6, pp. 272—275
2. Note 7, p. 275.
3. Note 8, pp. 275—276
4. Note 9, p. 276.
5. Note 10, pp. 276—277.
6. Note 11, p. 278.

or, if they please, to sell them[1]; though this is not often done without some good reason.

In cases of indigence, a Pulleah uncle and mother may sell a child, but not for more than 60 fanams, and if a higher price were to be given, it would be of no use to them, as the proprietor would take the overplus. The eldest born, whether son or daughter, of a Pulleah couple is the property of the owner of the father, and the other children belong to the owner of the mother, who has also a right of redeeming the first child for the sum of 16 fanams whether the possessor like it or not. Among Europeans these things are quite different, for the master of the mother has a right to all the children, there being no legal form of marriage among the slaves. With us, too, a master or mistress may strike or chastise, but not kill a slave. And if a slave were to complain of gross ill-treatment from his master or mistress and after a strict examination it were to be found that the alleged cruelties were true, he might obtain his freedom, or his master might be compelled to sell him to another. If a slave were to raise his hand to strike his master or mistress, or otherwise injure them, he might be punished by death. A freed slave may give evidence, but not one in servitude[2]. No one may sell his slave to a heathen, Jew, or Turk, for by so doing he would place his soul in peril.

To return to the Malabars; Rajahs and Princes may sell, besides Pulleahs, men of other castes, Nayars, Chegos, etc., who have committed any crime by which they have lost caste and are liable to capital punishment. No Rajah has power to sentence to execution a Brahmin or a Canarese, however heinous his crime[3], but he may cause his eyes to be torn out, or his hand to be cut off, by which he would be dishonoured and expelled from his caste. Capital punishment is executed in divers methods. The criminal may stand upright and have his head cut off; or he may be shot, for which purpose he is made to stand unfettered and free in an open field, and three or four shots are rapidly discharged at him. If he be not wounded and begin to run away he is pursued and fired at until he is killed, when his body is thrown into the river. Sometimes they empale criminals alive, piercing a sharp pointed stick right through the body, which soon puts an end to his life[4].

I shall conclude this letter with an account of the sales and loans[5] of the Malabars, which, though they are of various kinds, may be reduced under five heads.

1. Note 12, pp. 278—281.
2. Note 13, pp. 281—284.
3. Note 14, p. 284.
4. Note 15, pp. 284—294.
5. Note 16, pp. 294—323.

1. There is the complete sale, called *Ate Patta*, which does not often take place; when a person resigns all right over a garden or estate which he has sold; and the foundary of this deed runs thus; that he renounces stone and mud, splinters and thorns, snakes, great and small, and everything within the four corners of the estate to him and to his successors. If the estate is situated on the river bank, the number of feet to which it extends in the water is also certified.

2. There is a mode of loan called *Patta* which is very common, and can only be explained by an example. Thus, supposing a man has a garden worth 10,000 fanams, he sells it for 8,000 f. or 9,000 f., retaining for the remainder of the value the r.ght to the proprietorship of the estate; for these 1,000 f. or 2,000 f. the purchaser must pay an annual interest. If the seller wishes at the end of some years to buy back his estate, he must restore the 8,000 or 9,000 fanams, and pay in addition the sum of money that shall have been fixed by men commissioned to value the improvements made upon the property in the interim by fresh plantations of cocoa-palms or other fruit trees. But if the purchaser or tenant becomes weary of the estate and wishes to force it back on the original possessor, he can do so only at a loss of 20 per cent.

3. *Berampatta* is a complete lease, similar to those which take place among us.

4. *Kararna* is a species of exchange:—one man lends a garden to another worth, for instance, 6,000 f. and borrows that sum in return for an appointed term of years, during which the fruits of the garden serve for interest.

5. *Nierpatta*:—A landlord gives to some individual a piece of waste land for building or for planting with cocoa palms, and receives no interest for it until the trees are so high that a Carnak sitting on an elephant can reach a leaf of them with his stick. A small sum of money is however paid beforehand for the use of the land; when the trees have attained the height above mentioned the garden is taxed according to its value, and rent paid accordingly.

LETTER XI.

Revenues of the Rajahs of Cochin.—Their mode of Government.—Accounts of the National Assemblies collected in cases of emergency.

The Malabar States, in common with all others in the world, possess certain fixed revenues [1] and funds for replenshing the treasury, and maintaining royal pomp, and the welfare of the State; though here the Rajah's incomes are not very large or out of the common. Their chief profits are derived from their private estates, and the inferior princes are often richer than the reigning sovereign, being possessed of larger free and hereditary properties.

Merchandize is a source of great gain to monarchs whose territories are on the coast, for which reason these Malabar Rajahs have taken so eagerly to commerce. Why, when the Portuguese first visited these coasts, did the Moors possess much influence over the Zamorin? Because they, at that time the only maritime traders, procured him so much profit that he feared to disturb them by the reception of strangers.

Ten per cent is the duty levied on all goods imported into the kingdom of Cochin by private and native merchants, and the profits derived from it are divided between the Company and the Rajah. The latter obtained this privilege originally from the Portuguese[2], and since their expulsion the East India Company have confirmed him in the enjoyment of it, introducing however some changes in the rate of the duties—the Portuguese having imposed different amounts of duty on different nations, as appears from the following list, on the imports—

the Moors paid { 7 per cent to the Rajah
3 per cent to Portugal

the Benjanese paid { 5 per cent to the Rajah
3 per cent to Portugal

the Canarese paid { 5 per cent to the Rajah
3 per cent to Portugal.

but, now, these restrictions are done away with, all paying 10 per cent., of which 6 goes to the Rajah and 4 to the Company. The duty on exports is 6 per cent.

All goods imported by the Company, and those forwarded by them to their settlements and factories elsewhere, are free. There

1. Note 1, pp. 324—349
2. Note 2, pp. 349—351

C.

is no rate of tolls fixed for the merchandize of foreign nations, such as French, English, as they are not allowed to trade at the Company's factories. To the Portuguese alone has been conceded by long custom, permission to dispose of sweetmeats, eatables, etc., brought from China, when they put in here on the passage to Goa, paying on these a duty of 4 per cent to the Company and 6 per cent to the Rajah. The Company and the Rajah each appoint an officer to collect these dues.

The duty on native commodities, such as pepper, which amounts here to half a ducat per kandy, is paid by the merchant who sells them, and not by the Company. The dues are heavier in the south.

There are certain estates in Malabar, whose owners are obliged to pay an annual tribute [1] in recognition of their proprietorship to the Rajah; this is regarded rather as a free will offering than a tax.

All merchandizes conveyed by inland navigation pay a *junkara* [2] or toll of 1 per cent to the Rajah, the merchants entering the gross amount of their cargo at the *junkenaars* or custom houses [3] (which are curious edifices, built on piles in the water); small as this tax is, it presses heavily enough on the inhabitants, as there are a great many of these custom houses. All vessels bearing the Company's flag, are free and exempt from examination. The duties on tobacco from Coedenatti, Coechim, and Oediampoor [4] are a source of considerable emolument to the Rajah. The native tobacco is somewhat raw in taste, no doubt it would be much nicer if they understood the art of preparing it as they do in Europe; for here the leaves are tied up in bundles and sent off before they are properly dried. In Kully Quilon, Porcad, and Quilon, tobacco from Java is principally used which is brought by the natives in their annual visits to these shores. The Patterys [5] who are employed in the inland conveyance of goods, pay a fanam in every kingdom through which they travel, for the packs which they carry on their backs, but there is no charge on those which are carried on the head, so we always see them loaded with two packs, one carried on the shoulder and the other on the head.

All gardens situated in Carraparam [6] pay a tenth on their fruits to the Raja of Cochin, who is the sole lord (*volkomen meetser*) of the land. He receives a smaller proportion in other places.

1. Note 3, p. 351
2. Note 4, p. 351
3. Note 5, pp. 351—352
4. Note 6, p. 352
5. Note 7, p. 353
6. Note 8, pp. 353—354

On all debts discharged under sentence from the Rajah he receives 20 per cent. Mothers present an offering on the birth of their children. He is the inheritor of the property of all, whether Heathens, Moors, or Jews, who die without heirs, and this sometimes when there are blood relations living. He receives an acknowledgment in money for every office or dignity he confers. If he despatches any of his guards to the assistance of any one he expects a valuable present in return. The visits paid him by his subjects always bring in something, and this is especially the case on their first introductions to him, or if they have any favours to demand. The offerings which they bring, consisting of stuffs, money, fruit, or anything else, they must deposit at his feet; and this custom is so universal in Malabar that if the natives have any favour to ask of the Commandant, they always bring him presents of pigs, fruit or poultry.

We must also take into consideration the fines paid by criminals: for the right of passing sentence being vested in the Rajah of each State, they understand how to make the most of the opportunity of making the criminals bleed well in their purses, and there is hardly any crime which may not be expiated by money.[1]

All ruminating animals, such as oxen, cows, buffaloes, belong to the Rajah, as well as those that have five or six tents.[2]

All people, whether of high or low caste, who have transgressed against the distinctions of caste[3], belong to the Rajah, who generally sells them. No one may wear whiskers, except by his permission, for which a fine or acknowledgment must be paid, and then a great banquet is celebrated in honour of these whiskers.

All leases, renewals of contract, etc., bring him in a small sum, and all deeds of gift and sale must be renewed at the accession of every new monarch. On the death of a feoffee (*Leenman*) his heir must renew the deed of gift, purchase or fief (*gift koop endeen*) and pay for it.

A gift for maintenance (*gift tot on-derhoud*) conferred by the Rajah on any one who subsequently dies without legitimate heirs, reverts to the Rajah.[4]

All the chiefs of the Mocquas, Chegos, Cannekaas, etc., must pay an annual sum to the Rajah for their dignity.[5]

All Christians, Jews and Moors, wishing to obtain license to use drums and wind instruments at their festivities and merry

1. Note 9, pp. 354—355
2. Note 10, p. 355
3. Note 11, p. 355
4. Note 12, pp. 355—356
5. Note 13, pp. 356—368

makings must present an offering when they demand the Rajah's permission. Persons of low caste must do the same in order to obtain permission to wear the *roemal* or fillet round the head, gold rings, etc.

It would seem that the income derived from all these sources ought to be sufficient to maintain the regal state handsomely, but as their dominions are for the most part very limited, the petty Rajahs are generally poor. The greater Rajahs may amass a considerable fortune, the more as their expenditure is small.

I shall now add a few words on the mode in which the Government is conducted.[1] The Rajah is supreme in those dominions which are immediately subject to him, but not in the free inheritances which belong to the minor Rajahs and Caimals, for every one is sole lord in his own territories. They know little of assemblies, councils or parliaments. The Rajah chooses his favourites at his pleasure, consulting them in particular cases, but generally being guided solely by his own will, unless that will should run entirely counter to the customs of the country. Many keep near them a Brahmin to instruct them in the fundamental and long established laws and customs.

The only checks upon their arbitrary power are the general assemblies of the nation, which are however, but seldom held. These are of two kinds: one assembled under orders of the Rajah, the other by the spontaneous will of the people. Many years elapse between the recurrence of these assemblies. Those summoned by the Rajah are conducted as follows: He despatches messengers, who by birth and descent are entitled to this office, in all directions to summon the people. When collected, they sit down in a circle in the open air, a number of Nayars keeping guard around them. The propositions are then discussed and measures rejected or adopted by unanimous silence or clamour. But in affairs of minor importance not affecting the welfare of the whole community, the chiefs of the nation alone are summoned, and decide upon the question.

The assemblies collected by the will of the nation are conducted in much the same manner, but with more impetuosity. These are never held except in cases of emergency when the Rajah is guilty of extreme tyranny or gross violation of the law Then, all the land proprietors (*landesheeren*) are bidden to attend, and any one who dared refuse to obey the summons would be subjected by the assembly to the devastation of his gardens, houses, estates, tanks, etc., and, if he were to persist in his

1 Note 14, pp. 368—374

obstinacy would be liable to be deprived of his privileges and votes, or even to be sentenced to banishment. As the object of these assemblies is to thwart the will of the Rajah, we are not surprised to find that he does all in his power to obstruct their deliberations. He has no right to attempt to put them down by force of arms, and, besides, so many thousands flock to these meetings that he would find difficulty in so doing if he tried: so he sends a troop of lads called *Pandera Putte*[1] with instructions to provoke them with all manner of annoyances, and to pelt them with stones, sand and dirt. The Nayars on guard do all they can to keep off the assailants with their shields.

If any one, provoked past endurance, were to strike and hurt one of these youths, it would by their laws be regarded as a crime of treason (*geschondene majesteit*) the assembly would be involved in a heavy fine, and be deprived of its inviolability; and the Rajah might then proceed against them by arms ; if he were to fail in subduing them they would all desert their allegiance. Allies and neighbours do their best to remedy all the mischief thence ensuing, and endeavour so to intercede between the parties that every one is confirmed in his rights.

The guards (*Schuttsmannen*) are a body of men employed by the Rajah in the defence of any pagoda or estate to the possession of which their right is disputed. These guards are bound to defend such places at risk of their lives, and to attack the assailants, for whose death they are not held responsible. They do not fear death in the cause, knowing that the Rajah whom they serve is pledged by the laws to revenge their blood. So powerful is the love of revenge in these nations, that in hopes of obtaining it they are willing to encounter death itself, and no reconciliation can ever be brought about until full satisfaction has been taken for the offence.

Thus are public affairs conducted in Malabar[2] in a very different way from our proceedings in Europe, where each separate nation has its own laws. Meanwhile I pray the Almighty that he will endow you, who have a share in the management of the Netherland's Exchequer, with wisdom and trust—worthiness in your difficult employment; and subscribe myself.

---

1. Note 15, p. 374
2. Note 16. pp. 374—385
   Note 17, pp. 385—404. A Note on Mamamkam.

LETTER XII.

Of the coinage of India—Rupees, Pagodas, etc., and their value—Of the money current among the Europeans and its value—of the fanams, boeseroks, and cowries.

Sir,—As you have the superintendence of the State's mint, and the charge of that coinage which is used for the service of the world-famous Dutch trade as well as for replenishing the public treasury, you will not be displeased at my addressing to you in the present letter an account of the coins used by the East Indians.

Their current money is of three kinds, the European money, the Heathen and the Moorish; for, though there are many Jews there, yet as they possess no State of their own, so neither have they any peculiar coinage.

The Moorish pieces which are used in trade throughout India, are the Rupees, which consist of gold and silver, and whole and half rupees. They are stamped with letters on both sides; for the Moors have such a horror of all figures and images that they will not endure even the likeness of a beast—flowers only being admissible. This is soon discovered by traders, who consequently take care not to offer them wares of China or silk having patterns in which animals are introduced. And yet I have seen a set of gold rupees, twelve in number, bearing the twelve signs of the Zodiac; together with a small gold penny bearing the likeness of a man, and said to be a representation of Mahomet. Nobody could tell me when or where this last piece was struck: but with regard to the rupees, it is well-known that they were coined by order of a famous Mogul empress, who, possessing entire sway over the mind of the great Mogul, and being immoderately amibitious, desired above all things to perpetuate her name and glory by some extraordinary deed. Nothing was more suitable for this purpose than to strike a new coin: so she issued orders that throughout all parts of her extensive domains, stamps bearing the twelve signs of the Zodiac should be prepared under the care of certain of her faithful servants. She then exerted all her female arts of cajolery to induce the monarch to grant her absolute sway for one single day. This she obtained under certain conditions; and when the day arrived, she despatched swift messengers in all directions with orders that the rupees should be immediately struck, which was accordingly done. The following day when the emperor resumed his authority, he sent round counter orders, to prohibit the coinage, break up the stamps, and call in all the money that had already been struck; but the empress had been beforehand with him, and had caused many thousands of the rupees to be circulated and collected in cabinets, and thus it happens that to this day many collectors of curiosities, both Christians and Moors, have several of them in their possession. Indeed it is sometimes doubted whether their number has not been increased by false copies.

Of the rupees in actual circulation, the common gold ones are the least useful in trade, and not always maintain the same standard value beyond the Mogul empire. I have seen them exchanged here for 7½ rix dollars, according to the Indian reckoning. The silver rupee, both half and whole, is used in trade throughout the Indies, and especially in the Districts of Bengal and Surat. The Bengal coin is either the Sicca rupee or the bazaar rupee. Sicca rupees are of two sorts, the new and the old; both being good, but the old the most prized. Bazaar rupees are poor, and are worth at least three stivers[1] less than the others, in this part of the world. The Surat rupees are also good. They are much the same as the Sicca rupees, and are likewise much used in trade. The value of a rupee is less than its current price, which is five shillings.[2] But, beyond the Bengal territory, no one gives more than four shillings and a half for a Bengal rupee. The silver of the rupee is very fine, and of a better quality than that of the ducats. The English coin rupees at their chief place, Madras, but these are inferior to the rupees of Surat. A rupee is about the size of a shilling in circumference, but its thickness is greater.

The Pagoda is a gold coin struck by the heathens, in value about equal to two rix dollars. It weighs the same as a ducat, but is of inferior quality. It is called a pagoda because it bears the image of an idol on one side: a pagoda being the name for an idol temple. The most valuable are those bearing the impression of three heads. The pagodas with one head are less circulated. There is no image on the reverse, but an impression of holes, resembling the exterior of a thimble.

I have seen two kinds of Japanese coins; the Kobang and the Itzeboo. There are half and whole kobangs: the first equal to five and the last to ten rix dollars. Both are flat oblong pieces of gold, bearing no impression save a kind of sign in the middle, not unlike that with which our Vats are marked. The other coin, the Itzeboo is a small bar, and is seldom or never used by the Europeans in trade.

1. A Dutch coin, equal to about a penny.

2. A Dutch shilling is worth about six stivers.

The coins which Europeans make most use of are rix dollars, ducatoons, Spanish *matten* and ducats. The Dutch usually compute by rix dollars, and though salaries are counted by gulden in the company's books, they are generally paid down by the first named coin. Property also is taxed by rix dollars, and they are the medium employed in private commercial transactions. But a rix dollar here is equivalent to 48 stivers, only, instead of 50 as in Europe—hence people who put their money into the Company's funds to be repaid in Holland, make four per cent profit, or two stivers on every rix dollar.

The ducatoon is the coin chiefly circulated by the Company in the Indies and particularly at Batavia. It passes for thirteen shillings; thereby affording the Company a clear profit of 2½ shillings on each piece. I must add an observation as to the remarkable ingenuity evinced by the Company in their mode of paying their servants. It is a good specimen of that cunning thriftiness for which they are noted all over the world. In the first place they pay in ducatoons, which always pass current here for thirteen shillings, instead of 10½, and in the second place they pay their light money for heavy, so that their servants for one gulden receive no more than sixteen stivers. And, in addition to this, the inferior officers of the Company receive their pay half in money and half in kind, giving the Company a profit of 50 per cent, on Indian goods and 75 per cent on home commodities. From all which it appears very plainly that a soldier whose pay is nine gulden only costs his employers four.

This however does not alienate people from their service, for so artfully have they managed the whole concern that their officers, instead of feeling injured, are, on the contrary, well pleased with the treatment they receive. They are paid at the beginning of every month, so that no one is kept waiting, a punctuality which distinguishes the Dutch above all other Europeans in India. Moreover they give their servants a monthly allowance for board, varying according to their rank, and other compositions of like kind. A soldier receives about four shillings monthly, and rice sufficient for his consumption. An inferior merchant has four rix dollars, chaplains and upper merchants 10½ rix dollars, and also a house or lodging. At Batavia a permanent chaplain receives twelve rix dollars per month to provide lodgings, a pile (*stapel*) of firewood, two quarts (*Kan*) of Lisbon wine, four quarts of Dutch vinegar, six lbs. of cheese, twelve quarts of sack, twenty-four lbs. of Dutch butter, and other articles besides. The same is the case in other places, where, in lieu of money, they receive a house, seven quarts of wine, four lbs. of cheese. one lb.

of spices, consisting of cloves, cinnamon, mace and nutmeg (for the Company give or sell these articles, mixed, to their officers in order to prevent private trade in them) one quart of lisbon oil, eight quarts of cocoanut oil for their lamps, half a pile of wood, and drinking water. If to all this we add the 10 $\frac{1}{3}$ rix dollar for board, I cannot see that our chaplains have any right to complain. Further to obviate all discontent, the Company empower their servants to send over their accounts, signed by the Director-General, to Europe, where they may receive their whole salaries without any reduction ; but as this course is attended with peril, and persons at distant stations would have a long time to wait for their money, they prefer receiving their salaries with the before mentioned loss.

The Spanish matten, which are here reckoned worth 10 shillings, come from the Manilla or Philippine Islands, the Spaniards bringing them to Batavia for the purchase of linen and cinnamon, to be exported to the West Indies. The Company make considerable profit on this trade.

Ducats are also much used in the Persians' commerce, that nation circulating them in their payments to our Company. The Venetion ducats are the most valuable. The King of Persia receives heavy duties on the ducats, which the Company also are bound to pay. Consequently the price of the ducat is higher here than elsewhere, and as the Persians sell no great amount of goods to the Company, the latter are bound to receive the ducat at the fixed price, which rises as high as nineteen shillings, though more usually it is 18 or 18½. At Tutecoryn they are valued at 20 shillings. The settlements of Malabar and Ceylon are generally provided with these ducats, the pepper trade being always carried on with that coin, at a firm price of 18 s. the ducat.

But now to describe our Malabar specie. It has a good deal of variety, on account of the number of monarchs who possess the right of coinage[1]. The gold and silver pieces are generally called fanams, those of copper or lead, Boeserokken. They differ greatly in value in different places. A fanam of Calicut is worth one shilling, a fanam of Quilon two shillings and a half ; while those of Cochin are four to the shilling. It is my intention at present to describe only the Cochin mint, as being that in which the East India Company is concerned.

The Boeserokken are a mixture of lead and tin melted together and bearing on the one side the arms of the East India Company, and on the other a figure resembling a harp. They are

1. Note 1, pp. 405—416.

smelted in moulds, several being stuck together at the side, and then cut separate. Sixty of them are equivalent to a Cochin fanam or one stiver and a half, so that if a man were to reckon his capital in this coin he would find himself the possessor of some hundreds of thousands. The Cochin fanams are the common money of that kingdom, made use of both by the merchants and by the East India Company which pays its servants' salaries in this coin. The right of coining fanams appertains to the King of Cochin as supreme authority in the country : but these monarchs are apt to be defrauded by those whom they appoint to strike the coins, and the metal has been found to be adulterated both in the assay and composition of the metal ; consequently the Company have persuaded the king to allow the coinage to take place within the city, reserving to himself the appointment of the Mint masters, and having his own mark stamped upon the coin, but placing all under the supervision of the Dutch Commandant who sends Commissioners to watch the striking, mixing, and assaying of the fanams and to see that they have their due weight and value. There is always a deduction of 4 per cent; two for the king and two for the master of the mint, who pays all the expenses incurred in the coinage. These fanams are composed of gold, silver and copper, 10 lb. of the metal being made up of 1 lb. of fine gold of the highest test, 4½ lb. of fine silver, and 4½ lb. of fine Japan copper. This mixture being melted down is then moulded into little balls of the proper weight, and beaten flat with a stamp having certain Malabar characters on either side. The coin is small, and very inconvenient to handle. The East India Company derive a profit from this coinage, as supplying the gold, silver and copper material : but this is not their only gain ; for the present Commandant has discovered that the loss which always takes place in the smelting of the mixed metal and from which the old Mint masters made their profit, is not a loss upon the gold and silver, but upon the copper, and has to be made good by the addition of so much copper only.

Finally, I must speak of a kind of money cowries, used not only in Bengal, but also exported in quantities to the West Indies. These cowries are small shells found on the shores of the Maldive Islands. They are distinguished into the coloured cowries, which are those least priced, and the white cowries which are used instead of money in the aforesaid countries. The Hindoos in Bengal go about with bags full of cowries to purchase their daily necessaries : and the Europeans make their slaves carry them behind them, and use them on all occasions. From this we perceive that they may be made the means of a profitable trade, and indeed several

English private ships visit the islands to buy them. It is a dangerous voyage however, both on account of the adjacent deep and of the climate, which is often fatal to foreigners. The inhabitants are a wretched race, owing to the islands being small and frequently under water, and so barren that they afford scarcely anything but cocoanuts, which, together with a few fish, are the only sustenance to be procured. The boats of these people come annually to Cochin, bringing cowries for the Company, a few cocoanuts, and some dried fish which look like bits of wood, and are equally hard. In return for these commodities they take rice, the value of each cargo not amounting to more than 300 or 400 rix dollars. Their boats are strangely fashioned. The bottoms are made of wood, but without nails, being fastened together by wooden bars. A foot above water they are woven of reeds or straw, for I cannot exactly say what it is; and their anchors are pieces of wood: so that how they manage to cross the sea is a marvel. However they only sail in the fine season, when storms never occur.

The natives of the Maldive Islands are blacker than the Malabars, and of a good height. Their religion is the Mahometan. You may imagine the power of their monarch when I tell you that, at the annual voyage of his ships, he sends a royal present to the Commandant of Malabar, which is brought with all due ceremony into the city upon a silver salver lent for the occasion, and consists generally of two small mats, worth scarcely two shillings!

Cowries being the principal wealth of these islands, it is worth while to mention how they are collected. The natives take branches of the cocoanut tree on which they fasten stones to make them sink to the bottom. These they leave lying in rows from six to eight feet deep in the sea, round the island. At the end of some days they go out in their canoes, and taking up these branches gently, find their leaves covered on all sides with cowries which they shake off into their boats. They are then thrown into heaps and left to decay, till they are thoroughly dried and purified from animal matter, after which they are polished and either sold to the merchants who come for them, or carried by the natives to Malabar and Ceylon.

Here you have a brief account of the money to be found in India. There are many other kinds besides, current in particular provinces, but those I have mentioned are the most used in commerce, particularly in commerce with Europeans. Having thus fulfilled my promise, I will here conclude, etc.

LETTER XIII.

Ecclesiastical and temporal grandees in Malabar—Customary salutations between the higher and lower orders in their daily intercourse; and their modes of shewing respect.

I hope you will not object to my writing you a letter on "miscellaneous topics", tending to a more full acquaintance with the affairs of Malabar. First, I will mention the magnates of this country, who may be distinguished as the Spiritual and the Temporal grandees.

The Malabar Brahmans, or *Namboories* as they are called, in some cases exert secular authority[1], being the possessors of certain domains, with Nairs or soldiers in their service, and the power of capital punishment over their subjects; being amenable to no superior sovereign or rajah. They have also the patronage of all offices and dignities within their territories, so that in this respect also, they are independent in the same manner as some of the German bishops, only that their dignity is hereditary, whereas that of the German bishop is electoral.

The *Namboories* are also sometimes lords over certain territories, exercising the right of making war. The four principal *Namboories*[2] are those of Eincour, Manacaloa, Poenetoer, and Ella Enganare, who are very powerful. The Namboories are neither spiritual nor temporal sovereigns, but may be called half spiritual, half temporal. In order to understand this, we must remark that in the old times of Cheramperoumal, when that monarch had reigned twelve years, many people wished to summon a new emperor from Hindustan to fill his place, whilst others were desirous to keep him in power, on account of his sage government. Now, the first party, having introduced their new emperor into the country, some Brahmans of the other side went to meet him, cut off his head, and brought it to Cheramperoumal, who was then at Telepalc near Amkoer. In consequence of this deed they lost caste, indeed, but Cheramperoumal to shew his gratitude made them *Namboories* and gave them the lands of Telepale[3] for a perpetual possession.

The Caimals[4] are temporal potentates, also possessing the right of making war. Some of them are subject to the princes in whose territories they are situated; but others are independent: the difference depends on the privileges they received in ancient

1. Note 1, pp. 417—418.
2. Note 2, p. 418.
   Note 3, pp. 418—421. **A Note on the Nampadies.**
3. Note 4, pp. 421—422.
4. Note 5, p. 422.

times. The Malabars say that there are fifty Caimals in the Kingdom of Côchin.

The Rasidoors are lords who have been raised by the Rajahs to certain commands over the army or country. In many places they are appointed to govern a district or town in the name of the prince. Besides these, there is another class, namely the *Menons*, that is to say scribes, whose office it is to write the letters of their Rajahs and great people with an iron style on the *olas*[1] or leaves of cocoanut trees, to record public affairs, to make out business letters, and also to tie up and seal the Prince's letters, which may not be done by common persons. These Menons rise indeed to higher dignities, sometimes even becoming captains and chiefs of the army, when they acquire the title of *Menon Mare*.[2] The *Goeryps*[3] (who are the fencing masters) are likewise held in great esteem, some Princes and Rajahs bear this title, as for instance, the Goeryp of Travancore.[4]

And now to another subject. I will here describe the manner in which the lower classes shew respect to the higher and some other of their customary gestures, in which their manners bear a marked difference from those of the Europeans. While with us a shake of the head is a sign of refusal or denial, with the Malabars on the contrary to incline the head from side to side signifies affirmation and satisfaction.[5] A negative they express by opening and closing the thumb and first two fingers.

No greater affront can be shown to a Malabar than by striking him with the stalk[6] on which a cocoanut grows. A remarkable instance of this occurred not long ago. A Quilon-Kara (as the black Christians of Quilon are called), going to the house of a Chego to tap toddy, hard words happened to pass between him and the Chego's mother, and the Quilon-Kara, waxing impatient, struck the woman with one of the aforesaid stalks. She related the affront to her son who was not present on the occasion and he immediately threatened to take the life of the Quilon-Kara.

1. Note 6, pp. 422—425.

" They write on the leaves of wild cocoa trees, cut of the breadth of two inches, and two hands long: of these they lay together as many as they think fit, and put a small stick through them on the top, which done they fasten the stick or both ends to the leaves with packthread:—each of these leaves is called *ola*". From John Menhoff's *Remarkable Voyages and Travels into the best provinces of the West and East Indies.*

2. Note 7, pp. 425—426.
3. Note 8, p. 426.
4. Note 9, p. 426.
5. Note 10, p. 426.
6. Note 11, p. 426.

The latter perceiving the imminent danger he was in, fled to Quilon, thinking that the affair would be forgotten in time, but on his return, after seven months, the Chego discovered and murdered him, and then took flight and escaped punishment.

The modes of salutation[1] differ according to the quality of the parties. When a subject meets a Caimal Ragiadoor or any other grandee belonging to the Court, he lowers his sword placing it with its point to the ground; or if he has no sword takes off his head dress. Before Rajahs or Princes they must perform a peculiar mode of salutation. They re-cover their heads and joining the palms of their hands raise them to the forehead, then separate them and then open and close their fists thrice before their heads. The Princes must make the same obeisance to the Rajah as first Prince, but they are not obliged to uncover their heads. The petty Rajahs, subordinate to the Rajah of Cochin (those of Mangatti, Porcad, &c.) must thus show their respect to him, and they must remove their upper garment in his presence and remain bare shouldered till he gives them permission to resume it. The Princes of Porcad and Paroer, being Brahmans, have alone the privilege of being seated in the presence of the Rajah of Cochin. The former of these, who is superior both in sanctity and rank, may sit on the same couch with the Rajah who takes his hand and places it in his bosom. There is also a high seat prepared for him by the side of the Rajah when he visits him. These visitations are very expensive to the Rajah, who has to provide food for the princes and their retinues, amounting to more than 100 individuals, the whole time they last or to give money in place of food.

The women make the same obeisances as the men, letting fall their veils or coverings and folding their arms in front. If the Queen mother is older than the Rajah, on his first visit to her after his accession, he must bend his head down to the ground, and lay both his hands joined together on his head, which is the highest mark of respect. If the Queen mother or the eldest Princess of the Royal family is younger than the Raja she must perform the same reverence to him.

The ordinary grandees and others salute each other by an inclination of the head on one side: sometimes the common people fall on one knee before the Rajah, and join their hands over their heads. Others embrace each other with one or both arms. Subjects on their first introduction to the Rajah lay presents at his feet, as a token of respect. The Rajah rewards[2] a grandee or general who has done any special service by the gift of a

1. Note 12, pp. 426—428.
2. Note 13, pp. 428—429.

somereel, palanquin (a somereel in the Portuguese language means a sun screen made of the leaves of the cocoa tree or palmyra fastened in a slight wooden frame), or, a gold bracelet or ear-rings. These gifts, though themselves of little value, are regarded as marks of great honour.

The Rajah of Cochin in some respects ranks higher[1], and possesses more privileges than the Rajahs of Travancore, Colastri and the Zamorin. Thus, if these four Princes travelling together were to approach the house of a Pulleah, the Rajah of Cochin must be the first to enter ; and so if they were to bathe together no one must enter the water until he has first set foot in it, after which they must all imitate his proceedings. If a Nair lose caste in any kingdom, no one has power to restore him, except the Rajah of Cochin, who presents him with a *guide* or vessel of water to drink. It is not every one who is privileged to approach equally near to the Rajah. A Chego must keep a distance[2] of 30 paces, a Nayar may come near but may not touch him : but a Pulleah may never be seen in the place, where he is, while the Brahmans have free access and have the privilege of preparing every thing, even to his food, for him.

When the Zamorin writes to the Rajah of Cochin, or any of the superior Princes to each other, the letter[3] must be addressed not to the Prince, but to the chief Rasidoor, who in Cochin is called the Naicoviti, and the chief Rasidoor of the Zamorin is called the Mangàtatja. If a Nair brings a letter from his Rajah to another, or to the Commandant, he must prostrate himself thrice in token of reverence; a Brahman or Pattari is exempt from this ceremony. When the Rajah is employed in religious offices no one may speak to him[4], not even a Brahman ; but if any very important circumstance occurs which demands his attention, he must be informed of it by certain signs on the fingers .

And now having told you so much of manners of the Malabars in their intercourse together, perhaps you will like to hear how they conduct themselves in their dealings with the Europeans. In the time of the Portuguese, there was a quarrel between their soldiers and the Nairs about the right of way in their casual meetings. The dispute ran so high (according to the Portuguese) that at last it was agreed between the Rajah and the Portuguese General-in-Chief that it should be settled by a duel between a

1. Note 14, p. 429.
2. Note 15, p. 429;
   A Footnote on Malabar Untouchability on pp 429—434;
   Note 16, a note on the manner of eating, pp. 430—435.
3. Note 17, pp. 436—437.
4. Note 18, pp. 437—438.

member of each party, and that the conqueror should win the right for his associates. For this purpose the Rajah selected his most able fencing master, who was well versed in the use of sword and shield. The Portuguese also made choice of the bravest of his army for his champion, but dressed him in common sailor's clothes, so that if he were to lose, the disgrace might not fall on the army ; however he prostrated his adversary three times and the Rajah, unconscious of the deception, was very much surprised that a common sailor should display such dexterity. Since this time, the Nairs have always conceded the right of way to the Europeans, except in one or two instances in my time, when they have disputed that right with our soldiers, who resisted their incivility so valiantly that they have not had courage to repeat it.

When a Rajah visits the town, the Commandant receives him at his residence at the foot of the stairs, and leads him up by the right hand. If a Prince comes to visit him, he is received on the steps; a Caimal or other grandee, the Commandant receives in the hall, where he makes him take a seat. At their first entrance into the town, the Rajahs are conducted from the gate by two members of the political council, with the attendance of armed troops. One member of the council and the chief interpreter perform this office for an inferior prince. They are conducted out of the town in the same manner, the prince walks in the middle, or on the right hand of his conductor. They are also saluted with artillery, the number of discharges being proportioned to their rank. For the Rajah of Cochin, eleven salutes are fired, for the other Rajahs of the kingdom nine, for the petty Rajahs seven, and for other members of the Royal families, five or three.

When the Commandant goes to Court, he is received by the Rajah at the foot of the stairs, unless that Prince is in mourning, in which case the office is performed by the second Prince, or any other who may happen to be at Court. When deputies from the political council go to Court, they are accompanied by two servants, and may sit down with their heads covered; but the chief interpreter must stand uncovered.

When a new Commandant and Rajah meet for the first time, presents[1] are exchanged between them, the Commandant presenting gifts prepared by the Company for the purpose, while the Rajah loads him with gold chains and bracelets, and presents are distributed among his suite in proportion to their rank. The Rajahs fasten these bracelets with their own hands on the arms of those to whom they present them, which, as they are rather small,

1. Note 19, pp. 438—439.

often occasions pain, as I know by experience. Some of the bracelets are plain, others chased. The Company's gifts consist of stuffs, sugar, rosewater, spices, etc. But as the Rajahs generally sell them under their real value, they would be better pleased if money was given them instead, as they deem it no disgrace to receive pecuniary gifts.

LETTER XIV.

Customs and luxuries of the women in Malabar. Management of the children. Weddings, etc.

Dear And Honoured Mother,

Though it might seem hardly consistent with my respect for you to descend to a minute description of the costume, habits, etc., of the women of this country, yet since you have asked for it, I will devote this letter to satisfying your curiosity.

The people here are of a different colour from those at home, for the natives are either black, brown, or of a light tawny colour, and the Europeans themselves soon lose their beauty and become pallid, a fresh bright colour being never seen, because the delicate veins of the epidermis which give the rosy tint, are here destroyed by the heat of the sun. The women, however, are not deterred from seeking to make up for this loss, by the outward adornment of costly apparel. There is not one of any fortune who does not own as many as twenty or thirty chests full of robes, made of silk or some other valuable material, for it would be a disgrace in their eyes to wear the same dress two or three days in succession. Their necks are adorned with necklaces of diamonds, their ears with ear-rings, and their fingers with rings of the same precious stones. Pearls are very common with them, and gold chains are worn by the wives and children of tradesmen and soldiers. Perhaps you will say that this is a shocking luxury, and ask what is the use of all these clothes? But what would you say were they to remind you that many Dutch and Frisian women fill their chests with linen which is never used, but is kept carefully locked up, and never sees day-light except when it is grown so yellow with age that it must needs be washed?

In Cochin, the women go generally on foot, but at Batavia, people of even ordinary degree are often carried in sedans by their slaves, whilst the rich travel in coaches, and these are so common there that my own tailor rode in a calash. When the ladies go out to walk, it is generally by moon-light, and they are followed by a troop of slaves, male and female. India is certainly a

e,

luxurious country for women: for no sooner does any servant girl arrive from home in Batavia than she becomes a lady, marries a man with money, and is immediately surrounded by slaves who run hither and thither at her command. Even the women who are supported by charitable funds would be ashamed to go out without a slave. All persons of any pretension carry a parasol over the head, to ward off the heat of the sun, and no woman would like to be seen without a slave to hold it. The universal pleasure, both of men and women, is betel chewing, and when the women visit each other, a large silver dish of betel is brought out, with silver boxes and cups, in which the betel leaves are laid, with areca and lime. Cardamoms, ketchup, gambier and other condiments are often added to give the mixture a flavour. With persons of any rank, all this service must be of silver, indeed they would be ashamed to place their wine glasses upon any but silver salvers: the glasses are then filled with wine, and handed round to the company by a slave. Perhaps you will object to such pomp and luxury, but custom is second nature, and it is not the possession and use of such things, but their abuse, that signifies any thing. None but fools would feel any pride in them; as for myself, I am indifferent whether I have them or not.

The native women of European race are all dressed like the Dutch; but the mixed or half-white races have a totally different costume. They wear a vest over the upper part of the body, without sleeves and open in front: over this, a jacket of fine linen, descending below the waste, wide in the body and tight in the sleeves. Round the lower part of the body they twist cloths of various colours, and fasten them with pins in front. They wear also stockings and slippers, and hang a folded cloth over their shoulders, about a hand breadth in width, hanging down half way back and front. This garment they call a *tokes*: it is frequently made of fine stuff edged with gold. They wear no covering on their heads, and their hair is not plaited, but is done up in a stiff knot ornamented with gold hair pins sometimes set with precious stones. They wear ear rings and finger rings like our women.

I must add a word about the management of the children, which differs in many particulars from the customs of our country. They do not swaddle their infants in the way we do; and indeed the swaddling cloth is never used here, loose wrappers only being used. This custom merits approval, not only because the heat renders swaddling inappropriate to this climate, but because it is in itself a more healthy plan. This is the reason why so few men of dwarfish stature are found in India, whereas they abound in Europe. It is doubtless owing to the same system and the greater coolness and cleanliness it induces, that the infants here know nothing of convulsions, which affect nearly all our children, more or less. They are careful to wash themselves and their children very often ; and they laugh at our Dutch and Frieslanders, whose cleanliness is expended on their houses only : but I would venture a wager, that if they could but once feel the cold of our winters, they would not think washing so indispensable.

And now I will say something about their betrothals and marriages. In Batavia, these ceremonies are accompanied with what may truly be called princely pomp and expenditure. So extravagant is the outlay for carriages adorned with ribbons, for thrones, wedding fees and other accessories, that many incur ruin in consequence. A wedding which costs only 800 rix dollars besides clothes and ornaments, is considered quite shabby. Here it is even more expensive: so much so, that a wedding among the meaner sort of people would often put to shame a like ceremony among our grandees at home. At the betrothal, the youthful pair are attended by two couples as witnesses, who march behind the bride and bridegroom in a stately manner. Then follow a young man and maiden bearing the crown, which they place upon the bride's head and then another couple, carrying herbs, which they scatter over the betrothed pair. A feast is given, accompanied with music and for the two Sundays after the betrothal, the bride and bridegroom must be visited by all the persons invited. A crown is suspended before the door of the bridegroom to betoken his situation; and in the bride's house a throne is set up, over which hangs another crown; and here the young pair are to sit when they are married. On the evening before the wedding, the bridegroom's crown is carried through the streets on the points of two swords, a man carrying a naked sword in front : musicians follow, together with young men bearing torches. When they have finished their procession through the street, they bring the crown to the bride's door, where it hangs till the next day. On Sunday afternoon, the bride and bridegroom accompanied by their young friends proceed to the church, and on the completion of the ceremony, two soldiers, who with others are keeping guard in the church, stand at the door to present them with fire arms adorned with flowers, for which they receive presents in return. Outside the door stand the crown-man and crown-maiden, who fasten a small crown with a pin on the bride's head. They are met on their way home by the herb-man and maiden, who carry baskets of herbs and ornaments made of coloured paper, and strew them before the steps of the advancing pair. Seated on her throne, with a brides-maid on each side, the bride then receives the congratulations of the company. The rest of the night is spent in music, dancing and feasting : and as soon as the bridal dance is over in which all the company join, the bride is conducted to an elegantly adorned chamber, and the guests depart.

The women marry at a very early period of life, and are to be seen sitting with babies on their knees at an age when in our country they would be playing and running about with children. A girl is considered marriageable when she has attained her 13th year; and then all the suitors begin to flock around her. As she attains womanhood earlier, so her bloom is proportionably sooner over than in our country.

Such, dear mother, is a description of the women in India. I trust that God will support you, who have given birth to eight children, in your advancing years. I can assure you that my heart is always filled with true affection towards you and with all tenderness I subscribe myself, &c.

LETTER XV.

An account of the Topasses, their religious ceremonies, Priests, and Customs.

There are a certain Christian people to be found in this country of Malabar, and throughout the extensive coasts of India called Topasses[1], who cannot be reckoned as belonging exactly either to the Europeans or the natives, but form a third class. They are a mixed race: some are sprung from Portuguese settlers and slaves, whose children have intermarried with blacks; but the greater part are the offspring of enfranchised Portuguese slaves. With these we must also reckon freed slaves of all races: including Christian slaves, who are chiefly of the Romish persuasion. Their number is daily on the increase. These people have a very good opinion of themselves, as if they possess a little money, know how to make a fine show with it. They like to class themselves with the Portuguese, whom they call *our people* (Teur nossa genti), though these, owing to their native pride, despise them even more than we do, always styling them Negroes or Blacks. The Topasses however are no whit discouraged by this treatment and not only give themselves Portuguese names, but are in the habit of choosing those that belong to the noblest Portuguese and Spanish families. They affect very haughty airs, and teach their children always to address them as "*My Lord my father*" (Senhor mei Pai).

1. Note 1, pp. 440—442.

The name Topas is curious. It is supposed to be derived from two Portuguese words, *Tu Pai* (*thou boy*) because the Portuguese in early times, having taught their language to the slave born in their house, made use of them as interpreters in dealing with the natives, and were in the habit of saying "*Tu Pai falla aquel*" or " you boy say so and so". There seems to be a glimpse of truth in this account; for they still call the oldest and most respected slaves *Pai.*

Others refer this word to *Kocpaj*, which in the Malabar language signifies a coat ; for they wear coat, shirt and breaches, like the Europeans, as likewise a hat, in sign of their freedom, and the more wealthy among them wear shoes and stockings though more generally they go barefoot. Formerly, when the Company first obtained possession of this place, there was a rule that none of the Topasses might wear shoes and stockings, or that at any rate they must pay something to the *Diacony* (or charity fund) for the privilege of so doing. But this rule has fallen into disuse, as has also the tax that was paid for carrying a cane. But in my opinion the origin of this name must not be ascribed to *Kocpaj* (coat), but rather to *Toepay* (interpreter); because the race served as interpreters between the people of Malabar and the Christians; and to this day the same office is exercised by many of them, and is esteemed a very honourable profession.

There are a great many of these Topasses to be met with in Malabar, especially on the sea-coast, and in the neighbourhood of the European forts and settlements. Several are to be found in the city of Cochin, and its environs where they follow various trades, as bakers, cabinet makers, carpenters, shoemakers and in short all callings which furnish the necessaries of life. In the country they are often agricultural labourers. During the war they were employed by the Company as letter carriers. They are not to be found in our forts, except that of Chetwa where a company of them is stationed , the majority of the garrison however being European. They are more employed by the English who are usually deficient in European hands.

So bigotted are the Topasses to their religion, which is Romish, that it is a work of impossibility to convert them. Their superstition exceeds even that of the Portuguese and Spaniards,

Note.—The East Indian community which is here alluded to has undoubtedly undergone a great change since the days of our Author, consisting of numerous families in all parts of the country, most of whom are of high respectability and usefulness. The term Topass has fallen into disuse, but it is singular enough that to the present day, the Europeans in India invariably call 'boy' whenever they require their servant, East Indian or Native.—H. D.

otherwise the most bigotted of Papists. In accordance with the general custom of their church, they have several brotherhoods, as those of the Rosary, the Conception, etc. On Good Friday they repair in crowds to their churches, and flagellate themselves with scourges made of rope, until the blood runs down. The ends of these scourges are knotted with lumps of wax and bits of broken glass stuck in, to make the strokes more painful. Before applying them, they raise their courage by swallowing huge drafts of arrack, till they get intoxicated, and in a very unfit state for en tering on divine service, St. John the Baptist's Day, June 24th, is an occasion of great hilarity. The little children are then dressed up in gariands and green boughs. On the previous evening, called St. John's eve, they let off grand fireworks in honour of the Saint. (The Dutch at Cochin sometimes indulge in the same display, but they do it merely for a pastime.) On Good Friday, they appoint some one to represent Our Lord, and lead him outside the church carrying the cross in a sort of dramatic show. When ill, as a means for recovering their health, they make vows to the Holy cross, dressing it with flowers, and burning lamps before it all night. These crosses are set up in the public roads as well as in the churches. Some of them are held to possess miraculous powers, though since the arrival of the Dutch heretics it is granted that their efficacy has very much diminished. At the beginning of the rainy season in June, a priest goes round to every house, sprinkling it with holy water to keep off evil spirits. They have a hundred other superstitions, not worth mentioning.

Many of their priests are Europeans; but the vicars of their churches are mostly Topasses, and are not admitted to any higher dignity in the church; the Dutch call them parish priests. They are not eligible even to this office unless they possess property to the value of a hundred rix-dollars, for the clerical revenues being insufficient for their support, they must help to maintain themselves out of their own funds. They are mostly very illiterate, of Latin they know no more than enables them to perform mass. I was once told by one of them with whom I was conversing about the adoration of the Saints, that he could justify the doctrine by the adoration of the golden calf? This I willingly conceded him. Another coming to visit a church or parish, was asked by the Commandant, who first existed, Christ or the Christians? And in his simplicity made answer, the latter. But indeed most of the priests ordained at Goa are not much better. One of the Dominican parish priests, a white European, being advanced in years was waited on by one of our visitors of the sick, who, knowing no other language, began to converse with him in Dutch. The priest remarked:" I understand the Latin you are speaking very well, but I don't know it quite well enough to make answer in it."

The Topasses have many customs widely different from ours, and which they have probably learnt mostly from the Portuguese. At the birth of a child, the women keep on singing to it, or it would be considered unlucky. They have many peculiar marriage customs. The marriage is more commonly arranged by the parents than by the children, and it happens not unfrequently that the bridegroom has never previously seen the bride: within the company's jurisdiction the ceremony of betrothal takes place in the city, and must be conducted before the Committee of matrimonial affairs. The pair do not go thither together, but the bride goes alone, accompanied by an old woman, usually her mother if she is living; next follow several of her nearest male relatives and friends. Then the bridegroom arrives with a party of friends carrying shoes and stockings, and perhaps a sword, if he chooses to pay for it; which money, as also that which is paid for the somereel of the bride, goes to the poor. The appearance of the bride is somewhat strange. She walks generally very lame, being quite unused to the slippers which she now wears for the first time. Besides the tunic and the coloured cloth, in which articles of clothing her dress resembles that of the mixed races (*Mysticen*), she wears a silken veil, red or green, thrown over her shoulder from behind, and falling in front below the waist. Besides this, the bride is adorned with many gold chains and bracelets. On her head she wears a crown, within the circlet of which her hair is gathered into a knot, and from which several little chains depend. Hair pins set with various coloured stones are set in the plaits of her hair. The marriage ceremony is performed in the Romish Church, with a license from the Commandant. When the bridal pair reach the door of their house on their return from Church, they are sprinkled with rose-water, and then follows a marriage feast, when the guests eat in good earnest being generally a hungry set.

When a husband and wife go out together, they never walk side by side, as we do, but the husband walks first and the wife follows. I have observed this custom also sometimes among the Portuguese here. When a Topass dies within the city, his body is laid on a kind of litter covered with a cloth on which a large cross is embroidered, and is then carried out of the city, to be laid in consecrated ground in the island of Vypeen. When Topasses are in mourning, they not only wear black coats, but wear them inside out (having no lining to them) and let their beards grow.

They are idle as well as proud, and will seldom work as long as they have any money. Hence there are few wealthy men among them. They are naturally fonder of the Portuguese than of the Dutch, though the former abandoned them shamefully to our mercy when the city changed hands. The unanimity of religion, the resemblance of names, and the notion that they are sprung from the same stock, make these poor creatures cling to their former masters; and I have no doubt that in the event of a war they would side with the Portuguese rather than with us, although at present they are under our protection, and are shielded by the Company against any pretensions on the part of the Heathen, who have no jurisdiction over them, for when they commit crimes, they must be delivered up to the Company and punished according to our law.

This is all that is worth noting about the Topasses; and I hope this description will give you satisfaction.

LETTER XVI.

Description of the St. Thomas or Syrian Christians—Their Priests—means of bringing them back to the right way—Their antiquity, and history.

The Christian world in general, and you especially who write Church histories, take great interest in the progress of Christianity among the Heathen through the efforts of Gospel preachers: it will therefore be not inappropriate in the present epistle to give you a veracious account of the St. Thomas' Christians, such as I have been enabled to gather partly from personal enquiry and partly from their own writings, leaving out of sight the narratives of other persons.

To have a clear notion of the people in question, you must understand that all the Christians in Malabar are divisible into three classes[1], viz., the Europeans, the principal of whom are the Portuguese, the English, and the Dutch; the Topasses, who spring from mixed races of whites and Indians, and the Native Christians of unmixed race. These last are again divided into the new Christians, consisting mostly of converts from the low castes, made by the Portuguese priests after their arrival in this country, and known by the names of *Cascargas*, *Mocquas*, *Quilon Karas*, etc., and the old Christians[2] called Christians of St. Thomas, of whom it is my purpose here to speak. We must first notice their different appellations; for they are sometimes called St. Thomas' Christians, and sometimes Syrian Christians. The former name is derived without doubt from the Apostle St. Thomas[3], who is

1. Note 1, p. 443.
2. Note 2, pp. 443—444.
3. Note 3, pp. 444—479.

said to have preached the Gospel in these parts; a tale, in my opinion, not to be scoffed at; seeing that it is asserted in the traditions of the old Christians both of Malabar and of Coromandel, which agree in indicating a certain spot where he preached. These people are also frequently called Syrians because, for several centuries before the arrival of the Portuguese, their Churches have existed under the government of Syrian Bishops who have been sent out up to the present time, and they make use of the Syriac version of the Bible.

Among these St. Thomas' Christians may be distinguished, on the one hand, those who have remained constant to their first faith, and on the other hand the Apostates, not few in number, who have embraced the doctrines of Rome. The Papists call the first class schismatics, and place them in the same category with the Christians of the Greek Church: but we might with much more justice apply that term to the second class, who have abandoned the faith of their fathers.

The St. Thomas Christians living along the mountain range have many Churches there: but of these several were seized by the Roman Catholics in the time of the Portuguese, and in some the service is performed by Syrians and Papists indifferently, not a little to the grief of the former, who are scandalized at the multiplicity of images introduced by their rivals. Of this feeling I was myself a witness at Tekkenkoer, where on my entrance into the sacred edifice, the Bishop then in residence gave vent to his abhorrence of them. They resemble the other inhabitants of Malabar in costume, but wear more clothing[1]. A veil or cloth is often worn above the forhead, wound round the hair. Their dwellings are separate from those of the other inhabitants, consisting of hamlets or villages in which they live together, the houses being small and mean. It seems that they keep very strict genealogical records and they will neither marry nor in any way intermingle with the new low caste Christians being themselves mostly *Castade Nairos* that is, nobility of the Nair caste, in token of which they generally carry a sword in the hand, as a mark of dignity.

Their priests or teachers mostly wear white linen trousers hanging wide over the knee, and over them an ample robe of white linen or some other material, descending to the knees. On their heads they generally wear a black cap shaped like a sugar loaf. The neck is adorned with a rosary of white coral, and in the hand they carry a painted cane, much longer than our walking sticks. Like the heathen they generally go barefoot, knowing nothing of shoes and stockings. They are uncultivated and ignorant

1. Note 4, p. 480.

of the manners of society, being in this respect inferior to the Topass priests who have become accustomed to Europeans, and know something of the acts of courtesy.

Besides their priests, the St. Thomas' Christians have Bishops who exercise supreme jurisdiction over their churches. At present there are two, Mar Gabriel and Mar Thomas, who do not agree well together, as each of them, especially the latter, claims authority over the other. Mar Gabriel, a white man, and sent hither from Bagdad, is aged and venerable in appearance, and dresses nearly in the same fashion as the Jewish priests of old, wearing a cap fashioned like a turban, and a long white beard. He is courteous and God-fearing, and not at all addicted to extravagant pomp. Round his neck he wears a golden crucifix. He lives with the utmost sobriety, abstaining from all animal food. His house, rather a large one for the habits of the Malabar people, is situated on a hill in the kingdom of Tekkenkoer. He holds the Nestorian doctrine respecting the union of the two natures in our Saviour's person. Mar Thomas, the other Bishop, is a native of Malabar. He is a black man, dull and slow of understanding. He lives in great state; and when he came into the city to visit the Commandant, he was attended by a number of soldiers bearing swords and shields, in imitation of the Princes of Malabar. He wears on his head a silken cowl, embroidered with crosses, in form much resembling that of the Carmelites. He is a weak-minded rhodomontader, and boasted greatly to us of being an Eutychian in his creed, accusing the rival Bishop of heresy. According to his own account, he has forty-five churches under his own authority, the remainder adhering to Bishop Gabriel. And thus we see that these St. Thomas' Christians are divided into two parties, a circumstance of which the Romish priests do not fail to take advantage.

A closer examination of these people will convince us that they are Christians rather in name than in reality. The Priests themselves are stolid and ignorant, most of them unable to read more than certain formularies setting forth their times of prayer and other duties. Nor can any correct account be given at the present day, of their confession of faith, their services being a medley, partly borrowed from the heathens among whom they live and whose fellow countrymen they are ; partly from the Papists, to whom very many of them have gone over, and with whom they have several churches in common ; and partly from the Greek or Syrian Christians, by whose Bishops they are governed, and whose opinions they adopt. I have witnessed their celebration of the Lord's Supper. The consecration was performed in the native language, by a priest before the altar, with a number of ceremonies in this respect resembling the Romish mass; but in essentials they are orthodox, as they do not allow that the bread is changed with the body of the Lord, and affirm that it is broken only in remembrance of His death. They likewise give the cup to the laity, though their method of distributing the elements differs slightly from ours, the Priest taking the bread and dipping it into the wine, and then placing the pieces in the mouths of the Communicants one after the other. They receive kneeling, with napkins round their necks.

It would not be impracticable to bring over these people into the right way by suitable measures. But this is not a work to be accomplished by a Chaplain whose duties are assigned to the town of Cochin; for these people dwell in the mountains and are rarely seen except when they come in to procure necessaries. A knowledge of the Malabar language, the only one they speak, would also be indispensable, and this language is very difficult, and requires a man's entire devotion to it, having a great abundance of words and letters, of the latter no less than fifty-one. It is moreover divided into three dialects; the Tamil, which is the easiest, and is spoken in Ceylon and Coromandel; the common Malabar, spoken in the parts, and the *Twankerdamish* 1, the language of the learned, in which the Brahmins write the mysteries of their religion.

Should the East India Company at any time seriously undertake the conversion of these peoples, it would be requisite to send out two or three young students of Divinity, well instructed in the Syriac tongue, to reside among them, having with them interpreters, through whom they might acquire an adequate knowledge of the native language and be enabled to use it in their preaching. There should also be a Seminary at Ceylon for the instruction of native youths, and their training as preachers. It need not be supposed that the people would be averse to such a measure; for besides the claim it would give them to the Company's protection, they shew their favourable disposition even now, by offering their children to be educated by us. This I know from my own experience. When I had discussed the principal doctrines of our Faith with the Bishop of whom I spoke before, he was so much pleased that he wished to entrust me on the spot with two youths to be brought up in accordance with those doctrines. Some of these Christians, when they visit Cochin, offer me their customary salutations with every appearance of esteem. Perhaps too, the Company's interests might really be furthered by the course suggested; seeing that these people, besides being numerous, are generally speaking of a martial turn; not to mention that the principal pepper merchants who supply the Company, are to be found among them.

It will not be useless, nor will you take it amiss, if I include in this letter a somewhat remarkable account of the origin and spread of Christianity in Malabar[1], which has been sent me by Bishop Mar Gabriel, written in the Syriac language. The title runs as follows:—"The antiquity of the Syrian Christians, and Historical events relating to them."

"Fifty-two years after the birth of the Messiah, the Holy Apostle Thomas arrived at Maliapore on the coast of Coromandel preaching the Gospel and founding churches there. Passing from thence to Malabar, the holy man landed on the island of Maliankarre, (situated between Cranganore and Paroe), preached and taught, and built churches in that island, and likewise at Cottacay, Repolym, Gokkomangalam, Pernetta, and Tirocusngotta; and having finished his work in these parts and ordained two priests, returned to the land of the Pandies (as the natives of Coromandel are called) to teach the people there. But whilst he was thus occupied, the Apostle was pierced by the Heathens with spears and thus ended his life. In the course of a few years all the priests in Hindostan and Malabar, died; and many years afterwards, a *Tovenaar* called Mamukawasser, an enemy to the Christian faith, arrived at Maliapore, performing many miracles to hinder its progress. And many of the principal Christians giving heed to him, forsook Christianity and followed this false teacher Mamukawasser. In those days certain persons came from Hindowy or Hindostan, who were not disposed to abandon the people of Malabar, and who allied themselves with the believers, that is, the Christians, who had remained constant, in number about 160 families or tribes. These men taught for many years in Malabar, but there were few among them who had knowledge, because they were destitute of pastors; and therefore most of them ended in becoming heathens, and had all things in common with the other heathens. This caused a second apostacy; so that out of the 160 families, 96 adopted the heathen superstitions, 64 only adhering to the true faith. Now in those days there appeared a vision to an Archpriest, at Oerghai, in consequence whereof certain merchants were sent from Jerusalem by command of the Catholic authorities in the East, to see whether there were here any Nazarenes or Christians. These persons have arrived here with ships, joined all the Christians from Maliankarre, as far as Tierowangotta, treated them as brothers and strengthened them in the faith; and having taken leave of the 64 families, set sail and returned to Jerusalem, and related to the Catholics in that place their adventures in Malabar. After this,

1. Note 5, pp 480—491.

several priests, students, and Christian women and children came hither from Bagdad, Nineveh, and Jerusalem by order of the Catholic Archpriest at Oerghai, arriving in the year of the Messiah 745, in company with the merchant Thomas: and having made acquaintance with the 64 families, they became united and lived in concord one with another. At this time the famous Emperor Cheram Peroumal was reigning over the whole of Malabar. To him the new comers went, and when they informed him of the cause of their arrival, the king was well pleased, and gave them pieces of ground in the territory of Cranganore to build churches and shops upon, that they might pursue their trades, at the same time he granted the Christians royal marks of honour, and permission to carry on their trade throughout the whole country so long as the sun and moon should shine, as may be seen to this day in their documents written upon copper plates.[1] In consequence of this, the Christians possess in the territory of Cranganore East, West, North and South, several churches, besides 472 shops and dwelling houses built round them; and they lived in peace and unity for several years. In this period, by order of the Catholic Patriarch of the East, many great teachers arrived in Malabar, from Bagdad, Nineveh, Jerusalem and several other places, who assumed authority over the Christians of the country. This state of things lasted until a separation took place among the Christians of Cranganore, in the year of our Lord 823, and then Mar Saboor, Mar Botoe, and Seboor Isso, came to Quilon as teachers. They went to visit the King Sjak Rawiosti, with presents and built churches and shops at Quilon. In these and similar ways, the chief pastors came, teaching and instructing the people of Malabar. In the year 1500, when the Portuguese first appeared in Malabar, where they afterwards obtained a footing, there came, by order of the Catholic Patriarch, four teachers, by name Mar Mardina, Mar Jacob, Mar Thoma and Jene Allay, who governed the Christians and built many churches. After the death of these four teachers, another, called Mar Abraham came to Malabar about the year 1550, whereupon the Portuguese passed a decree that henceforth no Catholic teachers should come thither, and placed guards everywhere to seize and put to death all who should attempt it. Mar Abraham was captured, but escaped through God's mercy, and continued to teach for many years, and built several churches; after which, he went the way of all flesh. After that time the road was closed to the Syrian priests, and the Christians experienced a want of pastors; which the Portuguese perceiving, a Vicegerent and Bishop called Alexio, came to the city of Cochin in the name of, and with authority from the Pope of Rome. This Bishop took a great deal of trouble to bring the Syrian

1. Note 7, pp. 492—503.

Christians into subjection, and seeing no chance of effecting his object, the Portuguese gave to the King of Cochin 30,000 ducats, and with the help of His Highness persecuted the Christians who dwelt in his dominions, for three whole years. The Christians then, unable to endure the persecution longer, submitted to the Bishop, and thus became reconciled with the Portuguese. Shortly afterwerds the Syrian manners and customs underwent a change: the priests were forbidden to marry; and for about 55 years the Syrians followed the same customs as the Portuguese. In the meantime a priest called Mar Matti came to Maliapore sent by the Catholic Patriarch. The Portuguese apprehended him and brought him into the city, and afterwards dragged him to the harbour and cast him into the water. On hearing this, the Christians of Malabar assembled in the church of Mar Tancheri, took counsel together, bound themselves by oath, and thus threw off the Portuguese yoke from their necks; having first written and signed a letter declaring that from that time forward and for ever, they would have nothing more to do, for good or evil, with the Portuguese. Meanwhile the Portuguese Bishop went to Cranganore, wrote secretly to the Cassanarios and Christians, and sent messengers with presents consisting of fine silk stuffs, gold ornaments and jewels; and those who were allured by these things and also by fair words and promises, went over secretly to that Bishop. The Portuguese and those who belonged to their party, filled the hands of the Prince in whose country the Sryian Christians dwelt, with gifts and materially injured the latter by sundry vexations, confiscations and deeds of violence. And in the days of this persecution, the upright, God-fearing, justice loving, and peaceable Dutch were sent to Malabar by the inspiration of Almighty God and by order of the East India Company, under the command of the noble Lord Admiral Ryklop Van Goens, and like as the heathen were driven out of the land of Isso Biranon Kinan [Canaan ?] so have they driven the worse than heathen Portuguese out of Cochin and other cities and fortresses of Malabar; and through Divine Providence and Syrian Christians have been from that time forward protected and defended from them, and their pastors have again visited this country without let or hindrance. In the beginning of the year 1700, the Bishop Mar Symons, sent by the Catholic Patriarch of the East, arrived in India, being appointed to Malabar. This man gave notice of his intended arrival by letters to the Syrian Christians, which happening to fall into the hands of the Carmelites and Jesuits, they accordingly placed sentinels every-where, captured the Bishop, and led him prisoner to Pondicherry where they kept him in irons. After him, in the year 1705, the chief teacher, Mar

Gabriel, came to this land; and since that time most of the Syrians have adopted the church customs of the Portuguese, subjecting themselves to several ceremonies, and condemning the marriage of the priests; and that out of the 64 churches, twenty have remained on the side of the Carmelites, and 44 on that of the Syrians: but as we enjoy the favour of the Lord Commandant, we hope that all this will be restored to the old footing, and this is what we now humbly pray of His Excellency and his Council trusting that they will not turn away their face from us. And therefore we pray God to spare them in good health and all welfare and to give them blessing and prosperity."

LETTER XVII.

Of the Roman Catholic Priests in Malabar, and their Converts among the Heathen.

The Christians of Malacca, Coromandel and Malabar are mostly of the Romish persuasion, with the exception of a small number of our co-religionists, consisting chiefly of Dutch, and their descendants of mixed race. In each of these countries there is but one Reformed minister, while thousands of Romish priests are found along this coast, covering the land like locusts: most of them are very poor, as their churches here do not possess the incomes they enjoy in Europe, and their congregations are generally indigent. These priests are of two classes, the natives and the Europeans, of whom the last are most respected.

You may judge of their power in Malabar, when you hear that that country contains one Archbishop and two Bishops. The Archbishop has authority over the Christians in the mountain district, from which he derives his title; his residence is generally at Ambekatti, a few leagues from Cochin. The present prelate is a Jesuit, a Spaniard by descent, named Antonio Peimental. Another Jesuit enjoys the title of Bishop of Cochin; he lives at Quilon. These two prelates receive their appointments from the King of Portugal, the Pope confirming them; as we may suppose they are the craftiest spies of the Portuguese monarch, prying into the affairs of the company, and imbuing the natives with deep aversion to the Dutch. The company has no power to drive them out, not possessing any authority in these countries. We cannot but wonder at the manner in which our former commandants received these priests ; they saluted them with a display of arms and firing of cannon, shewing to them the same honours as to Kings, thereby grieving all true protestants, whilst the Romanist were extremely delighted, to see their Bishops so much more honoured than our chaplains. Any one can see with what purpose this was done, who remembers how selfishness and love of money prevail throughout the world. Another abuse existed under the government of Commandant Ketel, namely, that the Romish priests were allowed not only to visit condemned criminals of their persuasion in Cochin, but even to accompany them to the scaffold. The present Commandant, Hertenberg, who is a man of noble character, and extremely averse to such proceedings has done away with these irregularities, and restrains their insolence.

Besides these two Bishops there is another, who styles himself Bishop of Cranganoor, and the surrounding districts; he is a Carmelite, appointed by the Pope alone, and is under the Company's protection ; the States General having conceded to the Emperor the right to appoint such a prelate, which right he has handed over to the Pope.

There is no fear lest this Bishop should make common cause with the Portuguese. On the contrary, he has always been their enemy, for the Portuguese King having assumed the right of ecclesiastical patronage, cannot quietly see a Bishop settled here without his consent ; so that this prelate and his clergy shun the Portuguese, knowing that they would gladly get rid of them and send them back to Europe. The Portuguese, and the Jesuits combine also to intercept their letters from Europe, as well as the money which is sent them from Rome. In consequence these clergy are always at variance with the Portuguese Bishops, and a wise Commandant with due caution, might through them discover the measures of the Portuguese clergy. The residence of this Bishop and his Priests is at Warapoli, three leagues from Cochin, where they have a convent and a neat church.

There is no likelihood of their making many adherents, for their proverty causes them to be held in small esteem by the native princes ; whilst the Jesuits, on the contrary, are rich and astute in all their proceedings, and have consequently acquired great influence over that venal race.

From this description you will understand the present state of Christianity in Malabar, where superstition reigns supreme, and no human means can be devised to spread the Reformed faith among the native Papists ; partly, because they are stupid and incapable of understanding any reasoning , and partly because the Romish Missionaries have roused in them a mortal hatred against our religion, which they carry to such an extent, that they will not dignify us with the name of Christians, always meaning a Roman Catholic when they speak of a "Christiano". They invented a thousand calumnies against us, such as, that we deny the Divinity of Christ, etc., and tell all manner of fictions to mislead the ignorant people. Thus a certain Portuguese General, van Timor, who was at Batavia, had the effrontery to assert that he had seen there one of the greatest miracles in the world for the conversion of heretics ; namely how a stone cross grew on a bench outside a certain house in the Roemalakken, and as often as it was cut down, sprung up again of itself ; now it is certain that this is as great a lie as can be, for I and thou sands besides, have walked through that street every day, without seeing anything of the kind. In the same way, I was asked by a Lutheran merchant of Hamburgh, who had come from Portugal to Goa, and thence to Tellicherri, whether there was here a miraculous arch, for he had been told as a certain truth, that there was such a Portuguese building, which the Commandant had sent several men to destroy without success, and had at length placed guns before it to shatter it, but it still remained standing ; and when I made a face at the story, he answered that it was believed by the most intelligent people in the place.

You will wish perhaps to know the further reason why the Romish religion is spread so widely over the coast of India while our reformed faith has struck such small roots there.

First, you must observe, what I have mentioned before, the great number of Romish Priests in this country, both those who have been brought up here, and those who came from other places, especially Goa, which may be called the mother and seminary of the Romish Priests in India. Half the population indeed of the city consists of clergy, who are much more numerous there than soldiers, and are not only sent from Europe in ships each containing 40 or 50 of various orders, but are also ordained at Goa itself in great numbers ; and as it is impossible for them all to obtain a livelihood there, they spread themselves throughout the whole country. In the islands, on the contrary, where the East India Company are masters of the seacoast, few or no Roman Catholics are found ; and the Company have there several chaplains and seminaries, for the instruction of youth, which do not exist in these parts.

Secondly, we must take into consideration, that the Romish worship is much more attractive to those who are converted from Heathenism, than the reformed ; for where the latter commands men to worship God in spirit and in truth, the former has rites and ceremonies resembling those of the heathens. They both worship images, though those of the papist are beautiful, and those of the heathens frightful and monstrous ; both have their saints or minor deities, both have lights in their churches, both make vows to their images and adorn them with flowers ; and this great similarity, no doubt, makes the transition to the Romish persuasion easy to these people.

In the third place we must add, that except the St. Thomas' Christians, all those who are converted by the Roman Catholics are either the slave children of Christians, like most of the Topasses, or of the lowest sort of Heathens, none being higher than Chegos. Few Brahmins, Chetriahs or Sudras adopt their religion ; indeed, we might suppose that the low-castes do so generally in order to escape the contempt in which they are held by their nation, for when they become Christians they are more esteemed, and may even come to the palaces which they might never approach before. There are also many among these new Christians, who come over to that religion, because they have lost caste, and are dishonoured among their own people ; a class of persons who would not be lightly received among us. The priests also make very little circumstance about the baptism of these new Christians, for they merely ask whether they believe in Christ or in the Holy Church, or can say the Apostles' creed, and then baptize them at once ; and as the people know well enough that we should not act in that manner, but should ask them their reasons for wishing to become Christians, and teach them diligently, they do not come to us, Besides, seeing that the great mass of blacks are papists they follow their example, thinking blindly that to possess the mere name of Christian is enough. We may add another reason namely, that the Romanists baptize slaves and the children of slaves, thus making them nominal Christians ; whilst among us baptism is only administered to those whose parents are Christians.

LETTER XVIII.

Of the Jews, Black and White.

One of your letters, dated from Harlinger, has at length reached me. It seems that place is more favoured than West Kappel, for the letters you sent from thence have never come to hand, Perhaps they were sent by sailors who found no opportunity to deliver them safely, so that they were passed on from one ship to another without ever entering the bay, or perhaps the letters have been thrown into the great bay at Penang or elsewhere, where, after being kept a year unclaimed, they would be burnt.

Jews are found here, and in many other places on the vast coast of India, as they are almost all over the world. They are not, however, to be met with in the neighbouring islands, nor at Java, Sumatra, Celebes, Amboyna, Banda, or Ceylon. A colony of them is domiciled on this coast, who, according to their own account, came here after the destruction of the second temple, which is the era from which they date: thus this present year (1723), is with them the year 1657[1].

Since this period about a thousand Jews, men, women and children, have settled in Malabar, fixing their abodes at Cannanore, Nagorne, Malai, and Porivarem. For some centuries they were unfortunate enough; but their situation improved in the reign of Cheramperoumal, that Monarch having granted them certain privileges, which were inscribed on copper, and are still preserved.[2] I have seen a copy of them [3]; they consist of certain frivolous grants[4], such as permission to use trumpets and drums, sedans and similar trifles, which are much thought of in this country. He also placed over them a Jew named Joseph Rabban, who as well as his successors received the title of Chiramand Mappela; *i. e.*, the merchant whose office it is to furnish the Emperor's lamps with wicks, which must be regarded as a tribute paid to the monarch in acknowledgment for the dignity. The word *Mappela* does not express any supreme or independent authority.

I have been told, but I will not vouch for the truth of the story, that these merchants wished to purchase with a large sum of money, from one of the princes of Malabar, the entire supremacy over their own nation, and that the bargain was nearly completed, when the monarch hearing from other quarters that the Jews had no large independent possessions in any part of the world, refused their demand. These white Jews came to a place called by the Portuguese *Sinhora Savod'e*, about half a league distant from the town of Cochin, where they maintained themselves for fifty years; but being unable to endure any longer the offensive vicinity of the Moors, and still more of the Christians who keep unclean animals in their houses, they obtained from the Rajah of Cochin a piece of ground near his palace, on which to build their houses[5]. Here they have dwelt now for 202 years, but the place being small, their houses are poor and huddled together; they are chiefly built of stone, and covered with tiles.

1. Note 1. pp. 504—500.
2. Note 2, p. 506.
3. Note 3, pp 506—514.
4. Note 4, pp. 514—515.
5. Note 5, pp. 515—521.

At the present time they have a Jewish chief, appointed by the Rajah of Cochin with the title of Modeliar[1] who bears as a sign of his dignity, a wand with a silver knob; a kind of staff which both the Rajah and the Company give to any one whom they wish to honour, or who is appointed to certain offices, such as that of merchant to the Company. The Modeliar has power to enforce some punishments, and to impose and remit fines, subject to the Rajah's judgment; but great and capital causes are tried by the Rajah himself. The Company has however some jurisdiction over them.

I have enquired of the principal persons among these Jews the reason why they have kept so few records of the history of their nation here. Their answer has been that their records had been torn from them by the Portuguese in the year 1662, when that people devastated their synagogue, and deprived them of their privileges, because they had supplied the Dutch with provisions during their unsuccessful siege of the city.

The Black and White Jews[2] inhabit the same district, the latter occupying the banks of the river. The white are much richer and more powerful than the black, who are mostly of slave race, and amount, I have been told, to 2,000 souls in Malabar. The number of white Jews who have of late come here from Europe, Bagdad, and Cairo is small[3]; but there are some also who have been settled here for many centuries. They try as much as possible to prevent inter-marriages with the black Jews, although these sometimes take place. The two races possess also separate synagogues[4]; and the blacks have a dark coloured Rabbi who must stand back if a white one enters, and must resign to him the honour of performing divine service in the synagogue. On the other hand, when the black Rabbis enter the synagogue of the whites, which is a very superior one, they must only be hearers. There has been lately a great dispute between the two races: the black wishing to compel the white Jewesses to keep their heads uncovered, like their own women, and trying to persuade the Rajah to enforce such a rule. The dispute ended, however, with permission given to every one, both men and women, to wear what they chose.[5]

The Jews make no objection to selling their slaves who are not of their own religion to other nations, obliging them, however, when sold, to abandon the use of the Jewish cap, which they had

1. Note 6, pp. 521—523.
2. Note 7, pp. 523—527.
3. Note 8, p. 527.
4. Note 9, pp. 527—528.
5. Note 10, pp. 528—531.

before worn on their heads. But slaves, male or female, once fully admitted into their religion by the performance of the customary rites, can never be sold to a stranger. The black Jews trade chiefly in poultry, eggs and butter; but the whites, who trade with the Company, sell more valuable commodities.

Thus, my brother, you see the Divine prophecies confirmed in the far East, where the curse upon this stiff-necked people is heavy upon them, as it is in Europe, and the veil is still before their face; while they look in vain for a Messiah, and now begin to despair of their expectation, for there are some here who venture to say that possibly the Messiah for whom Isreal has been longing for so many centuries, was never promised at all.

And now, my worthy brother, I long sorely to see you and our dear parents once more. Oh, when will that day arrive! perhaps never. My desires to re-visit my beloved fatherland are ceaseless and all the enjoyments I have here cannot satisfy them. Others may say, our country is wherever we are well off, but the force of nature goes beyond all that. It would seem as though our frames have a perpetual attraction to the land where we first drew breath, and that being formed of the very dust which is found there, they seek it as their own element, and are mysteriously thus drawn to it. You will say perhaps that in some respects this ardent wish of mine is unreasonable, as I have here every requisite for temporal comfort. It would be ingratitude to deny it. Yet, my brother, our happiness does not depend on these things, as is sometimes imagined. It is true I find my house filled with slaves, my table loaded with delicacies: but I am not the happier for it, for the multitude of slaves breaks the head, and twenty do not now serve me so well as six or seven did formerly. And why? because they put their work off upon each other's shoulders. and those who are sent to put things straight only make matters worse. Can you expect anything else from savages? and yet, oh foolish vanity! the law of fashion forces us to submit to all this. Our food, delicately dressed in various ways, is generally insipid, and a dish from our old fatherland would be considered a banquet here. And how can any kind of food help us, when appetite, its only sauce, is wanting, as is the case with me and with thousands besides, for the heat of the sun and the climate is such that we seldom know the feeling of hunger. But of all these grievances I think but little, compared to that of the absence of my dear parents. You know that love despises everything but its object. Meantime may every Divine blessing attend you.

LETTER XIX.

Account of the Moors in Malabar.

As the population of Malabar, includes members of various religions, we are not surprised to find among them a race of Moors, who profess the faith of Mahomet [1]. They deserve our attention the more, that they were the chief foes the Portuguese had to contend with on their first landing on these coasts, for as commerce had hitherto remained solely in their hands, they disputed any share in it being usurped by the new comers [2]. They, being like the St. Thomas' Christians, born in this land, might be in one sense regarded as natives of Malabar, but as they have mingled with other members of their faith, Moguls, Turks and Arabs, who resort to the country for purposes of trade, they form in some sort a distinct people.[3]

Like the Portuguese here, their disposition is naturally inclined to cruelty and malice. In costume they resemble the natives, the beard, which they alone wear, forming their distinguishing mark, and they also usually carry some weapon, sword or cutlass. There are but few wealthy merchants among the Moors in the neighbourhood of Cochin, who are for the most part in small circumstances; their dwellings, which lie on the banks of the river, beyond the Jews' locality, are built of stone, and are mostly small and mean. The people are held altogether in small estimation here, and are but little employed in the commercial transactions of the East India Company.

On the other hand, they are very influential at Calicut, and indeed are almost the masters of the place. The chief merchant there is always attended by a large suite of his compatriots, who are armed with sword and shield, in imitation of the pomp and parade of the native princes [4]. The East India Compay make every year an agreement with him for turmeric, of which he usually furnishes 100 kandies to the Commissioners there.

The most powerful of all the Moors, who may be regarded almost as an independent prince, resides at Cannanore. He is entitled Ali Rajah,[5] king of the islands, being the lawful sovereign of all the Laccadives which were ceded to him by Colastri. Being descended from the ancient house of Colastri, he is indeed a scion of the royal family, but having embraced Mahometanism, he forfeited his right of successisn to the kingdom in Malabar. But he

1. Note 1, p. 532.
2. Note 2, pp. 532—533.
3. Note 3, pp. 533—537.
4. Note 4, pp. 537—538.
5. Note 5, pp. 538—544.

has sufficient territories in his possession, among which the Laccadives are the most considerable; and as a testimony of the above-mentioned cession to these islands a new Ali Rajah must always receive his crown from the reigning Rajah of Colastri. His Turkish or Moorish appellation is Mahomet Ali Caauw. Although he has embraced the Mussulman faith, the Malabar laws of succession hold good in his domains, the sister's son being his rightful successor.

Ali Rajah has a large and handsome bazaar, where most of the Moors in his dominions reside. This bazaar extends on one side nearly to the bay, and on the other is within reach of the Company's fort and cannon. It is itself sufficiently fortified with walls and artillery to enable it to resist the attacks of the heathens. The Moorish Rajah carries on a considerable traffic with Mocha, Persia, Surat and other places, and owns several vessels. The East India Company trade with him at Cannanore, in cardamom and turmeric. They indeed derived considerable benefit from his friendship on their first settlement in Malabar, when they were at war with the Portuguese ; and a treaty for mutual protection was entered into between them. Last year (1722), a great quarrel arose between Ali Rajah and the people of Colastri, which ended in open war. It originated in some private dispute ; a party of Moors slew some Nairs, and the latter in revenge killed as many Moors as they could lay hands on. At length the Moors, hearing that a prince of the house of Colastri was about to pass the bazaar on his journey to the Court of the Zamorin, intercepted him, put his retinue to rout, and inflicted disgrace on him by publicly flogging him in the Bazaar. An insult so gross offered to one of their own race so enraged the Rajahs that they laid siege to the bazaar, and several conflicts took place; the English always supporting the party of Colastri, and furnishing them with all necessaries of war, on condition, it is said, that if the bazaar was conquered and the Moors compelled, the English should have a factory there. Our Company remained neutral, only permitting the Moors to purchase ammunition, etc., in the city. The siege lasted a long time within sight of the fort of Cannanore, which retained its neutrality, merely warning the belligerents not to carry on their combats within reach of its artillery. But when the Malabars, finding their attempts on the opposite side fruitless, proceeded to assault the bazaar in a quarter where they were within range of the fort, our garrison finding their warnings disregarded, fired a volly among them, which destroyed numbers, and obliged the rest to beat a hasty retreat. After this occurrence the siege proceeded slowly, till at length the parties concluded a treaty, (through the mediation, it is said, of the

English Governor of Calicut, (Mr. Adams), which was highly disadvantageous to the Moors; they being compelled to pay a large sum of money to Colastri for the expenses of the war, leaving some gardens in pledge till this was done, and also to permit him to retain a fortified village on the further side, the guns of which would command the bazaar.[1]

The Portuguese and Moors nourish a rooted hatred towards each other,[2] which commenced at the first arrival of the former in India, and still endures. It is perceptible even when they are at peace. In the year 1720 the Portuguese, meeting a ship belonging to Ali Rajah which was conveying money and horses from Mocha, attacked it, under the pretext that no one had the right of transporting horses but themselves: and although the vessel had a Dutch passport, they captured it and brought it into the harbour of Cochin. On hearing this, Ali Rajah despatched twenty well-manned vessels to pursue the Portuguese, who were discovered in the harbour with the captured ship. The Portuguese Commander, or *Capitano di Marre Guerre*, overcome with terror, fell at the feet of the Dutch Commandant and implored his protection. The latter, moved to compassion by his deep humiliation, charged the Moors to refrain from hostilities in the harbour, and it was mutually agreed that an officer should be appointed by each party to report the event to their superiors, and that in the meantime no hostilities should take place. Shortly after this, a Portuguese named Alba Bordo entered the roadstead, without any salute, and in spite of this compact treacherously stole off with the captured vessel, taking the mate with him.

This treachery against all human laws so incensed the Commandant that he detained two Portuguese Captains who were on land, and not prepared for a sudden flight; and then sent word to the Viceroy, who was compelled to restore the ship and her merchandize in order to obtain his officers' liberty.

Another event happened at Tanoor last year, which arose from the following cause:—A certain Moor had invited some Danes to trade with him; the Portuguese Resident not approving of this, strengthened with a troop of Nairs, expelled the Danes, and caused the Moor who had called them in, to be bound to a stake and beaten. This so enraged the Moors that they resolved to take violent revenge. The Resident Bibero happening to die soon after, the Viceroy appointed in his place his son-in-law, Felisco dos Santos. The offended Moors took an opportunity one day when the

1. Note 6, p. 544

2. Note 7, pp. 544—548.

new Resident had gone out for a walk to enter his house secretly and to maltreat his two children in such a manner that they died within two days. Having made a complaint of this at Goa, a ship of war was despatched to his assistance in the beginning of January, conveying troops, who after landing put all the Moors they met to death, and proceeded to plunder and burn their houses. The Moors were obliged for the time to submit; but as soon as the Portuguese had departed they vented their fury on the native Christians, laid waste their houses and gardens, pulled down their church, and even compelled a slave belonging to the Resident to adopt their religion, which was an infraction of the treaty. Meantime the Resident and his wife retired to Cochin. The Zamorin however offers reparation and satisfaction, which will perhaps appease the quarrel.

The extension of the Mahometan doctrines on this coast took place in early times[1], if we are to believe certain Malabar records in the Arabic language. According to them, some emissaries came here so far back as the reign of Cheramperoumal, when Mahomet was in his 57th year, and so entirely persuaded the Emperor of the Divine mission of their Prophet, and he resolved to go in person to visit him. Cheramperoumal died, however, on his journey, but not till he had taken care by letters which he addressed before his death to the Rajas of Malabar, that all freedom should be allowed the Mahometan teachers to propagate their religion, make disciples and build temples through the whole country. This they did with equal zeal and success; so that within a few years their false creed had struck deep root here. The narration I have followed is however filled with trifles and does not hang well together, so I will not detain you longer with it[2].

---

1. Note 8, pp. 548—553.
2. Note 9, A note on the appearance, dress, ornaments, etc. of the Mappillas.

Visscher's
LETTERS FROM MALABAR.

LETTER IX.

Account of the royal houses of Malabar, Travancore, Cochin, the Zamorin, and Colastri—Disagreements existing between them.

In a previous letter, I have explained the laws of succession which obtain in Malabar, from which you have gathered that the supreme authority never rests with females, their laws in this respect resembling those of France. Great honour indeed is paid to the princesses, ample possessions set apart for them, and they are provided with a retinue of Nairs. And, as in case of a failure of heirs to the crown, the Rajah may not adopt a successor without the consent of the princesses, it has sometimes happened that by refusing this, they have for a time held the reins of Government. An instance of this occurred in the family of Signati, in which a Ranee reigned for several years: this, properly speaking, was but an interregnum. In some cases, again, the princesses and the other tributary Rajas cannot agree as to whom they shall admit into the royal family[1].

There are four principal royal houses in Malabar, those of Travancore, Cochin, the Zamorin and Colastri. In order to get a clear idea of the condition of Malabar, we must examine these in detail: for which purpose we must bear in mind the following rules[2].

First, that these four royal houses consist of princesses, whose sons are in the line of succession to the throne.

Second, that the eldest princess bears the title of queen mother, though it may happen that her son is not the reigning Rajah.

Third, that the minor kingdoms are called by the names of these families.

Fourth, that the first or superior Rajah being a descendant of the oldest princess, is designated by the name of the kingdom to which he belongs, though but a portion of it may be under his rule. The younger Rajahs, descended from the younger sisters,

1. Note 1, pp. 1—3
2. Note 2, pp. 3—5

Barbosa has not evidently grasped correctly the principles of succession to the Malabar kingdoms. Perhaps it is difficult for foreigners to understand a system which is altogether different from what they have ever before come across, and hence one need not be surprised at our author, as also many others, who had better opportunities to understand the system, giving an account of it sometimes altogether unintelligible. Succession, as we have already observed, is in the female line, *i. e.*, a deceased king is succeeded not by the issue of his own loins, but by the issue of his female relatives on the maternal side. The system may be styled the matriarchate in contradistinction to the patriarchate. The next point to be noted is that succession is regulated by *seniority in age among male* members, so long as there are any in the family, irrespective of their being the issue of the eldest female relation on the maternal side of the deceased king. There is nothing in the laws and customs of Malabar which prevents females from succeeding to the throne or governing the country. In default of male members, succession devolves on the eldest female member. Barbosa is wrong in saying that ladies who are not blessed with male children are not considered capable of inheritance. In their turn, they are as much entitled to succeed as any who have given birth to male children. These ladies, however, are not precluded from adopting some male relative of a collateral branch and investing him with the government. But they are not bound to do so. They may all choose to govern in turn till it comes to the last, when, to save the line from extinction, females of collateral branches with issue or with the possibility of having issue may be adopted, as also males, in which case the eldest male, if a major, takes up the reins of government. Neither is our author correct in saying that the period during which a Rāṇi, *i. e.*, a Queen, who reigned for several years in Signaty or Quilon was properly speaking but an interregnum.

The paucity of male members does not create any interregnum at all. The last male is at once succeeded by the eldest living female in full right. This was exemplified in Travancore when, on the death of the Raja Bāla Rāma Varma, in the year 1810, leaving only two ladies, who were themselves but adoptees into the royal house, the eldest of them, Rāṇi Gauri Lakṣhmi Bāyi, succeeded as "the direct and legitimate heir to the vacant musnad." Her right was disputed by a collateral uncle, but the claim was disallowed, "and the young princess was at once crowned under the auspices of the Madras Government, and the Honourable the Court of Directors of the East India Company." When, afterwards, in 1813, a Prince was born to the Rāṇi, the child was proclaimed Raja of Travancore, and the Queen mother continued to govern as regent on behalf of the infant Raja. The Rāṇi herself died two years after, and the Raja being a minor still, his aunt, the late Rāṇi's sister, who had not borne any children, male or female, succeeded as regent till the young Raja attained majority. All the while, and it is a significant fact, that there was no thought of adopting a male into the family to rule over the State. In fact, there has been no instance, so far as now known, in Travancore of male members being ever adopted into the royal family. On the other hand, there have been several instances in Cochin in which both males and females have been in a body affiliated with the reigning house. In Cochin, we have only a single known instance of a Rāṇi ruling the country, and she was set up by the Portuguese against other legitimate heirs to serve their own purpose. Her name was Gangāḍhara Mahā Lakṣhmi.[1]

2. **The Four Rules.** Of the four rules mentioned by our author, the first two are correctly stated. The third can scarcely be called a rule. Neither is it quite

1. A. D. 1665.

accurate to say 'that the minor kingdoms are, as a rule, called by the names of their families.' Of the several minor kingdoms enumerated by our author himself, the families that ruled over them seem to have taken their names from the names of the states. For instance, the maternal house of the Raja of Travancore derives its name from Āttingal, the state over which it ruled. Signati, the family that ruled over Quilon, took its name from Singnati, a Portuguese corruption of Ḍēśinganāḍ, which itself is a corrupted form of Jeyaṭunganāḍ, or Jayasimhanāḍ, the term by which the country ruled over by the family was known in early times. Similarly with respect to some of the other families and states. On the other hand, the States of Elayaṭaswarūpam, Ṭekkankūr, Vaṭakkankūr, etc., seem to have derived their names from the families ruling over them. So that, no general rule of the nature mentioned by our author can be stated with any degree of accuracy.

With regard to the fourth rule, it has to be observed that the first or superior Raja, *i. e.*, the ruling chief, need not necessarily be the descendant of the eldest princess, for, as we have observed, succession to the musnad is regulated by seniority of age among the male members of the family, whether descended from the eldest or the youngest princess. Proximity to the eldest or the youngest princess has nothing to do in the matter of succession. The ruling chiefs are always designated by the name of their kingdoms, as also by certain peculiar dynastic names. Thus, the King of Travancore takes his designation after his kingdom. So also the Kings of Cochin, Calicut and Chirakal. Travancove is also known as Vēṇāṭṭaṭikal and Kulaśēkhara Perumāl. His dynasty is called Vēṇāṭṭu Swarūpam and Śrīpāḍa Swarūpam which, in Malayalam, is corrupted into Ṭṛppāppi Swarūpam. The dynastic name of Cochin is Perumpaṭappu Swarūpam, that of Calicut, Neṭi-Viruppu Swarūpam, and that of Chirakkal, Kōla Swarūpam. The last two are also designated the Ṭāmūṭiri or Kuṅṅalakōnāṭiri and the Kōlaṭṭiri respectively.

The younger Rajas need not necessarily be descended from the younger sisters. They are juniors to the ruling chief in age and might be descended from the elder sisters also. They never lose their family name, but are styled prince so and so of such and such a family. In Travancore the princes are referred to as those born under particular stars of the lunar month.

3. **Molpad.** This term does not denote the 'head'. It is used to designate the eldest female member of the families of certain minor chiefs; for instance, the Punnaṭṭūr Mōlpāḍ.

4. **Attingal Kingdom.** Though the kingdom of Travancore comprehended the various principalities mentioned by our author, those of Āṟṟingal, Signati, Peritaḷḷi and Eḷayaṭa Swarūpams were ruled over by collateral branches of the Travancore Royal house. It is said that the Travancore royal family resided at different places and was commonly known by five different names, viz., Vānavanāṭ or Vēṇāḍ, Śrīvāḷumcōḍe or Ṭiruviṭāmcōḍe, corrupted into modern Travancore, Śrī Pāḍām or Ṭṛppāpūṛ corrupted into Ṭṛppāppi, Śrīwāye, or Cheravāi and Jeyaṭuṅganāḍ, Chenganāḍ, Ḍēśinganāḍ or Jeyasimhanāḍ—Swarūpams. All these Swarūpams, when collectively taken, was styled as Vēṇāṭ, Travancore or Ṭṛppāppūr, and sovereignty was assumed under these three designations only. It is difficult at present to definitely describe the relation between the various principalities above referred to. But there are circumstances which seem to indicate that the senior of all these collateral branches, or the most competent among them, ruled as Kulaśēkhara Perumāḷ.

The origin of the Travancore dynasty is buried in obscurity. Various conjectures have been hazarded for which there is little or no historical data. It is commonly believed that the State came into existence along with other Malabar States at the disruption of the Kērala Empire of Chēramān Perumāl. But the Syrian and Jewish Copper plates belie this. The Revd. S. Mateer observes, on the authority of some native tradition, that the Perumāl "bestowed on his son, Vīra Kērala, the southernmost part of his empire, lying between Quilon and Cape Comorin. This territory decended from Raja Kērala by nephews, according to the custom of Malabar for 300 years * * . The line of rulers descended from Vīra Kērala, son of Chēramān Perumāl, had by this time become extinct. About 1304 A. D., two princesses, said to have been decended from Chēramān Perumāl by another wife took up their residence at Āttingal and established that principality. From them were descended (or adopted according to Hindu Custom) the 33 sovereigns who preceded the present Raja".[1]

Fra Bartolomeo would have us believe that the Travancore Rajas had their origin in the Madura country, and Col Heber Drury endorses it. The Carmelite Father adds that "the Kings of Travancore had hitherto been insignificant princes, whose territories extended only about 15 or 20 miles up the country from Cape Comorin and were besides not very fruitful.[2]

Mr. Shungunny Menon, the author of *A History of Travancore*, claims for the Travancore Family descent from the Chēra dynasty of Kings who ruled over Southern India from very early times. He says that "Chēra is generally recognised as Kērala or Travancore. Many eminent authors, ancient and modern, indiscriminately use the one for the other. In his manuscript translations, Mr. Taylor often writes Chēra

1. *The Land of Charity*, pp. 14—15.

2. P. 171.

for Travancore and *vice versa.* In the collections from *The Asiatic Journals*, the same use of the term is made".[1] He then refers to various other indications, such as the existence of inscriptions on temple walls, in Erode, Coimbatore and Tinnevelly which were once in the kingdom of Chēra, commemorating the names of Chēra or Travancore Kings, etc. These inscriptions take us to comparatively recent times. The relation between the Āttingal and Travancore Princes is undoubted, and the country about Āttingal has been identified by Professor Sundaram Pillai with the *Kupadesam* (Kūpaḍēśam) of early times—a province of the early Chēra or Kēraḷa Empire. Mr. Sundaram Pillai says, "An inscription of Raja Raja Chōḷa, dated in the 30th year of his reign, claims for him a decisive victory over the King of the *Kupakas* (Kūpakas). The Tamil Poem *Kalingatta Parani* (Kalingaṭṭa Parani), of the days of Kulōṭṭunga Chōḷa, enumerates the *Kupakas* (Kūpakas) amongst the subject races that paid tribute to that Emperor. The identification of Āttingal with *Kupadesam* (Kūpaḍēśam) is rendered almost certain by an inscription in the *Apaneswara* (Apānēśwara) temple, about two miles from Āttingal, dated as late as 751 of the Malabar era (A. D. 1576), which speaks of the princess who repaired that shrine as the Queen of the Kūpakas". He also refers to an inscription, dated 389 M. E., to be found on the north-western wall of the temple of Mahāḍēva at Kaṭhinamkuḷam, a place distant by 20 miles from both Trivandrum and Āttingal, in which the Travancore Raja is designated as "Śrī Vīra Iraman Kēraḷa Varma Ṭiruvaṭi of Kīḷppērūr." Now Kīḷppērūr is an old and ruined village, unapproachable by cart or boat, about eight miles to the north-east of Āttingal. The name of Kīḷppērūr is found annexed as the house-name of the Vēṇāḍ princes in later inscriptions also.[2]

1. P. 33.
2. *Some Early Sovereigns of Travancore*, Part 1, pp. 35—37.

The accounts preserved in the archives of the great temple at Trivandrum contain certain entries which lead us to infer that the members of the collateral branches, already named, ruled over their respective possessions and maintained among themselves some sort of union, always submitting to the authority of the temple corporation or *Yogam*. These accounts lend support to the position that members of the various branches have at some time or other ruled over the various tracts indiscriminately. They seem to have formed a cofederacy of states with one or other being supreme at times. We see the term *Tiruvati* used throughout the accounts as an adjunct of the names of the reigning sovereigns of the several branches. It will be remembered that Ibn Batuta in the 14th century calls the King of Quilon simply *Tiruvati*. Another circumstance of some importance is that the house name of Kīlppērūr is also added to the personal designations of the Rajas of the Ṭṛppāppūr, Chervāi, and Ḍēsingaṅāḍ branches.

The chronicles of the Trivandrum temple and the collection of inscriptions made by the Travancore Archæological department bear out the suggestion made here with regard to the interrelation of the various houses that constituted the dynasty of Travancore.

The temple chronicles mention the following names of ruling Princes among others as doing something in connection with the temple on the dates given against them:—

(1) 550 M. E.—Śrī Vīra Iravi Varma Ṭiruvaṭi of Kīlppērūr ruling over Vēṇāḍ.

(2) 557.—Śrī Vīra Mārttāṇda Varma, senior Ṭiruvaṭi of Ṭṛppāppūr.

(3) 644.—Śrī Vīra Mārṭṭāṇḍa Varma of Ḍēsingaṅāḍ Kulasēkharaperumāl.

(4) 673.—Śrī Vīra Iravi Varma of Ṭṛppāppūr Kīḻpperūr, senior Ṭiruvaṭi of Ṭṛppāppūr.

(5) 674.—Along with the above name is mentioned the following, Śrī Vīra Iravi Varma of Ṭṛppāppūr, senior Paṇḍāram (ruler) of Cherawāi.

(6) 704.—Śrī Vīra Mārttāṇḍa Varma of Ḍēśinganāḍ, senior Ṭiruvaṭi of Ṭṛppāppūr.

(7) 713.—Śrī Vīra Kēraḷa Varma of Ḍēśinganāḍ Kīḻpperūr, senior Paṇḍāram of Cherawāi.

(8) 763.—Śrī Vīra Uḍaya Mārttāṇḍa Varma of Ḍēśinganāḍ Kīḻpperūr, senior Ṭiruvaṭi of Ṭṛppāppūr.

(9) 782.—Śrī Vīra Iravi Varma of Ṭṛppāppūr Kīḻpperūr Kulaśēkhara Perumāḷ.

(10) 807.—Śrī Vīra Iravi Varma of Ṭṛppāppūr Kīḻpperūr, senior Paṇḍāram of Cherawāi.

(11) 837.—Śrī Vīra Iravi Varma Paṇḍāram of Ḍēśinganāḍ Kīḻpperūr belonging to Ṭṛppāppūr Swarūpam (dynasty).

(12) 894.—Śrī Vīraḷa Unni Kēraḷa Varma of Ḍēśinganāḍ Kīḻpperūr, senior Ṭiruvaṭi of Ḍēśinganāḍ.

Coming to inscriptions: a Vaṭṭeluttu inscription at Ṭirunāvāykuḷam in the taluk of Chiraiṅkīḻ records that, in 614 M. E. (1439 A. D)[1], Śrī Vīra Rāma Mārttāṇḍa Varma Kulaśēkhara of Kīḻpperūr, the senior Ṭiruvaṭi of Vēṇāḍ, constructed a granite temple of fine workmanship with *Mandapam* (maṇḍapam) and the inner shrine roofed with copper plates. Another Prince, Chempaka Āḍittya Varma, the senior Ṭiruvaṭi of Cherawāi, is mentioned as a ruling King of the period. On the 20th

1\. കൊല്ലത്തില്‍ തരളാംഗത്തെ
കൂട്ടുമ്പോള്‍ കലിവത്സരം
കൊല്ലത്തില്‍ ശരജംകൂട്ടി
ക്രിസ്ത്വബ്ദം കണ്ടുകൊള്ളണം

This means that, if you add 3926 to the numbers that denote an year of the Kollam era, you get the corresponding year of the Kali-yuga; similarly, by adding 825 to the former, you get the corresponding year of the Christian era.

Edavam, 630 M. E. (1455 A. D.), he consecrated an image of *Gangadhara* (Gangāḍhara) in the Kṛshṇancōil at Vaṭaśśēri. An inscription in the temple of Śuchīnḍṛam records certain gifts made by Chempaka Rāma Varma of Jayasimhanāḍ, the senior Ṭiruvaṭi of Ṭṛppāppūr in the year 643 M. E. (1468 A. D.). There is an inscription to prove that Āḍiṭṭya Varma, the senior Ṭiruvaṭi of Jayasimhanāḍ, as well as *his younger brother* named Rāma Varma, the senior Ṭiruvaṭi of Cherawāi, reigned on the 14th Kumbham 659 M. E. (1484 A.D.). A pillar inscription of Paraśurāma Perinṭēru in Kōṭṭār records that, on the 1st Chiṭṭirai 661 M. E. (1466 A. D.), the crowned King of the Chēra family, Jayasimha Ḍēva, came on tour to Vaṭaśśēri and redressed the grievances of the inhabitants groaning under the oppressions of the Brahmans and the Piḷḷamārs. Regarding these inscriptions, Mr. Nagam Ayya observes: "Two or more Kings of the same dynasty are mentioned as ruling at the same time. It may be that both were independent chiefs ruling over small tracts. Or it may be that the senior associated the junior with him in governmental affairs * * * * or again it may be that one of them is the reigning sovereign, while the other is only a member of the family making certain gifts under his sanction."[1] But it is necessary to point out here that Princes who are described as members of one house or dynasty as Mr. Nagam Ayya calls it are seen to rule over lands that belong or ought to belong to the other houses. Again in one instance we see brothers of the same house described, the one as the senior Ṭiruvaṭī of Jayasimhanāḍ and the other as the senior Ṭiruvaṭi of Cherawāi.

The sweeping statement of Rev. S. Mateer that the Travancore line has all along followed the system of succession by nephews prevalent in all Malabar has also to be accepted with considerable reserve; for Archæological sheet No. 5, published by the Travancore

1. *State Manual*, Vol. I, p. 276.

Government, cites several instances of the prevalence of succession through sons. Inscriptions therein referred to as well as others make it also clear that the Chōlās, Chērās, and the Pāṇḍyās, intermarried at least till the 7th century of the Malabar era or the 13th century A. D. The notable instance of Jayasimha who "belonged to the family of Yaḍu and of the lunar race, and ruled over the Kēraḷa country with his wife Umā Ḍēvi of Kūpaka family"[1], may be cited as one exactly in point.

It is significant that, in an inscription on a large bell in the Ṭṛkkaṇāmkuḍi temple in the Tinnevelly District, dated Kollam year 644(1469 A. D.), King Aḍiṭṭya Vaṙma of Vanchi (Travancore) describes himself as an "ornament of the race of Jayasimha"[2]. Again an inscription at Kollam (Quilon) dated in the Kollam year 671[3] opens with the following Sanskrit verse:—

> Svasṭy asṭu Jayasimhasya
> Vīra Kēraḷa Vaṙmaṇa [1*]
> ṭa [th] ā ṭaḍvamśajānāncha
> rājyasya nagarasya cha [II*] [4]

The full text of the inscription on the Ṭṛkkaṇāmkuḍi temple is as follows:—"In the year *Bhavati* 644 of the Kolamba era, King Āḍiṭṭya Vaṙma, the ruler of Vanchi, born in Viśākha, the tenth asterism in the Hindu Calendar, who is a string of gems of virtues, and a master of all arts (Kala), who adorns the Jayasimha dynasty, and who has attained the sovereignty of Chiravāya-Maṇḍalam (Kingdom), hung up the bell which adorns the gate of Murāri (Vishṇu) enshrined in the Śrīkuranga (Ṭṛkkanāmkuḍi) temple".

It may be noted that this inscription fully supports the theory above put forward that the Travancore Rajas

1. Already identified with the family of Attingal.
2. *Ind. Anti.*, Vol. 2, p. 360 f.
3. No. 285 of *The Government Epigraphist's Collection for* 1895.
4. Note. Vol. 4, *Epigraphia Indeca*, p. 146.

belong to the Jayasimha dynasty of the lunar race, and that the members of the various branches have ruled over the tracts indiscriminately, the most prominent among them maintaining superiority over the others. The inscription describes Ādiṭṭya Vaṙma, the donor of the bell, as "adorning the Jayasimha dynasty" and calls him, "the ruler of Vanchi" (Travancore). He is further said to have "attained the sovereignty of Chiravāya-Maṇḍalam." We may take it that Ādiṭṭya Vaṙma had become, on the date of the inscription, the sovereign of Chērwāi also, i. e., of Cheravā-Swarūpam i. e., Kāyamkuḻam. Or can it be that Chiravā-Maṇḍalam refers to the Kingdom of Chēra? Sixty-nine years after this, we see a descendant of Ādiṭṭya Vaṙma living in the palace, at Ṭṛkkaṇāmkuḍi. The Trivandrum temple account mentions him as Ḍēśinganāḍ (Jayasimhanāḍ) Kīlppērūr Śṙi Vīra Kērala Vaṙma, the Mūṭṭa (senior) Paṇḍāram (ruler) of Chērawai (Kāyamkuḻam).

The penultimate Maharaja of Travancore, while First Prince, noticing the inscription on the Ṭṛkkaṇāmkuḍi bell mentions another inscription of the reign of this very Ādiṭṭya Vaṙma (644 M. E.) on a stone in the Śuchīndram Pagoda which gives the then boundaries of Ṭṛppāppūr or Travancore. They are:—" East, Paṅṅivāykal—(an old water course near Vaṙkkala)—South, Vaip̄ar, in the Tinnevelly District—North and West, the sea" The Prince remarks: "We must make allowance for the geography of those days, in judging of the correctness of the cardinal points here described. However, there is little room to doubt that Ṭṛkkaṇāmkuḍi, *now* situated in the Nanganneri Taluk of the Tinnevelly District, was then (and for some time after as we have shown) a part of Travancore".

On the data available at present, it would perhaps be not far too wrong to make the hypothetical statement that the Royal House of Travancore represents the early Chēra dynasty that held sway over the whole of Southern India. This statement is but provisional. It is not asserted with any degree of confidence that the descent of the Travancore Rajas can be traced in an uninterrupted line of succession from the old Chēra Kings. Nevertheless, there is ample reason to raise the inference that they are the modern representatives of the early Chēra Rulers. Political vicissitudes had, during the course of centuries, brought the Kēraḷaputṛa of the Aśōka inscriptions, the Cerobothras of Ptolemy, Strabo and Arrian, and the later Chēra rulers low in the category of sovereign rulers. The Chōḷās, the Vijayanagara and the Pāṇḍya dynasties successively trenched upon the independence of the Chēra or Kēraḷa kingdom and hemmed its sway within circumscribed limits.[1] The Chōḷa conquest of Southern India including Travancore is recorded in inscriptions[2] as well as in some Tamil historical texts.[3] In course of time, however, Travancore seems to have shaken off the Chōḷa yoke and gained a prominent position in the south. The celebrated missionary, Francis Xavier, describes the King as "the great King of Travancore", and speaks of him as having had authority over all South India. He adds that a near relative of the King resided at Kāyal on the Coromandel coast.[4] Two decades before this, Duarte Barbosa, a Portuguese Captain, who visited Kāyal in 1514, mentions the place as belonging to the King of Quilon, by which is evidently meant the sovereign of Travancore; for he calls

1. It is noteworthy that in the *Report on Epigraphy* for the year 1900 (Madras) it is pointed out that "early in the 14th century, a king of Travancore appears to have made the Pandyas and Cholas subject to the Keralas".

2. *South Indian Inscriptions*, Vol. II, pp. 2 and 236, E. Hultzsch.

3 No. 4, *Tamil Historical Texts. The Vikrama—Chola—Ula. The Ind. Anti.*, Vol. XXII, p. 141.

4. *Life and Letters of St. Francis Xavier* by Fr. Coleridge.

the ruler of Vēṇāḍ, Travancore, King of Benat-dery.[1] More than a century and a half before this, the Arab traveller Ibn Batuta (A. D. 1347) calls the King of Quilon 'Ṭiruvaṭi [2] which is a well-known designation of the Kings of Travancore. Barbosa mentions *Tiruvangoto* (Ṭiruvāncōḍu) itself as a town and territory lying on the coast towards the south of Quilon belonging to a lord, a relative of the King of Coulam. After noticing Coulam or Quilon, the Portuguese Captain proceeds southwards, points to Cape Comorin as the southernmost extremity of Malabar and observes "that the aforesaid Kingdom of Coulam, however, still goes on and comes to an end at the city of Kāyal where the King of Coulam made his continual residence." He is " very rich and powerful," says Barbosa, "on account of his many men-at-arms who are very good bowmen. He always has in his guard four or five hundred women, trained from girls to be archers: they are very active. He sometimes is at war with the King of Narasinga, who wishes to take his country, but he defends himself very well."[3] The summary of Kingdoms in *Ramusio* also describes the Kingdom of Coulam as extending on both sides of Cape Comorin.[4]

Thus the early Portuguese found the King of Travancore the legitimate sovereign of the whole of the south of Tinnevelly.[5] The Travancore King is said to have, at one time, levied tribute from Ceylon, and ventured even to challenge to battle the powerful King of Vijayanagar.[6] The power and influence of

1. *Description of the East Afr can and Malabar Coasts.* Hakluyt Society's publication, pp. 103 and 173.

2. *Cathay*, Vol. II, p. 420.

3. P. 173.

4. Friar Jordanus. *Wonders of the East.* Preface by Col. Yule, p. 16.

5. Caldwell's *Tinnevelly*, p. 67.

6. Logan's *Malabar*, Vol. I, p. 310.

the King, over the south, must have, however, by the beginning of the sixteenth century, become very much diminished, for, though he extended his sympathy, he was not able to protect his Parava subjects against the incursions of the Badages. Very soon the Badages invaded Travancore itself in great force, and it is said that the King was able to repel the attack only with the assistance of Xavier and his convert fishermen.[1] The Badages have been recently identified with the Vijayanagara ruler Vithala's officers and soldiers who seem to have invaded Travancore shortly before 1544, i.e., sometime about the arrival of Xavier on the coast.[2] Bishop Caldwell identifies them with the Nayakas of Madura.[3] But this can scarcely be correct. For the Nayakas themselves came into power and threw off the Vijayanagara suzerainty only later on. No doubt a Jesuit writer of the time describes the Badages as "the collectors of the royal taxes, a race of over-bearing and insolent men, commonly called Nairs". The writer evidently used the Malayalam term Nayar instead of the corresponding Tamil Nayk or Nayaka; for the Nayars could, under no circumstances, have invaded Travancore from the east. Xavier represents them as lawless marauders. Another important circumstance tending to show that the Badages could not have been the emissaries and representatives of the Nayaka rulers of Madura, is, that those rulers were very tolerant of Christianity, while the determination of the Badages was to "expel the Christians, both natives and foreigners, from the coast." The mission of the Badages was to collect the "Royal taxes." These were, no doubt, the dues payable to the Rajahs of Vijayanagara and the object of their invasion of Travancore is explained when we see that Achyuṭarāya (crowned King of Vijayanagara, Saka 1452 (1529—30 A. D.) received

1. *History of Tinnevelly*, p. 71.
2. *Archaeological Survey Report for 1896*, p. 31.
3. Caldwell's *Tinnevelly*, p. 70.

tribute from Travancore as mentioned in two inscriptions at Conjeevaram. Achyuṭarāya is said to have despatched armaments to the Kingdom of Ṭiruvaṭi, (Travancore), planted a pillar of victory in the Ṭāmraparṇi river, received tribute from Ṭiruvaṭi, taken in marriage the daughter of the Pāṇḍyan King, and brought Tumbichchi Naykan and Salva Naykan into subjection. Some time before this, Travancore had successfully invaded Pāṇḍya, and it is surmised that it was at the invitation of the Pāṇḍya King that Achyuṭarāya despatched armaments to Travancore and received in return the hand of the daughter of the Pāṇḍyan King. The King of Travancore of that period (Kollam 708=A. D. 1533—4), Bhūṭalavīra Vīra Uḍaya MārṭṭaṇḍaVarman, perhaps identical with the Mārṭṭaṇḍa Varman of the Travancore list, claims to have taken "the earth by conquest." Hence the Biruḍu, Bhūṭalavīra, prefixed to his name. His successor was also styled Bhūṭalavīra Ravi Varman. One of these or both seem to have over-run the Pāṇḍya country and issued coins with the legend Bhūṭala.[1] Thus there can be no doubt that Achyuṭarāya was invited by the Pāṇḍyan King to assist him against a Travancore invasion. The Vijayanagara arms not only repelled the Travancoreans but also exacted tribute from their King. This tribute must have been paid but grudgingly, for the enforcement of it required constant armed intervention. Thus the war against Travancore was continued during the reign of Achyuṭarāya's successor, Saḍāśiva. Shortly before, Saka Samvat 1466 (1544—45) i. e., just about the time Xavier came to the Western Coast, we see the Vijayanagara ruler Viṭṭala leading an expedition against Ṭiruvaṭi (*Tiruvati*) and fighting from *Anantasayanam* (Ananṭaśayanam) (admittedly Trivandrum) in the south to Mudugal (now in

1. *Annual Report of the Archaeological Department of Madras for 1896*, p. 18.

the Nizam's territories) in the north. The expedition against Travancore and its subjugation by the Vijayanagara King Viṭṭala receives confirmation from an inscription at Śuchīndram. It is of the year Kollam 722 corresponding to A. D. 1546—7, and records that the then King of Travancore described as the Senior (member) of Jeṭunganāṭu (Quilon) called Bhūṭala Vīra Iravi Varman, "who took the earth by conquest," provided for special offerings to be made to the Vishṇu shrine at Śuchīndram on the birthday of Viṭṭalēśwara Maharaja. This grant, indeed, establishes the subordinate political relationship of Bhūṭala Vīra Iravi Varman to Viṭṭalēśwara Maharaja in spite of his boast of having "taken the earth by conquest." In the face of this indubitable evidence, it is difficult to believe either that the Badages failed in their attempt to conquer Travancore or that the Raja was more indebted to Xavier than to his army of Nayars for deliverance from them. The story of the panic that seized the Badages on the sudden appearance of Xavier in full canonicals at the head of his host of convert fishermen and their subsequent flight is puerile and may be taken for what it is worth. The story goes "that whilest the Raja was collecting his military nobles and their retainers to oppose them (the Badages), Xavier took the field against them at the head of a small body of his converts. With a crucifix in his hand, he advanced to meet the invading army and forbade them in the name of God to proceed. Whether they thought that he was one of their own divinities come down to turn them from their purpose or feared the anger of the God of the Christians, we know not; a panic seized them and they fled. Great honour was paid to Xavier for his bloodless victory by the Rajah and nobles; but he besought them to give the glory to Jesus Christ."[1] The picture drawn is, indeed, sublime. But its sublimity

1. *The Church and the Churches in Southern India*, p. 22.

C

is a great deal marred by lack of probability. I is remarkable that Xavier himself is silent on the subject in his letters from the coast. We may therefore safely take it as a pious invention of the Catholic propagandists of the period, for we read that the immediate effect of the miracle was that "cries came continually to the ears of the missionary, beseeching him to go and teach," and that Xavier felt that he and his handful of helpers were not sufficient to meet the incessant demand, so much so that Xavier himself is said to have written in one of his letters—"that millions of idolators might be easily converted, if there were more preachers, who would sincerely mind the interests of Jesus Christ and not their own concernments" —a strange comment by no means complimentary to the missionaries of the day.

In A. D. 1553, the Portuguese found Travancore a powerful kingdom, "the king of which our people," says D'Barros, "called the *Rey Grande*," because he is greater in his dominions and in the state which he keeps than those of the princes of Malabar.[1]

In the year 1559 A. D., Madura fell finally into the hands of the Nayaka generals of Vijayanagara and Viśwanāṭha Naykar who had been sent by the Vijayanagara King to bring to reason his father Nāgama Naykar set up for himself an independent dynasty acknowledging, however, the suzerainty of the Vijayanagara sovereign. The assumption of sovereignity by the Naykars over the Pāṇḍyan Kingdom formed but a prelude to frequent invasions of Travancore, and it is recorded in the Tamil chronicles[2] that Viśwanāṭha Naykar overcame some chiefs of Travancore by his personal valour in single combat and acquired their territory. Naykars, representing their suzerain of

1. D' Barros, Fl. XI.

2. Taylor's *Oriental Historical Mss.*, Preface, p. VIII.

Vijayanagara, claimed the right of levying tribute from Travancore. The great Ṭirumala Naykar, not long after, reduced the Travancore Prince into absolute subjection, and we find the Malayalam Nānchi Nāṭu Raja heading, as the vassal, the list of the 72 Pālayams appointed to guard the bastions of the Pāṇḍyan capital[1]. Whether this is a historical fact or a mere boast, the cadjan documents recently published in the Travancore Gazette afford ample proof of Ṭirumala's invasion of Travancore. These incursions were, no doubt, intended to enforce the tribute payable by the State to the Vijayanagara Empire, for it is admitted that the king paid it only when compelled[2]. Thus another document, also recently published in the Travancore Gazette, shows that the Naykar's forces used to repeat their incursions often and that the king had to remit arrears of tax on land in the Nānjanāṭu country "owing to heavy losses sustained by the people on account of the Naykar's invasion" between the years 849 and 869 M. E., i. e., A. D. 1674 and 1694.

In the year 1697, an army of Vadukas was sent to Travancore to enforce the payment of the usual tribute which had long fallen in arrears and which had always to be levied by force. The king of Travancore skilfully availed himself of this opportunity to use the Madura forces to put down his rebellious ministers, the Eṭṭu Vīṭṭil Pillamārs. He then suddenly fell upon the Vadukas and almost destroyed them. To revenge this treachery, Queen Mangammāl entered upon a war with Travancore in 1698. The Queen's General, Dalaway Narasappaya, entered the country and conquered the Travancoreans after much hard fighting and returned to Trichinopoly laden with much priceless booty.[3]

1. Taylor, Vol. II, p. 161.
2. Caldwell's *Tinnevelly*, p. 70.
3. *Oriental Historical Mss.*, vol. II, p. 224; *The Manual of the Madura District*, Nelson, Part III, pp. 225—226.

We have now come to the period of the establishment of the Dutch on the Malabar Coast and the Dutch Captain Nieuhoff has supplied us with the following description of the kingdom:

"The kingdom of Travankoor (thus called from its capital city) begins at the Cape of Comory or Comorin, and extends all along the sea-coast as far as Koulang, comprehending a tract of ground 20 or 24 leagues in length; the famous village of Paru, belonging to the queen of Singnaty, being only in the midst To the east it borders upon the kingdom of Madura, and to the west upon the countries of Peretaly and Kotarkery. It has several considerable villages which are inhabited by the Moors, such as Tengepatnam, Kuletture, Koritypatnam and Allage. * * * *

"The chief cities lie deeper in the country, which is of a great extent all along the mountains to Naymar, near the Cape of Comorin and toward Travancore, in all 29 great cities and villages. About a league and half to the north of the Cape Comorin is the city of Kotate or Kottatti, a place of great traffick; the populous city of Siminitira and Matadavalur, famous for its bigness, being surrounded by six or seven other towns; Verrage is not above a quarter of a league distance from Kotate and Katikury, the two most considerable places of the whole country. Kalkolang is a very large city, being a league and a half long, upon the confines of the Neyk of Madura. It is situated upon a high hill, 3 leagues from Tengepatnam, and 12 from Koulang; being on one side strengthened by inaccessible mountains, on the other by a wall, the undermost part of which is of stone, the uppermost of brick-work, in all 24 foot high, the royal palace stands at the west end, being surrounded by a stone wall. On the east side you see the ruins of an old castle, built on the top of a hill, fortified with a triple wall. The city of Kalkoulang is the chief residence of the king, who constantly keeps a garrison of

10,000 Negroes (Nairs) here to secure it against the Neyk of Madura, whose power is much dreaded here[1]".

Captain Nieuhoff s account of the origin of the dynasty ruling over Travancore at his time is at once curious and interesting.

........."The ancient race of the kings of Travancore owed its origin to Attinegen, but for want of male heirs, one of the Princes of Cochin was placed in that throne ; the king who then reigned, being descended from the Cochin race of Rammerankoil, and elected King of Travankoor".

This receives support from an official document regarding the state of Malabar drawn up in 1677 A. D. by Van Rheede, then the Dutch Governor of Ceylon, and quoted at page 305, Vol. 1, of *The Travancore State Manual*. "The Prince (of Travancore) is an adopted son from a Cochin family called *Ramencoil*, this court has often solicited a Cochin Prince and Princess as heirs, but I have never been able to persuade the king to it, not but that he saw the great advantages which might result therefrom to Cochin, but because this would be from the Cochin family of *Tyaloor*, (Chālūr) which he will not suffer." Mr. Nagam Aiya, the author of the *Manual*, doubts that the "reference to Cochin is probably a mistake for Kōlaṭṭunāḍ from which Travancore made adoptions, or it may be that the Raja of Kōlaṭṭunāḍ was at the time a tributary of the more powerful Prince of Cochin." That these surmises are incorrect and that Van Rheede was writing from personal knowledge and cannot therefore be mistaken about the country of which he was writing is evident from the extract itself. He had been Governor of Cochin from 1673 to 1677 A. D. and was removed to the Governorship of Ceylon only in 1677, the year in which he wrote the extract quoted. He had been present at the Dutch attack on Cochin

1. *Voyages*, p. 228.

10 years before he became Governor of the place. He must have been sufficiently long in the country to know of its political affairs and the several families that ruled over the various principalities that constituted Malabar. What is more, the document itself was an official document regarding the state of Malabar, and it is extremely unlikely that a Governor of Cochin should, on the eve of his departure from the place, confound Cochin with Kōlaṭṭunāḍ or mistake the one for the other. Further, if an earlier adoption had not taken place from the Cochin family, it is impossible to conceive that the Travancore court would, as mentioned in the extract, solicit a Cochin Prince and Princess as heirs and that Van Rheede would exert his personal influence with the King of Cochin, who was the *protege* of the Dutch East India Company, to grant the request though without success. The suggestion that the Raja of Kōlaṭṭunāḍ might at the time have been a tributary of the more powerful Prince of Cochin has no foundation in history. Cochin had already lost its former power and had already come under Dutch suzerainty, whereas Kōlaṭṭunāḍ was still independent and, so far as historical evidence is available at present, Cochin was at no time more powerful than Kōlaṭṭunāḍ; neither was Kōlaṭṭunāḍ at any time dependent on Cochin, nor was ever a tributary of it. Between the two States of Cochin and Kōlaṭṭunāḍ lay the powerful kingdom of the Zamorin who, as we have seen, waged perpetual war with Cochin, and who, it would appear, held the king of Cochin always in subjection till the European powers attained supremacy in Malabar. It is significant that Nieuhoff speaks of the king then reigning in Travancore (Nieuhoff's voyages extended from 1653 to 1672) as being descended from the race of Ramerankoil. Fra Joseph A. S. Maria de Sebastiani, the first Vicar Apostolic of Malabar, who was appointed as such in 1659 and was present in Cochin when the town was captured from the Portuguese by the Dutch

mentions one *Ramancoil*, the brother of the reigning Raja of Travancore, as being opposed to the succession of the Mūṭṭa ṭāvali in Cochin and befriending the adoptees from the Ṭaṇūr family[1]. The Raja of Cochin whom the Portuguese Admiral Cabral first visited and with whom the Portguese made their first engagement is called by them Uṇṇi Rāmankōil Ṭirumulpāḍ. All old records designate the Raja of Cochin as Kōil Aḍhikārikal and the Raja still styles himself as such in documents issued by him such as the renewals of Kanam tenures etc. It is therefore altogether impossible to accept the suggestion of Mr. Nagam Aiya.

We have had occasion already to speak of the Dutch relations with Travancore, the disastrous war the Dutch East India Company waged with the King and the dishonourable peace with which it closed. The modern History of Travancore commences with the exploits of the great Mārṭṭāṇḍa Varma who extended the limits of his kingdom to the frontiers of Cochin in the north, and annexed all intermediate principalities. Of him the Dutch Governor Gollennesse observed that he was a "clever and untiring prince" and that he aimed "at nothing less than the supremacy over the whole of Malabar, and no doubt he would have obtained his end, had not the Honourable Company been in his way." His successor, the no less renowned Rāma Varma, consolidated his predecessor's conquests, withstood the advance of Tippu Sultan and placed his Government on a firm foundation by entering into a subsidiary alliance with the English East India Company which had by this time established its supremacy in India. His successor was a weak and imbecile prince whose tyrannical and oppressive rule under the guidance of low and cunning intriguers paved the way to insurrections and turmoils resulting finally in the rebellious war with the English and the

1. *Second Expedition of Fr. Sebastioni. India Oriental*, by Fr. Ginseppe.

complete conquest of the country by them. The opportune death of the Raja was availed of to avert annexation, and he was succeeded by an adopted Rāṇi who wisely entrusted the management of the State into the hands of the British Resident, Col. Munro, acting as Diwan also. Under the rule of Col. Munro, order was restored and government reorganised on almost a new system. The progressive administration thus inangurated continued during the reign of the Rāṇi and her successors. Under the rule of the Maharaja Rāma Varma (Āilyam Ṭirunāl), the State started on reforms on western lines and that distinguished statesman, the late Raja Sir. T. Māḍhava Row, K. C. S. I., who was then the Diwan of the State, brought the administration of the country to such a high level that it soon achieved the enviable reputation of being styled the "model State" and extorted the high encomium from Lord Salisbury, the then Secretary of State for India. When submitting his report on the material and moral progress of India, he wrote that "if all Native States in India were administered as was Travancore by Mr. Madhava Rao and Cochin by Mr. Shangunny Menon, then the British Government will have to look to their laurels". His Highness was succeeded by his brother (Viśākham Ṭirunāl Maharaja) who was an accomplished scholar, philosopher, scientist and statesman of rare merits whose very successful reign has effected lasting improvements. His Highness Śrī Mūlam Ṭirunāl Maharaja nobly pursued the progressive policy of his immediate predecessors. Treading out of the beaten path of routine improvements, His Highness conferred on his loving subjects the much cherished privilege of being summoned to an annual Popular Assembly at the capital to which representatives were elected, to submit to the Darbar the wants and grievances of the people. A Legislative Council was then constituted for the enactment of laws necessary for the State. The Council was composed of official and non-official members, the choice of the latter being left to the representative members of the Popular Assembly, subject to the veto of the Darbar. The constitution and powers of this Council have been enlarged. The power of electing representatives has been given to the people; and the members are now allowed, not only to assist the Darbar in making laws, but they have the right of interpellation, of discussing the financial budget and of moving cuts in it, and also to submit recommendations to the Government by means of resolutions on all matters of importance. The Ghauts have been pierced and the Railway now cuts across the mountains to Quilon, one of the most important towns of the State. Under the benign rule of the Maharaja, his subjects continued to enjoy a high degree of prosperity.

5. **Attingal.** This is the maternal house of Travancore; but it was originally a province altogether distinct from Vēṇāḍ and the origin of its relationship to Travancore, albeit obscure, may be said to be dimly visible through a long vista of ages. Professor Sunḍaram Pillai observes: "If Kūpa Rājyam (which we have seen is identical with Āṯṯingal) and Vēṇāḍ were thus at one time two co-ordinate provinces of Malabar, and if, in later times, we find the Princes of the latter appropriating to themselves, as their *House name*, the name of a locality (Kīḻpērūr) situated in the former, it cannot be a violent assumption to suppose that the two were originally independent principalities, and that their amalgamation took place under such circumstances as led to a compromise, the weaker party submitting to the stronger on the condition of the stronger appropriating, not only the kingdom, but also the family name of the weaker. In short, it looks not in the least unlikely that, when the power of Vēṇāḍ prevailed over Āṯṯingal, some matrimonial or other alliance was concluded which naturally led the blood of Āṯṯingal to prevail, in its turn, in the veins of the Vēṇāḍ Princes."[1] That

1. *Some early Sovereigns of Travancore*, p. 35.

this surmise is correct appears from the fact subsequently ascertained that Jayasimha, King of Quilon, married Uma Amma, Queen of the Kūpakās (Āṭṭingal) and ruled over Kēraḷa with Quilon as its capital until the year 441 M. E.[1] Their son, Ravi Varman Kulaśēkhara, being a minor at the time of the death of his father, the Pāṇḍyan King Kulaśēkhara Ḍēvar, the 'Kalis Ḍēvar', the Ruler of Malabar' of the Mahomedan historians, encroached upon and subdued his territories. But, on attaining majority, Ravi Varman Kulaśēkhara conquered the whole of Travancore during the last quarter of the 5th century M. E., defeated Vīra Pāṇḍya, the younger son of 'Kalis Ḍēvar' as also another Vīra Pāṇḍya of his own dynasty, i. e., Śrī Vīra Uḍaya Māṛṭṭāṇḍa Varma who reigned in 491 M. E. and married a Pāṇḍya Princess when he attained the age of 33. He extended his conquests up to Conjeevaram and subdued the Pāṇḍyas and Chōlas.[2]

Notwithstanding the close relationship indicated above, the two principalities continued to have separate existence for a long time. The *Travancore State Manual* refers to a queen of the Kūpaka family who was known by the name of *Kulasekhara Nambirattiyar* who built the temple of *Kariyamanekka Vinnavar Emperumal* at the village of Idaraikudi in the Taluk of Agasṭīśvaram with an additional *Sopanam* and *Mandapam*. This work was completed and consecrated by her on the 30th Meḍam 643 M. E. (May 1468 A. D). [3] The inscription on the Apānēśvara temple near Āṭṭingal records that, in M. E. 751 (1576 A. D.), the Queen of the Kūpakas repaired that shrine. In 1664, the Dutch captain Nieuhoff found the King of Travancore keeping his residence at Āṭṭingal when he visited His Majesty to transact business. In 1677, the Dutch Governor Van Rheede says:—

1. *Travancore Archaeological Sheet*, No. 5.
2. *Report on Archaeology for 1900*, p. 9,' Madras. Also *Archaeological Sheet*. No. 5, Travancore.
3. Vol I, p. 77.

"The princes of Āṭṭingah, who is not alone the mother of Travancore but the eldest of *Tippaposorewam* (Ṭṛppāppisvarūpam) has a large territory of her own, independent of Travancore, is also in alliance with the Hon'ble Company—along with the old Princess lives a younger one, but of such noble and manly conduct that she is both feared and respected by every one, some out of respect to her sex and others out of regard to the old Queen, which this youngest Princess knows so well how to turn to her advantage that she not only rules Āṭṭingah but Travancore itself within whose bounds no Princess may set her feet according to their laws, nor pass the river Canimani on pain of forfeiting their rights, but this young Amazon has lately violated those customs and made even the king fly before her."[1]

In 853 M. E., (A. D. 1678), the Trivandrum temple chronicles contain an entry on the 20th of Edavam that Śrī Vīra Iravi Vaṛma of Ṭṛppāppūr Kīḻpērūr, the Senior Paṇḍāram, being also Senior Paṇḍāram of Āṭṭingal together with Rāma Vaṛma, Junior Paṇḍāram, made donations to the temple.

The English, on establishing themselves on the Travancore Coast, obtained their grant for Anjengo from the Queen of Āṭṭingal. They built the fort with her consent. In 1723, we see the King of Travancore, on behalf of the Rāṇi, engaging himself to punish the murderers of the English officers who were killed while on a visit to the Queen at Āṭṭingal. In 1726, the English appear to have obtained a ratification from the Queen in regard to the Factory at Eḍḍava. In 1729, the Chief of Anjengo seems to have entered into an agreement directly with the Princess of Āṭṭingal "for the continuation of the union of the English Company". In 1731, however, the King of Travancore and the Queen of Āṭṭingal jointly confirmed the grant of the

1. See passage quoted from a document found among the old Huzur records—Travancore *State Manual*, Vol. I, p. 305.

gardens of Palatady and Cottudals to the English East India Company. Ives writing in 1757, observes: "Till of late the town and country of Āťťinga were quite independent of the King of Travancore, but now they are tributary to him. The eldest son of the Queen of Āťťinga is always heir-apparent to the Crown of Travancore." Walter Hamilton, in his *Account of the East Indies*, informs us that "the Ṭampurāṭṭīs of Āťťingara (Āťťingal) possessed the sovereignty of Travancore from remote antiquity, until Raja Māťṭāṇḍa Vaťma, who died in 1758, and was the son of one of the Ṭampurāṭṭīs adopted from Cherecal (Chirakkal) persuaded the reigning Ṭampurāṭṭi to resign the sovereign authority to the Rajas, both for herself and for all succeeding Ṭampurāṭṭīs. To perpetuate these conditions, a regular treaty was executed between the Raja and the Ṭampurāṭṭi which was inscribed on a silver plate, and ratified by the most solemn imprecations limiting the successors to the offspring of the Āťťinga Ṭampurāṭṭīs". From what Hamilton says after this, we may gather that the alleged treaty must have been entered into sometime before 1740. But no such treaty is forthcoming; neither is such an engagement referred to by any one else. M. Moens, in his *Memorial*, observes that "Āťťinga became dependant on King Māťṭāṇḍa Vaťma during the Dutch war with Travancore" which commenced in A. D. 1734. The history of Travancore before the year 1740 does not support the statement that the Rāṇīs of Āťťingal possessed the sovereignty of Travancore at any period. On the other hand, the two principalities were separate and independent of each other. Travancore had always been ruled by male sovereigns so long as there were male members in the family and the earliest Queen known to have ruled over the State was Uma Amma Rāṇi (1677—8 to 84) and the next one Rāṇi Lakṣhmi Bhai (1815) mentioned by Hamilton himself later on. What actually did take place was that the Ṭampurāṭṭīs of Āťťingal were induced to surrender their right of ruling over *their own* principality of Āṫṫingal to the male members who are Rajas of Travancore. And for this, no stipulation "limiting the succession (to the throne of Travancore) to the offspring of the Āṫṫinga Ṭampurāṭṭīs" was necessary; for, even before the alleged arrangement, so far as can be traced at present, succession to the Travancore throne was in the Āṫṫingal line. How this relationship was brought about will be discussed presently.

We learn from Forbes who arrived at Anjengo in February 1772, and who lived there for some time that a semblance of sovereignty was still kept up in the Rāṇīs of Āṫṫingal: For he says "There was still a nominal Queen of Āṫṫinga when I resided at Anjengo; who, like the Raja sovereign of the Maharattas, was little more than a state prisoner, while the King of Travancore, the usurper of her dominions, imitating the Peshwa of Poona, styled himself *Diwan* or minister to the Queen of Āṫṫinga."[1] From this, it becomes evident that the Rāṇīs could not have resigned their rights of sovereignty absolutely to Raja Māṙṭṭāṇḍa Vaṙmā as observed by Hamilton, for we find Māṙṭṭāṇḍa Vaṙma's successor, the Raja Rāma Vaṙma, styling himself as *Divan* or minister of the Queen of Āṫṫingal, thirteen years after the death of King Māṙṭṭāṇḍa Vaṙma. At present, the female members of the Travancore Royal House are known as the Rāṇīs of Āṫṫingal, and the village and country thereabouts are still regarded as their private property. These comprise the two *Adhikarams* or *proverthies* or revenue subdivisions of Āṫṫingal and Eḍacōde and a few gardens. These are wholly free from Government interference in matters of revenue administration.

It is difficult to ascertain precisely the nature of the peculiar relationship that exists between the two principalities, its origin, evolution and development till it has come to be regarded that the one is an adjunct of the other, the principality of Āṫṫingal being

1. *Oriental Memoirs*, Vol. I, pp. 269—60.

an appanage of the female members of the Royal House of Travancore who are all Rāṇīs of Āṯṯingal, while the State is ruled by the male members in succession, who are all styled princes of Travancore. The Rāṇīs are, no doubt, styled in English as the Senior and Junior Rāṇīs of Travancore; but, in all official communications and publications in the vernacular, they are styled as Āṯṯingal Mūṭṭa Ṭampurāṭṭi and Āṯṯingal Ilaya Ṭampurāṭṭi i. e., the Senior and Junior Rāṇīs of Āṯṯingal.[1]

If, as we have attempted to show, the relationship between the two houses had its origin in matrimonial alliance, we have to account for the change from the makkaṭṭāyam (system of inheriting through father) system of inheritance into the present one of marumakkaṭṭāyam (matriarchal system of inheritance) in the Travancore Royal family. The slide from the one to the other is not a difficult one. Later on we shall see how easily the Pāṇḍyan Princes who settled at Pūññār gave up their own customs and adopted the Malayāḷi form of marriage and inheritance. Even in our own day, we have instances of a mixture of the two working harmoniously among the Nāññanāṭ Veḷḷāḷars, the Īḻuvās, as also among some Ampalavāsis or temple servants, such as the Vāriars. In the last class of people, there are indeed cases where a marumakkaṭṭāyam Vāriar enters into holy wedlock, not sambandham as among the marumakkaṭṭāyam community, and begets children who lapse into marumakkaṭṭāyam once more, by the brothers and sisters living together as a joint family of the Nayar type. There are certain Nambiyārs who observe this custom. We have seen that Travancore had large possessions on the Madura and Tinnevelly side, and the Travancore Royal House must originally have been a non-Malayāḷi one. Later on we shall see that the Rajas of Panṭaḷam who were originally Pāṇḍyan Princes settled in Travancore on their being harassed by their enemies about the 4th

1. See the English and Malayalam Almanacs published annually by the Travancore Government.

century of the Malabar Era, under the patronage of the Travancore King *as they were related by marriage* with the Royal family of Travancore. The Travancore State did not extend further north of Quilon or Kāyamkuḷam. Though Kēraḷa extends to Cape Comorin in the south, all that part of the coast south of Quilon is commonly said to lie beyond Malabar. It will also be remembered that, according to the early division of the country, the portion in question lay beyond Kēraḷa proper. There are no Nambūṭiri villages to the south of the Quilon river. Nambūṭiri women going south of the Quilon river are said to lose caste. The Kings of Travancore seem to have found it almost impossible to induce this sacerdotal class to make settlements in their country, and Dr. Day goes so far as to say that it is the fourth or last class of Nambūṭiris alone, who are only Brahmans in name, (with one exception) who have Illams (houses) in Travancore. It is a matter of common talk in Malabar that the later Rajas used to protest too much of their being Malayālīs, and it is perhaps this anxiety that established such costly ceremonies as the *Murajapam* (Muṟajapam), *Tulapurushadanam* (Ṭulāpurushadānam), *Hirannyagarbham* (Hiraṇṇyagaṟbham), &c., almost exclusively for the benefit of the higher class of Nambūṭirīs. One is inclined to suggest that this change from a non-Malayāḷi house to a Malayāḷi house must have taken place not long before the institution of the above ceremonies by the Great Māṟṭṭaṇḍa Vaṟma (904 to 930 M. E). A Travancore King of the 7th century M. E. Bhūṭala Vīra Uḍaya Māṟṭṭaṇḍa Vaṟma (665 to 710 M.E.) seems to have married a Chōḷa Princess known as Chōḷakulavalli. Records available to the public at present do not carry us any further; so that we may reasonably suggest that the change must have taken place some time after 710 M. E. Even in the Protuguese times, the Rajas of Travancore seem to have remained a non-Malayāḷī power; for according to both Barbosa and St. Francis Xavier, their possessions lay more on the eastern side of the Ghauts than on the western. Van Rheede tells us that the Travancore Raja's "dominions formerly extended from Cail patanam on the coast of Madura to Poona", and adds that "he is a powerful Prince". The marriage customs in vogue in the Royal Family still point to a non-Malayāli origin. The Rāṇīs are married not by Nambūṭirīs, as in Cochin, but by Kōil Ṭampurāns or Kṣheṭṛyas, and it is no mere mock ceremony. The Royal Consorts receive State recognition and have well and clearly defined positions accorded them in the family. Long-standing precedent has indeed sanctioned second marriage, and then the alliance takes the form of *Sambandham* of the marumakkaṭṭāyam type but still only with a Kōil Ṭampurān and never with a Nambūṭiri Brahman. This is somewhat akin to the system prevailing among the Nāññanāṭ Vellālars. The Royal house at Āṭṭingal is at present held in such great estimation that each Travancore sovereign has to visit the place, soon after his coronation, to complete the ceremonies in connection therewith, and he is expected further to renew that visit every year of his reign for the ceremony known as *Ari Ittu Valcha* (Ari Iṭṭu Vālcha) in the month of Makaram (January—February).

6. **Signati.** This is the kingdom of Quilon. Signati is a corruption of the term Ḍēsinganāḍ, which again is a corrupt form of the real name of the country, Jayasimhanāḍ. It received this designation apparently from Jayasimhan who had married the Queen of the Kūpakās and who had ruled at Quilon. It was their son Ravi Varma Kulaśēkhara who had established his capital at Quilon, ruled over the Kērala country and extended his conquests to Cānjīvaram.

We have notices of the kingdom by Marco Polo, Ibn Batuta and other travellers which have been already referred to elsewhere.

With the arrival of the Portuguese on the Malabar Coast, we begin to be able to gather something of these Malabar principalities. Whilst the Portuguese

Admiral Cabral was at Cochin, he received a deputation from Quilon, inviting him to visit the Raja and promising to supply him with pepper and spices at a cheaper rate than at Cochin; but this offer was politely declined. Both Varthema and Barbosa describe Quilon then as a powerful kingdom. It was ruled by Gōvardhanan Mārttaṇḍan of Vēṇāḍ (Travancore) whose territory, known as Vēṇāḍ, extended from Quilon to Cape Comorin, a distance of 24 Kāṭams or 80 miles. His possessions on the Eastern Coast extended to more than 30 Kāṭams or 120 miles, the southern portion of the Pāṇḍyan country being subject to him. He had his residence at *Cael* also. Of this country, Varthema (1503-8) observes:—"At the end of three days, we departed from this place, (i. e. Kāyamkulam) and went to another city called Colon (Quilon) distant from that above mentioned 20 miles. The King of this city is a pagan, and extremely powerful, and he has 20,000 horsemen and many archers, and is constantly at war with other kings. * * * At that time, the king of this city was the friend of the King of Portugal; but, being at war with others, it did not appear to us well to remain here. Wherefore we took our way by sea, aforesaid; and went to a city which is called Chayel belonging to the same king, opposite from Colon 50 miles". Barbosa's (1503) description of the country and the power of its king is equally glowing. Speaking of the capital, he says:— It "is a great city and good seaport, which is named Coulam in which dwell many Moors and Gentiles and Christians. They are great merchants and very rich, and own many ships with which they trade to Cholamandel, the island of Ceylon, Bengal, Malacca, Sumatra and Pegu: these do not trade with Cambay. There is also in this city much pepper. They have a Gentile king, a great lord of much territory and wealth, and of numerous men-at-arms, who, for the most part, are great archers"[2]

1. P. 183.
2. Pp. 158—9.

In the year 1502, when Vasco da Gama was at Cochin on his second visit, the Queen of Quilon sent him a message, requesting him to send two of his largest ships to Quilon, and promising to load them with pepper on the same terms and conditions he had already established at Cochin. She also undertook to provide him with a similar quantity each year at the same price as might from time to time prevail at that place. Da Gama received the Queen's messenger with much honour, and, after consulting with his captains on the matter, fearing to run any risk in regard to the recently established friendship with the King of Cochin, he sent a courteous reply, excusing himself from at once accepting the invitation on the ground, that, owing to recent engagements with the King of Cochin, he could not enter upon this matter without His Majesty's concurrence. He, therefore, requested her to send a message direct to the King of Cochin, and should he raise no objections, he, Vasco da Gama, would be glad to entertain her proposals.

On receipt of this reply, the Queen at once despatched messengers to the King of Cochin with whom she was on friendly terms. The King had apprehensions that, should the Portuguese go to Quilon to load pepper, his revenues and the trade of his port would be prejudicially affected thereby, and therefore, it was with no great pleasure that he received the Queen's message. However, after consultation with the Portuguese and on the understanding that they would not trouble to send ships to Quilon so long as they could obtain all the pepper they required from Cochin, the King gave an apparently ready acquiescence in the proposal. The Portuguese undertook not to open a factory at Quilon but only to send ships when there was a scarcity in Cochin. But, as most of the pepper sold in Cochin was obtained principally from Quilon, the King was naturally much chagrined, but, having given his word, he felt himself unable to draw back and sent back the messengers of the Queen with the best grace he could assume under the circumstances.

On receipt of a favourable reply from the King, the Queen renewed her invitation and Vasco da Gama, after obtaining sanction of the King, sent two ships to Quilon. The Captains of these two ships were Diogo Fernandes Pereira and Francisco Marecos, whilst Joa de Sa Pereira went with them as factor. On arrival at Quilon, the latter went on shore and handed to the Queen a letter from da Gama, accompanied by a present of a handsome mirror, some coral, and a large bottle of orange-flower water, whilst to her ministers he presented 30 scarlet-caps and 30 dozen of knives with sheaths. The Queen in return sent as a present to da Gama several silk stuffs of various colours, together with some very fine white stuffs of great width, all being of native manufacture. The ships were taken to a river called Callecoulam (Kāyamkuḷam), which was five leagues south from the port (Cochin), were filled in 10 days and returned to Cochin loaded with pepper and spices.[1]

Soon after his arrival at Cochin, Alfonso de Albuquerque had sent two vessels to Quilon. At this time, the heir to the throne was a minor and the Queen Dowager governed as Regent. She generally lived in the interior of the country and appointed a Council of leading men to manage the affairs of the State at Quilon. These men had been bribed by the Zamorin to oppose the establishment of the Portuguese in that place. But, on the arrival of Albuquerque, the Kāriakār (Minister) of Vēṇāṭṭaṭikaḷ (the Travancore King) at Quilon, a Nambiāṭiri, gave him a hearty reception in the name of his sovereign, who permitted him to establish a factory there. On this coming to the knowledge of the Zamorin, he used every endeavour to induce the Nambiāṭiri to drive out the Portuguese from Quilon. He sent ambassadors to the Queen saying that she must beware of what she was about, for the Portuguese were a bad race, and that, if she admitted them into her

1. Danever's, Vol. I., p.

land, they would rise up against her. She however replied that not only had the people of Quilon received no insult or injury from the Portuguese, but the latter were believed to be men of their word, and that unless they were to act otherwise, it would not be possible to depart from what had already been agreed upon with them. "The king of Coulao" (i. e. the Nambiāṭiri) is described as "a man of such truthfulness that, in spite of all these arguments which the Zamorin advanced, he kept his word and established his friendship with Alfonso de Albuquerque".[1] One great cause of the success of Alfonso de Albuquerque at Quilon was that here there were no Moors, or other foreigners with whom the Portuguese were likely to come into serious competition in the matter of trade.

The State of Quilon at the time is thus described:—" At the time when Alfonso de Albequerque arrived at Coulao, it was a very large city, peopled with heathens, with not a single Moor in it, nor any foreigner except the brother of Cherinamercar of Cochin, who had gone thither just lately to reside. This city was a great sea-port of merchants, and anciently had in it many merchants stopping there from all parts of India, principally from Malacca. And as it was a port sheltered from the wind on every side, the ships which go to India, as well as those which passed the island of Ceilao (Ceylon) and Chale (Kāyal) made their enterport there. In those days, the island of Ceilao was subject to it and paid tribute to it and it possessed all the lands from Coulao to Chale, which is about sixty leagues, and the distance from Coulao to the island of Ceilao is eighty leagues. The King of Coulao was a very honest man, and very gallant, and in the war which he carried on with the King of Narsinga who had many soldiers, both horse and foot, he attacked him with sixty thousand archers and overcame him. Besides the Nambeadarim, who was the chief governor of the land, there were in the city thirty-six principal

1. *Commentaries*, Vol. I., p. 10.

men who governed it, so that it was the best ruled city at that time in those parts."[1]

Albuquerque himself visited Quilon soon after and had an interview with the 'King'. One of the ship's crew, Eupoli by name, gives us the following account of the meeting :—"We were then presented to the King, Nambiadora, who received us with great kindness and urbanity ; and having asked him if we could be supplied with spices, he answered that in twenty days he would engage to load us with every kind of spices, we could wish. We returned on board with the agreeable information, and immediately set about careening ships ; as soon as that was finished, we took in our lading complete, of most excellent spices, which were in such abundance, that we could not take the whole of what was offered us.

"As we now began to think of departing, a meeting betwixt the King and the captain was resolved on, and upon the day fixed, the captain ordered out six boats armed and elegantly decorated with velvet at the stern, Jack and flags flying, himself dressed in gold brocade, with gold-chains and other ornaments in honour of his sovereign; the crews were dressed also in form. The whole being arranged, were ordered to lay close in with the beach and wait the coming of the King. In an hour the King came down, attended by an innumerable concourse of people, all marshalled in procession, according to their several degrees the whole closing with the King, seated cross-legged on an ivory chair, and carried by four Brahmins. The King was dressed in silk embroidered, with an upper robe of gold muslin ; he wore rings of a considerable value, and had on his head a crimson velvet cap highly ornamented with jewels and long chains of pearls and brilliants hanging from the top of the cap, with his hair flowing loose upon his shoulders. There were a number of elephants, and Persian horses followed by the train, which made

[1] *Commentaries of Alfonso Albuquerque*, Vol. I, p. 11.

an elegant appearance. A number of various warlike instruments joined in the procession, playing as they passed. Soon as they arrived opposite to where the boats lay, they made a halt ; immediately the captain made the signal for a salute from the ships, the band playing all the time : he then was rowed to the shore, to have the honour of kissing the king's hand. The King perceiving this, ordered all his people to retire some distance in order to convince the Portuguese of the confidence he had in the captain by meeting him alone. Compliments being paid and the ceremony being gone through, the following compact was mutually entered into by each party: that the King should annually grant to the Portuguese all the spices which his territory produced, which we agreed to take at prices stipulated, paying for the same in goods at regulated prices. We also requested that whoever was left as agent for the King of Portugal, should have the right of punishing or trying any of His Portuguese Majesty's subjects who should remain on the land. This the King granted, though with reluctance, considering it as an interference with his judicial right. The whole being transcribed in silver letters, was properly signed and sealed; and thus the matter was concluded. The natives being desirous of seeing our priests, we landed the two friars, and had mass solemnly performed in their church, with a sermon preached afterwards and explained to the people by the interpreter."[1]

Albuquerque renewed the treaty of peace with the ministers of Vēṇāḍ who agreed to supply the pepper that was immediately required. The Christian inhabitants of the place also assisted in procuring the article. It was said that there were 6,000 Christian houses in the kingdom and several of the Christians came to Albuquerque and requested to intercede on their behalf with the ministers to protect them against the oppressive conduct of the Nairs. He did so and the privilege

1. *Collection of early Voyages*, Vol. I, Book III—*Voyage of Albuquerque.*

that they had enjoyed of being tried by their own castemen was restored to them. They pointed to the Portuguese their Church which they said was erected by St. Thomas the Apostle and wished them to take care of it. Albuquerque left Quilon on the 12th of January 1504 leaving behind him Antonio de Sa as factor with 26 men. Padre Fr. Rodrigues consented to stay there to educate the people in the Catholic religion.

In the meanwhile, a war had arisen between the Zamorin and the Cochin Raja, the Portuguese, of course, assisting the latter. Before its conclusion, a rumour reached Quilon that the Portuguese were worsted in Cochin and the Moors, who had by this time become strong, thinking that this was a good opportunity for them to strike a blow at the Portuguese trade at Quilon, rose and killed one Portuguese and loaded their own ships while those of their enemies were left empty in the harbour. In consequence of this, Duarti Pacheco was sent from Cochin. He remonstrated with the authorities who allowed the Portuguese to empty the Arabian vessels and fill their own.

Francisco de Almeyda had despatched from Cannanore a Portuguese Captain named Homan in advance to Cochin and Quilon to acquaint the Raja of his coming and to have cargo weighed and kept ready for shipment. On reaching Quilon, Antonio de Sa, the factor there, informed him that, though under the terms of the treaty preference ought to be given to the Portuguese, the Arabs had bribed the Raja's ministers to supply 32 vessels belonging to the Arabs with cargo without delay, so that it was extremely unlikely Almeyda would get any supply at all. Annoyed at this, Captain Homan had the sails and rudder of the Moorish vessels taken and removed to the Portuguese factory by force. The Moors complained to the king pointing out that if it came about that Vēṇāṭṭaṭikaḷ (evidently Quilon was then under Travancore suzerainty) was not able to protect foreigners trading in his city against such high handedness on the part of the Franks, it was time that they quitted his shores. One of the Raja's officers proceeded to the Portuguese factory and remonstrated against the conduct of the Captain who had by this time sailed away. The factor, de Sa, usually a prudent man, now put on airs in view of the expected arrival of Almeyda with his ships and began to abuse the officer and his men. Thereupon a tumult arose. The Moors and the Nairs drew their swords and set upon the Portuguese who retired to a neighbouring Bhagavaṭi temple for safety and shut themselves up there. There were 13 of them. The infuriated mob at once set fire to the temple and reduced it to ashes and in it perished the ill-fated Portuguese. This was on the 31st October 1505. On the 1st November, Almeyda arrived at Cochin. He received the sad intelligence that the factor at Quilon with all his men had been killed by the Moors; whereupon he sent his son Dom Lorrenco with three ships and three caravels to procure lading at that port, with orders to appear as though unaware of what had occurred there, but in case of any opposition he was to avenge the murder of the Portuguese. The messenger whom Dom Lorrenco sent on shore was received with a shower of arrows, and 24 ships from Calicut and other places that were in the port prepared for defence. Dom Lorrenco attacked the ships with vigour and having burnt them all, he returned to Cochin.

The Portuguese seem to have had their hands too full elsewhere to permit them to direct their attention to Quilon for some time. But, on Almeyda's arrival at Cochin in November 1508, he was met by messengers from Vēnāṭṭaṭikaḷ who intimated that their sovereign was very sorry for the destruction of the factory at Quilon and its inmates, that he was quite averse to enter into hostilities with the Portuguese and asked if the old relations could not be resumed if the Raja agreed to supply annually 300 Bhāram of pepper. Almeyda replied that that was not enough and that the

Ponnutampuran (Ponnuṭampurān) (the golden King),—a term still applied to the Rajas of Travancore—who had with him two very precious rubies of fame (Mānikkakkallu) should give them up, so that Almeyda may make a present of them to king Manuel of Portugal on his return home. Upon this the messengers went away saying that they had no orders from their master to agree to such terms. Soon after this, Almeyda was informed of the death of his brave son Lorrenco.[1]

This state of circumstances continued till the arrival of Lopo Soares de Albergaria as Governor in succession to Albuquerque. The new Governor thought it necessary to conciliate the Raja of Quilon before setting out on a course of adventure towards the north. He accordingly sent messengers from Cochin to Quilon offering terms of peace. The Raja was at the time a minor. His eldest sister, known as Alī Paṇdāri Rāṇi and styled as Āttingal Ṭampurāṭṭi (Rāṇi of Āttingal), reigned as Regent and was a friend of the Portuguese. She received the advances made with favour and a treaty was concluded with her and the Governors of the land, dated the 25th September 1516. The Rāṇi promised to favour and to protect the Christians as heretofore; to pay 500 *bhars* of pepper in three yearly instalments; to let the Portuguese have all the pepper and other spices they might require at the same prices as they paid for them at Cochin, and to export no drugs or spices without their consent. In case of war with a common enemy, each party agreed to assist the other. No ships from Quilon were to enter the straits of Aden beyond Cape Guardafuy, unless in the service of the Portuguese; and any of the King's subjects, whether natives or Moors, who might desire to become Christians are to be at full liberty to do so. Another treaty on much the same lines as above was subsequently concluded on the 17th November 1520

1. *Keralapazhama* (Kēralapaḷama), p. 99.

with the Queen of Quilon in which it was stipulated that all the pepper in the land was to be sold to the King of Portugal and to nobody else.[1]

Soares left Quilon appointing Captain Heytor Rodrigues as factor. He reached Quilon on the 1st of February 1517 and presented himself before the ministers to receive delivery of the balance of the pepper due. They delayed payment and the Captain represented matters to the Queen. She answered that she was starting the next day to wage war with her neighbour the Raja of Ṭiruviṭancōḍe, that there was a lack of funds then, that the dues to the church have not yet been realised and that she would make all payments on her victorious return from the war. Captain Rodrigues agreed to wait but requested that he may be allowed to build a house for the Portuguese to live in. This was only the thin end of the wedge. Soares had left instructions to secure a desirable site to build a fort. The Queen was rather disconcerted at the request. Nevertheless she selected a site for a house before leaving Quilon. The Moors were shrewd enough to suspect as to what was going to happen. They complained that the so-called house will soon be turned into a fort and remonstrated with the Rāṇi and induced her sister the junior Rāṇi to intercede on their behalf to withold permission. In the meanwhile, the Portuguesē gained over the ministers and put up a building at Ṭamkachēri on an eligible site near the sea-shore, with good water, and had it thatched with cocoanut leaves. The Moors set afloat all sorts of rumours regarding an alleged discomfiture of the Portuguese in the vicinity of Goa, that the Portuguese were beaten by the Moors, that Soares was killed, that Adil Khan had made up his differences with Vijayanagara and

1. *Tratados*, T. 1. p.38. *Report to the Secretary of State for India in Council on the Portuguese Records relating to the East Indies contained in the Archivo Da Torre Do Tombo and the Public Libraries at Lisbon and Evora* by F. C. Danvers, pp. 9 & 10.

that he and Kṛṣhṇa Rāyer were together beseiging Goa. Though the Captain was slow to believe all this, he warned his men not to stir out of the house or occasion any cause for quarrel till the Rāṇi returned from the war. He further took the precaution of conciliating the authorities and keeping them in good humour. By the time the Rāṇi was back, he got news that Soares had returned from Ormuz and that Adil Khan's attempt on Goa had proved fruitless. The neighbouring prince with whom the Queen of Quilon waged war was no other than her own relative who ruled over a tract of country known as Ṭiruviṭāncōḍe. Barbosa, after noticing the kingdom of Quilon, observes:—"Further on, along the same Coast, towards the South is a town of Moors and Gentiles called Tiruangoto which also possesses shipping. The town and territory belong to a lord, a relation of the King of Coulam; it is abundantly supplied with provisions, rice and meat."[1]

Diogo Lopo de Sequeira hastened to fulfil the wishes of Soares to build a fort at Quilon. He wrote to Rodrigues to offer to the Rāṇi and her confident minister, Chānai Piḷḷai, a bribe of 4000 Cochin fanams each, for permission to convert the house or factory into a fort. They received half the amount at once and observed that the matter required great circumspection; the junior Rāṇi would not like it and that her chief adherents, viz., Uṇṇēri Piḷḷai, Bāla Piḷḷai Kuṟup and Kolla Kuṟup, who each held command over 600 Nayars, should be gained over by whatever means. Rodrigues managed the business with great tact and, under pretence of repairing the factory, collected materials secretly and commenced the building of the fort. The junior Rāṇi and her brother, the minor Rāja, were very much annoyed at this and proposed to oppose it by force, whereupon the Queen and her

1. P. 163.

minister Chānai Pillai prevailed upon them to desist. The junior Rāṇi was still burning with fury. When Rodrigues with 27 Portuguese were building up the foundations, she employed 2,000 Nayars to obstruct them. But having the authority of the Queen behind them, they proceeded with the work despite the opposition of the junior Rāṇi. Rodrigues succeeded by evening in putting up a bastion and, as it was feared that by morning a more active and regular opposition may be expected, he had a few pieces of cannon placed in position by night. The moors and Nayars were dispirited at the turn events had taken and did not make any further attempt at opposition. By the month of September 1519, the fort was completed and armed and was christened Fort Thomas. It was a square building with five bastions.[1] The Fort would seem to have been subsequently rebuilt or strengthened, for Captain Nieuhoff tells us that " this castle is the strongest the Portuguese ever were masters of on the coast of Malabar, being built some hundred years ago, by the famous engineer Hector de la Casa ".

The Queen and her ministers went further. In spite of the increasing opposition of her subjects, both Hindu and Mussalman, the deluded Queen not alone encouraged the Portuguese Captain to restore the St. Thomas Church but materially assisted him in doing so to a great extent: all on the firm belief that she would get exemption from the payment of the annual subsidy in pepper. The Captain realised this and desisted from making any demand so long as the fort was being built, and contrived a means of supplying himself with the quantity of cargo required for shipment, and entered upon an enterprise which put an end once for all to the inland trade between the East and the West Coasts. Rodrigues got information that 5,000 bullock loads of pepper which certain traders from the

1. *Keralapazhama*, p. 154.

East Coast had collected in barter for as many bullock loads of rice were on the point of being taken across the ghauts *via* the Āriankāvu Pass. He demanded of the Queen to hand them over to the Portuguese. She excused herself saying that the convoy could not be stopped as the pepper was "*Brahmasvam*", the property of the Brahmans. Upon this, Rodrigues employed 500 Nayars to seize the bullock loads by force promising them Rs. 50 for every human head they produced. They succeeded in bringing the whole 5,000 bullock loads with the heads of 5 of the leaders of the convoy. From that time forward, East Coast merchants were afraid to cross by that pass for trade at Quilon and it gradually fell into disuse.[1]

Now that the fort was completed and fully armed, Rodrigues threw off the mask and disclosed the Portuguese in his true colours. Evidently the Zamorin was not wrong in asking the Queen of Quilon to beware of the Portuguese. Rodrigues sent a message to the Queen demanding immediate weighment of 280 *bhars* of pepper being the balance due under the factory accounts. She contended that the demand was preposterous and that the permission to build the fort was on the distinct understanding that no such demand would be made in the future. The Captain would not relent and hostilities were resolved upon. The junior Rāṇi and her son Mārttāṇḍa Ṭiruvaṭi ordered the Moors to prevent workmen from attending and caused various obstructions which disconcerted the Portuguese very much. Complaints made to the Rāṇi were of no use. The Moors began to load their vessels secretly and the Portuguese Captain caused 7 of their boat loads to be seized by force. An investigation followed, and the Portuguese and their adherents, fearing that the mob would rise against them, retired to the fort and sent information to Cochin. No aid came. Negotiations were opened and the three principal

1. *Keralapazhama*, p. 155.

adherents of the Junior Rāṇi already named proposed to meet the Captain at the St. Thomas Church. Rodrigues was apprehensive of treachery and put off the interview. The result was that an army of 1,500 Nayars soon appeared before the fort under the command of Bāla Piḷḷai Kuṟup. Fighting continued for some time. The inmates of the fort consisting of the Portuguese and their Native Christian adherents suffered much. A strict blockade was kept up; water and provisions fell short. They were reduced to very straightened circumstances. The 30 Portuguese who were within the fort were all laid up. For want of rice or other food-stuffs, they had to live upon rats. Meanwhile the Governor of Cochin got information of this and sent his nephew with 20 Portuguese, as also meat, bread, powder, etc. He succeeded in breaking through the blockade and provisioning the fort. The fighting now became severe. Māṟttāṇḍa Ṭiruvaṭi suffered severe losses. In the month of August, the Queen wrote to the Governor in Cochin seeking peace, and he despatched two messengers, Cherina Marakkar and Pathu Marakkar, to negotiate with Her Highness. Meanwhile, on the 8th of August, the Junior Rāṇi sent an envoy by name Kochikkāli, a well-known Christian lady, who pleaded that her mistress was not privy to what had happened and that she was willing to supply them with provisions, etc. Rodrigues replied that he could treat only with one of the Piḷḷays; so Chānai Piḷḷay met the Captain the next day with provisions, etc., and threw the responsibility of having commenced hostilities on the Queen of Quilon, denounced her conduct as treacherous and offered to withdraw that part of the besieging force which was under the orders of the Junior Rāṇi. The Captain agreed and a considerable portion of the army was withdrawn. The Queen herself finally gave up the siege soon after. From this account one is inclined to suspect that the Portuguese must have employed the wealth at their command to bring about defection in the enemy's camp and the withdrawal of the Junior Rāṇi and her adherents. At any rate we have already seen that Chānai Pillay was not above corruption and that the Portuguese were not averse to spend money in that direction to attain their object.

On the arrival of Pereira with the two Marakkars, Rodrigues was much concerned to see two Moors being employed by the Governor to negotiate the peace; for the Moors were notoriously the implacable enemies of the Portuguese. However, he thought it prudent to offer terms and the following proposals were sent:

(1) That, in addition to the annual subsidy of pepper, 72 *bhars*, being the balance due up-to-date, should be supplied by the Queen.

(2) All that had been plundered from the Portuguese and the Native Christians should be restored. The fort walls should be repaired.

(3) As the revenues of the St. Thomas Church had hitherto been allowed to be appropriated by the Mudaliar of the Muhammedans, the Queen should execute a deed by which the Church should be put in possession of them to endure so long as the sun and moon lasts. The Moors who had come from Cochin, Cannanore, and other places to fight the Portuguese should be excluded from Quilon.

(4) Bāla Pillai Kurup and his sister having proved themselves to be traitors should live 4 miles away from the fort. If they or any of the Changacheri people are found near the fort, those who kill them should not be found fault with.

(5) As a penalty for having commenced hostilities, the Rāṇis should, in addition to at once weighing 100 *bhars* of pepper, supply annually 2,000 *bhars* at the price current in Cochin.

(6) If these terms are not agreed to immediately, all the shipping in the harbour would at once be seized.

Pereira had a long conference with the Rāṇīs and their ministers. The Marakkars advised Pereira not to accept any terms which of course led to some delay, and Pereira, not liking their attitude, ordered them to go back to Cochin. The terms were however not agreed to and both parties retired without signing the agreement. But hostilities were not resumed.

On the 17th November 1520, a treaty was finally concluded between Diogo Lopes De Sequeira and the Queen much on the same lines with the treaty of 1516. It was stipulated that the pepper still owing under the former treaty should be paid at once; that all pepper in the land should be sold to the King of Portugal, and to no one else ; that all ships arriving at that port (not being enemies' ships or laden with pepper) should be allowed free access and be well received ; and that the Captain of the fortress should grant any reasonable assistance to the Queen as she might require.

For some time after this, the Portuguese seem to have got on well with Quilon. When St. Francis Xavier arrived on the Coast, Quilon formed part of Travancore. Xavier, in a letter to the King of Portugal, speaks of the 'Coast of Quilon' being under the authority of the King of Travancore. Fr. Coleridge in his *Life and Letters of the Saint* observes that the Kingdom lay on the western shores of the tongue of land which ends in Cape Comorin, and between the Fishery Coast itself and the Portuguese at Cochin. He adds that it is not easy to settle with perfect clearness the exact relation the Raja of Travancore held towards other princes of the south of India, and it is probable that the relations between them were continually changing. At this time the Raja of Travancore seems to have been a potentate of considerable magnitude and it is surmised that the whole Fishery coast was under his suzerainty. Xavier was a friend of the Great Raja as he is called, who, not simply supplied him with money occasionally but also allowed him ample scope for his evangelizing mission. In spite of the friendly relations then existing between the Raja and the Portuguese, the latter never hesitated to do high-handed acts that outraged the feelings of the Saint. The Portuguese authorities carried off one of the Raja of Travancore's servants and took him in fetters to Tuticorin. Writing to Francis Mancias, Xavier expressed himself thus:— "Any one can see how detestable the whole country and especially the Court itself must think it, that a foreigner should dare to lay violent hands on a servant of the Maharaja in a place under his dominion, especially when that prince is behaving so differently to us." Notwithstanding these occasional differences, the parties continued to pull on well till the arrival of the Dutch.

The whole of the Dutch fleet anchored two leagues to the south of the city of Quilon on the 7th of December 1661. By this time the state of affairs had changed. Travancore had ceased to hold any direct sway over Quilon, having lost her dominion over territories lying to the north of Parūr, though the Raja had still some influence in that direction.

The following extract from Captain Nieuhoff's *Travels* gives us an accurate account of the proceedings of the Dutch by a person who took no inconsiderable part in the capture of Quilon:— "We came to an anchor the 7th of October before Colombo, where we were employed among the rest to take the great train of artillery aboard of us. The Commodore Roodhaes, in the meanwhile, went out before the rest with seven ships only, ordering the rest to follow him to Manepara, one of the seven seaport villages on the Coast of Madura, where all our ships were to meet, which we did accordingly on the 15th of November. Mr. John Vander Werf, Mr. Symonson, and myself, were made not only supervisors, but also treasurers of the whole train of artillery; being provided with everything requisite for such an expedition, we set sail from thence, and came with the whole fleet the 7th of December to an anchor, about two leagues to the south of the city of Kolang or Koulang. The remaining part of the day was spent in landing our soldiers and other necessaries and bringing the ships as close as possible could be to the shore. The 8th we marched in battle array into the country, and the *Negroes* (Nayars) had thrown up a small redoubt within half a league from the city, from whence they fired thick upon our yachts, but without any great loss, yet they plyed us so warmly near the shore, that we were forced to cut our way through the woods to attack them from behind. Immediately all our carpenters were set to work to cut down the bushes and trees, whilst the seamen were employed in levelling the grounds to make way for our artillery. After we were advanced a little way to the wood, we came into a small plain, to the left of which leading to the seaside, we saw a stone house, where we halted a little to take breath, because the seamen had been hard put to it, in drawing the cannon through the deep sand along the seaside. The enemy at the same time kept within his stronghold but, as we advanced farther, they charged our vanguard, who were ordered to break in upon them; they bravely stood the first brunt, but afterwards retreated again to their fort. In the meantime, our cannon having joined us, we prepared for a general attack, which was carried on so vigorously, that the Negroes (Nayars) deserted the fort, in hopes of saving themselves by flight, but were most of them either killed upon the spot or in the flight. A strong party of them happened accidentally to fall in with Captain Polman's Company of firelocks, who were sent thro' the woods to attack the fort from behind: here you might have seen them fight like desperate men, the engagement was very terrible considering the number of men on both sides ; at last they were overcome with above 100 killed and as many wounded on their side; we had no more than three killed, but a great many wounded who were sent aboard the ships to be taken care of. We found two iron pieces of cannon in this fort, which we nailed up, and beat the carriages in pieces. After we had placed guards in all convenient posts thereabouts, the soldiers reposed themselves under the shadow of trees; but within two hours after we continued our march to the city of Kaulang, passing all the way by a great many fine plantations, surrounded on all sides with walls, the road betwixt them being very narrow. As we advanced to the city, the enemy fired briskly upon us from a small fort near the waterside, where they had set up the Portuguese standard, but perceiving us notwithstanding this to march undaunted towards the walls, their hearts began to fail, and betaking themselves to flight, left the city to our mercy, which we took without the least resistance.

"We rested the next day, but every one being animated by the last success in taking so considerable a city without opposition, longed for action, so that, before the morning, the whole body being put in battle array without the water-gate, the chief minister of the camp, Mr. Baldeus, made a short but very fervent speech, and the Commanders exhorted them to fight courageously for the honour of their country and religion; which being joyfully accepted by the soldiers who promised to hazard all for the service of the Company, the drums and trumpets began to sound the march. Mr. Ysbrand Goskeled commanded the van, and Commodore Roodhaes the rear, being both persons of known bravery; Mr. Rykloff Van Goens commanded the main battle; we carried some field pieces along with us to serve us upon occasion. We were forced to march thro' narrow ways, where scarce four could march abreast, and finding that the enemy galled us from an adjacent small fort, some companies wheeled to the right, and the rest to the left, whilst the seamen immediately approached with their scaling ladders, and mounting the walls, took the fort with little resistance. We found here no more than two iron pieces of cannon ready charged; notwithstanding all this, they skirmished briskly with our foremost troops as they were advancing beyond the fort, but gave way by degrees and retreated up to the royal palace, where they made another halt, and engaged our troops a second time, but with no better success, for being once seized with a panick fear, they soon gave ground, and left the palace to our mercy, which we plundered and destroyed. They had, however in the meanwhile, attacked our rear several times because our heavy cannon could not come up soon enough with us, by reason of the narrowness of the way; the enemy making use of this advantage attacked us very furiously, but were bravely repulsed by the help of our field pieces, which being charged with small shot, were discharged among them with such success, that many of them remained dead on the spot; and by this means we kept them so long in play, till we received a seasonable reinforcement, when they betook themselves to their heels, and left us absolute masters of the field. In the meanwhile, our troops were advanced to the river, where they made themselves masters of another fort in which they found 2 brass and 10 iron pieces of cannon. In a certain Pagode next to the royal palace, called *Matta del Reyne*, we found a great chest with gunpowder, which being set on fire, in an instant blew up and destroyed this ancient structure, covered on the top with brass. Then our troops beat the country both to the right and left, burning and destroying all they met with. In an instant we saw whole woods in a flame, the bamboo canes making a most terrible noise, and burning like brimstone, a miserable spectacle to the enemy, who from the other side of the river, saw the flame consume in an instant, what had cost them many years' labour. John Piccard, my nephew, a captain lieutenant, and William Van

Teylingin were sent with some chaloops up the river *Arwick*, to pursue the flying enemy on that side, but these took another way; most of them wading thro' the river, where they could not come near them with their chaloops. Mr. Piccard then landed his company on the other side, where he set 40 houses on fire, which occasioned a fresh consternation among the flying enemy. After we had thus ravaged the country, we returned to the before mentioned Pagode, where our troops reposed themselves for a while, and the same evening returned conquerors to the city of Koulang. The 12th (December) all the ships' carpenters were sent for ashore to cut down the trees that stood upon the city walls, and orders were given for breaking down part of it, and to bring it into a narrower compass, which was put in execution immediately. About the same time the natives sent some deputies to sue for peace".

In January 1662, Nieuhoff was appointed Chief Director of the Dutch East India Company at Quilon, and he arrived there on the 7th, after taking part in the capture of the Portuguese forts of Crānganūr and Pallipōrt. He gave orders for the repair of the fort and, in his own words, began "settling everything that might tend to the re-establishment of traffick with the Queen of Koulang, and other neighbouring princes, unto whom I was sent a deputy to treat with them and to enter into a confederacy with them for that purpose". The first treaty concluded was, of course, with the Queen of Quilon, which was on the following terms, viz., "That her palace and great guns should be restored to her and that the company would pay her a sum of money for the rebuilding of the palace and as compensation for other damages sustained". The Dutch Captain significantly adds that it was the Company's interest "rather to purchase peace upon reasonable terms than to be at the charge of war".

The Nayars or as Nieuhoff calls them "the Negroes" had expelled the Dutch once before from

Quilon, where they had made a settlement, murdering Captain Henry Glunning, their Governor, as he was taking a walk without the gates of the fort. They afterwards massacred all the Dutch; since which time the Portuguese got into possession of it. But now that the Dutch were once more masters of Quilon, they were not slow to get into the good graces of the Queen, for we see the Dutch soon after sending their *protegee*, the exiled King of Cochin, to the Queen so that he may be cured of an illness he was then suffering from. The Dutch were slow to fulfil the terms of their treaty with the Queen and we see frequent demands being made by her. Says Nieuhoff: "No sooner was I arrived, the 9th of February 1664 at Koulong, but the Queen of the same name, sent the next day her Chief Captain to receive the customs and cannon she pretended to be due to her by virtue of the late treaty. I was willing to surrender the cannon according to the agreement, but could not consent to the other". Captain Nieuhoff was about to go on a mission to the Court of the King of Travancore and nothing was done. While he was at the Court of Travancore, engaged with the ministers in settling the terms of a treaty with the King, an envoy from the Queen of Quilon arrived with a letter to the king complaining "that she had not received any share of the customs, nor were the cannon restored to her". The Queen was evidently under the suzerainty of Travancore, for Nieuhoff tells us that the Governor of the King of Travancore kept his residence in that part of Quilon known as Quilon-China. The ministers of the Travancore King remonstrated with the Captain and asked him "what the meaning of it was, and whether (the Dutch) would do less than the Portuguese had done". The Captain answered: "If we should follow the footsteps of the Portuguese, we must be guilty likewise of the same enormities, in murthering, plundering, etc., things not customary with us, the intention of our Company being to maintain every one in his right, and establish a free commerce without interruption". As the negotiations with Travancore were rather protracted, the Dutch managed to detach the Queen of Quilon from the king, but the Queen was afraid to enter into any separate arrangement with the Dutch so long as the King of Travancore was in the neighbourhood. Nieuhoff observes: "I very well foresaw that this negotiation (with Travancore) would meet with no small difficulties, unless something more was granted than had been offered hitherto. About the same time, the before mentioned Queen, sent me underhand word, that she was very inclinable to a farther treaty, but that it could not be done till the King of Travancore was gone."

On the next day, after Nieuhoff had signed the treaty with Travancore and other neighbouring princes, *i. e.*, on the 22nd February 1664, the Dutch Captain sent to the Queen a letter through Mr. Sebastian Ferdinandi, his interpretor, giving her "an account of what had been transacted with the Rasidoor (Kariakar or minister) of the king of Travancore and the Dutch". On the 2nd March, Nieuhoff met the Queen in person and he gives the following description of the interview. :—

"The 2nd of March with break of day, the vice-roy of the King of *Travankoor* call'd by them *Gorepe* (Kurup), the chief commander of the Negroes, call'd *Matta de Pulo*, (Mārttāṇḍa Pillay) and myself, set out for the court of the Queen of *Koulang*, which was then kept at *Calliere* (Kallada). We arriv'd there about 2 'o clock in the afternoon, and as soon as notice was given of our arrival, we were sent for to court, where after I had deliver'd the presents, and laid the money down for pepper, I was introduced into her majesty's presence. She had a guard of above 700 soliders about her, all clad after the *Malabar* fashion; the Queen's attirement being no more than a piece of callicoe wrapt round her middle, the upper part of her body appearing for the most part naked, with a piece of callicoe hanging carelessly round her shoulders. Her ears, which were very long, her neck and arms were adorn'd with precious stones, gold rings and bracelets, and her head cover'd with a piece of white callicoe. She was past her middle age, of a brown complexion, with black hair tied in a knot behind, but of a majestic mein, she being a princess who shew'd great deal of conduct in the management of her affiairs. After I had paid the usual compliments, I shew'd her, the proposition I was to make to her in writing; which she ordered to be read twice, the better to understand the meaning of it, which being done, she ask'd me, whether this treaty comprehended all the rest. and whether they were annull'd by it; unto which I having given her a sufficient answer, she agreed to all our propositions, which were accordingly sign'd immediately. * * * I then desired leave to depart, because I expected Mr. Hustart (Councillor of the Indies and Governor and Director of the Isle of Ceylon and the Malabar Coast) every hour at Koulong, which she readily granted, and at the same time took a golden bracelet from her arms, which she presented to me as a token of her good inclinations to the company. She order'd one of the *Residoors* (Governors?) to fasten it to my arm, but it being too straight she caused it to be fitted for me, she having once before, viz., when I first gave her notice of Mr. Hustarts' coming, presented me with another golden bracelet, for which and all other honours, I had received from her majesty, since my residence at *Kaulang*, I returned my hearty thanks, desiring her once more not to withdraw her favour from the Company". [1] Nieuhoff left the Queen's presence after recommending Mr. James Cherde Venne who was to succeed him at Quilon.

Apart from what can be gathered from Portuguese and Dutch writers, we have little or no means of information regarding these native principalities till we

1 Churchill's *Collection of Voyages and Travels*, Vol. II, p. 231.

come to the beginning of the 18th century. The Quilon branch of the Travancore Family seems to have secured its practical independence according as the power of the main Family declined in Travancore. With its separation from Travancore, Quilon began to decline. Its political and commercial importance seems to have gone down greatly during the succeeding century and a half, for Baldeus describes it as the least among the Malabar Kingdoms, while Captain Alexander Hamilton speaks of it as a "small principality" and adds that "its trade is inconsiderable". Incursions from the Madura and Trichinopoly side and civil tumults and internecine wars coupled with the growing power of the Eṭṭu Vīṭṭil Piḷḷamārs crippled the sway of the Travancore Kings, so much so that ere long they had to confine themselves to the small tract of land lying between Eḍawai in the north and Cape Comorin in the south. But towards the beginning of the 18th century, a more enterprising King reigned in Travancore in the person of Mārṭṭāṇḍa Varma, who set himself about compensating for losses on the eastern border by extending the boundary of the kingdom towards the north. The first country that claimed his attention was the kingdom of Quilon. Fra Bartholomeo tells us that the King encamped for ten years at Parūr, because the King of Changachēry or Collam disputed with him the passage of the Parūr River. The king at length found means to force his way over and to take prisoner the King of Quilon after a decisive battle with him.

We learn from the *History of Travancore* that, in the year 1731, the Raja of Quilon made an adoption of certain members of the Kāyamkuḷam family in opposition to the wishes of King Mārṭṭāṇḍa Varma, who had already made up his mind to annex the principality to Travancore on the death of the then Raja who happened to be the last member of the house. Enraged at the conduct of the Raja of Quilon, King Mārṭṭāṇḍa Varma

H.

invaded his country and took the Raja prisoner and removed him to Trivandrum. He however escaped after some time, was joined by Kāyamkuḷam, and the two princes marched on Quilon. The Travancore general withdrew after a pitched battle and the Quilon chief once more sat on his ancestral throne. Quilon now assumed the aggressive and attacked Travancore possessions about Māvēlikkara in conjunction with Kāyamkuḷam. Mārttāṇḍa Varma at once took the field. The enemy had formed a confederacy of the northern princes to withstand Travancore, but to no purpose. The Kāyamkuḷam Raja died in battle and his successor, seeing resistance useless, sued for peace. While negotiations were progressing, the Raja of Quilon died and Kāyamkuḷam took possession of the Quilon territories under pretence of the adoption made by the deceased Raja. King Mārttāṇḍa Varma remonstrated. But the Kāyamkuḷam Raja, backed by the King of Cochin and the Dutch, gave no ear to the remonstrances with the result that war was declared. This war ended in the complete overthrow of the Kāyamkuḷam King whose territory was annexed, the Raja himself flying towards the north.

7. **Three Co-heiresses.** The three princes mentioned were in no way related to one another. Our author's information as to these having had their origin with three co-heiresses appears not to be accurate. The Raja of Signati or Ḍēśinganāḍ belonged to the Kshetria caste, while "Poele Barriate" or Vaṭayāttu Piḷḷay was a Nayar to which class also belonged the 'Goeryp' or Kurup. We have seen that the Portuguese accounts of Quilon make mention of a *Kolla Kurup*, *Kollathu Kurup*, i.e., *Kurup* of Quilon, one of the chief adherents of the Junior Rāṇi. This chief had authority over that part of Quilon which was known as *Changacheri*, and we have seen that the Portuguese had stipulated with the Queen of Quilon that Bālappiḷḷa Kurup and his sister or any one from *Changacheri* should not be

allowed to approach their fort at Quilon on pain of being instantly killed by whomsoever, who finds them in the locality.

Poele Barriat. This stands for Piḷḷa of Vaṭayāṯṯu. Nieuhoff tells us that in his time 'Prince Barytter Poele' kept his residence in that part of the city called Quilon-China, where also lived the Governor of the King of Travancore. That he was a power in the kingdom is certain, and it is possible, and indeed probable, that he held territorial sway over some particular tract; for we see him mentioned along with the kings of Marta, Signaty, Travancore, &c., as entering into articles of agreement with the Dutch East India Company. Further we find it mentioned by the Dutch Governor Gollennesse of Cochin in the *Memoir* left by him in 1743 that the Raja of Travancore "had all the noble men of the State, both Piḷḷas and Guṟups, put to death or banished the country except the Pula of Bariatte." Of the Vaṭayāṯṯu Piḷḷay we read in Mr. Justice Kunju Raman Nayar's *Memo on Land Tenures*:—"He is a Malayāli Śūḍṟa, but his house is called Maṭhom and the estates owned by him are the estates of an ancient Swarūpom or Chiefship, probably conferred upon his ancestors by a former sovereign. Vaṭayāṯṯu Maṭhom is the recorded proprietor of lands in no less than eight Taluks: (1) Trivandrum, (2) Neyyāṯṯinkara, (3) Ceṟayinkīḷ, (4) Quilon, (5) Karuṅāgappiḷḷy, (6) Kuṅṅaṭṭūr, (7) Koṭṭārakkara, and (8) Ṭiruvella. The Vaṭayāṯṯu Chiefs style themselves as representatives of the Śṟēya Swarūpam—an ancient petty State in South Travancore. The selection to the Chiefship is subject to the confirmation of the sovereign, though the selection is always made from the members of four families or Ṭaṟawāḍs in the Quilon District."[1]

8. **Peritalli.** The identity of this State it is somewhat difficult to make out from the name mentioned. But our author tells us that it lies between

1. P. 61.

Quilon and the Mountains, and it has been suggested that the country referred to must have been Neḍuvangāḍ. But, according to Lieut. Horsley, the present district of Neḍuvangāḍ formed a small principality known as Ellavallūṙṅāḍ and not Peritalli. Visscher adds "that Kully Quilon (Kāyamkuḷam) is *at the present time* united to this country by adoption;" and, as he was making a record of events that had transpired in his time and within his personal knowledge, we may take it that he is correct. Day says that, in 1734, the Travancore Raja made himself master of the fruitful pepper Kingdoms of Peritali, and Eḷayaḍa Swarūpam which a few years previously had been united, owing to the demise of one of the Rajas without leaving a nearer heir than the neighbouring prince. Referring to the protest made by the Dutch Envoy, M. Van Imhoff, against the wholesale annexations made by Travancore, Day says that "the cause of the princess of Elleda Suruwam or Ellertoo Sooroopam *also designated* Peritalay was taken up and a protest sent in 1740 to the Raja of Travancore retaining her territory." Day seems to have derived his information from the Dutch official records preserved in Cochin, so that it is hazardous to say that he also is wrong.

'Perītalli' may possibly stand for Paṭṭaḷi.

9. **Ellidaseruwan.** This was the principality of Eḷayaḍa Swarūpam governed by a branch of the Travancore Royal House. According to the *Memoirs of Travancore* compiled by Lieut. Horsley, it lay to the north of Ellavallūṙnāḍ, i. e., modern Neduvangāḍ and was an extensive principality that included the two districts of Koṭṭārakkara and Paṭṭanāpuram. Mr. Shangoony Menon's *History of Travancore* adds to these Shencōṭṭa, Kaḷakāḍ, Keṙkuḍi and Vaḷḷiyūr on the Tinnevelly side. In the year 1734, King Māṙṭṭāṇḍa Vaṙma seized the country, and removed the reigning family to Travancore. The Raja died in prison in 1736. One princess alone escaped by taking refuge with the

Raja of Ṭekkenkūr. She sought the aid of the northern States, and the Dutch deemed this a fit opportunity to interpose as mediators and champions of the Malabar Rajas. Espousing the cause of the exiled Princess, the Dutch Góvernor presented a protest to the Travancore King through his Envoy M. Van Imhoff. It was not heeded and, in the year 1741, the Princess was forcibly re-instated in the regency of the kingdom. As a reward for this, the northern States gave the Dutch a large farm at Airūr at about 3 Dutch miles from Quilon, and also one at Bichoor (Vechūr) in the Vaṭakkankūr country, where they erected a strong redoubt. Their success was however of short duration. For the Travancore forces soon took the field with great success, every Dutch out-post in Travancore falling before them. The Princess was driven from her throne and the country annexed. The Dutch had also to give up their recent acquisitions. Thus the country of Elayadaṭṭuṅāḍ became part of Travancore in 1742.

Speaking of the States of Peritally and Elayaḍa Swarūpam, the Dutch Governor Gollennesse observes in 1743: " They bound on Travancore in the north-east. By the extinction of the families of former rulers, they have come under one ruler who is called the King of Peritalli, adopted from the princess of Ellerta Surowan, being of the Chiodircoor (Chovarakkūr) faction. The King of Travancore took possession of this State in the year 1734, led away the Royal Family into captivity and had them imprisoned in a Pagger where the King died two years ago. The other princess and princesses are still there with the exception of one princess, who was fortunate enough to escape from the hands of the usurper and to get safely to Ṭekkenkūr; in the year 1740, she was brought back from there by the Hon'ble Company to her State and made Regent; but, in the year 1742, she had again to leave, and she withdrew into the State of Cochin where she puts up with her relations, at Corporam, and she still receives

45 fanams daily from the Hon'ble Company towards her own support and that of her suite."

The States already named were once portions of the kingdom of Travancore and so Van Rheede, in 1694, calls the whole territory by the name of 'Tippopposorivan' or Ṭṛppāppūr Swarūpam. He observes that 'Tirivancore' (Travancore) could collect 100,000 soldiers; 'Attingan' (Āṭṭingal) which, being under the direct sway of the Queens of Travancore, is treated separately by European writers, 30,000; 'Elaiyathswarupan' 50,000; 'Peritalli' 3,000 and Quilon 30,000.

10. **Marta or Carnagopoli.** This principality was called *Marta* from its capital Maruṭukuḷangara. Nieuhoff says that it lay three leagues to the south of Cochin. According to him, the Kingdom was as large as Kāyamkuḷam extending to the north as far as Poṙaçāḍ, to the south it bordered on the Indian sea, and to the east it was surrounded by high mountains. "To the south of the Capital, near the seashore, was another city called by the inhabitants *Panderatoutte* and by the Portuguese *Pesse*." Māvēlikkara with its chief city Puṭiakāvu formed part of the Kingdom. He adds that this King possesses some parts in common with the King of Kāyamkuḷam. There were many rich Mahomedan merchants here. A Christian community had also existed here for a long time. Till the year 1581, they had no Church to worship. In that year, "the reigning King not only gave them liberty to build a Church but also to cut wood in the adjacent forests dedicated to the pagan idols. The Jesuits had full power granted to them to exercise the Church censure and to inflict it upon those that were baptized by them."

Nieuhoff visited the King who is described as a sovereign prince with whom the Dutch East India Company entered into an agreement. Of him Nieuhoff says, "He that then reigned (1662—4) was of about 60 years of age, very large of body and a stern countenance; he keeps constantly 1,200 Negroes (Nairs), in pay; his residence was at Carnopoly (Karināgappiḷḷi), a place surrounded with an earthen wall of 20 feet high, but appeared much decayed at that time." The demands that the Dutch made upon the King were:—"To forbid the importation of *amfion* (opium), the peeling of the wild cinnamon and the exportation of pepper. After being vigorously opposed by the Mahomedan Merchants, we overcame all difficulties, the king having granted us all we demanded except the peeling of wild cinnamon." This kingdom became absorbed with that of Kāyamkuḷam some time before the latter was annexed to Travancore. Regarding these two States we glean the following particulars from the *Memoirs* of Governor Gollennesse:—

"Marta comprises two small States, Carnapoly and Carimbalie or Betimene; the former stretches along the sea between Coi and Calicoilan, the latter lies on the other side of the river between Calicoilan and Porca. The King of Travancore against right and reason had caused a princess of his own family to be adopted there; she was called queen, but as a matter of fact the State was ruled by the King's Ragiadoors. In the year 1740, she was compelled to leave the State and to withdraw into Tekkenkoor to Nedoompuram, a desam or free place. But in 1742, when we had to leave the field owing to want of men, the State fell again into the hands of the Raja of Travancore; the latter still holds possession of it on condition that his claims on Peritally and Marta will be examined by impartial Kings."

11. **Kully Quilon.** This was the State of Kāyamkuḷam ranked as the second kingdom of Travancore It was closely related to the Royal House of Vēṇāḍ and was known as the Cheṛava Swarūpam. It was one of the 18 Nāḍs into which Vēṇāḍ was originally

divided and was known as Ohnāḍ or Ōḍanāḍ. The earliest mention we have of this dynasty is in the Kōṭṭayam copper-plate of Vīra Rāghava about the 8th century A. D. There the ruler of Ōḍanāḍ is cited as a witness along with that of Vēnāḍ. In the Trivandrum temple accounts already referred to, the dynastic as well as house name of Travancore is thus combined with those of the ruler of Kāyamkuḷam: Ṭṛppāppūr Kīḷpperūr Śri Vīra Āḍiṭya Varma, the senior member of Cheṛavāi.

Varthema says, "that the city of Caolan (as he calls it) lay 50 leagues to the south of Calicut and that the King thereof was not very rich. The manner of living, the dress, and customs are after the manner of Calicut. Many merchants arrived here, because a great deal of pepper grows in this country and in perfection." He found a large number of St. Thomas Christians who were merchants. Barbosa's account is the same as Varthema's; he however calls the place by its correct name *Caincoulam*. Baldeus, nearly a century and a half later, describes it thus: "The next adjoining Kingdom (to Poracca) is Calemcoulang of no great extant. Here the Dutch had a factory." Nieuhoff seems to have paid a visit to the ruler of Kāyamkuḷam. He says:—

"We arrived at Kalkolang on the 22nd January 1664. I gave notice of my arrival by our interpreter to the King, who soon after returned in company of a *Residoor* from the King to fetch me to court. Accordingly, I and Mr. Willing, who resided there as under-factor of the Company, were introduced by the said *Residoor* into the King's presence, whom we found surrounded with a great number of courtiers, that constantly attend his person. After the first ceremonies and compliments, such as are usual in this place, were passed, I surrendered my credentials to the King, who received them with a great deal of respect and seeming satisfaction. This prince had the character of a very sincere person which appeared both in his countenance and actions, but leaves the management of all affairs of moment to the before-mentioned Residoor."

Kāyamkuḷam appears to have attained some importance after the absorption of the kingdoms of Marta and Bettimeni or Karunāgappiḷḷi and Kārttigapiḷḷi. It managed to throw off its allegiance to Travancore and stood by the side of Quilon and Eḷayaḍa Swarūpam. Just before this, Hamilton describes it as "a little principality contiguous to Poracca." It was bounded by the kingdom of Poracad in the north, and Quilon on the south extending to a considerable distance inland stretching between Quilon and the southern limit of Kuttanāḍ. It comprehended the districts of Karunāgappiḷḷi, Kārttigappiḷḷi and Māvēlikkara.

Kāyamkuḷam came into prominence in the early part of the 18th century in connection with the confederacy of the northern States to oppose the advance of the Travancore King. The Cochin Raja put himself at the head of the confederacy and sought the aid of the Dutch who were only too glad to have an opportunity of curbing the rise of Travancore. The Raja of Kāyamkuḷam invaded the Marta country without any provocation, about the year 1730, and rendered material help to Quilon in the late war. He had further induced the Quilon Raja to adopt certain members of his family as heirs of the Quilon house, so that the two countries may be amalgamated on the demise of the Quilon Raja, who was the last of his line. Travancore took umbrage at this, marched an army into the Quilon country, defeated the Raja, took him prisoner and removed him to Trivandrum whence he escaped and was joined by the Kāyamkuḷam Raja. The allies then drove the Travancoreans from Quilon, and the Raja was reinstated. Not content with this, the allies assumed the offensive and attacked Travancore possessions situated at Kaḷḷaḍa and Māvēlikkara.

King Mārttāṇḍa Varma placed a strong army in the field, re-conquered Quilon and advanced towards Kāyamkuḷam. The Raja was alarmed and despatched his Kāriakār or minister, Ītchchara Paṭṭar, accompanied by two of the Cochin Raja's friends to seek the aid of the Dutch Governor in Cochin. This was in October 1733. The emissaries stated that the Raja of Travancore was making great preparations to attack Kāyamkuḷam on the 16th of that month and was also trying to persuade the Ṭekkenkūr and Poracād Princes to join in the war. Assistance was, therefore, most urgently wished for from the Dutch and the Cochin Raja. Just then the Dutch were disinclined to join the fray, and Governor Maten replied that the cause of the troubles was owing to the Raja of Kāyamkuḷam having wantonly invaded the Marta country and that he could give no assistance. He advised the Raja to join the Peritalli Chief who had refused leave to the Travancoreans to pass through his country to attack Kāyamkuḷam.

Early in 1734, Travancore made itself master of the Peritalli or Eḷayaḍa Swarūpam country, carrying away the reigning family as prisoners. All except a princess died in prison and she, as we have seen, escaped to the Ṭekkenkūr country. In the meanwhile, Kāyamkuḷam sued for peace, and hostilities were suspended. Soon after, the Raja of Quilon died, and the Kāyamkuḷam Raja proceeded to take possession of the kingdom under pretence of the adoption already mentioned. King Mārttāṇḍa Varma remonstrated without effect, and war was once more declared with Kāyamkuḷam in the year 1739. As the war was progressing, Kāyamkuḷam once more sought the aid of the Dutch and this time with better results. The Company interfered on behalf of the exiled Rāṇi of Eḷayaḍa Swarūpam and went to war with Travancore and got itself worsted. Finding that it was not possible to continue the war, the Kāyamkuḷam chief sought for peace, and a treaty was concluded between Travancore and

Kāyamkuḷam in 1742, the Raja ceding the greater portion of his country to Travancore and binding himself to be a tributary and ally, paying an annual tribute of a thousand rupees, besides an elephant. He also bound himself to treat the enemies of Travancore as his. Before two years had gone by, the Raja put forth every endeavour to shake off the Travancore yoke. He could get no assistance from Cochin, as the Cochin Raja was himself defending his country, at the time, against a sudden invasion by the Zamorin. Kāyamkuḷam then turned to the Chiefs of Ambalappuḷa, or Poṙacād and Changanāśśēri or Ṭekkenkūr, who promised their co-operation. Kāyamkuḷam now withheld the payment of the tribute due under the terms of the treaty and began to make preparations to resist any attempt to levy it by force. In 1746, the Travancore general, Rāma Iyen Ḍaḷawa, marched at the head of an army to exact the tribute. He met with little or no opposition. From Māvēlikkara, the Ḍaḷawa summoned the Raja to pay up the arrears in full. He asked for a few days' time either to pay up the amount, or to surrender his country. This was granted. He then sent his family and all available treasure in covered boats to the north, collected all that he could lay hands on, arms, silver and brass vessels, etc., in fact every thing of any value, removed them in big boats to the middle of the Ashṭamuḍi Lake and consigned them to the deep. After accomplishing this, he stole away by night leaving behind him his desk containing correspondence implicating the neighbouring Chiefs. When the time allowed for payment had expired, the Ḍaḷawa marched to Kāyamkuḷam to find that the bird had already flown away. He at once took possession of the country and annexed it to Travancore.

Writing of this Raja and his State, in 1743, Governor Gollennesse says :—" Calicoilan is a beautiful small State stretching from the sea far inland ; it lies between Pandalam, Thekkenkūr, Elleda Surowan,

Martencore, Porca and Tirkenapoly or Pagodingo. The King of this State also possesses the States of Coilan and Pannapoly. He is a man of understanding and courage, but his profligacy and fickleness mar all his other good qualities; he is not exactly avaricious but rather wasteful, and as his own means do not suffice, he gathers and scrapes together as much as he can, and for this reason he may rightly be called grasping. He has 15,000 Nayars who were formerly looked upon as the best in Malabar, but in the late war they behaved with unheard of cowardice; the strange conduct of the King no doubt contributed greatly to this; his people are far from loving him, and they do not think him worthy that they should risk their lives in his interests."

12. **Tercunapalli.** Tercunapalli, at present Ṭṛkkuṅṅappuḻa, is the possession of the Nambūṭiri Raja of Eḍappiḷḷi called by the Portuguese Rapolim. The boundaries given by our author tally almost exactly with the Raja's possessions on that side at present. It is, therefore, doubtful if the suggestion recently made that Visscher's 'Tricunapalli' was Kāṟṭṭikappiḷḷi is correct.[1] According to Governor Gollennesse, "Trikanapaly, which is better known among us by the name of Pagodingo, is a small piece of land situated along the sea; it stretches from Calicoilan to Poraca and belongs to the King of Repolim; it is governed by the King's Ragiadoors." The principality of Kāṟṭṭikappiḷḷi was known as Batimena or Venmaṇi and not Ṭṛkkuṅṅapuḻay. Of course at present, the Raja does not exercise any sovereign authority over the tract, but he is treated as the titular sovereign.

13. **Rapolim or Edappilli.** As our author has failed to notice Rapolim or Eḍappiḷḷi which occupies a peculiar position in Malabar, the king of which State being a Brahman of great sanctity, we propose to give an account of this chief.

1. *Malabar Quarterly Review*, Vol. III, p. 143.

The Rajaship of Eḍappiḷḷi has a peculiarity of its own. The State itself is but small and was never of much consequence; but the circumstance that it belongs to a Nambūṭiri of the highest class and of peculiar sanctity has invested it with an amount of significance out of all proportion to its extent or power. The dynasty claims to have had its origin from the days of Paraśurāma himself. After the colonisation of Malabar by the Nambūṭiri Brahmans, Paraśurāma, as the Kēraḷōlpaṭṭi says, organised a militia of 36,000 Brahmans, imparted to them a knowledge of the art of war and gave their Chiefs swords of office. The foremost to accept the sword from the warrior-sage was Eḍappiḷḷi Nambiāṭiri, i. e., the Eḍappiḷḷi Chief. The term *Nambiatiri* means a Brahman (Nambūṭiri) general and the Eḍappiḷḷi Chief is still styled as such, though it is pretty long since he has sheathed his sword. That at one time he did make a free use of it will appear from his conduct in the wars the Zamorin waged with the Cochin Raja and the Portuguese. The dynasty is known as *Elangallur Swarupam* (Eḷangallūṙ Swarūpam) which was distorted into *Elengol* by the Portuguese writers who appear to have mangled and distorted the name of the country, *Edappilli* into *Rapolim* and *Replim*. The Dutch have followed the Portuguese in the use of the latter terms.

Sometime before the advent of the Portuguese, the island of Cochin had belonged to Eḍappiḷḷi;[1] but when and under what circumstances the Raja of Cochin came to possess it is shrouded in mystery. In the early part of the 15th century, it must have belonged to the Cochin Raja, for the Chinese traveller, Ma Huan, mentions it to be so. The Eḍappiḷḷi Raja had allowed the Madura exiles, who finally established themselves at Pūññāṙ, to reside in the island and had conferred on them certain rights therein, which they exercised till they abandoned Cochin, resigning these rights and privileges to Maṇḍala

1. See *Note* on p. 89 of Day.

Muḍaliār, and moved on southwards as they found that the Eḍappiḷḷi Raja was harassing them. The exact period of this event is not certain. We can only say that between the date of this incident and that of the arrival of Ma Huan, Cochin must have been lost to Eḍappiḷḷi.

As to how the Rajas of Cochin came to possess the island, tradition says that it was a gift to one of them who was the son of the then Eḍappiḷḷi chief— a not unlikely event. We have in the Rajaship of Nīlīśvaram and Kaḍaṭṭanāḍ, instances of even States being carved out as a provision for the children of Rajas, an act which certainly derogated from the rights of their legal heirs, their sister's sons, under Marumakkaṭṭāyam law. The Cochin dynasty has been always known as Perumpaṭappu Swarūpam, and the country over which they rule, Perumpaṭappu Ṅāḍ. The Kēralōlpaṭṭi styles both the dynasty and the country as such. It is significant that the Cochin Sirkar *Grandhavari* (Grandhavari-chronicles) claims the appellation of Perumpaṭappu having been received by the dynasty because of the circumstance that one Perimpaṭappu Nambūṭiri had married in the family and had issue there to whom devolved his property and ṭarawāḍ as he had no legal heirs left.

At the advent of the Portuguese, they found the Eḍappiḷḷi Raja a strong partisan of the Zamorin ready to fight against their ally, the Cochin Raja. We have found that, in the earlier wars between the Zamorin and the Portuguese, the '*Elengol*' or the Eḍappiḷḷi Nambiāṭiri took a most prominent part. His sword was always at the service of the Zamorin. In the Zamorin's attack on Cochin, on the Raja's refusal to deliver up the few Portuguese who were left behind by Vasco Da Gama, the Eḍappiḷḷi Raja had taken part for which he seems to have received chastisement at the hands of Albuquerque who had recently arrived from Portugal. Faria Y Souza tells us :—" The Lord of Replim, his lands were wasted with fire and sword, and only four Portuguese lost in this action." Nothing daunted, the Eḍappiḷḷi chief joined the Zamorin in the subsequent attack on Cochin and commanded a large host, both at the attack on the fort and at the attempt to cross the fords at Kumbaḷam and Panangāḍ. Here again Faria tells us, "They (i.e. the Zamorin's feudatories) drew together 50,000 men, as well for land as sea; for the sea were 4,000 men, in 280 Paraos, Caturs and Tonees, vessels of several sorts with 382 cannons to batter the new fort; all the rest was for the land to attack the ford of a river that passed to the island; these were commanded by Nambea Dering, Nephew and Heir to him of Calicut and by Elancol, Lord of Replim." It would appear that, even after the Zamorin had made up his mind to retire, disheartend by defeat after defeat, the Eḍappiḷḷi chief cheered him on to the attack promising to carry everything before him. But the attempt finally failed, and the Zamorin and his allies had to beat a hasty retreat, having lost a considerable portion of their army. It was during this war that the sacred stone at which the Zamorin was made the Lord of the Southern Malabar States was removed from Cochin to Eḍappiḷḷi. It may be remembered that one of the Zamorin's many invasions of the Cochin kingdom was on behalf of the Eḍappiḷḷi Raja, claiming the island of Cochin as belonging to him.

Many of the allies and principal Chiefs subject to the Zamorin were now extremely anxious to make terms with the Portuguese, amongst whom was the Raja of Replim, who, alarmed for his country and himself, proposed to enter into a treaty. He, at the same time, sent Pacheco, the Portuguese Commander in Cochin, a present of a large quantity of pepper. An alliance between them was then entered into, being apparently the first formed between the Portuguese and any petty Indian Prince.[1] This was in A. D. 1504.

The next we hear of the Raja of Eḍappiḷḷi in the Portuguese annals is in the year 1536 when Martin Alfonso de Souza led an attack on the principality.

1. Day, p. 93.

For a long time after this, Eḍappiḷḷi drops as it were from the arena of Malabar politics; for, till the arrival of the Dutch, we see no mention of the Raja or of his State made by the Portuguese writers. The Dutch Governor Adrian Van Moens gives us a long and interesting account of the principality, its possessions, the method of its government and various other particulars regarding it, throwing a flood of light on the change that had come over the State in the interval between the days of the Portuguese and the Dutch. It will be noticed that, when the Eḍappiḷḷi Raja emerges from this period of darkness and obscurity, he does so no more as the militant general of the Zamorin, fighting the foreigner to the bitter end both by land and water, but as the mild Brahman whose sole vocation consisted in ablutions and prayers and whose sole companion was the idol to which he made offerings for his spiritual uplift. This change explains the preculiar position occupied by the Raja among the Princes of Malabar and the reason why he enjoyed immunity from molestation from his neighbours. Among all the Malabar sovereigns, the Rajas of Eḍapiḷḷi and Ambalappuḻa alone belonged to the highest class of Nambūṭiri Brahmans, and of these the latter could not boast of the same antiquity or ancestry as the former. While the State of Eḍapiḷḷi dates from the period of Paraśuṛāma himself, that of Ambalappuḻa had its origin in comparatively recent times. While the latter has been absorbed by Travancore, the former still holds its position, however shorn of its sovereign powers. M. Moens' account is as follows:—

"Repolim *alias* Ellengaloor is a little State about two miles in length and breadth, next to Angecaymal at the other side of the river in the territory of the king of Cochin. It is divided into three portions, named *Repolim*, *Peroendda* and *Illamacarre* and consists of gardens and fields.

"Besides this, this chief has many plots of ground in the kingdoms of Travancore, Cochin, Collastry and in that of the Zamorin; hence his properties are scattered all over Malabar and first of all:—

"In the eastern states of Travancore at Manjamal, Palottil, Nhatottil, Chakanatto, Cunattunatto, Basalacotta, Cottacarra and Oypenom, where palaces and houses have been built on account of Repolim.

"In the southern districts of Travancore, at Ezemalur, where Repolim also possesses palaces and houses; the same at Pattanacotta, where Repolim has erected a pagoda; besides at Cheramangalam, Oosua, Carcarapally, Bulambor, Carraporam and Trinconaposa, at which place Repolim possesses a very large piece of ground, almost as large as Repolim itself, on which several palaces and houses are built. Further more at Nallanikel, Chepatto, Chenitallo, Pandaloon, Tumbonam, Bettockanrom, Caddecatto, Malleapose, Caleoparra, Erowera, Ballancolam, Cacengaporom, Benekolottam, Balangare, Nertuncarre, Maddatumbagom, Calurcarre, Benattare.

"In Porca at Muttikel.

"In Teccencore at Wassapally, Perinellom.

"In the kingdom of Cochin, at Callore, Pallariwattam, Bennele, Paddiwattam, Poonurunny, Chalicodda, Cheramelur and Ninadacarre.

"In the kingdom of the Zamorin at Ballonattocare and Oerwenur and these places are at present in the power of the Nabob (Hyder Ali Khan).

"In Collastry, we are told, he had also here and there a piece of ground, but these places shared the same fate as his property in the country of the Zamorin, as Collastry has already been for a long time under the sway of the Nabob.

"From all these places, with the exception of those which are in the possession of the Nabob, the Chief of Repolim receives some taxes. While the inhabitants of those places are looked upon as subjects of Repolim, more properly they are the subjects of those kings in whose territories those places are.

"The Company concluded a contract with this chief for the first time in the year 1740.

"In that contract, dated 13th October 1740, this chief promised:—

1. To supply all the pepper, which grows in his territory.

2. To prevent smuggling therein and to confiscate undeclared goods in the interests of himself and the Company.

3. To arrest deserters and to hand them over to the Company.

4 The Company promised in return to protect his territory provided the chief did not wrong any one, or make war without the knowledge of the Honourable Company.

" This chief is a priestly ruler, being of the oldest and the first caṣte, viz., that of the Brahmans, and for these two reasons and for these reasons only, he is highly respected by all the heathen kings and rulers of these countries. His mode of living is very superstitious and lonely. His daily work consists only of spiritual ceremonies; he is bound to bathe every day before the rising of the sun in a cistern or bathing-tub, (tank or pond) and to perform ceremonies and to say prayers in it and to remain in it till the sun has reached its zenith. Then he retires to his private quarters and assorts flowers with which he decorates the idols of his temple. When he is performing the ceremonies, two Paṭṭeries or temple-servants, stand near him the whole time, and pay attention to everything he does, in order that the different ceremonies may be performed at the proper time. Various other superstitions and follies are performed which one would hardly believe.

"The high opinion the Native Kings have of his piety and of the effect of his prayers goes so far, that it is the reason why he finds it possible to exact from the kings of the four principal kingdoms of Malabar everywhere in their territories plots of ground, which he is able to keep. He gets these plots on the plea that he will pray for them more fervently and that their kingdoms, for the sake of his plots of ground therein, will be blessed. He was however not able to keep the places, which he had obtained in the kingdom of the Zamorin and in Collastry, because the Nabob, being a Mahomedan, does not take much notice of the customs of heathenism.

"It is for the above reasons that the King of Travancore, when in the last war he conquered the lands of Cochin in the neighbourhood, left alone the little state of Repolim with the reservation that the pepper which grows in Repolim was to be supplied to Travancore. The outturn of pepper however is very small. It is therefore surprising that in the year 1740 it has been thought worth while to make with this chief a pepper-contract; the more so as there are no proofs that a single grain was ever supplied. Moreover he never handed over to us any of the deserters.

"This chief does not grant audience to anybody. In case therefore necessity requires one to see him, one must do so at midday when he is on his way back to his palace and in order to be successful, one must coax the courtiers beforehand, for, without their favour, one cannot make use even of this opportunity.

"The affairs of this little state are managed by the ministers of the Chief, who must give account of their doings to the Chief on certain days of the week, fixed for that purpose. One can therefore easily understand that the administration of the State depends entirely on these courtiers, who are trying to outdo one another in getting the favour of the Chief and who chiefly seek their own interests.

"The Company has little to do with the Chief. However it is expedient for us to know that this little state is a kind of asylum, like a free town, to which people, who are afraid of prosecution and punishment, retreat and where they are safe; and more especially when they are able to reach a temple or pagoda there. This privilege is ackowledged and respected by all Malabar kings. However I never could find out on what right or grounds this privilege is based, unless it be that this state obtained this privilege as a matter of course on account of its ruler being priestly and very pious chief of the principal priestly caste among the natives. It is for this reason that at times he is called by a name that would signify as much as a 'priestly king, who on account of his royal dignity, makes a retreat to his altars safe'.

"Nevertheless I would never suffer the Native Christians who have committed crimes and retreated to that little state to be considered to be in an asylum, partly because the country would become full of thieves and murderers on account of the great number of Christians here, among whom murders are already constantly committed and thefts almost daily, and partly because it seems to me not proper that Roman Christians would have recourse to heathen idols and temples. If such a case occurred, I demanded the fugitive quietly back and pointed out at the same time that, on account of their being Christians, they could not take refuge there. As a rule they were then delivered to me.

"On the other hand, I once had a Canarese brought back from Repolim, who having greatly injured a Christian, had retreated to that place, partly because the crime was too great and too wellknown, and partly to show that we are not at all bound to respect this assumed privilege. However, the less this happens the better, because in case it was too often repeated, it would scandalise the native kings. If, on account of necessity, one has occasionally recourse to such a measure, one ought to give strict orders not to approach the temples, and still less to enter into them in order to arrest the fugitive. He should only be arrested when he is outside the pagoda's limits. A certain letter, which I wrote to the king on the 2nd January 1774, gives sufficient directions how to act in such cases. It may be referred to. It will be found among a pack of letters addressed to the native kings."

For the reasons given by M. Moens, Eḍappiḷḷi continued to be independent. Even Travancore, which had conquered all Cochin territories in the neighbourhood of Eḍappiḷḷi, spared that little State on the score of the Raja's sacerdotal character and perhaps on account of the vicarious spiritual benefits the Travancore king expected to enjoy by the prayers of this Brahman chief. However the Travancore king insisted that all the pepper grown in Eḍappiḷḷi should be delivered to Travancore and that Eḍappiḷḷi should be a subject State under the suzerainty of Travancore.

The Eḍappiḷḷi Raja continued to exercise sovereign powers for some time more. On the establishment of British supremacy over Travancore and Cochin we see Eḍappiḷḷi ruling over its little tract under the protection of the Travancore king. From the correspondence available between the various Diwans of Travancore commencing with Major Munro, who was both British Resident and Diwan, down to the present time, we see the Eḍappiḷḷi Rajas seeking and obtaining the assistance of the Travancore authorities in realis ing their dues from their subjects.

While so, in the year 1820, the Raja of Cochin, being desirous of bringing Eḍappiḷḷi under his government, induced the British Resident Col. Mc'Dowall to address the Madras Government to sanction the change. The Raja proposed to take the Eḍappiḷḷi Chief under his protection and undertook that he would "without making any diminution continue to grant the Eḍappuḷḷee Nambecatiri (Nambūṭiri Raja of Eḍappiḷḷi) the privileges at present he enjoys and besides if any change is found requisite at any future time, nothing shall be done without the consent of the British Government." In his letter to Col. Mc' Dowall, the Raja observed: "The Eḍappiḷḷi country which had been from ancient times amenable to my control was by the Travancore Government, in the year M. E. 974, when a dispute ensued between that State and mine, subjected to its authority." The Raja was not evindently seeking redress against a forcible act of the Travancore king and demanding restoration of what was his territory or territory over which he had suzerain rights. For he says in this letter:—"I will with much pleasure pay to the Travancore State for the Revenues of Eḍappiḷḷi annually the sum of Cully fanams 7579¼ (Rs. 1,000) *and in the event of this not being found satisfactory I propose to pay a Nuzzar in addition to the above amount by a written agreement.*" What prompted the Raja to propose this change was not his desire to come by his own, but the constant trouble arising from disputes between the two States regarding collections of dues in Eḍappiḷḷi lands which lay surrounded by those of Cochin. The Raja says: "From the Eḍappiḷḷi country being nearly surrounded by my territory many disputes arise between the servants of the two States both in the collection of the Revenues and in the sale of goods belonging to the sirkar of Travancore, consequently by your favour if Eḍappiḷḷi be hereafter subjected to my government as it was formerly and as no disputes such as the above are likely to arise." From the terms of this letter (letter from Raja of Cochin to the Resident Col. Mc' Dowall, dated 19th Eḍavam 995 M. E.) it is hard to realise that though Eḍappiḷḷi might have been under Cochin at some time or other it continued to be so till M. E. 974 or A. D. 1799.

The Resident Col. Mc' Dowall, before addressing the Madras Government, obtained the consent of the

Travancore Rāṇi for the proposed transfer; and of the Governor-in-Council, on the strength of the representation of the Resident that "having been formerly subject to Cochin His Highness is very anxious to regain it (Edapilly) and Her Highness the Ranee of Travancore accedes to the proposal in order to terminate the incessant disputes complained of arising from interference of the servants of the two States with each other on the monopolies of Salt and Tobacco. The Edapilly Rajah is likewise desirous of the change in order to free his residence from the scuffles which frequently occur and render it a scene of outrage and confusion—his rights being equally maintained as at present and in greater tranquility. Travancore at present derives in tribute and emolument from the monopolies the sum mentioned by the Rajah of Cochin which he is willing to pay."[1] On the recommendation of the Resident, the Madras Government sanctioned the transfer on the 20th September 1820.[2]

Thus Eḍappiḷḷi came under the government of Cochin, but its outlying possessions at Kallūppāṟa, Cheṅṅiṭala, Vāḷakkuḷam etc., continued to be subject to Travancore. This subjection to Cochin did not, however, continue long; for, once within her grasp, Cochin began to aggress on Eḍappiḷḷi territories and there were constant disputes between the two States. The Eḍappiḷḷi Chief complained to the Resident bitterly that it was against his wishes that he was transfered to Cochin and to quote the Chief's own words "the Rajas of Cochin have been hostile to my house from the earliest ages and the protection of the Sovereigns of Travancore has saved what remains to me of the possession of my ancestors from the encroachment of the Rajas of Cochin; under these circumstances and from strong feeling of respect and attachment to the Rajas

1. Letter from the Resident to the Chief Secretary to the Madras Government, dated 18th July 1820.

2. Letter from the Chief Secretary to the Madras Government to the Resident, dated 12th September 1820.

of Travancore, I request that my possessions may be replaced under the protection of Travancore." The then Resident was, however, quite unwilling to recommend the retransfer and, in forwarding the application of the Edappilly Chief to the Madras Government, observed that the change should not take place as "the arrangements proposed by the late Resident and sanctioned by Government have completely put an end to those disputes and scuffles which formerly existed between the servants of the two States regarding the monopoly of salt and tobacco." [1] The Madras Government did not agree with the Resident. In addressing him they observed:— "The Honourable Governor-in-Council has had under consideration your letter of the 5th April 1821 reporting that the Rajah of Edappilly strongly objected to the arrangement by which he was transfered from the authority of the Travancore Sirkar to that of the Rajah of Cochin. You are aware that your predecessor had misrepresented the Edappilly Rajah as being desirous of the change, and that it was sanctioned by Government under that impression. As it now appears that a total misapprehension of the Edappilly Rajah's sentiments had arisen on the part of the Resident, the Governor-in-Council is of opinion that the arrangements founded upon it is harsh and unjust and desires accordingly that that Tributary may again be re-transfered to the authority of the Travancore Sirkar. You will however use your endeavours to prevent the recurrence of any of those disputes and affrays with regard to the monopoly of salt and tobacco which in part led to the arrangement now set aside." [2]

The re-transfer was soon effected much to the chagrin naturally of the Cochin Raja. Thus we see that Eḍappilli which has been originally independent

1. Letter from the Resident to the Chief Secretary, dated 5th April 1821.

2. Letter from Chief Secretary to the Resident, dated 31st December 1824.

coming under the suzerainty, at one time or other, of three of the four important States of Malabar. Before the arrival of the Portuguese, Eḍappilli was an ally, if not a feudatory, of the Zamorin. When this allegiance was changed, it is not possible to discover. During the Dutch period, we may gather from the account given by Governor Moens, that all the four States respected the rights of Eḍappilli which had its possession within their respective territories. As the secular power began to assert its independence of the spiritual, and as the anathemas hurled by priests had to submit themselves to the more powerful and matter-of-fact argument of powder and shot, Eḍappilli found her position between two powerful neighbours, such as Travancore and Cochin, rather risky. She had to choose between the two, and she made up her mind to place herself under the protection of one of these. She changed her allegiance from time to time. Prior to 974 M. E. (1799 A. D.), she was, according to the Cochin Raja, under Cochin. From 974 to 996 she was under Travancore; again she came over to Cochin and was a feudatory of that State till 1000 M. E. Finally, with the approval of the Madras Government, she returned to Travancore. Ever since she has continued to be under the protection of that State.

Eḍappilli proper, the seat of the Raja, is a small territory about four miles in length by two and a quarter in breadth. Within this territory and in the villages of Vālakkulam, Ṭṛkkuṇṇappuḷa, and Kallūppāṛa, the Raja exercises *quasi*-sovereign rights. Elsewhere he has estates in two-thirds of the Taluqs of Travancore and in Cochin and in the British district of South Malabar, and there his position is that of a Jenmi. The sources of his revenue are:—where he is a ruling chief—salt, abkari, opium, tobacco, etc., which revenue is collected for him and paid over by the Travancore Sirkar. The land-tax and other royal dues are collected by his own agency directly. He has a great number of tax-payers or subjects and a very considerable number of tenants who hold his lands on various tenures ranging from Verumpāṭṭam to Aṭima and Śāśwaṭam. He has in all 44 devaswams with 71 temples of which 38 devaswams are situated in Travancore, while there are two devaswams with one temple for each in Cochin and four devaswams with five temples in British territory.

Sir A. Seshiah Sastri, a former Diwan of Travancore, speaking of the Eḍappiḷḷi Raja says: "He was, and still in some respects is, an independent chief and entitled to all sources of revenue, whether actually levied by himself or administered by this State for him, compensation being settled and paid every year. He pays no tribute excepting a sum of Rs. 1,000 per annum which is for Police service rendered. He has, however, no police, civil or criminal authority within the Principality."

Ever since Eḍappiḷḷi's return to Travancore allegiance, the Travancore Sirkar has treated the Nambūri Raja with marked kindness and consideration. Successive Residents and Diwans used to lend their sympathy and active aid in the Raja's administration of his territory and estates, and the Raja still enjoys the respect, sympathy and protection of the kings of Travancore due to his position both as a tributary and an ecclesiastical dignitary.

14. **Battimeni**. Battimeni stands for Wemmaṇi. Whitehouse tells us that Battimena, in old lists, is called Bemanil, and Bemmani—"B" used by Latin writers for "W" which leads to the identification of this place with Wemmaṇy. At one time the sway of Kāyamkuḷam must have extended to this place, for M. Du Perron includes Kāṛṭṭikapiḷḷi, Chēpād, Wemmaṇy, and Puṭiakāvu as lying within the territory of the Raja. This was a separate principality with Kāṛṭṭikapiḷḷi for its capital at the time of Nieuhoff. He says, "Upon the banks of the same

river, where the Kingdom of Marten lies, is also the Kingdom of Batyma, with its city called Katyapery (Kāṙṭṭikapiḷḷi)". The Dutch Captain speaks of a law existing in this kingdom of so abominable a character as scarcely to be believed of human beings. He says, "It is commonly reported in these parts that the King of Batyma made a law, by which a man is empowered to kill any woman that should refuse him a kindness." This law or custom is referred to by earlier writers also. Archbishop Meneses found it to exist when he visited '*Catiapilly*' in the dominions of the Raja of Batuniena. Hough says, "The men assumed the right of dishonouring any woman, whatever her rank or circumstance; and the laws permitted them to put one to death on the spot who should resist their brutal demands."[1]

15. **Panapoli.** It is difficult to identify this state. There is no warrant for the suggestion that it was Panṭaḷam. The Panṭaḷam family still exists and is in possession of the tract of land over which it once ruled. From the itinerary of Archbishop Meneses, as recorded by Gouvea, we see the Archbishop proceeding from 'Catiapilly' to *Corigo-Langre*; and the Rev. Whitehouse has pointed out that this latter name is a corruption of the native word *Kurien Kulangara*, modern Chēppād, a town situated to the south of Kāyamkuḷam. According to Du Perron, this was in the territory of Kāyamkuḷam. Meneses passed southwards still from Chēppād to Batimena or Wemmany, Pudiogabo or Puṭiakāvu and Narasian. The last was situated in the Ṭekkenkūr kingdom. It is, therefore, probable that there existed at one time a small principality of this name lying between Kāyamkuḷam and Kāṙṭṭikappiḷḷi and that it became absorbed with Kāyamkuḷam by adoption as mentioned by our author. This conjecture receives support from what Governor Gollennesse says of Pāṇāpaḷḷi. According to him, this" is a small inland state beyond Kalicollan

1. *History of Christianity in India*, Vol. II, p. 175

to which it was attached when its ruling family died out. The people of Malabar call the four states above mentioned Cherrievay or Oonaddu Carre, because formerly they were under one queen who divided them among her four daughters". The four states mentioned are Kariṅāgappiḷḷi, Kārttigappiḷḷi, Kāyamkuḷam and Pāṇapaḷḷi.

16. **Pantalam.** After Pāṇapaḷḷi, Gollennesse mentions a state called Panṭaḷam or Chembalanūr. He says: "It is a principality situated beyond Calicoilan, bordering on Pandise; it is of little importance. The Raja is a great friend of the Raja of Travancore and a great enemy of the king of Calicoilan; he allowed the former to march with his army undisturbed through his dominions when he was on his way to attack the latter. Without this permission the invasion would not have been so easy, because good fortifications had been constructed in the direction of Elleda Surowan. The Raja is a Kshetrya by caste and has 3,000 Nairs."

According to an old *Grandhavari* (Grandhavari) or chronicle, the Panṭaḷam Rajas had originally belonged to the Pāṇḍya country, of a part of which they were rulers. They were allied to the Travancore royal house by marriage. Being harassed by bands of marauders and unable to withstand their incursions, the family took refuge in Kēraḷa under the patronage of the Travancore Rajas and resided at Āchānkōvil, Kōṅṅiyūr and Panṭaḷam. The female members lived at Kōṅṅiyūr and Panṭaḷam, while the males resided at Āchānkōvil which was near to their principality in the Pāṇḍya country. From there they held a doubtful sway over their possessions till on the 17th of Meenam 345 M. E., (March—April 1170 A. D.) when their harassers attacked their residence at Āchānkōvil and killed one of the Rajas. His brother abandoned their possessions in Pāṇḍy as also their residences at Ṭenkāśi and Elaṭṭūr and finally settled down in

Travancore. We can, therefore, well understand why Panṭaḷam was so friendly to Travancore in its war with Kāyamkuḷam.

17. **Tekkenkur.** This was an independent state that interposed and acted as a buffer between the rival states of Travancore and Cochin. It comprised the modern Taluks of Ṭiruvella, Changanāssēri and Kōṭṭayam. The Dutch seem not to have had any factory in this kingdom. It fell a prey to the conquest of Travancore and was annexed to that state by king Mārṭṭāṇḍa Varma.

Of Tekkenkūr Gollennesse says: "It is a considerable state; it lies between Calicoilan, Berkencoor, the broad river of Carraporam and the hills; it exports much pepper and arrack. The State has 18 marambins (Māṭampīs or noblemen) and two powerful Caimals (Ḳaimals—Chiefs) in the east next to the hills called Nawacadda and also Nanojattoo Caimals who do not take much notice of His Highness. Most of the pepper is brought up-country to the Bazaars of Koon, Serepilly, Irataperha, Erunaloor and Irroony, and from there it is fetched by Pandise merchants with their oxen; this is done notwithstanding the contract of 16th July 1664 in which an express promise is made that of this produce no more and no less will be carried up-country than what is required for the sustenance of His Highness's subjects. The king resides at Cottatte (Kōṭṭayam); he is a man of between 50 and 60 years old, he is gentle by nature and his only aim is to keep his state in peace and prosperity. His Highness has always shown good-will towards the Company and although he even now makes, since he has noticed that the Company is determined to take serious steps to make itself master of the pepper trade, open profession of his warm regard for the Company, still it is quite certain that he is of one accord with the other chiefs of Malabar to undermine and reduce the Company's power underhand."

18. **Poonjar.** Our author has failed to make

mention of another small state referred to by Gollennesse and which still survives like Panṯaḷam as an Eṭavaka, viz., that of Pūññār. Gollennesse says: "In the east of this state, (i. e., Ṭekkenenkūr) next to the hills, is the principality of Poonjat Perumal; its ruler was adopted from the house of the princes of Charkara; much cardamom is found here."

The ancestors of the Pūññāṟṟ Raja were orginally natives of Madura and were kings of Pāṇḍya. The chief of the family then appears to have been called Kulaśēkhara Perumāḷ. From an account of the house prepared from old chronicles and records, it appears that it had to leave Madura on account of the unceasing inroads made by the Poligars and specially the Tondiman amongst them. So Māna Vikṛama Kulaśēkhara Perumāḷ, the then head of the family, (no date is given except that this must have been before 364 M. E. i. e., 1189 A. D.) went to the Rayor kingdom (probably Tanjore) and lived there twelve years. After many trials and tests, the Rayor was finally convinced that his guest was the Pāṇḍya King. Thereupon, on the latter's request, Viśvanāṯha Naicker was sent by Rayor as an ally to the Pāṇḍyan King; but, at the same time, he was warned that the Naicker might prove treacherous. So it happened too; for, as soon as Kulaśēkhara Perumāḷ, assisted by Viśvanāṯha Naicker had subdued his enemies, Naicker assumed sovereignty of the recovered kingdom, giving Ṯenkāśi alone to Kulaśēkhara. Disgusted at this act of bad faith, Kulaśekhara Perumāḷ determined to immigrate to the Kēraḷa country and so proceeded with his family and treasures to Pālakāṭśēṛi (Palghat) where they lived for three years. Thence they went to Karikat Grāmam and lived for 6 years in the Illam or house of Ākkōṭṭupuram Nambūṯiri. This was in the country of Ēṛāṭṭukara. The Ēṛāṭṭees, who apparently were masters of the country, being afraid that the new-comers may subjugate their own kingdom, interdicted them from salt and cooking vessels, a proceeding not dissimilar to what at present would be called *boycotting*. Leaving Kārikāt, Perumāḷ visited Kuṅṅalakkōnāṭiri, the Zamorin Raja of Calicut, at whose direction he took up his residence at Vaṅṅēri in the house of Muṇḍa Nambūṭiri, where the family lived for a period of three years. This was in the territory of Punnaṭṭūr Nambidi who was annoyed at a foreign ruling family being entertained in his country without his permission. He caused the house to be burnt and expelled the refugees. Kulaśēkhara, now a wanderer for the third time, proceeded southwards together with his family, accompanied by his devoted companion, Ākkōṭṭupuram Nambūṭiri, and came to Eḷangallūr Nambiāṭiri or the Raja of Eḍappiḷḷi. When he had resided six months in Eḍappiḷḷi, the unfortunate Kulaśēkhara was removed from his worldly cares. His faithful wife followed him soon after, leaving their little children and the other members of the family to the care of the Eḍappiḷḷi Raja.

The nephews of the deceased, that is the sister's sons, performed the obsequies of both the deceased. The Eḍappiḷḷi Raja, to whom the island of Cochin belonged, conferred on the Pāṇḍyan princes certain dignities in Cochin, where they were asked to reside and exercise the privileges attached to them. With Muṇḍa Nambūṭiri as Vāḍhyān or family priest and Ākkōṭṭupuram Nambūṭiri as Ṭēvāri or performer of ceremonies, the Upanayanam, or investiture with the sacred thread, of the eldest prince of the family was performed. An Ārya Paṭṭar celebrated the Ṭāli marriage of the princesses and the Eḍappiḷḷi Raja wedded one of them in the Malabar form of Sambandham. Here we see the family finally giving up its own customs and adopting those of Malabar. We have seen that it was the nephews who performed the funeral rites of the deceased Raja. They, at the same time, performed the rites for the Raja's wife also. More important than the performance of the uncle's funeral rites by the nephews is the fact that the princesses were *formally* married, i.e., had the Keṭṭu Kalliāṇam or Ṯāli-tying ceremony (a purely Malayali form of marriage) performed, by an Ārya Paṭṭar, before the eldest of them was wedded by the Raja of Eḍappiḷḷi. Thus the Pūññāṟṟ family became a Malayalee one. To return to the narrative, the young princes lived in Cochin for 12 years, when the Eḍappiḷḷi Raja died. His successor was not friendly to them and ordered them out of his country. Remonstrances made by the princes were of no avail, and they resigned their dignities and privileges in Cochin in favour of Maṇḍala Muḍaliār and left the place. By this time they had become disgusted with the bad faith of Malabar and made up their mind to fix their abode somewhere near their native country of Pāṇḍya whither they could not go having changed their customs, manners, modes of living, &c. On their way, when they came to Vaṭakkankūr in Venmalanāṭu, the eldest prince, Māna Vikrama Kulaśēkhara Perumāḷ, became unwell, being possessed of evil spirits. He was treated and restored to health by Neyṭaśśēri Nambūṭiri in whose house the family lived for six months.

While about to leave the place, Māna Vikrama received information that the Rajas ruling over the hill tracts of Kākkanād had been murdered, and that their country known as Pūññār lying to the west of the western Ghauts was available. Thinking that it would be well to secure the tract, he went in quest of it taking with him his informant Veṭiyūr Nambūṭiri and Neṭṭaśśēri Nambūṭiri. Coming to Eṟṟumānūr, he worshipped at the celebrated shrine there, made offerings and vows to the deity and left the place, leaving the princesses in the house of Poyka Nambūṭiri. Māna Vikrama and the Nambūṭirīs proceeded to Pūññār at which place they met the chief man of the locality, Vellūr Mūṭṭeṭaṭṭu Paṇikkar, who was soon won over with rich presents. The party remained at Maṇkompumkāvu to which place the Paṇikkar brought all the chiefs and headmen. On conferring with them, Māna Vikrama was told that the country was under the suzerainty of

Ṭekkē Eḷamkūṟṟil Kōvil or Raja whose capital was at Kōṭṭayam. The three Nambūṭirīs and the yaṭṟir were despatched to Kōṭṭayam to negotiate with Ṭekkenkūṟṟil Nairi for the purchase of the Pūññār country. The Ṭekkenkūr Raja, by name Āḍiṭṭya Vaṟma, was agreeable to the proposal, provided the people of the country would accept the new-comer as their sovereign, and he sent a message to this effect through Maṭappaḷḷi and Periñchēri who accompanied Māna Vikṟamā's messengers. The inhabitants of the tract were also informed of this, and they sent back a reply intimating their willingness through a special messenger of their own, Kuññaykāt Nambūṭiri who went to Kōṭṭayam along with Maṭappaḷḷi and others. On receiving this message, the Raja called a council of Brahmans, chiefs and noblemen and conferred with them. The proposal being acceded to by all, Kuññaykāt Nambūṭiri was deputed to bring together the inhabitants of the Pūññār country, the Nambūṭiri messengers of Māna Vikṟama and his minister. After all were assembled, the proposal that the tract was to be sold to Māna Vikṟama was placed before them formally, and they were asked if they were agreeable to it. After the people had expressed their willingness, negotiations were set on foot to settle the price which Māna Vikṟama was willing to give, and on the yaṭṟir informing the Raja that the Perumāḷ was willing to pay what was demanded, His Highness sent a deputation of the chiefs and noblemen of the country headed by Uḷḷāṭṭil Kaimaḷ and Nanṭikāt Paṇikkar to bring over Māna Vikṟama Perumāḷ. The deputation waited on the Perumāḷ at Pūññār and invited him to meet the Ṭekkenkūr Raja. Māna Vikṟama and party started taking along with them the priceless treasure his predecessor had brought with him from Madura. The Nambūṭirīs and the people of Pūññār also accompanied the party. On reaching Kummanam, the Nambūṭirīs of Ākkōṭṭupuram and Muṇḍa were sent to give intimation of the arrival of the party. The ministers of the two Rajas held a conference, and all terms being settled, the Rajas met each other at the portico of the Ṭali temple. The transfer was inscribed on a copper-plate witnessed by Elangallūr Nambiāṭiri (the Raja of Eḍappilli), Vaññippuḻa Paṇḍāraṭṭil, (a neighbouring chief), Veṭiyūr Nambūṭiri (the yaṭṛir already mentioned) and Mūṭṭımana Bhaṭṭaṭiri (a Nambūṭiri Smārṭṭa). The deed recorded the transfer by the Ṭekkē Eḻamkūṛṛil Kōvil of the country of Pūññār with all rights and dignities possessed by that Raja in that country to Māna Vikṛama. In return, Māna Vikṛama handed over two priceless gems and countless treasure which had to be measured out in measures; and these were received by the Raja, Āḍiṭṭya Vaṛma, and the other members of the family.

The two Rajas accompanied by their retinue then proceeded to Pūññār where the inhabitants of the country were called together and, in their presence and with their consent, Māna Vikṛama Kulaśēkhara Perumāḻ was installed as Raja of Pūññār with great *eclat*; the Ṭekkenkūr Raja invested Māna Vikṛama with the symbols of sovereignty, viz., a piece of silk and a sword of authority. The Ṭekkenkūr Raja was then sumptuously entertained by the Pūññār Raja at Mamkompukāvu, and the Raja's retinue were given rich presents.

In memory of their migration from Madura, the Pūññāṛṛ Raja still pays his homage to Sunḍarēśwara Swāmi and Mīnākṣhi Amman, the chief deities worshipped in the great temple at Madura and retains the figure of the latter on his seal with the words *Madhura Meenakshi Sahayam*, *i. e.*, "Mīnākṣhi of Madura is our protectress."

At the time when Kulaśēkhara Perumāḻ settled down at Pūññār after his wanderings, his family consisted only of a couple of members or so, and consequently it became extinct before long. This cast a gloom over the people. The chief men among them conferred together and informed the Ṭekkenkūr Raja of the state of circumstances. That Raja gave them the option of choosing any one who was able and willing to rule over them. The Paṇikkers (chiefs), headmen and representatives of the people proceeded to the north and requested the head of the Śarkara Kōvilagam (a branch of the present Cranganūr Raja's family) to become their liege lord. He readily assented to the proposal, and the members of the Śarkara Kōvilagam were formally installed as the sovereigns of Pūññār.

The Pūññār Rajas continued to exercise full rights of sovereignty till they became subject to Travancore with the conquest and annexation of Ṭekkenkūr and Vaṭakkenkūr about the year 1756 A. D. Since then they have been shorn of all state functions and are now no more than mere zemindars, possessing large estates in the hilly tracts which have become very valuable recently on account of the influx of rubber planters from Europe.

The above narrative, long as it is, is given from the old chronicles, not because there is any importance attached to the state itself, but because it throws some light on the practices of the period, how an east coast family following Makkaṭṭāyam or the Hindu Law of inheritance and succession could easily adapt itself to the Malabar system of Marumakkaṭṭāyam inheritance, how a state could be secured by purchase, how it was necessary for the sovereign who was making the sale to obtain the consent of the people before he could make a transfer and how, when the reigning house became extinct, the people were allowed the liberty of choosing their own ruler.

19. **Cochin.** Of the Cochin State we have had occasion to speak often. It together with its dependencies extended from Poṙakkād in the south to Cheṙṙuwāya in the north. The family claims direct descent in the female line from the last Cherāmān Perumāl. The Hebrew version of the Perumāl's grant of

privileges to the Jews of Cochin is said to contain a statement that the Raja of Cochin is not called to witness the deed because he was the Perumāḷ's heir. The Kērala Māhāṭmyam, however, gives a different story. In Chapters 59 and 78 of this work, it is said that Paraśu Rāma installed a Kṣheṭṛiya of the solar race, a descendent of Lava, son of the hero of the Rāmāyaṇa, at Ṭṛppūṇiṭṭuṛa which is still the capital of the Cochin State. The official account of the State says: "The oldest name of the State is Perimpaṭappu, for Cochin is that part of Kērala which came under the eldest son of Chēramān Perumāḷ's sister by Perimpaṭappu Nambūṭiri. The ruling house is still locally known as Perimpaṭappu Swarūpam and the Rajas of Cochin hold the territory by right of descent from Chēramān Perumāḷ."[1] The dynasty is also known as Māṭa Bhūpaṭīs by virtue of adoption to the Māṭaṭṭinkal family and the possession of their country.[2]

20. **Cochin and the Dutch East India Company.** The first treaty between the Cochin Raja and the Dutch East India Company was concluded soon after the capture of the fort of Cochin from the Portuguese. It was as follows:—

"Copy of treaty between the Perumpaṭappu Valia Ṭampurān and the (Dutch East India) Company inscribed on a silver-plate.

Treaty of perpetual alliance to endure as long as the earth shall last entered into between the Dutch Admiral, the Honourable Ryclof Van Goens on behalf of the Illustrious Governor-General of Batavia, the Capital of the United Dutch East India Company in India, and his Council on the one side and the Raja of Cochin, Vīrakērala Swarūpam belonging to the Mūṭṭa Ṭavaḷi of the Chaḷiyūr branch, for himself and his successors on the other side.

1. *Census Report*, p. 12.

2. For detailed information regarding Cochin, the reader is referred to this author's *History of Cochin* (Mal.) in two volumes, available with Mrs. K. P. Padmanabha Menon, Ernakulam.

1. Both parties agree that, as long as the earth shall endure, there shall be mutual friendship, union and confidence between the Raja and the Dutch Company.

2. The Cochin Raja gives his solemn assurance that, as long as the sun, the moon and the earth shall endure, he and his successors will not question the right of the company to hold the Fort, its outworks, and territories adjoining thereto, together with the islands ceded to the Company by the Portuguese and now in their possession, in the same manner as they had hitherto been held and enjoyed in the name of the illustrious King of Portugal.

3. The Raja of Cochin having been driven out of his Kingdom and since reinstated on the throne through the help of the Honourable Company, the Raja accepts the Company as his protector.

4. The Raja of Cochin agrees that all the pepper and wild cinnamon produced in his dominions between Poṙakkād and Cranganore shall be brought to this fort and weighed and delivered to the Company. And no quantity of either shall be given to any other nation hereafter.

5. The Cochin Raja agrees that the Company may prevent all ships and boats laden with opium from landing their goods or entering the Cochin bar. This is to guard against loss to either side.

6. The Cochin Raja gives his solemn assurance that the four conditions aforesaid shall be duly observed. The Raja also agrees to help the Company with men and provisions to the extent of his power. The Raja requests the Company to erect three more fortresses, one at Paḷḷippuṙam, to guard the Cranganore river, another in Chēppuṙam at Poṙakkād at a spot deemed most advantageous, to command the Poṙakkād river, and a third at Aḷīkkal for the security of the Cochin river. And the Company may build such other fortresses and at such positions as they shall deem necessary.

7. The Admiral promises in the name of the Honourable Company that, in order to carry out the terms of this treaty and for the safety of the Raja, the Company shall build fortresses at Cochin, Pampa, Pallippuram, Alikkal and at Porakkād in the Chēppuram country. If more fortresses shall become necessary, they shall build them.

8. All customs duties which have hitherto been levied and which shall hereafter be imposed shall be paid to the Raja.

9. All Christians living on the seashore who were subject to the jurisdiction of the Cochin Fort long since shall remain under the protection of the Company.

10. Should any quarrels arise between a Malayāli subject of the Raja and a Christian subject of the Company, the Raja shall be the judge of the Malayāli and the Company's judges of the Christian. If a Malayāli kills a Christian, he shall be promptly executed by the Cochin Raja. If a Christian is the murderer, he shall be promptly put to death by the Company's judges.

11. The Raja shall prevent the transport (smuggling) of pepper and cinnamon by land on bullocks.

12. In the open ground, outside the fort now cleared of all trees, no one shall plant cocoanut or other trees without the Company's permission.

13. Portuguese priests shall not be allowed to reside within the Cochin territory without the permission of the Company. The priests of Chempaloor (St. Paul's village) are to be sent out of the country beyond the frontier.

14. The coinage of fanams shall be carried out at a mint to be established in the Palace of the Raja outside the fort. The profits of the mint deducting all expenses shall go to the Raja. One or two captains shall remain there to supervise coining operations when it goes on. Those guilty of counterfeiting coins shall

be punished by the Raja, if caught by him, or by the Company's judges, if caught by the Company.

15. The Cochin Raja gives his assurance that the Company's officers may arrest any debtors of the Company resident within his territory. If any such debtors abscond and take to the hills, the Raja shall endeavour his best to arrest and deliver them over to the Company. That the Raja shall also endeavour his best to arrest and hand over to the Company any of the Company's servants, Europeans or others or their men who may have taken refuge in the State.

16. Merchants living in the State and trading with the Company shall not be subjected to any dues in excess of what they have hitherto been paying. They are to be under the protection of the Company.

17. This treaty is agreed to be written in duplicate, both in the Dutch and the Malayālam languages, on silver plate and on paper and signed by the parties.

The above terms were ratified from the Raja's palace at Cochin and from the fort at Cochin and reduced to writing and signed this day the 12th Mīnam 322 of the Puṭuvaippu Era corresponding to 20th March 1663.

Signatories herein. Vīrakērala Swarūpam, Raja of Cochin and Admiral Ryclof Van Goens representing the Honourable Dutch (East India) Company.

Witnesses. Cornelis Valkeniar and Hendric Van Rede of Drakensteyn.

Company's Seal.

According to ordinance of His Excellency in Council.

(Signed) Martin Hyisman,
Secretary."

21. **Company's arms on Raja's Crown.** Says Nieuhoff: "His brother (i.e., the exiled Raja's brother), being the next heir to the crown, was, after the taking of the city, crowned King of Cochin, by the Dutch, his crown which was of gold, having the Cyphre of the East India Company engraven on one side."

22. **Five families of Cochin.** The names of the five families were:— Mūṭṭa ṭāvaḷi, Elaya ṭāvaḷi, Paḷḷiviruṭṭi ṭāvaḷi, Chāḷiyūr ṭāvaḷi and Muriññūr or Māṭaṭṭinkal ṭāvaḷi. At the time of the arrival of the Dutch, three of these branches had become extinct.

Gollennesse describes the kingdom of Cochin as "lying along the sea coast between Porca, Tek and Berkencoor, Angikaimal and the territories of the Zamorin. Even by himself the king is very powerful and, as the result of adoption and decease, his power has been further increased by the addition of the territories of Mouton or Ellerta Surowan stretching from the south of Porca towards the north near the Manor of Paloirty, half a mile from the town of Cochin where the rightful princes of this State live in poverty. Cooricatty Tawasy was added to the State in the same way and there are also the territories taken from the Zamorin and handed over to His Highness by Admiral William Bakker Jacobtz. The King's chief power lies in his landed proprietors of whom there are very many besides the four most important ones who have already been mentioned.

"Cochin had formerly five dynasties, viz, Martingel (Māṭaṭṭinkal), Mootta, Palloorty, Elerta, and Chaloor; and adoption took place in the last mentioned in the year 1689 and it is still in existence but the other four have died out; the remaining dynasty counts several princes and princesses."

The territories handed over to Cochin by Admiral William Jacobtz comprised the conquered tract of Paponetty or Pāppinimaṭṭam ceded to the Dutch by the Zamorin by the treaty of 1717. It also included Trikonetty, Aerattu, Aratta Pala (Āṟāṭṭupuḻa), Moodele Coonattu and Pootenbare (Puttenchira)." Gollennesse adds that "by a secret despatch of 4th July 1740, Their High Worshipfuls have *returned* to the King of Cochin the so-called eighteen half-villages (Paṭineṭṭarayālam) which are situated there, because his claim to the same was judged to be legal."

Regarding these 18 half-villages, the following extract from Moen's *Memorial* will be found interesting:

"These lie between the northern limit of the kingdom of Cranganore and southern limit of Paponetty. They belonged formerly to the Zamorin, but in course of time came to the king of Cochin, how cannot be ascertained. He retained it till 1719 when a quarrel arose between the kings of Cranganore and Cochin about a piece of ground. Commander Hertenburg tried to settle the dispute. The king of Cochin took this amiss and wrote to the Commander that he had obtained the villages after a long war and, if the Commander so desires, he would renounce his rights to them and that the Company was at liberty to hand them over to the king of Cranganore. The king of Cochin had said this in peevishness. But the Commander took him at his word and assured him that he could not decline such a generous gift. The Company thus came into possession and kept them till 1740 when they were returned to the king of Cochin under the following deed:

'Julius Valentin Stein Van Gollenesse, Commander and Governor of the Coast of Malabar, Canara and Wingurla and Cornal.

'Whereas it has pleased His Excellency the Governor-General Adrian Valkenier and the Honourable

M.

members of Council of the Dutch Indies to write to the undersigned, Commander of this coast, in a secret letter of the 4th July 1740 and to command him to return to His Highness the King of Cochin with all the title-deeds, the so-called 18 half-villages, formerly accepted by the Commander John Hertenburg on account of the Company in the year 1719, and situate behind Paponetty in the regions of Edawillinga and Hadialipuram, on the good testimony of the Honourable Counsellor-Ordinary, Gustaf William Van Imhoff, for the good will of His Highness towards the Company we now restore in conformity with the express command of Their aforenamed High Worshipfuls, at the reiterated request of His Highness, the aforesaid 18 half-villages to His Highness the King of Cochin, with all the title-deeds, and we return them in such a way as they are given to the Company before. Besides, we renounce all rights whatever, properties and claims, which the Company ever have had on them or may have at present and in order that the same may be clear at all times, we resolved to confirm and corroborate the above transfer in a public document and by our signature.

'Cochin 22nd December 1740 was (signed) J. V. Steyn Van Gollenesse.'

"Since then the king of Cochin kept the villages till 1757 when His Highness in union with the Zamorin and other northern kings opposed the king of Travancore in his designs. The Zamorin then with his troops invaded the district of Paponetty. Thereupon the kings very soon realised their mistake, disagreed and dared not to continue their operations. The Zamorin desired compensation for his expenses, as he had marched up with his army at the request of the king and when this was not forthcoming, he invaded the territory of Cochin and took possession of the 18 half-villages.

" In the year 1758, the Zamorin concluded peace with the Company and restored the district of Paponetty, and also handed over to the company the 18 half-villages, but remained in possession of the other Cochin territories. Afterwards, when the king of Cochin again got possession of his northern districts, he claimed the 18 half-villages and insisted upon this more and more. This was reported fully to Batavia and the reply given in a secret despatch, dated 25th October 1763, was that they would like to see the king influenced in such a way that he would give up his claim. The king would not listen to anything but insisted more and more on the restoration and the authorities here were written to in a secret letter of the 17th September 1765 to try as much as possible to find excuses, or to offer him another piece of ground, but in case His Highness should have recourse to hostilities and there was no chance to put a stop to them, to give them back to His Highness.

" The Company remained in possession till 1769 when at the instance of the king of Cochin they were returned to His Highness which may be seen in a Malabar resolution of the 18th February 1769, the terms of which in connection with the subject I shall quote them below :—

'Finally His Excellency the Governor informed the meeting :—

'That His Excellency (the G—Seuff) and the Commander (Breekpot) had the pleasure to return to that king at his frequent and pressing instances and under the sanction of Their Worshipfuls, the 18 half-villages, bordering in the territory of Paponetty, and that as soon as the Palgetter (Pāliyaṭṭ Achchan) should return, envoys would have to be appointed, in order that the restitution be made officially to His Highness or his ambassadors, and certain boundaries be laid down to prevent disputes, which otherwise might arise in the future.'"

"Although now the whole territory, from Chetwai to Cranganur, is occupied by the Nabob Hyder Alychan, yet these villages are left alone and the revenues thereof are collected by the king of Cochin without interference. For this privilege however the king has to pay a tribute to the Nabob, at a fixed time."

23. **Paliat.** This stands for Paḻḻiviruṭṭi.

Montate Vise. This stands for Mūṭṭa Ṭavaḻi. Nieuhoff terms it 'Momadavil' and Tavernier 'Moutani.'

Shalour. This is Chaḻiūr. The branch is still existing and the present house is said to belong to it.

The events recorded in this para are all noticed elsewhere in detail and require no further consideration here.

24. **Moutan.** This is Maṭṭam or Cheṙṭṭala. This was a small territory known as Karappuṙam which devolved on Cochin by adoption. We have seen that according to Gollennesse 'the territories of Moutan extended from Poṙakād in the south to Palloorty in the north'. Our author tells us that to it belong also some districts on the other side of the Vembanād Lake. Within its limits lay Māṭaṭṭinkarai, the seat of the ruling house known as Māṭáṭṭinkal, which, according to Gollennesse, formed one of the five dynasties that went to make up the Perumpaṭappu Swarūpam. The Raja of Cochin is still known as Māṭa Bhūpaṭi. It is possible that the territory was originally an appendage of the "Ellerta" branch which devolved on the Māṭaṭṭinkal branch and became finally absorbed by the Perumpaṭappu Swarūpam. It was lost to Cochin during the war with Travancore. Family disputes drove the Ṭampāns of Chaḻiūr to seek the aid of king Māṙṭṭāṇḍa Vaṙma of Travancore who marched southwards and conquered Karappuṙam. The Chaḻiūr Ṭampāns were for some time left in possession of this territory. It was subsequently ceded to Travancore by Cochin under the terms of the treaty of 937 M. E. (A. D. 1762)

25. **Coernad** (Kuruṅād). This territory extended up to Eṙṇākuḷam opposite to the town of Cochin, the present seat of the Cochin Government.

26. **Seven.** This ought to be five, for the tract of country along the coast of the backwater is known as the land of the five Kaimals or lords, *Anjikaimal.* The District Court of Eṙṇākuḷam still bears the name of Anjikaimal.

Kuruṅād was overrun and conquered by Travancore along with Karappuṙam, Vatar Kuru Mala and Kuṅṅaṭṭuṅād in 931 M. E. Of the Anjikaimals we gather the following information from Gollennesse: "These Caimals are very powerful and would be able to make head against the King (of Cochin) if they were united among themselves, but they count five leading houses, viz, Cherally, Coonattanadu, Paloorgatte, Coroomalecoor and Badercoor; these again have many sub-divisions, and this is the reason of their powerlessness. The Angia Caimals are oppressed most of all because they live in the centre of his territories (Cochin Raja's) and right opposite to his palace on the other side of the river; but it is for this very reason that they ought to be protected by the Honourable Company against the greediness of the King and Their High Worshipfuls have ordered a police force to be stationed in the bazaar of Angiecaimal; for this fertile land has of old been looked upon as the storehouse of Cochin which indeed it is.

"The lands of Cherally (Chērāṅellūr Kaṙṭṭāvu) lie in front and this is the reason why he suffers most, but he is the strongest as he is also the chief of Cooremalecoor by adoption and I have advised him that he should occasionally show his teeth taking care that right is on his side; and in such a case it will be Your Excellency's business to stop those quarrels by the authority of the Company and act as mediator.

"I think this is the only way somewhat to moderate unbearable vexations of the King. Of these lands those of Cooremalcoor, Tachetta Moonencoor and Tattayet Paunicail export much pepper, but the Company has never had and will never get a grain of it except by determined measures. All I have been able to obtain from Cherally are promises to grow pepper in his lower lands for the Company on the pretext that it would be too expensive and difficult to have the grain brought down from the higher lands along the main road. This cannot be denied, because while we were in Kismalanaddu, which land borders on Cooroomalecoor, we were at a loss how to bring down the pepper without heavy expenses, great trouble and waste; for this reason Their High Worshipfuls by secret letter, dated 22nd June 1741, have proposed that this product should be sold, on the spot with 75 per cent advance.

"Caimal Cherally (Chērāṅellūr Kaimal who is also known as Kaṛṭṭāvu) is a gentleman of 50 or 60 years old, particularly cautious and shrewd and devoted to the Honourable Company. His heirs are not great courtiers but good soldiers, and when they take up the government they will probably not put up with the injustice of the King of Cochin but rather follow the example of their neighbours, Moorianatty Nambiar and Codachery Caimal, two powerful landed proprietors of the King. Being tired of his extortions they sent home the King's messengers, or rather marauders with bleeding heads; by this they incurred the great hatred of the grasping King; however since that time they are living unmolested."

27. **Other Kaimals.** Besides the 'Angecaimals,' Gollennesse mentions the following powerful landed proprietors as being the principal ones under the King of Cochin, viz., (1) 'Moorianatty-Ṇambiar', (2) The 'Paljetter', (3) 'Coddachery Caimal', (4) 'Caimalieone of Coretty', (5) 'Changera Codda Caimal', (6) 'Panamoocattu Caimal'. The last four are called the four 'Caimals of Nandietter Naddu'.

Of the above, the lands of Murianād Nambiār, also known as Muriassu Nambiār "lie between Cochin, Paponetty, Belossa Nambiar and Codacherry." Gollennesse observes: "This Nambiar is between 40 and 50 years old, very proud and conceited. He has no heirs and owing to old disputes the king is unwilling to validate the adoption which he would like to make from Belonga(Vellāngallūr). He has several times requested the Company to support him in this matter and we have promised him to do so provided he is prepared to sell his pepper to the Company". "It is to be feared that if that gentleman comes to die without an heir, the King of Cochin will try to swallow up that beautiful land; so in time we shall have to disregard all considerations and so compel the King to allow the adoption."

By the term *Paljetter* is meant the Pāliaṭṭ Achchan. Of him Gollennesse says: "He is the Principal Ragrodoar and hereditary general of the State of Cochin, resides at Chenotty quite near Cranganore; he is chief of the island of Bypin and sometime back he became by adoption a sovereign prince of Manacotta or Mooloorcarre which lies to the north of Chetwai. He possesses also a right to the old State of Williar Waṭṭaṭṭa; this however is merely nominal."

The country of Kōṭaśśēri Kaimal lies between Paru (Paṟūr), Cranganore, the Cochin territories and the hills.

"The territory of the Caimalinne (feminine of Kaimal) of Coretty situated on the same neighbourhood is of no great importance, still it exports 120 candies of pepper; but this worthless woman has the pepper carried elsewhere. In the year 1730, she was adopted into the state of Mangatty; for she maintains that one of her cousins will have to be adopted into the state; this would take place if she herself had children and if her adoption were legal, but it does not extend to her cousins. And as there are in that state plenty of princes and princesses of the family of Walluanatty, we have always opposed her in order to prevent the great harm that would result."

28. **Cranganor.** This is a small principality, subject to Cochin, situated at the southern end of the Chēťťwāye island possessed by the Paṭinnāťťiēṭaṭṭu Swarūpam. At present it covers an area of 18¾ square miles. Day says that the Crānganūr Rajas base their claim to this tract of land as having been granted to their family by Chēramān Perumāl, the chief of whose guard was their ancestor. The Cochin Census Report, however, refers to a tradition, which, the reporter says, may be taken for what it is worth, "that one Paṭinnāřēṭaṭṭu Bhaṭṭaṭiri had married a sister of one of the Perumāls and that, on the extinction of the Bhaṭṭaṭiri's family, his issue (by the Kṣhe-ṭriya wife) succeeded to his estates, and gave rise to Paṭinnāťťiēṭaṭṭu Swarūpam". It is doubtful if the Crānganūr Rajas were ever independent rulers of the country. Their right to regal authority they have long been forced to waive either before the superior power of the Raja of Cochin or that of the Zamorin. In the early wars of the Zamorin with Cochin, specially during the time of the Portuguese, Crānganūr always sided with the Zamorin. Later on, Crānganūr seems to have entered into an agreement with the Dutch East India Company. We learn from Gollennesse that, by the treaty of peace made with the Zamorin on the 17th of December 1717, Crānganūr was placed under the Dutch. He observes that "the king is called the father of the Zamorin family because he has to live in wedlock with the princess of that state". Even now the two families are allied by marriage. During the progress of negotiations between Hyder Ali, the Dutch and the king of Travancore, we find the Dutch Commandant of the Crānganūr fort complaining

that he had allowed the Zamorin's family and armed followers flying before Hyder to take refuge in his territory. The Dutch Governor pointed out to the Raja "that according to a lawful contract between him and the Honourable Company, all the land from Chetwai to Cranganore was under the ownership of the Company and also that His Highness and his whole country were under the protection of the Company; that therefore his request to send away the Zamorin's family and followers was not unreasonable, and that, hereafter, His Highness must abide implicitly, by the good advice given him by the Company." Subsequently when Hyder captured the whole island of Chēṭṭwāi, the Dutch allowed the princelings who had ruled over small tracts small allowances and the Raja of Crānganūr among them got Rs. 50 a month. This was in 1761. Hyder then directed his forces against the Raja of Cochin who submitted without a blow, finding resistance impossible. He accepted Hyder's suzerainty and undertook to pay an annual subsidy. The Crānganūr Raja who had recently enjoyed the protection of Cochin and who also seems to have benefited by the arrangement made with Hyder was called upon to contribute the subsidy. The Raja agreed to pay 5,000 pagodas annually, and this tribute began to be levied in 1777. This amount was, in the year 1791, reduced to Rs. 6,857-2-3, which has not been since altered. The internal administration of the state continued to be in the hands of the Crānganūr Raja till the time of Col. Munro, the British Resident of Travancore and Cochin (1810-1819), when it was taken from him in consequence of the tribute having fallen in arrears. It was afterwards restored to the Raja on his tendering security for the regular payment of the tribute in the future, but remained with him only for a short time; for, soon after, it was again placed under the direct administration of the Cochin Sirkar. His present position is thus stated in the *Cochin Census Report*: "Although outwardly the fiction is kept up that the Chief

N.

is a feudatory in political alliance with His Highness the Raja of Cochin, he is now practically in the position of a pensioned Chief."

Governor Moens gives the following account of the administrative system of the kingdom of Cranganūr in his day:—

"The king himself is of a specially kind-hearted character, simple and meditative, being very devout on account of his caste. The affairs of the kingdom are not settled by him, but by two of his ministers, whom he likes most. This lasted until they were dismissed and replaced by others.

"When important and embarassing affairs have to be settled, which they feared would have had bad consequences, all the ministers would then come together. Usually they used to quarrel all the time, for every one insisted that his opinion should be taken, without considering the public good. When they could not agree, they had recourse to their idol in the big pagoda. A decision was then asked for from this idol who is supposed to be interrogated secretly by one of the most prominent and cunning ministers of the pagoda. This decision was then told outside, and was usually of an ambiguous nature, more or less in accordance with the nature of the case, but especially framed to fit in with the general opinion. The decision was then looked upon as an oracle even as the oracles of the ancients."

29. **Iyroor.** Airūr formed a small principality lying between Cranganūr in the north and Chettwai in the south. It was ruled by a branch of the Cranganūr house under the suzerainty of the Zamorin. It was also known as Pāppanimattam or Papanietty as the Europeans called it. In 1717, the Dutch took it from the Zamorin. Gollennesse claims it as a Dutch dependency and says that "the prince is poor and is without power."

Governor Moens makes some observations regarding the inter-relation between the families of the Rajas of Cranganūr and Airūr. He says that "Ayroor is the most ancient; after that follows Cranganore and the principality of Cartamana. The kings of Ayroor belonged to the highest and most noble family among the people of Malabar. The country was the gift of Cheraman Perumal. The Raja received some estates, most of which are situated between the territories of Cranganore and Chetwaye in the district of Papanotty. The other estates are situated on the other side of the river opposite to Papanotty in the northern part of the kingdom of Cochin. The kings of Ayroor used to reside and keep their courts on these latter estates known as Belanga (Vellāngallūr).

"The Ayroor family became reduced in numbers, there remaining but two brothers and a sister and the estates were divided among them on account of differences. The elder brother lived in Belanga and the younger brother and the sister settled themselves on the other side of the river in the district of Papanotty. He looked after his estates as a common land-owner, whilst the eldest brother remained in possession of the kingdom and the privileges belonging to a king.

"Now it happened that a chief of Cranganore, also of a noble family, and who had free access to the princesses of the Zamorin bequeathed his estates in Cranganore to the aforesaid younger brother of Ayroor. Hereupon he went to Cranganore, built the present palace, settled down and obtained finally from the Zamorin, to whom the deceased prince was also subject, the title of King. Besides, he and his heirs not only received the right of life and death, but also the privilege to marry the princesses of the Zamorin's family. Hence the Kings of Cranganore are up till now called Fathers of the Zamorin.

"The possession of the eldest brother was once more divided (perhaps between the issue of the sister) between two brothers, the eldest of them remaining in Belanga, and the other taking the estates in Papanotty.

The latter came to be known as Cartamana. These petty kings are, therefore, according to Malabar geneological reckoning, brothers of the dynasty of Ayroor; and the present king of Ayroor, so to speak, is in possession of one-fourth, Prince Cartamana of one-fourth and the king of Cranganore of half of the former estates of Ayroor, besides those he inherited. When treaties of peace were concluded with the Zamorin in the years 1710 and 1717, these kingdoms came under the protection of the Company."

In 1792, the Raja of Cochin laid claim to the whole island of Maṇappuṙam, comprising the three principalities of Cṙānganūr, Airūr and Chēṫṫwāī, while Cṙānganūr was claimed by the English East India Company as forming part of the island which was under the direct administration of the Company. The commissioners appointed by the Bombay Government to investigate and settle disputes regarding territories ceded by Tippu under the last treaty, rejected both claims. Airūr now forms part of the Ponnāni Taluk of South Malabar. Gollennesse mentions "Cranganore Ayrur or Belanga (Veḷḷāngallūr), Beloota Nambiar, Changaracanda Caimal, Chittur Nambudiri and Payanchery Nayar as vassels of the Dutch East India Company under the treaty of 1717 with the Zamorin."

Of these, Beloota Nambiar, also known as Veḷḷōss Nambiār was lord of Māppṙāṇam. His property bordered on the lands of Murianād Nambiār, the tract of Paponetty and Trichur.

"Formerly, he was under the Zamorin, but, in the previous war, he lost his lands, and the king of Cochin appropriated them. However, to the great chagrin of the king of Cochin, this proprietor of the house of Wengenatta was restored in his former position by Commander Joannes Hertenburg. The terms may be found in the contract concluded with him, dated 27th June 1709. The king of Cochin has not ceased to give trouble every now and then, but he always found the Honourable Company in the way. This Nambiar is between 50 and 60 years old; he pays the Honourable Company annually 90 bushels of rice, but the *palam* which he paid the Zamorin before and which he consequently owes to the Honourable Company, he has never yet been willing to pay. He is an irritable gentleman who often mixes up in affairs which do not concern him at all, and, when he finds himself embroiled, he would like the Honourable Company to come to his assistance; this however is not our intention."

"Changaram Canda Caimal and Chittur Nambudiri whose lands lie to the south of Enammam and near Aerattu and Arattupuzha are two proprietors who were formerly under the Zamorin but were placed under the Dutch by the 24th Article of the above-mentioned treaty."

Of Payanchēri Nayar we shall have to say something presently.

30. **Four Tributary Rajas.** The four states of Ampalappuḷa or Poṙakkād, Vaṭakkenkūr, Paṙūr and Mangāṭṭy or Ālangād were considered the four pillars of the Cochin State. Though they had independent jurisdiction over their respective principalities, they were all subject to the jurisdiction of Cochin. They had a voice in the election of the Raja of Cochin. All the four states were conquered by and annexed to Travancore and now form part of the present Kōṭṭayam or northern division of Travancore.

31. **Porcad's Spiritual Prince.** The tradition referred to by our author is thus related in the first volume of the Travancore *State Manual*:[1] "An interesting local tradition exists as to the origin of the Chempakachery Rajahs. The tract of the country known as Kuttanad was in the rule of a powerful oligarchy of Nambudiri Brahmins, their head-quarters being Ampalapuzha, where the ancient temple dedicated to

[1] P. 345.

Sri Krishna stands. This temple owned most of the lands there. The managing trustees of the temple property formed the oligarchy who ruled the state. The business of state used to be transacted in the Council-hall still known as *mantrasala* of the Ampalapuzha temple, where the proud Brahmins met every day for business as well as for recreation. One day, while engaged in chess after business was over and rioting and revelling and chewing to their heart's content, a ship-wrecked crew of a few hundred Europeans, probably Portuguese, arrived with their arms, related their adventures by the sea and begged of the chess-playing Brahmins to give them food and shelter. The thoughtless Nambudiris mad with the fatal game of dice and revelry told the hungry crew in a vein of cruel jest pointing to a pious old man coming from his ablutions and noonday prayers to worship at the temple that they themselves were poor and humble and could not help the unfortunates, but 'here comes the greatest man of the village who will feed and clothe you, if you seek his help.' The distressed crew took it in right earnest and applied to the old man, explaining their miserable condition by signs and symbols and seeking immediate succour at his hands. That pious old Brahmin, be it remembered, was the poorest man in the village and lived on one meal a day, spending himself wholly in prayers and religious exercises and keeping himself aloof from his noisy but opulent neighbours. When he saw the supplications of these Europeans distressed by thirst and hunger and saw also the jesting reference made to him by the proud dice-players at the *mantrasala*, he comprehended the situation in an instant, discovered that there was no escape for him and took it as a sign from the God Krishna, and thereupon handed over to the hungry crew one of his very few golden rings which formed the sum-total of his earthly possessions. Even to this day Nambudiris of all grades and ranks carry in their fingers a number of gold rings, each of a pound sterling value, a point of special vanity with that class of people. The poor Nambudiri directed them by signs to go to the bazaar and sell that ring and buy their food and drink, which being done, they came back to his house and mounted guard there to do his bidding. Next day he gave another gold ring and that sufficed for their second day's meal. The armed aliens had now become his faithful retinue. So runs the story. The Nambudiri had now reached the depth of his pocket and was afraid he had not the wherewithal to maintain his new regiment for the third day. Necessity is the mother of invention, and he hit upon a happy idea. His genius turned the situation to his advantage. He sent the armed retinue with a servant boy of his own to one of the oligarchist's houses with orders to remove the inmates without offering any violence or insult to them and bring away the whole of his goods to his own quarters. Day after day, all the richest houses in the village were similarly dealt with and the spoils brought to his house maintained him and his army in great affluence. He next sent men to collect the temple dues. He took charge of the Devaswam itself and managed it on behalf of the God. He appointed officers and collected taxes. By one stroke of fortune he became King. Thus came into existence the line of the Chempakachery Rajahs at Ampalapuzha."

The origin of the state of Poṙakkād, as given by our author, fairly indicates the political condition of Malabar at the time. Bodies of fighting men seeking service under a leader who could carve out a principality roamed about the country.[1] Mercenary soldiers offered their swords to whomsoever would pay them amply, and such men used to be entertained by the various Rajas. It was a body of soldiers of fortune belonging to this class that assisted one of the twelve Nambūṭiri messengers of the well-known

1. Mr. Nagam Ayya's version of the tradition that the adventurers were Europeans, probably Portuguese, receives no support from European writers.

Ampalappuḷa pagoda to carve out a state for himself. The principality of Poṛakkāḍ is known also as Ampalappula and Chempakaśśēri. Chempakaśśēri is said to be the house name of the hero of the episode mentioned by our author. The ruler is sometimes called Poṛakkāṭṭaṭikal, just as the ruler of Travancore or Vēṇāḍ is called Vēṇāṭṭaṭikal. By the Portuguese he is called the Arrel of Porca. Barbosa notices the state and observes that it had a lord of its own with a small territory where "many fishermen reside who do nothing and have no other occupation than that of fishing during the winter and of plundering on the sea during the summer." The way they set to work at this has been noticed elsewhere. "The booty," he says, "they divide with the lord of the country who countenances them."

The Raja was a great friend of his Christian subjects who were permitted to build Churches all over the state. It is said that, under the workings of remorse of having killed his fellow Brahmans, the first sole ruler of the state erected an altar in the Christian Church at Koḍamālūr, a strange procedure for a Hindu and that a Nambūṭiri Brahman. The Church at Poṛakkāḍ which was visited by Archbishop Meneses is said to have been erected by a Raja of Poṛakkāḍ who attributed a victory he had gained to the cross displayed on the banner of his Christian subjects who fought for him. The Archbishop was visited by the then Raja who is described by him as "a young man of short stature, but well-proportioned, and distinguished among the Rajas of Malabar for his valour and courtesy." He was gorgeously apparelled, and covered with gold and jewels. The conversation that followed between the Brahman Prince and the Roman Catholic Prelate indicates the relations that existed between the Portuguese and the country powers at the time. It is thus related by Hough: "After courteously saluting him, and taking to himself the credit of protecting the commerce of the Portuguese from pirates and performing other services for that people, he (the Raja) said that he hoped these good offices would be deemed sufficient to entitle him to the honour of being called '*Brother-in-arms* to the king of Portugal', as the Raja of Cochin had been. The Archbishop's answer showed that he knew how to make the Raja's ambition available for his own purpose. After returning civilities, he said, "that what he had asked for was an honour that the King of Portugal never conferred on any sovereign until he had merited it by some signal service. However, he promised to do what he could to obtain for him the distinction to which he aspired." A similar distinction was sought for and obtained by the Raja of Gundara. The hankering for honours, stars and ribbons that even the present Rajas have, in spite of their enlightenment and education, is thus no new development, their ancestors before them having done what they could to secure these baubles at the hands of foreign powers.

Though the Raja of Poṙakkād managed to keep the Portuguese in humour at first, circumstances led him about the year 1528 to join the Zamorin, the sworn foe of the Portuguese. They resolved to teach him a wholesome lesson. Taking advantage of the absence of the Raja with a considerable portion of his army from Poṙakkād, the Portuguese resolved to raid the city. Lopo Vaz was sent for the purpose. The city was assaulted by 1000 men. Though the Raja was not there, the Moors and Nayars defended the place courageously, until the majority of them being killed, the rest fled, whereupon the Portuguese entered the city and plundered it. The wife and the sister of the Raja, besides other persons of note, were taken prisoners. Quantities of gold, silver, jewels, silks and other stuffs, a number of cannon, and 13 large vessels were also taken. All inhabitants found in the city were slain, and the place was then burnt. It is said that those who fought on that day got 800 gold pagodas per head as their share of the plunder and that their leader's

O.

share came up to almost a hundred thousand pagodas. Before leaving for Cochin, Lopo Vaz had all the cocoanut trees in the city cut down. Such was the inhuman and cowardly conduct of the Portuguese. They did not wait for the return of the Raja, but skulked away with their booty soon after the plunder. This took place on the 15th of October 1528. It is said that it was out of the wealth plundered from Poṙakkād that the Portuguese were able to pay the arrears of salary due to Pero Mascarenhas for three years at the rate of 10,000 mohurs per annum. Finding the sorry plight in which he was placed, the Raja, on his return to his capital, begged the Portuguese Governor, Nuno de Cunha, to restore to him his wife and sister, offering to pay a heavy ransom. The Governor agreed and the princesses were restored to the Raja.

Troubles again arose with the Portuguese some time after. About the year 1540, news reached Dom Christovao da Gama, brother of the Viceroy, who was then wintering in Cochin, that the Raja of Poṙakkād had attacked some Portuguese vessels commanded by Sebastiao de Sousa while on a voyage from the Maldives. He sent a message to the Raja demanding the return of all he had taken. The Raja replied that the vessels which attacked the Portuguese were not his, but belonged to a Kaimal over whom he had no control. But Dom Christovao, having received what he thought was authentic information that both the Raja and the Kaimal were joint perpetrators of the robbery, again demanded the return of the stolen property, but, as the Raja only made further excuses, Dom Christovao determined to obtain redress by force of arms. He accordingly invaded the Kaimal's territories situated between those of Poṙakkād and Cochin with a company of 600 men. The Kaimal resisted, and a fierce fight ensued in which his army was completely routed. The Kaimal fled, and the Portuguese pursued their usual course of indiscriminate plunder and pillage. His city was wholly burnt, and about 2,000 palm-trees were cut down. On perceiving this wholesale and wanton destruction, the Raja went in person to the Portuguese Commander and requested him to desist, telling him at the same time that the erring Kaimal had repented. Peace was agreed to, but during the course of the negotiations and while the Portuguese were resting, the Kaimal with some of his followers treacherously rushed on a party of them unawares, whereupon other Portuguese came to their assistance and the Kaimal and all his followers were slain. The Raja of Pořakkād then agreed to a treaty of peace and friendship with the Portuguese, notwithstanding that the king of Cochin, who was not friendly to Dom Christovao, did all in his power to prevent it.

We have no further information regarding this kingdom till the arrival of the Dutch in Cochin. At the siege of Cochin, the king of Pořakkād seems to have played an important part. He brought up contingent after contingent to the aid of the Cochin Raja on behalf of the Portuguese and threw supplies into Eřṇākuḷam. His troops fought fiercely at the landing place at Eřṇākuḷam. On the fall of Cochin, the Pořakkād chief, like other Malabar chiefs who were ready to worship the rising sun, turned his allegiance to the Dutch, and a tripartite treaty was entered into between the Dutch, the Raja of Cochin and the Raja of Pořakkād.

Copy of a treaty entered into between the Perumpaṭappu Valia Ṭampurān (Raja of Cochin), the Honourable the Dutch (East India) Company and Chempakaššēri Swarūpam (Pořakkād) on 14th Meenam 838 (March 1663):

"1. Forgetting all that has taken place between the parties in the past, there shall be perpetual alliance and confidence in the future, so long as the sun and moon shall endure.

2. The Pořakkād Raja shall not in future do any act of hostility towards the Cochin Raja and the

Company. And if at any time the Portuguese or any other neighbouring state shall proceed against them as enemies, the Porakkād Raja shall put himself forward as the enemy of such power or powers.

3. The Porakkād Raja shall crush the power of Kōḍavarma and keep him out of the country for ever.

4. The Porakkād Raja shall have faith in the Company, as hitherto in the Portuguese, and shall entertain greater confidence in the Company.

5. The Raja shall not allow pepper or cinnamon to be weighed in Porakkād, nor exported from it, without the permission of the Raja of Cochin and of the Company. All rights and dues regarding these articles shall enure to them as already settled by custom.

6. It is resolved that the Honourable Company shall erect a fort for the protection of the Porakkād Raja and his country.

7. The Porakkād Raja shall not permit any one else except the Company to bring elephants to his territories or to take them out of it.

8. All Portuguese vessels in Porakkād shall be given up to the Company by the Raja. The money spent for this shall be given to the Porakkād Raja by the Company.

9. To mark the sincerity of his friendship, the Porakkād Raja will dismantle a fortified wall 100 *Koles* long and very broad, constructed in his territories; and it is agreed, according to the wishes of the Company and the Cochin Raja, that this wall shall not be repaired and shall be allowed to go to ruin untouched by the hand of man.

10. If any enemy invade Cochin or Porakkād territories, the Company shall render all available help to the Rajas according as truth and justice require and drive out the invaders.

11. The Cochin and Poṙakkād Rajas agree to give the Company all powers and privileges enjoyed by the Portuguese."

Six copies have been taken of this treaty, all being signed and sealed by the parties—that is, three copies in Dutch and three in Malayalam—each party to retain two copies, one in Dutch and one in Malayalam.

The Cochin Raja and Admiral Ryklof Van Goens representing the Company, signed their names and the Poṙakkād Raja affixed his royal mark—a *Shank* or conch-shell.

Captain Nieuhoff has left us an interesting account of the kingdom of Poṙakkād whither he went along with Mr. Willing to have an interview with the Raja. On arrival at Poṙakkād, the Captain was informed that the Raja had some ten days before left for Koḍamālūr where he has been building a palace for the last 20 years. Nieuhoff proceeded at once thither and was granted an audience with the Raja. "After the usual respect paid," says Nieuhoff, "I delivered to him my credentials which he having received, he ordered all his attendants and my interpreter among the rest to withdraw, because he had a mind to discourse with me alone in Portuguese, which he understood very well. I told him that I was sent on purpose by my masters to His Majesty, to assure him of their friendship, and to pay the money stipulated by the last treaty which sum, though it much exceeded the value of the thing received, yet notwithstanding all this my masters had thought fit not to recede from what had been promised in their name. The king gave for answer, that it never had been a custom to weigh the pepper at Cochin, (which I had desired should be done) and that therefore he hoped the Company would not introduce any novelties in his territories; assuring us withal, that he would be ready to assist the Company and their officers upon all occasions; besides several other assurances too tedious to be inserted here. I soon understood his meaning, to wit, that he would not have the pepper trade transferred to Cochin, which was a matter of no great consequence, so I did not insist any longer upon it, but agreed that the pepper should be received and weighed at Porka; assuring him that the Company had never had the least intention to impair anybody's right, as His Majesty might easily be convinced as well by this as several other transactions and treaties made lately with other kings and princes. The king appeared to be highly satisfied thereat, desiring that a factor might be sent thither forthwith, to buy and receive the pepper, which I having promised to the king, he ordered the Residoor to receive the money, and granted me leave to depart."

The Raja appears to have been a good diplomatist and tried his best to ingratiate himself into the favour of the Dutch. He told Nieuhoff that "he had caused the flags of the English and some other nations to be taken down and the Dutch flag to be set up for which they threatened him with open war in his own territories and refused to quit the country which made him to be looked upon but with a very indifferent eye by all the neighbouring princes." Apparently he wanted to impress on the Dutch envoy that he had made great sacrifices to secure the interests of the Dutch East India Company and expected adequate recompense.

Of the kingdom of Porakkād, Nieuhoff gives us the following description: "The kingdom of Porka, or Porkah, otherwise Perkatti, has borrowed its name from its capital city; it borders to the north upon the kingdom of Cochin, to the south upon that of Kalkoulang; it has Takken Berkenker to the north-east, and the sea to the west, being about 12 leagues in length. * * * It was not till the year 1590 that the Romish religion was openly professed here with consent of the king, tho' many years before the Christians called of St. Thomas lived in these parts. The king granted considerable privileges to the jesuits; such as the building of churches with crosses on the top of them, and the necessary bells, near unto which no pagodas, Jewish synagogues or Mahometan mosques were to be erected; they had also liberty to baptise as many as were willing to embrace the Christian religion, all which was punctually observed. * * In the year 1640, one *Siam Baatshery Vaubaar* (Chempakaśśēri Nambūṭiri) reigned over Porka. They claim a superiority over the king of Cochin, against whom they waged heavy wars in former ages; but now-a-days the kings of Porka are under the jurisdiction of the Dutch East India Company, being forced thereunto by their victorious arms; the chief strength of the king of Porka consists in his small frigates, of which he has 500, and are made use of when the fields are overflown with water. Formerly the Portuguese were masters of the pepper trade here, with the king's consent; but finding that they intended to fortify themselves in several places, he engaged in war against them, which lasted three whole years. The Dutch never came to Porka till 1642, under the reign of *Siam Baatshery Vaubaar*, being then not above 24 years old; they were very kindly received by him, a treaty being concluded betwixt them at that time, by which the Dutch had the pepper trade granted to them. * * * During the rainy season most of the rice fields hereabouts, as well as all along from the Cape Comorin, as far as Pokare Biarbar, lay under water. This countrey also produces a considerable quantity of pepper yearly, which is for the most part bought up by the English, who have had a factory here many years ago. Deeper into the country live abundance of Christians who were formerly converted by the Portuguese; these buy up the pepper in the countrey, which they are obliged to deliver to a certain merchant, appointed for that purpose by the king."

Nieuhoff also gives us a pleasant account of the prince with whom he had an interview and of his administration of the state. "The king then reigning at Porka was a person of 30 years of age, very stately and well-made. He was adorned with many jewels of diamonds and rubies, which he wore on his hands, arms, and ears, according to the Malabar fashion. He is a most absolute prince, acknowledging no superior, every foot of the countrey being his own, and at his disposal. Justice is administered here with extraordinary severity, especially on the account of theft, which makes this crime scarce ever to be heard of here * * which surprised me not a little knowing that the Malabars in general are the earrantest thieves in nature."

Gollennesse describes the kingdom of 'Poraca' as lying, in his day, "on the sea-coast to the north of Pagodingo (Ṭṛkkuṅṅappuḷa) and to the south of the province of Moutan; towards the interior it bordered on Tekkenkoor and Calicoilan; and so looking from Coddemaloor—a piece of land with a court walled in and situated in Tekkenkoor where the queen resides—it borders on Berkenkoor." The Raja, "a Brahman by caste, is a man of 32 years of age. He is not very intelligent but his State is more or less wisely governed according to the salutary laws of his grandfather. * * * * The Raja has for some time been on very good terms with the King of Travancore, nor does he make a secret of it and to please him he has offered insults and affronts to the Honourable Company for which however he will have to pay dearly one day." The Raja seems to have had his complaints against the Dutch for not paying the full value of pepper supplied, for allowing the Raja of Quilon to seize his vessels in the Bay of Quilon and for firing by the Dutch on the Raja's vessels on the broad river. The Dutch justified the first by saying that the Raja and his merchants failed to supply the full quantity of pepper within the contract time and so had to forgo the full contract price. As for the second, as soon as Governor Gollennesse heard of the seizure, he ordered their release, but this being delayed by the

Raja of Quilon, the Governor himself released the vessels "almost forcibly to the great chagrin of a ruler with whom the Company was on good terms." With regard to the third complaint, the guilty were punished as the firing had been expressly forbidden. Notwithstanding this, the Raja continued sulky and the Governor says: "Meanwhile, as this little potentate insists upon showing his temper, we must treat him coolly and refuse the Company's passes to his subjects until he has come to his proper senses and until he has given fitting satisfactions to the Honourable Company."

We next hear of Poṙakkād in connection with the Travancore conquests. The Raja took a prominent part in the confederacy of the northern states, under the presidency of the king of Cochin, to oppose the advance of Travancore. With the powerful aid of the Dutch, the northern princes set themselves up to make a firm stand against King Māṙṭṭāṇḍa Vaṙma. During the war with Kāyamkuḷam, the Rajas of Poṙakkād, Ṭekkenkūr and Vaṭakkenkūr had rendered material help to the Kāyamkuḷam Raja who, on his flight from his country, had left behind him his writing desk which fell into the hands of the Travancore Ḍaḷawa. Its contents disclosed the confederacy that had been formed against the Travancore king. Besides this, a number of swords were found heaped in a corner of a room in the Raja's palace which bore the name of the Poṙakkād Chief. Upon this, the Travancore Ḍaḷawa, Rāma Iyen, was ordered to march against Poṙakkād. The Raja had a well-trained army which, under the command of Māṭṭūr Paṇikkar, advanced to oppose the Travancoreans. The two armies met at Ṭōṭṭāppiḷḷi, where a severe conflict ensued. Māṭṭūr Paṇikkar, the general, and Ṭekkēṭaṭṭ Bhaṭṭaṭiri, the family priest of the Raja, both proved false. Treachery was at work. These chieftains deserted their master and went over to the enemy and were amply rewarded. Nothing daunted, the Raja continued the fight, but resistance was useless, and the

Raja was forced to yield. He was taken prisoner and removed to Trivandrum, while his state was annexed to Travancore. This was in the year 1746.

32. **Chanamangolam** (Chēṅṅamangalam). This is the seat of the Pāliaṭṭ Achchen, the premier nobleman of the Cochin State. It is also known as Chēṅṅōṭṭ and is remarkable as one of the old Jewish settlements. The famous Jesuit College of Vaippucōṭṭah was also here. It has disappeared, and the Jesuit fathers who once ruled there have deserted the place. It was here that Dr. C. Buchanan "was surprised to meet the Jews and Christians in the same street" * * * and "a Jewish Synagogue and a Christian Church standing against each other."

33. **Berkenkoor.** This was the Vaṭakkenkūr state. Vaṭakkenkūr and Ṭekkenkūr were together known as Bimbāliṅād or Vempāliṅād, and the broad lake, along the eastern coast of which and mountains to the further east Bimbāliṅād lies, is also known as the Vēmbaṅād lake. According to Gollennesse, Vaṭakkenkūr was bounded on the west by the broad river, on the east by the country of Pāṇḍya, on the south by Ṭekkenkūr and on the north by Cōṭomangalam. "This State," says he, "comprises eight provinces called Badeatty. Among these are Tallia-parambu, Cardutty, Mangoor, Ballachery, Pudicalu Manatty, Kilnoor, besides the large province of Kismalanadu in which lies the well-known bazaar, Toddopale or Carcotty. These provinces export a considerable quantity of pepper, and of this 1,000,000 candies must be supplied annually to the Honourable Company in accordance with a contract made in 1740, but what we said before in our general remarks regarding the limited power of the rulers in Malabar must be noticed here, for the prince-regent, who owes all to the Honourable Company and who is powerless without the Company's protection, would take care, as it is certainly in his own interests, that the contract is complied

with if it were in his power, because His Highness has been given to understand in very significant terms that if he fails to fulfil his promise, the expelled prince will again be made regent. He has done whatever was in his power but without success. For this reason it has been necessary to raise the price of the pepper if we wished to buy it at all. However this expedient will not prove successful, because the natives secure still higher prices by smuggling the pepper."

At first, the Dutch had no foot-hold in the Vaṭakkenkūr territory. But they were afterwards allowed to build a factory at Vechchūr as a reward for the aid they rendered to the northern princes against Travancore. But this they had to abandon soon after. The states of Vaṭakkenkūr and Ṭekkenkūr touched each other, running inland eastward from the shores of the Vempanāḍ lake or backwater, till they reached the territories of the Pūññāṟṟii chief lying along the foot of the western ghauts. Ṭekkenkūr lay to the south of Vaṭakkenkūr. The rude fortifications or lines intersecting the country at Muvvāṟṟupuḷa and Ēṟṟumānūr both defined and defended their territories. The Vaṭakkenkūr state was known to the Portuguese as Piementa or the pepper kingdom, because pepper of a very fine quality grew there in abundance. The queen of Piementa figures prominently in connection with the endeavours made by Archbishop Meneses to subdue the Syrian Christians and to bring them to the Roman fold.

The Vaṭakkenkūr Raja was one of the members of the confederacy that attempted to withstand the king of Travancore. But when the Raja found that Kāyamkuḷam, Quilon, Poṛakkāḍ and Ṭekkenkūr had fallen, and that resistance was of no avail, he abandoned his kingdom and fled northwards, taking refuge with the Zamorin. The state was annexed to Travancore. The Raja's family was, however, invited to come back some time after and was allowed a pension on which it still subsists.

34. **Parur.** This was a small principality ruled over by a Nampūṭiri chief. It comprised almost the present Taluk of Pařūr in the Travancore State, lying on the northern side of the Periyār river. Gollennesse says that this state is situated between Bardella (Vaṭuṭala), Cheralli (Chērāṅellūr), Mangatty (Ālangād), Chenotty (Chēṅṅamangalam) and Baypin (Vypīn) "It is a beautiful piece of land and there are warlike Nairs there. It produces annually 150 candies of pepper which according to contracts should come to the Company, but it is still conveyed elsewhere. The king is a Brahman of high caste, about 30 years old, handsome but a strange and desperate character, having fairly ruined this valuable state; the second prince, a brother of the king, instigated by his mother, opposed his brother's conduct and indeed made himself master of the state; but the king with his own hand murdered the first minister, the shrewd Ragiadoor Tekkanetta Mēnon, and so the whole government fell again into the hands of the king. The royal family is partly Chodircoor, partly Pandircoor and is divided into two branches."

The Rajaship of Pařūr was also known as the Pindniweṭṭaṭṭu Swarūpam and enjoyed extensive privileges under the Cochin Raja. In the year 1764, the Raja surrendered himself to Travancore, and his state was annexed by the Travancore king. Pařūr, the capital of the state, lies about five miles south of Crānganūr in a direct line, and about one mile inland from the shores of the backwater. It possesses one of the oldest churches in Malabar, as the church there is said to be one of the earliest of the seven churches founded on the coast. Paoli as well as some Portuguese writers call the place Puttona Paroor. It is also called Kōṭṭakkāyal, i. e., the fort-backwater, perhaps on account of a fort having stood on the shores of the backwater.

35. **Mangatti.** This was the principality of Ālangād, governed by a Sāmanṭar chief and was

situated on the side of the Periyār river at Ālwaye. His rule extended over the woody tracts skirting the river on the east up to Malayāṫṫūr. It comprises the modern villages of Ālangād, Ayrūr, Chengamaṅād, Kōṭakuḷangara, Maññappara and a portion of the village of Pāṙakkaṭavu. The state surrendered itself and acknowledged the supremacy of Travancore in the year 1764, and the Raja is now a pensioner. In the treaty of surrender, the boundaries of the state are set forth as follows:—To the west of Maññappara, to the north of Varāppuḷa, to the east of Ṭaṭṭampiḷḷi and to the south of Kochukaṭavu. Gollennesse gives the following particulars regarding this principality: "Mangatty or Puddingattu Eddattu is situated between Cranganore, Chennotty, Paro and stretches as far as the hills. It consists of three small states, Mangatty, Carta and Belta dawil (kaṙaṭṭa = black and veḷuṭṭa= white ṭāvaḷi = branch) which formerly had their separate kings, but since the death of the late Caratadawil in 1735, they have been governed by a prince who was adopted by the Honourable Company from the house of Walluvanatty and who owes everything to the Honourable Company. The late king was in the house of Murianatty Nambiar and died in the year 1741 after having fairly plundered the State. The country exports about 150 candies of pepper and is for the rest of little importance. Among the nobility, the family of Cooriloonise excel in power but still more in mischievousness and when an opportunity offers ought to receive some chastisement. The royal family have pressed strongly for a contract with the Honourable Company and although there is no necessity for this because the country is under Cochin, still as contracts have been made with the other three States and so it may be of some use we have granted the same in Council 15th December ultimo."

This state had originally belonged to one Mangāt Kaimal whose family became extinct about M. E. 875, when the present family came into possession and continued to be styled Mangāt Kaimals. The state is said to have been known as Jangamanād or Chenganād of which Mangād and Mangāṭṭi are corruptions. The eldest member of the family or the ruling Raja was styled Mūṭṭērippād.

36. **Fierad Alva.** This is the Ālwaye river, a well-known summer resort for bathing for people living about Cochin, Erṇākulam and other places. The town of Ālwaye is situated on the southern bank of the river and is distant about 18 miles from Cochin. Several bunglows are built on the banks of the river which are in great request during the hot months of March, April and May, both on account of the cool temperature of the place, compared to Cochin, and the wonderful salubrity of the water, which induces all who frequent the place to enjoy the luxury of bathing. In general, each bunglow is furnished with a temporary covered way leading down the bank to a comfortable booth jutting into the river and screened off by mats. We have a fine description as to how the officers of the Dutch East India Company resident in Cochin enjoyed in the hot weather the waters at Ālwaye given us by Captain Alexander Hamilton in his *New Account of the East Indies*. The popularity of the place has gone down a good deal of late, on account of the quantity of water flowing down the river having been considerably affected by the Periyār irrigation works at its head. The great mass of water which used to come down, and which was of the utmost benefit to the people, not only for bathing and drinking, but also for irrigation of lands lying in its vicinity almost up to Cochin, has been diverted to Madura. The British Government obtained a concession from the Maharaja of Travancore who gave them the land necessary for constructing a reservoir, a tunnel etc., for which Travancore was compensated in money. But the material loss to the people both of Cochin and Travancore is

immense and irreparable, and one need not be surprised to find that they are complaining bitterly. It is to be regretted that, while the Paramount Power put forth its endeavours to benefit its own subjects, it did not apparently take over-much care to see that the interests of the subjects of the Native States did not suffer. Whether unable to resist the demand of its suzerain or unmindful of the wrong perpetrated on its subjects, the Travancore State seems to have loyally submitted to the behests of its liege lord. Anyhow the opening of the Periyār works synchronises with the woeful diminution of water coming down the Ālwaye river.

37. **Bettitte and Kartatavyd.** These stand for Veḷuṭṭa Ṭāvaḻi and Kaṟuṭṭa Ṭāvaḻi, two branches into which the family of Mangāt Kaimal was divided. One of these branches was in possession of Angamāli. The Kaṟuṭṭa Ṭāvaḻi was known also as Vaṭakken-Kūṟṟil Swarūpam and the Veḷuṭṭa Ṭāvaḻi as Paṭiññāṟṟen Kūṟṟil Swarūpam. Of these, the first resided at Aḻakam in Kōṭakuḷangara and the other at Ālangād Kōṭṭappuṟam. About the year 870 M. E., the Veḷuṭṭa Ṭāvaḻi had become almost extinct, while the other one continued for a few years more. In view of this, a few members of the family of the Raja of Waḷḷuvanād were brought over and adopted into the Kaimal's family with the assent of the Raja of Cochin and the Dutch East India Company.

38. **Talappilly Nad.** Visscher has altogether failed to notice the Ṭalappaḷḷi Nād. According to Gollennesse, it consisted of four principalities called Ainikkūṟṟ, Punnaṭṭūr, Maṇakkuḷam and Kakkāṭṭ. Gollennesse observes that "the last having died out, that country was to be divided among the remaining three and indeed Poonnatur, secured his share; but Ainecootty and Mannacolam made a treaty that the remainder of Cacattu should be governed by them n turns; this has been done ever since and at present it is governed by Ainecootty.

"Ainecootty Nambeddy is in reality under Cochin, but he cares little for him owing to the Zamorin being in the neighbourhood; to-day he is a good Zamorin, to-morrow a good Cochin, according as his own interests require. The king has often requested to support him against this man, and this no doubt is very necessary; but if we did so, the Zamorin would surely meddle in the matter, hence we have thought such interference to be too dangerous and we have asked His Highness to exercise patience until the hands of the Honourable Company are somewhat free.

"Poonatur Nambaddy is under the Zamorin. He is a restless and irritable ruler, and the cause of much trouble between the kings of Cochin and the Zamorin. Three years ago he attempted to bring the French into his land and to make himself independent of the Zamorin; but he was forestalled and those friends had courage enough, but not sufficient power to put this matter into execution and had to take their departure without accomplishing anything. He has apparently now dropped the matter entirely, at least for some time past, Poonatur has become a great deal more manageable.

"Manaculam is the smallest of the two rulers in Talapally; he is under the Zamorin and the king of Cochin. He gives by no means as much trouble as the other two. He has always shown in the late war that he was faithful to the Company and since that time he has done nothing that could displease the Honourable Company."

Within Ṭalappaḷḷi is "Manacotta or Moolloorcarre, a freehold estate inherited by Paljettor (Pāliaṭṭ Achchen); it lies to the east of Peratobiddy (Pērāṭṭuvīṭhi) and hard by the lands of the Zamorin."

39. **The Zamorin.** The first mention we have of this prince is in the Kōṭṭayam copper-plate of Vīra Rāghava Perumāḷ where he is cited as a witness to the grant as the ruler of Ēṛnāḍ. The Kēraḷa Māhāṭmyam also mentions him as a Sāmanṭa prince. There can

be no doubt that, from very early times, the Zamorins cut a conspicuous figure in the political arena of Malabar. The Kēralōṭpaṭṭi assigns their origin to the gift of a small bit of land by the last Perumāl to two Ēṛāḍi brothers with the injunction that they may extend it by the aid of a sword with which they were invested. The Zamorins appear to have subdued all the neighbouring princes and for a long time held the Cochin Raja in subjection. The Kēralōṭpaṭṭi relates how the Zamorin became the most famous of the Malayāli Rajas. He seems to have adopted the high sounding title of Kuṅṅala-Kōnāṭiri or 'King of the hills and waves.' The Sanskrit form of this title is Sāmuḍri and Sāmūri or Ṭāmūṭiri is the Malayālam corruption of it. Hence the term Zamorin used by the Europeans to designate the prince. The dynasty is also called the Nēṭi Viruppu Swarūpam or the greatly extended dynasty.

The Zamorin's first act of aggression after the departure of the Perumāl was to dispossess the chieftain of Polnad—the country round Calicut. He fought with this chief called Pōṟlāṭiri for 48 years, but was not able to conquer him. At last, what he failed to obtain by force of arms was achieved by treachery. Pōṟlāṭiri's minister and mistress were bribed, and his troops won over; the Zamorin's forces were admitted to Pōṟlāṭiri's fort treacherously, whereupon that prince fled and took refuge with Kōlaṭṭiri, and from one of the females of this family is descended the present Raja of Kaṭaṭṭaṅād in North Malabar. About this time, the Mahomedan Moors arrived at Calicut and built the city. The Kēralōṭpaṭṭi asserts that it was through the aid of these settlers that the Zamorins made their next great encroachment on the neighbouring chiefs. With the aid of these Arabs, the Zamorin subdued the Raja of Waḷḷuvaṅād who had hitherto presided at the Mahāmakham or the great Assembly held at Tiruṅāvāya once in 12 years, and got himself installed in that office. The

Cochin Rajas were also despoiled about the same time of the Kūṭṭanād and Chāvakkād portions of the Ponnāni Taluk. It is impossible to say exactly when these events happened. The Gangās, the Rāṣhṭrakūṭas and the Chālukyās seem to have at one time or other invaded the Zamorin's dominions and conquered him. With the founding of the Vijayanagara dynasty, a new political force was brought into existence in Southern India. The Vijayanagara kings in the 14th century seem to have brought into subjection the Zamorin who more than once succeeded in getting himself free from the Vijayanagara yoke. It was about this time that Ibn Batuta visited Calicut and he found the Zamorin a powerful monarch. About the end of the 14th century, Mahomedan influence was on the increase, and we see Sha Rokh of Persia sending an embassy to the court of the Zamorin in the person of Abdur-Razak to secure the goodwill of that potentate. It is said that the Zamorin's embassy to the Shah cut a shining figure at the Persian Court. Half a century later, the Portuguese arrived on the coast, and the first Malabar sovereign of any magnitude with whom Vasco da Gama treated was the Zamorin. The Portuguese Admiral found the Zamorin a powerful ruler and almost lord paramount over Malabar. Regarding the Zamorin, Faria Y Souza tells us:—"The King of Calicut is the most powerful of all the coast and therefore for distinction called Zamorin as much as Emperor. The Kingdom took its name from the metropolis, in which are many stately buildings of the Natives." Though well received at first, the Moors managed to create ill-feeling between the king and the new comers. The Zamorin was at no time a friend of the Portuguese; from first to last, the two powers were inimical. The various wars which the Zamorin waged with Cochin have been noticed, in all of which the Portuguese appear to have taken part on the side of the Raja of Cochin.

On landing at Calicut, da Gama had an audience with the king who, on receiving him, "bowed his head and body a little, extended his right hand and arm, and with the points of his fingers touched the right hand of the Captain Major and bade him sit down upon the dais upon which he was." In delivering his message, da Gama pressed for freedom to trade in the produce of the kingdom, explaining what he could give in return. The Portuguese were permitted to put up a factory and were asked to land their goods. One boat-load was landed and taken to the factory, but was soon robbed. The treatment that da Gama received at Calicut was far from encouraging, and he sailed away. Running up the coast, he was met by boats sent by the Kōlaṭṭiri Raja who invited him to his country. Da Gama accepted the invitation, had an interview with the king, exchanged presents with him and carried a message to the king of Portugal engrossed on a gold leaf and the expedition returned to Europe. The profits realised on the cargoes taken back by da Gama were so enormous that, in the following year (1500 A.D.), Pedro Alvarez Cabral was sent out at the head of a larger expedition with secret orders to negotiate with the Zamorin, if he was favourably received, and to endeavour to induce him to banish the Moors from his country. On the 13th of September, the fleet arrived off Calicut and, on hostages being sent to the ships, Cabral landed and had an interview with the Zamorin at which rich presents were exchanged, and a treaty of friendship "as long as the sun and moon should endure" was entered upon. A factory was also established at Calicut, in which 70 Europeans were stationed. The Moors seem to have effectually prevented the Portuguese from obtaining any large supply of pepper. Cabral pressed the Zamorin for cargo sufficient [to load his ships, and finding that his demands were met with evasion, he attacked and seized a Moorish vessel which was loading in the harbour. The Moors retaliated by wrecking the factory on shore and slaughtering 50 of the Portuguese; the remaining 20 contrived to escape by swimming off to the ship's boats. Cabral demanded satisfaction, but not receiving any, bombarded the town killing 600 of the inhabitants. He seized 10 of the Zamorin's ships and sailed for Cochin. On the 10th December 1500, he reached Cochin and sent on shore Micheal Jogue, a Syrian Christian, to visit the Raja. Cochin, though at this time a tributary of the Zamorin, did not hesitate to receive the foreigners favourably, at which Cabral was very much pleased. Hostages were sent to the ships, and the Admiral and his men landed. A treaty of friendship was entered into with the Raja, the Portuguese promising at some future time to instal him as Zamorin and to add Calicut to his dominions. A factory was established, and seven factors were placed there to sell their merchandise. Cabral then left Cochin and sailed for Portugal. The king of Portugal was extremely indignant at the treatment meted out by the Zamorin to Cabral and determined to exact further retribution. Da Gama was, therefore, despatched a second time at the head of a large expedition, followed soon after by his cousin Stephen da Gama. When he reached Calicut, the Zamorin sent a message by a Brahman that he had arrested the 12 Moors who had been guilty of the outrage to the Portuguese. Da Gama detained the Brahman with him. Out at sea, he met a large Calicut fleet which he destroyed, after which he left for Europe. Da Gama's departure was the signal for outbreak of hostilities between the Raja of Cochin and the Zamorin, an account of which is given elsewhere.

Again, in January 1504, before Albuquerque sailed for Europe, he concluded a short-lived treaty with the Zamorin, the conditions of which were:—(1) 900 candies of pepper to be given as compensation, (2) Moors to give up trade with Arabia and Egypt, (3) permanent reconciliation between the Zamorin and Cochin, and (4) the delivery up of two Italian deserters. These terms, except the last, were accepted by the Zamorin, but the peace was of short duration. For the Portuguese captured a vessel bound for Crānganūr laden with pepper and killed and wounded those on board. The Zamorin resumed his war with Cochin, but was not able to subdue the Raja who had the powerful aid of the Portuguese. The war lasted for five months, and the Portuguese exhibited prodigies of valour in the course of it.

In the year 1506, seeing the Portuguese were establishing their position in India firmly, the Zamorin sought the aid of the Soldan of Cairo, in conjunction with whom preparations were made on a large scale, and with much secrecy, for a great naval attack, with a view to drive them from the Eastern Seas. A travelling European, however, named Ludovico of Bologna, disguised as a Moslem Fakir, visiting Calicut, fell in with the two Italians who had deserted the Portuguese and sought service with the Zamorin and soon ascertained the secret. He escaped to Cannanore and was thence sent to Cochin to lay his information before the Viceroy. The Viceroy sent his son, Dom Lourenco, with 11 sails, and he, on learning that there was a large fleet gathered in the roads of Cannanore, proceeded thither on the 16th March 1506, just in time to intercept an armada of Turks and Moors which the Zamorin had launched against Cannanore. This armada consisted of large vessels gathered from Ponnāni, Calicut, Kappāṭṭ, Panṭalāyani Kollam and Dharmapaṭṭaṇam. Lourenco steered his ship straight between two vessels carrying Turkish troops, and soon dispersed the enemy whose armada retreated towards Dharmapaṭṭaṇam. Adverse winds, however, drove them back again to Cannanore. They protested that they had not come to fight with the Portuguese but only wished to pass northwards. To this Lourenco was not disposed to listen; he again closed with them and nearly 3,000 Moslems, it is said, fell in battle and the ships that survived the attack were scattered in all directions.

In 1507, the Zamorin made one more attempt to regain his power at sea and, to attain this purpose, proposed to Melique Az, lord of Diu, Captain of the king of Cambay, to seize the Portuguese ships carrying pepper and drugs to ports in Cambay and to make war with the Portuguese in every way, the Zamorin undertaking to afford him every assistance. Melique Az, however, refused to entertain this proposal. These negotiations coming to the knowledge of the Viceroy at Cochin, he fitted out a squadron of ships to take the offensive under the command of Dom Lourenco. Dom Lourenco proceeded to Chaul and thence to Dabhol where he discovered the Calicut fleet a short distance up the river and proposed to give battle at once, but was overruled by his Council of Captains, who, considering the narrowness of the stream, deemed that it could only be undertaken at great disadvantage and risk. In the meanwhile, Gonsalvo Vaz had sunk a ship off Cannanore, and the body of a nephew of Mammāli Marakkar, a rich merchant of Cannanore, who was on board the ship was washed ashore. The Cannanoreans, not knowing the real facts, attributed the destruction of the ship to Lourenco Britto, and this was made an excuse by the king of Cannanore to break the peace with the Portuguese, being incited thereto by the Zamorin who supplied the king with 21 pieces of cannon and 20,000 Nayars. These, with 40,000 Nayars of the king, laid siege to the Portuguese fort but were gallantly repulsed. The Portuguese, in their turn, attacked the Zamorin's port at Ponnāni, killed all the people there, burnt the ships in the harbour and captured a large quantity of artillery.

As soon as Alfonso de Albuquerque assumed the office of the Captain-General and Governor of India (5th of November 1509), Marshal Fernando Continho informed him that the King of Portugal had ordered him, in his instructions, to destroy Calicut, a measure to which the kings of Cochin and Cannanore (Kōlaṭṭiri) had urged on the king of Portugal; Albuquerque was so wearied with the Zamorin that he expressed himself pleased with the idea. Preparations were commenced at once. The king of Cochin who was informed of the enterprise sent two Brahmans to Calicut to spy out the state of the city and the extent of its resources to sustain a defence. He also wrote to certain lords of the mountainous country, his vassals and friends, instructing them to commence a war with the Zamorin on the interior frontier country and so draw off his armies from Calicut. The Brahmans, on their return, reported that the Zamorin had gone into the interior of the country to a war which was raging there, that in the city itself there were but few Nayars, that the shores were defended by having six large *bombards* on as many wooden stages and that, all along the beach, many holes had been dug to serve as pitfalls.

The expedition consisted of twenty ships of war, besides paraos, twenty of which was supplied by the king of Cochin, carrying 2,000 Portuguese. It left Cochin on the last day of December under the command of Marshal and accompanied by the Governor and a large and brilliant array of fidalgos, secretaries and interpreters and anchored off Calicut on the 3rd of January 1510. The Zamorin was absent, and the Portuguese landed on the 4th and speedily drove away the Moors from the stockades, capturing the six *bombards*, whereupon the defenders retired to the city. The Marshal pursued them, burnt a mosque on the way and pressed on to the Zamorin's palace. It was defended by the Koṭṭuvāl and three Kaimals who were slain. The palace was ransacked, its various rooms being emptied of all their valuable contents. Treasure accumulated for ages together with valuable images of gods set with precious stones and the regalia of the Zamorin were rifled.

Hitherto but little opposition was met with, but now the Nayars increased in numbers and threatened to cut off the retreat of the Portuguese. The Marshal made several violent attacks on them but with little effect. At last, he ordered a retreat, Albuquerque leading the vanguard and the Marshal bringing up the rear, but before retiring he set fire to the palace. The Nayars were furious and violently attacked the rear guard and put them to flight. The Marshal and his lieutenant, Manuel Pacanha, Vasco da Silveira, Lieonal Continho, Filippe Rodrigues and 80 others were killed, whilst Albuquerque who had hastened to assist the Marshal received two wounds in the shoulder and had to be carried down to the ships. At this juncture, Dom Antonio de Noronha and Rodrigo Rebells hurried up with reinforcements and kept the Nayars at bay. The Nayars now abandoned the pursuit and enabled the Portuguese to reach their ships, and the expedition returned to Cochin the next day, leaving Jorge Botelho and Smioa Alfonso in their caravals behind. The Zamorin returned to Calicut four days after the Portuguese had sailed away and was much chagrined at his absence. He was, however, pleased at the result but found fault with the Moors at their conduct in the fight and rewarded the Nayars who had secured the victory though at great cost.

It would appear that a league had been entered into between the Adil Khan and the kings of Calicut and Cambay with a view to drive the Portuguese out of India with the assistance of the Grand Soldan. Albuquerque deemed it necessary to counteract the effects of this league and proposed to his Council of Captains an expedition to capture Goa. The project was opposed by several of the captains, but was insisted on by the Governor who soon after accomplished his purpose. As soon as Zamorin heard of the capture of Goa, he sent ambassadors to solicit the Governor's friendship and offered a site for the construction of a fortress. Albuquerque gladly accepted the offer and sent Simao Rangel along with the ambassadors with instructions to accept no other site for the fortress but at Calicut, in front of the Zamorin's own landing stage. This, however, the Zamorin refused to grant and limited his offer to a site at Chāliyam. Simao Rangel doubted whether the Zamorin was sincere even in this offer, and the matter was allowed to lie over.

In a letter of the date of the 20th of August 1512 to Albuquerque, the king of Portugal had commanded him to enter into treaties with all the native Powers with the exception of Calicut. Albuquerque in his reply, while informing His Majesty that he was at peace with the whole of Malabar except Calicut, pointed out that there was nothing to be gained by prolonging the war with Calicut, that the Zamorin would not then refuse to enter into a treaty if requested to do so and that a far larger trade was to be obtained by peaceful means than by war. However, while writing so to the king, Albuquerque was much annoyed at the failure of Simao Rangel's mission and determined to execute vengeance at the Zamorin's alleged duplicity in the matter. He accordingly sent his nephew Dom Garcia de Noronha to go up against Calicut, to do as much harm as he could to the Zamorin, and to institute a rigorous blockade of the coast so as to prevent any vessels leaving that port for Mecca.

Dom Garcia set sail for Calicut with all his fleet; but no sooner had he arrived off that city than the brother of the Zamorin, who was friendly to the Portuguese, sent word to say that the Zamorin was desirous of peace and was prepared to grant a site in Calicut for the proposed fortress and would pay a tribute to the king of Portugal. To this message no reply was given, and the blockade was continued, so that not one of the ships that were then ready to sail for the Red Sea could venture out. This blockade was continued till January 1513, when Dom Garcia was ordered to join Albuquerque. On being informed of the overtures of the Zamorin, Francisco Nogueira and Goncalo Mendes were despatched to Calicut to conclude terms with the Zamorin, but with instructions to accept no site for a fortress, unless it were within the reef in front of the Zamorin's landing pier, in the harbour pool. These officers, however, met with no better success than others before them, and, as soon as the Zamorin knew that the Portuguese fleet had sailed from the coast of India, he prolonged the negotiations with complimentary communications, so that the officers at length returned to Goa without achieving the object of their mission.

Albuquerque was very indignant at receiving this news and resolved to have a fort built at Calicut at any cost. He arranged a fleet to be prepared in order that he might himself go and carry out the business. Before starting, however, he sent in advance Dom Garcia to demand of the Zamorin the following conditions:—

First, that he should grant space in the roadstead in front of his jetty, on which to build a fortress capable of protecting the Portuguese factors from the troubles they had hitherto suffered at the port; secondly, that he should give whatever pepper might be required for the lading of the ships bound to Portugal in exchange for merchandise of various kinds, according to the weights and prices current at Cannnanore, and that the Portuguese factor should be allowed to purchase the ginger, which the producers brought down for sale to the market place, in accordance with the custom of the country; thirdly, that he should repay all the property which the Moors had taken from the Portuguese in times past; and fourthly, that he should pay a yearly tribute towards the expenses of the fortress and those in charge of it, equivalent to one-half of the payments compulsory on the Moorish merchants for the safe conduct of their shipping.

The kings of Cochin and Cannanore were averse to the Portuguese coming to terms with the Zamorin, lest by that they and the trade of their cities may come to be neglected. Albuquerque had a stormy interview with the king of Cochin on the subject at which the Governor insisted on his right to do as he pleased in the matter without consulting others. The Cochin Raja was alarmed at this and addressed the king of Portugal on the subject direct, being instigated thereto by a priest named Juan Fernandez. As soon as Albuquerque got information of this, he had the erring cleric shipped off to Portugal. While yet in Cochin, he received a despatch from Dom Garcia that the Zamorin was still putting off final settlement with his usual procrastination, acting under the advice of the Moors. The failure of his latest adventure along with Marshal Continho to take Calicut by force was still rankling in his bosom, and he resolved to attain his object by having recourse to a method abhorrent to all principles of humanity. We have already seen that the brother of the Zamorin was a devoted friend of the Portuguese. Albuquerque wrote to the Prince suggesting that he should cause his brother to be poisoned, promising, as a reward for such service, that he himself shuld succeed him on the throne of Calicut. The Prince assented to these base proposals, and having by these means raised himself to the throne, he wrote to Dom Garcia, acquainting him of the fact and stating that he would be happy to make peace with the king of Portugal and to give him a site in any part of Calicut for the erection of a fortress.[1] The new Zamorin also ordered the native Moors who opposed the admission of the Portuguese to be killed in his presence, and the recalcitrant foreign Moors were sent out of the kingdom.

Albuquerque now set sail for Calicut, where he had a highly favourable interview with the fratricide Zamorin. A fort of the same size as that of Cochin was built with two towers on the sea-side, and in the wall between them was placed a wicket-gate, in order that the fortress might receive assistance whenever

1. See *Commentaries of Alfonso Albuquerque*, Vol. IV, p. 72. Also Morse Stephen's *Albuquerque* in the *Rulers of India* Series, p. 131.

necessary, without the Moors on the land being able to prevent it. On the sea-face, there were erected a keep of three storeys, and two others were built on the side towards the city, between which was placed the principal door of the fortress, defended by a bastion.

Writing about this time to King Dom Manoel, Albuquerque strongly advised him to secure Calicut. He recommended to His Majesty to cling fast to the ports of Cochin and Calicut, which places were capable of supplying cargoes to the Portuguese fleets "until the day of judgment". He went on to say, "Now that the treacherous Zamorin is dead, is the opportunity to cultivate a trade with those two ports which are the emporiums of ginger, of the whole of the pepper from Malabar, and of the precious stones of Narasinga. In spite of the war which Your Majesty has waged for years against Calicut, it is even this day the wealthiest place in India."

On the 24th of December 1513, Albuquerque entered into a treaty with the Zamorin, under which the latter agreed to supply the Portuguese with all the spices and drugs the land produced, for the purpose of landing their ships. Besides favourable terms of duty and facilities for their shipping, it was stipulated that, in case of any war the Zamorin may engage in, provided that it was not against any friendly power, the Portuguese would help him, whilst the Zamorin undertook to help them with men on the same condition, should occasion arise. The revenue of the land was to be equally divided between the king of Calicut and the king of Portugal. The Portuguese were to pay for all pepper etc., purchased by them in kind but the duties thereon in coin. This was the blood-money that His Most Christian Majesty, the King of Portugal, paid to the barbarous heathen king of Calicut for poisoning his brother, so that he may remove a thorn from the side of the Portuguese. The step that Albuquerque took to get the inimical Zamorin out of the way, and the language used by him about that great potentate would indicate the depth he was prepared to descend to gain his end. On Albuquerque's departure after the the conclusion of the above treaty, he was accompanied by two ambassadors from the Zamorin who were to convey to Dom Manoel, king of Portugal, rich presents of precious stones etc., and also a letter of peace signed by the Zamorin and the principal men of his kingdom, and sealed with a golden seal, begging that the king would, on his part, send him an ambassador in return, to confirm the treaty of peace which he had made with Albuquerque and a royal safe conduct for all his harbours. On the same day the treaty was concluded, Albuquerque addressed a letter to King Dom Manoel informing him that the Zamorin was sending ambassadors to Portugal, and pointed out the advisability of giving them a grand reception and of continuing on peaceable terms with their king. He also stated that the Zamorin had said that, if the king of Portugal wished to build ships etc., there was plenty of cheap wood in his river and port of Chāliyam, which was at his disposal for that purpose. The ambassadors duly arrived in Portugal and were magnificently entertained by the king, who, after receiving their message, sent them back to their own country handsomely rewarded with presents, and deeply impressed by the magnificence of his hospitality. One of them had become a convert to Christianity while in Europe and received the name of Cruz.

The Zamorin, now on the throne, reigned for ten years, and there was peace between him and the Portuguese for that period. But he found his hands so tied up by the terms of the treaty that he was no longer able to send out a single ship for trading purposes. When, in the year 1515, he asked permission to despatch two ships to Aden, Albuquerque objected, not simply as contrary to the treaty, but also because he was himself on the point of making a voyage to Aden and did not wish that the Zamorin's ships should go before him and acquaint the king of his coming. He, however, at last yielded at the importunity of the Zamorin on the express condition that the ships did not carry pepper, and also that the merchants of Calicut should make for him, at their own expense, two large galleys These terms were agreed to, and the ships were allowed to sail. On their part, the Portuguese themselves seem to have set at naught the terms of the treaty; for, in the year 1521, when the Cochin Raja, smarting under the recollection of former defeats sustained at the Zamorin's hands, massed an army of 50,000 Nayars, they did not hesitate, notwithstanding treaty obligations, to send forty men, thirty of whom were musketeers, to assist the Raja.

On the arrival of Dom Duarte Meneses as Viceroy (January 1523), he found that the protēgē of the Portuguese who reigned at Calicut was dead and another reigned as Zamorin. He found that the new king was made of a different stuff, and that he had resolved to try conclusions with the foreigner. Repeated insults offered to the inmates of the fort by the Moors and Nayars in the city had to be patiently endured. Dom Joao Lima who was commandant at Calicut smarted at the insulting conduct of the people, but the Governor would not come to his aid. At last, in August 1524, the Moor, Kuṭṭyāli of Ṭānūr, after despatching a fleet of 200 vessels, with 40 others to escort it, to Arabia, appeared off the fort at the head of 160 vessels and began to fire on the fort. All appeals to the Zamorin failed. An attempt was made by a Nayar on the life of the commandant but was foiled. Meanwhile, a party of 12 Portuguese and two messengers who had been despatched to the Zamorin were way-laid and murdered by the Moors, who began also to carry away Christian women. A rumour spread that the fort was to be attacked, which received some sort of confirmation from a message secretly sent to the commandant by 'Pūnachen', brother-in-law of the Zamorin. The Nayar soldiers employed under him began to desert, and altogether the aspect of affairs looked serious. But there was no immediate rupture.

Not long after, Lopo Vaz de Sampayo accompanied an expedition against a fleet of the Zamorin which was commanded by Kuṭṭyāli and defeated it in the river of Baeanor. On the arrival of Dom Hendrique de Meneses at Calicut, he found that the Zamorin had employed 15,000 Nayars under the command of Ṭinayancheri Elayaṭu and the Raja of Kurumbarnād to attack the fort and that, having failed to make any impression, had sent Pūnachan and others to Lima to make up all differences. The commandant had replied that he would open negotiations only on the Zamorin surrendering to him the traitorous Moor, Pāṭṭu Marakkār of Cochin. Before leaving Calicut for Cochin, Dom Henrdique demanded further that the Zamorin should agree to pay the expenses incurred by the Portuguese in defending themselves against his attack. The Zamorin protested friendship and offered to give up his vessels then lying in his harbour of Ponnāni. The Governor doubted the Zamorin's sincerity, suspecting that he was simply delaying for the monsoon to set in. He accordingly called on the Rajas of Cochin and Porakkād to support him in his expedition against Calicut. The latter Raja came up with 50 sails. The Zamorin's commander at Ponnāni was called on to surrender his fleet, and he answered that he had no definite instructions from his master. When the Portuguese landed to take water, they were set upon by the Moors. The Governor found the place well-fortified, armed with cannon and commanded by a Portuguese renegade, and, as it was late in the day, the attack was deferred to the morning, the 26th of February. A number of Portuguese were landed, and a fierce engagement took place both by sea and land The fortifications were captured, the city burnt and looted. Kuṭṭyāli's vessels were also burnt and the Portuguese renegade killed. Dom Henrique proceeded next day to Calicut and burnt all the ships that were in that port, after which he proceeded to Panṭalāyani Kollam which was defended by a garrison of 20,000 men and a fleet of 150 ships. After a stubborn fight, the Nayars fled having suffered severe loss, and the Portuguese thereupon entered the town, which they burnt, and took a large quantity of booty including 360 cannon and a vast number of muskets. The majority of the ships were destroyed, being either burnt or sunk, and 53 were captured, most of which were laden with spices. During the course of the fight, while the Portuguese were landing, fighting against odds, the Governor found the Poṙakkād Raja keeping back and sitting at ease in his ship watching the opportunity for plunder. Burning with indignation, he ordered a musketeer to "aim at that idler" and the Raja's leg was at once 'blown off'. He, however, escaped with his life and joined the Zamorin.

The king of Calicut ever kept in mind the inhuman tactics resorted to by the Portuguese to secure the site for the Calicut fort and to build it, and resolved never to rest till he had dislodged them from the fort. He swore vengeance on those who had so basely instigated the foul murder of his uncle and was determined not to leave the fortress long in peace. But, before taking hostile measures, he sent an envoy to the Governor at Cochin offering peace. The Governor proposed that the Zamorin should give up all his war-ships, also the Moors who had burnt the St. Thomas Church at Crānganūr and killed a number of Christians there, pay the amount required to rebuild the Church, and make terms with Kalluruṭṭi Kaṇāran who had sided with the Raja of Cochin. These terms were not accepted, and hostilities were resolved on. Ṭinayanchēri Eḷayaṭu and Kuṙumpyāṭiri, i. e., the Raja of Kuṙumbaṙnād, were sent to invest the fort with an army of 12,000 Nayars. With them was a clever engineer, a Portuguese convert to Islam. The Portuguese outside the fort sought shelter within and shut themselves up there, removing all goods and other things and burning their houses in the city. The Nayars now proceeded to dig a trench round the fort, commencing at Vaṇṇaṭṭānparamba to the south and carrying it all round, erected batteries and brought forward guns with which to bombard the fort. The battery opened fire on the 13th of June 1525, and the next day a messenger was sent off to the Governor to demand assistance, as Dom Joao de Lima had only 300 men with him for the defence of the fort. The messenger reached Cochin on the 10th of July. Dom Henrique at once called for volunteers who would undertake to go to the defence of Calicut, to which 150 men responded at once. They were sent in two caravels and succeeded in getting into the fort. The Nayars brought forward scaling ladders and attempted to scale the walls, but were repulsed and thrown down; de Lima sent an urgent message for further reinforcements, and an additional force of 500 men was despatched to his relief, but these were unable to land on account of the surf and so returned to Cochin. The Zamorin renewed his attempt, promising his engineer rich rewards. One of the towers of the fort was almost falling, and the powder magazine had to be removed. The trenches dug by the Sicilian and the tunnel made by him had almost approached the walls, when information of the course adopted was conveyed to the besieged by a Portuguese convert to Mahomedanism. The Portuguese on their side tunneled, met the Nayars half way and drove them off. Famine now began to do its work. Provision had become scarce; there was no meat to be obtained; sickness increased; and the besiegers were pressed hard from outside. The Governor now recognised the seriousness of the position at Calicut and despatched thither two squadrons under the command of Heytor da Silveira and Pero de Faria. Subsequently, Dom Henrique himself hurried up with twenty sail and 1,500 men, besides small craft. He reached Calicut on the 15th of October and succeeded in landing all his men a few days after. But before he himself landed, he succeeded in throwing 150 men into the fort under Heytor da Selveira on the 4th day of his arrival, and as many more the next day, under Dom Duarte de Lima. Dom Henrique himself landed with the remainder of his force and violently attacked the Nayars in the trenches, early next morning, the garrison within the fort also making a sally. Being taken by surprise, the Nayars lost some 3,000 men with the Sicilian, their engineer, and the remainder retreated.

The Zamorin sent the son of Kaja Pakki to sue for peace and offered to give up all his guns and warships as also to pay the expenses of the war. But the Governor was not satisfied with this and demanded that the Zamorin should surrender into his hands the Raja of Poṙakkād who had deserted the Portuguese, so that he may be hanged for his treachery. This the Zamorin firmly refused, and the negotiations which had lasted for four days were dropped. The fort was demolished, in accordance with instructions received from the king of Portugal, and having placed on board the vessels all that was of value within the fort, the walls were razed, and all the Portuguese withdrew to the fleet. As soon as they had all retired, the enemy rushed in to pillage anything they could find there, when, the powder igniting, the fort was blown up, and many Moors perished.

The above account of the siege of Calicut rests on the authority of the Portuguese writers, and it may be interesting to know what a Mahomedan historian has to say about it. The author of the *Tohfut-ul-Mujahideen* has the following account about it: "Now at the time when the fracas took place in Calicut between the Franks and certain of the Mahomedans of Fundreeah, and in consequence of which the Zamorin had resolved to attack the former, he himself was absent from Calicut, being engaged in carrying on war against certain other enemies of his at some distance; at this time, therefore, he was content with despatching the prime minister, who was called Baluz, against the Franks, with instructions to attack them. Thus commissioned, this person began to act against them with great vigour, taking his measures with prudence, and collecting together the Mahomedans and the Nair soldiers of the Zamorin, the former flocking to his standard (to fight for their religion and the cause of God) from various towns. And the Zamorin himself setting out for Calicut, and the provisions of the Franks at this time being expended, they did not await his approach, but evacuated their fort and embarked all that it contained on board their ships; to facilitate their doing this they made an opening in the wall from within the fort, and in a part which was not visible to those who were without, and abandoning the fort, they set sail in the ships and went away, which event happened on the 16th day of Mohurrum, in the year 932. And there were slain, from the commencement of the war up to the victory of the Nairs, of the Zamorins and soldiers, officers, and of the Mahomedans, upwards of a thousand persons! Nevertheless, the rage of the Franks increased ten-fold, whilst their animosity towards the Mahomedans was heightened to the last degree from this capture of their fort."[1]

The fort at Calicut having been thus pulled down, the Portuguese wanted to erect a stronghold in its vicinity to hold the Zamorin in check and, therefore, approached the king of Chālieṭṭ, with a request that they may be permitted to erect a fort and a factory at the mouth of the river. As the king was afraid of the Zamorin, he wanted to ascertain his views. He, however, arranged matters in such a way that, with the assistance of the king of Ṭāṇūr, the Governor was enabled to build a fortress which contained also a church and dwelling house for 120 men. The fort which was armed with heavy artillery was named Santa Maria de Castello and Diogo Pereira was appointed Captain,

1. Pp. 121—123.

The Mahomedan historian's account of this transaction is that a Portuguese Captain who "was master of the greatest subtility and cunning and capable of employing the deepest stratagems" ingratiated himself with the Raja of Ṭāṇūr and effected a reconciliation between him and the Zamorin. "Now the Zamorin who captured the fort of the Franks at Calicut, was weak and possessed of but a limited under-standing and of few mental resources, being, moreover, addicted to habits of inebriety. But his brother, who during his reign resided at the ports, and who succeeded to the government of the Zamorin after his death, was one who commanded respect, being a man possessed of great courage and resolution, and not one, who considered himself tied down to the observance of forms, however ancient their institution By means of these qualities, he obtained the Rayship of Ṭāṇūr before he became the Zamorin, and succeeded to the sovereignty (of Calicut), which, with all its dependencies, he bequeathed with an undisputed authority to his successor. And it was during the reign of this prince that the Franks erected their fort at Shaleeat, in the vicinity of which the Zamorin, his troops, and indeed all travellers of whatever description, were obliged to pass; it thus commanded the trade between Arabia and Calicut, since between the last city and Shaleeat the distance was scarcely two parasangs. The Zamorin had given them permission to build this piece of fortification, after his accommodation with the Ray of Shaleeat; and in consequence of this permission, the Franks setting sail in a large vessel laden with all the necessary materials and instruments for building this fort, arrived in the Shaleeat river at the end of Rubi-al-Akhir, in the year 938."[1]

In building the fort, it is said that the Portuguese demolished the Jamie Mosque and used its materials, the complaints of the Mahomedans to the king of Shaleeat being left unheeded. The historian adds: "Before it

1. P. 128-130.

was finished, however, the Zamorin died, when his brother (of whom some account has been before given) succeeded him, and he, putting an end to the armistice, commenced hostilities against the Ray of Shaleeat, and laid waste his territory. So that at length he was compelled to submit to the Zamorin, and to implore such terms from him as that chieftain was disposed to dictate."[1]

We learn from Sheik Zinuddien that, in A. D. 1533, the Zamorin made peace with the Portuguese upon condition of permission being given him to send every year four vessels from Calicut to the ports of Arabia. After this arrangement it was, that the Zamorin sallied forth to punish the king of Ṭāṇūr. Shortly after, peace being made between these chieftains, Khoajeh Hossien Sanjakdar, the Turk, and Kanjee-Alee-Murkar arrived in certain grabs, bringing with them vast presents from the Sultan Bahadur Shah to the Zamorin, besides money; the Sultan being desirous of engaging the Zamorin's influence towards inducing the Mahomedans of Malabar to fight the Portuguese.

The Zamorin marched an army to Crānganūr and Vypīn to drive the Portuguese out of Cochin. The king of Cochin joined the Portuguese with 20,000 Nayars and succeeded in defending the passes. Alfonso de Sousa set out from Goa with reinforcements and, on arrival in Cochin, was joined by a fresh supply of men from Lisbon, whereupon the Zamorin retired, making an attempt, however, on the pass of Cambalam, but after being defeated in six battles, he retired. He then fitted out a naval expedition and, thus drawing off their forces from Cochin, advanced against that place with a large army, but had to retire once more on Martin Affonso hurrying up for the defence of Cochin.

While the Viceroy was at Diu, he despatched his son Dom Alvaro, with instructions to proceed to Calicut

1. P. 132.

if the Zamorin sent him any message desiring to treat with him, but on no account to land. But though he passed Calicut and Cr̄anganūr *en route* to Cochin, he heard nothing from Calicut. Zinuddien says that the Portuguese, about the end of 1539, prayed for peace and met the Zamorin at Furran (Ponnāni), and that the kings of Cr̄anganūr and Ṭāṇūr, who were also at the place, were instrumental in bringing about an understanding. On the other hand, the Portuguese writers say that the king of Calicut along with others were struck with awe at the success of the arms of the Portuguese, especially at Cambay, and sent an ambassador, Chinna Cutiale, with a splendid retinue to Goa to sue for peace. The ambassador was accompanied, however, by Manoel de Brito, Captain of the fort of Chālieṭṭ, to act as intercessor. The embassy was received with great courtesy and pomp. The Zamorin requested that the Viceroy, Dom Garcia, himself should meet him to negotiate the terms; but the Viceroy sent his son, Dom Alvaro, excusing himself on the plea of ill-health. Dom Alvaro sailed in great state and, on reaching Chālieṭṭ, sent his ambassadors over to the king who, proceeding to Ponnāni, requested Dom Alvaro to meet him there. A treaty was concluded in January 1540, the principal terms of which were :—No rowing boat in the kingdom of Calicut to have more than five oars a side; no vessel to navigate to or from Calicut without having first obtained a pass from the Captain of Chālieṭṭ; no vessel to trade with Mecca, in pepper or drugs, without the special permission of the Viceroy or Governor of India; the king of Calicut to restore all the Portuguese artillery which might be in his territory, and to return all slaves and fugitives who might have escaped into his dominions; the king to supply all the pepper in his dominions at the Cochin prices, and to deliver it at a specified place, and to sell all the ginger at the rate of ninety-two fanoes (fanams); the Zamorin to be the friend of the Portuguese' friends, and to assist the Viceroy with men whenever he might require them. The terms are so one-sided that one may be pardoned in doubting if these comprised the whole, seeing the anxiety evinced by the Viceroy in coming to peace with the Zamorin. Anyhow it is significantly remarked that this treaty proved one of the greatest blessings the Portuguese experienced in India, and that it lasted for 36 years.[1]

There were constant misunderstandings between the Zamorin and the Portuguese still, especially in connection with disputes arising between the king of Cochin and other country powers. In 1549, the king of Piementa attacked the king of Cochin, and the Portuguese had to assist the latter, while the Zamorin came to the assistance of Piementa with a large army. The storm, however, blew over after some time. Zinuddien informs us that the Zamorin interfered only after the king of Piementa, his protēgē, had been slain, and that a pacification was agreed upon in 1555. As years passed, a new treaty had to be negotiated, and, early in December 1562, the Viceroy went from Goa with 140 sail and 4,000 men in order to meet the Zamorin at Ṭṛkkoṭi, to ratify the treaty already agreed to between their respective representatives. The relation between the two parties could never be peaceful, since each of them never failed to lay violent hands on ships laden with cargo belonging to the other whenever there was an opportunity. Thus, during the course of the war with Cannanore, many such occurrences took place. Once Dias de Meneses fell in with three paraos, attacked the largest of them, captured it and slew almost all the crew. The two others came to the rescue, and Dias was hard pressed but succeeded in escaping. The Viceroy complained to the Zamorin who replied that "those vessels must have been pirates and whoever should fall in with them was at liberty to punish them." The Viceroy was very much dissatisfied with this answer and, hearing that over 80 ships were sailing from

1. Danvers, p. 443.

Calicut, sent Domingos de Mesquita, a man of great daring but no conscience, to destroy them. He committed great devastation, and the result of his action was a very tedious war.

The Zamorin sent ambassadors complaining of the harm which Domingos de Mesquita had done to his subjects. The Governor answered that the misdeeds must have been committed by some Portuguese rebels, and that the Zamorin was at liberty to punish them if he could. But before the ambassadors left, the erring Captain appeared, and the Governor had him arrested in their presence, but as soon as their backs were turned, he was released and rewarded. The Moslems, however, swore vengeance and took up arms and laid siege to the fort at Cannanore. Thus commenced the Malabar war already referred to. It lasted for two years, during which there was some violent fighting and the capture of many Malabarese ships.

The next step the Portuguese undertook was the destruction of the towns on the coast of Malabar. For this purpose, Dom Diogo de Meneses was deputed, and he with 42 sails carried fire and sword along the whole Malabar coast, to the terror of all the inhabitants there. The towns of Panṭalāyani Kollam, Ṭṛkkoṭi, Capocate, Padrarigab (Puṭiyangāṭi ?), Ponnāni and Calicut fell victims to this fury, and above 1,000 men were either killed or made prisoners, more than 60 vessels were captured and many more sunk and burnt. The Zamorin, with the view of putting a stop to this wanton act of ruin and desolation to his territories, sued for peace, but the Portuguese, exulting in their superior power, turned a deaf ear to his proposals. But the weather, however, effected what he desired, as it was no longer practicable on account of the violent burst of the monsoon, to lay off the Malabar coast.

The ferocious and tyrannical conduct of the Portuguese roused the ire of several of the Princes of India who entered into a league to expel the Portuguese from India. The Zamorin was a party to the league along with Adil Khan, Nizamulco and others. The Zamorin's share in the spoils was to be Cannanore, Mangalore, Chālieṭṭ and Cochin. In pursuance of their object, Adil Khan proceeded to besiege Goa, while Nizamulco marched against Chaul. While the fighting before these places was going on, the Zamorin offered to withdraw from the league and made proposals for a treaty of peace, but his sincerity was doubted, and his proposals were rejected. The sieges of Goa and Chaul were vigorously kept up, and the fight was furious on both sides. Towards the close of 1571, Adil Khan resolved to retire from Goa and did so without coming to any arrangement. Later on, however, on the 17th December 1571, a treaty was concluded between him and the Viceroy.

The Zamorin had, at first, acted in a half-hearted way and had made advances to the Portuguese. But, when he found that these were rejected, he despatched a fleet about the end of February 1570 under command of Kuṭṭi Pōkkar Marakkār who soon made his appearance before Chaul with 21 ships and a large number of men. He succeeded in passing through the Portuguese galleys and galleons without encountering any opposition. The men were landed, but the ships had, after a hard fight with Liolel de Sousa, to scuttle away unseen during night.

Towards the end of June, when Adil Khan and Nizamulco were on the point of retiring from the siege, the Zamorin arrived before Chālieṭṭ with 100,000 men most of whom were musketeers. The fort was then commanded by Dom Jorge de Castro. The Zamorin planted 40 brass cannon and completely surrounded the fort, so that when relief was sent from Cochin under Dom Antonio de Noronha, he was quite unable to get the supplies into the fort, so closely was it hemmed in, and so incessant and deadly the fire of the Zamorin's cannon. A party from Cannanore succeeded in bringing some relief, but it was of small account. The Viceroy sent Dom Diogo de Meneses with 18 sails to carry supplies to the fort. With great difficulty, he reached it in September, when the besieged were reduced to the last extremities, there being at least 600 souls in the place, of which number not more than 60 were capable of bearing arms: Dom Diogo succeeded, after some heavy fighting and amid great danger, in getting a large quantity of provisions and ammunition into the fortress, in which action he lost 40 men. After the treaty with Adil Khan, the Viceroy sent two galleys, one galleon and four ships under the command of Dom Diogo de Meneses to relieve Chālieṭṭ and subsequently two more galleys and three other vessels followed. These reliefs reached too late, as the fort had already been surrendered to the Zamorin on certain conditions by Dom Jorge de Castro, for which act he was subsequently tried, found guilty and beheaded in the market-place of Goa. Curiously enough, a year later, a commission arrived from Portugal appointing Dom Jorge de Castro to another post.

Zinuddien's account varies somewhat from the above. According to him, the Zamorin's assistance was sought by Adil Khan or, as he calls him, Adil Shah, some time after the sieges of Goa and Chaul had commenced. "At this time also," says he, "Aodil Shah sent a messenger to the Zamorin with his royal credentials, informing him of his having commenced his attack upon Goa, and calling upon him for his co-operation, in prohibiting all provisions from being carried from his dominions to that place. Now the Zamorin and his subjects, as has been shewn, had been carrying on hostilites against the Franks for many years, when this envoy of Aodil Shah arrived; the former being indeed at that very time at Shaleeat, employed in concerting plans to attack them".[1] Again, the means adopted to make Adil Khan retire from Goa is, to say the least, not honourable to

1. Pp. 162—3.

the Portuguese. We read in Danvers that the Viceroy "even corrupted the Adil Khan's favourite wife, and through her succeeded in obtaining information regarding his most secret designs and intentions." We learn from Zinuddien that treachery was at work, and that the Viceroy had tampered with Adil Khan's ministers, "desiring to surrender him up to them (the Portuguese) and promising to bestow the sovereignty of Beypore upon one of his relations who was with them in Goa." The conspiracy was discovered, and Adil Khan privately withdrew from his troops, called the treacherous ministers to him and punished them. Ferishta makes no mention of this. But Faria-y-Souza confirms the Sheik's account, informing us that the Viceroy, Louis de Ataide, made overtures to Noor Khan (a Beypore General) to assassinate Alee-Aadil-Shah, on promise of his being supported by the Portuguese in ascending the throne. The treachery, however, was discovered and prevented, Alee-Aadil-Shah raised the siege after being ten months engaged in it and losing 12,000 men. The conduct of Louis de Ataide was altogether of a piece with that of his distinguished predecessor, Alfonso de Albuquerque, who felt no qualms of conscience in having the then Zamorin removed by means of poison administered by the hands of the Zamorin's own brother.

With regard to the siege of Chālieṭṭ, we gather from the Sheik that, some time after the siege had commenced, the Zamorin himself came to conduct it in person "and with such extreme vigour and activity did he pursue his measures, intercepting all supplies, that the stock of provisions of the Franks became entirely exhausted, and they were compelled to devour dogs, and to feed on animals of a similar vile impure nature." Many civilians deserted the fort and were allowed to pass on unmolested. "Now, although the Franks sent supplies to their countrymen shut up in Shaleut from Cochin and Cannanore, yet these never reached them, their convoys having been attacked and destroyed. During the blockade, the besieged sent messengers to the Zamorin, offering to capitulate and deliver up to him certain large pieces of cannon which were in the fort, and also to indemnify him for the expenses of the war, besides some other concessions. But he refused to consent to these terms, although his ministers were satisfied with them; shortly after, when the Franks perceived their condition desperate, from the failure of their provisions, and that they could make no easier terms, they sent messengers to the Zamorin, offering to deliver up the fort, with its arsenal, and all its cannon, provided that a safe passage was afforded them, and protection for their private property guaranteed: and he consenting to these terms, the garrison marched out at midnight on the 10th of Jumadee Al-akhur, safe egress being afforded them". They were, then, sent on to Cochin. The Sheik adds that "shortly after, the Zamorin, having taken possession of the ordnance and stores contained in this fort, demolished it entirely, leaving not one stone upon another. And he made the site, where it had stood, a barren waste, transporting to Calicut the greater part of the stones and masonry of which the fortifications had been composed, whilst he gave the remaining portion of it to be appropriated to the re-building of the ancient Jamie Mosque, which the Franks had demolished for material to build their fort'—an act of retribution of which the Sheik exclaims, "This, by the permission of God most High, and through His gracious aid."

The Portuguese were, of course, much chagrined at the loss of their fort at Chālieṭṭ which, as we have seen, commanded the trade route to Arabia. They proceeded to harass the Zamorin, and Dom Joao de Casta, Admiral of the Malabar seas, destroyed an island of the Zamorin in the Chālieṭṭ river, proceeded further up and laid waste the city of Parappanangāṭi. The Zamorin's heir who had come to its relief was slain together with

200 Moors. At Capocate, 300 were killed. The town of Nīlīśvaram was burnt to ashes. Several ships were also captured or destroyed. This was in 1575.

About the year 1582, Mathias de Albuquerque, pursuing the Malabar pirates, followed them up into the territory of the Zamorin and destroyed several of the villages of the Zamorin. The latter sued for peace, but, owing to incessant delay in coming to terms, hostile measures were adopted, and Mathias destroyed many of the smaller places on the coast and bombarded Calicut, Paracale, Capocate, and Chēṛṛwāye. The Zamorin, tired out by the destruction caused and urged on by the demand of his subjects, at last agreed to accept the terms dictated by the Viceroy. We learn from Zinuddien that, in the year 1578, the Portuguese met the Zamorin who was then at Cṛānganūr for the purpose of treating with him for peace. He consented to permit them to build a fort at Calicut again, but they wanted to have it erected at Funan (Ponnāni) to which the Zamorin could not consent, and the attempt at negotiations failed. The Zamorin, however, sent his men along with the Portuguese who had come to meet him at Cṛānganūr to confer on terms of pacification with the Viceroy at Goa. They were received with great respect and courtesy but had to return without having effected anything, the conference having been broken off on the question of building the fort at Funan (Ponnāni). Of the treaty concluded in 1582, the Sheik observes:—"However, towards the end of the season of the latter year, a treaty was entered into between the Zamorin and the Franks, whereby the latter were permitted to build their fort at Funan, which accommodation was followed by a general exchange of prisoners, the Mahomedans delivering over to the rulers of the Franks their captives of that nation and the Franks delivering over to the Zamorin those of his subjects that they had taken, and also receiving from that chieftain the prisoners that he had made. Further, the Franks delivered up to the Zamorin, the Mahomedan captures that they had made, but these last were but few; and there was an agreement entered into between the Franks and the Zamorin regarding the building of the fort before mentioned, which was to be commenced when the Viceroy of that nation should come to visit the Zamorin in the following year."[1]

These treaties seem, however, not to have stood in the way of either party resuming hostilities when it pleased him, and in 1591-2, we read that, in consequence of the Zamorin allowing a subject of his, known as Kuññāli Marakkār, to scour the coast and commit acts of piracy, himself sharing in the booty, a fresh engagement was entered into between the Portuguese and the Zamorin through Friar Francisco da Costa, who was then a prisoner at the court of the Zamorin. Under this treaty, the Zamorin not only released all the Portuguese slaves in his kingdom, but even permitted the Jesuits to build a Church within his territories of which he himself laid the foundation stone.

Notwithstanding the peace, the fleet under the command of Andro Furtado did not hesitate to attack, on the 1st of August 1594, three ships belonging to the Zamorin carrying valuable cargoes. Over 2,000 men and women were killed, and the vessels captured. They proved rich prizes to the raiders. Soon after (1596), when Pate Marakkar obtained leave from the Zamorin to build a fort at Puṭupaṭṭaṇam, under cover of which he and his successor, Mahomet Kuññāli Marakkār, carried on extensive piracies, the Portuguese turned to the Zamorin for aid. Kuññāli had made the place strong, and the Viceroy sent Dom Alvaro de Abranches as an envoy to the Zamorin proposing a joint expedition against Kuññāli's fort. The Zamorin assented, and a fresh engagement was entered into with

1. Pp. 178—9.

the Portuguese, wherein it was agreed that the Zamorin should provide a force to attack Kuññāli by land, whilst the Portuguese should send a naval expedition to act in conjunction with it for the expulsion of Kuññāli and the razing of his fort.

A joint expedition was undertaken. The allies appeared before Kuññāli's fort. The king of Cochin feared that this association of the Zamorin with his patrons might be detrimental to him and so circulated a rumour that the Zamorin had agreed with Kuññāli to suddenly fall upon and cut off all the Portuguese as soon as they should be engaged in the assault on the fortress. But it was not credited. The attack commenced, and the fight was furious. The first attempt ended in complete failure, and Dom Louis de Gama returned to Cochin. The Portuguese Commander left behind Francisco de Sousa, persuaded the Zamorin to make another assault which he did with 10,000 men, which too was repulsed. On receipt of the news of this second defeat, Gama was sent back to conclude an arrangement with the Zamorin not to raise the siege, but to maintain his position before the town during the winter and until the Portuguese fleet could return to renew the attack. The arrangement was effected. In the following year, 1599, the Viceroy sent a new expedition under Andre Furtado de Mendoca, who, after an interview with the Zamorin, concluded a treaty with him in December, under which the latter was to supply, as long as necessary, 1,000 workmen for the camp and siege and 15 elephants for so long as the siege should last; to provide all necessary timber, carpenters, sawyers, etc.; to find 5,000 men-at-arms for the siege; to supply four ships with sailors and lascars, to watch and protect the river, besides 30 smaller boats for the same purpose; and 200 axes and 1,000 baskets for the siege; Andre Furtado, on his part, undertook that directly the fort of Kuññāli was captured, it would be destroyed, and that the Zamorin should receive half the money, goods and artillery found in the place, whilst all the other arms there were to be the property of the finders. The Zamorin further undertook to erect a church and factory for the Portuguese at Calicut.

After the conclusion of this agreement, the Portuguese brought up further reinforcements; batteries were erected in which battering cannon were placed. Andre Furtado then directed his attacks on the outworks from which the Moors were driven, but Kuññali himself came up and expelled the Portuguese. A second attempt was more successful, but an attack on fort Blanco ended in failure. Kuññāli, now opened negotiations with the Zamorin with a view, it is said, of bribing him by means of large presents to accept the surrender of the place on the condition that all the men's lives should be spared. The Zamorin seemed disposed to agree to this, but, seeing that the Portuguese were averse to it and were attacking one side of the fort, broke off all communications and seconded the efforts of Andre Furtado by an attack with 600 Nayars on the other side of the fort. Both parties did good execution, and Kuññāli being unable to offer any further resistance, surrendered upon the single condition that his life will be spared. He marched out of the fort with a black veil over his head carrying his sword point downwards, which he handed to the Zamorin, by whom it was given to Andre Furtado. Kuññāli was made prisoner and carried to Goa, where, in spite of the conditions of his surrender, the Portuguese condemned him to death as a traitor to his king, a pirate and a persecutor of the Christians, and he was beheaded with many of his companions. They forgot for the moment that Kuññāli had obtained leave of his king before starting on his enterprise, and that he had given up his sword to his suzerain on the express understanding that his life would be spared. They forgot that most of their own enterprises were not less piratical than his, and that they were less tolerant of Mahomedanism than he of Christianity. The fort of Kuññāli and all the adjoining works were levelled to the ground in accordance with the agreement previously made.

About the year 1614, the Zamorin possessed himself of the kingdom of Upper Crānganūr and was desirous of getting hold of the town of Crānganūr from the possession of the Portuguese, so that he may have his coronation performed in the pagoda in which the Perumāls used to be crowned. The king of the neighbouring island of Paṛūr commenced, at this time, a series of attacks on the Portuguese shipping in the river between Cochin and Pallippuṛam, and it was believed that the king of Cochin who was, at this time, not well disposed to the Portuguese, incited his brother of Paṛūr in this direction. The Zamorin also was a particular friend of Paṛūr. The Viceroy despatched an expedition to Paṛūr under Dom Lopo de Almeida, defeated the king and obliged him to conclude a peace. An embassy, with presents, was then sent to the kings of Cochin and Calicut who received the presents, but evaded entering into an agreement with the Portuguese.

Before two years had passed, the Zamorin had again attacked Crānganūr. By this time, the Dutch had appeared on the Malabar Coast, and a fleet under Dom Bernardo de Noronha appeared just in time to prevent three Dutch ships that were in the neighbourhood from sending any assistance to the Zamorin whose Nāyars were soon forced to retire.

The star of the Portuguese was now on the wane. Other nations from the west had appeared on the scene, and the race for empire was being run on different lines than on those hitherto. The enemies of the Portuguese in the East had become powerful. There was disintegration going on within and disruption without. In spite of all these unfavourable circumstances, the gallant nation, true to their instincts, stood their ground well for some time more. So early as the 16th of October 1608, the Zamorin had entered into a contract with the Dutch admiral, Peter William Verhoven, in which he insisted that the admiral should besiege the town of Cochin which was still in the hands of the Portuguese.

A treaty of peace was concluded by the Portuguese with the Zamorin on the 2nd September 1696, under which the latter agreed to provide a site for a Church in Calicut; to permit the re-erection of the Church of St. Antonio de Parulla; to reimburse to the Church all the losses sustained through the robberies committed by the Moors in Calicut; and that none of the Zamorin's vessels should trade with Muscat, or with any other port belonging to the enemies of Portugal.

The last we hear of the Portuguese relations with the king of Calicut is in an account of the state of India during and at the end of his administration left by the retiring Viceroy, the Marquiz de Castello Novo de Alorna, in 1750 for the benefit of his successor. Therein the Viceroy says: " The Samory (Zamorin) was formerly the most powerful king on the Malabar Coast and the greatest enemy the Portuguese ever had. To-day, however, he is considerably weakened and almost ruled by the Moorish inhabitants of his kingdom. In Calicut we have a factory."

We have already referred to the treaty entered into between the Zamorin and the English Captain, Keeling, at Cranganūr.

Towards the close of the 17th century, the English had made settlements at Anjengo in the south and at Tellichery in the north. Calicut would probably have been selected as the head-quarters of the northern settlement, but the Zamorin, after his bitter experience of the Portuguese, was naturally averse to allow the English, another foreign nation, to hold a fortified position at his capital.

We have seen that the Dutch had to give up Chettwaye to the Zamorin in 1691. He was not slow to take advantage of the position he had secured and used it with great effect against his hereditary enemy, the Cochin Raja. War broke out shortly afterwards and, from 1710 to 1715, the Dutch were drawn into it. The Dutch set about the erection of a fort at the northernmost point of the island of Chēṙṙwāye, and the English at once set up the Zamorin to recover possession of the island. In the year 1715, the Zamorin allowed the English to open a warehouse at Chēṙṙwāye, and what occurred after this have been related elsewhere. Our author has given us a short account of this war in his fourth letter.

Here we may interpose with an extract from the *Memoir* of Gollennesse, which gives us some information regarding the Zamorin and his country about the time that the Dutch Governor wrote. He says:—

"The Zamorin or Errenaddecarre (Ēṙaṅāṭṭukara) and Neddoo Wiripoo is the third Chief King of Malabar and a powerful prince, although his influence has been a good deal diminished by the late war. His extensive lands lie bteween the countries between Cochin and Colastry. He is the head of the Pandicoor Faction. His power is divided among his nobles of whom the principal are Mangattyaatja (Mangāt Achchen), the hereditary general, Tinanchery Elleaam, (Ṭinayancherri Eḷayaṭu), Paranly (Pāṙa Nambi) and Dhermoottu Ponnical (Ḍhaṙmōṭṭu or Ḍhaṙma Guṇaṭṭu Paṇikkar), the influence of the last named has been greatly checked by the loss of a large portion of his lands which were taken from him by the Honourable Company.

"The King is a prince of between 30 and 35 years old, adopted from the house of Neleseram; he came to the throne last year (1742) and seems to be a man of a good disposition, but a little too gentle to oppose adequately the passionate nature of his second prince who boasts that he intends to live and die a mortal enemy of the Honourable Company. Some months ago, we heard something of the effects of this boast when this foolhardy prince, without any previous declaration of war and apparently without the slightest reason, suddenly, with about 1000 men, made a raid upon the Kingdom of Cochin and burned the land of Mangalam (Maṭilakam?). At the same time, the English of Madras received information of the return to these regions of His Excellency Van Imhoff, and they spread the report. On hearing this news, he abandoned his wicked designs, and he thought it advisable to sheath the sword very quickly. The Zamorin declared that all this had been done without his orders; we did not fail to profit by this, and a peace was concluded on the 3rd of December ultimo in the presence of our deputies, the undermerchants Francois Terburg and Guilliaune Gerard Franchimont. It is to be hoped that this peace will be lasting. At any rate, we have seriously warned the King of Cochin to avoid carefully every occasion of new disturbances and to bear and swallow a small injustice rather than to bring upon himself greater wrongs, inasmuch as the Honourable Company cannot help him at present. The King holds his court at Panany (Ponnāni), where the Honourable Company has a resident, viz., the book-keeper Gerrit Van Dorpen, who has only to watch the stratagems of the Court. Ever since the late war, very little is heard in those quarters about the Honourable Company; the reports from there are generally of a dangerous nature. Such a state of affairs should neither disquiet Your Excellency too much, nor should it be altogether disregarded; but prudence demands that enquiries be made, and that you ever hold yourself well on the defensive. At present, the Zamorin is celebrating the famous feast of Mamanga (Mahā Māgham) at Tireneway (Ṭiruṅāvāya) with much pomp and not without heavy expense."[1]

In 1753, the Dutch had, by their treaty with Travancore, basely thrown over their native allies and especially the Raja of Cochin. The Zamorin found

1. This was the last time the festival was held. For its history and description, please see appendix to this Volume.

this his opportunity to subdue Cochin. In the year 1755—56, he marched along the Coast from the north, attacked Chēṫṫwāye, drove the Dutch outposts and rapidly possessed himself of Cṙānganūr, Paṙūr and Varāppuḷa and stationed himseil at Trichur.[1] In his extremity, the Cochin Raja turned to Travancore for assistance, though Cochin had but recently suffered at the hands of Travancore. Cochin entered into an alliance with Travancore,[2] under which

1. When he was residing in the palace at Trichur, the Zamorin tried to win to his side the *mutts* (Brahmaswam Matams) of that place. The response that he got to his offers was not complimentary to him and showed the loyalty and devotion of the *mutts* to the ruler of Çochin. This was the reply :

മാടക്ഷ്മാവരണബാഹുബലാഭിഗുപ്താ
സേയം സഭാ പരവശേതി ന ശങ്കനീയാ
ഏകാകിനീ നിശിചരാലയ മദ്ധ്യഗാപി
കിം രാമഭദ്രദയിതാ ദശകണ്ഠമാപ.

This, when freely rendered in English, would mean that this Sabha, protected as it is by the power of the ruler of Cochin, would never be defeated by anybody, just as Sita, the wife of Ramabhadra, was never overcome by Ravana, though she was alone in the home of the Rakshasas and surrounded by them.

The author of this *slokam* was honoured and rewarded by the Raja of Cochin.

2. The ultimatum sent to the Zamorin on this occasion was couched in this graceful but firm way:

മാപ്രാണം ത്യജ മാപ്രാണം
മാപ്രാണ മമ സന്നിഭ
മാനവിക്രമ സൌജന്യ
മാനവിക്രമ ഭൂപതേ.

(Māpṙāṇam ṭyaja māpṙāṇam
māpṙāṇa mama sannibha
mānavikṙama saujannya
Mānavikṙama bhūpaṭē.)

Mapranam, by the way, is the name of a small village to the south of Trichur, the primeval capital of Kerala, and still a small beautiful town in the State of Cochin.

the latter undertook to expel the Zamorin out of Cochin limits. In 1762, the Travancoreans launched themselves under their General, Eustachius Benedictus de Lanoy, in three divisions on the Zamorin's garrisons, extending in a long weak line into Cochin territory at Cr̄anganūr, Par̄ūr and Varāppul̄a. The defeat of the Zamorin was rapidly achieved, and his troops were completely and finally driven from Cochin territory.

The Zamorin was actively aggressive in another direction also. Some time previously, he had driven a wedge through the territories of his other hereditary foe, the Wal̄luvanād Raja, and had cut the dominions of the latter in two by annexing a broad band of territory, extending from his own country of Ēr̄nād in the north to the previously conquered Wal̄luvanād territory of Neṭunganād in the south. And by adopting similar tactics with the dominions of the Palghat Raja, his neighbour on the east, the Zamorin had, about 1756—57, driven a similar wedge, to which he gave the name of Naṭuvaṭṭam through the Palghat territory and cut it in two with a view, no doubt, to eventual absorption of the whole.

The Palghat Raja turned, in his extremity, to Hyder Ali, thus enabling him to make his appearance in Malabar for the first time. In 1757, a deputation was despatched to Mysore, and Hyder in response sent his brother-in-law, Mukhadam Sahib, with 2,000 horse, 5,000 infantry and 5 guns to assist the Raja, and this force, aided by the Palghat Nāyars, carried their arms as far as the sea coast. The Zamorin's force retreated, and the Zamorin bought off his opponents by agreeing to restore his Palghat conquests and by promising to pay, in instalments, a war indemnity of 12 lakhs of rupees. The Zamorin then opened negotiations with Deo Raj, the puppet Raja of Mysore, on whose behalf Hyder, his Foujadar, was ostensibly acting. Hyder relinquished his claim to Deo Raj, who, thereupon, sent a Rajaput corps under Hari Singh to collect the money. Before he was able to collect anything, he was informed of the death of his master, and he at once returned to Avaṇāśi in Coimbatore. There he was surprised and treacherously murdered by a force sent by Hyder under Mukhadam Sahib. The claim to this war subsidy was never relinquished, and to recover it was one of Hyder's avowed objects in invading Malabar.

In 1766, Hyder invaded Malabar from the north and, after subduing the northern Rajas, despatched, on the 6th of April, an army of 6,000 men against Calicut. The invaders met with little resistance, and, as they proceeded, they secured the country in the rear by a series of block-houses, called *lakkadi kotta* or wooden forts. The Nāyars, in their despair, defended such small posts as they possessed most bravely. Col. Wilks says: " One of these (lakkadi kottas) which my manuscripts name Tamalpelly, was surrounded by Hyder in the following manner: first, a line of regular infantry and guns with an abbatis; second, a line of peons; third, of cavalry. This disposition was made for the purpose of striking terror by not allowing a man to escape destruction. The Nairs defended themselves until they were tired of the confinement, and then leaping over the abbatis and cutting through the three lines with astonishing rapidity, they gained the woods, before the enemy had recovered from their surprise." [1]

On the 11th September, Āli Raja, at the head of 1,000 men, appeared before the Zamorin's palace near Calicut and summoned him to surrender it, which he refused. Another account says that " the Zamorin himself met Hyder Ali, who demanded a contribution of a crore of gold mohurs, which was so extremely extravagant that the Zamorin protested his inability to find such an enormous sum. He is said to have offered the whole of his treasure and all his property, but this did not satisfy his greedy adversary. He was

1. Vol. I, p. 291.

sent under a guard of 500 horse and 2,000 infantry to the fort of Calicut; the Raja was confined to his own house without food, and was strictly prohibited from performing the ceremonies of his religion; and as he thought that Hyder might inflict some further disgrace upon him, either by causing him to be hanged, or blown from a gun, the Raja set fire to the house with his own hand and was consumed in it."

Hyder had now possessed himself of the whole of the Zamorin's dominions, and, for the present, he turned homewards. Before he reached Coimbatore, he received information that Malabar had revolted. Raza Sahib whom Hyder had left at Mādakkara with 3,000 infantry, being apprised of what was going on in the south, marched to Ponnāni, in spite of the inclemency of the weather and the inundated state of the country. He was, however, stopped at the junction of the Tutka and Ponnāni rivers, whence he could neither advance on account of the streams, nor retreat on account of the ravines strongly held by the Nāyars in the rear. On receiving information of the revolt, Hyder marched down with a strong force and once more subdued the country. He took effective measures to crush the Nāyars and ordered that a fort be built at Palghat as an advanced post and depot to facilitate communication with the newly subdued province.

Hyder had despatched a force for the invasion of Travancore, seeking a passage through the mountains. On the 10th January 1767 came the news that this force had been defeated, and this reverse seems to have been the signal for another general rising in Malabar. Hyder, of course, came down once more in great force, and, in the conflict that followed, the English had also to take part. In December 1768, Hyder had made arrangements with the Malabar chiefs much to his advantage, the result of which was, in the words of Wilks, "Hyder's provincial troops, whose escape would otherwise have been impracticable, not only retreated in safety but loaded with treasure—the willing contribution of the chiefs of Malabar—the purchase of a dream of independence."

The peace, concluded between Hyder and the English in the meanwhile, was not of long duration. First through the country powers and then through the French and afterwards directly, hostilities were commenced by Hyder. At first, the fight in Malabar was confined to the north, but it soon spread itself to the south. In December 1780, the Travancore and Zamorin Rajas were addressed to assist in crushing Hyder's force on the coast as soon as the Tellicherry siege was raised. Fort George at Māhê surrendered itself to Major Abington on the 8th of January 1782. The Nāyars rose all over the country and rushed to support the English. Major Abington pushed on southwards and took Calicut on the 13th February. The war in the south continued till the 12th of December when, on the eve of Tippu's attempt to resume the attack on Ponnāni, he received news of his father's death on the 7th December, and he marched back to secure his father's throne. Col. Fullerton marched on Palghatchery, which surrendered after a severe assault in November 1783. "The heir-apparent of the Zamorin left his retirement in the woods and remained with Col. Fullerton during the siege. In answer to his urgent solicitation that the Zamorin family should be restored to its possessions, he told the prince that he would do so on moving by Calicut; but that, in the meanwhile, he would be put in possession of the Palghat country, requiring only that the prince should supply grain to the army. A large body of Brahman Haricārāhs were also left with him."

Palghat was occupied by the Zamorin as soon as the British force retired. Col. Fullerton applied for and received four battalions of Travancore sepoys, which he despatched to Palghat to help the Zamorin to hold it till further assistance could arrive; but before the Travancoreans could arrive, the Zamorin's force, despairing of support, abandoned the place and retired into the mountains. Tippu's forces speedily reoccupied all the south of Malabar as far as the Koṭṭa river.

Peace was concluded on the 11th March 1784 between Tippu and the English, in which the Malabar Rajas were recognised, strangely enough, as Tippu's "friends and allies." Early in 1788, Tippu made one more descent into Malabar, and the usual excesses followed his train. The Sultan broke faith with all Malabar princes and drove them to desperation by his barbarities. The Nāyars, the Coorgs and even the Māppilās rose in rebellion. The movement was headed by Ravi Varma of the Zamorin's house, on whom, to quiet him, a jaghir had already been conferred by the Mysoreans. Ravi Varma, between July and November 1788, took the field, and being victorious, made himself master of the open country. He then proceeded to invest Calicut. Tippu, in December, sent down Lally and Mir Asr Ali Khan, who succeeded, with 6,000 native troops and 120 Europeans, in driving Ravi Varma away from Calicut, but never quite succeeded in driving him out of the field.

The exodus of the Malabar families to Travancore, unable any longer to suffer the persecutions of Tippu, had already begun, and the Zamorin and his family too fled and sought refuge in Travancore like so many others. Incensed at the Travancore Raja's conduct in affording an asylum to his Malabar subjects, Tippu marched an army to invade Travancore and attacked the 'Travancore lines', which he finally carried. This caused the English to declare war with the Sultan, during the course of which the Malabar Rajas were invited by the English to join them.

On the 27th of September 1790, General Medows, the Governor and Commander-in-Chief of Madras, entered into an agreement with "Kishen, the Zamorin Raja of Calicut," "investing him with the sole management of all the countries heretofore included in the province of Calicut, which are or may be conquered by the English troops."

On the cession of Malabar by Tippu to the English, an agreement was entered into on the 18th August 1792, in pursuance of the terms of General Medows, by Cowl, with the fourth Raja of Kiḷakke Kōvilakam, on behalf of, and as surety for, the Zamorin for Rs. 4,16,366¼, being the peishcush payable for the districts leased to him for one year. As a mark of respect and superiority, the Rajas of Beypore, Parappanāḍ and Veṭṭaṭṭunāḍ were required to pay their revenues through the Zamorin, who was also temporarily vested "as in the ancient times" with power to administer justice "over all these petty Rajas." The mint was also leased to him for Rs. 15,000.

The Paṭiññāṟe Kōvilakam branch of the Zamorin's family possessed considerable influence in the country, in consequence of which the collection of the revenue of the district of Neṭunganāḍ was entrusted into the hands of the head of this branch who was also the heir-apparent of the Zamorin. On the strength of this, he attempted to make himself independent of the Zamorin, and the dispute waxed so great that his person had to be secured by Captain Burchall at Cheṟplaśśēri. He died there a day or two after and, at the instance of the Zamorin, the brother and nephew of the deceased had also to be put under restraint, but were released on the Kiḷakke Kōvilakam Raja standing security for their good behaviour.

Various agreements followed regarding the payment of the revenue of lands leased to the Zamorin. Finally, on the 11th October 1798, the Company resumed the management of the country leased to the Zamorin," the revenues of 971 (1795—96) due from the Samoory's Talooks having been misappropriated or withheld from the said Raja or his Agents.' The Taluk of Ēṙnād had been already resumed in 1797. On the assumption of the district, the Zamorin's family had allotted to them 20 per cent of the net land revenue *plus* 10 per cent of the customs gross collection *plus* 50 per cent of the profits of the Calicut mint. By an agreement dated the 15th of November 1806, the amount of mālikhāna payable to the family was fixed and confirmed in perpetuity on certain conditions. In 1857, the Government agreed with the Revenue Board and the acting Collector of Malabar "that the allowances are perpetual during good conduct and are not revocable at pleasure." The total amount annually paid is Rs. 1,32,163—4—0, and this sum is distributed in the following manner :—

	Rs.
The Zamorin	69,663-4-0
The Ēṙālpād or 2nd Raja	15,000-0-0
The Mūṅṅālpād or 3rd do	7,000-0-0
The Eṭaṭṭarālpād or 4th do	5,000.0-0
The Neṭuṭṭarālpād or 5th do	4,500-0-0
Ampāṭi Kōvilakam Ṭampurāṭṭi (female)	4,000-0-0
Puṭiya Kōvilakam Valia Ṭampurāṭṭi (do)	9,000-0-c
Paṭiṅṅāṙe Kōvilakam Valiya Ṭampurāṭṭi (do)	9,000-0-0
Kiḻakke Kōvilakam Valiya Ṭampurāṭṭi (do)	9,000-0-0
Total	1,32,163-4-0

Before concluding this account of the Zamorin, we may give here extracts from the *Memoirs* left by the Dutch Governor, Moens, relating to the Calicut country and its rulers.

"The Zamorin" says Moens, "was the *most powerful* and the *most wealthy* of the four kingdoms of Malabar—the *most powerful* first on account of its many and brave Nairs, for it is known, that the Nairs of the Zamorin have always been the most daring and resolute among all the Nairs of Malabar, and secondly on account of the extensiveness of this kingdom, because its milestones, in the north border on the kingdom of Collastry, and on the south reached the mouth of the river of Cranganur, and in the east were placed against the mountains and the kingdoms of Palcatcherry and Mysore. It was therefore much larger and more extensive than the then kingdom of Travancore. The *most wealthy*, on account of the extensive trade carried on by the Moors of the Zamorin with the Red Sea, Persia and Surat and especially their trade in that ancient and famous free commercial town, Calicut.

"The Portuguese crippled the trade of Calicut. Besides this, the kingdom itself lost much of its power and wealth and was at last reduced to the state it is now. This was chiefly brought about by its subjects, the Moors, and the bad system of Government, as the Moors as a rule domineered over everybody and continually caused dissensions at the Court. They managed this in such a way that their party was usually the strongest and hence this kingdom had many a time to defend itself against its own subjects and had therefore, as the saying is, its enemies in its own bosom. The kings on their part were as a rule cowards who were unable to maintain themselves and their authority sufficiently, allowed almost all the courtiers to meddle with the affairs of the kingdom, yea even suffered women to have their say in State affairs especially the mothers of the crown princes."

The Dutch Company had much trouble with the Zamorin and had often to wage expensive wars. "The Company also found out that they were the most untrustworthy of all the Malabar kings. Besides they intrigued occasionally with the English, French and Portuguese. These aforesaid troubles were chiefly caused by Cochin, for between them there was always an irreconcilable hatred, as we were more or less obliged to take the part of Cochin for well-known political reasons, as it is of great importance to the Company that the latter State should remain in existence."

Hyder subdued the Zamorin in 1766. "Possibly it would not have come to this push, if they had dealt with the affair better at Court. For when the Nabob sent messengers to the Zamorin to ask for a contribution, he sent them scornfully away." He should have, as others did, negotiated about the amount of contribution and tried to lower the amount as much as possible. This embittered the Nabob, who conquered the country, took the Zamorin prisoner who committed suicide by setting fire to the house in which he was confined. "In the meantime, the Nairs continued harassing the troops of the Nabob till he recalled them to meet the Maharattas who were giving him battle. The Crown Prince was allowed to rule on condition of paying an annual tribute. The Zamorin had expected that the Maharattas would consume the Nabob and so failed to pay the tribute; but it happened otherwise and Hyder after making peace with them returned in 1775 and conquered the Zamorin's dominion." "The indifference of the Zamorin, when the Nabob marched against him the last time is surprising to me." State after state fell before him, and, at last, the Zamorin's time was sure to come, and yet he kept himself engaged with trifles instead of concerting measures for protecting his kingdom. He was once more conquered "and without having made any resistance worth speaking of, took to his heels after having first been nicely dressed up by the French Governor of Mahe and left his kingdom a prey to the Nabob." "This is the end of this kingdom. It was chiefly brought about by the intrigues of its Mahomedan subjects who had better opinions of the Government of the Nabob (as being a Moor himself) than they experienced now to their regret."

40. **Palingery Nairs.** A Nāyar chief who was lord of a portion of Ayruṅād comprised in the island of Chēt't'wāye, now a part of the Ponnāni Taluk of the collectorate of South Malabar. Tradition says that one of the Ayrūr Rajas once went on a pilgrimage to

Benares and, not returning for a long time, was given up as dead. His obsequial ceremonies were performed by his relatives. While so, he returned and found that he would not be admitted into the family. He was, therefore, allowed to hold a portion of Ayrunād with a following of 3,000 Nāyars. After his death, his issue by his Nāyar-wife was allowed to possess this portion, and thus arose the family of Pal̈anchēri Nāyar. Their modern representatives are the Bl̈āhayil and Mannal̈āvil Nāyars, who are still large land-holders in South Malabar. We have the following account of this chief given by Gollennesse: "Paynechery Nair is an important proprietor; his lands lie to the north of the kingdom of Cochin. They were formerly under the Zamorin, but, according to article 17 of the often-mentioned treaty, they have now been placed under the Honourable Company. The Honourable Company has in this country the important fortress of Chetwai. The family of the Paynechery Nairs consists of four houses, subdivided into many branches; they are involved in endless quarrels and disputes among themselves. In the capacity of supreme ruler, the Honourable Company has to settle these disputes, but as this cannot be done according to our ways of thinking, each contending party brings two good men to enquire into the matter and settle it. If they cannot come to an agreement, the first Paynechery is bound to add two impartial men. But as the first, second and third of the family being old men with one foot in the grave are not competent, the Honourable Company must sometimes add two Brahmins. Most embarrassing of all is the fact that the losing party of this petty clan (the worst on the Malabar coast) does not submit to these arrangements, but runs off to the Zamorin who does not fail to mix himself in a matter which is no business of his. Sometime ago this was permitted in a quarrel between Ittiteyen and Oolattu Nairs owing to the dangerous state of the times, but in future such interference ought to be politely prohibited with the assurance that the

Honourable Company never refuses justice to its subjects.

"This land belonged formerly to the Prince of Charkare (Śarkara), who lost it because the last owner made a voluntary donation of it to the Paynechery Nairs, his illegitimate sons; he did this from a dislike of his nearest of kin who at present live there as private individuals and in very poor circumstances."

We have a fuller account of the family of the Palancheri Nayars and of the government of their territory given us by the Dutch Governor, Van Moens. It is as follows:—

"The district of Payenchery is usually called by the natives 'the sandy land.' In the Company's records it is as a rule called the sandy land of Chettua. However at times the whole region from Chettua to Cranganore is also called by the natives 'the sandy land' without any addition.

"It has amused me to trace their origin as far as it has been possible from old documents of the peoples of Malabar, and also from notes and traditions of the families themselves.

"This territory was from ancient times a subordinate kingdom Charcarre. Its last proprietor having begotten a natural son from a woman of the aforesaid house of Payenchery, got into great trouble with his family on that account. They made so much unpleasant commotion about it, and embittered him to such an extent that he bequeathed this landed property, besides Nairs to the number of 2,500, to this natural son and disinherited his natural heirs. In this way it happened that this territory came in the possession of the family of the Payenchery Nairs.

"When now the notorious Emperor Cheram Perumal divided his territory into four principal kingdoms he presented also several estates to kings of less importance, and so it came to pass that he presented to the eldest of the Payencheries who was at that time a life-guard of the Emperor, a certain Manattaparambatto and also some fields in the districts of the Zamorin. Besides this, he put also under him 500 Nairs from that same district. Hence this Manattamparambatto came into possession not only of the district of Chettua, but also of the above-named estate in the Zamorin's kingdom and was at the same time the head of 3,000 Nairs.

"This dynasty, comprising many families, was later on, with the approval of all, broken up into three chief families. One family was that of the aforesaid Manattamparambatto, whilst for the two others were selected Panangatto and Ulatto, whereby there were three chief families. I say three *chief* families, because the family of Manattamparambatto was again divided into two branches and the family of Panangatto into as many as four branches as appears from the following.

"The first chief family, named Manattamparambatto, is now divided into two families, viz., Tekkentale and Masyaly Baddankentale.

"The second chief family, named Panangattu, is now divided into four families, viz:—

Panangattu	Tahelli
Blaga	Cherierto

"The third chief family named Ulattu is still to this day known by that name and no other.

"Each of the abovementioned families has under it many more families of less importance. When one wishes to speak about these three chief families together, they are called by the general name of Payenchery Nairs.

"From of old, this territory has been governed by these chief families. The eldest member of each family has the special governance of his family in the manner of Patriarchal rule and these three eldest members are considered to be the eldest of the people. Again

W.

the eldest of these three has the general management of everything, governs the country as he pleases and exercises the right of life and death.

"I mentioned above that this dynasty obtained from the Emperor Cheram Perumal some territory in the kingdom of Zamorin. In connection with this, I must also mention that this has been the cause of the great hatred and envy, which since that time the Zamorin has displayed. This went at last so far that, although they remained in possession of their states, and privileges, he began to levy heavy taxes and imposts. This gave rise to great disturbances and he would have made these families entirely tributary to him if the company had not taken them under its protection. For this kindness however the Company stipulated a fair remuneration. In a contract made with the Zamorin in 1717, they were for the first time publicly acknowledged to be under the protection of the Company. Nevertheless, these families had also to pay something to the Zamorin, in order to possesss their estates in peace in the territory of the Zamorin. But, notwithstanding this, they were often oppressed by him and the Company was more than once obliged to intervene.

"These families, in order to make more sure of our protection, offered to the Company in the year 1755 the half of a certain land revenue, which yearly amounts to 492½ golden fanams equal to 98 rupees and 523 paras of rice.

"Again in the year 1764 they offered to the Company the half of the tithes of the whole of their territory. The annual amount of those tithes comes to 960 paras rice and 1709½ golden fanams or about 341 rupees. These tithes are collected at Chettua. But there is a difference between the tithes of corn and the tithes of other things, because the tithes of corn may mean either the tithes of what has been sown or what has been reaped, which is not the case with the tithes of other things, and is quite self evident, because all tithes except those on arable land consists of revenue. It may be observed that in the agreement the words 'tithes of arable lands' are mentioned without any further explanation. The Payencheries almost of their own accord have promised the half of the above-mentioned tithes of what has been sown and not of what has been reaped, and this explanation has been accepted by us. The fields which they cultivated themselves, besides those belonging to the pagoda and those belonging to some other prominent people, were exempted from these tithes; on the whole the fields which had come in their possession through sale or in other ways in the district of Popanetty, were, together with other properties situated in that district, subjected to tithes of what had been reaped for the benefit of the Company.

"The object of these families in offering us the gift of the aforesaid half of the tithes of their district seems to have been to make themselves more and more sure of the protection of the Company. And it cannot be gainsaid that since that time they have possessed their estates in peace as nobody gave them any trouble. During the last revolution in Malabar, they have not sustained any loss. On the contrary, all the kings, rulers and chiefs together with their subjects have felt the inconveniences and consequences of war and had to pay military contributions. Hence the Payenchery Nairs have been the only ones of those who had been favoured by the Emperor Cheram Perumal, who have kept their former privileges through the protection of the Honourable Company. Recently, however, Nabob Hyder Alychan has conquered the whole region from Chettua to Cranganore. The Company has not been able to prevent this on account of his superior force. In compensation for this, they receive for the present, until further order from the Company, a monthly allowance of Rs. 30 as may be seen in a resolution passed on the 14th July 1777.

"A ttimes these families have been quarrelling among themselves and even have tried to countermine one another, but I always backed up the eldest, even if at times the other party had more or less right on his side, which I would then point out to the eldest privately at a tete-a-tete. This proved to be the best means of maintaining equilibrium among the families, for otherwise one would be constantly worried by them.

"I have inferred from old documents, that at times they were on good terms with the Zamorin, if it served their purposes, but now they seem to have broken all connection with him. Granted that this has been formerly the case, I am of opinion that the reasons of this intimacy had their origin in state-interests or more particularly to please the Zamorin a little, who being their neighbour could in a dexterous way constantly create disturbances among them, without its always being possible to prove that he had a hand in them. For these reasons and for the sake of their estates, situated in the territory of the Zamorin, they remained friends with him.

"I have to remark still another thing with regard to these families which is rare with heathen or at least with Malabar kings, viz., that, in the management of their affairs, no violence or extortions take place, and that when they administer law, the offering of gifts and presents is not much in vogue. I said 'not much' because, however tolerably this district is ruled the Governors have not sufficient strength of mind to be able to decline always and at all times gifts and presents, although I have to confess that I have heard the people complain very little about it. Hence the inhabitants of this district in comparison with others have been fortunate in their rulers and always thought it best to interfere as little as possible with their form of government, and allow them to settle their own affairs themselves. I intervened only when they went to extremes and then I took direct cognisance of the matter and acted according to justice."

41. **Repoecoil.**—Pappucoil ruling over Chālyam, Parppucoil ruling over Beypore and Pappucoil ruling over Parapanangady.

This is probably the country or Rajaship of Parapanangāḍy known to the Portuguese as Pappucoil. A branch of this now lives in Travancore, and that distinguished Sanskrit and Malayāḷam Scholar, gifted poet, and generous patron of letters, the late Kērala Varma, C. S. I., M. R. A. S., F., R. H. S., F. M. U. &c., the Valia Kōil Ṭampurān of Travancore, brother-in-law of the late Śrī Mūlam Maharaja of Travancore, belonged to that branch. Gollennesse mentions the countries of Bettatta *alias* Tanur, Parappoor Kovil, Pappu Kovil as bordering on the lands of the Zamorin and adds that the Dutch had no dealings of importance with these.

42. **Walluvanad.** It is surprising that our author has failed to notice one of the oldest royal houses of Malabar viz., that of the Raja of Walluvanād. Gollennesse speaks of it as Walluanatty *alias* Arangolla, "a kingdom situated next to Bettette." He adds: "The king has the right to send every twelve years notorious marauders to the feast of Mamanga[1], which right, so he says, has been taken way from him by the Zamorin, contrary to all right and equity. A few weeks ago, he caused two elephants of the Zamorin to be carried off. By this he has provoked the Zamorin to such an extent that the latter intends to make war upon him after the feast of Mamanga; but as this is a matter in no way affecting the Honourable Company, we may look forward to the results with equanimity."

It was perhaps because the Raja had no political or commercial relations with the Dutch that our author has not mentioned this country.

The first authentic mention we have of the Raja is in the Jew's copper-plate (A. D. 700). There he is called "Rairan Chāṭṭan, owner of Valluva province, the Ārangōṭṭūr Swarūpam," and one of the Syrian

1. Vide appendix to this Volume.

Christian deeds named his country as Vaḷḷuvanād. He is generally known as Vaḷḷuva Kōnāṭiri, or the Vallabhan or Veḷḷaṭṭiri Raja and is styled the Ārangōṭṭ Uṭayavar. Evidently, Gollennesse's Arangolla is a misprint for Ārangōṭṭa. The term Ārangōṭṭ Uṭayavar means the chieftain who holds the country on the other side (Mal: angōṭṭu) of the river (Mal: ār), his dominions lying to the north of the Ponnāni river. The Vaḷḷuva Kōnāṭiri is still known by this title. He is also called Vallabhan, and it is significant that he styles himself Vallabhan or Vaḷḷuvan Chāṭṭan in his royal writs. Mr. Logan conjectures that Vaḷḷuva may be another form of Pallava, and that Vaḷḷuvanād may stand for the Valluvar (Pallava) country. Mr. Logan says that "besides the Chēra, Chōḷa and Pāṇḍya dynasties, one other dynasty, that of the Pallavas, stands most prominently in the early history of Southern India. It is proved by inscriptions that the dynasty was in existence in the 4th or 5th century A. D., and at a still earlier period in the 2nd or 3rd century. When and how far they invaded Malabar and, whether having taken the country, it was the Cherumars or Kurambars, or partly the one and partly the other that they displaced, is at present matter for speculation. It is quite possible that the dynasty is still represented in Malabar by the *Vallodi* or *Vulluvanadi* caste of Nairs. There is also a servile caste of *Valluvar*, who are labourers, fishers, ferrymen and sorcerers. Of these two classes, the former inhabit *Valluvanad* (i. e. the country of the Valluvar), which to the present day gives its name to one of the taluks of the district ; while the latter are usually regarded as of superior rank to the huntsmen who abound on the western ghauts and in Wynad. The latter are called *Kuramber*, or *Kuruchiar*, *Kurassiar* and they too have a local habitation in the low country, in the name of one of the present taluks of the *Kurambarnad* or the country of the *Kurambar*. The *Kurambar* were originally, and are to the present day in districts east of the ghauts, shepherds and herdsmen, and from their having given their name to such an impastoral portion of the district as *Kurumbarnad*, it is perhaps safe to conclude that it was only occupied by them under compulsion and that there they made a stand for some considerable time. The *Vulluvar* country, on the other hand, is a fine pastoral country lying close to the south-west slopes of the Nilgiris, just such a country as shepherds and herdsmen would select.

"It is not improbable, therefore, if the *Chermar* (agrestic slaves) are, as suggested, the real aborginies of the ancient *Chera* kingdom, that they were displaced to some extent at least, by a more independent race of shepherds, who in turn gave away to the *Valluvar* (Pallavar ?). The fact that the *Kurumbars* preferred a roving life in the jungles to a sedantry one in subjection on the plains, proves them to have been a superior race, and indeed to the present day they very markedly retain this characteristic."[1]

Mr. Logan pursues the argument further by remarking that, from inscriptions recording the conquests of the Western Chalukyan King, Pulakēśi II, it may be inferred that Pallava influences had become paramount in the south at some time previous to the early part of the 7th century A. D. He refers to the fact of a deed (albeit forged) of the 10th century A. D. recording that Chēra was distinct from Kērala, both of which were overrun by Pulakēśi, and observes that this opens up ground for remark. "It has already been noticed [2] that the traditionary limits of the original *Kerala* extended from *Puthupattanam* on the *Kotta* river to *Kannetti* in Travancore. If this was Kērala, where then was Chēra ? Could it be that the forger was referring to the *Gangas* or Kongas ?" Mr. Logan points out that a genuine deed nearer to the time of the occurrences specifically says that Pulakēśi II

1. Logan's *Malabar*, pp. 256—7.

2. P. 224.

in his southern raid was "closely *attended* by the Gangas", so that the forger could not have been referring to the Gangas. If so, there must have been a *Chera* dynasty distinct from the Kērala dynasty at the time; and this argument leads to the suggestion that "perhaps the Pallavas still held that part of Malabar where their name still seems to linger—the Valluvanād." We have seen that the official or regal designation of the Raja of Walluvanād was Valluva Kōnāṭiri, and Mr. Logan says that "it is certain that the Valluva Kōnāṭiri, after the last Perumal's departure in A. D. 825, became the protector of the *Maha Makham* feast at Ṭirunāvāya, and this looks as if he had held a distinguished place among the Malayāli chiefs before that time—a place so distinguished that he appears to have superseded the last Perumāl's lawful heir (Cochin) as protector at this festival." The Kēralōṭpaṭṭi says that the last Perumāl assigned a *nad* (or country) to Valluva Kōnāṭiri together with the privilege of conducting the Maha Makham festival at Ṭirunāvāya. Of the latter, he was deprived by the Zamorin with the assistance of the Mahomedans,

The Valluva Kōnāṭiri did, at one time, exercise suzerain rights over a large portion of South Malabar. But his territory had been gradually broken up by the Zamorin. At the time of the Mysorean conquest, there remained to the Raja only a few of the modern *amsams* of the present Taluks of Walluvanād and Ērnād. He had been, a little while before, deprived by the Zamorin of some other *amsams* of the Walluvanād Taluk. His possessions in Neṭunganād had been lost earlier still. On the cession of Malabar to the British by Tippu Sultan, the Raja entered into an agreement, on the 30th July 1792, with Mr. William Gamul Farmer and Major Alexander Dow deputed by the Bombay Government to settle the ceded districts, whereby the Raja was allowed to hold his former countries as manager of the East India Company in consideration of the services rendered by him to the Company in assisting their armies, on paying to them the revenues collected from the said countries. But, subsequently, owing to the inability of the Raja to preserve the peace of his district, which was disturbed by Māppiḷa freebooters, the Bombay Commissioners concurred in the order sent by the Supervisor to the Southern Superintendent to assume the immediate management of the country, especially "as he and his family had come into the country from their place of refuge in Travancore and, on the expulsion of Tippu's troops had, under the auspices of the Rama Raja's (Travancore) Dewan, been reinstated without (as far as it appears) awaiting or asking the permission of the Company's Government." He was granted an annual pension.

43. **Ponnani**. A town of some importance where the Zamorin usually held his court, now the head-quarters of a Taluk. Zinuddien writes it Funan.

44. **Tamares Gerya**. This was Ṭāmaraśśēri Ṅād, which was subject to the Kōṭṭayam Rajas. It now comprises nine villages in North Malabar. The origin of this Rajaship is thus explained in the Kēraḷōṭpaṭṭi. The chiefs of Puḷavai and Kuṛumbuṛnād quarrelled and caused much mischief in the country. Thereupon the Kaimals or lords of Puḷavai with 3,000 Nāyars and seven of the elders threw up their allegiance of their Raja and swore fealty to the Raja of Kōṭṭayam who was installed as Raja of Ṭāmaraśśēri. The tract over which he was appointed to rule was contributed by the two Nambūṭirīs of Ṭāmaraśśēri and Eṭamaram Illoms. A fort was built within which was installed Bhagavaṭi and Śāsṭha as titulary deities, and a guard of 500 Nāyars was also constituted. An offensive and defensive alliance between Puḷavai and Ṭāmaraśśēri was formed. Ayyāyira Pṛabhu Kaṛṭṭa or the lord of the five thousand, together with a section of 10,000 Nāyars of the militia, were appointed *Jangadas* (guards).

45. **Cottesal**. This is the Kōṭṭa river. We have had occasion to speak of the Malabar pirates

generally and of the destruction by the combined forces of the Zamorin and the Portuguese of Kuññāli, their stronghold. Even after this, they plied their trade freely, often with the connivance of the neighbouring chiefs who shared in their plunder. Those of Kōṭṭakkal seem to have directed their attention to vessels engaged in inland navigation only.

46. **Cotta Mariakkere.** This term is a compound of Cotta=Kōṭṭa or fort (also name of a river) and Mārgakkāran, literally 'doer' or 'follower of the law', a convert from Hinduism to a foreign religion; in this case, a Mahomedan.

Mr. Logan observes: "At the mouth of the Kōṭṭa river was a famous port for pirates in former days. They made prizes of all vessels not carrying the pass of the Kaṭaṭṭanād Raja, their sovereign, who was styled 'the lord of the seas.'" Again, "Famous among the pirate chiefs who commanded these fleets stands out the name of the Kōṭṭakkal Kuññāli Marakkārs. The family originally hailed from Panṭalāyani Kollam. Probably at the time when Henry Meneses destroyed the Moorish settlement, the family moved to Ṭṛkkoṭi, and thence again to Kōṭṭakkal at the mouth of the Kōṭṭa river. They obtained the title of Kuññāli Marakkār from the Zamorin. *Kunhe* means a youth, a title of distinction: *Ali* is the name of the Prophet's son-in-law, and *Marakkar* means the doer or follower of the law—*Marggam*,—and is applied, as a title, to persons of a foreign religion like the Christians and Mahomedans. Some of the remains of the fort at Kōṭṭakkal are still to be seen. It was situated at the northern extremity of a spit of sand extending from the south across the Kōṭṭa river-mouth, and it completely commanded the bar of the river and the shipping which lay inside it. The position was one of great strength against ancient artillery, as it was protected on two sides (north and east) by water, on a third side (the west), by a swampy salt marsh, through which the river, encumbered by another sand-spit stretching from the north across the mouth, has now (1885) forced its way. On the south, the narrow neck of land was easily protected by a rampart. This fort lay just opposite to Puṭupaṭṭaṇam, the ancient seat of Ṭekkenkūr (Southern Regent) of Kōlaṭṭnād. It would occupy too much space to relate the history of this family whose descendants still live in comparative poverty."[1]

Governor Gollennesse tells us that the northern portion of the Zamorin's country "is called Cottica after the river of that land; it is inhabited by Moors; they are pirates and are able to do much harm to small traders, but they do not lightly venture to attack ships or large vessels. It is true that the Samorine does not exactly openly approve of this, but there is not the slightest doubt that they obtain his full permission secretly by means of gifts and presents."

47. **Colastri.** It is the Europeanised form of the word Kōlaṭṭiri, the Malayālam designation of the Raja of *Cherakkal* or Kōlaṭṭunād. The Kēraḷa Māhāṭmyam says that Paraśurāma installed a Sōma Kṣheṭṙya as king of Kōlaṭṭunād and assigned to him the tract over which he was appointed to rule, whereas the Kēralōṭpaṭṭi attributes this assignment of territory to Chēramān Perumāḷ. There is a tradition that Kēraḷa had existed in the preceding *Kalpa*, that is, the period before Paraśurāma reclaimed it from the sea, but had been submerged in the general deluge, and Paraśurāma had only restored the land to its old position. Three girls belonging to the early Kēraḷa Rajas had been saved by a Ganḍhaṙvan (angel) named Mōhanan from the general destruction, and he kept them in a cave near Ēlimala (Mt. D'Eli), the particular spot being called Rāmanṭaḷi. By divine intervention, these three girls were consigned to the land of Kēraḷa as progenitors

1. Note, p. 332.

of the three Royal Houses, which, in future, were to rule over the country. One of them, so goes the story, became the ancestress of Kōla Swarūpam and lived at Ṭalipparamba. A variant of this tradition, related by Mr. Logan, says "that three women (one Kṣheṭrya and two Śūdras), strangers from some northern land, being stranded in a boat on Mount D'Eli, Chēramān Perumāl took all of them to wife, apparently, and on the descendants of the Kṣheṭrya woman, he conferred the title of Ēlibhūpan (king of Ēli) with 'heirdom to the kingdom', and he built for her the Ellot King's house at the foot of Ēli Mala (Mount D'Eli.)". This tradition, says Mr. Logan, relates undoubtedly to the northern Kōlaṭṭiri family, the second most ancient seat of the family having been at this particular king's house under Mount D'Eli.[1]

The dynasty is known as Kōla Swarūpam or the Kōla family. Bishop Caldwell, speaking of the origin of the Tamil dynasties of Southern India, observes that Tamil traditions as well as the *Harivamsa*, and other Purāṇās say that Pāṇḍya, Kērala, Kōla and Chōla were the sons of Akrīḍa or Ḍuṣhyanṭa, the adopted son of Ṭurvasu, a prince of the Lunar line of Kṣheṭryas. The learned Bishop then asks who the Kōla referred to here was—"Was he supposed to be the ancestor of the Kōlas or Kolarians of Central India? This is very improbable. Kōla is said to be identified by the Kērala Māhāṭmya with Kōlam or Kōlaṭṭunāḍu, North Malabar. The derivation involves difficulties, but it is the only reasonable one I have met with."[2]

It is significant that the Jewish and Syrian copper-plates do not mention the Kōlaṭṭiri among their attestors, and it is difficult to surmise why he is omitted, if he was then under the hegemony of the Perumāls. It is very probable that his kingdom lay outside the limits of the Perumāl's empire. Dr. Gundhert conjectures, and with great reason, that the north

1. P. 235.
2. *Hist. of Tinnevelly*, p. 12.

Kōlaṭṭiri was, at the dates of the execution of these documents, independent of the Perumāl.[1] Mr. Logan, however, questions this and observes that there is no evidence forthcoming that the north Kōlaṭṭiri dynasty had a separate existence in the eighth century A. D., and he attempts to support this by relying on the Mahomedan tradition about the introduction of Islam into Malabar, which, he says, renders it probable that the last of the Perumāls had sufficient influence over the north Kōlaṭṭiri to induce him to grant a site for a mosque at Māṭāyi and to endow the institution. This presumes that the Mahomedans were hospitably received and were allowed to build a mosque at Māṭāyi by the Kōlaṭṭiri under orders of the last Perumāl, an assumption without authority. The Mahomedan tradition, as recorded by Zinuddien, only says that the apostate Perumāl "wrote for them (his missionaries) in the character and language of Malabar, a description of his territories and kindred, detailing also the names of the different governors who had been appointed by him throughout his kingdom"[2] This writing, of course, is not forthcoming, and, in its absence, it would not be right to surmise that the Kōlaṭṭiri was one of of the governors appointed by the Perumāl, or that the Kōlaṭṭiri country had formed part of the Perumāl's dominions. Looking to the graceful way in which the Kōlaṭṭiri welcomed the Portuguese and allowed them to build churches, it is not difficult to understand his welcoming their predecessors, the Mahomedans, with pleasure and granting them site for a mosque. Both were bent on commercial enterprises, and, the Kōlaṭṭiri country producing the best quality of pepper in all Malabar, the Raja was only glad to find a means of converting the spices of his country into money.

Another explanation offered by Mr. Logan as to why the Kōlaṭṭiri was not an attestor to the deeds, while

1. M. J. L. S. X III, Part I.

2. P. 53.

his cousin of the south (meaning Travancore or Vēṇād) had attested it, is altogether imaginary, resting on absolutely no basis. After making a reference to the system of inheritance and succession in Malabar which makes a Malayāli king's natural heirs the issue of his sister or aunt or female cousin he points out that it was likely that from natural affection, a suitable provision would be made for the mother of the king's children and her offspring; and this provision, it is added, often took the shape of a grant of territory. After giving some instances of such grants made by the Kōlaṭṭiri, Mr. Logan says, "It is not at all improbable therefore that the northern Kōlaṭṭiries are descended from matrimonial alliance between the last of the Kērala Perumāls and a lady of the stock of the great southern feudatory, the Travancore (south Kōlaṭṭiri) Rajas." Of course, any surmise of this nature may be said to be probable. For aught we know, the last Chērmān Perumāl may have been a much married man and a uxorious husband. The many princes amongst whom he is said to have divided his realm may have been the issue of his many wives, who might have induced the Perumāl in his old age to part with portions of his territory to their children. All this and more is probable. But the question is, is there any evidence to show that it *was* so? Mr. Logan tells us that "the two families have always observed pollution, when deaths occurred in their respective houses and, as a matter of fact, the southern family would have ceased to exist long ago but for the adoption of heirs on several occasions from the northern family." It is not possible to say with any certainty when and how the ruling families of the extreme north and the extreme south came to be so related as to have *Pulasambandham* or community of pollution by birth and death; so that upon the basis of this relationship, any hypothesis may be started that may appear to be plausible. But the Kērala Māhāṭmyam tells us that the kings of Travancore and Kōlaṭṭunād, installed as such originally by Paraśurāma, were cousins, being sons of sisters married according to the Marumakkaṭṭāyam system, which, to a Malayāli, is a natural explanation for the relationship aforesaid. So far as known at present, this relationship cannot be traced beyond the fifth century of the Malabar era when, for the first time, it is believed, an adoption from the Kōlaswarūpam appears to have taken place. It would appear that the advances made by the Travancore Raja met with rebuff at the hands of the Kōlaṭṭiri, who was naturally unwilling to send any members of his family to Travancore, and the Raja of Travancore was forced to have recourse to stratagem before he could attain his object. Negotiations between the two Rajas having failed, Travancore arranged, through a Kōil Ṭampurān of Ṭaṭṭiri Kōvilakam (now represented by the Kilimānūr family to which belonged the distinguished Travancore artist, the late Raja Ravi Varma), to bring, by stealth, two princesses for adoption. Foreseeing the ire of the Kōlaṭṭiri in this undertaking, he sent his own family to Travancore and then brought away all the members of the Puṭuppiḷḷi Kōvilakam under pretence of taking them on a pilgrimage. The first adoption to Travancore was from this family, and from this apparently dates the *Pulasambandham* between the two Royal Houses. We have already shown that the Travancore Royal House was most likely a non-Malayāli one in its origin, and that it had gradually evolved into a Malayāli one, the first step of which was perhaps this one of adoption from Kōlaṭṭunād. If it was so, one can easily understand why the Kōlaṭṭiri should have evinced such marked dislike for the proposed adoption.

The first authentic information we get of the kingdom of Kōlaṭṭiri is from the *Travels* of Marco Polo. After describing the "kingdom of Coilam" (Quilon) and the "country called Comari" (Comorin), a short chapter is devoted to the "kingdom of Eli" (Kōlaṭṭunād).

"Eli is a kingdom towards the west, about 300 miles from Comari. The people are idolaters and have a king, and are tributary to nobody; and have a peculiar language. We will tell you particulars about their manners and their products, and you will better understand things now because we are drawing near to places that are not so outlandish.

"There is no proper harbour in the country, but there are many great rivers with good estuaries, wide and deep. Pepper and ginger grow there, and other spices in quantities. The king is rich in treasure, but not very strong in forces. The approach to his kingdom however is so strong by nature that no one can attack him, so he is afraid of nobody.

" And you must know that if any ship enters their estuary and anchors there, having been bound for some other port, they seize her and plunder the cargo. For they say, 'you were bound for somewhere else, and 'tis God has sent you hither to us, so we have a right to all your goods'. And they think it no sin to act thus. And this naughty custom prevails all over these provinces of India, to wit, that if a ship be driven by stress of weather into some other port than that to which it was bound, it is sure to be plundered. But if a ship come bound originally to the place they received it with all honour and give it due protection. The ships of Manzi and other countries that come hither in summer lay in their cargoes in 6 or 8 days and depart as fast as possible, because there is no harbour other than the river-mouth, a mere roadstead and sandbanks, so that it is perilous to tarry there. The ships of Manzi indeed are not so much afraid of these roadsteads as others are, because they have such huge wooden anchors which hold in all weather.

" There are many lions and other wild beasts here and plenty of game, both beast and bird ."[1]

1. Vol. II, pp 385—6.

Mr. Logan observes that Marco Polo's Kingdom of Ēli can be no other than the kingdom of Kōlaṭṭiri "whose original settlement was at Karippāṭṭ in Kuṟummāṯṯūr amśam in Cheṛakkal ṭālūk. The second most ancient seat of the family was at the foot of Mount Deli (Ēli mala), and the site of one at least of their residences at the time of Marco Polo's visit is probably still marked by a small but very ancient temple—with a stone inscription in Vaṭṭeḻuṭṭu characters—not very far from the big Rāmanṭali temple on the banks of the river near Kavvāyi, and lying close in under the mount on its western or sea face. While residing at this Ēli Kōvilakam or king's house, the family seems to have split up—after the fashion of Malayāḷi ṭaṟavāḍs—into two branches, one of which (Uḍayamangalam) settled at Aḍuṭṭila in the Māṭāyi amśam, while the other (Paḷḷi) had various residences. The head of both branches, (that is, the eldest male) was the Kōlaṭṭiri for the time being. He, as ruling prince, lived apart from the rest of the family and had residences at Māṭāyi, Valaṛpaṭṭaṇam, and other places. Māṭāyi was probably, as the Kēraḷōṭpaṭṭi seems to indicate, the more ancient of the two seats of the ruling prince, for, down to the present day, the Māṭāyi Kāvu is looked on as the chief temple of the Kōlaṭṭiri house-hold goddess Bhagavaṭi, and the next most important temple of the goddess is at the Kaḷarivāṭukkal (Fencing School gateway) temple at Valaṛpaṭṭaṇam." [1]

Ibn Batuta also refers to Hili or Eli and localities around it. He mentions *Jarkannan*, which he afterwards writes *Jarfattan* and *Dadkannan* afterwards written *Badfattan*. He speaks of the king as an infidel and mentions a mosque built by the then king's grandfather and of a tank also excavated by him. He relates the wonderful story of the conversion of the king's grandfather to the faith of Islam. Mr. Logan thinks that the

1. Vol. I, p. 284.

mosque at Hili mentioned by Ibn Batuta refers probably to the one at Paḷayangāṭi (lit—old bazaar), the town of *Dadkarman* to Vaḷaṙpaṭṭaṇam and the pond the king had dug to the "magnificent tank at the Cheṙakkal Kōvilakam of the Kōlaṭṭiri family where the Cheṙakkal Raja now usually resides." Col. Yule identifies Batuta's *Badfattan* with Puṭupaṭṭan, north of Calicut, mentioned also in the *Tohfut--ul—Mujahideen* as well as by Cosmas and Nicolo Conte. Ibn's reference to *Fattan* (Dhaṙmapaṭṭaṇam) and *Pandarina* (Panṭalāyani Kollam, North Kollam) before Calicut places it beyond doubt that he is speaking of the kingdom of Kōlaṭṭiri.

We may pause here to say a few words about the extent of the kingdom of the Kōlaṭṭiri and the constitution of its government. The late Raja Ravi Vaṙma, M. A., B. L., a scion of the Māvēlikkara branch of the Kōlaṭṭiri family, observes:—

"The kingdom of the Kōlaṭṭiri Raja extended from Kāsercōde in the north, to Kōrappuḷa in the south. The eastern boundary was Kuṭakumala, and the western, the sea. Within this territory were included the jagirs of Kōṭṭayam (north), Nīlīśwaram and Kaṭaṭṭanāḍ. The first was given as a present to the Kōṭṭayam Raja, and the two latter to the children of Kōlaṭṭiri Raja. Marriages (Ṭālikeṭṭu) in Nīlīśwaram family are even now performed by Kōlaswarūpam Rajas.

"The sovereign was styled Kōlaṭṭiri. There were, besides, four Kūṙvāḷchakkārs or dignitaries, Ṭekkeḷamkūr, Vaṭakkeḷamkūr, Nālāmkūr and Anchāmkūr The eldest of the male members reigned as sovereign, Kōlaṭṭiri. The next in succession, the heir-apparent, was the Ṭekkeḷamkūr. The residence assigned to him was the Vaṭakara fort. The third in succession was the Vaṭakkeḷamkūr in charge of Vekkolāṭ fort. The fourth was the manager of the household, and the fifth, the personal attendant or A. D. C. of the sovereign. Each of these peerages had large estates attached to it. These dignities even now obtain in name. But the large estates which were once appurtenant to them were sold away, except those of the Nālāmkūr, the present incumbent whereof has nearly an annual income of Rs. 500. The Nālāmkūr was usually the dispenser of all honours under the command of the sovereign. The dignities or Sṭhānams so given were "Nāyar", "Kuṙupp" and "Nampiyār" to Sūḍrās, and "Paṇikkar", "Perumalayan", "Kōmar", and "Velichappāṭu" to low caste-men. The eldest female member of Kōlaswarūpam was called *Achamma*, and the eldest lady of the family is called by that title even to-day. The estates attached to her dignity yield an income of nearly Rs. 700 per annum to its present holder.

"By hereditary right, the post of minister belonged to the members of Murukanchēri house, of Commander of the forces to Chiṫṫōṭṭu Kuṙukkal and of Financier to Māvila Nampiār, though the affairs of State were actually conducted by others. As already stated, the office of Purōhit belonged to Areppan Nampūṭiri and of the chief priest of temples (Ṭanṭri) to Kāṭṭumāṭas Nampūṭiri".1

After Ibn Batuta, till the arrival of the Portuguese, we have not been able to gather any references to this kingdom. After da Gama's rebuff at the Zamorin's court, the Admiral left the shores of Calicut and sailed away refusing the invitation of the Zamorin to land again. Da Gama appears to have remained for about seventy days at Panṭalāyani Kollam and to have left the place about the 4th November 1498.

Running up the coast, the Portuguese ships were met by boats sent out by the Kōlaṭṭiri to invite da Gama to land. He decided to visit the place but, warned by his experience at Calicut, declined to land. The king sent him provisions and, as a free gift, more

1. *Malabar Quarterly Review*, Vol. I, pp. 295-6.

spices and merchandise than the vessels could hold, so that some had to be declined; and da Gama sent in return large quantities of the goods he had on board—branch coral, vermilion, quicksilver, and brass and copper basins—being almost double that which he had received from the king. He also sent Nicolas Coelho with a present of a green cloth, brown satin, velvet crimson damask, a large silver basin, thirty scarlet caps, two knives in sheaths and five ells of darker scarlet cloths to the king. These were graciously received, and the king expressed his great desire to see da Gama. As the Admiral would not land, the king had a narrow wooden bridge, a sort of pier, constructed jutting into the sea to the distance of a cross-bow shot, and, at the extremity of it, he had a small chamber made of planks prepared. The brothers da Gama and the captains proceeded thither, had a conference with the king, exchanging valuable presents and talking of the vile treatment received by da Gama at Calicut. Da Gama entered into a treaty with Kōlaṭṭiri on behalf of the king of Portugal. The engagement was engrossed on a golden leaf and was signed by the king and his ministers. It was accompanied by handsome presents to the king of Portugal. On behalf of Dom Manoel, da Gama presented Kōlaṭṭiri with a handsome sword. He then sailed away from Cannanore on the 20th November, once more distributing presents to the ministers of the king and exchanging courtesies generally.[1]

Whilst Cabral was in Cochin, he received a deputation from the Kōlaṭṭiri, promising to supply him with pepper and spices at a cheaper rate than at Cochin. The offer was politely declined. But, as Cabral was about to leave Cochin, he descried a fleet belonging to the Zamorin and prepared to attack it at once. But the Calicut people held off. Cabral chased them, but was overtaken by a violent storm, which carried him out to sea. He put into Cannanore, where he arrived

1. *Danvers*, Vol. I, p. 60.

on the 15th January 1501, and received on board an ambassador from the Kōlaṭṭiri king to the king of Portugal together with presents and the offer of a free trade to that port. On the following day, Cabral left on his homeward voyage.

Before the return of Cabral, King Manoel had sent another expedition under Joas da Nova, who called at Cannanore and was well received, where he arranged to take goods on his return from Cochin whither he was going. On his return, he found that, owing to the interference of the Moors, he could not get goods without cash. On entering the port of Cannanore, da Nova took a ship off Calicut, which he plundered and burnt. Besides many valuable jewels, there were found in this ship three silver navigating instruments, which were quite unknown to the Portuguese astronomers and navigators. The Zamorin, on hearing of the loss of the ship and the valuable instruments, equipped a large fleet of 180 vessels to punish the Portuguese. The Kōlaṭṭiri offered any assistance in his power, which was, however, civilly declined. When the attack came on, da Nova was able to sink a number of the Zamorin's vessels, and the remaining Moors did not continue the action. Owing to the generosity of the Kōlaṭṭiri, the Portuguese ships were soon loaded, and da Nova departed, leaving his European merchandise for disposal in Cannanore under the charge of a factor and two clerks.

On his second voyage, da Gama visited Kōlaṭṭiri and delivered to him a letter from the king Dom Manoel together with the presents which he had brought out, consisting of six pieces of satin and coloured velvets, a piece of brocade, an arm-chair with cushions of brocade, and a sword of gold and enamel. This latter was greatly admired by the king, who, in return, delivered to da Gama a necklace and two bracelets, together with ten rings, all of considerable value, as presents for the queen of Portugal, besides some rich jewels for himself. A treaty of commerce was arranged with the king, the goods to be supplied at fixed prices. The king allotted to the factor at Cannanore, Goncalo Gil Barbosa, a *Jangada* or guard of ten Nayars. The Moors who ventured to oppose the king were severely punished, and the acts of barbarity, committed by Vincent Sodre in punishing Koja (Mohmed Marakkār, the principal Moor, for using insulting language to the king, struck terror into them. For the service rendered by de Sodre on this occasion, the Kōlaṭṭiri began, it is said, the custom of giving a gold *pardas* daily for their table supplies.

Returning from Cochin whither he had gone, da Gama buried most of his artillery at Cannanore. He also persuaded the Kōlaṭṭiri to have a high stone wall erected round the factory palisade, with a gate to fasten with a key, and to send some one to shut the gate, and to keep the key himself. This the credulous king agreed to, and forthwith had the work executed, thinking that, in making this request, da Gama desired that the Portuguese left in the factory should remain subject to him. After regulating the factory affairs, da Gama sailed for Europe on the 28th of December 1502.

Not long after, the old Kōlaṭṭiri died, and there were disputes about the succession, which were referred to the arbitration of a Brahman nominated by the Zamorin, so that the new king came to be attached to the Zamorin's cause and turned out to be no friend to the Portuguese. One of the numerous acts of barbarity of which the Portuguese were all along guilty was perpetrated at about this time, and this incensed the Kōlaṭṭiri and his people very much and with great reason. The minister of the Kōlaṭṭiri, Chenchēri Kuṟup, had addressed the king of Portugal on the subject of the passes granted by the Portuguese to native vessels and had prayed that orders may be issued to permit ten native vessels to go annually to Hormuz or Guzaret to purchase horses. He had also prayed that the petty islands belonging to the Laccadive group belonging to his master may not be molested. The reply was favourable. But, in the execution of the order, all sorts of obstacles were thrown by the Portuguese captains. It so happened that, at this time, a Portuguese captain, Goncalo Vaz, meeting with a vessel near Cannanore, overhauled her papers, and declaring a pass which she carried from Lourenco de Britto, the Commandant at Cannanore, to be a forgery, seized the rich prize, and, to avoid discovery, plundered and sank her, after sewing the crew up in a sail and throwing them overboard. The stitching had not been firm, and the corpses of the crew were washed upon the beach. One of the bodies was identified as that of the son-in-law of Mammāli Marakkār, and the father, a very influential merchant, came to the Cannanore fort and indignantly up-braided the Commandant for this breach of faith. Britto protested his innocence, but was not believed. And the murdered man's family went in a body to the Valaṟpaṭṭaṇam palace of Kōlaṭṭiri and demanded vengeance. The populace was greatly incensed, and the king reluctantly consented to hostilities. The Zamorin also advised him towards this and promised material aid.

The Zamorin supplied Kōlaṭṭiri with 21 pieces of cannon, and the fort of Cannanore was invested by an army of 40,000 Nāyars. All communication between the town and fort was cut off by a trench. The attacking force was increased before long by the addition of 20,000 Nāyars sent by the Zamorin. One morning, the besiegers advanced against the fort in 12 columns of 2,000 men each, tom-toms beating, rockets and blue lights blazing and doughty champions dancing in front of the array, performing wonderful athletic feats. They were not allowed to reach the wall, being driven back by the Portuguese pouring in a destructive fire. The water of the garrison came from a well situated outside the fort, and, each time they came out to draw water, they had to fight for it, until an engineer named Fernandez hit upon the expedient of mining a passage as far as the well and so drawing off the supply under ground. In a sally subsequently made, the Portuguese filled up the well with earth to hide the device. The Moors constructed ramparts of bales of cotton, and, against these, the ordinary cannon used had but little effect ; but the Portuguese planted a large piece of ordnance on their ramparts, and one lucky shot from it sent the cotton bales flying, and killed no less than 22 men. After this, no attempt was made to take the fort, and the besiegers hoped to starve out the garrison. The latter were thus reduced to the greatest straits, and lived on lizards, rats, cats and other animals. To bring the siege to a termination before the Oṇam festival, a grand final assault both by sea and land, was planned. The boats and catamarans were easily enough driven back by the besieged garrison, but the Nāyars gallantly stormed the wall and effected an entrance. So steady however was the Portuguese fire that they were soon checked and they finally retreated. Nearly every one of the garrison was wounded in that day's fight; and de Britto, to conceal the exhaustion of his resources, kept up a bombardment of the town after the enemy had been repulsed and succeeded in destroying a mosque in which the Moors had congregated for the Friday service. But relief came; for, on the 27th of August, a fresh fleet of 11 ships under Tristao da Cunha arrived from Europe, and their Commander with 300 of his men drove back the besiegers and relieved the fort. The Kōlaṭṭiri then sued for peace, which was granted on terms advantageous to the Portuguese.

In the year 1510, after retreating from Goa, Alfonso de Albuquerque arrived at Cannanore on the 15th of September. There in a large tent erected in front of the fort, a grand durbar was held attended by the Kōlaṭṭiri, his minister, Chenchēri Kuṙup and Mammāli Marakkār, the chief Moor of Cannanore. After this durbar, Albuquerque decided on a second expedition against Goa. The Zamorin attempted to draw off the Kōlaṭṭiri from the Portuguese allegiance by sending to him a force under the command of the Cochin Prince whose claim to succession to the throne Albuquerque had rejected. There was mutiny amongst Albuquerque's own men. He, however, was equal to the occasion. He persuaded the Kōlaṭṭiri's minister, Chenchēri Kuṙup, to join his expedition at the head of 300 picked Nāyars, and this, it is said, shamed his own men into facing the dangers in front of them. On the 6th of November 1510, Goa fell into the hands of the Portuguese after a contest of barely six hours' duration. Henceforward, Goa supplanted Cochin and became the capital of Portuguese India.

Soon after da Gama had arrived in India as Viceroy, he went to Cannanore and stayed for 3 days, during which time he insisted on the Kōlaṭṭiri surrendering a notorious pirate chief called Bala Hassan, who was thereupon thrown into a dungeon in the Cannanore fort. One of the first acts of Henry Meneses on his assuming the government after the death of da Gama was to order the execution of Bala Hassan. He was related to the Aṙakkal (Māppiḷa) Raja of Cannanore, and bribes to a large amount were offered for his release, but in vain. The Kōlaṭṭiri also offered a visit to the Viceroy to intercede for him, but the execution was not stayed. The Moors were greatly disgusted at this and decided that, in future, they should act independently of the Kōlaṭṭiri altogether. And the Kōlaṭṭiri, on his part, asked the Viceroy to punish those Moors who had taken refuge at Ḍhaṙmapaṭṭaṇam island. An expedition was accordingly organised, and the towns, bazaars and shipping at Ḍhaṙmapaṭṭaṇam and at Māhe were destroyed (January 1525).

After the destruction of Panṭalāyani Kollam, the Viceroy dealt with the Laccadive Islands, 18 in number. Orders had come from Portugal that, if the Kōlaṭṭiri would supply all the coir (for which the islands are famous) required by the Portuguese at a cheap rate, he might keep the islands. The Viceroy, Meneses, at an interview with the Kōlaṭṭiri, demanded a thousand candies of coir *per annum*. He replied that he could not underdake to supply such a large quantity and said he would prefer giving up the islands, which was accordingly done.

After this, we get very little information regarding the dealings of the Portuguese with the Kōlaṭṭiri, as also between him and the Dutch. The disruption of the family and the disintegration of the kingdom had been already going on for some time past. To quote Mr. Logan :—

" Family quarrels were not infrequent in the Kōlaṭṭiri Chief's house, and the reasons therefor are in operation in all Malayāli families down to the present day, and more especially in North Malabar. The head of a Malayāli house has two conflicting sets of interests to deal with—first, those of his legal heirs, the children of his female relatives of various degrees; and secondly, those of his natural heirs, his own wife and children. The latter have no *legal* claim on him, but natural affection comes into play, and to provide suitably for his own children and their mother, a man not infrequently trenches upon the right of his *legal* heirs. Hence arise bitter quarrels and jealousies.

" There can be no doubt that the Kōlaṭṭiri family's dominions had become greatly curtailed by such provisions having been made for the natural heirs of the chiefs, out of the territories belonging of right to the legal heirs. And at the period when the Tellicherry factory was established, somewhere about 1694-95, one of the natural offshoots of the family, the Kaṭaṭṭunād Raja, known to the early English as the

Boyanore or Baonor of Badagara, was in semi-independent possession of Kaṭaṭṭuṅād, that is, of the territory lying between the Māhe and Kōṭṭa rivers. And another such offshoot was in similar semi-independent possession of the Malayāḷam terrritory lying to the north of the Kavāyi river. And of the territory lying between the Kavāyi and Māhe rivers, various portions had come, whether by family alliances of the kind described or by grants, it is difficult to say, into the possession of various chieftains who were all more or less dependent on the Kōlaṭṭiris. Randattara, otherwise called Pōyanād, was under the Achchanmār (fathers), four houses of the Nampiār caste; Kōṭṭayam was under the Puṙanāt (foreign) Rajas, and Iruvaḷinād (including Kurangōth) was ruled by six houses of Nampiār caste and by one house of the Nāyar caste. Besides the above, the two houses of Nampiārs still continued to rule, in some subjection to the Kōlaṭṭiris, the territories assigned (it is said) to them by Chēramān Perumāḷ himself along the foot of the Western Ghauts in the present Chiṙakkal Ṭālūk, and there were other houses of Nampiārs (though of lower rank) located in different places in what is now the Chiṙakkal Ṭālūk. Lastly the Māppiḷa Chief of Cannanore (the Āli Raja) or Raja of the sea, had secured to himself a small slice of territory at and about Cannanore. The original Kōlaṭṭiri dominions were, therefore, broken up into a large number of petty principalities at the time of the founding of the Tellicherry factory, and the territory which remained under the direct rule of the Kōlaṭṭiris was of comparatively small extent".[1]

It will be well to notice here the several branches into which the family broke up and their present location to enable us to understand more clearly what follows. The late Raja Ravi Vaṙma, M. A., B. L., has given us an account of the break-up, and the following table is prepared on the basis of that account.

1. Vol. I, pp. 345—6.

Kolaswaroopam
(The Kōlattiri Family)

- Udayamangalam
  - Mēttale
    - Kottārakkara (Travancore) (extinct) 1029 M. E.
    - Mariappilli (Travancore)
    - Tiruvella (Travancore) (extinct) 1068 M. E.
  - Kuññi (extinct) 665 M. E.
  - Natuvile (Travancore)
  - Cheriya (2) (Travancore)
- Palli
  - Putuppilli (1) (Travancore) (extinct) 1030 M. E.
  - Palli
    - Chirakkal
    - Chenga (3)
      - Ennakkāt (Travancore)
      - Prākkara (Travancore)
      - Māvēlikkara (Travancore)
    - Kōnnissēri
    - Tēvanangōtu
    - Patiññāra Kōvilakam

(1) Migrated to Travancore, 5th century M. E.
(2) Do do between 920 and 930 M. E.
(3) During the invasion of Tippu, all the Kovilakams found shelter in Travancore. When peace was restored, all the Palli Kovilakam families except Chenga Kovilakam returned to their original homes.

About 1680, a disruption took place in the Kōlaṭṭiri family, and Captain Hamilton, who had been voyaging along the Coast and who paid a visit to the reigning Kōlaṭṭiri in 1702, gives an account of it:—"There were three princes of the blood royal who conspired to cut him (the reigning Prince Uṇṇiṭṭiri) and his family off, to possess themselves of the Government of Callistree (Kōlaṭṭiri); but, being detected, they were beheaded on altars built of stone. About two miles from Cannanore, the altars were standing, when I was there. They were only square piles of hewn stone, almost three yards high and four yards each side."

Of the five Kūṟvāīchās or dignities already mentioned, the first, i. e., the Kōlaṭṭiri, ruled over the whole kingdom, but retained the immediate executive charge of only the middle portion. The Ṭekkeḷamkūr or the Southern Regent had separate charge of the southern portion with his head-quarters at Puṭupaṭṭaṇam on the Kōṭṭa river, and tradition says that it was by marriage with one of the Southern Regents that one of the Kaṭaṭṭanād Raja's female ancestors acquired the territory of that family. The Vaṭakkeḷamkūr or the Northern Regent had separate charge of the northern territories, and, from a marriage with one of them, the Nīlīśvaram Rajas acquired their territory, forming, at present, the southern portion of the Kāsergōde Ṭāluk in South Canara. The other dignitaries were, as we have already seen, on personal attendance on the king, rendering him any assistance he required.

Mr. Logan observes that, on examining the records, it is found that, as a rule, the ablest member of the family, sometimes peaceably with the consent of all the members, sometimes by force, seized the reins of power at the earliest possible opportunity, and the rest of the family, although perhaps senior to himself, were mere puppets in his hands.

It was from the Vaṭakkeḷamkūr that the English East India Company obtained permission to settle at

Tellicherry and build a fort and factory there. On the 20th of August 1708, Prince Vaṭakkeḷamkūr of the Paḷḷi Palace gave the Honourable English Company the following grant:—

"The fort of Tellicherry has been built at the request and entreaties made by me as a friend. To acknowledge the love and friendship which the Company bears towards me and my palace, I give and make over the said fort with its limits to the Honourable Company, where no person shall demand, collect and plant. Our custom house will be obliged to give us what has been settled."[1]

The English entered into commercial and *quasi* political relations with chiefs subordinate to the Kōlaṭṭiri, such as the Kurangōṭ Nāyar, the Nampiār chieftains of Iruvaḷinād, the Raja of Kaṭaṭṭnād etc.

In 1722, the Kōlaṭṭiri himself granted the English Company "all the trades and farms * * * from Canhorotte down to the river Pudupatnam * * * save that granted to the Dutch Company", and the English were authorised to carry on their commerce and "if any other European or any other stranger come to this our country, the English Company can, in our name, punish, prevent and drive away." This was confirmed two years later by "the Prince Regent and Governors of the two palaces of Odeoculom, Nadduyteculotu Odeavarmen and Baddacaculotu Codormen, and of the palace Pally and Prince Odeavarmen." On the same date, 24th February 1724, the above Princes on behalf of their "uncle Colasteri" promised "to remain united with the Company". Six years later, the English Company stood in need of further guarantees against the admission of other European nations to commerce, and the Prince Regent gave the following grant:—

"Royal writing to protect the trade of the English Company.

1. Logan's *Malabar*, Vol. III, p. 2.

"For the greater security of the English Company and their Trade and Dealings of our Dominions, Be it known to all whom these presents may concern, That I Ode Ormen, Prince Regent and Governor of the Palace of Pallee by this our Royall Grant, do promise free Liberty to, and authorize the aforesaid English Company (and not do any other European nation whatsoever) for to Trade and Traffick in, buy and sell the severall goods and products of our Dominions. I likewise promise them not to admit either the Dutch or French nation to make any establishment or carry on any Trade in the Country of Erbenadoo, Trentapatam nor Randoo Tarra. That in case either the Dutch or French nation should hereafter pretend to Traffick or settle themselves in any of the aforesaid Countrys, We do hereby give full Liberty to the English Company to Hoist their national Flag either on Trentapatam or Randoo Tarra in such Place as to them shall seem convenient.

"Given under our Royall Sign Manuall this 2nd of November in the Malabar year 906 and the Christian year 1730.

"Note.—From the Diary of the Tellicherry Factory, dated 3rd November 1730."[1]

In the year 1734, the English Company was given "the island of Ḍharmapaṭṭaṇam, with the Grounds, Bars and Rivers thereunto belonging." Two days after this, on the 27th of May 1734, the Prince Regent wrote:—"In consideration of the kindness, with which we are treated by the English Company, and of the regard evinced towards our Palace, we, of our free will, cede and give to the said Company, the Tellicherry Fort, as also all the other Forts subordinate to it and the limits of each. In the place above alluded to, no one shall demand, collect or plant; but our Custom House must give us what has been written and settled down."

In the meanwhile, the French were making great exertions to obtain a firm footing in Malabar. In 1725,

1. *Malabar*, Vol. III, p. 18. XIX.

a French squadron made a descent on Māhe "in pursuance of orders from the Directors with a view to secure on the Malabar Coast a post that would indemnify the French for the loss of Surat." The French came into conflict with the Kaṭaṭṭanād Raja, who was then at war with his neighbouring Raja of Kōṭṭayam. Mr. Adams, the English Agent at Tellicherry, brought about a reconciliation between the latter with a view to turn the Kaṭaṭṭanād Raja unhampered against the French. But this was of little use. On the 14th of August, the French seized a small hill lying between them and the Raja's forces, and, notwithstanding smart firing, the Raja failed to dislodge them. On the 15th, one hundred Nāyars were sent to assist Kaṭaṭṭanād. The Raja stood in need of money, and, when aid was solicited, Mr. Adams asked him, first of all, to settle his accounts. Unable to find funds, the Raja preferred to come to terms with the French and was told by the English Agent that he was unreasonable. The French did not stop here, and the English factors resolved to assist Kaṭaṭṭanād with money, etc., as being cheaper than war. However, matters were soon adjusted between the two nations in Europe.

After the Portuguese reprisals on the Moorish commerce, the relations between the Āli Rajas and the Kōlaṭṭirīs had become strained, and the Dutch who had captured Cannanore from the Portuguese now began to take advantage of this. The Āli Raja was set up to seize Codally. He and the English came into conflict: a detachment belonging to the Company sent to protect the English warehouse being stopped at Ḍharmapaṭṭaṇam by the Āli Raja's people and turned back with insults, aid was sought from the Kōlaṭṭiri and the Kōṭṭayam Rajas. The fight between the parties continued for some time. The Kōlaṭṭiri stood in need of money. On the 1st of November 1730, Mr. Braddyle, the English Chief, had an interview with the Prince Regent, and, on the next day, grant of the monopoly of trade in Iruvalinād already noticed was obtained in return for

20,000 fanams worth military stores to enable the Prince to carry on the war with the Māppiḷās. Further loans were given on the 13th of January and the 10th of May. On the 9th of June, peace was agreed to between them, the Māppiḷās agreeing to pay an indemnity of 100,000 fanams at once and a similar sum in four months' time. Mr. Braddyle promptly applied for re-payment of the loans, but was informed that "The present Treaty is only to give me a Breathing for four months."

But before the four months passed away, the Kōlaṭṭiri had to face a stronger enemy from the north. On the invitation of a discontented member of his family, Sōmaśēkhara Nāyaka, the ruler of Bednore, appeared in the north and pushed his forces across the boundary of Kōlaṭṭunāḍ. On the 16th of January 1732, the factors reported that the Prince Regent's army had been routed by the Canarese, who had, they said, "gott as farr as Mounty Dilly." The country about Vaḷarpaṭṭaṇam was "altogether unsettled" and "in utmost confusion by reason of the great progress made by the Carnatick army against his kingdom." Finding it impossible to make head against the Canarese, the English being apparently unwilling or unable to render assistance with men or money, the Kōlaṭṭiri came to terms with the Bednore Raja's general "Ragonatt" (Raghunāth). These were:—The Prince to hold the country north of Vaḷarpaṭṭaṇam river as far as Nīlīśvaram as a tributary of Bednore. Bednore to have three forts in the said territory—one at "Madacarro," another at "Cavi" and the third at Nīlīśvaram in South Canara. The country south of the river to be under the Prince Regent who was to receive assistance against his rebellious subjects, first of whom were the Māppiḷās of Cannanore.

The position of the English at Ḍharmapaṭṭaṇam island and at Tellicherry had become serious, in view of the attitude of the Canarese and the divided authority that prevailed all around them. The Bībi of Cannanore and the Raja of Kōṭṭayam were prevailed upon to allow the English flag to be hoisted on the island. As soon as a solid footing was obtained on the Ḍharmapaṭṭaṇam island, the English proceeded to form a combination of the native powers to drive out the Canarese. An engagement was concluded between the English, the Prince Regent and the Kōṭṭayam Raja on the 29th of January 1736. On the 24th of February, the Canarese were peremptorily ordered to move back to the north of the Vaḷarpaṭṭaṇam river. On the 29th, the first hostilities commenced. The incursion of the Canarese had been disastrous to the Dutch trade at Cannanore, and, after some hesitation, the Dutch were induced to join the combination on the express understanding that, if the Canarese stronghold of Caṭalāy was taken, the English would not retain it so as to intercept the Dutch trade with the pepper country lying up the Vaḷarpaṭṭaṇam river. On the 30th of March, the Dutch forces were landed, and, on the 1st of April, the combined forces of the allies delivered a well-planned attack on the fort of Caṭalāy. The Canarese made a stubborn resistance, but were defeated and compelled to give up the fort. Other Canarese forts surrendered one after another, till, at last, peace was concluded on the 9th and 20th of February, by which all grants previously made by the Kōlaṭṭiri were recognised, a monopoly for pepper and cardamoms in all the Kōlaṭṭiri territory that might thereafter be conquered was assigned to the English, and the Canarese were prevented from coming to the south of the Vaḷarpaṭṭaṇam river. The rest of the Kōlaṭṭiri dominions was left to be overrun by the Canarese as they might think fit, though one of the English Chiefs in writing to the Bednore Raja on the 11th of May had expressly said that one of the causes that had contributed to hostilities between them was the conduct of the Canarese general Gōpālayyā's creating dissensions in the Kōlaṭṭiri family. The English Chief had offered to negotiate terms of peace between Bednore and the Prince Regent.

The Prince Regent, thus left in the lurch, applied for a loan of money to enable him to resist the Canarese, but was told that no advance could be made, unless securities were given. To add to the difficulties of the Kōlaṭṭiri, on the 16th of February, the date on which the terms of the treaty were ratified by the English Chief, orders were given to evacuate the fort of Ālikkuṅṅu protecting the mouth of the Nīlīśvaram river. The English garrison at once withdrew, and it was immediately occupied by the Canarese. It gave them the command of the Nīlīśvaram river and of the northern portion of the Kōlaṭṭiri's dominions. The Canarese, of course, made the best of their opportunity and busied themselves within the limits allotted to them in the treaty. In April 1737, they came up as far south as Māṭakkara. The Prince Regent was alarmed and flew to seek the aid of the English Company. This was exactly what the English Chief had desired. He was certain that the Kōlaṭṭiri will have to turn to the English Company in his extremity, and that that would be the opportunity to exact from him whatever terms the Company wanted. So the Prince was promised Rs. 5,000, if he would decline to deal with any other European nation than the English, and if he would consent to give an authentic deed ratifying the English Company's hold on Eṭṭakkāt and Māṭakkara. Of the amount promised, Rs. 1,000 was sent to him in advance, the remainder to follow the execution of the deed. In pursuance of this, two deeds were executed, one in March and the other in July 1736. By the first, the Company was empowered to erect a fort " at the entrance of the river Baliapatam, on the spot called Maddacara," and another " to enjoy the sole traffic of pepper and cardammams produced in those parts," and it was added that the grant was made with the intent that the Company may "prevent the

Canarese frequenting with their vessels molesting me that way." In the second deed, the Prince undertook to maintain the privileges already granted to the English Company, not to "enter on any terms of amity with any European nation whatever in prejudice of them," and "in all things give the strongest proofs of my sincerest attachment to Saib English Company." "Hoping at the same time they will contribute what is in their power towards the prosperity of this kingdom."

The English factors, having obtained all what they had aimed at, now interposed and arranged articles of peace between the Kōlaṭṭiri and the Canarese. By August 1737, the Canarese had overrun the whole of the country as far south as the Ṭalipparamba river, but Māṭāyi fort still held out against them. The English Chief, his assistant and the Prince Regent met the Canarese Governor Śūrappayya, near Māṭakkara on the 30th August. The terms arranged were as follows:—

"That from the fort of Maddy, (Māṭāyi) westward, to Urbelly, southward, and as the river winds to the fort of the Hills, eastward, with all the country, northward of the said river, shall hereafter appertain to the King of Bednure, and from the parts aforesaid, southward, the King of Colastri (Kōlaṭṭiri) shall enjoy what appertains to him; and it is moreover agreed that neither of the aforesaid powers shall enter with an armed force for invading or molesting in any wise the assigned territories of either."

These terms were, however, not acceptable to the king of Bednore, who refused to ratify them, and Śūrappayya was superseded by Ragonatt, a person not acceptable to the English, as Governor of Mangalore and Commander of the army. The new Governor, on reaching the camp at Māṭāyi, peremptorily ordered the English Chief, on the 1st of January 1738, to proceed forthwith to the camp to talk of important matters. A deputation was sent, however reluctantly, to ascertain the intentions of the Canarese general, which returned on the 4th of January and reported that the Canarese wished the Company to remain neutral in the war about to be commenced with the "Malabarrs."

War commenced and continued for sometime. In October 1738, the Prince Regent appears to have been so far pressed that he delivered Rs. 30,000 to the factors to prosecute the war, and the agreement come to with the factors at this juncture "to make war against the insolence of Canara" and "to drive out Canara", stipulates that "the Company should bear the expenses as well as the pay and expenses of the Company's soldiers who fight on land," and "the expenses for ball, powder, Nairs, Tiers, Moquas, Dhoneys and Manchuas, as well as other expenses, will be defrayed by the Prince." The Prince also promised to pay any amount required over the Rs. 30,000 already paid, and, if the money was not forthcoming, "the Company may retire (from the war) and seek any other means beneficial to themselves." In case of success, he promised to pay the Company "the expenses both on sea and land defrayed from its coffers." Hostilities continued till the 10th of January 1739, when prospects of peace began to dawn, the Canarese being defeated at the obstinate defence of the line of Valaṙpaṭṭaṇam river, but the actual terms were not definitively settled till February 1740. The chief points were :—the permission to export a definite quantity of rice without duty from Mangalore, and the omission of the clause stopping the Canarese from making conquests to the south of the Valaṙpaṭṭaṇam river. The Canarese do not appear to have subsequently attempted to force their way to the south of the Valaṙpaṭṭanam river which was securely guarded by the Company's fort at Māṭakkara. "The fact seems to have been," observes Mr. Logan, "that besides the opposition which the factors would have made, had they (the Canarese) attempted to pass to the south of the river, the invaders had pretty well exhausted the resources of the country to the north of it and found a difficulty in supporting the large force they had there, and which, it is said, was costing them in January 1749 as much as 12,000 pagodas per month."

It will have been observed that, by the treaty between Kōlaṭṭiri and the king of Bednore, the former had ceded to the latter a considerable portion of his territory. The remaining portion was now given up to Prince Uḍaya Varman of Palli Kōvilakam under the following grant entered in the Diary of the Tellicherry Factory on the 1st of September 1737 :—

"The Canarees having entered my kingdom, some time since, with an armed force, and proceeded as far as Durmapatam, our heir, Odearmen, of the Palace of Pally, with the assistance of an European Power, by loans and force, did expel them as far as Neleasarom, but it has since happened that they re-entered the country, being joined by the Fifth King of the *Palace of Ody*, and thereby subdued all to their obedience, as far as Madday, where the English Company mediated a Peace between us, and with which I acknowledge to be fully satisfied. Declaring by these presents that I do commit the Government of my Kingdom, remaining to me, unto my heir, the aforesaid Odearmen of the Palace of Pally, to which you are to bear witness."[1]

It will be interesting to note the popular belief regarding the facts above narrated. The story current in the country is that in the year "914 M. E. (i. e. 1739 A. D.), a Mahomedan adventurer by name Ikkerian invaded Kōlaṭṭunāḍ with a force for brigandage. The then Kōlaṭṭiri—Uḍaya Varman of Kuññi Kōvilakam—was a weak sovereign, much addicted to chess play. The Moslem invader found hardly any resistance offered, and he established himself accordingly as sovereign at Cannanore. This humiliation touched the minor members of the family to the quick. But to think of giving battle was impossible. For, neither the men, nor the sinews of war necessary for such an

1. *Malabar*, Vol. III, pp. 34—5, XXXVIII.

undertaking were forthcoming; the state revenues remained uncollected; and the salaries of servants were in arrears. Then a member of Chenga Kōvilakam branch, generally known as 'Kaṙkaṭaka Māsaṭṭil Ṭīppeṭṭa Aṇṇan,' (the brother who died in the month of Kaṙkaṭakam) treated with the Moslem conqueror, and the latter agreed to quit the country on his being paid a ransom of a lakh and twenty thousand Surat rupees. The Kōlaṭṭiri had not this at the time in his coffers. It was borrowed of Rāma Vaṙma Raja, a member of Chiṙakkal Kōvilakam, and the kingdom was given in fee for the amount. Thenceforward, the then Kōlaṭṭiri became a name bereft of its royal prerogatives, all semblance of which was finally detached from that dignity, when, after the fall of Seringapatam, the country was annexed to British India."[1]

The Ikkerian of the above narration was no Moslem; neither a brigand. The Rajas of Bednore were known as the Ikkeri or Keladi Rajas—and Ikkerian means only one who belonged to the Ikkeri family. These Chiefs were Canarese and obtained independence on the breaking up of the Vijayanagara Empire after the battle of Talikkotta in 1564. The Uḍayavaṙman who is said to have bought off the Ikkerian belonged to the Paḷḷi Kōvilakam. Perhaps this refers to the heavy payments the Kōlaṭṭiri had to make to the English factors, and it is most likely that the amount was advanced by the Chengal branch.

The dissensions of the Kōlaṭṭiri family still continued and the party of disorder appears to have been headed by a prince called "Oekoo,' who, in consequence of the peace with the Canarese, seemed to have turned his attention to creating trouble in the south. In an attempt to reach Kōlaṭṭunāḍ by sea in November 1739, he was taken prisoner by the factors and confined in the Māṭakkara fort, whence he effected his escape and created further disturbances.

1. *Malabar Quarterly Review.* Vol. I, p. 297.

The factory Diary of the 23rd of July 1740 records that the English Company had a grant from the Kōlaṭṭiri empowering them to hoist their colours at any time and anywhere in the kingdom consisting of seven provinces.—

" 1.	Pallartuta	5.	Edevadu Nadu
2.	Choulsaroun	6.	Carta Nadu
3.	Neliotusaroum	7.	Porovenadu. "
4.	Alerta Naddu		

Meanwhile, dissensions in the family became rampant, and these continued disintegrating the kingdom. The English and the French interfered in the family concerns very much, obtaining such advantages as they were able to secure from the rival parties. There was war between the English and the French from 1744 to 1749, and the Kōlaṭṭiri of the period happened to be jealous of the English and interfered very much with the rights and privileges of the Company. After cessation of hostilities with France, an arrangement was arrived at between the parties on the 10th January 1749. It is said that Mr. Byfeld, the English Chief, also siezed the opportunity to obtain from the Prince (Vaṭakkeḷamkūr) and who belonged to the Uḍaya Mangalam branch a deed dated 9th of May 1749, transferring absolutely to the Prince Regent of the Palli-branch all the property of his family lying to the south of a line drawn " from the river Quilānṭy to Urbelli." Of course the other members of the family would not consent to part with their birth-right in this way and as the Chief was unable to bring them to terms resolved to assist the Prince Regent against them.

The Prince Regent wanted to carve out a fief for his son who was nephew, being sister's son, of the Kaṭaṭṭanād Raja. The semi-independent Nampiārs, the nobility of the Kōlaṭṭiri, had to be brought round to consent to this. The Chief of Tellichery assented to the proposal, as he thought that this would give him an opportunity to counteract the French influences, but Mr. Byfeld had to give place to Mr. Thomas Dorril as Chief in January 1750, and the new Chief being a weak and narrow-minded man, a change for the worse came over the management of the Company's affairs at Tellicherry. Mr. Dorril fell out with the Prince Regent and set his face against the design of providing the Prince's son with an appenage, and, what was more serious, the factors openly acknowledged an elder Prince of the line as the proper person to rule by virtue of his age. The Nampiārs at once took sides. The *de facto* Prince Regent, finding himself thrown over by the English, naturally turned to the French for assistance. Mr. Dorril then took the extraordinary step of placing himself in communication with the Kōlaṭṭiri Raja himself, " a frail old man, who had no power in the country." Mr. Dorril persuaded the old man to supersede the Prince Regent by appointing a junior by name Ambu Ṭampān to his place. The English Chief on proceeding to have an interview with the elder Prince *regnant*, the latter abruptly withdrew within his fort and prepared to fire on the Chief's party. The Chief's guard opened fire at this threat. It was returned from the fort, and the Chief withdrew to Valaṛpaṭṭaṇam, where he got information that the *de facto* Prince Regent was advancing with an army against him. The Chief withdrew to Māṭakkara and was again fired at. Incensed at this, Mr. Dorril took the aged Kōlaṭṭiri and Ambu Ṭampān prisoners and carried them away to Tellichery.

The whole country now stood up against the English Chief who, finding no friend nearer home, turned towards Bednore. He advised the Canarese Governor of Mangalore to at once seize Nīlīśvaram. This was on the 7th of July. But, before the Governor could move, he was forestalled by the French, who hoisted their flag at Nīlīśvaram on the 17th of July and were busy fortifying the mouth of the Kavvāyi river. On the 25th of September, the Prince Regent visited

Māhe and was received with a salute. Even before this, he had assumed the aggressive, and the contests that ensued were mostly unfavourable to the English. By the end of the month, matters assumed a rather serious turn, and Mr. Dorril, as already observed, turned to Bednore for help. The Company's Canarese linguist, Antonio Pires, negotiated two treaties which, however, were of little use except that these prevented the French from concluding terms with Bednore. Mr. Dorril succeeded, however, in creating a split in the Prince Regent's camp by drawing off the Kōṭṭayam Raja, with whom a treaty was concluded. Soon after, the Prince Regent laid seige to the Māṭakkara fort, and the Morakkum redoubt within the Tellicherry limits was also attacked. The fight was kept up for sometime; meanwhile, the Raja of Kōṭṭayam was mediating between the parties. In December, the Canarese met with a severe reverse which had the effect of putting off negotiations for some time more. On the 19th of March 1752, the French attacked Māṭakkara fort. The duel continued up to the 13th of May. A week later, an armistice was concluded and, on the following day, the terms of peace were ratified by the Prince Regent. These consisted of two parts: those that were mentioned in the written engagement and those that were privately arranged. The terms of the written deed were, for the most part, very general. The Hon'ble Company and the Kōlaṭṭiri Princes were not to meddle in each other's affairs, the grants of the Company being confirmed. They were to give each other mutual assistance if attacked. Those that did not appear in the treaty itself were:—Rs. 50,000 was paid to the Prince Regent as compensation, and Rs. 10,000 to Kōṭṭayam for mediation. Māṭakkara fort was, given back to the Prince Regent, and the Prince was on his part, to destroy his redoubts on the outskirts of Tellicherry on the hills of Andolla, Ponolla and Putinha. Mr. Dorril objected to the insertion of these terms in the treaty, because they were disadvantageous to the Hon'ble Company, and because the Prince did not wish to have the facts entered on his records[1].

Mr. Dorril still conspired against the Prince Regent. He brought about a combination of the country powers consisting of the Zamorin, Kōṭṭayam Raja and the Iruvaḷinād Nampiārs; and his object was "to ward against the growing power of the Prince Regent (Kōlaṭṭiri) and Kaṭaṭṭanād backed by the French." The Prince's offer to visit Mr. Dorril at the English Factory was declined, but he was received with open arms by the French at Māhe. In 1753, Kaṭaṭṭanād commenced hostilities against the Iruvaḷinād Nampiārs, and the Prince desired very much to go to his brother-in-law's assistance; but the English factors and the Kōṭṭayam Raja effectually blocked the way. He once more endeavoured to make friends with Mr. Dorril and went to the factory on the 17th of November 1753.

On the 3rd of January 1754, a Commission arrived from Bombay to enquire into Mr. Dorril's administration, which completed its enquiry by the 15th of March, on which date Mr. Thomas Hodges, one of the Commissioners, took charge of the office of Chief from Mr. Dorril.

In the quarrels between the English and the French which resulted in war, the Prince Regent intervened in favour of the latter and arranged that, if Maṭṭalāi fort were restored to the French, they would evacuate Nīlīśvaram and some other places, and the Prince Regent was to be recompensed by the return of his bond for Rs. 60,000 advanced to him by the French in the war with the Tellicherry factors. The Prince Regent guaranteed on oath that the French would perform their part of the contract and surrender Nīlīśvaram and other places. On the 22nd of July 1756, Maṭṭalāi was restored to them: but they deliberately broke their promises of evacuating Nīlīśvaram

1 *Malabar*, p. 391.

and other places and of returning the Prince Regent's bond to him. This, as remarked by Mr. Logan, was not unnaturally the turning point in the Prince Regent's friendship with the French.

Mr. Hodges set himself about attempting to come to a reconciliation with the Prince Regent. Disgusted at the conduct of the French, the Prince paid a visit to the Chief at which the Prince promised to assist the factors against the French. At a subsequent visit paid by Mr. Hodges to the Prince, on the 21st of April 1757, the agreement was reduced to writing.

The Prince Regent died in May, and there were, as usual, disputes about the succession, which led to misunderstandings. The Chief put forward the Vaṭakkeḷamkūr or Northern Regent in opposition to a junior prince named Uṇṇāman who had married the late Prince Regent's daughter and who was, therefore, likely to fall under the influence of the French, who were the friends of his uncle-in-law, the Raja of Kaṭattanād. A combination of the Northern Regent, the Kōṭṭayam Raja and the Āli Raja of Cannanore was formed. Hostilities commenced on the 23rd of September, the allied forces ousting Prince Uṇṇāman from place after place. Prince Uṇṇāman sued for peace. By the 17th of October, the Northern Regent was in full possession of the country, and he, in return for the services rendered him, transferred "for ever" to the Honourable Company the "whole right of collecting the customs in all places in our dominions" for the sum of 21,000 silver faṇams to be paid annually.

In the meanwhile, complications had arisen between the English and the French. The French fort of Māhe was invested and, on the 3rd of February 1762, M. Lovet, the Chief, was called on to surrender the place. He refused, and a siege proceeded. On the 9th, the French delivered over all their forts in the north except Mount Deli and Ramdilly to prince Kāppu Ṭampān, a recalcitrant member of the Kōlaṭṭiri family. On the 13th, Māhe surrendered, and three days after, Major Hector Munro proceeded towards the north to recover the French forts in the possession of Kāppu Ṭampān. By the 19th of March, he was able to accomplish his task, though after some severe fighting. He then demolished them, as their retention was of no great use for the Company's trade in those parts.

On the 11th of March 1761, the Kōlaṭṭiri Regent had written to the Chief to say that the Āli Raja of Cannanore had given the greatest affront possible to the Hindu religion by putting up a golden spire on the top of one of his mosques, it being contrary to their established rules to have a spire of gold on any edifice throughout the Coast except on the principal pagodas; and only those of Ṭalippaṟampa, "Turukacoonoṭu", in Kōṭṭayam and "Urpyachy Cauvil at Agarr" were entitled to the distinction. War ensued. The Factors interfered only to mediate, and a hollow peace was patched up between the parties on the 28th of August 1762.

It was now time for Hyder Ali to appear on the Malabar arena. On the 8th of October 1764, the Nawab sent his emissary, Ananṭa Row, with a letter to the English Chief. Ananṭa Row intimated that it was his master's intention to invade Malabar, and that he expected the English not to oppose him in his conquest of the Kōlaṭṭiri, the Zamorin, the Cochin and other Rajas of Malabar. Upon this, the Chief invited Hyder Ali to enter into a previous engagement with the Company.

Āli Raja of Cannanore, in view of the impending invasion, proceeded to better himself by siding with the irreconcilable party of Kāppu Ṭampān in the Kōlaṭṭiri family. The Prince Regent applied to the Factors, and they tried to bring Āli Raja to reason, but without much success; for notwithstanding his previous engagement to give back what he had unjustly seized and not to interfere further in Kōlaṭṭunāḍ affairs, the war went on, and on the 18th of August 1765, the Ramdilly (Aïikkunnu) fort was taken by a party sent from Tellicherry under Captain Lytton Leslie, to aid the Prince Regent. The irreconcilables under Prince Ambu Ṭampān still kept the field, and it was in ostensible aid of this prince and also to collect an old Bednore debt of 20,000 pagodas due by the Kōlaṭṭiri, Hyder having conquered Bednore, that the Nawab eventually crossed the frontiers. Another avowed object was to recover the subsidy due by the Zamorin under an arrangement with Mysore consequent on Hyder being invited by the Palghat Raja to aid him against an attack by the Zamorin, of which mention has already been made.

When the English Factors heard of this event, two members of the Tellicherry Board were sent under orders of the Bombay Government to Hyder Ali's camp "to point out to him what powers were in alliance with the Company and should not be molested". But, when it came to the execution of "a grant" at Māṭāyi on the 23rd of February 1766, the Factors did not discreetly press the inclusion of a clause stipulating that these allies should be let alone and not molested. They satisfied themselves with securing the ratification of "all the several Grants and Privileges made over to them by the several Malabar Powers." They took care also to obtain a "promise to grant and confirm the same wheresoever my arms may prove victorious." Thus, in the presence of the most formidable enemy the Malabar Rajas had ever to encounter, the Honourable English Company threw them overboard, crippled as they were by the exhausting wars they had already to fight. And this was done in spite of the many engagements entered into by the Company, specially with the rulers of Kōlaṭṭunāḍ, that "if any enemy whatsoever come against the said princes of Cherica (i. e., the

Kōlaṭṭiri of the time), the Honourable Company is to assist them against such enemy to the utmost of their power as formerly practised and observed." 1

While negotiations were still progressing, on the 21st of February, the factors heard that Hyder's force had taken possession of a temple, probably that of Kuññimangalam and had laid seige to Māṭāi, which the officer in command offered to deliver up. Hyder would, however, consent only to an unconditional surrender. On the following day, news came that the fort had been evacuated.

Forsaken by their friends on whose support they had calculated in the hour of danger and abandoned to the enemy who had given "a general instruction to his army to grant no quarter," the Kōlaṭṭiri family made no resistance. Simultaneously with Hyder's advance, the Āli Raja and his men seized their palace at Chiṙakkal, and the old Ṭekkelamkūr prince with his attendants flew to take refuge at the Brass Pagoda within Tellicherry limits. They were followed by numerous other refugees. Hyder objected to the protection given by the English to those who were flying before him. The Bombay Government kept on counselling the adoption of a conciliatory policy, which, of course, meant that the Malabar Rajas in their last extremity were not to be assisted in terms of treaty stipulations. Hyder kept on steadily and did not show much respect for the English Company. The Company's territories themselves were threatened, and then came the order from Bombay, when it was too late, to repel force by force; and that only *if the invaders attempted to pass the Tellicherry limits, or to invade the Company's immediate property.* Still the factors were not to lend a helping hand to their allies, the Malabar Rajas. Hyder soon overran the territories of the Kōlaṭṭiri, the Zamorin and the other Malabar Rajas. Upon the Zamorin, he heaped such enormous indignities that it is said that he set fire to his palace and perished in its flames.

Having accomplished this, he called on the Rajas of Cochin and Travancore through the Dutch Commissioners who met Hyder at Calicut to acknowledge his suzerainty. The Dutch pleaded hard for the Rajas. Hyder agreed not to molest Cochin on certain conditions, but he would guarantee nothing in regard to Travancore. As there was delay in replying to Hyder's proposals, he modified his terms somewhat and demanded four lakhs of rupees and eight elephants from Cochin and 15 lakhs and 20 elephants from Travancore, in default of receiving which, he said, he meant to visit those countries. Cochin placed itself unreservedly in the hands of the Dutch, but Travancore replied that Hyder had not commenced the invasion of Malabar to please the Raja or with his advice. Both the Rajas, however, said that they were willing to contribute something towards his war expenses, *if he would reinstate the Kolattiri and the Zamorin Rajas in their dominions*. This was indeed remarkable, seeing that the Zamorin had only so recently as 1761 invaded Cochin and deprived the Raja of a great part of his territories, and that it was with the aid of Travancore that the Zamorin was finally driven out of Cochin. Cochin eventually obtained immunity from invasion by agreeing to pay an annual subsidy of two lakhs of rupees and eight elephants.

Hyder had now to go back to Mysore, and so he secured his new possessions by means of fortified posts and proceeded eastwards, leaving behind him the Āli Raja at the head of a moveable column of 3,000 Māppilās at Calicut and Madanna as Civil Governor of the province of Malabar. At Māṭakkara, he left Raza Sahib in quarters with 3,000 infantry. Āli Raja's brother, Sheik Ali, was left Military Governor of Kōlaṭṭunād.

No sooner had Hyder turned his back against Malabar, the Nāyars rose in revolt *en masse*. The attempt was so secretly organised and executed that before information could reach him in his camp, his forces were driven back and his stronghold captured one after another. Retribution, of course, followed and that with a vengeance. Hyder once more established his power in Malabar.

The Āli Raja failed to pay the stipulated tribute and, towards 1757, the Prince Regent of Chemkal (Kōlaṭṭuṅād) was allowed to rule over his territory but with a Mysorean officer to administer the revenues. The Prince Regent, while continuing to be friendly with the English Factors and supplying them as usual with pepper, administered the country under Mysore.

The recognition of American independence by France brought on a war between the English and the French, and Pondicherry was captured by the English on the 18th of October 1778. Soon after this, Māhe was threatened. As Hyder used to obtain his military supplies through that port, its reduction would have cut him off from his base of supplies; so, though not yet prepared to break off with the English, Hyder ordered the Prince Regent of Kōlaṭṭuṅād to join the French at Māhe with 1,500 Nāyars. Similar orders were given to the Rajas of Kaṭaṭṭanād and Kōṭṭayam and the Zamorin. But the Tellicherry factors had exerted their very best to secure the alliance of these chiefs. The Prince Regent of Kōlaṭṭuṅād alone joined the French as ordered by Hyder. In the hostilities that ensued, Kōlaṭṭuṅād did not fare well. He found all his neighbours opposed to him, and the Prince effected his retreat from Māhe through Nittur after suffering defeat from Kōṭṭayam and sustaining considerable loss. The Prince returned, however, to the Kōṭṭayam country after joining the Mysorean officer, Bulwant Row, dispersed the Kōṭṭayam force and proceeded to Kaṭaṭṭanād, where the senior Raja who was an adherent of the English was deposed in favour of a young prince. The war that followed between the English and Hyder and which was

AC.

continued by Tippu after his father's death, need not detain us, as the Kōlaṭṭiri had not much to do in connection with it. Though still a vassal of Tippu, the reigning Kōlaṭṭiri appears to have joined in 1782 General Mathew's forces. All the Malabar Rajas, such as those of Kōṭṭayam, Kaṭaṭṭanāḍ and the Zamorin, not to mention the minor ones, had stood steadfast allies and friends of the English during the war. On the 11th of March 1784, peace was concluded between the English and Tippu, and, notwithstanding the strenuous efforts of the Tellicherry factors, no mention was made in the treaty of the Malabar chiefs and, what was more strange, the peace plenipotentiaries, Messrs. Staunton and Huddleston, explained this by saying that they have been included by Tippu among *his* "Friends and Allies."

Towards the beginning of 1788, Tippu set up the Kōlaṭṭiri, or as he came now to be called the Chiṙakkal Raja, to put forward pecuniary claims against th Tellicherry factory. On the 27th of May, the Prince de manded a settlement of accounts and presented a claim for one lakh of rupees, though, according to the factors, he was indebted to them to the extent of four lakhs. The Prince sent his minister with instructions to remain at Tellicherry till the amount was paid. The English Chief stopped the minister's "diet money," and the minister after protest departed. On the 7th of June, the Prince occupied the Ḍhaṙmapaṭṭaṇam island which had been in the Company's undisputed possession since 1733. Three years previously, he had occupied the Randattara district over which the Company had a mortgage. Soon after the occupation of the Ḍhaṙmapaṭṭaṇam island, the Chiṙakkal Prince was accorded an honourable and flattering reception by Tippu at Coimbatore. The prince was sent back with orders to molest the English. His nephew was appointed by Tippu Governor of Iruvaḷināḍ and Kuṙamgōt.

The Prince accordingly proposed to seize Mīncara on the south-east of Tellicherry. But this was frustrated by his sudden death at Palghautchery on his way back from Coimbatore. His brother and successor was not inclined to be aggressive against the factors. Between July and December, the Nāyars once more revolted against the authority of Tippu, and the tide of religious persecution rolled over the length and breadth of the land.

On December 23rd, the Chief demanded from the Raja of Chiṙakkal the restitution of Ḍhaṙmapaṭṭaṇam island within 10 days, failing compliance with which he said, "I shall be under the necessity, conformably to my orders, to resume possession of the said island by force." No heed was taken of this threat and, on the appointed day, the factors took possession of the island by force, the Prince's Nāyars giving it up without any resistance. The Chief then intimated that he was now ready to come to liberal adjustment of accounts with the Raja.

While matters were so, Tippu's marauders came upon the country like an avalanche crushing everything before them. Malabar was offered the honour of Islam. Thousands and thousands were forcibly converted and compelled to eat beef, the highest sin a Hindu can commit; 30,000 Brahmans with their families took refuge in Travancore, where they were entertained at great expense. All the Malabar Rajas fled to find a safe asylum there. On the 22nd of March, the Chiṙakkal Raja claimed the protection of the factors of Tellicherry. But his recent conduct with regard to the district of Randattara and the island of Ḍhaṙmapaṭṭaṇam was made a pretext to refuse him admission within the Company's limits. The English feared that, if he were admitted, the whole force of Tippu would be directed against them. The next day, the Raja's sister and the rest of the family came in uninvited to the island and prayed for protection. They would not listen to any refusal and continued to be there for two days. Being pressed again to leave the island, they set sail in a boat to Travancore in the night on the day following. Some 10 to 15 thousand Nāyars with their families had followed them to the island, which was crowded with refugees by the evening of the 26th of March; but during that night, after their chief's family had sailed, "they most mysteriously disappeared and the Commanding Officer of the island, who had received orders to send them away, found, to his surprise on the morning of the 27th, that they had already gone."

There are different accounts of what befell their unhappy prince. Wilks says that he "had been induced by the most sacred promises to pay his personal respects to the Sultan, and was for several days treated with considerable distinction, and dismissed with costly presents to his little principality." But after his departure, malign influences came into play; he was accused of a secret conspiracy to revenge the cruel indignities committed on his country-men; two brigades were sent to take him; his attendants prepared to defend themselves; and, in a skirmish, he was killed. The Tellichery Factory Diary records that "he was killed in attempting to escape." Another account says he shot himself on finding that escape was hopeless. However that may be, it is certain from Tippu's own account as well as from the Factory Diary record, that his body was treated with the greatest indignities by Tippu. He had it dragged by elephants through his camp, and it was subsequently hung up on a tree along with 17 of the followers of the prince, who had been captured alive.

The tension between the English and Tippu was becoming greater and greater every day. Passing southwards, Tippu visited Cannanore, made friends with the Bībi and solemnized the preliminary ceremonies of a marriage between the Bībi's daughter and one of his sons, Abdul Khalic, and handed over to the Bībi a portion of the Chiṙakkal district. He then passed on still to the south, his mind being bent on the conquest of Travancore. The attack on the Travancore lines, in the beginning of January 1790, was the signal for a declaration of war between the Honourable East India Company and the Sultan. The Malabar Rajas and their Nāyars were invited to take part, and they at once flocked to the standard of the Company and, in the arrangements made with them, Mr. Taylor, the Chief of the Tellicherry factory, on the 4th of May, assured, under his hand and seal, the Chiṙakkal Raja who is styled as "Reviwarma, King of the house of Pallikulam of the Kingdom of Colastri," that, if he heartily entered into the war against Tippu and fulfilled his contracts for supplies granted to him, he would, in any future treaty with that prince, "be included and considered as an ally of the Honourable Company." The war with Tippu was vigorously conducted by the Governor-General, Lord Cornwallis, himself taking the field at the head of a powerful army having the Nizam and the Maharattas for his allies. On the 16th of February 1792, the allies effected a junction under the walls of Seringapatam and, on the 22nd, Tippu was forced to yield submission. By the treaty that was subsequenly concluded, on the 18th of March 1792, Tippu ceded Malabar to the English East India Company.

On the 4th of May, a temporary arrangement was entered into between the Raja and the government of Bombay for the future Government of the country. The Raja's administration proved unsatisfactory. The revenue payable to the Company fell into arrears. There were quarrels in the family, some of the junior members openly revolted, and the authority of the Company had to be used to reduce them to submission. The exactions of the Raja created much discontent and. on the 18th of October 1799, on the expiration of the lease under which the Raja had held the district, the Honourable Company assumed its direct administration.

The family is paid an allowance or as it is termed a *Malikhana* (Mālikhāna) of Rs. 24,000 per annum, which is still paid.

Before closing this note, it is necessary to point ont that the old name of the dynasty, Kōlaṭṭiri, has become well nigh forgotten. We have seen that there had been a split in the family at the time of the Bednore invasion (1733—40). Soon after the treaty with the Bednore Raja, under which a portion of the kingdom had to be ceded to him, the Kōlaṭṭiri had conferred heirship on "Odeorman of the Palace of Palli," and ever since the Princes of this Palli branch of the family had been recognised as having taken the place of the head of the family—Kōlaṭṭiri. In fact, the Uḍayamangalam branch had been shut out from the Kōlaṭṭiri sovereignty altogether, though one of that branch, if the eldest in age of all the branches, could still claim the empty title of Kōlaṭṭiri. The title having fallen into disuse, the ruling family, the Palli branch, gradually began to be known as that of Chirakkal from the Kōvilakam of that name, which was the head-quarters of that branch of the family. The Palli branch claimed "such part of the kingdom as had not been dismembered" by the Bednore Raja and, as the ruling family, they obtained and still enjoy Rs. 23,500 out of the Rs. 24,000 Mālikhāna allowance from the British Government. The remaining 500 is enjoyed by the Uḍayamangalam branch.

48. **Cananoor.** Directly after the capture of Cochin, the Dutch proceeded to Cannanore. They found that place well-fortified, especially on the side facing the sea, so that it was deemed advisable to make an attack principally on the land side. The town was without walls, but the fortress was strongly built. A force was landed, and an attack immediately commenced, but the cannon balls made only a slight impression on the walls of the fort. After the seige had been carried on for some days, the Portuguese commander, having heard of the fall of Cochin, and entertaining no

reasonable hope of relief, capitulated to the enemy on the 13th of February 1663. Most of the Portuguese garrison retired to Goa, and Antonio Cardosa, who had been Commander of Cannanore, was decapitated by order of the Viceroy for having, in his judgment, surrendered the fortress without reasonable cause or excuse.

Soon after the loss of Cannanore, news arrived that peace had been concluded between the States-General and the king of Portugal. The treaty had been signed on the 6th of August 1661, and was ratified by the king of Portugal and the States-General on the 24th of May and 4th of December 1662, respectively. On the ground that the towns and fortresses of Cochin and Cannanore had been captured subsequently to the signing of the treaty, the return of those places was afterwards claimed by the Portuguese from the Dutch; to which, however, the latter replied that hostilities only ceased when both parties had assented to and ratified the treaty, the publication of which did not take place till the 14th of March 1663. This question was again raised in 1666 by the Portuguese Ambassador to Holland, but he was unable to obtain any satisfaction for Portugal.'[1]

If the above statement of events is correct, one fails to see wherein lay the craft of the Dutch referred to by our author. It might be that Antonio Cardosa was induced by 'craft' to surrender the place, and his execution by the Viceroy certainly lends colour to our author's statement.

49. **Balenor.** This is the territory of Kaṭaṭṭanād whose ruler was known as 'Balenor' a corruption of the Malayālam word Vāḷuṅṅavar, or "one who rules or governs"—a governor. The territory extended from Māhe to Vaṭakara. Its extent was three kāṭams and it had a force of 3,000 Nāyars. Its capital city was Kuṟṟippuṟam. We have already referred to the origin of the family which is said to have been established there in A. D. 1564. The Tellicherry Factory Diary

1. Danvers, *Portuguese in India*, Vol. II, p. 329.

records : "The Kings(Kōlaṭṭiris) heretofore appointed a governor in Cartua Nadu, but some few years before the French settled at Māhe, the Governor (called Boyanore) paid little regard to the present king (Kōlaṭṭiri) who was then also embarassed on the war."

Hamilton speaks of "Ballanore Burgarie" as "a formidable Prince. His country produces Pepper and the best Cardammoms in the World." Hamilton appears to have visited the Prince in January 1703. "This Prince and his predecessors," says he, "have been Lords of the sea, time out of mind and all trading vessels between Cape Comorin and Daman were obliged to carry his Passes. Those of one Mast paid for their Passes about 8 shillings yearly, and those with three paid about sixteen, but when the Portuguese settled in India, then they pretended to the sovereignty of the seas which occasioned a War between him and them that has lasted ever since. He keeps some light Gallies that row and sail very well, which cruize along the Coast from October to May to make Prize of all who have not his Pass. In our discourse I asked him if he was not afraid to venture his person on board of a Merchant ship since he himself was an enemy of all merchants that traded on these Coasts. He answered that he had heard of my character, and that made him fearless and that he was no enemy to trade, but only vindicated the sovereignty of those seas before-mentioned, and that our own King was invested with the like sovereignty not only on his own Coastes but on those of France, Holland and Denmark and could have no greater right than he had, only he was in a better position to oblige transgressors of his Laws to obedience than he was. However he would maintain his claim and right the best way he could, and whoever lost their ships or vessels for contempt of his authority might blame their own obstinacy or folly and not him." On parting with Hamilton he gave him a bracelet and made him "a free Denizen in all his Territories." Of the extent of this Prince's territory, Hamilton says: "I do not certainly know how far southerly this Prince's Dominions reach along the sea Coast, but I believe to Tecorie (Ṭṛkkoṭi) about 12 miles from Meali (Māhe) and in the half way is Cottica (Kōṭṭakkal), which was famous formerly for privateering on all ships and vessels that traded without their Lord's Pass."

It is not necessary to dwell upon the history of this Prince, for it is of a piece with that of other Malabar principalities—internecine quarrels, wars eternal with neighbouring princes, concessions to foreign nations, disagreements with them, alliance with the Portuguese, the Dutch and the English in turn, quarrels with them, the Mysorean invasion, flight to Travancore, war between the English and Mysore, return from Travancore and joining the English, cession by Mysore to the English, revenue leases and engagements with the English, the falling of the revenue into arrears and final assumption by the English and settlement of a Mālikhāna allowance in perpetuity of one-fifth of the land revenue on the family. Kaṭaṭṭanād also had the common lot and is now receiving an annual allowance of Rs. 26,441.

50. **Perreveacocil.** This is Puṙavālya Kōvil or Puṙanāṭṭukara Raja, i. e. the Raja of Kōṭṭayam, or as it is called by European writers, "Cotiote." His territory was formerly a part of Kōlaṭṭunād. The Raja is styled Puṙanāṭṭu, because his family is believed to be a foreign Kṣheṭṙiya-Rajaput—Puṙanāṭṭ in Malayālam means a foreign country. Kōṭṭayam differed from ordinary Malabar families in not theoretically recognising the eldest female as the head of the family. They held independently, as it seems, of the Kōlaṭṭiris the country lying inland from Tellicherry, and their influence extended still further inland over the mountainous jungly country of Wynād. The family is divided into three Kōvilakams or branches, called respectively the Eastern, Western and Southern, from the position which their

AD.

chief dwelling places occupied round the big tank at Kōṭṭayam. Their three dignities (*Stanams*) are:—Mūṭṭa, (2) Eḷaya and (3) Mūṅṅāmkūr Rajas. The family is alleged originally to have received their territory from the Kōlaṭṭiri. This event took place centuries ago, and, when the English settlement was formed at Tellicherry, "the Cotiote" was one of the first with whom the Company came into formal relations. He steadily supported the English in the wars with Hyder and Tippu, first in 1780—82 and again in 1791—92. On the cession of Malabar to the British in 1792, some unfortunate misunderstandings arose, and the Paḷaṣṣi or Pychy Raja, the *de facto* head of the house, rose in rebellion against the English and maintained a sort of independence for some time. The joint Commissioners had made the initial mistake of leasing his territory to an uncle of his, the Kuṙumbaṙṅād Raja, who had no right to or influence in the district Naturally the Paḷaṣṣi Raja resented. The mistake was repeated, which led the chief to openly revolt against the Company and, in November 1795, his conduct seemed to Mr. Richards to be "distinguished by a contempt for all authority." He succeeded in completely setting aside the authority of his uncle of Kuṙumbaṙṅād. An attempt was made to seize the Raja in his house by Lieutenant James Gordon at the head of 300 men who surrounded it on the morning of the 19th of April. To his great chagrin, Lieutenant Gordon found that the bird had already flown away. Finding it unsafe to loiter in the low country, the Raja retired into the mountains along with his family in May 1796. Later on, he wrote to Colonel Dow in whom he seemed to have confidence a penitent letter and offered to surrender on promise of pardon. Though the Commissioners were not agreeable to this, Col. Dow promised the Raja an "act of oblivion." He returned and was conducted to Paḷaṣṣi by Lieutenant Walker and his property, except the treasure carried away from his house, was restored. He gave security for his future good behaviour pending the final orders of the Government. In due time, the orders of the Bombay Government came ratifying the pardon given by Col. Dow and approving his reinstatement. The "restoration to his district and property' was distinctly ordered. But strangely enough, these orders were not communicated to the Paḷaśśi Raja direct. They were sent through his adversary, the Raja of Kuṛumbaṛnād whose agents omitted both to communicate them to the Raja and to pay over to him the money taken at the sack of his house, which the Government had ordered to be restored to him. The Raja, of course, felt himself deceived. A majority of the Commissioners were determinedly set against him. So he suspected that a fresh attempt would be made to secure his person, which might be successful. He, therefore, thought it prudent to keep away and "retired to the most impenetrable part of the jungle."

The orders of the Bombay and supreme Governments regarding his restoration had by this time reached the Raja and the Northern Superintendent, and the Commissioners felt that something should be done in the matter. They resorted to the expediency of referring to Government as to what was meant by the "doubtful phrase" "restoration to his districts and property," though the meaning of the Government was clear enough that the Kuṛumbaṛnād Raja should be made to disgorge all that he had obtained by false pretences. Meanwhile, troops were sent to Wynād to protect the ingathering of the cardamom crop, and this appears to have excited the gravest suspicion of the excited Raja.

The Northern Superintendent arranged a meeting with the Raja to arrive at an amicable settlement. The Raja came to it attended by 1,200 to 1,500 armed men. A week's conference ended in nothing; for the

Superintendent's aim was to bring about a reconciliation between the rival Rajas. It is said that nothing resulted because of "duplicity" on the one side and "intolerable insolence" on the other. The Superintendent could very well have foreseen that the sturdy independent spirit of the Palaśśi chief will be met by the duplicity of the Kuṙumbaṙnād Raja, which was the sole means by which he had ingratiated himself with the English authorities. After this failure at negotiations, matters drifted from bad to worse. The Commissioners wrote to the Raja that "not a sepoy shall rest in this province till you and all your adherents are utterly extirpated." His subjects were informed that, unless they threw up allegiance to him within 15 days, they would be considered as "irreconcilable enemies of the Company's Government, their lands and property will be immediately confiscated, never again to be restored, and the Raja and his friends, pursued to their utter extirpation from the Company's dominions." Once more, an attempt was made at reconciliation. On the 30th of December, the Raja met the President of the Commissioners and pressed for the fulfilment of the order restoring him. Once more was this just request refused, as his rival, the Kuṙumbaṙnād Raja, would not agree.

The Commissioners then proceeded to overrun the district by a display of force and directed the Superintendent to act on the proclamation already mentioned. Thus was the gauntlet thrown, and the Raja did not hesitate to pick it up. The fight was bravely kept up by the rebel chief who inflicted reverse after reverse on the Company's forces. It assumed such a serious aspect as to call forth the energies of the Duke of Wellington, then Colonel Wellesley. Of course, the Raja and his adherents could not be expected to hold out for long. At last in 1805, driven from place to place, deserted by most of his people, and having no means of subsistence and hiding in the jungles, this the almost only Raja in Malabar who had the temerity to raise his arm against the English East India Company was effectually cornered by Mr. Baber, Sub-Collector of the Northern Division of Malabar. On the 30th of November, he wrote to Government that "this forenoon, after having been out 15 hours, I had the good fortune to come up with the Cotiote Kerala Varma Raja *alias* the Pyche (Paḷaśśi) Raja, and with the assistance of Captain Claphan and 50 sepoys and 100 kōlkārs (armed peons) to chastise the rebel chieftain, by destroying him and five of his followers, one of whom was the notorious and proscribed rebel leader of Cotiote (Kōṭṭayam) Aralet Cooty Nampiār." With what difficulty the final consummation was effected becomes clear, when we see that it required 50 sepoys of the regular army and 100 irregulars under the command of a Captain assisted by Mr. Baber as Civil Officer to hunt down the fugitive chief and five of his followers. One cannot help remarking that, but for the obstinacy of the Commissioners and the Northern Superintendent, and their persistence in perpetrating an act of utter injustice, in spite of the repeated endeavours of the Raja to compose all differences, this brave chieftain might have continued a sturdy and ardent supporter of the Honourable East India Company.

Leaving the Paḷaśśi branch to its fate, the Company had made arrangements with other branches of the family, and, on the 26th of December 1797, the senior Raja, "Ravy Varma of Kawanchey Culote" agreed to accept a monthly allowace of rupees 500, the Company undertaking to settle allowances for the junior Rajas. The Kōṭṭayam family now draws an allowance of Rs. 5,900 in all.

Before concluding this note, it will be interesting to cite here the terms of a treaty that terminated a war between the Kaṭaṭṭanāḍ and the Kōṭṭayam Rajas as a specimen of the arrangements made by the Native

Powers during those times. The peace was negotiated by Mr. Adams, the English agent of Tellicherry, as mediator. The terms demanded by Kōṭṭayam and accepted by Kaṭaṭṭanād were these: (1) the districts of "Bellata" with absolute command thereof to be delivered to the former; (2) an elephant to be given to Tellicherry pagoda by the latter with an offering of butter tied round its neck; (3) a piece of ground and a house for Brahmans to be given up by the latter; and (4) a house in the latter's country to be burnt.

51. **Welliapatam**. Valaṙpaṭṭaṇam. This was the residence of the Kōlaṭṭiri after Māṭāyi had been forsaken. Mr. Logan says that this port has a fair amount of coasting trade. Craft of considerable size enter the river of the same name and take in the country produce brought to market at Valaṙpaṭṭaṇam by the rivers Valaṙpaṭṭaṇam and Ṭalipparamba which here unite their streams.

52. **Marravy**. This is the town of Māṭāyi, or more correctly, Māṭaēli, the third most ancient of the king's houses of the northern Kōlaṭṭiris. It is said to have been built by Māṭan Perumāl or the Bouḍha king Naśanga of the Kēraḷa Māhāṭmyam as his capital. It is in the immediate vicinity of Paḷayangāṭi or old bazaar. The word has been spelt in various ways: *Murawee*, *Marabia*, *Maravia*, *Maravi*, etc.

53. **Kurumbarnad**. Our author does not profess to give the names of all principalities in Malabar. It would certainly have been difficult for him to do this; for there were so many of them that as the Malayāḷam saying goes: " Every second step would take you to a separate chiefship. " There were, however, some principalities which were of sufficient importance to deserve mention, such as those of Kuṙumbaṙnād and Vaḷḷuvanād, both in South Malabar, under the suzerainty of the Zamorin,

We have already given an account of Valluvanād, and here we shall try to give a short account of Kuṙumbaṙṅād.

The Kuṙumbaṙṅād, literally the country of the Kuṙumbar, was subject to the Kuṙumbaṙṅād family connected with that of Kōṭṭayam. It consisted of parts of the modern Tālūks of Kuṙumbaṙṅād and Calicut. The family is said to be of Kṣheṭṙiya descent and was in alliance with the Zamorin. They were at one time very influential, having at command 30,000 Nāyars whom they could bring into the field. They are now, and have been for some considerable time, in impoverished circumstances. The head of the family is styled Kuṙumpaṙāṭiri or Kuṙumpyāṭiri and had, as his official property, the Rāmangalaṭṭ Kōvilakam with a residence at Nankot. The family is divided into two branches, viz:—(1) Mēkollaśśēri with nine, and (2) Ṭuvayāṭṭ with three, subdivisions.

It is difficult to obtain any detailed information regarding the family. We have noticed elsewhere the account of a visit which Captain Alexander Hamilton paid to the then Raja. The Kuṙumbaṙṅād Rajas seem to have been always ready to go to the aid of the Zamorin, and we see the Raja personally leading his men on behalf of the Zamorin against the Portuguese. On the settlement of Malabar after its cession by Tippu, the British Commissioners had to deal with the Kuṙumbaṙṅād Chief's country. They dealt with one Vīra Vaṙma Raja who put himself forward as the Raja of Kuṙumbaṙṅād. Mr. Logan has the following note on the subject, which gives us some idea of the person who was the prime cause of the Palaśśi rebellion already referred to: "There are at least two contradictory accounts given of him in the records. That he belonged to the Kōṭṭayam family[1] originally is beyond doubt He seems, however, to have led the Joint Commissioners to understand that he had been adopted into

1. *Note* to Part I, XXVII.

the family of Kuṙumbaṙn̄ād proper and had succeeded by such adoption to the Raja of Kuṙumbaṙn̄ād; [1] whereas, some years later, on the 9th of August 1796, Colonel Dow seems to have satisfied himself that he was not Kuṙumbaṙan̄ād at all!! On that date, Colonel Dow wrote to the second Commissioner as follows:— 'It may be necessary here to remark that the person whom we commonly call the Coorimnad Raja is more properly the Raja of Cotiote and is considered in this relation by the country-people. He is the regular representative of the Cotiote family, whose ancestor obtained the Talook of Coorimnad for some services he performed to Rama Mungelah, the native Raja, about 10 years before Hyder's invasion. Here there is no invention of any adoption, and it seems improbable that any such adoption took place, for the Kuṙumbanad family proper is and has long been strong in numbers'. [2] Moreover, "Rama Mungelah, the native Raja", mentioned by Colonel Dow, evidently refers to the Rāmangalaṭṭ Kōvilagam or official property of the senior Raja of the true Kuṙumbaṙn̄ād family. And it may be suggested that Vīra Vaṙma was really the local representative of the Kōṭṭayam family in direct management of the tract of country ordinarily called Ṭāmaraśśēri[3] which was probably acquired by the Kōṭṭayam family from the Kuṙumbaṙn̄ād family in the manner described by Colonel Dow. The possession of this bit of Kuṙumbaṙn̄ād seems to have given colour to the title by which Vīra Vaṙma was known to the British authorities. Vīra Vaṙma appears to have been an intriguing sort of individual, always ready to grasp at personal advantage. It was probably in this way that he set himself in communication with Hyder Ali's General, Sirdar Khan, during the seige of Tellicherry (1779—82) with a view to the drawing off of his

1. *Joint Commissioner's Report* of 11th October 1793, paras 30 and 92.

2. See *Note* to Part II, *Supplementary* No. CCLXXXVIII.

3. See *Malabar*, Vol. I, p. 647.

uncle of Kōṭṭayam from the English alliance.[1] And it was certainly a self-seeking arrangement which he now[2] made with the Bombay Commissioners. They and the Bengal Commissioners who joined them subsequently found him to be a very convenient stalking-horse (so to speak) for bringing the Zamorin and the other Rajas to terms ; for he was apparently willing to accept the management of any districts *belonging to other people* on any terms, so long as these promised to be of advantage to himself personally. His subsequent engagements with the authorities[3] were all, more or less, entered into in this spirit, and his equivocal conduct must be regarded as having been mainly the cause of the very unfortunate estrangement between the British authorities and his high-spirited relative, the Paḷaṡṡi (Pychy) Raja, which ended in the rebellion and death of the latter."[4]

The Kuṙumbaṙnād Raja, like his brethren, is now in the pension list.

54. **Nayar Militia.** Our author does not seem to have furnished his correspondent, as promised in this letter, with "a list of the Nāyars, whom all the lords of Malabar, both small and great, retain in their service." Captain Alexander Hamilton has preserved a list of them. Hamilton says: "I have a list of them, as they were given in to the ingenious and curious Heer Van Rede, Commissory General for affairs of the Dutch East India Company in Anno 1694, who died off Bombay in his voyage to Surat.

"Each province can raise forces by its clans, as follows : —

Tipoposoriwars	*Men*
Terivancoa	100,000

1. *Joint Commissioner's Report*, Para 30.
2. Part II, Nos. VII and VIII.
3. Part II, XXXI, XLII, XLVII, LXXXIV, LXXXVI, XC, XCI, CXVII, CXVIII, CXXXVI, CLXXXII, CXCV.
4. *Malabar*, Vol. III, pp. 149—50.

Tipoposoriwars.		*Men*
Attinga	..	30,000
Eledasoriwan	..	50,000
Peritalie	..	3,000
Seigenatie	..	30,000
Teirewey	..	15,000
Odenadie Carree.		
Coilcolong	..	50,000
Pana Pollie	..	15,000
Martin Gallie	..	15,000
Carimbalie	..	15,000
Teiom Balanore Koilie	..	3,000
Reubanie Aregalie	..	3,000
Chitaw Canaar		
Tellicherry Baakie Elependre May Porombo	..	3,000
Dedamaadie Peneretta Moeterte Manka Polie	..	15,000
Perombara Corma		
Arregatte Calgampolie Mamalie Madome	..	15,000
Bambellendada.		
Kilpolie Chitway	..	75,000
Martingalie Coer	..	37,000
Tikellenore	..	37,000
Poonjatte Perumal	..	3,000
Cottenadie.		
Zembagacherry	..	30,000
Tesegidin Genatie.		
Elertecore	..	10,000
Moutere Coree	..	10,000
Ambada Coree	..	10,000
Rapolin		
Elengoly Serewan	..	5,000
Courour Nadie.		
Corour Mouta Coil	..	15,000
Billiatte Serewan	..	15,000

Badecancore.		*Men*
Manne Tellum	..	30,000
Moda Callic	..	3,000
Boy Pilcore	..	15,000
Kilmall core	..	15,000
Perimba Daponadie		
Martingaly Tavil	..	3,000
Moute Tavil	..	3,000
Palombe Tavil	..	3,000
Teilor Tavil	..	3,000
Ela Tavil	..	3,000
Tesieragatta Nadie.		
Teiragalle Caymaal	..	15,000
Padanarie erte Caymal	..	8,000
Pindereretol Nade		
Pinderetel Nambi Deri	..	15,000
Coil Pade	..	1,000
Mangela Nade		
Belatte Tavil	..	10,000
Carata Tavil	..	15,000
Nambouries, or Priests.		
Bay Pinade	..	6,000
Aaron Ade	..	2,000
Merinade Nambori	..	3,000
Nanderetti Nade.		
Coroseir Cymal	..	30,000
Cories Cymal	..	5,000
Siangrande Canmal	..	5,000
Panna Makettas Cymal	..	3,000
Tollapoli Nade.		
Amacotta Nambedi	..	15,000
Manacotta do	..	15,000
Cacatte do	..	15,000
Tistul do	..	15,000
Terratekin Nair	..	15,000

Nambiar; or Priests of the second order.		*Men.*
Relolaste Nambiar	..	3,000
Relo Canadarie	..	30,000
Erenaden Caree:		
Cannal Canadrie	..	40,000
Rete Coil	..	5,000
Paro Pachoil	..	3,000
Ropo Coil	..	2,000
Tomera Serinade.		
Iregale Nade, a priest of the first order	..	3,000
Candette Nayer	..	10,000
Omnitric	..	10,000
Palangier Nayer	..	3,000
Mangalacka	..	3,000
Dana Seirllicrda	..	10,000
Ramenatte Corie	..	15,000
Polletti Nade.		
Callistree Odirose Coilan, Palle Coilam, Zierck Coilan	..	23,000
Balianore Burgary	..	30,000
Tellicherry Mota Naire	..	15,000
Zitre Caymal Mar	..	30,000
Alarte Tere Cymal	..	30,000
Alarte Nade Adovodie	..	15,000
Paravia Coil	..	60,000
Bayella Nade.		
Mangalette Naire	..	1,000
Manetane do	..	do
Callepatte do	..	do
Teyka Patte do	..	do
Motrel do	..	do

"Making in all 1,262,009 men fit to carry arms."[1]

Our author arrived in Cochin in 1717, a few months before Councillor Extraordinary, William Bakkar Jacobtz, had been sent down to Cochin, where

1. Pinkerton's *Voyages and Travels*, Vol. VIII, pp. 366—7.

he arrived on the 28th of November 1716. One of his first acts was to send letters announcing his own arrival and that of Joannes Hertenberg to the powers of Malabar. The list of addresses given hereunder supplies us with a list of Malabar chiefs holding power during our author's time.

"To the Rajas of Porca, Repolim, Calicoilan, De Marta, Signatty, Travancore, Tekenkore, Berkenkore, Peritaly.

To the Ameens of Atinga, Cochin.

To the Rajas of Cartadavil, Ayrore, Palacatchery, Valuvanatty, Colastry, Cranganore.

To the Second Prince of Mangatty and of Bardella.

To the Pula of Bariatta, Gurip of Travancore, 7,000 of Carapuram, 30,000 of Cururndada, the Palyet, the 3,000 of Bypin, Codachery Caymil, Coratti Caymal, Changara Codda Caymil, Mangatta Atsjar, Torttachery Talachenore, Murianatty Nambiar.

To the Ayinicutty Nambeddy, Raja of Paru, Balanore of Baragara, Ade Raja of Cannanore, Cymal of Cunnattunadu, Tevengul Nairo, Parra Elledam, Palurgatty Cymal, Tachetta Munancur, Cymal of Anjecymal, Payencheri Nairs."

Commander Gollennesse, writing in 1743, notices the following Kings, Rulers and Landed Proprietors of Malabar in his *Memoir*:

Beginning from the south: "Travancore or Tripapu Surawam, Peritally and Ellada Surowan, Coilan or Signatty, Marta comprising the two small states of Carnapoly (Kariṅāgapil̄l̄i) and Carimbalie (Kāṝṭṭikapil̄l̄i) or Betimene (Weṇmaṇi), Calicoilan, Pannapaily, Pandalam or Chembalanoor, Trikenapoly or Pagodingo, Tekkencore, Poonjatti Perumal, Repolim or Ellengaloor, the King of Cochin (Perimpaṭappu) and his four States, viz., Porca (Chempakaśśēri or Ampalappuḻa), Berkencore or Bembellanaddoo, Mangatty or Padinjattu

Edattu, Paro or Pindinawattatta, Angia Caimal, Murianatty, Codacherry, Paljetter (Pāḻiaṭṭ Achchen), Bardella or Cheroolly, Twengal Nairs in the Maliatoor, Corretty, Chengara Codda, Cranganore or Paddinjattu Soorowan, Airoor or Belanga (Vellāngallūr), Paponetty, Beloota Nambiar, Changara Canda Caimal, Chittoor Namboory, Payanchery Nairs, the Tallapallynad consisting of four principalities, Ainecootty, Poonatur, Mannacolam and Kacattu, Manacotta or Moolloorcare, Walluanatty *alias* Arangotta, the Zamorin or Earrenaddecarre and Neddoo Wiripoo, the Cottica robbers, Bettetta *alias* Tanore, Parapoor Cowil, Reppu Cowil, Palicatchery, Colastry called Colamwasitraja by the Malabar people, Coonja Nairs, Balanore of Baragara, Adi Raja and King of Cottatte."

LETTER X.

1. **Administration of Justice.** It is rather difficult, at this distant date and in the present paucity of authentic records, to give an adequate description of the way in which justice was administered in Kērala before the advent of foreigners, whether Christian or Mahomedan. But traditions extant in Malabar, understood in the light of observations made by mediæval travellers, and such customs as have still a hold on the communities that inhabit the country, enable us to have some idea regarding it. Speaking of the customs of Kērala, Mr. Logan observes:—"If it were necessary to sum up in one word the law of the country, as it stood before the Mahomedan invasion and British occupation, that word would undoubtedly be the word 'custom'. In Malayālam, it would be Maryāḍa, Mārgaṃ and Āchāram—all signifying established rule and custom and all of them Sanskrit words.". *Custom*, it may be said, then ruled the land of Kērala. In this sense, the observation made by an Italian traveller that "the King in this country is the absolute arbiter in everything" will be correct. The king was, indeed, in one sense. absolute master of the lives and properties of his subjects; but this was as the head of a great military organisation and not, in fact, as chief magistrate. It would be a mistake to say that, in those ancient days, every grievance of a subject, whether of a criminal or of a civil nature, had to be laid before the king or his minister, and that it was heard and disposed of by him in any manner he thought fit. The early institutions of the country drew a clear distinction between the king as the absolute head of a great military organisation and the king as the head of the civil government. The king as the head of the military state was, indeed, despotic, while as the head of the civil government, he was not more than a mere ornamental figure-head.

The times were such that, as the head of the military organisation, his hands were always fully occupied with the suppression of rebellions and intrigues and in the defence of himself and his country against aggressions from outside. He had scarcely time left, even if he had the inclination, to take part in the details of the internal administration of the country. That was in the hands of the lesser chiefs and the heads of the communities, who had their own organisations for the purpose. We have seen, when speaking of the national assemblies, their constitution and working, that the king had many prerogatives in connection with them. He had, indeed, a controlling voice in the administration of the internal affairs of the country. We have also seen that the king was not slow to meddle with the civil organisation and desisted not even from attacking it, when he found it necessary to do so to gain his own ends. But never did he try to destroy it, nor could he do so if he were so minded. The co-existence of the civil organisation under the direction of the community with the military organisation under the headship of the king was deemed a necessity, each serving to support the other.

The Ṭaṙa organisation, already described, takes an important place in the mechanism of the early administration of justice in Malabar. The Ṭaṙa or village formed, as we have observed, the *unit* of civil organisation. A number of such Ṭaṙās formed a Ḍēśam, and two or more Ḍēśams constituted a Nāḍ. Each Ṭaṙa had its own elders or Kāraṇavērs, who really were the administrators of justice in that village in all matters of civil judicature.

The Ṅāṭuvālīs and Ḍēśavālīs had each their share in the dispensation of justice in the Nāḍs and Ḍēśams under their control. Captain Burton has pointed out that there does not appear to have been any limitation to the powers of settling disputes vested in these feudal superiors, nor were they prohibited from realising fines and costs of suits. The village elders or Kāraṇavērs, as also the Nāṭuvālīs and Ḍēśavālīs, who performed the functions of judges and magistrates, were no paid officers. They held their offices hereditarily and used to receive certain fees and emoluments at certain festivals in the village and at certain ceremonies at the village temple. This, however, was not in connection with their functions of administering justice.

The Kāraṇavērs do not appear to have had under them any establishment except a functionary designated the village accountant. The parties brought their witnesses with them, and the defendants were summoned by word of mouth through the domestic servants of the Kāraṇavērs. As for matters connected with caste disputes, offences against religion, the public morality also, the Kāraṇavērs were judges, when the offenders happened to belong to any class inferior to the Brahman. In the disposal of such cases, the Kāraṇavērs sought the help of the learned Brahman priest, and, if any corporal punishment was deemed necessary to be inflicted on the offender, the king's ministers were also asked to join the elders and the Brahmans as part of the investigating tribunal. As for criminal justice, in so far as grave crimes against property and person are concerned, the Kāraṇavērs, after taking cognizance of such offences and investigating the truth of the charges, submitted the cases to the king for disposal, who ordered his minister to try the offenders with the help of the village elders, and pass such sentences as appeared necessary after consultation with the learned Brahman, and carry them out subject to the king's approval. The decisions of the Kāraṇavērs in civil cases were generally submitted to by the parties, and it was seldom that any force had to be used in the execution of their decrees. Fear of social ostracism prevented the parties from showing any contempt of the authority of the elders. No corporal punishment was, therefore, necessary to induce the parties to obey the decisions of these Kāraṇavērs in civil matters. Usually, not less than three village elders constituted a civil tribunal to try civil and caste disputes. The number of the judges should, it appears, always be uneven. For the trial of civil disputes, the judges assembled in front of the village temple, or under the shelter of a big tree, ordinarily the banyan, and there, in the presence of the villagers, they investigated matters coming before them for disposal. Their procedure in investigations was extremely simple. Land disputes were but few. The village accounts contained a correct registry of the holdings of each village, and, whenever a dispute arose, there was the village accountant, a great functionary in those days, ready with his accounts before the tribunal of the elders. There were, it appears, occasionally disputes between the villagers about boundaries of lands—encroachments when embankments or new ridges were put up for paddy-lands—as to the appropriation of water for dry cultivation, etc. Such disputes were speedily and satisfactorily settled by the village elders. They always went and personally inspected the boundaries and lands in dispute, and, after examining witnesses on the spot, pronounced their decision, which were carried into execution at once. Whenever the tenant failed to pay his rent punctually, and the landlord had no reason to think that such non-payment was owing to any bad season or failure of crops, the landlord used to have resort to the following curious remedy. According to the then prevailing custom of the country, the landlord had the power of preventing the tenant from cultivating the land without taking the extreme step of evicting him from his holding. He had only to send his servant with a bundle of leaves of some trees and a handful of clay, which the servant was to place in the middle of the land or garden from which rent was due and then swear as follows:—"Here, the landlord has forbidden you (tenant) from cultivating this land or enjoying the fruits or any crops from this land, until you shall have paid the rent due to him from this land. I am deputed to, and do hereby, swear upon the landlord, your master, that you shall obey this injunction." The oath had a great superstitious value in those days. The tenants in this predicament complained to the village elders, who interfered and adjusted matters between the landlord and tenant. Where immediate payment was not found possible, the elders settled the time and condition of payment, and saw that everything was faithfully adhered to by both landlord and tenant. The manner in which debts were realised by creditors will be referred to later. It is also said that the creditor had the right of seizing and detaining the cattle, and implements of agriculture of the debtor, driving the latter to complain of the seizure to the village elders, who inquired into the matter and gave their decision about it without delay.

Mediaevai travellers give us a pleasant account of how and with what effect justice was administered in Malabar in their time. All laws proceeded from the king and were administered by the officers appointed by him with such good effect that the person and property of every individual of whatever race, caste or creed was perfectly safe. Ibn Batuta tells us that "thieves were unknown among them (the people of Malabar) and, should anything fall from a tree, none except its proper owner would attempt to touch it"—and this he attributes to the stern way in which justice was administered and the severity of the punishments awarded. "They put a thief to death for stealing a single nut, or even a grain of seed of any fruit." Ibn gives us a striking instance of the impartial way in which the slightest act of dishonesty was punished, even when the delinquent happened to be a man related to the king.

Calicut was, at the time, the foremost state in Malabar, and the methods and forms obtaining there give us an idea of the system in vogue in the states round it. According to Joseph the Indian, "the Egyptians, Persians, Syrians, Arabians, Indians, yea even from Cathay the space of 6,000 miles journey from here had their trade and traffic." Joseph informs us that "in the Palace of Calicut, which resembled a theatre, there were four courts of justice, for the Hindus, Mahomedans, Jews and Christians respectively, in which the causes of these different races were judicially investigated."

"All these Malabar kings," says Purchas, "have a special man, which is the chief administrator of justice, who in matters of government is obeyed no less than the king."

2. **Fees levied.** According to the Hindu law, five per cent is leviable from the plaintiff and ten per cent from the defendant, if the latter fails in his defence; otherwise he is exempt from any tax. Captain Burton says that some of the Rajas of Malabar were by no means content with such a moderate perquisite; the ruler of Cochin, for instance, never took less than double the sum above specified. [1]

3. **How debts are realised.** The method adopted, though rather summary, is very effective, and is available to all alike, whether prince or peasant, not simply with regard to the realisation of debts as between themselves, but also as between themselves and the Rajas. The Rajas are also authorised to levy their debts as against one another without having recourse to bloody wars. The idea that pervades the system is that every one should be in a position, without having recourse to never-ending law suits, to realise what is due to him. This method will, of course, be available only as long as all are ready to respect the "*Rama*" or arrest of the Raja. But custom, as already observed, was king in Malabar, and custom was so powerful an element in the constitution of Kerala that no one dared to violate so sacred a symbol of justice as the "Rama,"

1. *Goa and the Blue Mountains*, p. 204.

till foreign nations with foreign ideas gave a rude shock to the primitive beliefs of the people. We have it from accounts given by early travellers that the primitive system of administering justice worked with conspicuous success and rendered Malabar a secure and prosperous resort for merchants of all classes and creeds. Al Idrisi says, "Justice is a natural instinct among the inhabitants of India, and they hold nothing in equal estimation. It is stated that their numbers and prosperity are due to their integrity, their fidelity in fulfilling engagements, and to the general uprightness of their conduct * *. It is, moreover, on this account, that visitors to their country have increased, that the country flourishes, and that the people thrive in plenty and in peace. As a proof of their adherence to what is right and their abhorrence of what is wrong may be instanced the following usage. If one man owes another money, the creditor finding him anywhere draws a line in the shape of a ring round him. This the creditor enters and also the debtor of his own free will, and the latter cannot go beyond it until he has satisfied the claimant, but should the creditor decline to force him or chooses to forgive him, he, the creditor, steps out of the ring."

Varthema gives a similar description: "And if any one ought to receive money from another merchant, there appearing any writing of the scribes of the King (who has at least a hundred of them), they observe this practice:—Let us suppose the case that some one has to give me 25 ducats, and the debtor promises to pay them many times and does not pay them. I, not being willing to wait any longer, nor to give him any indulgence, shall take a branch in my hand, shall go softly behind the debtor, and with the said branch shall draw a circle on the ground surrounding him and if I can enclose him in the circle, I shall say to him these words three times: "*Bramini raza peratha polle*,"[1] i. e., 'I

[1] Brāhmaṇarāṇe Rājāvāṇe puṛaṭṭu pōkolla, which only means, I swear by the Brahmans and the Raja, do not go out.

command you by the head of the Brahmans and of the king, that you do not depart hence until you have paid me and satisfied me as much as I ought to have from thee'. And he will satisfy me, or truly he will die there without any other guard, and should he quit the circle and not pay me, the king would put him to death."

Barbosa's testimony is to the same effect: "If a debtor break day with his creditor, and often disappoint him, he goeth to the principal of the Brahmans, and receiveth of him a rod, with which he approacheth to the debtor, and, making a circle about him, chargeth him in the name of the king and the said Brahman not to depart thence till he hath satisfied the debt, which if he do not, he must starve in the place, for if he depart, the king will cause him to be executed."

Three centuries before Varthema and Barbosa, Marco Polo says that he saw the method carried out against the person of the king of Malabar. "And the said Masser Marco, when in this Kingdom (Malabar), on his return home, did himself witness a case of this. It was the King, who owed a foreign merchant a certain sum of money, and though the claim had often been presented, he always put it off with promises. Now, one day, when the King was riding through the city, the merchant found his opportunity, and drew a circle round both King and horse. The King, on seeing this halted, and would ride no further; nor did he stir from the spot until the merchant was satisfied. And when the bystanders saw this, they marvelled greatly, saying that the King was a most just King indeed, having thus submitted to justice."[1] This custom is also referred to and described, much in the same manner, by the Arab-Persian, Al Kaswini, who ascribes it, however, to Ceylon.

Captain Alexander Hamilton, at the commencement of the 18th century, mentions this method of realising debts. He says: "They have a good way of

1. Vol. II, p. 343.

arresting people for debt, viz., there is a proper person and with a small stick from the judge, who is generally a Brahman, and when that person finds the debtor, he draws a circle around him with that stick, and charges him in the King and Judge's name not to stir out of it till the creditor is satisfied either by payment or surety, and it is no less than death to the debtor to break prison by going out of the circle."

Dr. Caldwell, in a note to Yule's *Marco Polo*, observes, "The custom undoubtedly prevailed in this part of India at a former time. It is said that it still survives amongst the poorer classes in out of the way parts of the country, but it is kept up by school boys in a serio-comic spirit as vigorously as ever. Marco does not mention a very essential part of the ceremony. The person who draws a circle round another imprecates on him the name of a particular divinity whose curse is to fall upon him if he breaks through the circle without satisfying the claim". It will be remembered that, according to Varthema, Barbosa and Hamilton, the circle is drawn and the party prevented from leaving it in the name of the king and the judge who is generally a Brahman.

It will be observed that the method adopted to compel the payment of a debt is to stop the debtor from moving beyond circumscribed limits by means of an interdict before the claim of the creditor is satisfied. There are also other forms of interdicts resorted to for purposes other than the levying of debts. "A tuft of three green twigs tied to a door-way precluded persons from crossing the threshold of a house, and a similar tuft tied to the end of a staff stuck in the ground was, and still is, in some parts a sign that there is an interdict on the crops there growing."[1]

4. **How oaths are taken.** The manner in which these oaths are taken is referred to by Bartolomeo.

1. *Malabar*, Vol. I, p. 172.

He says that "Oaths are always taken before the gate of a temple; and the person who swears places both hands on the head, and invokes Mahādēva, that is, the great God, the avenger, to punish him as a perjurer, if he violates the truth." Such oaths are still taken, and the law accepts them in cases of civil disputes if the parties agree to abide by the oath, and decrees follow such adjustment.[1]

5. **Ordeals.** This was not an institution peculiar to Malabar and altogether unknown to other parts of Asia, Africa and Europe. It had existed in early Chaldea and was practised by the Egyptians. Profane history abounds with ordeals, and the bitter water of chastity and many similar trials in the Bible prove their prevalence among the Jews. In England, as Dr. Wharton tells us, there were four kinds of ordeals, viz., 1. camp fight or combat, 2. fire ordeal, 3. hot water ordeal, and 4. cold water ordeal. In Malabar, it had a firm hold till almost the early part of the 19th century. Fra Bartolomeo, writing in 1796, observes: "In former times, if a suspected person waded through the stream infested by a crocodile, or put his finger into boiling oil, melted lead, or a cocoanut shell in which a snake was concealed and drew it out unhurt, he was declared to be innocent." He adds: "This practice, however, is no longer in use."[2]

It was practised throughout the district, and the princes of the country stuck to the institution with a degree of tenacity which, at any rate, demonstrated the *bona fides* of their belief in its efficacy as a means of detecting crimes. Forbes observes that, in his time, ordeal trials were frequently practised in Tellicherry, even under the sanction of the British Government. In the English districts, the trials used to be conducted in the presence and under the superintendence of the

1. See the *Oaths Act* in British India.
2. *Voyage to the East Indies*, p. 312.

English officers, the seal of the East India Company being used on the wax-cloth covering of the hand and the prisoner placed under a European guard. Grose also refers to the practice at Tellicherry in his day under the Governorship of Mr. Adam. In Travancore, such trials continued longer, especially in cases of adultery committed on a Nampūṭiri woman, till it was finally put a stop to about 1844. In Cochin, it was abolished by a 'Hooknamah' or Royal Proclamation about the same date.

Walter Hamilton, in his description of Travancore, says that, "when, in a scheme of judicial reorganisation, Col. Munro, the then British Resident of Travancore, proposed to abolish trials by Ordeal, the assembled pandits and the Queen stoutly opposed it. They clung to the practice with such remarkable pertinacity that it became necessary in compliance with their united supplications to admit in certain cases such trials under the express sanction of the Diwan.

These trials were not always confined strictly to the Hindus. Barbosa points out that, when the culprit happens to be a Moor, " he passes through the same examinations only that, instead of putting his fingers in oil, they make him lick with his tongue a red hot axe, and if he burns his tongue he suffers death." So late as the early part of the 19th century, this species of trial was applied to other sects also in Travancore, and an unfortunate Hebrew complained to the British Resident that he, having incurred suspicion, had been obliged to plunge his hand into a vessel full of boiling oil and, not being able to sustain the fiery scrutiny, lost the cause and the use of his hand. That Christians also were subjected to these trials appears from the 16th Decree of the Synod of Diamper Session IX (1599 A. D.), where they were warned against submitting thereto.

Trials by ordeal were originally resorted to mostly in criminal cases and seldom for adjudicating disputes in civil matters, with perhaps an exception in the case of the denial of a debt. But the practice gradually found favour in the settlement of civil disputes also.

It was only in respect of heinous crimes, such as murder, theft, conjugal infidelity, etc., that ordeal trials were practised, and that only in "dubious cases in which no proof can be obtained." In such cases, the accused takes a solemn oath and the truth of the oath, is tested by the ordeal.

The various forms of ordeal practised in Malabar may be classed under the following heads:—

(1) The water ordeals, (2) fire ordeals, (3) ordeals by poison, (4) ordeal of the balance, and (5) other minor forms. These forms were not applied to all classes alike. Each of the different castes had assigned to it a distinct form of ordeal, e.g., the Brahmans were tried by the balance, the Kṣheṭṟyas by fire, the Vyŝyās by water and the Ŝūḍras by poison. But these distinctions seem to have fallen into disuse in very early days, and the stronger classes so managed matters that only those below the Nāyars came to be usually subjected to trials by ordeal.

The water ordeal.—There were several forms of this. The suspected being was made to swim through a river full of reptiles before the chief. Baldeus says that he found "a kind of oath common in Malabar, and the person who takes the oath is obliged to swim across the river between Cochin and Cṟānganūr which is full of crocodiles and, if he who has taken the oath escapes, he is supposed to have taken a just oath." Tradition points to the temple of Ṭṛkkaṭakkapiḷḷi situated on the western bank of the backwater to the south of Paḷḷippuṟam or Paliport as the place from which the culprit had to swim across the backwater to the eastern bank, a distance of about half a mile. Baldeus is not correct in saying that the culprit had to swim across the river between Cochin and Crānganūr; for both Cochin and Crānganūr are situated on the same coast almost in a line and the distance between the two places is about 18 miles.

In the latter half of the 17th century, Faria-y-Souza gives the following account of this form of trial: "They make another trial in the river that runs from Cochin to Crānganūr, where is the Pagod of Crocodile. The Brahmans by their sorceries bring one of them to the shore; the person accused leaps upon his back; if he is carried over safe, they account him innocent, if devoured, guilty. Both these (refering also to the oil ordeal) experiments have been made use of in presence of our people of late." We see this form mentioned in Decree XVI, Session 9, of the Synod of Diamper. Dr. Day, in 1863, observes that this form had been tried in the Cochin State during the last 50 years.

(2) Another form of this ordeal consisted in the accused standing up to his waist in water, a Brahman holding a stout stick in his hand, being stationed near him. A sepoy on the shore then shot three arrows from his bow, then a man was sent to bring back the arrow which had gone the farthest; as soon as he had picked it up, another person was despatched for the middle arrow, and when that was taken, another for the nearest; as soon as this last was picked up, the accused grasped the Brahman's foot, or the end of the staff, and dived under water. If he raised his head or body above the water before the arrows were brought back to the sepoy, it was considered a clear proof of his guilt.[1]

(3) A third form, most commonly used in cases of theft, consisted in the names of all the inmates of the house from which any article was lost being written on slips of paper, each enclosed in a ball of wax and all thrown into a vessel full of water. It was believed that the ball containing the name of the guilty

1. Day, p. 386.

individual would float on the surface while the other balls of wax would sink to the bottom. Dr. Day observes that this form of trial was implicitly believed in by natives, and is at times practised in European houses also. Forbes gives a singular instance of it in his own household. He says:—"Residing in a family at Surat, my sister lost a gold watch stolen on which she set a particular value. Several modes of divination were practised to discover the thief. One was similar to that used among the ancient Chaldeans and Egyptians and perhaps not unlike the cup of divination belonging to the Viceroy of Egypt found among the shepherds of Canaan. On this occasion the name of every person in the house was placed in a separate ball of wax or paste and thrown into a vessel of water. One only swam on the surface; the rest fell to the bottom and there remained. On opening the floating ball, it contained the name of an unsuspected female, who immediately confessed she had stolen and secreted the watch. Supposing this to be like other Asiatic juggles, I thought little about it, but afterwards at Broach I attended minutely to an ordeal in which myself and my head gardener, Harrabhy, were more immediately concerned." Of this more later on.

(4). A fourth form, said to have been used more in criminal cases, was for the accused to take three draughts of water, in which the representation of some Hindu Deity had been washed for the purpose. If he remained quite well for 14 days, he was considered innocent; but if any sickness or internal pain occurred, he was proved guilty.

(5). Yet another form consisted in both plaintiff and defendant, or, in their place, their advocates trying to ascertain as to who could remain longest under water, holding fast stakes placed for the purpose in sanctified pools of water or tanks. He who remained longest vindicated the truth of his cause. Dr. Day remarks that the last case ended in both the advocates being drowned; and, as both could not have been wrong, (not an impossible contingency however) this method fell into disrepute.

(6) One more form of the water ordeal may be mentioned. An image of the God of Justice was made of silver and another of iron or clay. These were then thrown into a vessel of water, and if the accused picked up the silver one, he was adjudged innocent.

Fire Ordeal.—Of all forms of ordeals, that by fire was the most important and was observed from the earliest times till but recently.

Barbosa gives a fair description of it in the following words. Speaking of the trial of persons accused of theft, he says : " If the thief denies the robbery, they keep him eight days in prison making his life uncomfortable, to see if he will confess, and throwing him his food, and when the eight days are passed without his confessing, they call the accuser, and he is told that the accused does not confess, and they ask him if he requires him to take his oath, or will let him go. If the accuser then requires the accused to swear, they make him wash and commend himself to his Gods, and eat no betel, and cleanse his teeth from the blackness caused by the betel, in order that he may swear next day, and that he may prepare himself for it. Next day they take him out of prison, and take him to a pool of water where he washes, performing his ceremony and from there they take him out to a house of prayer where his idols are kept, before which he takes his oath in this manner. It must be known that, if he is a Gentile, they heat a copper-pot full of oil until it boils, and they throw in leaves of trees, and with the great heat of the pot the leaves fly out, and this is in order that the parties may see that the oil is hot and boiling, and then two scribes come near, and take the right hand of the accused and look if he has any wound or itch or other disease, and write down in what condition his hand is, in the presence of the party. Then they bid him look at the idol and say three times, 'I did not commit this theft of which I am accused, nor do I know who did it', and then put his fingers up to the middle joints in the oil, which is boiling upon the fire, and he does so ; and they say that, if he did not commit the theft, he does not burn himself, and that if he did it, he burns his fingers, and then the scribes, and governor and party look at him again, and the scribes write down the condition in which his hand is, and they tie it up with a cloth whether it is burned or not, and put a seal on the fastenings of the cloth, and sent him back to prison, and three days later all return to the same place where the oath was taken, and they untie his hand before the Governor and party, and if they find it burned they kill him, but first give him so many torments that they make him confess where he has got the stolen property, or that he did it. And even if he did not confess, all the same he suffered the penalty, because his hand was burned, and if they find his hand not burned, then they let him go, and he who accused him pays a certain sum as a fine to the Governor."

Faria also makes mention of this form of trial. It continued to be practised in the days of Grose and Forbes. Grose (1750—64) gives the following account of the trial as observed in his time. "The ceremony is however performed with great solemnity. The party to be tried, on appeal to it for his innocence * * is brought in public to the side of the fire, on which is set a cauldron or ladle full of boiling water or oil, but most commonly lead; the prince or magistrate of the country assisting. His hand is previously clean-washed, and an *ola* or leaf of the wild brab-tree, with the matter of the accusation written on it, and girt round his waist, when on a solemn invocation of the Deity by a Brahman, the culprit plunges his hand in, scoops up the boiling fluid, and, if he draws it out unhurt, is absolved; otherwise, he receives the punishment prescribed by the laws for the crime on which the accusation lay."

Forbes mentions in more detail the rituals observed at such trials. He says that "the ground appropriated for the trial is cleaned, and rubbed with cow-dung; and the next day, at sunrise, the pandit worships Gaṇēśa, presents his oblations, and pays adoration to their deities, conformable to the Śāsṭra, then, having read the incantation prescribed, he places a round pan of gold, silver, copper, iron or clay with a diameter of 16 fingers, and four fingers deep; and throws into it a seer, or 80 sicca weight of clarified butter, or oil of sesamum. After this a ring of gold, or silver, or iron, is cleaned and washed with water and cast into the oil, which they proceed to heat; when it is very hot they put into it a fresh leaf of *pippala*, or *bilwa*; when the leaf is burned, the oil is known to be sufficiently hot. Then having pronounced a manṭra over the oil, they order the party accused to take the ring out of the pan; and if he takes it out without being burned, or without a blister on his hand his innocence is considered as proved, if not his guilt."

Both Forbes and Grose seem to have been somewhat impressed with the supposed efficacy of the test. In speaking of a trial by boiling oil conducted in his presence as Judge at Dhuboy, Forbes says: "The accused person without showing any anxiety, dipped his hand at the bottom, and took out a silver coin which I preserve in rememberance of the transaction. He did not appear to have sustained any damage or to suffer the smallest pain." Grose assures us "that so much at least is certain, that these ordeals are not in the least managed by any priest-craft, unless it could be supposed, combined with the whole governing laity, against the interests of justice, and their own having been for ages practised as the criterions of innocence, through the various provinces on the Coast. I never saw one of these trials myself, but believe that numbers of eye-witnesses to them are now in England, who can better ascertain the nature and manner of them than I dare pretend to do. It has, however, been assured to me that several of the English chiefs of settlements on the coast have used their utmost care and precaution to detect whatever fraud might be in this method of trial; that they have caused the party that was to undergo it, not only to be locked up in their own guard-room, or prison, but seen the hand that was to be plunged into the boiling lead or oil, bound up with a handkerchief closely tied round the wrist, and sealed with their own seals, which remained unbroke till the instant of the public ceremony of it. Notwithstanding all which precaution, and every other that the most determined incredulity and suspicion of the fraud could devise, they could never discover that there was any trick or juggle in it, to say nothing of the improbability of so many princes of different and discordant dominions, for so many ages joining in a cheat of no sort of use but to screen abnoxious criminals and to baffle that justice, by which alone any government can subsist. Some unable to deny the fact itself, have endeavoured to account naturally for it, by averring that neither water, oil, or lead, when boiling can affect a hand dipped into it so as to burn it. If these were true, the whole of this pretended miracle of the Gentoos would fall at once to the ground, and the miracle would be that it could ever pass for one."[1] He even invokes the aid of the Royal Society in starting an inquiry to ascertain the truth of the "miracle". Dr. Day, in attempting to explain the matter, remarks that "it was supposed that, if highly paid, the Brahmans continued to rub some substance on the arm to prevent any scalding taking place." "But no doubt," he adds, "that in many cases, the immediate and total exclusion of the atmospheric air from the surface would tend to heal the arm without leaving any, or at all events, only a very slight scar. If this is so, it may be taken to explain away many cases. But an incident mentioned by Grose as having taken place at Tellicherry about the period of our author is not calculated to inspire much faith in

1. Vol. I, pp. 198—9.

Dr. Day's theory. "An English lady," observes Grose, "however, could have contradicted this from her own experience, for at Tellicherry, where she then resided, and where scandal had not entirely respected her, happening to be present at one of these ordeal trials, where an Indian culprit drew his hand unharmed out of a cauldron of melted lead, she said, she was sure it was all a jest, and that it could not burn, but, on putting her finger in to prove it, screamed out with pain. 'That trial' (said the then Governor Adams humorously), 'I suppose, Madam, was for your virtue.' "1

The Zamorin, in the year 1710, entered into an engagement with Mr. Adams, the Chief of the Tellicherry Factory, to subject to the oil ordeal those who disputed with the factors as to the value of articles agreed to be supplied for money received. The agreement is thus recorded in the Tellicherry Factory Diary :. "A grant that any Malabarr having accounts with us must put his hand in Oyle to prove the verity thereof given Anno 1710," and the engagement itself says, "If his hands come out clean, he will be held innocent, and you will have to pay him, as usual, the expenses he may incur (in taking oath)."

Another form of fire ordeal consisted in making the accused lick or hold a red hot piece of iron. In the latter act, seven leaves of the peepul tree were placed on the palm of the accused over which is put the red hot iron, and he had to walk up and down for some specified time. There were yet other forms where molten lead was poured over the palm of one hand, or where the accused was made to walk seven paces over a blazing fire made by burning peepul wood. In the ordeal by fire, before the accused proceeded to take it, he addressed the fire thus: 'Thou, O Fire! pervadest all beings. O cause of purity, who givest evidence of virtue and of sin, declare the truth in this, my hand."

1. P. 199.

2. *Malabar*, Vol. I, p. 172; Vol. III, p. 3.

Latterly, this form of trial to prove one's innocence by plunging one's finger into boiling oil or ghee was confined to persons accused by a Nampūṭiri woman of having committed adultery with her. If the suspected persons were Nampūṭirīs, the ordeal was applied in the temple at Ṡuchīndṛam near Cape Comorin in Travancore, and in the case of other classes, in a temple at Kāṛṭikappiḷḷi, also in Travancore. The adulteress was, of course, excommunicated on her own confession, and her partners in crime were given an opportunity of proving their innocence by submitting themselves to the oil or ghee ordeal. If they came out scatheless, they were retained in the caste, but if their fingers were burned, they were excommunicated, and became outcastes. The last of these trials seems to have taken place at Ṡuchīndṛam about 1844—45, when, it is said, two Nampūṭirīs came out unhurt.

Ordeals by poison.—Of these, there were two kinds. In one, the Brahmans, after their oblations and manṭṛās, mixed three barley-corns of a poisonous root or of white arsenic in 32 times its weight of ghee, and the accused had to eat it from the hands of a Brahman. If it did not injuriously affect him, he was innocent; otherwise he was declared guilty.

The second form consisted in putting a cobra or any other venomous snake into a deep earthen pot or a cocoanut shell, or even wrapping it in a mantle, and the accused had to draw out of it either the snake itself or a coin or some other thing which had been dropped in along with the reptile. If he was bitten, he was considered guilty; otherwise he was declared innocent. In the ordeal by poison, the accused pronounced the following exhortation before he submitted to it: 'Thou, O Poison! art the child of Brahman, steadfast in justice and in truth! Clear me from this heavy charge, and if I have spoken truly, become nectar to me!"

Ordeal of the balance.—This consisted in the accused being weighed in the balance to ascertain his guilt or innocence. He and a Brahman fasted for 24 hours before the ordeal. These then bathed in a sacred pool, and the accused, after making his offering to the Deity, was weighed and his weight recorded. The accusation was then written out, and fastened to the forehead of the accused, and the Brahman, after exhortations before the scales, got into them. After the lapse of six minutes, the accused was once more weighed, and if he showed greater weight, he was condemned; if lesser, he was considered guiltless. The following interesting description of the performance of an ordeal of the balance by the late Mr. O. Chandu Menon, Sub-Judge of Canara, who witnessed it at Calicut about the year 1876, will be found interesting and instructive:—

"I myself witnessed an ordeal of this kind. Some 18 years ago, at Calicut, there took place 'Dhata' or the weighing ordeal. It was in connection with a suit then pending before the Sub-Court at Calicut, in which one of the questions to be determined was whether a Nampūṭiri Brahman, who was party to that suit, had lost his caste for breach of some caste rules. I do not well remember now the grounds of accusation, but I heard the parties agreed, with the concurrence of the Sub-Court, that, should the Nampūṭiri Brahman undergo the weighing ordeal, and succeed in establishing his innocence, before the Vyḍīkās or priests according to the rules prescribed on that behalf, the question as to the caste status of the accused Nampūṭiri Brahman might be decided in his favour. I purposely came down to Calicut from a distant place to be present at the ordeal. I have a vivid recollection of the very imposing ceremony I witnessed on that occasion. It took place in the temple of Śiva in Ṭali at Calicut, in the midst of a vast concourse of people, Brahmans and Śūḍrās—and the presence of the late Zamorin Maharaja Bahadur of Calicut, whose presence, it was said, was necessary to validate the procedure of the assembly of the Brahmans. The king or his accredited minister, it is said, should witness the ceremony. Accordingly, the Zamorin officiated as the king. There was a large assembly of the most respectable Vydīka Nampūṭirīs, Nampūṭiripāds and many learned Brahmans from all parts of South Malabar. A big weighing machine, made of copper, was hung to a thick wooden beam placed on two strong wooden pillars planted in the inner court-yard of the temple. Before the actual weighing ceremony, there were, as usual in all ceremonies conducted by the sacerdotal order, various preliminary ceremonies performed. Some Brahman priests of high order sat for making hōmams in the sacrificial fires kindled around the scales, some sat to perform pūjās, and some to recite manṭrās and Vēḍic hymns. The weighing apparatus was decorated with garlands and wreaths of flower and sandal paste and formally sanctified by manṭras. The temple music was going on all the time, and occasionally the kaṭināś or temple guns were fired. As usual at all Brahman ceremonies, a muhūrṭam or auspicious hour had been fixed beforehand for the actual performance of the weighing ceremony. About some half an hour before the appointed hour, a quantity of clay taken from the bed of the temple tank was brought and put into one of the scales, and the accused Nampūṭiri was made to sit in the other scale in order to adjust the weight beforehand. Many people examined the adjustment and said that it was exact, the clay and the Brahman weighing exactly the same weight. I believe I myself was one who examined and testified to this fact. The accused Brahman then left the scene to reappear for the ordeal. When the wretched man re-appeared, all who saw him were moved to pity. The Nampūṭiri looked about 50 or 60 years of age. The 24 hours' fasting which he had to undergo previously to purify him for the ordeal and the great mental anxiety made him look a very miserable creature indeed. Add to this the fact that he had just then plunged in the tank and was coming directly from the tank without wiping off the water from his body and with his wet clothes on, as he was directed to do. It will be observed that not only was his body, but his wealth, his reputation, his caste, in fact, everything he cared for in this world, were—as it were—to be put in the balance, and if he failed in the ordeal, his life was of course not worth living. You can imagine, gentlemen, under such circumstances what should have been the great mental perturbation of the poor old Brahman as he approached the scales slowly, trembling with fear, and with tears running down his cheeks. As he approached the scales, he was made to prostrate before the weighing scales and repeat a stanza which was, I think, to the following effect: "O Dhata, or weighing scale, thou art the great Judge of guilt or innocence, O mother Dhata, if I am innocent, let the scale in which I sit, go up, if guilty, let it go down." With these words he got into the scales. Great was the anxiety of the on-lookers to know the result which was however soon pronounced by the Brahman priests (who officiated as judges of the ordeal) to be in favour of the poor Brahman. As soon as the Brahman got into the scale, the surging crowd around the weighing machine became so uncontrollable and so disorderly, and there was so much confusion and uproar that many officials, including myself, were unable to see exactly how the scales stood; but the judges loudly and vehemently declared in favour of the poor accused and we were all much pleased. A rich banquet followed this ceremony, at which the Namputiri's innocence was formally declared by the Vydīkas, and he was allowed for the first time, after a long period of suspension from caste,—I believe nearly 30 or 40 years—all the privileges of a Brahman.

"It appears, however, that the Namputiri was not long allowed to enjoy the fruits of his victory, for some other zealous castemen and high priests, whom he had failed to propitiate and to invite for the ceremony sent a protest to the Zamorin Maharaja that the ordeal was not properly conducted, and the meaning and purport of the stanza which this unfortunate Nampuṭirī was made to recite on entering the scale was misunderstood by the priests who conducted the ceremony, and that the innocence was proved not by the Brahman's scale going up, but by weighing more than the weight opposite, or in other words, by his scale going down. There was a good controversy among the educated Nampuṭirīs, but I don't know how it terminated finally. I know, however, the poor Nampuṭirī who spent nearly ten thousand rupees in connection with this ceremony and underwent such a painful ordeal in public, was for a long time again under suspension and disallowed to enter temples or mess with other Nampuṭirīs on account of the controversy in respect of the meaning of the stanza."

There were other minor forms of ordeal practised, the most common of which consisted in giving those suspected of theft some raw rice to chew, and if, on spitting, the grain came out dry, the person was declared guilty, but if of a milky white form, he was innocent.

We may quote here with advantage the personal experience of Forbes regarding some forms of ordeal trials in which he himself seems to have had taken a prominent part. Says Mr. Forbes: "On removing from our country house at Broach to Surat, we packed up most of our things and placed them in the front verandah, where the peons slept on their movable beds. An iron plate chest was for greater security deposited in an inner room, near that where the family slept. We saw it there when we retired to rest, and in the morning it was missing. The contents being valuable, and the time for our departure near, we used every means to discover so extraordinary a robbery, in which, from the weight of the chest, three or four persons must have been concerned. Promises and threatenings were of no avail, the delinquents were concealed. I suspected an individual, but not knowing how he could have accomplished the robbery, I was silent. The public officers belonging to the court of Adwalat not being able to discover the robber, at the earnest solicitation of all our servants, Hindus, Mahomedans and Parsees, we had recourse to divination by balls in the water; our own names were included with the rest. On forming a circle round the vase, I observed the man I suspected, to change colour, and become a little agitated; no other person remarked it, until the balls being immersed in water; only one rose to the surface; his confusion was then evident, still more so, when, on opening the ball, it contained the name of Harribhy. He had lived with us several years as head gardener without our having any reason to suspect his honesty; he positively denied the robbery, and we had no other proof than the ordeal which, although fully satisfactory to all the Indians, was not so to us. They requested that neither Harribhy nor any other person might leave the spot until we had gone through the rice ordeal; to this we submitted though by no means palatable to Harribhy. He reluctantly complied and with all the rest of us put a few grains of unboiled rice into his mouth; it was previously intimated that from the mouth of the innocent after mastication it would come out a milky liquid, from the guilty a dry powder. We were all the milky party except Harribhy: mingling with the saliva it became a white fluid; with him it remained a dry powder, notwithstanding a number of fruitless attempts to liquify it. He was compelled thus to spit it out: his complexion changed from a rich brown to a sort of livid blue, his lips quivered, and his altered countenance plainly indicated guilt: he would make no confession, and on the evidence we could only put him in confinement under the court of Adawalat, until we obtained further proof. The next day a little slave boy, whom I afterwards brought to England, discovered the iron hasp of the plate-chest just appearing out of the deep bank of the Narbudda at the end of our garden about twenty feet above the river, and as much below the summit of the cliff; there we found the chest; buried in the earth. The robbers had attempted to wrench it open, and the clasps fastened by padlocks had given way but the locks occasioning greater difficulty, they awaited for a more favourable opportunity. When the culprit found that the chest had been discovered, and restored to the owners, and had no prospect of benefiting by its contents, he confessed that in concert with three other men, he had carried it off in the night, while our people were asleep, and was in hopes we should have departed without finding it."

6. **Slavery.** The institution of slavery in Malabar, like all other institutions there, is attributed to Paraśu Rāma, who is said to have organised the slave caste as a provision for agriculture, when he gave the country to the Brahmans. Historically, there can be no doubt that it rose out of the conquest of the original owners of the soil by invaders and settlers from the north. The term Cheṙamakkal or Cheṙman, the caste name of the slave class, clearly denotes the origin of predial slavery in Malabar. It means "sons of the soil-" chēr=soil and makkal=issue. Once they were conquered, and debased by the more refined northerners, whether Dravidian or Aryan, they were condemned to be tillers of the soil, whence they claimed to be sprung.

Slaves in Malabar were, originally, exclusively agrestic, domestic slavery being almost unknown. On account of the law of caste-pollution, they could not enter the houses of their masters and minister to their wants personally. The sources of slave supply were various; (1) by birth; (2) by operation of law or custom; and (3) by purchase.

(1) Certain castes are considered to be born slaves, such as the Pulayērs, Paṙayērs, Veṭṭuvās, Vēṭārs, &c. These are all attached to the soil and are said to be

born in bondage. "Of agrestic or predial slavery," says Mr. Baber, a former Collector of Malabar, "the origin is of very remote antiquity; the general term of the description of slavery is *atima* or literally, as I understand the term, serf, aborginal or indigenous, being held previously under the same tenures and terms as the land itself throughout, under some slight modifications."

(2) Slavery was imposed as a form of punishment. It was principally reserved for females reprieved from execution. Before the Mahomedan and Christian proselytizing agencies began their operations in Malabar, those of higher castes who were convicted of caste offences of a serious nature were put out of caste and condemned to be slaves. A Brahman woman found guilty of adultery becomes the Raja's slave. So also a low caste woman and her high class paramour if found guilty. A Brahman convicted of theft had to go into bondage.

A curious custom existed, which often added to the number of slaves. Barbosa refers to it as practised by the Pulayars. "These low people," says he, "during certain months of the year, try as hard as they can to touch some of the Nair women, as best they may be able to manage it, and secretly by night to do them harm. So they go by night amongst the houses of the Nairs to touch women; and these take many precautions against this injury during these seasons. And if they touch any woman, even though no one sees it, and though there shall be no witnesses, she, the Nayar woman herself, publishes it immediately, crying out, and leaves her house without choosing to enter it again to damage her lineage. And what she most thinks of doing is to run to the house of some low people to hide herself, that her relations may not kill her as a remedy for what has happened, or sell her to some strangers as they are accustomed to do.

AI.

It is not necessary that there should be actual contact. It is enough if the person is hit by a stone or stick and then that person remains touched and lost." [1] Similarly, when the various castes met annually at fighting grounds, such as at Paḷḷam, Ochiṙa &c., it was supposed that low caste men were at liberty to seize high caste women spectators, if they could manage it and to retain them. From this custom arose a popular error that, during the months of February and March, if a Pulaya meets a Śūḍra woman alone, he may seize her. This time of the year was called Pulapiṭi kālam (season during which Pulayas may seize). According to Dr. Gundhert, the time during which high caste women might lose caste, if a slave happen to throw a stone at them after sunset, is the month of Kaṙkaṭakam (15th July to 15th August). In the South Travancore, the season is known as Paṙapiṭi kālam.

(3) Felons and criminals liable to capital punishment were sold into slavery. A low caste woman allowing any improper intimacy with a Brahman was sold to the Mahomedans. In times of famine, parents sold their children for the sake of sustenance to those who were able to support them. Forbes refers to this practice in his day. "The number of poor people who came down to Anjengo and the other sea-ports, from the inland country during a famine, either to sell themselves, or to dispose of their children as slaves, is astonishing. During my residence at Anjengo, there was no famine, nor any unnatural scarcity of rain, but during the rainy season many were weekly brought down from the mountains to be sold on the coast They did not appear to think it so great a hardship as we imagine. I must and do think the feelings of a Malabar peasant and those of a cottage family in England are very different: the former certainly part with their children apparently with very little compunction; the latter are united with very tender sympathetic ties."

1. P. 143.

Trade in slaves was also carried on to a very large extent, in which even the early Europeans took great part. Barbosa says: "If it should happen any year not to rain, Chormendel falls into such a state of famine that many die of it, and some sell their own children, for a few provisions, or for two or three fanams, (6 d), and in these times the Malabars carry rice and cocoanuts to them, and return with ships laden with slaves." Later on, Bartolomeo also speaks of the trade in "Cafre slaves from the coast of Africa." At the period that Bartolomeo wrote (1787), he speaks of "the slave trade by which several thousands of men are sold annually, like cattle, and sent out of the country" as one of the obstacles that impeded the growth of population. Trade in slaves continued to be carried on to an almost appalling extent even under the eyes of the English East India Company's Government and sometimes with the active connivance of its officers, as in the case of the slaves of Mr. Murdoch Brown of Ancharakkaṇḍi, till it was finally suppressed and slavery altogether abolished. The Portuguese and the Dutch were also great sinners in this respect. Even so late as in 1812, Col. Munro, British Resident at the Court of Travancore, discovered a number of half starved and naked natives in irons as slaves at the Dutch Settlement at Changanāśśēri.

7. **Privileges of slaves.** To speak of the rights and privileges of these poor and degraded classes is altogether meaningless. Of rights and privileges in their true sense, they had practically none. Indeed, they were not allowed to perish, i. e., to die of starvation—so long at least as they are able to work for their masters—and there their so-called rights and privileges ended.

8. **Maintenance of slaves.** Captain Burton says that "the proprietors were bound to feed their slaves throughout the year; their allowance on workdays being double the proportion used at other times;

but it was never less than two lbs. of rice to a male and about three quarters of that quantity to a female." This is also the testimony of Mr. Baber, who observes that "when not regularly employed, the *vallie* (wages) is seldom more than half of what it is in working seasons, and very often even that scanty allowance is withheld, which obliges the slaves to seek work from strangers." So their condition may be said to have improved a little within the century after our author wrote.

9. **Work of slaves.** According to Mr. Baber, their employment is always in agricultural pursuits. These, however, were not confined to manuring, ploughing, sowing, harrowing, hoeing, reaping and thrashing, but they are likewise employed in fencing, tending and watching the cattle, and even in carrying the agricultural produce, it being not customary to use carts or cattle in the transportation to market; and when the harvest is over, in felling trees, and preparing materials for house-building, etc., and this without intermission of a single day, so long as the master can find employment for them. In some places on the coast, where the slaves were generally in better condition, and near large towns, they were permitted to employ themselves in carrying grass, firewood, and other articles to market.

10. **Slaves' wages.** What these are our author does not tell us. But Commissioner Mr. Graeme, reporting on the 14th of January 1822, almost a century after our author, says that it varied from one and a half to one and three-quarters seers of paddy (rice in the husk) to the male and from one to one and a quarter to the female slave: nothing is there stated as allowed to the young or aged; but Mr. Baber adds that it was within his knowledge that these were generally allowed half what able-bodied men and women received, provided they did some work. The wages above mentioned were a third less than what was generally given to free-men field labourers who work only till noon, whereas the slave had to toil from morn until

evening, with no other sustenance than his morning coññee (rice water) and evening meal, after which he had to keep watch by turns at night in sheds erected on an open platform in the centre of the field, exposed to the inclemency of the weather, to scare away trespassing cattle.

In 1854, just one year before the abolition of slavery in Travancore, the Church Mission records supplied the following information in the form of questions and answers:—"What are your wages? Three-quarters of an eḍangaḹi (measure) of paddy for adults over fifteen years of age, men and women alike." "What are the wages in other districts? Half an eḍangaḹi with a trifling present once a year at Ōṇam". "How do you get salt?" "We exchange one-sixth of our wages in paddy for a day's supply of salt." "And for tobacco?" "We give the same quantity for tobacco."[1]

There are other payments made to slaves which also require mention. Mr. Baber points out: "First; with respect to clothing; the allowance consists of a waist cloth, called muṇḍu to men, and muṙi, signifying a fragment, to females; it is just large enough to wind round their loins, and is of the value of from one to two fanams, equal to from 6 d. to 1 sh. In some districts this is given but once a year, but more generally twice, or at the festivals of Ōṇam and Viṣhu which fall in September and May * * On occasion of marriages, deaths, boring of ears, first signs of puberty in girls, as also on ceremonial observances, presents are made by their masters, of money from 2 to 4 fanams, of cloths called poṭava, or coverings for the bride, or corpse of the value of 2 to 3 fanams as also of articles such as oil, pepper, *nellu* (paddy), salt and tobacco." Captain Burton adds that, at harvest time, they were entitled to a certain portion of the produce as a compensation for watching the crop, and the proportion according to our author is a tenth.

1. Mateer, pp. 302—3.

11. **Master's power to kill slaves.** By the ancient laws of Malabar, a master was accountable to no person for the life of his own slave, but was the legal judge of his offence and might punish it by death. He had, however, to obtain the sanction of his feudal chief or, more generally, of the sovereign, before executing the sentence. He could inflict corporal punishment upon the slave, but old established custom limited the extent as effectually as law would. But, in course of time, with the disruption of the old constitution of things, masters became more cruel, as they found that they could do with impunity what they would not otherwise have been permitted before.

12. **Sale of slaves.** A proprietor in Malabar could always sell his serfs with or without the soil, but to remove them far from their houses would have been considered a cruel and unwarrantable measure, sufficient to cause, and almost justify, desertion. Only in some castes, the wives of slaves might be sold to another master, and generally speaking, parents were not separated from their children. They might, however, be let out on simple rent or mortgaged under certain deeds. Even after Malabar came under the English East India Company, slaves continued to be a marketable commodity. They were sold for the realisation of land revenue as also for decree-debts. On the 15th of November 1836, the Government ordered the remission in the Collector's accounts of Rs. 927-13-0, which was the "annual revenue" from slaves on the Government lands in Malabar.[1]

The following document will be found interesting with regard to the right of passing slaves from one owner to another. Translation of a Ṭīṭṭūram (Royal writ) from the Raja of Cochin— "To our Ayyanāṭṭ Kṛṣhṇan.—You are hereby authorised to hold and enjoy, on Anubhōkam tenure (a perpetual one), the following landed properties, etc., * * and to exercise the

1. *Malabar*, p. 149.

right of proprietorship over the *slaves* named Chāṭṭan, son of Iṭṭippēngan and Kuṙumba * * Dated Chiṙakkal Kōvilakam, 957 M. E. (1782 A. D). Written in the handwriting of Cheṙupaṙampaṭṭ. * *"

According to Burton, the price of a slave varied from £ 3 to £ 8. Mr. E. B. Thomas, the Judge at Calicut, writing on the 24th of November 1841, to the Sadr Adalat, said that the average cost of a young male under 10 years was about £3-8-0, of a female somewhat less. But in some Ṭālūks, women fetched higher prices in order to *breed* slaves. An infant, ten months old, was sold in a court auction, on 10th August 1841, for Re. 1-10-6, independent of the price of its mother. And in a recent suit, the right to 27 slaves was the "sole matter of litigation, and it was disposed of on its merits." Again, according to Mr. James Vaughan's report quoted by Commissioner Graeme, in the 35th para of his report, the largest sum the highest class slave will fetch is 250 old gold fanams equal to £6-5 sh. and the highest rent, 7½ fanams per annum, equal to 3 sh. 9 d.; but the average selling price of all castes (of which Mr. Vaughan enumerates 20) is 132 old gold fanams equal to £3-6 sh. ; and average annual rent 5 fanams, equal to 2 sh. 6d., while the prices of the 'lowly Pulyar Chermars' who compose more than half the aggregate slave population are still less than the lowest of the other castes and are for a man 48 fanams, equal to £1-4sh., a woman, 36 fanams, equal to 15 sh., a boy (average), 20 fanams equal to 10 sh. and a girl (average) 15, equal to 7sh. 6d.; while the annual rents of the two first are 2½ fanams, equal to 1sh. and 1sh. 3d. In Travancore, before emancipation, George Mathan wrote that the price of a slave was usually Rs. 6, but in Malappelly it was Rs. 18.

Lieutenant Conner says, in his *Report of the Trignometrical Survey of Travancore*, 1820: "Husband

and wife sometimes serve different persons, but more frequently the same. The females of this class are given in usufruct, scarcely ever in complete possession. The eldest male child belongs to the master of the father; the rest of the family remain with the mother while young, but being the property of her owner, revert to him, when of an age to be useful, and she follows in the event of her becoming a widow." In the Calicut district, half the children belonged to the mother, or rather to her proprietor, and the other half to the father's master; the odd number was the property of the former. When both parents belonged to one owner, he, of course, claimed all the offspring.[1]

The Dutch used to buy slaves in large numbers. So also the Portuguese. Dr. Day observes: "Report says that the church (in Cochin) was occupied as a slave godown on special emergencies, and that, in the week days, when the sacred edifice was not required for religious purposes, it was employed to keep these unfortunate creatures in, who had usually been carried off by the Moplas, and sold to the Dutch, who shipped them to Ceylon, Batavia, the Cape and other places." Numbers of poor innocent children used to be kidnapped by gangs of Mahomedans, who sold them to the super cargoes of European vessels, more especially to the French at Mahe, and the Dutch at Cochin. The English Government, on attaining supremacy in Malabar, endeavoured their best to suppress this by severely punishing those who trafficked in slaves. They wrote to the Dutch Government in Cochin requesting them to abolish the practice of buying children for slaves· but they declined, stating that they realised large sums of money by it. "When Cochin was taken, almost every servant in the place was found to be a slave."[2] These slaves, as a rule, appear not to have been treated badly.

1. *Goa and the Blue Mountains*, p. 277. *Note*
2. Day, pp. 183—4

They were employed even at the Governor's house. Forbes tells us that "3 female slaves, neatly dressed, attended each of the guests, before the dinner was put on the table; one of them held a silver basin decked with flowers to contain the water, which another poured upon his hands from a silver vase, and a third offered a clean napkin on a salver."

As already observed, the slaves do not appear to have been treated badly by the Dutch. But when any very grave offences were proved against them, they were unmercifully punished. Impalement and more rarely the nail torture, and that by fire or water were employed. If a European killed a slave, whether by an accidental blow or otherwise, he was severely punished but rarely by death. The law laid down was that slaves might be corrected by their masters, in any way short of causing death. To obviate the chance of an exasperated master giving a fatal blow, there was an official, who, amongst his other duties, received complaints against slaves, and on payment caused them, if males, to be beaten before their master's door, if females, within his house. [1]

13. **Abolition of Slavery.** One of the first acts of the British Government on their assumption of rule in Malabar was to put down slavery and the slave trade. In the year 1792, a proclamation was issued by the Commissioners against dealing in slaves. The slave dealer was treated as a thief. The slave was to be forfeited, and the dealer fined five times his value. The purchaser was also to be similarly treated. Houses suspected of being used as slave depots were to be watched and entered and searched. Fishermen and Moplas conveying slaves were to be "severely flogged and fined at the rate of ten rupees each slave;" vessels used in the slave trade were to be confiscated. On the 23rd of December 1819, orders were issued "stopping the practice of selling slaves for arrears of

1. Day's *Land of the Perumals*, pp. 170—1.

revenue." On the 15th of November 1836, the Government was "pleased to accede to the recommendation in favour of emancipating the slaves on the Government lands in Malabar." Between this date and 1842, correspondence passed between Mr. E. B. Thomas, the Judge at Calicut, and the Government, which disclosed a state of affairs that was considered very undesirable; and, on the 27th of July of that year, the Board of Directors sent out directions to legislate on the subject. The Government of India, thereupon, passed Act V of 1843, abolishing slavery altogether. The Collector of Malabar, however, explained to the Cherumar that it was their interest as well as their duty to remain with their masters, provided that they were treated kindly. He proclaimed that "the Government will not order a slave who is in the employ of an individual to forsake him and go to the service of another claimant; nor will the Government interfere with the slave's inclination as to where he wishes to work." It was also observed that "any person claiming a slave as Jenmum, Kāṇam or Paṇayam, the right of such claim or claims will not be investigated at any of the public offices or courts." The Court of Directors, approving these measures, wrote in their despatch of the 30th of July, 1845, as follows:— "It would defeat the very object in view to create any estrangement between them and their masters, and moreover would be an act of injustice and bad faith of which the masters would be entitled to complain." Slavery and the slave trade still lingered till the final and real blow was dealt to it by the Indian Penal Code.

It was not till 1854—5 that slavery was abolished in the States of Travancore and Cochin. At the instance of the British Resident, a proclamation was issued in Travancore, on the 30th of Kanni M. E. 1029, corresponding to 1853, declaring free the *children* of the slaves of the State who may be *subsequently born*, forbidding the seizure of private slaves in satisfaction of debts;

recognising the right of slaves to possess property and to enjoy the protection of the law; directing the emancipation of slaves connected with property escheating to the State; prohibiting without consent, the sale and separation to a greater distance than 15 miles of slave parents and children; and prescribing regulations intended to preserve that unhappy class from oppression. Upon this, Mr. Thornton remarks, in his article on Travancore, in the *Gazetteer*, "How far these rules will be effective against the opposition of both prince and people remains to be seen". So far as the prince who issued this proclamation was concerned, the justice of the historian's remark is somewhat questionable. No doubt, the force of long established custom sat oppressively on the mind of the naturally humane prince, and, however inclined he himself personally was to emancipate the slaves, he seems to have felt misgivings so far as it affected the old order of things which he thought it his duty to maintain intact. Major Heber Drury, the editor of our author, who was at the time Assistant to the British Resident at the Court of Travancore, bears testimony both to the humane inclinations of the Raja and to the trammels of custom that held him bound. "The Resident," says Major Drury, "has been for some time taking measures for abolishing slavery in Travancore and, with this view, he pointed out to the Raja, among other forcible arguments, the esteem he would be held in not only by his neighbouring states, but even in Europe and other parts of the world. 'True,' argued the prince, 'but the landed proprietors do not wish it, and I could never do anything that was not agreeable to all my subjects.' 'But,' replied the Resident, 'they will incur no loss. My desire is to free the next generation, and to emancipate children yet unborn; an act which I am sure your Highness will approve of. It is hardly fair that any child, before it can distinguish right from wrong, should be born and live in slavery, without choice.' 'Most assuredly,' rejoined the prince, 'and *as far as I am concerned, I should wish to abolish the practice at once.* But it has never been done before, and I should not like to make any alteration myself in the existing state of affairs'. The everlasting *but* did not eventually prevail and, after a little pressure from the higher authorities, the blot of slavery was wiped out from the land."[1] Several Royal Proclamations were issued from time to time which led up to the final abolishing of slavery altogether. So also in Cochin.

14. **Capital punishment.** In the States of Travancore and Cochin, no female is liable to capital punishment, however heinous her crime may be. It was so all over Malabar from the earliest times. Barbosa tells us: "No death sentence is inflicted on women, only fines."

Bartolomeo observes: " To touch a woman against her will is allowed to no person, not even the king's ministers and officers, unless the king expressly commands it. If women are guilty of anything that deserves punishment, they may be deprived of their liberty and sold as slaves; but to hang them, or put them to death in any other manner, is contrary to the laws of India."[2]

15. **Administration of Criminal Justice.** Five great crimes were held as heinous offences. These were—(1) the murder of a Brahman, (2) the drinking of spirits (probably a crime only among Brahmans); (3) theft; (4) disobeying a teacher's rules and (5) cow killing.

" They put a thief to death, " wrote Ibn Batuta regarding the Malayalees in the fourteenth century A. D., "for stealing a single nut, or even a grain of seed of any fruit: hence thieves are unknown among them, and should anything fall from a tree, none except its proper owner would attempt to touch it."[3]

1. *Life and Sport in Southern India*, pp. 213—14.
2. P. 288.
3. Lee's Translation, p. 167.

"The Nairs," says Faria Y Souza, "show no mercy to a thief though the thing stolen be of no value. They impale the criminal, and leave him to be eaten by the birds. An Indian that had turned a Christian stole a knife, the Nairs apprehended him, and sent to acquaint the Judge of the Portuguese at Cannanore. He returned answer, they should kill him. They instantly cut off his head, thinking it was a piece of civility, being he was a Christian, to kill him our way. Our Commander, Nicholas Soveral, sent some soldiers to fetch the body, and revenge his death on the Nairs, as if they had not obtained leave for what they did. The soldiers killed a Nair which provoked them in great numbers to besiege the Fort with great threats if satisfaction was not given them. Our Commander made show of hanging one of Soveral's servants to appease the Nairs; and being cut down, put him into a coffin, as if he were really dead. The Nairs were satisfied, and our men as well pleased that this fiction had passed upon them, as if the condescension had not been equal, whether the act was feigned or real."[1]

We have the following account of the administration of Criminal Justice in Malabar given by Barbosa in the early part of the 16th century:—

"Justice is administrated by an officer called *Talaxo* appointed by the king who has 3,000 gentlemen under him to whom he pays their salaries from revenues assigned for the purpose. Justice is administered according to the qualities of the persons, because there are diverse sects and laws amongst them. If any of the low people commit robbery and a complaint is made, they send to take the robber, and if they find the thing stolen in his hands, or if he confesses that he did it, if he is a Gentile they take him to a place where they carry out executions, and there they set them on high posts with sharp points and a small stand, through which passes one of those points; and there they cut off his head with a sword, and spit him through the

1. Tom, III, pp. 254—5.

back and the pit of the stomach, and that point comes out about a cubit, and on it they also spit his head. And they tie ropes to his legs and arms, and fasten them to 4 posts so that the limbs are stretched out and the body on its back upon the stand. And if the malefactor is a Moor, they take him to a field, and then kill him by stabbing him; and the stolen property is appropriated to the Governor without its owner recovering anything, because their law so disposes, doing justice on the thief. And if the stolen property is found and the thief escapes, it is for a certain number of days in the charge of the Governor; and if during that time they do not catch the thief, they return the stolen goods to the owner, a fourth part of it, however, remaining for the Governor; and if the thief denies the robbery, they keep him eight days in prison, making his life uncomfortable, to see if he will confess, and throwing him his food, and when the 8 days are passed, without his confessing, they call the accuser, and he is told that the accused does not confess, and they ask him if he requires them to take his oath or let him go." Then follows the ordeal of boiling oil.

"For other offences, whether committed by Moors or Gentilers, a pecuniary penalty is inflicted which goes to the Governor and this produces much revenue to him. He also lays hold of vagabonds and sell them as slaves at a price of from 4 to 5 ducats.

"The Nobles cannot be taken and put in irons for any offence. If a noble were to rob, or kill any one, or kill a cow, or commit adultery with a low caste or Brahman woman, or if he eats in the house of a low caste man, or spoke ill of his king this being established by his own words— 3 or 4 honorable gentlemen are given a warrant signed by the king to find out the offender and kill him wherever found. After the offender is killed, he is laid on his back and the warrant is pinned to his breast. If he is killed in the country he is left where he is dead, no one comes near him, so that the fowls and dogs devour him. If he is killed in the city, the people who live round beg the king to order its removal which is allowed sometimes as a favour, sometimes with a fine.

"If one noble accuses another of having committed robbery, murder, or any other evil, the Governor reports to the king and the accused is summoned to appear. If he absents himself he is held guilty, and is ordered to be executed without further investigation. If he presents himself the accuser is summoned and examined both of them together. And the accuser takes a small branch of a tree or green herb in his hand, and says, such a one did such a thing; and the other one takes another branch and denies it. The king then bids them return 8 days thenceforward to the house of the Governor to take oath and prove that which each one asserts, and so they depart and return on the day fixed to the house of the Governor, where the accused swears in the manner already described with boiling butter." The process already described is then gone through. If, on untying, the finger is burned, the accused is killed. If not, the accuser is killed. If the accused is not of great value and his finger is not injured, they inflict a fine on the the accuser and banish him. If a nobleman is accused of robbing the king's property, he is closely imprisoned before he is led to take the oath.

"In Calicut there is another officer like the Chief Justice of all the kingdom, excepting the city of Calicut. He is called *Coytorotical Caranavar*; he has lieutenants in all the villages, to whom he farms the administration of justice: that is to say, the fines; not capital penalties. And people come to this Chief Justice for any injury, and he gives an account of it and reports to the king, and renders justice in the manner followed at Calicut.

"No death sentence is inflicted on women, only fines. Nair women offending against the law of their sect are sold to Moors and Christians if the king knows of it before her male relatives. If they know of it before the king, they shut her up and kill her with dagger or spear, saying that, if they did not do so, they would remain greatly dishonoured. And the king holds this to be well done." 1

Varthema writing about the same time observes:—"With respect to the laws which are in use among them.—If one kills another, the king causes a stake to be taken 4 paces long and well pointed at one end, and has two sticks fixed across the said stake 2 spans from the top, and then the said wood is fixed in the middle of the back of the malefactor and passes through his body, and in this way he dies. And this torture they call *uncalvet*.2 And if there be any one who inflicts wounds or bastinadoes, the king makes him pay money, and in this manner he is absolved." 3

As to the method of administration of Criminal Justice in olden times, we have already observed that all grave crimes against person and property were tried by a court of enquiry constituted under the authority of the king or his lieutenant, the Ṅāṭuvāḷi, with the help of learned Brahmans, and the elders of the village of the accused. The place where the court assembled was called Koṭṭil or Maṇḍapam. The examination of witnesses and of the accused was conducted *viva voce* and was not reduced to writing. The punishments awarded were:—death, slavery, mutilation, confinement in prison, banishment, and corporal punishment. Forfeiture of property followed conviction for major offences. No punishment was awarded except on the confession of the accused, however extorted.

Persons found guilty by the court of enquiry of the following offences were punished with death:—

(1) Swāmidrōhi or he who excites insurrection or meditates the death of the king;

1. Pp. 116—120.

2. 'Celvete, Caloete, S. The punishment of impalement. Malayalam *Kalvekki* (pron: *etti*). *Hobson Jobson*, 1st ed., p. 114

3 P. 147.

(2) Brahmahanṭa or he who kills a Brahman;

(3) Māṭṛhanṭa or he who commits matricide;

(4) Piṭṛhanṭa or he who murders the father or paternal uncle or any other paternal relation;

(5) Manuṣhyahanṭa, all murderers in general;

(6) Gōhanṭa, he who kills a cow;

(7) Kshēṭra Sṭhēna or those who steal the property belonging to a place of religious worship;

(8) All those belonging to an inferior class, who steal anything from the house of a person of rank;

(9) Those who rob the royal treasure or Bhaṇḍāra;

(10) Those who hold illicit intercourse with the king's consort; or

(11) Those who counterfeit the current coin;

(12) Those who commit adultery with the wife of a Brahman, or the wife of their *Guru* or preceptor.

At one period, drunkards and persons who sold arrack, opium or bhang were condemned to lose their property.

The offenders were always hanged on the spot where the crime was committed. The gallows consisted only of beams and could with great ease be transported from one place to another. A hook is fixed to one end of the rope, and this hook the executioner forces, with all his strength, into the flesh below the criminal's chin; and he is then hoisted up, and the other end of the rope made fast to the gallows. The delinquents sometimes were hanged also in the European manner, so that they were instantly suffocated. Lesser crimes were punished by cutting off the nose and ears; by hacking off the right hand, banishment from the country, imprisonment, hunger and thirst, sequestration or confiscation of property, and sometimes by a pecuniary fine.

AK.

The sentence of death had, in general, to be subscribed by the delinquent's own hand, after he had been heard and convicted of the crime laid to his charge. The place of trial or Maṇḍapa, a sort of court of judicature, was at times in the magistrate's habitation. Of such magistrates, there were a great many, and they always lived in the neighbourhood of a temple. As soon as a delinquent was convicted, the magistrate repaired to the *Mantrasala* (mantŗaśāla) or judgment hall, where all the other magistrates, together with some Brahmans, were assembled. On their opinion and sentence, the life and death of the delinquent depended. He was, however, at liberty to appeal to the king, and on such occasions, he was never executed till the king confirmed the sentence. In doubtful cases, the superintendents and elders of the caste were consulted. In these assemblies, the first object of the members was to enquire into the laws, customs and usages formerly established in the caste, or in the town or city where the trial took place; and according to these old precedents, the point in question was determined. [1] Bartolomeo assures us that during the whole time that he resided in Malabar, he never heard of a criminal being beheaded, but sometimes that one or two had been run through with a lance.

Forbes who wrote about the middle of the 18th century, speaking of the method of inflicting punishment on criminals and debtors in Travancore, observes:—

"The method of inflicting punishment on criminals and debtors in Travancore is in some respects singular; for capital crimes the culprits generally suffer death; although, as in most oriental governments, money and interest may purchase a pardon: except for the dreadful sin of killing a cow, or selling one for slaughter: this subjects them to a most cruel death. For debts and non-payment of fines, inflicted as

1. Bartolomeo, *Voyage to the East Indies*, pp. 310—311.

a punishment, they are confined by the Sirkar, or chief of the district; who draws a circle round the prisoner, from which he dare not move; then, gently laying a sharp stone on the crown of his head, demands payment of the sum required: on a refusal, he places a flat stone over the other, and ties it firmly on; additional weights are gradually accumulated, with a repetition of the demand, until the sharp stone, penetrating the head, either ensures payment, or causes a painful death."[1]

Says Mr. Logan:—"The manner of carrying out capital punishments was sometimes barbarous in the extreme. Criminals were cut in half and exposed on a cross-bar in the manner still adopted with tigers and panthers slain in hunting expeditions and offered as a sacrifice to local deities. Thieves were similarly cut in two and impaled on a stake, which probably had a cross-bar. The word for it and that for an eagle or vulture (Kaḻu) are identical. But impaling alive was also known and, in June 1795, by the orders of the Paḻaśśi (Pychy) rebel chief, two Māppiḻās were thus treated after a pretended trial for alleged robbery in a Nair's house at Venkād in Kōṭṭayam Ṭālūk. Finally, great criminals were at times wrapped up in green palm leaves and torn asunder probably by elephants."[2]

The following account of the administration of justice in the native State of Cochin was supplied by the Raja to the Joint Commissioners from Bengal and Bombay sent to Malabar by Lord Cornwallies for the settlement of the districts then recently surrendered to the East India Company by Tippu Sultan:

"The laws of our realm are thus set forth:

First: As to how questions regarding the adjustment of legal relations between persons, the rights and duties of vendors and purchasers, and disputes

1. Vol. 1, p. 253.
2. P. 173.

concerning lands and tracts are settled: When such disputes are brought before the Darbar a few) Brahmans together with four or eight other learned men of age and experience, well versed in the laws relating to landlords and tenants, impartial in their conduct and possessing discretion and firmness, are assembled together to hear the parties and to recommend a settlement which, if approved of by the Darbar, the dispute will be adjusted accordingly. The decision will be explained to the parties, and counterparts of documents embodying the same, agreed to by both parties, and attested by witnesses will be executed and exchanged between them. If fresh disputes arise concerning the same transaction and the parties appeal to the Darbar, the terms of the document which had been exchanged will be enforced after hearing the parties and witnesses once more. When disputes concerning land arise, some 4 or 8 Brahmans of learning and a similar number of other men of intelligence, firmness and experience of the locality are assembled who, after hearing both parties, submit their decision to the Raja (Kōima) who, if he is satisfied with the decision as just and equitable, will confirm it and enforce it.

"*Secondly*: As to how grave crimes such as causing death or hurt, highway robbery and theft, injuries and offences involving loss of caste are dealt with:—In cases of homicide, the accused person is arrested and tried before Brahmans and 4 or 8 other learned men and, if found guilty, he is punished with death. In cases of hurt, if, on trial of the offender, the offence is proved, and if the complainant was of caste below the Ṡūḍra, the offender is condemned to pay a sum required to get the wounds healed. He is further fined and ordered to report himself every day before the authorities so that he may not repeat the offence. If the wounds inflicted are serious, the offender is kept in custody and if his victim dies of the wounds, the offender is punished. If the hurt was caused to a Brahman or a Nair and blood appears, the offender is punished. In the case of highway robbery and theft as also in the case of theft from the treasury of the palace or of temples, the culprit is brought before the king and, if the offence is brought home to him, the stolen property found in his possession or traced to the possession of anyone else through him, is secured and the offender punished.

"The punishment in the case of highway robbery is that fixed by the Brahmans and other learned men called togther to try the offence. The usual punishments inflicted for petty thefts and other miscellaneous offences are imprisonment for terms of six months and periods of years, whipping, fines, the loss of a limb or organ, &c., in proportion to the gravity of each particular offence.

"In the case of caste offences, in castes below the Śūḍra down to Chanḍālās, the accused persons are tried by the 6 Vaiḍīkas by whom those who have to be put out of caste are excommunicated according to the nature of their offence. The others are treated according to the rules of caste. In the case of those belonging to castes below the Śūḍra, subject to a Kșheṭṛiya king, the delinquents are purified by the king giving a vessel with water and by the Vaiḍīkas performing certain purificatory ceremonies. If a Brahman is accused of any caste offence, he is tried by the Smāṛṭṭa of the kingdom And if it is a Brahman woman who is accused, the Smāṛṭṭan, a representative of the king and a few learned Brahmans assemble together to perform a certain ceremony, after which the woman is put out of caste and is handed over to the king. In the case of the Brahman male, a like ceremony is gone through by the Smāṛṭṭan, the representative of the king and four virtuous Brahmans, and if made an outcaste, he is expelled from the country The remaining members of the family of the guilty person are re-admitted to all caste privilege on the 6 Vaiḍīkas performing a ceremony. If the person outcasted belongs to any caste below the Śūḍrās down to Chanḍālās, the remaining members of his family are purified after the person excommunicated is turned out. In the case of the Brahman outcaste, the 6 Vaiḍīkas have to perform certain rites before the members of the family can be readmitted to caste.

"*Thiraly*: As regards the question how the laws specified above are ascertained: In cases which are investigated by the 6 Vaiḍīkans and the Smārṭṭan, the rules and observances governing them are those prescribed by their law-books. In all other cases men of discretion and firmness are summoned to investigate causes and the king acts on the result of such investigation. A Chōgan, Māppiḷa, Pulayan or Pārayan condemned to death for any crime is hanged. If the condemned man is a Śūḍra or Māppiḷa, he is beheaded with the sword or impaled. Usages vary in different localities."[1]

16. **Sales and Loans.** It need hardly be pointed out that our author's classification of land tenures is altogether faulty; most of those mentioned by him are not loans, while one only is a complete sale. His description of the tenures mentioned is also not altogether correct.

1. *Atte-Patta.*—This stands for Malayalam Aṭṭipēr, and is the last of a graduated series of transfers of property which effects a complete alienation of proprietorship.

2. *Patta.*—If by this Pāṭṭayōlakkaraṇam or, as it is now called, Kāṇam is indicated, its description is hardly correct. A correct definition of the tenure will be given later on.

3. *Berampatta,* or more correctly, Veṟumpāṭṭam, i. e., simple lease.

4. *Kararna.*—There is no tenure known as such in Malabar. The term Karaṇam, not Kararna, in

1. This communication is dated M. E. 968 (A. D. 1793).

Malayalam means a document or deed. From the description given, we may take it that our author is speaking of Paṇayam, or mortgage with possession.

5. *Neir Patta.*—If this is Nērpāṭṭam, the description is altogether incorrect. There is a species of improvement lease extant in Malabar which would answer very much to the description given here. But these are known as Kuḷi Kāṇam. In a Nērpaṇayam tenure, land is given possession of as security for the money advanced, and the proceeds thereof will be sufficient only to pay the interest of the loan, without leaving any surplus to be paid over to the mortgagor.

To give a correct idea of the tenures above enumerated, it is perhaps necessary to give a short account of the system of land tenure extant in Malabar.

All land in Malabar is, in these days, being claimed by the Nampūṭiri Brahmans as their jenmum or birth right, something equivalent to the *plenum dominum* of Roman Law. According to tradition and the Kēralōṭpaṭṭi, Paraśu Rāma, after reclaiming Kēraḷa, made a gift of the land to the Brahmans for the expiation of the sin of the murder of Rēṇuka, his mother. Hence according to them, all land in Malabar, theoretically, belonged to the Brahmans, and their absolute right to it dated from Paraśu Rāma's advent or pre-historic times.

This contention of the Nampūṭirīs as to the proprietorship of landed properties in Malabar is not accepted by all, and is stoutly opposed by the Nāyars. The opponents of the Nāmpūṭirī theory say that the tradition as to the creation of Kēraḷa by Paraśu Rāma has considerably receded before the advance of geological science, while no one seriously thinks it worth his while, for various and some obvious reasons, to give much credence to Kēraḷoṭpaṭṭi and works of that sort on matters of importance. If all lands belonged to Nampūṭirīs, how comes it, the other party asks, that the several ancient rulers of different tracts of Kēraḷa, the

Nāṭuvālis and the Ḍēṣavālis, the many Kaṟṭṭāvūs, Kaimals and others, owned and possessed extensive properties from very early times. And most of these were Nāyars.

"What is more important in this connection is the fact that the Nampūṭirīs and Pōṯṯis who claim absolute ownership of all landed property in Malabar have, nevertheless, allowed centuries to roll away without asserting or exercising a semblance of title to lands, which were dealt with and controlled by Nāyar chiefs, called Sāmanṭas, Maṭampīs or Nāṭuvālis. It cannot be that the chiefs had no ownership of lands—many of them are even to-day full proprietors of ṭanaṭu holdings. In North Malabar, there are more numerous Nāyar Jenmies than Nampūṭirī Jenmies. There are several ṭālūks in Travancore, where Jenmum property of Nampūṭirīs is the exception rather than the rule."[1]

It is not proved beyond doubt as to who came first to this part of India, the Nāyars or the Nampūṭiris. The chances are that the former came first or, at any rate, they came together. There is nothing in history or, for the matter of that, in tradition from which to infer that, when they came, the Nampūṭirīs were considered to be on a plane higher than that of the Nāyars. On the other hand, the days of advent must necessarily be days of trouble and turmoil, and, as the Nāyars, even if, in those remote times, they formed a class separated from the other were the fighters, they must have had the predominant voice in the disposal of lands occupied or acquired by the show of fight or force of arms. Thus the contention of the Nāyars that the Nāyars were the original proprietors of lands in ancient Kērala is not without an logical or historical foundation. As they formed the military class and so became the retainers of most of the chiefs and kings of Kērala, they had to be off and on in fields of battle.

1. P. 51 of the *Report of the Jenmi Kutiyan Commission of Travancore*—Government Press.

Consequently they found that their other fields were uncared for and even unprotected. Gradually, when it came about that the Ḍēvaswam and Brahmaswam properties were left unmolested by the combatants, and had not to pay any tax, the Nāyars thought it to their benefit to clothe their properties with some halo of sanctity, so as not to be interfered with by others. Thus, probably, they took very small amounts from neighbouring temples over which they had control or from Nampūṭiris allied to their families or to the families of some chieftain under whom they fought, and made a show of surrender of the lands to them, to be taken back again as perpetual leases on nominal rents which would just cover the low interest on the money advanced. In those days, the parties had so much confidence in the high integrity of one another that they never dreamt that these transactions would be considered as outright sales, but only as shifts to tide over bad days.

Whether this statement of facts is approved by the Nampūṭiri theory or not, it goes without saying that the kāṇam tenure had a military origin.

"The Kāṇam which, in its inception, was a perpetual lease, changed its complexion when the Nāyars increased in numbers and their services as soldiers became less necessary with the advent of peaceful and settled times. The theory (about the right of the Jenmi to eject or redeem the Kāṇakkāran) was not enforced against old Kāṇakkārans, but when once it gained currency, the Jenmi was enabled to renew the leases periodically (and to add privileges and other dues), pressure being first brought to bear on the weaker Kāṇakkārs under threats of ousting them. The British rule strengthened the Jenmi's pretensions, and the theory became applicable to all Kāṇakkārs."[1]

Mr. Thackeray, reporting to the Madras Government in 1807, observed that "it is almost certain that the lands originally belonged to the pagodas and, at a

1. P. 59 of the above *Report*.

very early period, were largely alienated ; and from the pagodas, the present Jenmakkārs, or proprietors derived their title''.[1] To a certain extent, Mr. Thackeray is supported by the Kēralōṭpaṭṭi which expressly says that the land was given in *Jenmam* to the Brahmans for the support of the temples and religious ceremonies. The word *Jenmam* means 'life' or 'birth' and denotes technically a hereditary right to freehold lands subject to no state-tax at all. This right of the *Jenmi* in Malabar to hold his lands absolutely free of all burdens has been accepted, more or less, by all those who have had occasion to inquire into the origin and history of Malabar land tenures. The Joint Commissioners from Bombay regarded the *Jenmi* as owner. Mr. William Gamul Farmer, one of the Commissioners, speaks of the 'Jehn kaars' as 'Free holders.' Dr. Buchanan, writing in December 1800, says : "I have already mentioned that the Nampūṭiris pretend to have been possessed of all the landed property of Malayāla, ever since its creation, and, in fact, it is well-known that, before the conquest of Hyder, they were actual lords of the whole soil, except small parts appropriated to the support of religious ceremonies, and called *Devastanah*, (Ḍēvaswams) and other portions called Chērikkal, which were appropriated for supporting the families of the Rajas. All the remainder, forming by far the greater part, was the *Jenm* or the property of the Nampūṭiri Brahmans, and this right was, and by them is, still considered unalienable: nor will they allow that any other person can with propriety be called a *Jenmcar* or proprietor of land."[2] There is considerable truth in the observation of Mr Justice Kuññu Rāman Nāyar that "the Brahmans in Kērala were, at a very early period, shrewd enough to foresee that the halo of sanctity which encircled themselves might not be proof against the gradual degeneracy of religious feelings which time must produce, and they constitutionalised

1. *Report* dated 4th August 1807.
2. Vol. II, p. 60.

that sanctity by assigning large tracts of land and their revenues to certain temples built and consecrated by them. The actual Governors or Rulers of several villages (Ḍēśams) and latterly of Nāṭūs (Provinces), imitating the example of Brahmins, founded and endowed other temples. Other persons also did the same."[1]

Their anticipation that the integrity of temple lands would be respected was realised to a large extent, for, Hyder let them alone, and it was only when his fanatic and tyrannical son, Tippu, appeared on the scene that these lands were subjected to tax for the first time in the history of Malabar when the Brahman landlords had to fly from the country. Mr. Warden, in 1801, speaks of the same class "as the principal original landlords of the country."[2] Major Walker, reporting about the same period on the land tenures of Malabar, observed:—"The Jenmakāran possesses the entire right to the soil and no earthly authority can with justice deprive him of it. But his right is confined to the property and he possesses neither judicial nor political authority."[3] In 1803, the Board of Revenue at Fort St. George admitted that "individual proprietory right generally prevailed throughout the province" (Malabar). They were not prepared to admit the "allodial right (as the native proprietors maintained it to be) which recognizes no superior, renders no service, nor contributes any portion of its profits to the common wealth," for the reason that "such a right can appertain to the sovereign or lord paramount of the soil only." But they held that "it is a fee-simple or hereditary right of possession, subject to some of those various conditions from which no subject can be exempt."[4] In 1807, we have a full and well-considered *Report* of Mr. Thackeray, Collector of Malabar, dated 4th of August,

1. *Memo on the Land Tenures of Travancore*, p. 10.
2. *Report*, dated 19th March 1801.
3. P. 29.
4. *Fifth Report*, Vol. II, p. 440.

wherein he says:—"Almost the whole of the land in Malabar, cultivated and uncultivated, is private property, and held by jenm right, which conveys full absolute property in the soil. * * There are rules established, time out of mind, for the transfer, lease, and mortgage of land; and where a regular system of common law has been established and observed time out of mind, and where it appears in general reasonable and applicable, it may be inferred that the object for which such a system was formed must exist. There is obstinate opinion, and general tradition, to confirm the validity and antiquity of the title. The neighbouring countries of Travancore, Bednore, and Canara, have the same institution, and nearly the same rules regarding private property, which seem never to have been called in question. Every public and private authority, except Tippu, appears to have admitted this right; the British Government appears to have recognized it, and the people of Malabar have shown that they are able and willing to defend it, with stronger arguments than words: and, at all events, whether the right existed or not, it would be now impolitic, and unjust, to call it in question. So that I think it will be admitted that the Malabar Jenmakars do possess the full property in the soil. * * The Jenmum right conveys full absolute property in the land, and is not liable to become extinct by laches or desertion. The jenmkar, or proprietor can dispose of his land, as he pleases; by executing the deeds of transfer, he transfers it to an individual; by treason, he forfeits it to the sovereign. If he dies intestate without heirs, it escheats to the State; but as the jenmkars claim to the right of adoption, and the power of devising their lands to whom they please, but chiefly to pagodas, lands seldom reverts to the State for want of heirs."[1] In the *Fifth Report*[2] the following passage occurs :— "In Malabar, where private property has also

1. See passage quoted in Appendix VII. Sir Charles Turner's *Minute on the Land Bill*, Madras.

2. Vol. II, p. 81

existed from most ancient times, it is distinguished by the word Jenm signifying birthright." We gather from Col. Macauly's "excellent reports" on the land tenures of Travancore that, in that country also, the right to private property was fully recognised. Col. Macauly, who was British Resident in Travancore, (1800-1810) observes that such property was distinguished by the emphatical word *Junmum*, "a term having the express signification of *birthright*. '[1] In Travancore, the Nampūṭiris only are still recognised as original Jenmies, and their lands known as Brahmaswams, as well as lands belonging to pagodas known as Ḍēvaswams, are still absolutely exempt, in their normal condition, from taxation.[2] In December 1812, the Court of Directors referred to the Jenmakkārs as "the hereditary proprietors of the soil."[3] Once more, in 1815, Mr. Warden, Collector of Malabar, in reporting to the Board of Revenue, pointed to the resemblance between the Mirasi right in Tanjore and the jenmam right in Malabar and observed: "The resemblance is precisely similar in that prominent and essential qualification which vests in the holder an absolute property in the soil." Mr. Ellis, writing in 1816, took the same view of the Jenmies' position and rights,[4] and Sir Thomas Munro mentions the Nampūṭirīs as "the ancient proprietors of the whole country." He also observes that the Ḍēśavāli and the Nāṭuvāli, i. e., the head of the village and of the district, both claimed to have obtained their offices with all the privileges appurtenant thereto from the Nampūṭirīs.[5] In a minute of the Board of Revenue of the 5th of January 1818, we read:— "In the province of Malabar, the exclusive right of the ryot to the

1. See passage quoted by Wilkes, Vol. I, p. 98.
2. See *State Manual*, Vol. III, p: 316.
3. See Sir Ch. Turner's *Minute on the Land Tenures of Malabar*, Chapter II, para 30.
4. Mirasi Papers, p. 179.
5. See Report on Malabar, 4th July 1817, paras 7 and 15.

hereditary possession and usufruct of the soil is known by the term Jenm, or *birthright*, and originally belonged exclusively to the natives of that province, being vested partly in the Nampūṭirīs or Brahmans peculiar to the Western Coast, *but chiefly in the Nayars*, who, though Śūḍrās[1], constituted at once the chief landed proprietors and the principal military tribe of Malabar".[2] Again: "The jenmakkārs, free from all interference of this kind (payment of land revenue), were the independent owners of the land. They held by right of birth, not of the prince, but in common with him, and therefore may be considered as having possessed a property in the soil more absolute than even that of the landlord in Europe." [3]

In a memorandum drawn for Government in 1850 by the Collector of Malabar, he remarked "that all land in Malabar is strictly private property and the rights of the Jenmakkār or proprietor are held to be inalienable, whether it be cultivated or whether it be laid waste. So far is this carried that it is laid down by the standard authority on all matters relating to the land tenures of Malabar (Major Walker) that, should a person bring into cultivation a piece of waste ground which appeared to have no claimant, the owner, on making his appearance after any lapse of time, would have a right to resume his property, paying for the improvements that had been made." In short, as observed by Wilkes, "the hereditary right to landed property in Canara and Malabar was, and continues to be, indefeasible, even by the longest prescriptive occupancy: the heir may at any distance of time reclaim his patrimony on paying the expenses of such improvements as may have been made in the estate." [4] Of course, this right is now subject to the provisions of various enactments of the Legislature.

1. They are not.
2. Para 21.
3. Para 23.
4. Vol. I, p. 95.

Wilkes, referring to Sir Thomas Munro's Reports of the 9th of November 1800 and of the 15th of August 1807, says:—" Sir Thomas Munro who assures that the lands of Canara have for ages been private property, and that the landed property of that province is both more ancient and more perfect than that of England, has stated with equal confidence that 'private property *has never existed* in India, *excepting on the Malabar Coast.*' " Wilkes proceeds to point out that "in ancient royal grants of land in Canara and Malabar, the revenue, or king's share, is specified to be the thing given; in other parts of India, the *land itself* is given." [1]

The people of Malabar were, indeed, very tenacious of their rights regarding landed property and, as remarked by Mr. Thackeray, they were able and willing to defend them, with stronger arguments than words. Wilkes has explained how the nature of the country has made this possible. " The strength of the country," says he, "has enabled the people to defend their rent and remain landlords. Perhaps the strength of the country along the ghats is the true cause of the existence of private property in the soil, which the inhabitants of Bednore, Canara, Malabar and Travancore not only claim, but have been generally ready to support by force of arms. It would most likely have existed everywhere, but in other parts of India, armies of horse could carry into execution the immediate orders of a despot, who never admitted of private property, because his own wants incited, and his power enabled, him to draw the whole landlord's rent." [2]

"This much is certain," says Major Walker, " that in no country in the world is the nature of the species of property better understood than in Malabar, nor its rights more tenaciously maintained. It is probable * * that the possession of Jenmam land was originally inalienable, and confined to one or two castes." [3]

1. Vol. I, p. 79.
2. Vol. I, p. 97.
3. P. 41.

Sir Charles Turner, late Chief Justice of Madras, after reviewing all the literature available on the subject and after fully considering the nature and effect of early documents, has arrived at the following conclusion:— "It appears to me impossible to resist the conclusion that whatever the origin of the title, the Jenmies were, and for centuries before British rule had been, owners of the soil in full proprietory right, and that their rights were recognised even by the class that would have been most hostile to them, the Moplahs, who, owing to the persecution of Tippoo, had for some years been the masters of the situation." [1]

We have seen with what persistent tenacity the landlord holds to his proprietory right in land. That is perhaps the last thing that he would part with in this world. The giving up of the Jenmam right or its alienation is held to be sinful in the eye of man, and is said to incur divine displeasure. But the necessities of human beings compel them often to give up their dearly cherished rights. When such necessities arise, the proprietor gradually divests himself of his interest in the land by a graduated series of transactions parting with his rights inch by inch. He feels the wrench rather keenly and the nature and *quantum* of rights thus given up at each transaction fully discloses the extreme reluctance with which he divests himself of them. The final deed of surrender is called Aṭṭippēr and is known by that name from Karwar in Canara to Cape Comorin in Travancore, the whole of Kērala. There are three or four intermediate stages, besides others to be noticed later on, to be gone through before a Jenmi makes up his mind to execute a deed of final surrender, the Aṭṭippēr. These are (1) Kaiviṭu oṟṟi (2) Oṟṟikkumpuṟam (3) Nīr mutal or Kuṭima Nīr and in some places (4) a Jenma Paṇayam.

(1) Kaiviṭu oṟṟi, literally, the deed received from the hand, is that which must be first executed.

1. *Minute*, Chapter II, para 37.

It is a species of mortgage. "In this Karaṇam" (deed), says Major Walker, "the sum of 1,000 fanams will appear paid to the Jenmakar (landlord) as the value of the paramba (garden). The 500 fanams, which remain to complete the purchase, (the garden being valued at 1,500 fanams) are in compensation for the Jenmam right always estimated as worth one-half of the real value of the estate." In Travancore, the tenure is known as Kaippaṭa oṫṫi, and it is said that the mortgage amount would be almost the value of the land. The mortgagee obtains possession of the paramba, but he is not complete owner and, therefore, can neither cut a tree nor burn nor bury the dead in it nor sell it to another without giving the first option to the jenmi. The amount advanced will be mentioned in the deed.

(2) Oṫṫikkumpuṙam. If the jenmi is pressed with the necessity of a further loan, the mortgagee advances a further sum, calculated at 20 *per cent* on the original amount, and the jenmi has to execute this deed. The term Oṫṫikkumpuṙam means 'over and above the oṫṫi'. By virtue of this deed, the mortgagee assumes two-thirds of the jenmam rights and dispossesses the original jenmakar of so much authority. Some of the jenmam rights are suspended or left divided between the parties, that is, they cannot be exercised without mutual agreement or previous permission; neither the jenmi nor the mortgagee who is, to some extent, raised to the same rank, can burn or bury a corpse on the premises, or cut a tree in it without the consent of the other. No witnesses to this deed are necessary, but the heir whose consent is absolutely necessary should be present at the time of executing the deed. The amount advanced may be shown.

(3) Ṅīr muṭal or Kuṭima Ṅīr. If the wants of the jenmi should still continue, he may take a still further advance of 20 *per cent* on the Kaivīṭu oṫṫi amount and execute this deed. By this he loses seven-eighths of his authority over the paramba which, of course

goes over to the mortgagee. "It is thus," says Major Walker, "that he surrenders the Jenmam rights by degrees, and the tenacious manner in which he quits them is the strongest proof of the high value at which they are valued. In this state, however, the power of the Koḷḷuṅṅavan(mortgagee) preponderates, and he may now perform funeral obsequies without asking permission: a privilege which the Jenmakar cannot in this situation of the property exercise. But the liberty of cutting trees is still balanced." Under this tenure also, the jenmi has no method of recovering the right he has parted with, but by the offer of the alienee. The term Ṅīr Muṭal is a compound of two words, (Nīr=water and Muṭal=property) meaning "that the property is conveyed into the body and attached to it by means of water." Kuṭima Nīr, (Kuṭima=a family and Ṅīr=water) implies "that the water of this paramba is thus secured for the use of himself and his posterity." The consent of the heir is also necessary on this occasion, and he must be present. No other witnesses are necessary. The amount may be shown in the document. This is the last step which can be taken by the jenmi without parting with his rights for ever. Major Walker says that his Malabar informant observed to him with a pious fervour: "It is now that the divine superintendence will in its goodness look with an eye of compassion on the situation of the Jenmakar. Through the favour of *Ishwara* (God), he may still keep possession of an estate created for his support."

(4) Jenma Paṇayam. According to some, the jenmi has yet another chance of taking an advance and thus avoiding an absolute alienation of his jenmam right. Up to this point, he has only pledged the usufruct of the land. By the Jenma Paṇayam, he makes a mortgage of his jenmam whereby he relinquishes the power to redeem and has nothing left in him but the nominal right of proprietorship. According to the late Sadar Court at Madras, "On executing this deed, the land-lord

casts a few drops of water from his hand, indicating that he has yielded up all right of further interference in the land. He has also deprived himself of the power of sale to any one but the mortgagee."

The last and final deed which completes the sale and transfers the full freehold to the purchaser is called the Aṭṭippēr or Aṭṭippēṟṟ ōla. Of this term, Major Walker says: "Aṭṭippēṟṟ ōla—Aṭṭipora, to pluck up by the root, implying that the Jenmakar is entirely dispossessed of his estate; ōla, a cadjan, writing; hence the Karaṇam (document) is called the Aṭṭippēṟṟ ōla, a name strongly expressive of its meaning." Others derive the word Aṭṭippēr from peṟu = birth; hence equivalent to jenmam, birthright. The execution and delivery of this, the last and final deed of transfer, is attended with great formality. At the execution and delivery of this deed, six persons must be present, viz.:

1. One of the caste of the jenmi.
2. One of his near relations.
3. The heir.
4. A person on the part of the Raja who must have been apprised of the transaction.
5. The person who draws out the deed.
6. The Ḍēśavāḷi or headman of the village.

Neither the rent nor the jenma ḍravyam (the price of the jenmam) are specified in the deed.

Where the previously mentioned three or four preliminary deeds had not been passed, and the exigencies of the jenmi call for an immediate transfer of all his rights by the execution of an Aṭṭippēr, all the four or five deeds have to be executed simultaneously; for the last one cannot be executed without going through the other stages in regular succession. In this case, all the deeds are signed just before their formal delivery: the purchaser then pays four fanams to the jenmi: this is called oppu kāṇam, signing fee.

When the four deeds have been signed, the six persons who were present at the drawing up of the Aṭṭippeṭṭ ōla assemble and the jenmi brings a kinṭi (a bell-metal vessel with a spout) of water from the paramba (garden) which is under disposal, with some rice and flower put into it. The purchaser then puts two fanams as Ṅīr Kāṇam or water-fee: the jenmi then standing facing to the west and the purchaser eastwards informs his heirs and those assembled that he is going to make over his jenmam rights to such and such a person and with their consent pours out the water saying, "I give you the water of such a compound to drink". The purchaser standing, his left hand supporting his right which is held close to his mouth, receives a little of the water in the hand and drinks it. If he be of a higher caste, he washes his face and feet with it. At the time of drinking the water, the heir is given four fanams called Ananṭiravan Naṭu Kāṇam (a present to the heir for his consent). A Ṭūśikāṇam (a fee for the use of the instrument of writing, Ṭūśi or iron style) of eight fanams is paid by the purchaser to the person who draws up the deed. A present of two or three fanams should also be paid to each of the six persons for their attendance. This is called ṅaṭu, meaning middle, alluding to the position or agency of the parties as middle-men or advisers between the jenmi and the purchaser. The transaction is brought to a close by the payment of a fee both by the seller and the purchaser to the Raja, the amount being 10 *per cent* on the jenmam value of the property. If the heir of the jenmi objects to the sale, the business cannot be further proceeded with. The pouring of water by the seller and the drinking of it by the purchaser is a symbol of delivery and taking possession of the property sold and purchased, and such symbols are by no means peculiar to Malabar. The English common law requires delivery of a clod of earth to make a conveyance complete and this ceremony is known as the "livery of seisin."

After the ceremony above described is gone through, the purchaser is confirmed in all the seignorial rights of the jenmi, and the entire freehold of the property is transferred to him. We have already referred to the great respect, almost reverence, with which the jenmam right is looked upon. Major Walker has observed that it is "the case in Malabar * * * * that the land, after the mere property of it is gone, continues to acknowledge the feudal rights of a superior. The possessor is bound to perform certain services; he attends the jenmakkaran into the field, he appears on nuptial celebrations, and he presents his offering at the feast of Ōṇam."

The ceremony above described as well as the forms in which the deeds are drawn up are no longer required after the Stamp and Registration laws have come into operation. They have now been cast into the limbo of oblivion; but they are still of value as curiosities of antiquity showing the origin and development of property and rights in land in Malabar, and are still of use in ascertaining the incidents of various tenures.

The rights granted by the Aṭṭippēr deed are minutely specified, and certainly nothing can more forcibly define the ownership to the soil, or be exhaustive of all possible rights in it, than the words in which they are expressed. [1]

They are:—"The properties named and the produce thereon, either on the surface or in the subsoil, the stones, the rugged rocks, the nux vomica tree stump, thorns, rough surfaces, the ferocious snakes, the paths therein used by the public, the water courses, the deer forests, the groves of bee-hives, water, treasure troves, wells, the sky above and the nether strata below etc." These words are those generally used in Aṭṭippēr deeds

1. "വസ്തുക്കളെും അതിലുള്ള മേലുഭയം, കീഴ്ഭയം, കല്ല്, കരട്, കാഞ്ഞിരക്കുററി, മുള്ള്, മുരട്, മൂക്കൻപാമ്പ്, ആൾപോകുംവഴി, നീർപോകും ചാൽ, മാൻപെട്ടം കാട്, തേൻപെട്ടം ചോല, നീർ, നിധി, കിണറ, ആകാശം, പാതാളം മുതലായ്ക്കു."

in the south, and Mr. Nagam Ayya observes: "The list is complete and exhaustive giving no room for the quibbles of lawyers of later days and corresponds to the *esque ad caclumoe esqus ad solum* of English conveyance, meaning "from the centre of the earth to the heavens above."[1] "The general words in a Malayālam deed," says Sir Charles Turner, "exceeded in number even those that were formerly employed by English conveyancers." He adds: "Now if these words had any meaning, and we may presume they had, they point to an ownership in the soil as complete as was ever enjoyed by a free-holder in England."

A more complete and exhaustive enumeration may, however, be found in an Aṭṭippēr deed hailing from the north. The deed of sale No. 15 in Appendix XII of Logan's *Malabar*, conveys to the purchaser the following:—

1. Good stones.
2. Charcoal (probably a mistake for Karaṭu —bad stones.
3. Stumps of strychnos nux-vomica.
4. Thorns.
5. Roots.
6. Stupid, bad, wicked, snakes.
7. Holes.
8. Mounds or foundations.
9. Treasure.
10. Wells.
11. Skies.
12. Lower world.
13. Water-courses.
14. Boundaries.
15. Field ridges.
16. Canals.
17. Washing places
18. Foot-paths.
19. Streams.

1. *State Manual*, Vol III, p. 323.

20. Deer forests.
21. Shady places where bees make honey.
22. Ḍēśam.
23. Authority in the Ḍēśam.
24. Amśam (share).
25. Rank.
26. Battle wager.
27. Import, export and transport, custom.
28. Everything else.

There are a large number of tenures extant in Malabar at present: a larger number still has gone into desuetude. The Proceedings of the Court of Sadar Adalat at Madras, dated 5th August 1856, notices about 24 tenures. In Travancore, Mr. Justice Kuññu Rāman Nāyar says that there are more than 100 tenures in use to designate tenures subordinate to Jenmam.[1]

Some of the tenures now in use may be mentioned hereunder. They will be seen to extend from the most simple, such as the Veṙumpaṭṭam or simple lease, to the most absolute alienation of all rights, the Aṭṭippēr.

I. Leases.—Leases are either (a) temporary or (b) perpetual (Śāśvataṃ).

(a) Temporary leases. Under this class come the following:—

(1) Veṙumpāṭṭam, Veṙumkari, or Veṙum Koḷu, meaning a bare lease, i e, one unaccompanied by an advance (Veṙum=bare and pāṭṭam=lease). The simplest mode of transfer is the Veṙumpāṭṭam or simple lease. Where no term is fixed, it enures for one year only. Under this, after deducting the bare cost of seed and cultivation, the whole of the estimated net produce is payable to the landlord. The tenant is in fact a labourer on subsistent wages, liable to be turned out when the landlord chooses. The old custom was to reserve one-third of the net produce, after deducting the cost of seed and cultivation, for the tenant, and the

1. Para 2, *Memo.*

remaining two-thirds went to the landlord and the tenancy continued for some time. In such cases, the arrangement was beneficial to both parties, and the tenants always aimed to convert verumpāṭṭam into kāṇappāṭṭam, which gave them a better fixity of tenure.

Sometimes a year's rent, called muppāṭṭam, will be paid in advance at the commencement of the tenancy, as security for the annual payment of rent, which will be refunded on the determination of the lease, when all the accounts, such as value of improvements due to the tenant, arrears of rent due by him &c., are adjusted between the parties. The lease is then termed Muppāṭṭam, Ṭalappāṭṭam or Kaṭṭakkāṇam.

(2) Mēlpāṭṭam is a lease of trees and enures only for one year unless any special term is fixed.

(3) Kuḷi Kāṇam and (4) Kuḷi Kāṇampāṭṭam— These are improvement leases, the former applying to waste land and the latter to land partly cultivated and partly not. The lease runs for 12 years and the tenant has to be paid the value of improvements made by him on ejectment. Neglect to cultivate and denial of landlord's title forfeits the tenure.

(5) Verumpāṭṭam-Kuḷikāṇanm-Kuṭiyiruppu is a lease akin to Kuḷikāṇam and is in use only in the Calicut Taluk.

(6) Kuṭṭikāṇam is a lease for a term of the right to cut trees, generally a stipulated number, in a forest: a fee is charged for each tree cut. On account of these fees, the contractor usually pays a sum in advance as security and agrees to pay the balance by instalments.

Under class (b) i. e., Perpetual lease or śāśvaṭam come the following:— (1) Aṭima or Kuṭima—a service tenure. In this case, the land is made over in perpetuity to the grantee, either unconditionally as a mark of favour, or on condition of certain services being performed. The terms Aṭima and Kuṭima mean a slave or one subject to the landlord, the grant being generally made to such persons. A nominal fee of about two fanams (8as.) a year is payable to the landlord to show that he still retains the proprietory title. Land bestowed as a mark of favour can never be resumed, but where it is granted as remuneration for certain services to be performed, the non-performance of such services, involving the necessity of having them discharged by others, will give the landlord power to recover the land. The non-payment of the annual fee will form no ground for ousting the grantee; but it will be recoverable by action. The hereditary property of Native Princes cannot be conferred on this tenure, the ruling princes having only the right of enjoyment during life without power to alienate.

(2) Anubhavam—is both a service grant and a grant of land to support a Sṯhānam or dignity. It was customary for princes, when conferring a title on any person, to grant him at the same time sufficient land to enable him to maintain the dignity of his position. Grants under this tenure were also bestowed upon persons for special services rendered, or for the future performance of certain services. The tenant cannot be ejected, except where there are conditions imposed, and he fails to fulfil them ; but, on the other hand, he and his heirs have only the right of enjoyment, and cannot alienate their title. A trifling annual fee is generally paid to the landlord to show that he has not surrendered the proprietory right.

(3) Karam kari or Jenma Koïu.—a grant of land for services rendered or for future services. In this case, the land is made over for permanent cultivation by the tenant in return for services rendered. Where the proprietory title is vested in a pagoda, the grant will be made for future services. In some cases, the land is mortgaged on this tenure, the kāṉam mortgagee paying the surplus rent produce to the landlord after deducting the interest of the money he has

advanced. The tenant has, in north Malabar, only a life-interest in the property which, at his death, reverts to the landlord. In the south, the land is enjoyed by the tenant and his descendants until there is a failure of heirs, when it reverts to the proprietor. Except where the land is granted for special services, an annual rent is payable under this tenure. The tenant's right is confined to that of cultivation, but it is permanent, and he cannot be ousted for arrears of rent, which must be recovered by action, unless there be a specific clause in the deed declaring the lease cancelled, if the rent be allowed to fall into arrears.

(4) Kārāima—grant of land to temple servants for performing offices therein.

(5) Ari Jenmam—a grant of land by temple trustees, the tenant being bound to daily supply a fixed quantity of rice to the temple to be offered to the deity and, after the usual offerings, he is allowed to take back the cooked rice for his own use. The incidents which are common to all śāśvaṭam lands are :—

(1) the rent is nominal ;

(2) the tenants cannot be ousted in default of payment of rent which may be recovered by an action ;

(3) the land reverts to the grantor only on failure of heirs to the grantee ;

(4) in the case of those tenures burthened with performance of certain services, their non-performance would forfeit the tenure, except when the service has become unnecessary.

II. Mortgages.—There are various kinds of mortgage tenures in use, ranging from the simple mortgage redeemable at will, to those that leave but very little, if any, right subsisting in the mortgagor. Some of these may be mentioned here :—

(1) Chūṇṭippaṇayam—is a simple mortgage without possession. The land is here pledged as

security for the re-payment, with interest, for certain sums advanced, but the lender has no right to interfere in the management of the property.

(2) Ṭoṭupaṇayam—is where the mortgagor agrees to put the mortgagee in possession of the property mortgaged in case of default of payment of interest according to the stipulation in the deed. Where such stipulation exists, the lender can sustain an action for possession. In other cases, he must sue for the recovery of principal and interest of the loan, the land being liable in the event of the money not being paid.

(3) Ṅilamuṙi or Kuṭiyirumpād—is a simple mortgage without possession; the creditor under an arrangement with the mortgagor agrees to receive the rent produce of the land leased by the mortgagor to a tenant, in lieu of interest. Should the tenant fail to deliver the rent produce to the creditor, he can sustain an action only against his debtor, the landlord.

(4) Karippaṇayam, Koḷuviṙakkampaṇayam or Kaivaśampaṇayam—is a usufructuary mortgage, the mortgagee enjoying the usufruct or part thereof of the property in lieu of interest and accounting for the remainder to the mortgagor.

(5) Uṇṭaṙuṭippaṇayam—is a mortgage which redeems itself within a fixed period, the principal debt being liquidated by the surplus usufruct after payment of interest only.

(6) Oṫṫi—is a mortgage with possession, the mortgagee enjoying the entire produce of the land, the landlord merely retaining the proprietory title and the power to redeem after the lapse of 12 years. It carries with it a right of pre-emption in favour of the mortgagee. In Travancore, an oṫṫi does not differ from a usufructuary mortgage.

(7) Peṙumaṙṫham—is a mortgage in which the mortgagor receives the then full market value of the property, retaining the empty title of jenmi, and, in redeeming it, he repays, not the amount originally

advanced to him but the actual market value at the time of redemption.

Between the oṯṯi mortgage and the final surrender of proprietory rights by an aṭṭippēr deed, we have seen that four other mortgages, already described, have to be gone through, viz.,

(8) Kaiviṭu oṯṯi,

(9) Oṯṯikkumpuṟam,

(10) Ṅīr muṭal or Kuṭima Ṅīr,

(11) Janmapaṇayam.

III. We now come to the third class of tenures, viz., those which are of the nature of a lease and mortgage combined, and of these, the tenure known as kāṇam is the most prevalent and the most important.

(1) Kāṇam.—This is one of the most important tenures in Malabar on which a large portion of land is held by tenants. It partakes of the character of both lease and mortgage. Major Walker observes that "few of the tenures in Malabar are simple; they unite in almost every case the consideration of mortgage and rent. In this instance they discover that distrust and want of confidence peculiar to infant societies when a pledge is the most natural security for property." He treats the kāṇam as a lease. He says that " the kāṇam is a sum of money deposited in the hands of the jenmakār as a security in case the kuṭiyān (tenant) should pay his yearly rent; should the kuṭiyān (tenant) neglect his payment, the jenmakār reimburses himself from the kāṇam money; should the kuṭiyān have neglected the estate and the produce by that means be diminished, the loss will be made good to the jenmakār from the kāṇam money." Messrs. Farmer and Graeme seem to agree with this view, Mr. Farmer saying distinctly that the kāṇakārs were not mortgagees. But the Board of Revenue at Madras, in 1803, and Mr. Warden, Collector of Malabar, in 1815, as distinctly say that kāṇam is simply a mortgage, the latter adding that the mortgagee, after

entering into possession, is invested with every right of proprietorship, except that of alienating the land by sale.

Mr. Thackeray, however, described kāṇappāṭṭam, in 1807, thus:—

"Kāṇa-pāṭṭam is when the landlord lets his lands receiving a sum in advance from his lessee which may be considered either as a loan or as security for the due payment of rent. The tenant retains so much of the rent as will discharge his claim for interest and pays the remainder to the proprietor."

The position of the kāṇam tenant in Malabar, until the East India Company's Courts interfered in his behalf, was an anomalous one. In law, he was little more than a tenant-at-will and liable to capricious eviction; in practice, so long as he kept on good terms with his landlord, he had a permanent right of occupancy. "Mr. Strange," says Mr. Moore, "must be looked upon as the author of the 12 years term now enjoyed by kāṇam tenants." Mr. Strange observed in his Report, as special Commissioner, as follows:—

"It is obviously highly essential that the tenant should not be disturbed from possession arbitrarily and at unduly short periods, and the recognised rule is that if he should have paid a fine for his lease, it should endure for 12 years under certain reservations, as when the landlord, if a Raja, dies when he should renew with his successor, or when the landlord requires more money on the land and the tenant will not provide it, and it is obtainable from another; or when rents are not paid."

On the 27th of February 1856, the Sadar Court at Madras observed, in the course of a judgment, "that a mortgagee is not liable to be displaced until after a tenure of 12 years, such being a recognised usage of the country having the force of law." Ever since, the 12 years term has been adopted and is now the recognised period of a kāṇam tenure.

Mr. Justice Kuññu Rāman Nāyar of the Travancore High Court accounts for the term of 12 years, and the right of renewal at the expiry of the period, in the following manner :—

"Kāṉa-pāṭṭam is a combination of two words, kāṉam and pāṭṭam and has been taken in Malayāḷam to mean a tenure, by whatever terms known, under which the rent due is secured by an advance, and the advance is treated as a charge on the land and carrying interest.

" The kāṉa-pāṭṭam lessee was put into possession by a writing given to him by the jenmi which originally specified that the lease was to run only for a period of three years (kālam mūvvāṉṭāl) and it is probable that the three years' period was originally fixed with reference to the period of the duration of the administration by Rakṣha Puruṣhans or protectors, of Kēraḷa Uṭppaṭṭi. It was an understood thing, in ancient days, that every muniment of title to land should be renewed at the change of each administration. and, when the period of administration was extended to 12 years in the time of Perumāls, the term of such leases was extended to 12 years or, at least, the documents were not renewed until 12 years, although the ancient phraseology of kālam mūvvāṉṭu was still retained in some deeds, the people being conservatives to the core and reluctant to change anything prescribed by their ancestors. There are not wanting instances in which old and unmeaning formulas are still kept up simply because they were ordained by our ancestors ."

Nature and incidents of Kanam.—A sum of money or paddy is deposited with the landlord, on which the tenant is entitled to interest, which varies from three to six *per cent.* The rent payable to the landlord—kāṉam pāṭṭam—will not be more than one-half of the net-produce after deducting the cost of seed and cultivation,

1. P. 29.

The tenant is entitled to be left in possession undisturbed for twelve years, and to be reimbursed for all unexhausted improvements when evicted. If, at the end of 12 years, the tenant renews the kāṇam, he must pay a fine or premium, which, according to ancient usage, ought not to exceed 20 to 25 *per cent* of the kāṇam, or one year's rental at the option of the landlord, but which, in the present day, is usually fixed according to custom or the landlord's caprice.

Renewal fees consisted in the olden times of :—

(1) Aṭuṭṭaṭu, i.e., a sum of 10 to 20 *per cent* of the kāṇam amount as the case may be.

(2) Saujanyam, i.e., money value of one year's jenmi pāṭṭam mentioned in the kāṇam deed.

(3) Oppu, i. e., three to five *per cent* on the kāṇam amount paid to the jenmi for signing the deed.

(4) Ṭūśi, i.e., two *per cent* on the kāṇam amount paid to the writer of the deed.

After renewal, the tenant is entitled to hold the land for another term of twelve years.

(2) Puṙamkaṭam. If during the term of a kāṇam, a further sum of money is advanced by the tenant, it is termed a puṙamkaṭam or puṙavāippa, and he is entitled to deduct from the rent the interest on money so advanced.

(3) Mēlkāṇam. If the tenant is not prepared to make the advance, the landlord will have recourse to a stranger in whose favour he will execute a mēlkāṇam. The mēlkāṇam-holder will be entitled to redeem the kāṇam holder at the expiry of his term. The mēlkāṇam or mēlchārṭ is also a recent innovation, though it is nothing more than a second mortgage.

In Travancore, "the essential idea of a kāṇapāṭṭam is that of a lease on payment, immediate or future, of a fee or fine over and above the money advanced or lent as security for the repayment of rent. In North Ṭravancore, kāṇapāṭṭam was originally a transaction between landlord and tenant to regulate the holding of land for agricultural purposes and, in South Travancore, in most cases, a transaction between creditor and debtor having for its object the mortgage of land as security for the debt."[1]

In Travancore and Cochin, legislation has secured to the kāṇam tenant fixity of tenure, the tenancy being declared permanent and irredeemable on condition of the tenant forfeiting his rights under specified circumstances. At the same time, the right of the landlord to enhance rent and reduce the rate of interest and levy periodical renewal fees and certain fixed perquisites by summary process is also declared.

These perquisites are known as Āṙaṭiyanṭaram fees, i. e., fees payable to the jenmi on six ceremonial occasions such as:—

(1) Annapṙāśanam, i. e., the ceremony of the giving of rice for the first time to the jenmi's child.

(2) Upaṅayanam., the ceremony of investing the child with the sacred thread.

(3) Samāvaṙṭṭanam, the ceremony closing the Brahmachārya period.

(4) Vēli, marriage ceremony.

(5) Piṇḍam, funeral ceremony celebrated with a feast on the 11th day after death.

(6) Māsam, festival celebrated at the end of a year after death.

The six tenures that gradually eat up the jenmi's right to absolute ownership are said to be:—

(1) Kuḷikkāṇam, which is said to take away one-eighth of his rights.

(2) Kāṇam, which takes away one-fourth.

(3) Oṫṫi, which takes away one half.

(4) Oṫṫikkumpuṙam, which takes away three-fourths.

1. *Memo on the Land Tenures of Travancore*, Part I, para 25.

(5) Jenmappaṇayam which takes away seven-eighths and

(6) Aṭṭippēr which extinguishes all his rights to the above-said ownership of the property.

The mode of fixing the pāṭṭam or landlord's share is as follows:—

A land is said to sow 15 paras of seed.

	Paras.
Its estimated yield is seven-fold or	105
Deduct for seed 15 paras and for cultivation 15 paras	30
And the balance or maximum veṟumpāṭṭam is	75
The minimum veṟumpāṭṭam would be	50
The kāṇapāṭṭam would be	37½
Interest at 5 *per cent* on a kāṇam of rupees 100, would be Rs. 5 equivalent	15
And the net rent payable would be	22½
Interest at 5 *per cent* on an oṟṟi of Rs. 250 would be Rs. 12½ or	37½

And the interest would exactly extinguish the usufruct. The saleable value of such land would probably be about 12 years' purchase of the net yield, i. e., 75×12=900 paras or Rs. 300.

In summing up his consideration of the land tenures of Malabar, Major Walker observes:—" It is obivious from * * the tenor of the deeds that considerable provision has been made in Malabar for the security of landed property. Its limits and rights are ascertained in almost every situation, with no small degree of exactness. There is great attention paid to protect it against encroachment, and to preserve all its privileges inviolate. In all the stages of conveyance, the most watchful jealousy is observable to prevent the possession being loaded with additional engagements, and to save it from total alienation. The conditions of each step are the subject of a new writing, in which they are recorded with precision. The allodial right is the one last parted with. The final act which is to make a complete transfer of the land and its privileges, must be executed before a number of witnesses, with the consent of the heir, with the knowledge of the sovereign, and concluded by an impressive ceremony. The whole cannot fail to convince us of the high estimation in which this species of property was held in Malabar. It must also prove the early and positive rights that attended it; for nothing so likely as an ancient origin could render honorary privileges hereditary and valuable. It is more than probable that they supported some political consequence in the State.

"In the inferior tenures, which only convey a temporary possession, there appears an equal attention to the interests of the proprietor and of the tenant. While the cultivator is severely punished for any loss in the produce sustained by his neglect, he is fully rewarded for his improvements. By a wise provision, the kuṭiyān is fined when he returns, before the period of his lease expires, his paṟamba into the hands of the jenmkār. The jenmkār suffers a similar mulct when he deprives his kuṭiyān, by an untimely resumption, of the lease. The heavy penalty attending this at the season of produce is next to a prohibition. The tenure by which waste lands are brought into cultivation holds out no small inducement to industry."

Sir Charles Turner says:—"In no country with which I am acquainted had the land tenures been more minutely systematized than in Malabar. Looking to the deeds which bear dates antecedent and subsequent to the Muhammadan invasion, and to the treatises on Malabar Law, which have survived that event, we find the jenmakkārs in dealing with all subordinate holders of land, resorted to the use of documents. These documents declared the rights it was intended to convey, and if they did not express specifically the incidents of the several tenures they created, they were prepared in such a form as to leave it beyond dispute that they involved the incidents which the custom of the country attached to the tenures. These incidents were generally of a highly equitable character."

The art of conveyancing was all but perfect in Malabar before the Stamp and Registration Laws came into force. These Acts or Regulations, not taking into account the various tenures extant in the country, prescribed Stamp and Registration fees for documents embodying certain specified transactions into the denomination of which parties had to reduce the original tenures. The *Vyvahara Mala* (Vyvahāra Māla), and *Vyvahara Samudram* (Vyvahāra Samuḍram), among the earlier, the *Kshiti Ratnamala* (Kṣhiṭi Raṭnamāla) and others among the later treatises, contain rules of conveyancing and forms of deeds. In former times, these used to be learnt by heart by every boy attending the village schools. But, for the last half a century or so, the ancient system of education has been much neglected, and with the exception of a few old men to be met with here and there, no one knows at present exactly what the ancient forms were. The rules of conveyancing and the forms of deed contained in the Vyvahāra Māla were thought to be so good by Colonel Munro, British Resident in Travancore, who was also for some time in charge of the administration of the State, that he considered the Vyvahāra Māla as fit for introduction into the courts of Travancore. It is, however, a sealed book at present. The result is that, there being no legislative provisions which require definiteness and exactness in lease deeds which are of a complex nature, the writing really contains but part of the contract, the parties taking it for granted that custom will regulate everything for them and that local customs must be known to any and every body who may at any time be called upon to decide any disputes between them. The result is perennial and distracting litigation which ruins both parties.

LETTER XI.

I. Sources of Revenue. Mr. Graeme, Special Commissioner in Malabar (1818-1822), has, in his Report, preserved a curious list of items which brought revenue into the coffers of the Malabar Rajas. To these may be added other sources left out by Mr. Graeme. A somewhat detailed account of the chief items may be given hereunder, as these illustrate indirectly some of the customs and manners of Malabar in ancient times. The main sources from which revenue was derived were:—

(1) Aṃkam. (2) Chuṃkam. (3) Ēḷa. (4) Kōḷa. (5) Ṭappu. (6) Piḷa. (7) Purushāntaram. (8) Pulayāṭṭu Peṇṇu. (9) Kāḷcha. (10) Daṭṭukāḷcha. (11) Ponnarippu. (12) Aṟṟaṭakkam or Aṟṟālaṭakkam. (13) Aṭimappaṇam. (14) Chērikkal. (15) Aimula. (16) Mummula. (17) Chenkompu. (18) Chenkāmp or Pūvālu. (19) Kaṇṇaṭa Puḷḷi. (20) Ānappiṭi. (21) Uṭañña Urukkaḷ. (22) Kinaṟṟil Paññi. (23) Kompu. (24) Kuṟavu. (25) Vālu. (26) Ṭōlu. (27) Talappaṇam. (28) Precious metals and stones discovered. (29) Cardamoms. (30) Valappaṇam. (31) Changāṭam. (32) Rakṣhā Bhōgam.

(1) *Amkam* (Aṃkam). Battle-wager.—Of this Captain Burton remarks: "Quarrels and private feuds were frequent amongst Nāyars, especially when differences on the subject of the fair sex, or any of their peculiar principles of honour aroused their pugnacity. It was not indispensable that the parties who were at issue should personally fight it out. Champions were allowed by law, and in practice were frequently substituted. The combatants undertook to defend the cause they espoused till death, and a term of 12 years was granted to them that they might qualify themselves for the encounter by training and practising the use of arms. Before the onset, both champions settled all their

worldly matters as the combat was *al'outrance.* The weapons used were sword and dagger ; a small shield and a silk turban being the only articles of defensive armour. This system of duelling was a source of considerable revenue to the Raja, as he was umpire of the battle, and levied the tax in virtue of his office. The amount of the fee varied according to the means of the parties. Sometimes it was as high as 1,000 fanams.[1]"

Mr. Graeme observes that women were the chief origin of the quarrels which occasioned these combats. They were confined to the Nāyars. They were thought necessary to prove or disprove the charge of seducing women under particular protection. The right to levy this revenue was sometimes transferred by a chieftain along with other privileges appertaining to the tenure of the soil.

(2) *Chumkam* (Chuṃkam).—Customs duties.—The Rajas levied customs duties onimports, exports and transports both by land and sea. The earlier Rajas, it is said, did not claim duties on articles of inland trade. The amount of duty is variously specified as 2½—3 and even 10 *per cent.* According to the *Tohfut-ul-mujahideen,* in the 16th century, the Rajas exacted a tenth part upon all articles of merchandise.[2] Nāṭuvāḷīs were also entitled to inland customs.

(3) *Ezh* (Ēḷa).—Dr. Gundhert defines the term as a fine, penalty, or a forced present. Under this head, Burton observes it is "the systematic usurpation of territory belonging to the neighbouring rulers or chiefs, whom poverty or other causes incapacitated from holding their own." Sheik Zeenuddeen says that the Rajas levied "penalties and deodands, also when any one has subjected himself to them."[3]

(4) *Kozha* (Kōḷa.)—The right to force, by violence, if necessary, contributions on occasions of emergency according to the circumstances of the subjects.

1. Equal to Rs. 250.
2. P. 73.
3. P. 73.

(5) *Tappu* (Ṭappu).—Mulcts imposed by Rajas upon those who were convicted of accidental and unintentional offences. It means also fines levied by Nāṭūvāḷīs and Ḍēśavāḷīs from their inferiors.

(6) *Pizha* (Piḷa).—Fines imposed on criminals according to the magnitude of the crime and the circumstances of the criminal. They sometimes extended to a total confiscation of property.

(7) *Purushantaram* (Puruṣhānṭaram).—Succession duty.—The word literally means "the death of the man" —a relief or sum of money claimed by the ruler from Nāṭuvāḷīs (chiefs of provinces), Ḍēśavāḷīs (chiefs of villages), heads of guilds, holders of land in free gift or under conditional tenure, and generally from all persons enjoying sṭhānam or official position in the State, whenever an heir succeeded to a death vacancy. The chiefs of provinces and districts, like the private proprietors, were exclusively entitled to receive Puruṣhānṭaram from their own tenantry, as a price of entry paid upon the decease of either party, lessor or lessee. Sometimes the chiefs claimed the privilege of levying this tax from the Raja's subjects, they being under their immediate protection. "It is supposed that the Hindu rulers were entitled under the head of Puruṣhānṭaram to a certain share of the property left by deceased Moslems, but the prevalent opinion seems to be that, in such cases, there was no fixed sum payable; and moreover, that it was not claimed from all, but only from those individuals who held situation or enjoyed privileges dependent upon the will and favour of the Raja. This tax, so similar to one of our feudal sources of revenue in the West, often reached the extent of 1,200 fanams."[1]

Dr. Day points out that a succession tax was levied in Malabar, under the native Princes, on the estates of all Moplas who died leaving heirs, and varied from 1/6 to 1/20 of the amount bequeathed. The origin of this impost, he says, is lost in obscurity, but

1. Burton, *Goa*, pp. 196—97.

legends assert it to be coeval with the advent of the Arabs to the Coast, although it was occasionally held in abeyance. The English abolished it in 1792. To prove a sovereign right over a territory, it is necessary to bring evidence that the person has received "either customs or Puruṣhānṭaram (the essential attributes of dominion in Malabar for the country).

(8.) *Pulayattu Pennu* (Pulayāṭṭu Peṇṇu).— i. e. Lewd, adulterous women convicted by the caste of offences against their virtue passed over to the Rajas who were at liberty to sell them. The Rajas used to exact various sums, as far as 600 fanams to Rs. 150, chiefly from rich Brahman families from which the degraded women came, for their maintenance and for the trouble of preventing their going astray again. The chiefs, however, used to dispose them off for money thus making a double profit out of them. But their future condition was not exactly that of a slave. They were generally bought by the coast merchants called Chetties by whom they had offspring. These married among persons of the same caste and, in a few generations, their origin was obliterated in the ramifications of new kindred into which they had been adopted.

(9.) *Kazcha* (Kāïcha).—This is another feudal tax answering to the Nuzzarena of Mussalman India. It consisted of presents made by all ranks of people to the Raja and Nāṭuvālīs on such occasions of congratulation and condolence, as his ascending the throne, opening a new palace, marrying and dying. The amount expected varied from two to thousand fanams.[1] Presents had also to be given at the two great festivals of Ōṇam and Viṣhu.

(10) *Dathu Kazacha* (Daṭṭukāïcha).—Persons desirous of making adoptions into their families have to obtain the sanction of the Raja and to pay a fee which is a fixed proportion of the estate to which the adoptee would

1. Burton, 197—8
2. Day, *Land of the Perumals*, p. 66.

become entitled. In the Native States of Cochin and Travancore, this source of revenue is still kept up, being confined, however, to Malayalīs only. In Cochin, the Ḍaṭṭukāīcha is fixed at one-fifth of the value of the adoptor's properties. In Travancore, "when the adoption is of one's own children * * * * the aṭiyaṙa fee (or Ḍaṭṭukāīcha) was to be equal to one-third of the gross value of the property possessed by the adoptor; but when the person or persons to be adopted or affiliated belong to a strange ṭaṙavād, the fee is even higher, being equal to the value of one-half of the property of the adoptor, an extra additional fee being also levied by the Sirkar where the adoptee belongs to a lower grade in the Śūḍṙa caste than the adoptor." [1]

The following is a specimen of a writ of adoption granted by the Raja of Cochin. "To our Chanṭūr Cheṙukoṅṅen—We do hereby appoint and constitute Ṭēvalaṣṣēri Iṭṭūli and her offspring as your lawful ananṭaravērs ; and they shall, as such ananṭaravērs, be answerable for all your debts—be heirs to all your wealth—possess the right of performing all *post obit* ceremonies on your remains including your funeral obsequies, inherit likewise your gold and utensils, wearing apparel, weapons and instruments and also all your immovable properties, and the right of assigning them, and your boxes and documents and all other things. Dated Chiṙakkel Kōviḷakam, Kanni 928 M. E. (1753—A. D.) Written in the handwriting of Pauvaṭṭi Ampāṭi."

(11) *Ponnarippu*=the sifting for gold.—Gold dust generally was a perquisite belonging to the Raja or Nāṭuvāli within whose territory it was found. It is well known that certain rivers in Malabār, specially those that flow down the ghats at Wynad, used to wash down gold, and the quest for gold was not allowed without the payment of a royalty. M. Dillon in his *East Indies* mentions how the process is gone through

7. T. L. R. 66 at page 68.

at Calicut: "Among the sands of the shore, there is good store of gold dust, which is very fine; and everybody has the freedom to gather it at pleasure; the biggest piece that I ever saw was not worth above 15 pence, and commonly they are not worth above 4 or 5 pence a-piece: abundance of people get a livelihood by it, and with the consent of the Governor (which is to be purchased by a certain set price for the maintenance of a hundred poor people), you may have as much sand as you please carried to your dwelling place in order to separate it with the more convenience."

(12) *Attatakkam* (Aťťaṭakkam) or *Attalatakkam* (Aťťālaṭakkam) is the right of escheat. When a man died without heirs, the chieftain took his property; specially when the lands were held in free gift. The feudal chief had similar privileges with respect to their tenants. The estates of extinct Brahman families were not, however, claimed as escheat by the Rajas. These were handed over to some Brahman, a practice still, or, at any rate till but recently, adhered to in the Native States of Travancore and Cochin. Dr. Gundhert defines this term as the right of succession to another branch of the family when that has failed of descendants. The following is a specimen of a royal letter by which the properties of an extinct Brahman Illom (house) were conferred on another in the Cochin State.

"Royal letter addressed to Cheřuvaṭṭūr Nampūṭiri.—Eḷēṭaṭ Uḷḷannūr Illom in Perumpiḷḷiśśēri Ḍēśam of ūrakam Přavirṭṭi having become extinct, that Ṭařavād together with the property, rice-lands, persons (probably retainers, guards), slaves, chest of documents and all Ampalappaṭi and ūrāyma rights and everything of whatever description with the exception of the ūrāyma of Changarāyil Kṣhēṭřam (temple), are hereby granted to you, Cheřuvaṭṭūr Nampūṭiri, for exclusive enjoyment (literally without any question from any one). Written in the month of Vṛschikam 1020 M. E. in the hand of Pavvaṭṭil Kṛshṇan, in the presence and under the orders of Kaṇayannūr Kōvilakam Raja."

AP.

(13) *Atimappanam* (Aṭimappaṇam).—The yearly payment of one or two fanams levied by the lord or prince or patron from his bondsman.

(14) *Cherikkal* (Chērikkal).—These are the private domains which the Rajas possessed in proprietory right acquired either by purchase, lapse, or escheat.

(15) *Aimula* (Aimula).
(16) *Mummula* (Mummula). } Cows with five or three dugs belonged to the Raja.

(17) *Chenkompu* (Chenkompu).—Literally "red horn," i. e., cattle that had killed a human being or any animal. According to Dr. Gundhert, this term meant primarily a victorious fighting bull kept by kings, and secondarily an old tax on them. It is probable that the old Malabar Rajas sought amusement in bull fights, and that they claimed all such animals as came out victorious in the encounter.

(18) *Chenkampu or Puvalu* (Chenkāmpu or Pūvālu).—Dr. Gundhert gives the meaning of the former term as "some peculiar mark on cattle which was an old source of revenue to the Malabar Rajas." The latter term he defines as "cattle with marked tail—a source of royal income."

(19) *Kannata Pully* (Kaṇṇaṭa Pulli).—Beeves born with a peculiar white spot near the corner of the eye.

(20) *Anapiti* (Ānappiṭi).— Wild elephant caught in the jungles—still a royal monopoly.

(21) *Utanja Urukhal* (Uṭañña Urukkal) or *Atinja Urukhal* (Atiñña Urukkal).—The former term imports ship-wrecked vessels which became crown property, while the latter means vessels drifted ashore. All ships which came ashore were annexed by the local chieftain. Another ancient custom which was a source of revenue is thus referred to by Marco Polo, respecting the kingdom of Ēli, i. e., Kōlaṭṭiri; "And you must know that if any ship enters their estuary and anchors there, having been bound for some other port, they seize her and plunder the cargo. For they say, 'you were bound for somewhere else, and 'tis God has sent you hither to us, so we have a right to all your goods.' And think it no

sin to act thus. And this naughty custom prevails all over those provinces of India, to wit that, if a ship be driven by stress of weather into some other port than that to which it was bound, it is sure to be plundered. But if a ship come bound originally to the place, they receive it with all honour and give it due protection."[1] Two centuries later, Abdur-Razak assures us, that this "naughty" custom did not exist at Calicut. "In other ports," says he, "a strange practice is adopted. When a vessel sets sail for a certain point, and suddenly is driven by a Decree of Divine Providence into another roadstead, the inhabitants under the pretext that the wind has driven it there, plunder the ship. But at Calicut, every ship, whatever place it may come from, or wherever it may be bound to, when it puts into this port is treated like other vessels, and has no trouble of any kind to put up with."[2] It was, perhaps, because Calicut was a safe port in this respect that it was more resorted to, for even before Marco Polo wrote, Ibn Batuta informs us that all maritime and mercantile nations used to take their ships to this port. Mr. Logan observes that the custom of taking ships and cargoes wrecked on the coast continued down to recent times, for the English factors at Tellicherry entered into engagements with three of the country powers, for exempting English vessels from such seizure. It was a custom which the Malayāli chieftains broke through with extreme reluctance. The kings of Bednore were the first to grant immunity in 1736—37, and thrice afterwards ratified it; then followed the Kōlaṭṭiri Prince, on 8th May, 1749, ratified in 1760; and finally the Kaṭaṭṭanād Raja gave similar immunity in 1761. No others followed their example.

(22) *Kinattil Panni* (Kiṉaṟṟil Paṅṅi), i. e., wild hogs that had fallen into wells—"an occurrence," remarks Mr. Logan, "which must have been

1. Vol. II, pp. 385—6.
2. P. 14.

frequent to judge by the wide area in which the right of the chieftains was recognised." It perhaps includes all wild animals that happen to fall into pits or deep holes.

(23) *Kompu* (Kompu) (24) *Kuravu* (Kuṙavu) (25) *Valu* (Vālu) (26) *Tolu* (Ṭōlu)	These were royal perquisites. All these refer to the successful results of hunting parties. Hunting was a national institution in ancient Malabar.

Of these, kompu denotes the tusks of dead elephants, which still belong to the Rajas in the States of Travancore and Cochin. Kuṙavu means the hind quarter of any wild hog, deer or other eatable animal slain in hunting—still a source of revenue in Native Cochin.

Vālu and Ṭōlu—the tails and skins of all tigers similiarly slain. These too are the perquisites of the Rajas or local chieftain. These perquisites are retained in the Cochin State under the head of kuṙavupōkam. Having regard to the local chieftain's right to appropriate to himself specified portions of each wild game animal slain in hunting, it will be interesting to know a little more of the national institution of hunting.

The **hunting season** opens on the 24th of October, which day is known as Ṭulāppaṭṭu, i. e., the 10th of Ṭulām, and is celebrated as the end of the monsoon, the day for review of troops and for starting on hunting expeditions. This day is still considered important and observed with festivities in places in the interior where wild game is still found. In olden days, the permission of the chieftain to hunt on his territory was not required and was never sought. There were no game preserves. The forest tracts were open for hunting purposes to all. The idea of an exclusive personal right to hunting privileges in certain limits is entirely foreign to the Malayāli customary law. Such an idea was only imported into Malabar with English courts and English law and lawyers. The hunting parties assemble at certain prescribed localities, and go forth in great glee. Forbes, in the 18th century, refers to these hunting parties as he found them in Travancore. "The Malabars, and especially the Nairs, form large hunting parties to destroy them (the wild buffaloes) as also the wild elephant, tiger and leopard. They assemble by hundreds, armed with strong spears, and large bows and arrows: forming a circle round the thickets frequented by the wild beasts, they make a loud noise to rouse them from cover and drive them towards the centre; then gradually contracting the circle, they unite in an armed phalanx, and fall upon their prey, of which very few escape; but they sometimes wound each other in their furious onset, and often sustain dreadful attacks from their enraged foe."[1]

Having secured their prey, they proceed to divide it in a systematic manner according to certain rules and forms prescribed by custom; and first they carry the game to the ūṟpaḷḷi or the privileged building for the hunters of the locality to divide the game; for the ūṟpaḷḷi was the place where the game must be broken up.

The ūṟpaḷḷi is usually erected in a jungle close to the village and is duly consecrated to the hunting deity, Ayyappan or Śāsṭa, and the formal ceremony of dividing the game takes place in front of his shrine. The person who officiates at the ceremony has the hereditary right to do so, and he alone can officiate. He is known as the Kaikāran (trustee) and is in charge of the building and its appurtenances. To him belongs, of right, the other hind-quarter of the animal, the first being already claimed by the local chieftain. The hunter who had the good fortune to kill the animal gets the head and one fore-quarter. Each of the hunters who took part in the hunt gets a share of the flesh, and three pieces are distributed among those who had come to the ūṟppaḷḷi to see it cut up. The

1. Vol. III, pp. 222—3

animal was methodically cut up into 18 customary pieces.[1]

(27) *Talappanam* (Ṭalappaṇam).—A species of poll tax levied on occasions "from poor classes" to meet emergencies [2] amounting to "five paṇams for each head." [3]

(28) All precious metals or stones which might be discovered were royalties. So also were—

(29) Cardamoms, teak, jack, and black-wood trees, ebony, bamboos, honey, and wax.

(30) *Valappanam* (Valappaṇam).—This means net-money, being a tax paid by fishermen for exercising their profession, and consisted of a rāśi or 10 Chakṛams, equivalent to 5 as. 10 ps. The fins of sharks are also a royalty, still retained in the Cochin State under the head kāppu kuṭṭaka. The Fisheries Department now controls this branch of revenue and the rates with the system of levying them have been altered and modernised.

(31) *Changatam*(Changāṭam) or protection.—Whenever a man wished to place himself under the safeguard of one of consequence, he paid from 4 to 64 fanams annually for the privilege. He might also make an assignment of particular lands for the payment. The sum was devoted to the maintenance of a kind of sentinel, similar to the belted official peon of the Anglo-Indian settlements, furnished by the protector to his dependents. In cases of necessity, however, the former was bound to aid and assist the other with a stronger force [4]. In this sense, Changāṭam has some analogy to the tribute paid by the Native States of India to the British Government, as Paramount Power in India, for the purpose of protecting them against external and internal attacks and commotions. Under the system of Subsidiary Alliances, the Native Princes of India have entered into treaties with the British Government promising to pay a prescribed tribute and to abide by the

1. *Malabar*, p. 171.
2. Day, *Land of the Perumals*, p. 66.
3. Bartolomeo, *Voyages*, p. 310.

advice given by the representative of the Paramount Power accredited to their courts in matters of administration, the British Government on its part undertaking to station a subsidiary force in the Prince's territory to protect him. In some cases, as with the Nizam of Hyderabad, assignments of territory are made to the Paramount Power for the upkeep of the subsidiary forces.

(32) The next item of revenue, Rakṣhābhōgam, however, bears a closer resemblance to the tributes paid by Native Princes.

According to Yule, the name Jancada, as the Portuguese termed it, was given to certain responsible guides in the Nāyar country who escorted travellers from one inhabited place to another, guaranteeing their security with their own lives, like the Bhats of Guzerat. The term imports companionship and, therefore, confidence. Sometimes the institution is called in Malayālam Kāval Changāṭam, i. e. guard-companion. The early practice of detailing an escort by chieftains to take care of travellers passing through their territory on payment of a consideration was not altogether peculiar to Malabar. The Chinese traveller Fa Hian (A. D. 400), seems to have been prevented from passing through South India, as he was not in a position to pay his protection money. According to him, "those who desire to proceed thither should first pay a certain sum of money to the king of the country who will then appoint people to accompany them and show them the way."

Pyrard di Lavel (1610 A. D.) observes : "I travelled with another captain * * who had with him those *Jengai*, who are the Nair guides, and who are found at the gates of towns to act as escort to those who require them. * * Every one takes them, the weak for safety and protection. Those who are strangers and travel in great companies and well-armed take them only as witnesses that they are not aggressors in cases of any dispute with the Nairs".[1] Half a century after, Vincenzo Maria (1672) has the same account to give. "The safest of all journeyings in India," says Vincenzo, "are through the kingdom of the Nairs and the Zamorin, if you travel with *Giancadas*, the most perilous if you go alone. These *Giancadas* are certain heathen men, who venture their own lives and the lives of their kinsfolk for small remuneration, to guarantee the safety of travellers."[2]

Protection money was levied not simply from travellers but also from neighbouring chiefs who stood in dread of molestation from others, more powerful than themselves, when it assumed the nature of tribute or Rakṣhābhōgam. Later on, it was not only chiefs who levied the amount as such, but companies of Nāyars undertook, on payment of a sufficient consideration, on their oath, to protect those who stood in apprehension of another. Barbosa says that such a one takes "some of these Nairs, as many as he pleases, into his pay, and they accompany and guard him; and on their account, he goes securely, since no one dares molest him; because if he were molested, they and all their lineage would take vengeance on him who should cause this molestation. These guards are called *Jangada*, and there are some people who sometimes take so many of these Nairs, and of such quality, that on their account they no longer fear the king, who would not venture to command the execution of a man who was guarded by these, in order not to expose many Nairs to danger for it. And even if the Nairs were not in his company, when the man they guard was killed, they would not the less revenge his death."[3] The Portuguese took advantage of this trait of absolute fidelity in the character of the Nāyars and employed them both as guides on a journey and to guard property. They had, for instance, a *Jangada* for

1. Chap. XXV.
2. P. 127.
3. P. 129.

each of their forts in Malabar. It was the duty of the *Jangada* to defend anything entrusted to him with his life, and it was a serious matter to kill him, as it involved a blood-feud with all his relatives.[1]

The Portuguese Governor of Cochin, Martin Alfonso de Sousa (1542–45), once led an expedition to plunder the temple of Ṭēvalakara, a few miles inland from Quilon, which local information reported to be full of gold. There were two *Jangadas* attached to this temple, but one with almost all the guards had gone to the south, when the movements of the Portuguese attracted attention. The plunder was effected in the course of the night. When, in the morning, the plunderers started on their return journey, a Nāyar, dressed with scrupulous care with all his ornaments followed by ten or twelve others, flung himself on the Portuguese ranks and died fighting desperately. "This man," says Correa, "who so resolutely died was one of the *Jangadas* of the Pagoda. They are called *Jangadas*, because the kings and lords of those lands, according to a custom of theirs, send as guardians of the houses of the Pagodes in their territories, two men as captains, who are men of honour and good cavaliers. Such guardians are called *Jangadas*, and have soldiers of guard under them, and are as it were the counsellors and ministers of the affairs of the pagodes, and they receive their maintenance from the establishment and its revenues. And sometimes the king changes them and appoints others."[2]

(32) *Rakshābogam* (Rakşhābhōgam).—This is another form of protection-money—a tax differing from Changāṭam only in one point, viz., that the engagement to protect was a general one, not limited to any specific aid in the first instance.[3]

We have now enumerated in detail the main sources from which the ancient Rajas of Malabar derived

1. Whiteway, p. 12.
2. IV. 139.
3. Burton, p. 198.

their revenue. Their system was one of aid and perquisites and forced contribution rather than of fixed taxes and assessments. Extraordinary emergencies called forth extraordinary contributions. Such a system was indeed open to abuse for purposes of personal aggrandisement, but, as observed by Burton, "the influence of the Brahmans and the jealousy of the chiefs generally operated as efficient checks upon individual ambition." A land-tax *as such* was altogether unknown in Malabar till the year 913 M. E. or A. D. 1736—7. Though the writer in the *Asiatic Journal* says that "it is suspected that, besides these sources (enumerating the above), the Raja levied a land-tax equal to about one-fifth of the produce on lands, except those belonging to the Brahmans and pagodas" and that "if the tax was not regularly levied, there is reason to believe that contributions were occasionally imposed upon the landholders to that amount;"[1] yet we have the assurance of the Mahomedan writer, Sheik Zeenuddeen, of the 16th century that "they (the Rajas) demand no land-tax from the tenants of the lands and gardens, although they are of great extent"[2] "We may account for the peculiarity," says Burton, "by remembering that the country belonged to the Brahmans, in a religious point of view; moreover, the avowed and legitimate sources of revenue were sufficient for the purposes of a Government that had no standing army, and whose militia was supported chiefly by assignments of land." Captain Burton here accepts the legend of the grant of the country to the Brahmans, and think that it accounts in part for the non-existence of a land-tax as such in ancient Malabar. But the legend of the grant is discredited, though the possession of the land by the Brahmans from time out of mind is admitted; and the non-existence of a land-tax may be explained from the circumstance that the entire property in the soil, the *plenum dominum*, vested in the Jenmies

1. Selections from the *Asiatic Journal*, Vol. II, p. 661.
2. *Tohfut-ul-Mujahidin*, p. 73.

who, as Brahmans, were exempt from taxes under the Hindu system. The remarks of Col. Wilkes, already quoted, may also be considered in this connection. The contention that there was no land-tax in Malabar prior to the introduction of the same by the Mysorean Mussalmans is somewhat vehemently contested by Mr. Logan after a full examination of the land tenures of Malabar from the earliest times whereof records could be obtained. His conclusion is that "there *was* a public land revenue in Malabar originally, just as in every other Indian province, but, with the extinction of the supreme *Kon* or king in the 9th century A. D., the share of the produce due to him did not pass to those (the present Rajas) who supplied, in some measure, his place but to the great bulk of the people—the Nāyars, the six hundred—*with whom, in the corporate capacities, all powers rested.*"[1] Mr. Logan thinks that "it was probably different in Cochin—the territory left to and still ruled by the last Perumāls heirs—and in that territory the Mupṟa, (the 3 paras per 10 paras [bushels] of produce in wet lands) and the Eṭṭukkoṅṅu (the one in eight produce in gardens) do probably still represent what was the *Kon's* share or, in other words, the public land revenue of the State. This holds true also of the Cochin territory usurped by the Travancore Maharajas in the 18th century A. D. and perhaps also of their other territories in the south." In Travancore, the fact that conveyance of hereditary property at once broke the allodial character of the holding and made it liable to pay land revenue (Mupṟa and Eṭṭukkoṅṅu) leads Mr. Logan to remark that the purchaser of the Jenmam right does not hold it in Jenmam any longer, but only as an ordinary ryot of the State. Not so in Malabar, where the conveyance conferred on the buyer the hereditary position that was sold. This difference between the usages observed in the two countries is attributed to the fact that the Travancore Rajas were

1. Pp. 602—3.

stronger in their dominions than the Malabar chieftains. They are said to have been able to insist on conditions which the Malabar chieftains were powerless to enforce. Travancore had a standing army drilled by a European, the Fleming, Eustachius D' Lanoy, which made that State, during the first half of the 18th century, independent of the protector guild of Nāyars.

This view has not been left unchallenged. Mr. Arthur Thompson of the Madras Civil Service has critically examined in the pages of the *Malabar Law Reports* Mr. Logans' derivations of the words Jenmam, Kāṇam, Pāṭṭam, Aṭṭippēṟu, etc., on which he has based his theory and, in the result, observes: "Mr. Logan accounts for the fact that, prior to the Mysorean invasion, there was no regular public land revenue in Malabar by the theory that, on extinction of the supreme *Kon* or king in the 9th century, the share of produce due to him passed to the Nāyars or 'Six hundred'. No facts are adduced in support of this theory, and it seems to me to be much more probable that the real cause of the apparent absence of land revenue was that such revenue was practically collected in the form of transit and export dues."[1] Mr. Thompson is inclined to think that the picture drawn by Mr. Logan of ancient Malabar society and its methods of government and land tenure is more idyllic than historical, and seems to be based on mere hypothesis, without a single fact to support it.

Mr. Logan admits that it is an idea hitherto generally received that, in ancient times, there was no such thing as a land assessment in Malabar. The result of the enquiries made by the British officers soon after the cession of Malabar by Tippu entirely confirms this idea. Their reports fully substantiate the statement made by the Mahomedan writer, Zeenuddeen, in the 16th century that the Malabar Rajas never realised land-tax from their subjects.

1. *Malabar Law Reports*, Vol. I, pp. 77—83.

Speaking of the early land system of the country, Mr. Justice Kuññu Rāman Nāyar observes, in his learned *Memorandum on the Land Tenures of Travancore*:—"Land-taxes were unknown in Kēraḷam in ancient days. The Ruler, be he Rakṣhā-Puruṣhan, Avarōḍha-Nampi, Ḍēśāḍhipaṭi, Nāṭu-Vāḷi, or Raja—derived his income from other sources than land-tax. The Rajas and Perumāḷs also do not appear to have exacted regular land-tax until a period when necessity for war-like preparations ceased, though when powerful enough, they levied forced contributions from land-holders in cases of emergency."[1]

The Joint Commissioners reported in 1793 that "the Raja's rights in general did not extend to the exaction of any regular settled or fixed revenue from their subjects, the original constitution of their Government only entitling them to call on their vassals, the Brahmins and Nāyars, for military service; but although this general exemption from any land-tax is stated to have thus universally prevailed in the early times of the Rajas' Government, it is, however, allowed that they were occasionally subject to some contribution for the extraordinary emergencies of defence against the invasions of foreign enemies, such as the Canarese and Portuguese; and in Chērikkal and also in the Samoory's (Zamorin's) dominions the custom was at length introduced of the Rajas levying from lands (excepting perhaps those belonging to temples) a settled revenue or income in money or kind equal to one-fifth of the produce."[2]

Mr. Murdoch Brown informed Dr. Buchanan in 1800 that the Rajas could neither exact revenue from the lands of their vassals nor exercise any direct authority in their districts. Speaking of what happened in Malabar, on its conquest by Hyder, Buchanan says:—"Under the Government of the Rajas, there was no land-tax; but the conqueror soon found the necessity of

1. Para 23.
2. Para 10.

imposing one, as the expenses of his military establishment greatly exceeded the usual revenues." 1

Major Walker reported in 1801 that the burdens on the land were personal and military and he continued: "It is but recently that it was subject to any tax. The Rājākkanmār, it is true, before there was a regular assessment, in proportion to their strength, levied contributions on the landed proprietors. But the Jenmakkāran never considered himself under an obligation to support the Rajas or defray the expenses of the State from the produce of his Jenmam." 2

Mr. Thackeray (1807), after alluding to Hyder's invasion in 1760, says:—"There is no proof that any regular land-tax existed in Malabar, previous to that event; tradition and general opinion seem to deny it. The State of Travancore, where it was said that there was no regular land-tax, gives probability to this opinion, while the former State of Canara, where there has been a regular land-tax for many centuries, renders it somewhat doubtful. The proprietors of land were certainly bound to render military service, and were liable to contribute 20 *per cent*, in case of invasion. The pagodas and the Rajas had lands of their own. The Rajas had other sources of revenue, from fines, royalties, imposts, personal taxes, and plunder, which were sufficient to support them. There was no army besides the militia, nor any expensive establishments to support; so that there does not seem to have been any necessity for a general land-tax; nor had the Rajas power perhaps to collect one. It is only great States that want, or in India, can collect the land revenue easily."

The following statement appears in the *Fifth Report* to the House of Commons:—"It was represented by the Natives that, previously to that period (the conquest of Hyder), the lands were not subject to any

1. *Canara and Malabar*, p. 65.

2. P. 62.

assessment, and although no positive evidence has been adduced to disprove this fact, it seemed to be negatived by tradition and general belief. It is concluded that the proprietors of them must, at all events, have been liable to occasional contribution in time of war and invasion, bound, as they appear to have been, to military service."[1]

Sir Thomas Munro visited Malabar in 1817 to ascertain how far the Regulation Law could be introduced into that country. He made an enquiry into the existing conditions, examined a large number of documents and sent in his report on the 4th of July, 1817. He pointed out that "all lands excepting those set apart for religious purposes, were held by military tenure. The land owners were exempted from the payment of rent, and every little sub-division of territory, instead of being called a district of so many thousand pagodas, was called one of so many thousand men." He enumerates the sources of revenue possessed by the Rajas. The principal of these were:—

1. Extensive domains.
2. Customs.
3. Escheats of Hindu estates without heirs.
4. Fines, where no heir, for leave to adopt,—usually one-third of the property.
5. Fines from the estates of all Māpiḷās deceased, usually from one-twentieth to one-fifth of the value.
6. Fines from younger brothers on succeeding the elder in the sister's house.
7. Fines for offences, and heavy fees on law suits.
8. All cattle having particular marks.

He observes:— "Though denied by the landholders in general, it is asserted by some of them that, besides the above sources of revenue, the Rajas levied in money or kind a land-tax for all lands, excepting those of Brahmins and Pagodas, equal to about one-

1. Vol. II, p. 81.

fifth of the produce. There is reason to believe that, if this tax was not regularly collected every year, contributions were occasionally imposed upon the land-holders to at least an equal amount." But it has to be noted that these contributions were personal and not a burden on the land and that the land-holders never felt it an obligation to pay them and that they had to be levied by force. Our author observes in this Letter that "there are certain estates in Malabar whose owners are obliged to pay an annual tribute in recognition of their proprietorship to the Raja; *this is regarded rather as a free-will offering than a tax*." It is significant that Sir Thomas Munro notices that there were no Karṇams in the villages, which circumstance points to the absence of a land-tax. He says:—"The Desway had no village Curnam: the nature of the revenue did not require an officer of that kind."

The Board of Revenue at Madras, in 1818, declared it to be "a most remarkable circumstance that, until the conquest of Malabar by the Mussalman princes of Mysore, this right (i. e, the Jenmam right) seems to have been held by the Jenmakars, free from any condition of a payment, in money or produce, to the Government; for until that period, a land revenue appears to have been altogether unknown to the people." Again the Board says: "Nothing, therefore, could be more complete than that the property in the soil thus vested in the Jenmakars. After defraying the expenses of cultivation, the produce of the land, or its value, were their own, free from tax." * * * * "Hence, in Malabar, there were none of those hereditary village registers who, under the denomination of Conicopilies (Kaṇakkappillays) or Shambogues, were elsewhere universally found necessary by the Government to keep detailed accounts of the occupation and cultivation of the soil. The non-existence of a land revenue in that province rendered the employment of such persons unnecessary; and the Jenmakars, free from all interference of this kind, were the independent owners of land." The Board also notices the significant fact that this "absence of all accounts of the land revenue in Malabar, proceeding from the non-existence of such a tax, necessarily left the assessors of Hyder without any other alternative for their guidance, in fixing the amount of the land-tax, than the scanty and the interested information to be gathered from the people themselves or from a local inspection of the country."

From the extract given from Mr. Thackeray's *Report* as also from a passage in Buchanan's *Canara and Malabar*[1], we see that there existed no land-tax in Travancore in former times, and this receives confirmation from what we read in the *Travancore State Manual*. There it is said: "Taxation in the modern sense of the term did not exist in early Travancore or the whole of Malabar. The original Jenmam lands were free from tax, and it was long before Sirkar or Paṇḍāravaka lands came into existence or the alienated Jenmam properties were made liable to Rājabhōgam" (king's share). The first settlement of which there is any record in Travancore was that of 948 M. E. (1772—73 A. D.)[2]

In Cochin, in the words of the Superintendent of Census (1901): "Whatever might be the extact period from which a land-tax began to be levied and collected, it does not seem to have existed prior to 1760." With regard to the origin of the land-tax in Cochin, the *Report* says: "No land-tax appears to have been levied during the time of the Brahman rule, or in the period of the Perumāls, or even for many centuries after the dismemberment of Kērala into several States. Like other Rajas of the Coast States, the Cochin Raja made up his civil list by means of income derived from what is known as Kaṇṭukṛṣhi (Crown lands), monopolies, customs, escheats, protection fees collected from rich

1. Vol. II, p. 127.
2. Vol. IV, p. 342.

proprietors or temples, succession tax and various minor items. From some old papers, it is seen that a land-tax was first levied in 937 M.E. (1762), chiefly to meet the increasing expenditure consequent on the wars with the Zamorin and Travancore. This is corroborated by the treaty with the Dutch in 1785, in which the Christian subjects who, at first, refused to pay the taxes agreed to abide by the rule, which applied to other classes of the population, and the Raja, on his part, consented to remit all arrears due from them up to 1784. According to another version, it was during the occupation of the country by Hyder and his men (about 950 M. E.) that a tax was first levied on land. A third suggestion is that taxes were first imposed by the Raja himself to pay up the subsidy demands of the Mysore Suzerains." The earliest attempt at a survey and settlement of lands is said to have taken place at some period between 950 and 960 M. E., that is, after the Mysorean conquest"[1].

Our author dealing with the revenues of the Cochin Rajas of the period, when he was writing, does not say that they derived any tax from the land, though he mentions that the gardens situated in Karappuṟam, of which they were sole lords, (volkomen meester i. e. Jenmi) fetched a tenth on their fruits. From other places of which the Raja was Jenmi, he received a smaller portion.

The earliest instance we have of the payment of a land-tax in Malabar occurs in 1731-32, when the dominions of the Raja of Kōlaṭṭiri were invaded by the Bednore Raja's forces, and the Kōlaṭṭiri Raja in consequence imposed a tax of 20 *per cent* on the pāṭṭams of all rice lands. This was perhaps an imitation of what was in vogue in the Canara country of which Bednore formed a part, where a regular system of land-tax had existed "from the remotest times of which there is any record."

Speaking of that part of Canara which had formerly belonged to Malabar, Dr. Buchanan mentions

1. Introduction, p. lxi.

that it was not until 1729-30, when they had themselves become tributaries, that the Nīlēśwara Rajas established a regular land-tax in lieu of their claims on the moveable property of all persons dying in their territory.[1]

There is no means at present so far as our enquiries have gone, of knowing when it was that the Zamorin imposed a land-tax in his kingdom. Of course, from what has been said, it is clear that a land-tax as such could not have existed in early days, at any rate, before the Mysorean invasion in the Zamorin's country also.

All evidence hitherto collected renders it impossible to hold with Mr. Logan that there was a land-tax in Kērala in early times. Mr. Logan's theory is based on his rendering of the word Pāṭṭam which he derives from Pāṭṭavāram. Referring to deed No. 3 of Appendix XII, he says "that the Kon (shepherd, king) and the Paṭi (Lord, master) had shares of the produce due to them as the persons of authority in the land. And the specific words used in the ninth century A. D. to denote these shares have probably survived to the present day, and are still in common use in a contracted form as pāṭṭam. For pāṭṭam seems to be a compound word signifying the pāṭu (authority's) vāram (share) and it was perhaps used in the uncontracted form in this clause (i) of deed 3." He thinks that "it was the duty of the Kaṇakars or" Supervisors" to collect " the Kōn or king's share of the produce—*the public land revenue.*"[2]

Mr. Logan's derivation of the word is not accepted by competent Malayālam scholars as having an etymological basis. The late Mr. K. R. Kṛshṇa Mēnon, who was no mean Malayālam scholar, asserts that the word is derived from *Bhattakam*, signifying the price paid for the use of anything, wages, hire or rent. He

1. Vol. II, p. 209.
2. P. 602.

shows by what linguistic changes the word assumed its present form, and notices that it was applied to designate the hire of a house, the hire of an elephant and also the hire of slaves. Dr. Gundhert, the eminent Malayālam scholar, thinks that the word is perhaps derived from the Sanskrit *Bhalam*. Mr. Justice Kuññu Rāman Nāyar, another eminent Malayālam scholar and lawyer, observes:—"The word Pāṭṭam has been supposed by some to denote the Pāṭu's (authority's) share, or revenue demand, and theories founded upon this meaning of the term have been propounded to the prejudice of the Jenmies' right to the *plenum dominum* in the soil, but Pāṭṭam is really a corruption of the Sanskrit word *Bhatakam* signifying[1] price paid for the use of anything, i.e., hire or rent. Another corruption of the same word is Vāṭaka, or rent of houses, shops etc"[2].

Sir Charles Turner, in noticing Mr. Logan's theory that the *pattam* was received by the Jenmi as land revenue, which theory seems to have had the support of Sir William Robinson and the Committee of which the late Raja Sir T. Mādhava Row was president, observes: "If this were so, it would point to the existence at some time or other of a Brahmanical oligarchy which had constituted itself the sovereign of the soil and had retained the land revenue after it had lost other rights of sovereignty, or to a very general dedication of the land revenue as an Inām to the Brāhmins, but I cannot say that I find any sufficient evidence to support either suggestion."[3]

Regarding the meaning of the word Pāṭṭam, Sir Charles Turner says: "I do not venture to offer an opinion on this point, but I am satisfied that for some hundreds of years the term *pattam* has been used in Malabār as meaning neither more nor less than rent, while the land-tax is invariably termed *Nigadi*, and

1. See Max Muller's *Sanskrit Dictionary*.

2. *Memo*, para 78.

3. *Minute*, p. 34.

this is a further argument as to its origin, for *Nigadi* is a corruption of the Mahomedan term Nakd."

It becomes clear from what has been said above that a land-tax as such never existed in Kēraḷa till it was introduced somewhere about the Mysorean conquest.

2. **Cochin Raja got the Privilege from the Portuguese.** It would seem from what our author says here that the Raja of Cochin did not originally exercise the right of levying duty on goods imported into the kingdom, and that, after the Portuguese had begun to do so, they conferred on the Raja the privilege of sharing with them the profits arising from this source, and that, since the expulsion of the Portuguese, the Dutch continued or confirmed this privilege. Seeing that the levying of customs duties was one of the most important sources of revenue, and looking to the extent of the trade in exports and imports carried on by the Mahomedans on the Coast, it is impossible to believe that the Raja had contended himself with the levy of inland duties alone. The more so that the levy of customs duties has been all along regarded as one of the essentials of sovereignty in Malabar. We know from Faria that, about the year 1584, the Portuguese made an attempt to get the Raja to assign to them all the customs and that "the people rose to the number of 20,000, swearing on a book to die in defence of their liberties hereby infringed. D. George de Meneses Baroche, who commanded there (Cochin), finding the tumult too high to be opposed, suspended the execution of the Viceroy's orders relating to this affair." D. Giles Yanez Mascarennas was appointed by the Viceroy of Goa to go to Cochin and to endeavour to suppress the tumult in which, however, he did not succeed. Meanwhile, the Viceroy had been changed, and the first thing that the newcomer, Duarte de Meneses, applied himself to "was the appeasing of the tumults in Cochin. The Viceroy, D. Francis, had sent commissioners to treat with the heads

of that people, and they had reduced them to hearken to an accommodation. D. Duarte, now arriving, admits their proposals, so that the affair of the Custom House was settled."[1]

The following extract from Moens' *Memorial* gives us some idea as to the right of the Cochin Raja to levy customs duties and the policy of the Dutch with regard to the same: Governor Moens observes:—

"We are obliged to give annually the half of the customs to His Highness, i. e., of all the goods which are brought and sold here at the river. From the time the Portuguese were here, he got this revenue, and later on it was left to him by contract.

"I have once, for political and mercantile reasons, suggested to Their High Worshipfuls that they should buy the right from the king for a fixed annual sum. Their High Worshipfuls approved of this, and gave leave to do so, but the 'Honorable Majores' have made well-grounded objections against such a plan. This may be seen in detail in special letter to Batavia, dated 10th February 1775, 4th January 1776, 7th March 1777 and 5th June 1779. Also in special despatches from Batavia, the dates of which are 20th September 1775, 20th September 1776, 11th November 1776 and 15th September 1778, besides in general letter from the Council of the Seventeen, dated 8th October 1777.

"However we must not lose sight of this affair, although I am at present inclined to think that it will be very difficult to obtain this right from the king. For it is almost the only remnant of his former greatness. But in case the Company would later on be of opinion, that it would be better to have the whole of this revenue instead of dividing it with the king, the best plan would be to offer His Highness a good round sum down once for all. Such a proposal should be made to him at a time, when he is in the utmost difficulties, and this is often the case with him. Now

1. Tom, 3—pp. 17, 18, 20, 21.

that he has to pay tribute to the Nabob (Hyder) also, opportunities would often present themselves. I am of opinion that, if *he were allowed* to accept such a proposal, he certainly *would* do so as soon as he found himself in great distress. I remarked 'if he were 'allowed' because that the king of Travancore would prevent him, as it is well known, that the king of Cochin is only king of his territory in name and the king of Travancore king of Cochin in reality. However the scheme could be tried and if it was noticed, that he had a liking for it, but that the king of Travancore was likely to interfere, then it would be best according to circumstances to approach the king of Travancore directly about it and try to insist upon it with some force."

This policy was adopted later on by the British Government and, though physical force had not to be used, the Raja of Cochin was induced to give up his right to levy customs duties within his territory on an annual payment of a fixed amount by the Paramount power.

3. **Annual Tribute.** This was what was paid by Jenmies (proprietors who had absolute right in the soil), and was known as Rājabhōgam or Raja's share in recognition of the Raja's right of sovereignty. It is significant that our author mentions that " it is regarded rather as a 'free-will offering' than a 'tax'; for there was no burden laid on the land as a land-tax in Malabar though frequent contributions were either willingly paid by or were exacted from the proprietors.

4. **Jenmakara** stands for Chuṃkam, a Malayāḷam word to denote customs duties.

5. **Custom Houses.** At present, there are no custom houses in Cochin territory, as the revenue under this head has been commuted into a fixed sum to be paid to the Raja annually by the British Government under an interportal arrangement. The Travancore

Sirkar, however, retains its customs revenue and maintains customs houses. But they are no longer built on piles in the back-water, being located in substantial buildings at fixed points on the shores along the line of the back-water. Curious edifices of the kind described by our author still exist in the back-waters and are used as guard-houses to protect passengers from being molested by pirates and to prevent smuggling.

Towards the year 1785, the Cochin Raja claimed tolls on the back-water upon rice and other dutiable articles going into Cochin, for which purpose he had Chowkays (Custom houses) at Anjikaimal *i. e.* Eṛṇākuḷam, Vypin, Balghatty and Paḷḷuruṭṭi, but produce which had once paid custom was exempt from further toll.[1] Till the year 1836, transit duties were levied upon all articles which passed from one taluk to another. Chowkays were placed in all directions and peons stationed in them to examine boats. This tax was abolished in 1847, and the customs were made exclusively frontier and sea-duties, while British produce going from one British possession to another passed toll-free. This again was modified by an interportal arrangement with the British Government in the year 1865, by which the Raja agreed to take annually Rs. 1,00,000 in commutation of the customs revenue. This amount is subject to increase in proportion as the net revenue increases.

6 **Coedenatti**=Caṇṭanād.
Coechin=Cochin.
Oediampoor=Uḍayampērūr.

This last is the Diamper of the Portuguese noted for the Synod held there in 1599 by Archbishop Meneses to bring the Syrian Christians under the Roman yoke.

Tobacco. The Cochin Sirkar has abolished its tobacco monopoly, and the revenue from that source

1. Day pp. 66—7.

is now realised by the issue of licenses authorising to sell the article on payment of fixed rates for licenses. This was done on the 15th of August 1862. The Sirkar has, owing to financial difficulties, recently adopted a system of selling to the highest bidder licensed shops divided into classes. These shops alone being entitled to store or sell tobacco.

7. **Patterys** or Paṭṭers or Brahmans from the East Coast. They enjoyed the privilege of not paying for packs carried by them on their heads.

8. **Carapuram** (Carappuṙam), the tract lying between Alleppey to within a couple of miles south of Cochin, belonged to the Raja of Cochin, not simply in sovereignty but also in jenmam (proprietorship), and here he exacted as his share a proportion of the produce of the land. The Rajas never failed to exact contributions from the produce of lands which belonged to them in jenmam. This was in time extended to other lands over which they were sovereigns only. Thus a settled revenue in money or kind came to be levied from all lands excepting those belonging to the Brahmans and the temples. This source of revenue was resorted to mainly to meet the heavy expenses incurred in expelling the Ẓamoṙin from the country with the assistance of Travancore, and was instituted about the year 1762, when all lands were subjected to a tax known as Muppaṙa and Eṭṭil oṅṅu, which varied in different places as to rates. At the same time, a poll-tax was also instituted. About the year 1778, large tracts of waste land which belonged to the State in jenmam were cleared, reclaimed, and planted by private persons, who were allowed to hold them rent-free, until the trees began to bear when a small ground rent was imposed. This was continued till 1793, when the Raja, after consultation with the Dutch on the best means of raising money to pay his subsidy, placed a tax of 12½ *per cent* on the produce of the trees and 30 *per cent* on that of rice cultivation. In 1802, money was again

urgently needed, and the Raja resumed these lands, which were, however, re-farmed, not long after, at a lower rate than before.[1] In 1785, according to a treaty between Mr. Van Angelbeck, Dutch Governor of Cochin, and the Raja, dated 11th of October, the Raja levied tax according to the following scale around the fort of Cochin: 1/8 of cocoanut and other fruit-bearing trees; 3/10 of the paddy. The cocoanut trees were estimated at two puṭṭans (1 anna and 8 pies) rent; betel-nut trees at a quarter of a puṭṭan; jack trees at 8 puṭṭans. Free-hold properties which were untaxed were not subject to this rate. This treaty also shows that Christian subjects, who at first had refused to pay the taxes, agreed to abide by the rule which applied to the other classes of the population. Some time previously to this, in the year 1775, Hyder had succeeded in pushing on his conquests in Malabar towards the south, and his general, Sirdar Khan, effected the capture of the Fort of Trichur and established his Government there. The Mysorean administration would allow no land to go untaxed, not even that set aside for the maintenance of temples or charities, and Sirdar Khan proceeded at once to set about establishing a system of land assessment. The Raja seems to have followed the example of the Mysorean Sirdar in the southern portion of his dominions, in order to procure money to pay the subsidy demands of Mysore and get exemption from further harassment. For the same purpose, the Raja assessed also lands lying to the north of the Travancore lines at the rate of four old fanams per para of land, while those lying to the south of the lines had to pay four puṭṭans. Cocoanut trees growing in gardens situated to the south of the lines were assessed at the rate of one fanam per tree. These rates were, however, revised and increased later on.

9. **Fines paid by criminals.** Fines imposed on criminals were a permanent source of income to the State. The scale of imposition varied with the

1. Day, p. 67.

heinousness of the offence and the means of the culprit. Of course, only a portion of the amounts realised went into the State coffers, while a portion was appropriated as the legitimate perquisite of the officers sitting in judgment, and a considerable portion slipped through the fingers of the minions of justice. Apart from the payment of fines as punishment for crimes committed, immunity from prosecution itself was not infrequently purchased at heavy cost.

10. **All ruminating animals.** This is scarcely a correct statement. Only such of the ruminating animals as had an abnormal number of dugs or peculiar marks belonged to the Raja.

11. **Out-castes.** Those who are outcasted become slaves and are at the disposal of the Raja.

12. **Death without heirs.** This item would come under Aṟṟālaṭakkam or escheat.

In the report of Mr. Warden, Collector of Malabar, dated 10th September 1815, we read, "Among the Rajas the practice was to require their tenants to renew their deeds at the accession to the Raj of every new head. In the Cochin territory, such renewals have occurred three times in the last seven years and must have been severely felt if strictly enforced."

After a large portion of land covered by the State had fallen unto the Raja by escheat, forfeiture or seizure, they were let out to tenants either on Veṟumpāṭṭam or simple lease, Kāṉapāṭṭam or lease and mortgage with an advance of money taken, and other cognate tenures. As the necessities of the State increased, in view of the large expenses incurred in expelling the Zamorin, in buying off the Mysoreans and in the war with Travancore, the Raja had to borrow large sums from the people to whom lands were demised on favourable tenures. These sums had amounted in time to a large sum.

At the last Survey and Settlement, the very first one attempted on a scientific basis, these tenures were placed on an altogether new footing. The State treated the amounts originally advanced on the demises only as a "sum of money supposed to have been advanced." It further held that "it is almost impossible to ascertain accurately for each field its proportionate share of the Kāṇam amount, its share of interest and its renewal fees". In view of this, the State repudiated its liability to pay back the amounts advanced and resolved to place its Kāṇam tenants on what it considers to be an "equitable footing". The Settlement Proclamation issued by the Raja on the 10th of March 1905 therefore says:—"We accordingly command that, in case of all lands falling under Paṇḍāravaka (State) Kāṇam and cognate tenures, by whatever name known,

(1) a deduction of 33⅓ *per cent* shall be made in each case after assessing the properties at Verumpāṭṭam (simple lease) rates,

(2) the practice of subjecting the properties to renewal, once in 12 years, shall be altogether abandoned,

(3) the proprietorship to the soil shall hereafter vest in the Kāṇamḍār, and

(4) no amount shall be recognised as due to the Kāṇamḍār."

13. **Payment for dignity.** Various offices, dignities and distinctions were conferred by the Rajas, which brought in an annual payment from the recipients thereof; who by virtue of such dignities had to perform certain duties, and were entitled to enjoy the privileges and emoluments annexed to those dignities. Many of them have been since abolished, but there are numerous others still existing, an enumeration of which will be found interesting as well as instructive. They indicate the directions in which the State interfered and still interferes with private rights, individual

freedom, and even personal convenience. The conditions of life and the state of society which necessitated, or even tolerated, such interference have long ago ceased to exist, and yet the system still lingers, and operates as a heavy encumbrance in retarding progress in many directions.

The chief sṭhānam or dignity conferred on Nāyars, apart from the conferring of titles such as, Mēnōn, Mēnōkki, Paṇikkar, etc., is that of Karamēl Āśāima or Āśān, i. e., headman of a village. Sometimes personal privileges are conferred by royal writs, which are also sources of revenue to the State. Nāyars have to take out a sort of license for the use of musical instruments, drums, etc., at marriage celebrations, for a certain form of worshipping the sun at such ceremonies, for the wearing of particular gold ornaments by their women, for the use of certain eatables at feasts, etc. Even the privilege of being offered particular kinds of seats when invited to festivities at a neighbour's house is regulated by royal grants which have to be paid for.

The following is a specimen of a grant, in this instance by the Raja of Cranganūr, by which certain privileges were granted to a Nāyar family:—

"To our Kāṭṭollil Achyuṭan and Ananṭiravars (heirs). We have by this Ṭeet (Royal writing) permitted the females of your house to wear Kāṭila (ear ornaments) and Vaḷa (bracelets), to celebrate your Ṭālikeṭṭu Kallyāṇam (marriages), with the accompaniment of music and to worship the sun from a raised platform (Ṭaṭṭu) put upon posts".

Of the dignities or sṭhānams conferred, the following among others, may be mentioned as those conferred on classes below the Nāyars:—

(1) Among the caste of Īluvās, Chōgans, or Tīyās were conferred the titles of :—

(*a*) Ṭaṇṭān. (*b*) Paṇikkan. (*c*) Punampan. (*d*) Nālupurasṭhānam. (*e*) Maṇṇāli Paṇikkar. (*f*) Vīṭṭukārasṭhānam, etc.

(2) Among Kaṇakkans :—
Eḷaya Kaṇakkan.

(3) Among Vēlans:—
Vēla Paṇikkan.

(4) Among Vālans :—
(*a*) Mūpan. (*b*) Valia Aravan. (*c*) Punampan.

(5) Among Pulayans :—
(*a*) Ōmana Kuṙuppu. (*b*) Vaḷḷoan or Vaḷḷōn.

(6) Among Pāṇḍi Vānyars :—
Mūppan.

(7) Among Kallans :—
Chonnār.

(8) Among Musalmans :—
(*a*) Kāzi. (*b*) Musaliar.

(9) Among Jews :—
Muṭaliar.

The sṭhānams conferred entitled the holders to be headmen of the community to which they belonged and, by virtue of their office, they had the privilege of presiding at ceremonies such as marriage, burial, etc., and deciding caste disputes, etc. In some cases, they had also to procure men and supplies for State purposes. They are entitled to be remunerated by the levy of fixed fees from those at whose ceremonies they have to preside etc.

The following scale of fees levied by Ṭanṭāns show the nature of the income to which they are entitled :—

(1) At ṭāli marriages :—

For each girl......	12 Puṭṭans	Total Rs. 1-0-8.
For presiding at the ceremony	....4 Puṭṭans	
For rice placed in the plate..........	4 Puṭṭans	

(2) At marriages :—

(*a*) For the bride....	12 Puṭṭans	Total Rs. 1-0-8.
For presiding at the ceremony	..4 Puṭṭans	
For betel and nut..	4 Puṭṭans	
(*b*) For the bride-groom...............	12 Puṭṭans	Total Rs. 1-0-8.
For presiding at the ceremony	..4 Puṭṭans	
For betel and nut ..	4 Puṭṭans	

(3) At funerals :—

For burial....	12 Puṭṭans	Total Rs. 1-4-0
Pollution money	12 Puṭṭans	

(4) Fees paid at the first menses of a girl	Rs. 0-10-0
(5) At the purification of a house ..	Rs. 0-6-8
(6) At the ceremonial bath after first menses....	Rs. 0-10-0
(7) On occasions of death pollutions where no festivals take place	Rs. 0-10-0
(8) For betel to be presented for obtaining permission to celebrate festivals generally......	Rs. 0-3-4

The privileges that are appurtenant to the sṭhānams in general are as follows :—

The sṭhānam holders are entitled :—

1. to wear certain ornaments, such as :—(*a*) ordinary ear-rings; (*b*) others of a peculiar make—long ones. (*c*) they and their wives and other female relatives may wear golden bracelets, plain or chased, on one or both arms according as the grant authorises them; (*d*) they may wear a badge of honour on one arm or both arms according to the grant; (*e*) they may wear gold bangles of a peculiar make—chain work pattern—on either or both arms according to the terms of the grant; (*f*) their females may wear anklets; (*g*) they may wear gold ornaments strung on the waist band.

(2) To use arms, sticks and other personal accessories, such as:—(*a*) gold-hilted swords, (*b*) silver-hilted swords, (*c*) shields covered with tiger skins. They may have the shields carried by another in front of them, (*d*) gold-knobbed sticks, (*e*) silver-knobbed sticks, (*f*) gold-handled knives, (*g*) silver-handled knives chased in gold. (*h*) iron styles used for writing on cadjans chased in gold.

(3) To use certain kinds of wearing apparel, umbrellas, etc.—(*a*) white jacket or robe, (*b*) turban, (*c*) handkerchief or head cloth, (*d*) damask rich silk stuff, (*e*) scarlet cap, (*f*) umbrellas, (*g*) long umbrellas of a peculiar make, both made of palmyra leaves. (*h*) silk umbrellas, (*i*) sun shades, (*j*) to plant an umbrella at the starting point of a procession, i. e , to mark the place of assembly.

(4) To the use of certain kinds of lights, etc.—(*a*) brass lamp, (*b*) light by day, (*c*) lamp with a long handle, (*d*) torch, (*e*) royal torch with brass handle, also an oil vessel for torches.

(5) To erect particular sorts of buildings, etc.—(*a*) to build gate houses, (*b*) bath rooms, (*c*) to erect barricades at the entrance of houses.

(6) To the use of conveyances.—(*a*) to ride on horses, (*b*) to use mañchel, a light kind of litter.

(7) (i) other honours on ceremonial occasions.—(*a*) at marriages :—

(i) to erect sheds on 6 posts,

(ii) to worship the sun standing on platforms raised on posts,

(iii) to employ an Īḷavāṭṭi (barber of Īḷuvas) of one's own choice to sing,

(*b*) at funerals.—

(i) to have pop-guns fired, and music played at purificatory bath after pollutions consequent on death of relatives,

(ii) to offer funeral oblations and bathe at particular places.

(8) Other honours:—

(*a*) to have cloth spread in the streets at processions to walk on as at a king's coronation;

(*b*) to use descriptive sounds at processions—to have forerunners shouting;

(*c*) to use a particular form of shouting, specially of women;

(*c*) to use a fan in the shape of an umbrella, made of peacock feathers—generally a sign of royalty;

(*d*) to use the brush or whisk of a yak-tail—a royal ensign;

(*e*) to use flags;

(*f*) to have pop-guns fired on occasions other than funeral processions;

(*g*) to have rice cooked in large copper vessels at ceremonies;

(*h*) to dance on a platform erected on piles.

The information set forth above has been gathered from a careful examination and analysis of about 50 grants made by the Rajas of Cochin and Crāṅganūr between the years 998 and 1075 M. E., i. e., A. D. 1823 and 1900.

We may, with advantage, compare the dignities and privileges enumerated above with those conferred by the Chēramān Perumāls on the Jewish and Syrian Christian colonists, at the least a thousand years ago. The privileges conferred on the headmen of the Syrian community, Joseph Rabban and Iravi Corttan, along with their rank of *Utayavar* were:—

"(*a*) The *seventy-two Viduper, attaching to lordship over the land.*

What these were cannot now be fully stated, as the only information regarding them is contained in clause (b) of No 1 and in clause (k) of deed No. 3

AT.

(Appendix XII). From the instances there given, they appear to have been generally of a sumptuary character, such as the *use of elephants carrying earth and water in marriage or other processions, tribute from subordinate landholders*—the *revenues of the land* granted, the *light by day*, a well-known privilege still highly prized by the ruling houses of Travancore and Cochin and other chieftains, the *spreading cloth* to walk upon, the *litter* or palanquin, still in common use, the *umbrella*, another privilege still highly prized by Malayāli chieftains, the *Vaduca drum*, the *trumpet*, that is, the conch-shell, which still figures in the emblazonments of the Travancore and Cochin rulers, *the gateway with seats*, that is, probably the power of administering justice, *ornamental arches and similar awnings and garlands*, still thrown across the paths taken by members of the ruling houses—"*and the rest.*"

(*b*) *Remission of tribute* to the Supreme Government.

(*c*) *Remission of taxes* to the king's house due from townspeople.

(*d*) The *privilege of receiving presents* when townspeople receive them.

(*e*) *Feast cloth*.

(*f*) *House pillars* or pictured rooms.

(*g*) The *carved sword or dagger*, that is, probably, the right to make war armed with the distinctive Nāyar weapon, the *Ayudha Katti* (war-knife), or, as it is sometimes called, the *Kodunga Katti* (curved knife).

(*h*) *Sovereign merchantship* over the four classes (*cheri*), who were probably all foreigners ; Jews and Christians were certainly two of the classes, another of them may have been the Islanders or Cingalese (*Dvipar, Divar*, Ṭīyar, and *Simhalar, Sihalar, Ilavar*); the fourth were Chetties (East Coast merchants) or Arabs, or perhaps Chinese.

(*i*) *Right of proclamation.*

(*j*) *Forerunners* in processions.

(*k*) The *five musical instruments.*

(*l*) *Lordship over the oil-makers and the five kinds of artificers,* that is, the carpenter, blacksmith, goldsmith, brazier, and tanner.

(*m*) *Brokerage and customs of all general classes of goods.* The phrases used[1] in describing the articles to which this privilege extended are noteworthy: "all that may be measured by the *para* (bushel), weighed by the balance, stretched by the line, of all that may be counted or carried." This is almost an exact reproduction of the phrase so famaliar to Roman jurists, *Quoe pondere, numero, mensurave constant*[2].

It is, indeed, a matter for gratification that the Cochin Darbar has deemed it necessary to abolish some of the restrictions noticed above by a Proceedings of the Diwan, dated 20th January 1914, published in the Official Gazette, Part I, p. 538. By this order, the system of appointing by means of Ṭīṭṭūram "certain persons as headmen of the Īḻuvās, Vālans and other non-caste Hindus known as Ṭaṇṭāns, Paṇikkans etc., has been abolished, as the Darbar was ' convinced that in the present condition of society this institution may with advantage be dispensed with" and as the Darbar had "also ascertained by careful enquiry that the majority of these communities desire that the system may be discontinued". It also says that H. H. the Raja has been pleased to withdraw the restriction imposed on the Īḻūvās, Vālans and other non-caste Hindus against their celebrating marriages with pomp and performing funeral obsequies with solemnities without previously obtaining Ṭīṭṭūrams from His Highness." Let us hope that before long the Darbar will find its way to extend this boon to caste-Hindus, such as the Nāyars also, so

1. Deed No. 2, Appendix XII.

2. *Malabar* Vol. I, pp. 268—269.

that the last vestige of restrictions against personal freedom in these matters may disappear altogether.

Before closing this part of the note on the revenues of the Cochin Raja, it may be useful to refer to the major heads of the source of revenue at present with some details regarding certain heads. This will enable the reader to compare the former and present sources of revenue.

The major heads of revenue at present are:—

(1) Land
(2) Forest
(3) Salt
(4) Excise { Abkari, Opium and Tobacco }
(5) Customs and Marine
(6) Judicial { Stamps, Registration, Law and Justice }
(7) Tribute and Interest
(8) Temples and Ūṭṭupuras
(9) Education
(10) Miscellaneous { Post Office, Jails, Police, Medical, Stationery and Printing, Public works and Miscellaneous }

Land—All lands in the State may broadly be divided into (1) Paṇṭāravaka and (2) Puṙavaka lands, i. e. (I) lands over which the State has the jenmam right or ownership, and (II) lands of which the jenmam right is vested in private individuals and in religious or other institutions. These lands, whether Paṇṭāravaka or Puṙavaka, may be classed as *Nilams* (wet-lands used for paddy cultivation) and *Parambas* (dry lands and gardens).

Paṇṭāravaka lands were, till recently, subject to a number of minor imposts, apart from the land-tax, the most important of which may be mentioned hereunder:-

Those relating to wet-lands :—

(1) Muṭalkaṭam paliśa—interest on advances made by the State on the security of lands. These were due from all Ṭālūks except Cochin.

(2) Aṙṭṭhappaliśa, Changāṭam—similar demands but differently styled, due from all Ṭālūks except Cochin and Kaṇayannūr.

(3) Rakṣhābhōgam, Changāṭam.—these have been already explained, due from all Ṭālūks except Cochin.

(4) Kōymabhōgam,—dues of sovereignty, due from the Kaṇayannūr Ṭālūk.

(5) Kōyma Jīviṭam.—due from the Mukunḍapuram Ṭālūk.

(6) Manuṣhia Jīviṭam do.

(7) Ari Jīviṭam do.

(8) Mēlvāram—revenue derived from fugitive cultivation, due from the Ṭālūks of Trichur, Ṭalappiḷḷi and Chiṙṙūr.

(9) Chiṙanīr vaka—water-cess due from all Ṭālūks.

(10) Kuṭiyirimpāṭu. do.

Dr. Gundhert defines the term to mean a deed by which the proprietor transfers any payments made by the tenant to a third party. This cannot be the sense in which it is used here.

(11) Kāval palam—Mukunḍapuram.

(12) Enni palam do.

(13) Ṭirunāl Ēṙṙari—Kaṇayannūr.

(14) Ūrāyma ari—Kaṇayannūr.

(15) Upakari—Ṭalappiḷḷi.

(16) Kiḷa ṅellu Vallīāl pāṭṭam in Talappiḷḷi.

(17) Paṭivāram—Chiṫṫūr.

(18) Veṙumkaṭam paliśa.—due from all Ṭālūks.

(19) Lēlaṭṭil Aḍhika pāṭṭam.—due from the Mukuṇḍapuram, Trichur. and Ṭalappiḷḷi Ṭālūks.

(20) Ninṭa pāṭṭam.—due from all Ṭālūks.

(21) Annyam ṅiṅṅa vaka pāṭṭamichavāram—Kaṇayannūr and Chiṫṫūr.

(22) Imposts on improvements made by squatters.

(23) Kāppu kuṭṭaka, Kāppu kūli.—due from the Mukuṇḍapuram, Cochin, and Kaṇayannūr Ṭālūks.

Those relating to, or brought under the head of, dry lands :—

(1) Āṇṭu ṭirumulkāīcha or annual presents—due from all parts of the State.

(2) Nilakkūli, ground rent.—due from all Ṭālūks except Ṭalappiḷḷi and Chiṫṫūr.

(3) Ūṅṅipāṭ.—fishing-stakes, Cochin.

(4) Hire for Sirkar ware-houses, shops, etc.,—Cochin.

(5) Sṭṭhāna kāīcha.—dues for the enjoyment of dignities. Kaṇayannūr and Cochin.

(6) Palappaṇam.—probably a corruption of fruit or produce. Mukuṇḍapuram.

(7) Kuṭippaṭṭōla.—Cochin.

8) Ēīara upakari do.

(9) Vēlippaṇam do.

(10) Koṭṭakkāśu do.

(11) Veṙaku naṭaṭṭu kuṭṭaka.—Cochin.

(12) Imposts payable for cultivating lands not assessed to any fixed revenue. Due from all Ṭālūks.

(13) Ṭūkku paṇam.—Kaṇayannūr.

(14) Kaṭuku Ṭirumulkāīcha.—Kaṇayannūr.

(15) Nāyāṭṭu bhōgam.—hunting dues. Kaṇayannūr.

(16) Manuṣhya Jīviṭam. do.

(17) Kāval bhōgam.—guarding dues. do.

(18) Eṙappaṇam.—Kaṇayannūr.

(19) Ṭaṇṭāyma sṭṭhāna kāïcha.—dues payable by Ṭaṇṭāns for dignities conferred on them. Due from the Mukunḍapuram, Trichur and Ṭalappiḷḷi Ṭālūks.

(20) Muṭaliyār sṭṭhāna kāïcha.—Mukunḍapuram.

(21) Chūḷappaṇam.—Kaṇayannūr and Mukunḍapuram.

(22) Ālappaṇam.—Kaṇayannūr, Mukunḍapuram and Trichur.

(23) Chūṭṭālappaṇam.—Trichur and Ṭalappiḷḷi.

(24) Jenmi bhōgam.—Cochin.

(25) Changāṭam.—Mukunḍapuram, Trichur and Ṭalappiḷḷi

(26) Kūli ēkkam.—Trichur.

(27) Kāṙṭṭika paṇam—do.

(28) Kuṭṭakappāṭṭam Ṭirumulkāïcha.—Ṭalappiḷḷi.

(29) Mēlkūṙ.—Trichur.

(30) Koṭippaṇam.—Kaṇayannūr.

(31) Ṭoṭṭakula.—Ṭalappiḷḷi.

(32) Panappāṭṭam.—Chiṫṫūr.

(33) Karimpanappāṭṭam—do.

(34) Ṭirunāl kāïcha—do.

(35) Māṭumēkkuṅṅa Vakekku.—Chiṫṫūr.

(36) Maka kāïcha—do.

Another class of imposts may also be mentioned, which come under the head of miscellaneous.

Kuṙavabhōgam.

Kinaṫṫil paṅṅi.

Most of the above except those relating to personal dignities and such as are not attached to land have been, at the recent settlement, commuted into a payment of half-an-anna per rupee of land-tax paid by the Paṭṭaḍārs. By this measure, while professing to give up imposts which are at the very sight vexatious, but the burden of which fell only on particular classes, the Sirkar has succeeded in augmenting its revenue very largely by spreading the imposts on the whole land and making all Paṭṭaḍārs pay at a rate largely in excess of what they were paying hitherto. By this process, while the inequity of exactions is successfully veiled, the revenue has been disproportionately increased. The subjoined figures may be taken as rough averages of assessments till the present system was introduced very recently.

Paṇṭāravaka Nilams, 0 10 0 per para, i.e., Rs. 7-13-0 per acre.

Purавaka Nilams, Rs. 0 4 0 per para, i. e., Rs. 3-2-0 per acre.

		Rs.	A.	P.
Assessment	on a cocoanut tree	0	2	0
Do	on an areca tree	0	0	4
Do	on a jack tree	0	6	0
Do	on a palmyra tree	0	0	10
Do	on a house.	0	3	6

14. **Mode of Government.** The authority of the Raja was, no doubt, supreme within the limits under his direct rule. But the State was parcelled out among many feudatory chiefs, bearing various designations as Kaṛṭṭāvu, Paṇikkar, Kaimal, etc., who were sovereigns, within their contracted limits, and who warred not only amongst themselves but also ventured to set at naught at times the authority of their liege lord. The names of some of these have already been mentioned.

The following extract from the *Cochin Census Report* of 1901 will give us an idea of the early form of Government in Cochin and its development into its present state.

"In the earlier pages of this sketch, we have said that during what may be termed the dark ages, this State, like other kingdoms in Kērala, was governed on feudal principles. By the period at which we have arrived (the period of the introduction of the English supremacy), a fundamental change seems to have come over the Governmental system. We note the prevalence of a fairly uniform standard of administration directly controlled by the Raja, or by the officers commissioned by him. This was, perhaps, the natural inevitable outcome of centuries of incessant warfare, in which the State was involved, especially in the 18th century, when the feudal system became clearly discredited, owing to the constant conflicts and feuds among the vassals themselves and by their overtures to the Raja's enemies. Even during the prevalence of that original system of Government, there were the Raja's officers to look after his interests in the several parts of the State. They were the several grades of Kāriakkārs, and the Provēṛṭṭikkārs under them. They had the supervision of the State or crown lands, and also collected and transmitted to the State Treasury in the Raja's palace the transit duties, seigniorage and other dues, by which the treasury used to be replenished in ancient days. In fact, they controlled the collection of the revenue from different sources, and also took cognizance of all important civil and criminal causes. The feudal chieftains had, we know, the ordering of the militia and exercised also a measure of local authority. The power of these chieftains was gradually undermined by the personal rule of the Raja, who appointed his representatives in every centre of importance, minimising the familiar risk of internal dissensions and foreign invasions. In each Provēṛṭṭi, the Provēṛṭṭikkār's authority was increased by his being entrusted with all the duties and responsibilities of government, subject to the control of the Kāriakkārs, who, in their turn, were subordinate to the Sarvāḍhikāriakkārs, all of whom were under the orders of the Valia Saṙvādhikāriakkār, or the head kāriakkār of the Rāja. In regard to the military system, the brigades in the several ṭālūks were placed under the Commandants appointed by the Raja, and under the immediate orders of Pāliaṭṭ Acchan, for long the hereditary Prime Minister of the Raja, and the Commander-in-Chief of his forces. The gradual growth of the power of the Raja's officers led to the final emancipation of his authority from all feudal limitations and restrictions. In district administration, the land-tax was gradually taking shape, and the feudal chiefs, who were ceasing to be the centre of any public authority, were slowly brought to yield obedience to the new system, and to contribute towards its support. The establishment of the British supremacy increased the stability of the State, and strengthened the personal authority of the Raja."[1].

It was in the year 1762 that the country was first sub-divided into Kōvilakaṭṭumvāṭals or Ṭālūks, a designation still subsisting, and Pṙoveṙṭikkāṙs and Chanṭṙakkārs or revenue collectors and treasurers were appointed.

At present, the Government is, for all practical purposes, an absolute monarchy, the people having no voice whatever in the administration. The only checks upon the arbitrary power of the Rajas, the general assemblies of the nation, referred to by our author in the next paragraph, have been long since a thing of the past. The *pax Britannica* has taken their place, and the controlling authority of the British Resident,[2] the representative of the Paramount Power, is now the only check to the arbitrary power of the Rajas. That control is exercised by way of supervision, the Resident giving what is euphemistically called advice, but really commands which the Raja dare not neglect to listen to and carry out. The position of the British Resident at the Raja's

1. P. XXVII.

2. Now Political Agent of the Governor-General, as the State is at present directly under the Indian Government.

court is rather unique. He is the accredited agent of the Paramount Power invested with full authority to control and direct the administration of the State under certain given circumstances. Ordinarily, he is a friendly adviser, but one whose advice has necessarily to be conformed to. The Raja has to consult him in all important matters relating to the administration of the State. His sanction has to be obtained before any sentence of death can be executed; he has to be consulted before any legislative measures are undertaken; his advise should be taken before budgets are sanctioned or appointments to offices above a certain grade are made ; in short, he has to be consulted and his views ascertained and conformed to before any new step in the administration is taken. He is the final court of appeal in the country, though he does not profess himself to be such. His right to advise the Darbar enables him to interpose between the victim of an unjust act and the administration, where a gross miscarriage of justice occurs. But he takes care in no way to directly interfere with constituted authority so as to give rise to an impression that he sits supreme over all in the State. He does not, of course, allow the authority of the Raja to be thrown into the shade.

The administration is carried on under the personal directions of the Raja through the Diwan, or minister, who is responsible for his good conduct to the Raja and the British Resident. For some time past, the office of Diwan has come to be held by officers of the British Indian service whose services are lent by the Indian Government at the request of the Raja.[1] For administrative purposes, the state was divided into two divisions, the Northern and Southern, presided over by divisional officers called Peishkars, who were also District Magistrates. These divisions are now amalgamated into one and placed under an officer styled

1. From 1099 (M. E.) Medam, it is a native of the state and one who was, till then, the Chief Judge that has filled the place of the Diwan.

Diwan Peishkar, who is the "lieutenant of the Diwan." Under the Peishkar, there are Tahsildars and Deputy Tahsildars, who are in charge of sub-divisions known as Kōvilakaṭṭumvāṭils or Ṭālūks. The Tahsildars, who had hitherto exercised the functions of Sub-Magistrates also, were relieved of their magisterial duties, a separate magisterial department being constituted under the supervision of a District Magistrate for the whole State. The Ṭālūks are again sub-divided into villages or Ṗroveṙṭṭīs, under officers called Ṗroveṙṭṭikkārs, whose chief function is the collection of revenue. For purposes of administration of criminal justice, the Sessions Courts exercise appellate and revisional jurisdiction over the District Magistrate and Sub-Magistrates, while the Chief Court sits in appeal over the Sessions Courts, and exercises revisionary powers over all subordinate Criminal Courts. Civil justice is administered by a gradation of Civil Courts commencing with the Munsiff, whose jurisdiction extends to suits of the value of two thousand rupees and below. Next above comes the District Judge, who has appellate powers over the Munsiff, and whose original jurisdiction is unlimited. Over these two grades of courts sits the Chief Court composed of three Judges, which is the highest court of civil and criminal jurisdiction in the State. Of Munsiffs there are seven, and of District Judges two who are also Sessions Judges. There is a Police force, under a Commissioner of Police, that keeps the peace of the country. A number of Regulations have been enacted for the guidance of the various courts. In fact, every effort has been made to bring the State into line with the progressive administration of British India. In its extreme anxiety to imitate British Indian forms and methods and even to assimilate its own ways with the British system, Cochin is steadily sacrificing its individuality and giving up its national characteristics. While, in Europe, the Hungarians and the Irish are clamouring for official recognition of their own dialects, the

Cochin Sirkar is allowing Malayālam, the mother tongue of the country, to give way to English as the vehicle of official correspondence. In some instances, the use of the English language is insisted upon even in the lower grades of the service, all chalāns or receipts of money being required to be drawn up in that language. Malayālam official terms are superseded by English. The term Provertti used hitherto to designate the smallest sub-division for purposes of revenue collection has been dropped. In the official records, these subdivisions are henceforward to be called *villages*. English numerical figures have been substituted for Malayālam, and English years, months and dates, uniformly adopted. The Survey and Settlement records do not show the measurement of lands in Dannu and Kōle, but in English *feet*, *links* and *chains*; and the capacity of the land is measured by the English *acre* and *cent*, not by the Malayālam Para and Edangali The coin current in the State has been abolished, and the British Indian currency adopted. The Matriculation Examination of the Madras University and the School Final of the Educational Department have been officially declared to be the only passport for access into the superior grades of the Public Service, that is, offices to which a salary of more than Rs. 20 *per mensem* is attached. A knowledge of the language of the country is no longer insisted on as a *sine qua non* for office, with the result that almost all the departments of the State had, till some time back, to be presided over by foreigners, whose only tie with the country is the pay they draw from the State, and their own good sense of fellowship and sympathy with those over whom they are placed. All this may be progress, but scarcely progress on national lines or the result of a patriotic ambition to advance the country in the scale of civilized political societies. For this state of things, the apathy of educated men contributed not a little. When patriotism works on selfish lines and, at times, reduces itself to a race for lucrative posts, one cannot expect the development of the country in the proper direction.[1]

15. **Pandera Putte.** This stands for Paṇṭāra Pillēr or pages of the Raja. The personal attendants of the Raja are still, or were till recently, known as Paṇṭāra Pillēr.

16. **Conduct of Public Affairs in Malabar.**—Our author has given us some idea of the civil and political organisation of the kingdom of Cochin. It will be well to know how the rest of Malabar was organised for political, social and administrative purposes and also what the system of government pursued was.

We have seen that Paraśu Rāma, the reputed conqueror and coloniser of Kēraḷa, is credited to have handed over the government of the country to the Nampūṭiri Brahmans. Whatever truth there may be in this, it is clear that the organization of the country for social and political purposes was of the pure Hindu type. The unit of the social system was the joint family, suited to an infant stage of society. A number of such joint families of the early settlers in, or colonists of, Kēraḷam associated themselves for political and administrative purposes and established village communities, the Brahman village communities being designated Grāmams, and the non-Brahman, Ṭaṙa, Kara, Piṭika, Chēri, Muṙi and Ḍēśam as localities varied. According to tradition and the Kēraḷōṭpaṭṭi, the Brahmans who had been prevailed upon by Paraśu Rāma, to colonise his new land and who, it is said, were rewarded by him with the gift of the whole land, after fixing the ṭaṙas (Nāyar villages) and Sankēṭam (literally 'appointed place' or a division of the Brahman dominions answering somewhat to the English Pale in Ireland), established 64 Grāmams or Brahman villages and introduced a sort of republican government.

1. It is hoped that the Village Panchayats and the Legislative Council will, instead of accentuating sectarian differences, read the past aright, work steadily and honestly in the present so as to evolve a glorious future for the State of Cochin.

The actual government was vested in four Kaḷakams or Councils elected as representatives of the 64 Grāmams, assisted or presided over by an officer styled Rakṣhā Puruṣhan (Protector) who was to be elected by the whole body as their Executive Officer and to remain in office for a period of three years each. Each Kaḷakam further elected an Avarōḍha Nampi to serve as a sort of Councillor to the Rakṣhā Puruṣhan, and lands adequate for the support of these officers were assigned to them severally. The office of Rakṣhā Puruṣhan subsequently fell into disuse on the appearance in the country of certain foreign Hindu Princes, who came either on the invitation of the Brahmans who found themselves unable to carry on the Government, or as invaders, bent on conquest and aggrandisement. The office of Rakṣhā Puruṣhan, however, was, after some time, revived; it is not possible to say whether at the instance of the conqueror or on his expulsion or retirement from the country. It would appear that these foreign princes themselves were allowed to rule over the country only for 12 years each, with the designation of Perumāḷs, at the expiry of which term they had to give up their government. Even during their term of office, the Brahman Kaḷakams or Councils seem to have retained large powers and the Perumāḷs (literally great men) had to consult them and take their advice on all important matters. This leads one to think that the Perumāḷs were the nominees of the Brahmans who, as the ruling community, stood in need of external aid. Anyhow, the office of Rakṣhā Puruṣhan seems to have been revived at a later period with increased powers, such as those possessed by the Perumāḷs. After a while, we meet with another set of Perumāḷs on the scene, the first of whom was installed in office on Puṣhya Nakṣhaṭṛa (8th Lunar Asterism) in the month of Māgha in Karkkaṭaka Vyāḷa which, as may be ascertained from the Kali year given, was 216 A. D. It is expressly said that this Perumāḷ came on invitation and that his rule was subject to certain conditions stated. He was followed by two others at the expiry of the 12 years' term for which each was appointed. The third of them shook off the Brahman yoke and established an absolute monarchy, for the first time in the annals of Kērala; but it is doubtful whether his sway extended throughout Kēralam. Early records make it clear that, even during the sway of the Brahmans and the Perumāls, there were Kṣheṭṛiya princes ruling over tracts, perhaps as feudatories. At the close of the last Perumāl's reign, there was a disruption of his petty empire, when the petty chiefs and subordinate princes are said to have come into independent possession of their various tracts.

The administrative system inaugurated originally continued to be the same under the Nampūṭirīs, the Perumāls and the Rajas and was worked with success till the Mysorean conquest.

According to that system, the country was divided, for the purpose of internal administration, into Nāḍs (Districts or Provinces), which again were sub-divided into Ḍēśams (villages). The most successful of village head-men, Grāmādhipaṭīs or Māṭampīs, ripened in a few instances into Chiefs of Nāḍs in some places, and their domain came to be styled as Swarūpams and Eṭavakays. The village headmen were known in some places as Ḍēśavālīs and in others as Māṭampīs. The Ḍēśavālīs were at one time the sole proprietors of the land in their respective villages and they enjoyed in addition the following rights, viz.—

(1) The Ampalappaṭi or the direction of the ceremonies of the village pagoda.

(2) The Urāima or the management of pagoda lands.

(3) The Aśāima or the control of all the ceremonies in the families or houses that go to form the village.

(4) The Ḍēśāḍhipaṭṭyam or the general superintendence as headman of all affairs of the ḍēśam or village.

If he, i.e., the headman, enjoyed only part of the rights belonging to the chief of the ḍēśam, i. e., all except the first two, he is known not as Ḍēśavāḷi but as Jenmivāḷi. The direction of the civil, religious and military affairs of the village were always vested in the same person. The Jenmivāḷi had in his own village all the authority of the Ḍēśavāḷi but, not having the honors attached to the supremacy of the pagoda, his office was not considered so respectable. Some Ḍēśavāḷis had one and some two or more villages. There was a Ḍēśavāḷi to every village except where the village was the private property of the chief of the district i. e., the Ṅāṭuvāḷi, or of the Raja, when the rights of the head of the village belonged to the Ṅāṭuvāḷi or the Raja; but in most of the villages which the Rajas had acquired by purchase, the old Ḍēśavāḷis still retained their office. Where there was no Ḍēśavāḷi, the Raja employed an officer, called the Pṛavaṛṭṭikkār,[1] as the manager of one or more villages according to their size.

The Ḍēśavāḷi had the direction of all the affairs of the village; all orders regarding them were sent to him to be carried into effect. When there was no regular land-rent, he could not have much employment as a revenue officer, but he assisted in the collection of occasional contributions as well as of fines, forfeitures and other dues of Government. He was the military chief of the village, and marched at the head of its quota, when ordered to the field, and he had the direction of the police and the power of deciding petty suits. In police and judicial matters, he was aided by two or three respectable inhabitants, who were called Pṛamāṇis in the north and Ṭaṭasṭhars in the south.

1. The village officer in the States of Cochin and Travancore are still called Proverthikkars and the office Parvattyam. AV.

There were usually from one to five or six Pṙamāṇīs to a Ḍēṡam or village, but in some villages none. They had no regular appointment, nor were they hereditary. They were generally of the superior castes—Nampūṭīries and Nāyars, chiefly the latter. But other castes were not excluded altogether. Any respectable man in the village who was considered as more intelligent than his neighbours, and who was on that account resorted to by the inhabitants for the adjustment of their little differences, gradually acquired among them the title of Pṙamāṇi. The plaintiff, in the first instance, generally applied to the Pṙamāṇi, who assembled the other Pṙamāṇīs in the village, if there were any, or if not, he sent for those of the neighbouring villages, who always came as he would, in his turn, answer their summonses. Those who were called in were such as were acceptable to both parties. No writing was employed in the proceeding, a Kaṙāṙnāmah founded upon the decision was all that was necessary. The Pṙamāṇīs, where no opposition was made, acted on their own accord without any reference to the Ḍēṡavāḷi. If the defendant refused to attend, they applied to the Ḍēṡavāḷi, who sent for the defendant, directed the Pṙamāṇīs to try the cause in his own presence, and decided upon their report. If the parties required it, he associated two or three of the inhabitants with the Pṙamāṇīs to the court or Panchāyat. His authority was so much respected that the defendant scarcely ever refused to attend his summons, or to abide by his decision; but when this happened, the Ḍēṡavāḷi applied to the Nāṭuvāḷi, the chief of the ṅād or district, who ordered the parties to attend and settled the cause himself, by means of the Ḍēṡavāḷi and Pṙamāṇīs of the original village, or of those of any other village within his jurisdiction, who were most agreeable to the parties. Where a village had no Pṙamāṇi, the inhabitants carried their complaints to any neighbouring village in which there was one.

In case of theft, complaint was made to the Pṙamāṇi, who informed the Ḍēśavāīi and both together investigated the matter and reported to the Nāṭuvāli. If the thief was apprehended, he was taken to the Nāṭuvāli. If it was the first offence, the punishment was fine and restoration of the stolen property; if the third, severe punishment of death. If the offender absconded, he was outlawed.

The Ḍēśavāīi and the Pṙamāṇīs received fees in all suits decided by them. The amount was not fixed ; but when the parties could pay the fees, the rates were, to the Ḍēśavāīi, one rupee, to the Pṙamāṇi, half a rupee, and to the witnesses, four, two, or one anna *per* day, according to their rank ; but the whole never exceeded ten *per cent* of the claim. Where the parties were poor, not more than a fourth or a fifth of the usual rate was taken. Some of the more respectable Pṙamāṇīs were enabled by their fees to keep two or three servants for the purpose of summoning parties and witnesses, etc. The fees were not paid by the party who lose the cause, but in equal shares by both parties.

The Ḍēśavāīi derived, besides fees on settlement of suits, some other advantages from his situation. He received yearly from the owners of gardens the produce of one plantain tree, ten cocoanuts, one jack, one chest of *supari* or betel-nut, and from all ryots the value of four to eight annas in ghee or sugar, and a small poll-tax of eight annas from carpenters, smiths and washermen.

The Ḍēśavāīi had no village accountant, as the nature of the revenue did not require an officer of that kind. The accounts of the collections were kept by district servants employed by the Nāṭuvāīi or by any, acting immediately under the Raja. The few revenue accounts which were requisite for the Ḍēśavāīi's information were kept either by himself or by a servant of his own. The conditions of the landowners made it easy for the district servants to collect such occasional contributions as were required from them along with the other articles of public revenue. The collection is still more facilitated by the military nature of the tenures, and by the Government placing every man in the village under the orders of the Ḍēśavāḷi and at his disposal, either for revenue or police duties. He, of course, usually employed the lower classes, but no individual, even of the higher, ever hesitated in performing whatever services he commanded. None of them sat in his presence without leave, and he was obeyed rather as the chief of the clan than the head of a village.

The office next above the Ḍēśavāḷi, and placed between him and the Raja, was the Ṅāṭuvāḷi or chief of the Ṅāḍ or district. He was a kind of district Ḍēśavāḷi, for he enjoyed the same powers and privileges in the district as the Ḍēśavāḷi in the village. He claimed to hold office by a tenure as ancient as that of any of the Rajas, and to have derived it from the same conqueror, Paraśu Rāma, from whom the Nampūṭiries alleged that they derived their rights. He was sometimes the Ḍēśavāḷi of every village in his district, and sometimes of only one or two, the rest being held by separate Ḍēśavāḷīs, or by the Raja as part of his dominions.

The Ṅāṭuvāḷi had a small share of almost every branch of the Raja's revenue. He had customs of an inferior rate, all fines under four rupees, the property of all persons on his own lands dying without heirs not exceeding thirty rupees, and on the lands of others when it did not exceed fifteen rupees, and a variety of other dues which it would be tedious to enumerate. He was the chief police and judicial officer of the district, and, in these capacities, he had a share of all confiscations of the property of offenders, and of the fees of all suits brought before him.

The Ṅāṭuvāḷīs collected the ordinary and extra revenues, and in this duty, he was assisted by one, two, or more accountants, according to the extent of his district. The accountant kept all accounts of the Nāṭuvāḷi's collections and records of transfer of land. He was paid by the Nāṭuvāḷi an allowance of three or four rupees monthly. He received a fee of half or quarter of a rupee for every bond or other deed which he wrote for the inhabitants, for he was their conveyancer. He had service lands, rent free, yielding paddy that will fetch from fifty to eighty paṟas of rice, which had been granted by the Ṅāṭuvāḷi, who appointed him when he received his own.

The Ṅāṭuvāḷi was the military chief of his district and was bound to attend the Raja in the field, or march wherever he was directed, with all the fighting men of his district, under the Ḍēśavāḷīs or heads of their respective villages. It was also his duty, in times of peace, to assemble the Nāyars of his district every two or three years, in order to exhibit in the presence of the Raja, a mock, or rather real fight, with the Nāyars of another district; for these combats never terminated without the loss of a few lives. Ōcheṟa Paṭa and Vaḷuṭayil Paṭa, etc., are modern representatives of the sham-combats of ancient days. These combats were, as already pointed out, instituted with the view of keeping up the martial spirit of the Nāyars. It may easily be conceived that the Nāṭuvāḷi, with such followers at his command, was sometimes tempted to rebel; but, even when reduced, though he was himself punished, his office and estate were not confiscated, but went to his heirs.

The Raja, as has already been observed, besides getting his revenue from the customs, licenses and other fluctuating sources, was possessor of extensive domains. Of some villages, he was the owner of the lands and also of the Ḍēśavāḷi rights; of others, he was the proprietor of part or whole of the lands, while the Ḍēśavāḷi rights were still retained by the original land-lord. The revenues of the Raja's own villages were collected by temporary officers appointed by him. All appeals from the decisions of Ṅāṭuvālīs and Ḍesavālīs were decided by a court or Panchāyaṭṭ, in his presence or in that of his minister. The office of minister was, in some of the Rajaships, claimed as the hereditary right of particular Ṅāṭuvālīs, and though the Raja might appoint another person to discharge the duty, the title remained with the Nāṭuvāli. Thus the Zamorin's ministership was hereditary in the family of Mangāṭ Achchen, while the Pāliyaṭṭ Achchen was the hereditary minister of the Cochin Raja, till he forfeited his right to it for rebellion against the British Government.

The system of internal administration, of which an outline has been given above, was that which prevailed throughout Malabar, when that province was invaded by Hyder Ali in 1766. But, as the country could never be reduced to complete subjection while it existed, it was destroyed and another substituted in its room, resembling as nearly as the circumstances of the country then permitted, that which was established in the other provinces of Hyder's dominions; and though wars, in other quarters, compelled him to leave some of the inferior Rajas as his agents in the management of their territories, what he left undone was completed by his son, Tippu Sultan, who expelled them all. The military tenures were abolished; regular land-rent, founded on inspection, though not on actual survey, was imposed on the country. The administration of its affairs was entrusted to Subhadars and Fouzdars sent from Seringapatam instead of Rajas, and the Nāyars were overawed by a large body of troops from Mysore stationed among them. [1]

We gather the following account of the administrative system of the Zamorin from Buchanan:

1. Sir Thomas Munro's *Report on Malabar*, 4th July 1817. See also *Selections from the Asiatic Journal*, Vol. II, pp. 661—63, and Mr. Justice Kunju Raman Nayar's *Memo on Travancore Land Tenures*.

"During the Government of the *Tamuris*, the business of the state was conducted, under his authority, by four *Savadi Carigars*, whose offices were hereditary, and by certain inferior Carigars, appointed and removed at the pleasure of the sovereign. The *Sarvadi Carigars* are, 1st *Mangatachan*, a *Nayar* of the tribe called *Sudra*; 2nd, *Tenancheri Elliadi*, a *Brahman*; 3rd *Bermamuta Panycary*, also a *Sudra Nayar*; and 4th *Paranambi*, a *Nayar* of the kind called *Nambichan*. The inferior *Carigars* managed the private estates, or *Chericul* lands, of the *Tamuri*, and collected the revenues. These consisted of the customs, of a fifth part of all the movable estates of every person that died, and of fines: of course, the *Carigars* were the administrators of justice, or rather of what was called law. They were always assisted by four assessors; but, the selection of these being left to themselves, this provision gave little security to the subject. Eight-tenths of all fines went to the *Tamuri*, the two-tenths to the judge. For capital punishments, the mandate of the *Tamuri*, was required. The defence of the country rested entirely on such of the *Nayars* as received arms from the *Tamuri*. These were under the orders of *Nadawais*, who commanded from 200 to 3000 men, and who held their authority by hereditary descent. The *Carigar* says, that these *Nadawais* had lands given them, in proportion to the number of men that each commanded; but how that could be, when the whole lands belonged to *Nambudiri* landlords, I do not understand. The soldiers, when on actual service, received a certain small subsistence.

"In cases of emergency, certain tributary or dependent chiefs were also summoned to bring their men into the field. These chiefs, such as, *Punetur*, *Talapuli*, *Manacollatil*, *Ayenceutil*, *Tirumanachery*, and many others, acknowleged the *Tamuri* as their superior; but they assumed the title of Raja, and in their respective territories possessed full jurisdiction. They were merely bound to assist the *Tamuri* with military service. He never bestowed on any of them the title of Raja, either in writing or conversation, and treated with contempt their pretension to such a dignity".[1]

"In Malabar," says Bartolomeo, "the following royal officers are still in existence. The *Torakaren*, intendant of the sea coasts and rivers; the *Senabadi*, generalissimo of all the military forces; four *Sarvadis*, or Governors, each of whom has the superintendence of four provinces; a great many Kariakarer, or superior magistrates; the same number of Adhigari, or overseers of districts; together with a multitude of Pravartikarer or tax-gathers, and Pullas or writers"[2] Apparently Bartolomeo was referring to the administrative officers of Travancore.

Regarding the administrative system of Travancore in the early part of the eighteenth century, we have the following sketch given by Lieutenant Arthur:—"Under the Dalawah or Diwan, there is a chain of officers, all dependent on each other in regular gradation, for the management of the revenue and all other affairs of Government; thus the whole country is parcelled out into a certain number of grand divisions over each of which a principal officer termed Valia Sarvadhikariakar presides and his authority extends to all matters of a revenue, commercial and judicial nature. These great portions of the country are again divided into a certain number of parts, each under the secondary controlling management of a Sarvadhikariakar and these again are subdivided into districts, under the management of a Kariakar, who has a residency in certain principal places in his district. Other officers termed Proverticars are the last in gradation among the managing officers of respectability: but under them again there are several inferior officers called Chundracars, Toracars and

1. Vol. II, pp. 83—4.

2. P, 302.

Villakkārs or peons, who have each a distinct and separate office. Besides the above, there is an officer appointed in each of the three great divisions who is entitled the Mēluvijārippukār and the nature of his office is partly judicial; but in what particular cases his interference is required I have not learned. Each of the principal officers named above has an office establishment of writers, etc., for keeping the accounts of his cutcherry. The Head writer in the cutcherry of the Kāriakār is entitled Theroomukompedecha (Ṭirumukhampiṭichcha) Pillay and all those inferior officers, Pillays".[1]

17. **Mamamkam.** The Mahāmākham or Māmāmkam was the greatest national festival of Malabar which has, owing to political vicissitudes, ceased to be celebrated now, for the last 160 and odd years. Of the national assemblies or Kūṭṭams of Malabar, the most important was the one that gathered at Ṭiruṅāvāye, once in 12 years, on the occasion of the Māmāmkam festival, where all Kēraḷa was expected to be represented. The festival was held on the banks of the Periyār river at Ṭiruṅāvāye, near the pagoda of Śiva, and it was believed that the sacred waters of the Ganges appeared in that river on the Mākham day. The festival itself lasted for 28 days. The tradition is that the ceremony was instituted by Paraśu Rāma. In Kēraḷa, a Vyāḷavaṭṭam or cycle of Jupiter, a space of twelve years, is a period of great importance. All offices were held only for that period; all tenures of land subsisted only for that period; all transactions, appointments, contracts and tenures had to be renewed at the end of 12 years; all feudal ties were broken at the end of that period, and the Māmāmkam was the occasion when all parties assembled in solemn conclave at Ṭiruṅāvāye and readjusted all existing relations among themselves. In the early government of Malabar, whether republican or monarchical, the ruler was changed at the end of 12 years. The removal of the reigning incumbent and the installation

1. Lieutenant Arthur's *Report*, p. 16.

of the new one was also effected at this national festival with the consent and approval of the entire nation. The Kēralōṭpaṭṭi, a so-called historical account of Malabar in the Malayāḷam language, attributes the institution of this festival to Paraśu Rāma, who ordered the Brahmans of the 64 grāmās (villages), when they found it not possible to govern the country themselves any longer, to instal a Raja to rule over them for a period of 12 years. The day chosen for the installation of the sovereign was the festival day at the Śiva shrine at Ṭiruṅāvāye.

There are various versions as to the manner in which the ruling chief was removed at the close of this period. Early records show that the rulers brought their career to a tragic end at a jubilee they celebrated at the end of the 12th year of their reign. Though the strange custom seems to have died out sometime before the advent of the Portuguese, we have descriptions of it left by early travellers. We read in Purchas that the "King of Travancore's dominions stretched beyond Cape Comorin (where Malabar endeth) on the East Coast for a score and ten miles as far as Cael (Kāyal) which divers great lords held under him. Among the rest is the 'signory of Quilacaray'." Purchas then gives an account of the festival at which the king of the country brings his career to a close by publicly cutting his own throat. Evidently Purchas derived his information from the Portuguese Captain, Barbosa, and it would be better to quote from the latter on the subject. Speaking of 'Quilacare and of the lord who lives in it (the country of the king of Colam or Quilon) subject to him', Barbosa says:—"And in the province of Quilacare there is a gentile house of prayer, in which there is an idol, which they hold in great account, and every 12 years they celebrate a great feast to it, whither the gentiles go as to a Jubilee. This temple possesses many lands and much revenue: it is a very great affair. This province has a king over it, who has not more than 12 years to reign from Jubilee to Jubilee. His manner of living is in this wise, that is to say: when the 12 years are completed, on the day of this feast, there assembles together innumerable people, and much money is spent in giving food to Brahmans. The king has a wooden scaffolding made, spread over with silken hangings: and on that day he goes to bathe at a tank with great ceremonies and sound of music, after which he comes to the idol and prays to it and mounts to the scaffolding, and there, before all the people, he takes some very sharp knives, and begins to cut off his nose, and then his ears and his lips, and all his members, and as much flesh off himself as he can, and he throws it away very hurriedly until so much of his blood is spilled that he begins to faint, and then he cuts off his throat himself. And he performs this sacrifice to the idol, and whoever desires to reign other 12 years and undertake this martydom for love of the idol, has to be present looking on at this: and from that place they raise him up as king." [1]

It is not possible to know if the Chēramān Perumāls or rulers of Kērala or Chēra sacrificed themselves in this fashion at the end of their 12 years' term at the great Mahā-Mākham festival. The Kēraḷōṭpaṭṭi does not certainly support the tradition of their self-immolation mentioned by Dr. Day. [2] For it records that the Perumāls retired to their own country on vacating their viceroyalty. [3] The late Sub-Judge, Mr. K. R. Kṛṣhṇa Mēnōn, however, says that, as the influence of the Perumāls increased, they refused to vacate their office quietly, and offered to be cut down by those who were desirous of winning a crown. [4]

The last Chēramān Perumāl, in distributing his country among his relatives, dependants and friends,

1. *Description of Malabar and the East Coast of Africa*, pp. 172—173.
2. *Land of the Perumals*, p. 43.
3. See Mangalore Edition.
4. *Transactions of the Bombay Literary Society*, Vol I., p. 4.

is said to have entrusted the presidency at the Mahā-Mākham festival to the Waḷḷuvanāḍ Raja, which dignity carried along with it the over-lordship of Malabar, from whom, according to Mahomedan accounts, the Zamorin wrested it with Mahomedan aid. Mr. Kṛṣhṇa Mēnōn observes that this was effected by the Zamorin challenging the Waḷḷuvanāḍ Raja to celebrate the feast, at which he succeeded in killing the Raja in the manner prescribed, and thus secured the Mēlkōyma or right of supremacy over the other Malabar Rajas. At any rate, we have reliable record to show that, in the 17th century, the Zamorin, as the asserted supreme ruler in Malabar, acted as President of the ceremony. And what is more, we know that the old custom of the Zamorin, or the ruler for the time being, whoever he be, having to cut his own throat, had given place to a custom by which he who is able to cut down the king who sits well-guarded in a prominent place, is installed in the king's throne for a term of 12 years. Captain Alexander Hamilton, in his *New Account of the East Indies*, describes the custom as observed in the year (1695 A. D.) in the following words[1]:—

"It was an ancient custom for the Samorin, (Zamorin, then the local potentate) to reign but 12 years and no longer. If he died before his term was expired, it saved him a troublesome ceremony of cutting his own throat on a public scaffold erected for that purpose. He first made a feast for all his nobility and gentry, who were very numerous. After the feast, he saluted his guests, went on the scaffold, and very neatly cut his own throat in the view of the assembly. His body was, a little while after, burned with great pomp and ceremony, and the grandees elected a new Samorin. Whether the custom was a religious or a civil ceremony, I know not, but it is now laid aside and a new custom is followed by the modern Samorin, that a jubilee is proclaimed throughout his dominions at the end of 12 years, and the tent is pitched for him in a spacious plain and a

1. Vol. I., Ch. XXV.

great feast is celebrated for ten or twelve days with mirth and jollity, guns firing night and day, so that at the end of the feast any four of the guests that have a mind to gain a crown by a desperate action in fighting their way through 30 or 40 thousand of his guards, and kill the Samorin in his tent, he that kills him succeeds to him in his empire. In Anno 1695, one of these jubilees happened when the tent was pitched near Ponnany (Ponnāni), a seaport of his about 15 leagues to the southward of Calicut. There were but three men that would venture on that desperate action, who fell on with sword and target, among the guards, and after they had killed and wounded many, were themselves killed. One of the *Desperadoes* had a nephew of fifteen or sixteen years of age, that kept close by his uncle in the attack on the guard, and when he saw him fall, the youth got through the guards into the tent and made a stroke at His Majesty's head and had certainly despatched him, if a large brass lamp which was burning over his head, had not marred the blow; but before he could make another he was killed by the guards, and I believe the same Samorin reigns yet. I chanced to come that time along the coast and heard the guns for two or three days and nights successively."

Mr. Francis Wrede, writing in the year 1793, gives the following account of the festival:—"This feast is celebrated every twelve years at Terunavaye, near the pagoda of that place dedicated to the god Sheevan; it lasts twenty-eight days, and attracts a prodigious concourse of people from all parts of India; it consists in a great many religious rites, military games, comodies, etc., and a splendid fair. The institution of this feast seems to be of the most remote antiquity, at least prior to the Government of the Perumals, who used to preside over it; after Cheraman the last Perumal's abdication, Tirunavaye made part of the *Velleterra* Raja's country, and the Mamangom was, of course, celebrated under the auspices of *Wallavuna dircis*, who were to protect it with the fourteen thousand Nayars under their command, agreeable to Cheruma's disposition.

"But the Zamorin, after having established his power in that part of the country and attained the summit of his grandeur, assumed to himself the prerogative of his presiding at and conducting the Mamangom. The princes of the house of Vellaterra could not brook this usurpation of the Zamorin; they made an attack on his life when he presided at the first time at the Mamangom, and several princes of Vellaterra and Nayar chiefs fell in the fruitless attempt; and since that time, this tragedy has been repeated as often as the Mamangom was celebrated, the most resolute of the Vellaterra family and their followers devoting themselves to an almost certain death; for they appear armed with bows and swords and attempt to pave their way to the Zamorin's throne, who surrounded by a strong guard, is prepared to receive them, and they are, of course, overpowered and cut to pieces before they can reach the successful usurper; which attempt is repeated every day as long as the Mamangom lasts and each day some fall a sacrifice to their enthusiasm. It happened, however, towards the middle of the present century, that the Zamorin was in imminent danger of being murdered by a Nayar chief, who after having cut down with incredible bravery every man in his way, had already ascended the steps of the Zamorin's throne, when a Mapilla priest (Coyo) threw himself in his way, and gave the Zamorin time to save himself. It is a very remarkable circumstance that the Zamorin used to be accompanied during the celebration of the Mamangom by the chief Mecta or headman of the Mapilas on one side, and by the Portuguese factor on the other. It is not above forty years since the last Mamangam was celebrated".[1]

1. *The Transactions of the Bombay Society*, Vol. I, pp. 2—3.

Mr. Logan has given us, in his excellent work on Malabar, a graphic and authentic account in detail of the festival, gathered from the archives of His Highness the Zamorin's palace. In giving that account, Mr. Logan remarks :—"The Kērala Māhāṭmyam (a work in Sanskrit verse on Malabar), so far corroborates Hamilton's story that it declares that the king used to be deposed at this festival, but there is no mention of self-immolation; although it is quite possible that the deposed king may have occasionally adopted this mode of escape from the chagrin of not being re-elected by their adherents."

We have in the First Volume of the *Transactions of the Bombay Society* an account of the festival with reference to its origin by the late Sub-Judge, Mr. K. R. Kṛṣhṇa Mēnōn, himself a native of the country of the Zamorin, which does not differ from the above.

A variant of the tragedy is given by Mr. Elie Recles in his *Primitive Folk*. He says :—

"Precautions were formerly taken in Malayalam against the danger of the State falling into senile hands, and against its most important affairs being decided by a maniac. The constitution demanded that a prince who had reigned for twelve years should not govern a day longer; the child of the sun must enter upon his rest after having laboured for a whole cycle. At the last hour he presented his successor to the people and thereupon stabbed himself.

"To close the Monarch's career with due dignity, a grand jubilee and magnificent festival was announced at Calicut. On the great day the king himself inaugurated his own obsequies, and walking at the head of a procession of the highest officers of the State, descended to the sea-shore. When his feet touched the water, he flung down his arms, laid aside his crown, stripped off his garments and seated himself with folded arms upon a cushion. Whereupon four Nairs, whom he had specially entrusted to do him that last service, i. e., to cut his throat, bathed in the sea just beside the prince. Brahmins purified them, clothed them in gala costume, powdered them with saffron, sprinkled them with perfumed water, and then restored to them sword and buckler. To the shout of 'upon them'! the champions flung themselves upon the guards ranged around the king in close battalions, thrusting right and left and striving to force a passage to the man seated on the cushion. Credible or not, the legend affirms that more than one of these mad men plunged his sword into the royal bosom. It only remained for the conqueror to mount the throne, he had so dearly bought. After all, if the prince were unpopular, the regiments disloyal, and a convenient awkwardness in defence previously decided on............?[1]

The custom of killing the king or compelling him to commit suicide is of primitive origin and is traceable to most primitive societies of the old world. All primitive people regard their kings as human incarnations of the divinity. The gods themselves are conceived to be human in their bodily shape, human in their passions and human in their fate; for, like men, they were born into the world, and,like men, they lived and fought and even died. The Hindu gods incarnate, such as Rāma, Kṛshṇa and others, are similarly conceived. In the Hindu temples, the course of worship is adjusted according to human requirements.

In our temples, the daily routine of worship is adjusted to the requirements of human beings of position, such as royal personages and others of the kind. Early in the morning before day-break, the god in our shrines is awakened from his supposed sleep to the tune of music; the image representing the deity is anointed, washed and clothed carefully, incense and perfume are offered in the form of Ḍhūpam (incense) and sandal paste, it is decorated with flowers and precious jewels and a morning collation is offered in the form of

1. *Primitive Folk*, Contemporary Science Series, pp. 148-9.

fried rice and puddings. After resting for a while, the idol is taken round the temple for its morning constitutional with music and tom-toms. It then has its morning and mid-day meals and afternoon rounds. In the evening, the whole temple is illuminated, the god is shown lights attended with music and tom-toms, has its supper, after which it once more sets forth on its rounds and then retires to sleep. The Uṭsavams or annual festivals are more or less an elaboration of the daily worship, and it is significant that, on one of the festival days, the god goes on a hunting expedition, after which there is the grand bath to purify the image after the excursion overnight. All this, it will be observed, is conceived on the idea that gods incarnate are but human beings writ large and have to be attended to as such. I do not, of course, mean to speak with irreverence of our religion. Believing as I do fully in the teachings of our religion in its most authoritative form, I wish only to point out that we have, in our conception of our gods, not gone beyond the anthropomorphistic stage.

Thus likening their kings unto gods and regarding them as incarnations of the divinity, primitive people took the utmost care of the life of their king. But they never suffered their man-god or king to exhibit the slightest symptoms of mental or physical weakness and allow him to grow old and feeble and, at last, die a natural death. For, that would certainly be detracting from the virtue of his exalted divinity, inspired position and personality. This danger was averted by taking away his life as soon as he showed symptoms of failing power. The idea is that his soul must be transferred to a vigorous successor before the decay of senility sets in. And this was effected by putting him to death while yet in possession of all his mental and bodily powers in their vigour.

Some of the reasons that induced these savages either to compass the death of their king or to actually kill him may be gathered from instances of the custom set forth by Mr. Frazer in his *Golden Bough*.

(1) They believed that if the king were to die a natural death, the world would perish and the earth which he alone sustained by his power and merit would immediately be annihilated. This is the belief of the people of Congo with regard to their pontiff, Chitome.

(2) Serious illness, break-up from old age.

(3) Incompetency or unfitness to reign.

(4) Personal defect, such as any bodily blemish.

(5) Ill-government.

In Congo, when the pontiff, the *Chitome*, fell ill and seemed likely to die, his successor-elect entered the pontiff's house with a rope or club and strangled or clubbed him to death.

The Ethiopian kings of Meroe, who were worshipped as gods, were bound to kill themselves as soon as a messenger arrived from their priests ordering them to die, alleging an oracle of the gods as their authority for the command. This system continued till one of their kings, Ergamenes, a contemporary of Ptolemy II, king of Egypt, ventured to disregard the command of the priest and put the priests themselves to death.

In the kingdom of Unyoro in Central Africa, custom still requires that, as soon as the king falls ill seriously or begin to break up from age, he shall be killed by his own wives. When the king of Kabanga, on the upper Congo, seems near his end, the sorcerers put a rope round his neck which they draw gradually tighter till he dies. It was the custom with the Zulus to put the king to death as soon as he began to have wrinkles or grey hairs. It is said that it is one of the barbarous customs of the Zulus in their choice or election of their king that he must neither have wrinkles nor grey hairs, as they are both distinguishing marks of disqualification for becoming a monarch of a warlike people. It is also equally indispensable that their king should never exhibit those proofs of having become unfit and incompetent to reign.

A slight bodily blemish, such as the loss of a tooth, was considered sufficient reason to put to death a king of Sofala. It is said that a prince named Sedanda, a neighbour of the king of Sofala, being affected with leprosy, resolved to follow implicitly the laws of the country, poisoned himself, conceiving his malady to be incurable, or at least, that it would render him so lothsome in the eyes of his people that they would with difficulty recognise him. In consequence, he nominated his successor, holding as his opinion that sovereigns who should serve in all things as an example to their people, ought to have no defects whatever, even in their persons, that when any defects may chance to befall them, they cease to be worthy of life and of governing their dominions ; and prefering death, in compliance with this law, to life, with the reproach of having been its violator. A subsequent king of Sofala, however, took upon himself the role of a bold reformer like Ergamenes of Ethiopia, refused to kill himself on his losing a tooth, inveighed against the brutal custom followed hitherto, and published his resolve to continue to govern.

Mr. Frazer conjectures that the ground for putting the Ethiopian kings to death was, as in the case of the Zulus and Sofala kings, the appearance on their person of some bodily defect or sign of decay; and that the oracle which the priests alleged as the authority for the royal execution was to the effect that great calamities would result from the reign of a king who had any blemish on his body ; just as an oracle warned Sparta against a " lame reign, " that is the reign of a lame king. In Sparta as in Malabar, it will be observed that the heirs of the king were not his sons but the sons of his sisters. It is some confirmation of this conjecture that the kings of Ethiopia were chosen for their size, strength and beauty of person long before the custom of killing them was abolished. To this day, the Sultan of Wadai must have no obvious bodily defect, and a king of Angoy cannot be crowned if he has a single blemish, such as a broken or filed tooth or the scar of an old wound. It is only natural, therefore, to suppose , especially with the other African examples before us, that any bodily defect or symptoms of old age appearing on the person of the Ethiopian monarch was the signal for his execution.

In the kingdom of Eyeo,near Dahomey, when the people had conceived an opinion of the king's ill-government, which was sometimes insidiously infused into them by the artifice of his discontented ministers, they sent a deputation to him with a present of parrot's eggs as a mark of its authenticity to represent to him that the burden of the Government must have so far fatigued him that they consider it full time for him to have repose from his cares and indulge himself with a little sleep.

He thanks his subjects for their attention to his ease, retires to his own appartment as if to sleep and there gives directions to his women to strangle him. This is immediately executed, and his son quietly ascends the throne upon the usual terms of holding the reins of Government no longer than whilst he merits the approbation of the people. This custom was abrogated only about the year 1774 by a king of Eyeo who refused to take a nap on the representation of his ministers, who thereupon raised a rebellion, but were defeated with great slaughter, and thus was the king and his successors freed for ever from the tyranny of the councillors.

In Europe, the old Prussians acknowledged as their supreme lord a ruler who governed them in the name of the gods and was known as god's mouth (*Kirwaido*). When he felt himself weak and idle, if he wished to leave a good name behind him, he had a great heap made of thorn-brushes and straw, on which he mounted and delivered a long sermon to the people, exhorting them to serve the gods and promising to go to the gods and speak for the people. Then he took some of the perpetual fire which burnt in front of the holy oak-tree, and lighting the pile with it, burned himself to death.

In some countries, the king was killed even before he showed visible symptoms of failing health or advancing age or any bodily defect, blemish or incapacity or unfitness to govern. He is suffered by his people to hold his office only for a certain fixed term. We have seen that in Malabar the king was allowed only a term of 12 years, at the end of which he had to cut his own throat. Mr. Frazer believes that the reign of the Dorian kings of old was limited to 8 years, at the close of which, or whenever at a certain time a meteor flashed in the sky, the kings were deposed. We have seen that a twelve years' cycle was of great importance in Malabar; so was the eight years' cycle in early Greece. The sovereign of Toltecs succeeded in obtaining very reasonable latitude before causing him to perish, his people allowed him a reign of fifty-two years, the whole duration of the Mexican cycle. The Bull Apis enjoyed his divinity for twenty-five years.

In some countries, the kings were not suffered to enjoy their real position for more than one year or even one day, while in other countries, even in the course of the same day, more than one might have to sit on the throne. In Babylonia, at the end of an year's reign, the king was put to death, and a new king appointed to reign in his turn a year and suffer death at the end of it. In Nogio, a province of the ancient kingdom of Congo in West Africa, the rule obtains that the chief who assumes the cap of sovereignty one day shall be put to death on the next. The right of succession lies with the chief of Musurongo, but we need not wonder that he does not exercise it and that the throne stands vacant. " No one likes to lose his life for a few hours' glory on the Nogis throne."

The Old Portuguese historian, de Barros, remarks with surprise that no wise man would wish to be a king of Passier, a kingdom on the northern coast of Sumatra, since the monarch was not allowed by his subjects to live long. From time to time, a sort of fury seized the people and they marched through the streets of the city chanting in a loud voice the fatal words "The king must die." When the king heard that song of death, he knew that his hour had come. The man who struck the fatal blow was of the royal lineage, and, as soon as he had done the deed of blood and seated himself on the throne, he was regarded as the legitimate king, provided that he contiuned to maintain his seat peaceably for a single day. This, however, the regecide did not always succeed in doing. When Fernao Peresd Andrade, on a voyage to China, put in at Passier for a cargo of spices, two kings were massacred, and that in the most peaceable and orderly manner, without the smallest sign of tumult or sedition in the city, where everything went on in its usual course as if the murder or execution of a king were a matter of every day occurrence. Indeed, on one occasion, three kings were raised to the dangerous elevation and followed each other on the dusty road of death in a single day.

Looking to the custom of the king of Quiloncare (Quilon) cutting his own throat at the end of his twelve years' term spoken of by Barbosa, Odoric and others, it is very probable that the early kings of Malabar and notably the Zamorin or king of Calicut sacrificed themselves at the end of their term of office. It will be noticed that the old Prussian custom of the king burning himself to death has some resemblance to the Malabar custom of the king publicly cutting his own throat. This barbarous custom would seem to have been considerably modified in later days. The description of the Māmāmkam ceremony given by Hamilton in the 17th century points the direction in which the modification was effected. The Zamorin had no longer to cut his own throat. But he celebrated the great national feast of Māmāmkam at Ṭiruṅāvāye and offered his throne to any one who was able to force his way by desparate fight through his guards who surrounded him, and succeeded in cutting his throat. It is significant that, at one time, a custom arose of the Zamorin retiring for life to a pagoda and leading the life of a recluse, the second in succession acting as regent, who, in his turn, had to retire when his time came [1]. Similarly the Raja of Cochin followed the custom of retiring in old age to a temple and there leading a life in seclusion leaving the management of the State to the heir-apparent. This custom was abrogated at the instance of the Portuguese Governor-General Almeyda [2].

The custom of the king offering his throne to one who should succeed in cutting him down was not peculiar to Malabar. "It is a similar custom in Bengal," says an old historian, "that there is little of hereditary descent in succession to the sovereignty. There is a throne allotted for the king ; there is, in like manner, a seat or station assigned for each of the Amirs, Wazirs and Mansabdars. It is the throne and these *stations alone* which engage the reverence of the people of Bengal. A set of dependents, servants and attendants are annexed to each of these situations. When the king wishes to dismiss or appoint any person, whosoever is placed to the seat of the one dismissed, is immediately attended and obeyed by the whole establishment of dependents, servants and retainers annexed to the seat which he occupies. Nay this rule obtains

1. Day's *Land of the Perumals*, p. 43,

2. *Keralapalama*, pp. 10-79, Mr. Whiteway's *Rise of the Portuguese Power in India*, p. 107.

even as to the royal throne itself. Whoever kills the king and succeeds in placing himself on that throne is immediately acknowledged as king; all the Amirs, Wazirs, soldiers and peasants, instantly obey and submit to him as being as much this sovereign as they did their former prince, and obey his orders implicitly. The people of Bengal say: ' We are faithful to the throne. Whoever fills the throne, we are obedient and true to it' " [1]

A similar rule appears to have obtained among the old Slavs. When the captives, Gunn and Jarmerik, contrived to slay the king and queen of the Slavs and made their escape, they were pursued by the barbarians who shouted after them that, if they would only come back, they would reign instead of the murdered monarch.

As already observed, the origin of this tragic custom may be found in the belief that the kings are gods incarnate as men and that they should, so long as they rule on earth, have no blemish whatever, whether mental or physical. The divinity that hedges round the king is no mere Eastern idea. If Śrī Kṛṣhṇa and Śrī Rāma were claimed by the Hindus in the Epic age to be gods incarnate on earth as men and kings, amongst the Pagans of the West, at a much later period, the early Roman Emperors laid claim to divine authority and their apotheosis is a matter of known notoriety [2]

1. *The History of India* as told by its own Historian, Sir Henry Elliot, Vol. IV, p. 260.

2. Long before the Romans, the Greeks believed that the great heroes, Achilles and Agamemnon, were of divine parentage. Achilles was a sea-god, son of Thetis, goddess of the sea. Agamemnon was likewise a god. The former was worshipped at his temple Lurce, the " shinning Island, " near the mouth of the Danube, while the latter was worshipped as Zeus Agamemnon at Sparta. Later, Alexander the Great claimed to be the son of the god Zeus Ammon. To obtain an official assurance of this from Ammon himself, Alexander undertook a journey to the

The first two Caesars allowed themselves to be worshipped during their life-time, though not at the Capitol. Malabar itself is said to have once possessed a temple of one of them ; for, according to the Peutingerian Tables, there was at one time a temple of Augustus at Crānganūr with a garrison of two cohorts or one thousand two hundred men.[1] The difference between the Orient and the Occident, with regard to the attribution of divinity to men, is that, in the East, the gods are supposed to descend to the earth and become incarnate as men, such as Rāma, Kṛshṇa, Paraśurāma and other Hindu Avatārs, while, in the West, men are made to ascend towards heaven and are held to partake of divinity, such as in the case of deified Roman Emperors and the Saints of the Christian church who are canonised and are made to look like something more than mere heroes[2]. A halo of divinity is supposed to surround them. It may be remembered that the Saints themselves and even their relics are supposed to work miracles—acts which set at naught or, at any rate, transcend the laws of nature. The invocation of Saints is an accepted practice in the Roman Catholic churches.

In Kērala itself, in the southern extremity, Travancore, within the last two hundred years, we had the unique instance of the Great Mārttāṇḍa Varma dedicating the State to Śrī Paḍmanābha Swāmi, making

oracular sanctuary of Ammon in the oasis of Sirah. Later still, the Romans believed that Romulus, the founder of the 'Eternal city', and his twin brother, Remus, were the sons of the God Mars. It may be remarked here that, while the Hindus believe in the incarnation of Gods as human beings , they do not attribute divine parentage to them as the early Greeks and Romans.

1. *List of Antiquities of Southern India*, Vol. I, p. 257

2. It is urged that this theory does not suit the divine origin of Christ. It must be remembered that Jesus, having had his birth in Jerusalem, was an oriental, a son of the East. It is remarkable that all the great world religions, Christianity, Hinduism, Mahomedanism, Buddhism, and Zorastrianism, had their origin in the East.

over the kingdom to god and declaring himself to be the vassal or agent of the deity, in virtue of which he assumed the title of Śrī Paḍmanābha Ḍāsa, a title borne by the sovereigns of Travancore to this day. The astute king found the idea of divinity in kings losing hold on the people, and he hit upon the ingenious device of dedicating the State to God and acknowledging himself to be the God's agent. This but crystallized once for all the hitherto nebulous notion of the divine right of kings in Travancore. The idea that underlay the dedication was neither peculiar to Travancore or Malabar, nor even to India. So late as in the early part of the 17th century, i. e., long before the Travancore dedication, we read that Louis XIII of France put his crown and kingdom under the protection of the Virgin Mary by what has been called "*le voeu de Louis* XIII." Great festivals were held in honour of this. His more renowned son, the Grand Monarch, also countenanced the idea. He regarded himself as the vicegerent of the Almighty upon earth and responsible to Him alone. He went to the length of allowing himself to be openly worshipped. Versailles was decorated with the Apotheosis of Louis, and it is said that the family of Law Fenellade burnt incense before his statue till pious scruples urged him to abolish the practice.

Most countries of Europe have their patron Saints, St. George for England, St. Patrick for Ireland, St. Andrews for Scotland, St. Dennis for France, St. Mark for the quondom Republic of Venice and so on.[1] In Spain, at the commencement of the decline of their great empire, the Cortes gravely proposed as a remedy to change the patron Saints. Their proposal

1. The English court is known as the court of St. James. That of France under the monarchy was called the court of St. Germain. The English Parliament used to sit at St. Stephen's. St. Peter's at Rome and St. Paul's in London are instances of the places of worship being called after their patron saints.

to hand over Spain to the protection of Saint Teresa de Jesus was opposed on the ground that their former patron, St. Iago, " under whose protection they had seen the whole world at their feet and the nation enlightened by science and virtue might take offence".[1] The claim to the divine right of kings in England was not finally given up till after the flight of James II, and his consequent deposition. In 'Holy Russia', the Tzar was, to many, the divine figure from the north. In China, the Emperor was the 'Son of Heaven'—Heaven was his father and Earth was his mother. In Japan, the Mikado is believed to rule by divine right. Thus the recognition of the divine element in kings may be said to be the common heritage of humanity all the world over, [2] a burden which man is successfully seeking to get rid of under the stress of progressive ideas of civilization, freedom and individual liberty.

The theory of the incarnation of Gods as human beings is radically different from the theory of deifying human beings as gods, and, in so far as the one theory differs from the other, the tragic custom of the suicide or murder of kings with mental or physical blemish on them obtained amongst those who held the one theory, as it was eschewed by those who held the other. Hence, perhaps, we fail to find any parallel or analogue of the tragic custom amongst races and countries other than those of which instances have already been given.

1. Dyer's *Modern Europe*, Vol. III, pp. 235—342—43.

2. Even amongst some races inhabiting parts of the New World, the belief in the divine origin of kings was extant. In Peru " the sun was the accepted ancestor of the sovereigns and the sun was the deity worshipped by Incas and other people." Sir Clemento Markham observed that "like the Ptolemies, the Incas resorted to the method (of marrying sisters) of making their family a race apart from the rest of mankind and almost divine." *The Incas of Peru*, 3rd Impression, 2nd Edition, pp. 64—103. For a similar reason, the Burmese kings too appear to have married their sisters.

We may thus have some idea of the origin and evolution of the curious custom that enjoined on the reigning sovereign to cut his own throat, or have it cut for him by some one else, to pave the way for a new and more vigorous and robust monarch to succeed him on the throne after he had reigned for a fixed period—a custom in no way peculiar to Malabar, but prevalent all over the old world. Here I believe we have the genesis of the Māmāmkam festival at which the tragedy was enacted at the close of a round of festivities of unsurpassed magnificence, whereat all Kērala was represented. Māmāmkam is but the corrupt Malayālam form of the Sanskrit word, Mahā Makham, meaning 'the great sacrifice', truly an apt designation for the ceremony which ends with the sacrifice of the life of the king who presides over its celebration.

LETTER XII.

1. **Coinage.** The Portuguese historians report that, on the arrival of the Portuguese in Malabar, the Zamorin alone possessed the right of coining money. They say that it was a peculiar privilege conferred on him by Chēramān Perumāl. Barbosa observes: " He (Chēramān Perumāḷ) instituted three kingdoms in the country of Malabar and commanded that no one should coin money except the king of Calicut."[1] Purchas also makes a similar statement on the authority of Barbosa, Castenheda, and other Portuguese writers. Barbosa further observes : " And there are many other lords in the country of Malabar who wish to call themselves kings; and they are not so, because they are not able to coin money nor cover houses with roofs (with tiles) under penalty of all the others rising up against whomsoever should do such a thing or of having to destroy them. And these kings of Coulam and Cannanore afterwards struck money for a certain time in their countries without having the power of doing so." Till Cochin secured the powerful aid of the foreigner, its Rajas had to submit themselves to be ousted from their throne periodically by the Zamorin, and then restored as the Calicut king's vassal. Barbosa refers to this practice thus: "And the king of Cochin could not coin money nor roof his house with tiles under pain of losing his State. And now since the Portuguese went there, the king of Portugal made him exempt from all this. So that he lords it over absolutely and coins money according to his custom."[2] Thus the Portuguese, having placed the Cochin Raja in a position to coin money, while the Rajas of Cannanore and Coulam (Travancore) had already begun to do so, we can account for the statement of Vincenzo Maria, who

1. P. 104.
2. P. 157.

visited the coast in 1657, i. e., more than a century after Barbosa, that the privilege of coining was at that time confined to the four States of Cannanore, Calicut, Cochin and Travancore.

Fanams.—Yule and Burnell say that "it is the denomination of a small coin long in use in Southern India, Malayālam and Tamil, *panam* (money) from Sanskrit *pana* * * *. The fanam was anciently a gold coin, but latterly of silver or sometimes of base gold. * * * Fanams are still met with on the West Coast, and as late as 1862, were received at the treasuries of Malabar and Calicut."[1] The following references show that the coin had been known from comparatively early times to foreign travellers.

A. D. 1344.—"A hundred *fanams* are equal to 6 golden dinars (in Ceylon)." [2]

A. D. 1348.—"And these latter (the Malabar Christians of Quilon) are the masters of the public steelyard, from which I derived, as a perquisite of my office as Pope's Legate, every month a hundred gold fanam, and a thousand when I left." [3]

A. D. 1442.—"In this country, Vijayanagar, they have three kinds of money made of gold, mixed with alloy * * * the third, called *fanam*, is equivalent in value to the tenth part of the last mentioned coin (partab vid-pardo o)." [4]

A. D. 1553.— "In the ceremony of dubbing a knight, he, the Nāyar, is to go with all his kinsfolk, and friends in pomp and festal procession to the house of the king * * * and make him an offering of 60 of those pieces of gold which they call *Fanoes*, each of which may be worth 20 *reis* of our money." [5]

A. D. 1582.—In the English translation of *Castenheda* is a passage identical with the preceding.

1. *Hobson Jobson*, 1st Ed. p. 265.
2. Ibn Batuta.
3. John Marignolli in *Cathay* p. 343.
4. Abdur Razak, in *India in the 15th Century A. D.*
5. Dr. Barros, Dec. I, liv. IX, Chap. III.

Fanams were of different sizes, values, and weights, each country having its own standard. The Zamorin had his old Vīrarāyan paṇam (gold—4 to a rupee. 12½ Malabar pice to one fanam.)

New Vīrarāya or gold - 3½ to a rupee; 14½ Malabar pice to one fanam.

Silver fanam = 5 to a rupee and each fanam worth ten Malabar pice.

In Trāvancore, there were the following coins:—

The Ananṭarāyan paṇam, a gold coin of the same value with the new Vīrarāyan, the device only being different. The Kalian, also gold, now a nominal coin, as such silver coin of equivalent value has never been struck.

The Chakram in silver and Cāsh in copper may also be mentioned. The value of these coins are:—

The Rāsī, worth 10 Chakrams, is also a nominal coin at present.

16	Copper Cāsh	=	1 Chakram
4	Chakrams	=	1 Kali paṇam
2	Kalians	=	1 Ananṭarāyan
3½	Ananṭarāyan	=	1 British rupee

The most ancient of the indigenous fanams in Malabar is the Rāsi supposed to have been coined by Paraśurāma for the use of his people in Kērala. The specimens sent to Sir Walter Elliot were found to weigh five and eight-tenths grains each, "with an obliterated form on the obverse, probably a śhankh." Mr. M. J. Walehouse has an interesting notice of them in the third volume of the *Indian Antiquary*. He says: "The small spangle like gold coins, so frequently found throughout the south of India, are called by the Natives Shannar Cash: I have twice known Chatties containing some hundreds to have been ploughed up in the District of Coimbatore. In the Travancore country they are called *rashis*, and along all the western coast the approaches to fords over large rivers which have been used for centuries are specially prolific of them. After heavy bursts of the monsoon, people often regularly resort to, and minutely scrutinise, the tracts leading to the fords. In Travancore, the Hindus say that Paraśurāma, when he had created Kērala, sowed it all over with *rashis*, and buried the surplus in the cairns which occur sparingly on the Travancore mountains. On the higher ranges, there are three of Paraśurāma's cairns, where the mountain tribe, the Mala Āryans, still keep lamps burning. Stone circles are very rare; one much dilapidated was called a *Rashi* hill of Paraśurāma."

The Rāśi *fanams* are of gold and have 14 dots on them. Rāśi means a sign of the Zodiac, and it is supposed that the 12 dots are the 12 signs of the Zodiac and that the two separate dots represent the Sun and the Moon. The 12 Zodiacal signs are divided into four good, four middling, and four bad signs, which may account for the appearance of the dots on one side of the coins: the four prolonged dots being the good, the four ordinary sized ones the middling, and the four tiny dots placed separately in a corner by themselves, the four bad signs. The other emblems are not understood.[1]

"The history of Travancore coins", observes Mr. Nagam Aiya, "mounts up to remote antiquity. Sir Walter Elliot, the eminent numismatist, is of opinion that the Travancore mint "is the only Hindu ṭankaśāla still maintained in its original form." Of gold coins, besides the Ananṭarāyan fanam already mentioned there were the Kaliyuga Rājan or Kaliyuga Rāyan Paṇam, as also the Ananṭa Varāhan. The first, as its very name implies, was probably issued by the sovereign who reigned in the beginning of the Kaliyuga. It has a faint resemblance to the Rāśi coin. According to Sir Walter Elliot, it was at one time current over the whole of Kērala.

1. *Malabar*, Vol. II, p. c. l. XXIX.

Ananṭa Rāyan Paṇam and Ananṭa Varāhan were two gold coins issued subsequently. Ananṭa is the appellation of the God Śrī Paḍmanābha, the tutelary deity. Their values were Re. 0-4-7 and Rs. 3-15-5 respectively. In 1052 M. E. (1877 A. D.), two gold coins called *Travancore Varahans* and *Half Varahans* were struck and declared legal tender by State legislation. The obverse contained the inscription "R. V.". (the initials of the Maharaja) and the words "Travancore Varāhan" or "Half Varāhan" as the case may be, in Malayālam, with the years of issue both of English and Malayālam; the reverse contained a śankha and a flag. The two coins weighed $78\frac{4}{10}$ and $39\frac{7}{10}$ grains and their values were $7\frac{1}{2}$ Rs. and $3\frac{3}{4}$ Rs. respectively. The new currency failed in its object, as there was hardly any circulation, and was discontinued.

Gold chukṙams are stated to have been minted at one time, but nothing is now known of these coins, though rare specimens are to be met with.

With regard to silver coins, silver chukṙams were issued from the earliest period, and they were stated to have been current even in the Pāṇḍyan kingdom. This, by repute, is the earliest silver coin of Travancore.

Later coinages were of three different sizes:—

Double chakṙam	weight $11\frac{6}{10}$	grains.
Single chakṙam	,, $5\frac{7}{10}$	,,
Small or chinna chakṙam	,, $2\frac{8}{10}$	,,

The exact date of their coinage is not known, but all accounts agree in assigning to them a period of more than 200 years. In the year 985 M. E. (1809 A. D.), double and half chakṙams were coined by the order of the then Diwan, Ummiṇy Ṭampi, and it is said that their coinage was immediately discontinued. From some specimens now available, it is found that, on the obverse of the double chakṙam was a śankha or shell and on the reverse was the chakṙam, resembling what is called a Solomon's seal with the inscription

"Paḍmanābha" in Malayālam. The impression on the chakram represents on the obverse a head ornament of Śiva, a curved line representing the moon with a star above it. The moon appears also on the reverse with the twelve signs of the Zodiac above, marked by dots and an ear of corn below. The representation is, of course, primitive and rude. The chinna chakram resembled the chakram in all respects, and it was perhaps the smallest silver coin in the world.

In 1035 M. E. (1860 A. D.), a new silver coin of the value of 4 chakrams and known as the paṇam was introduced. These coins were minted in Trivandrum with the aid of stamping presses got down from Madras.

In 1065 M. E. (1889 A. D.), quarter rupees and half rupees, equal in value to 7 and 14 chakrams, respectively were coined. They have the device of the śankha and the name of the coin on one side and the inscription "Rāma Varma, Travancore" with the year and the name of the coin in English on the other side.

In 1076 M. E. (1900 A. D.), the silver chakrams were discontinued, and an improved silver coin of the value of 2 chakrams was minted instead and declared part of the currency of the State.

The coin known as Kāśu or *cash* is the earliest copper coin minted in Travancore. It is valued 1/1,456 of a British Rupee and is undoubtedly the smallest copper coin in the world. It was first minted in 991 M. E. (1815 A. D.). The cash issued in 1006 M. E. have a different stamp, which was again changed in the coinage of copper cash made in 1014 M. E.

In 1024 M. E. (1848 A.D.), three varieties of copper coins were minted, viz:—

Cash = $\frac{1}{16}$ of a chakram.
Double cash = $\frac{1}{8}$ do.
Four cash = $\frac{1}{4}$ do.

On the obverse of all, there was the figure of Kṛshṇa and on the reverse the chakram. The double cash contained in addition the numeral "2" in Malayāḷam below the figure of Kṛshṇa. In the four-cash pieces, the numeral "2" was replaced by "4" also in Malayāḷam, and there were two floral sprigs in addition. The last two coins were, however, subsequently given up.

In 1076 M. E. (1900 A. D.), copper coins of the value of one, half and quarter chakṛams were issued. At the same time, an improved copper cash was also struck with the inscription "one cash" in Malayāḷam on one side and the śanka in an ornamental circle on the other side. These coins form the present copper currency of the State.

In 988 M. E. (1812 A. D.), zinc coins of the value of one cash were issued from the Travancore mint. This was the first 'cash' coined, but it was soon replaced by copper coinage. Specimens of the zinc cash are not available. It is not, therefore, possible to give any description.

A large number of foreign coins, both European and Indian, appear to have been current in early times, and numbers of them have been subsequently unearthed in different parts of the State. Of Indian coins, the earliest are the punch-marked coins current at the time of Buddha. Specimens of these when first found were sent to Mr. Edgar Thurston of the Madras Government Museum, and he identified them as the punch-marked coins "which are found all over India from Kabul to Cape Comorin." According to Sir A. Cunningham, "they were certainly current in the time of Buddha, i. e., in the fifth century B. C. But I have no difficulty in thinking that they might mount to as high as 1,000 B. C." [1]

Other Indian coins which once circulated in the country were—

Sultan Varāhan
Sultan cash.
Kumbhakōṇam Varāhan.

1. *Coins of Ancient India from the Earliest Times to the 7th Century*—1891—p. 43.

Ṭarangambāḍi Varāhan.
Parangy Varāhan.
Calicut Fanam.
Rāmanād Chuṭṭi Paṇam.
Madura Velli Paṇam.
Cochin Puṭṭan.

From a South Travancore inscription dated 98 M. E. (922 A. D.), it is found that Ceylon gold coins were once current in that part of the country.

Of European coins, the earliest that are met with are Roman ranging from 30 B. C. to 547 A. D. Mr. Cunningham asserts that these coins were current in Southern India in the early years of the Christian era. Of the later ones, the Venetian Sequin is met with in large numbers and are in great demand for jewelry.[1]

With regard to the coins current in Cochin, the *Census Report* says: "Confining our remarks to Cochin, it may be stated that, in the earliest days, the gold coins or Rāśi paṇams (so called from the dots on them supposed to stand for the 12 signs of the Zodiac and said to have been coined by Paraśurāma), and later on, Vīrarāyan faṇams on almost the same model (supposed by some to have been so named after one of the rulers of Vijayanagara and by others as being called after one of the Zamorins of Calicut), the Dutch copper coins, several species of Varāhans, the elephant cash, Sultan cash, &c., the English Surat Rupee, the Company Rupee, and all small silver and copper coins belonging to them, were at one time or another in circulation in the State." [2]

The Dutch copper coins long continued to be current in the bazaar, even after the expulsion of that power by the English. With regard to these, Dr. Day says: "The most common copper coins now (1863 A.D.) current in the bazaar, next to those of the English East India Company, are those of the Dutch, which have a large V on one side, with an O on the right arm of the V and a C on the left. These coins have

1. *Travancore State Manual*, Vol. I, pp. 170-175.
2. P. Liii.

various emblems on the other side, generally with a crown surmounting one or more lions, or a coat of arms. The only ones, with inscriptions, are those of 1791 and 1792, on which is the inscription *In des est spes nostra*. The earliest date to be found on them is 1731, but specimens of almost every year from that time until 1792, may be procured. In 1757, a half cash appears to have been coined, whilst some of those minted in 1746 are of the thinnest description. There cannot be a question as to whether these cash are of European manufacture, as they have evidently been minted in Europe, and subsequently despatched to India. Antecedent to that date, good Dutch money cannot now be discovered in Cochin, but a curious specimen like lead, covered over with a brown amalgam, exists, on which is the VOC of the Dutch East India Company meaning *Vor ost Indian Compagnie*."

Varāhans.—Of these, there were several species current, and they were all of gold, e. g., Bahadir Varāhan=Rs. 4-50 reis, Varāhan=Rs. 3¾-40 reis, Parangi Varāhan=Rs. 3¼, Ikkēri Varāhan=Rs. 4, &c.

Elephant Cash.—These were Mysorean coins of the pre-Mahomedan Era of Mysore with the device of an elephant with cross lines on the obverse. Subsequently, a moon was placed over the elephant.

Sultan Cash.—Tippu added dates and letters to the above and placed an Hindustani B (Bangalore) over the elephant. These came to be known as the Sultan B Cash.

Clause 14 of the treaty between the Dutch East India Company and the Raja of Cochin, dated 20th March, 1663, stipulated that, "the coinage of money shall be done by the King's own mint situated outside the Fort (of Cochin), and within the precincts of the royal palace, under the supervision of one or two Captains to be appointed by the Dutch. All profits arising from

1. Pp. 575—6.

this, after deducting expenses, are to be enjoyed by the Raja." Under this clause, coins seem to have been minted under the supervision of the Dutch Commandant, who used to send Commissioners to watch the striking, mixing, and assaying of the fanams, and to see that they had their due weight and value. But no specimens of these coins are obtainable or have been obtained, and the Census Reporter observes that, "so far as is known, the first coin issued by the State was the *Kaliyameni puthan* without the *sankh* or conch mark, which ceased to be current at least a hundred years ago." The term *puthen*, which in Malayālam literally means something new, bears testimony to its later origin, and there must, therefore, have been earlier coins with other denominations. In 1780, a fresh supply of single puṭṭans was minted by a Master of the Mint appointed by the Raja, the work being done under the supervision of the Dutch Commandant. It is a small silver coin valued at 10 pies, and is supposed to be made of an alloy of five metals—gold, silver, copper, lead and iron—though, according to a Dutch authority, the coin was made of gold, silver and copper. They have a *sankh* or conch, and four dots representing a discus with festoons and the ūrḍhwapunḍram (the Vaiṣhṇava mark) on the obverse, and a figure somewhat like a horizontal J, with three rows of four dots in each row on the reverse, in almost exact imitation of the early Rāśi faṇams. The conch is the most important of the heraldic emblems of the Raja's "Coat of arms," so much so that it is used as the Raja's 'Sign Manual.' The figure that has been likened to the letter J turned upside down is a sword, which is either an emblem of royalty or a symbol representing a family Deity, a scythe-shaped sword being pre-eminently the symbol of Bhagavaṭi or Goddess. Though the whole device on the reverse is an exact imitation of the earlier fanams, it is not at all improbable that the sword on the Puṭṭan is symbolic of Paḷayannūr Bhagavaṭi, the family Deity of the Ruling family. The dots seem to represent the 12 signs of the Zodiac, and the circle and the semi-circle within the loop of the sword and by the side of its handle seem to stand for the Sun and Moon."[1]

Fra Bartolomeo, who lived in Cochin about this time, speaks of "the Cochinies Panam, a very small round coin of tin or lead, which has on one side a horn (and) is called Ciangupanam (śankhupaṇam), the horn fanam. This horn represents the arms of the King of Cochin. Six Cochinies Cembu Casha, a copper coin bearing the stamp of the Dutch East India Company, are equal to one Cochinies Panam. There are also small coins of tin called Jaja casha."[2]

Double puṭṭans were coined in the years 1820, 1821, 1856 and 1857. The device on those minted in 1820—1 was the same as before, but on those minted in 1856—7, the obverse side contained a distinct image which has been variously interpreted to represent the God Śiva or Viṣhṇu. The device on the reverse side remained as before. These continued to be current, further supplies being minted in 1896—7, till the 1st day of Miṭhunam 1075, i. e., 14th June 1900, "when," the *Census Report* says with considerable naivete, "the British Indian coins were declared hence forward to be the sole currency of the State." Thus, as regards one important prerogative of sovereign rights, Cochin stands at present just where it stood before the Portuguese enabled them to exercise the right of minting money. Then the might of the Zamorin prevented the exercise of the sovereign prerogative. Now the Raja has given it up of his own accord unable to withstand the persuasions of a masterful minister invited from the British Indian Service.

Lieutenant W. A. Horsley, writing about 1839, gives the following table of coins current then in Cochin:—

1. C. IV.
2. P. 85.

"2 Rasi Shelle
2 Sheiles.............1 Doodie.
2 Doodies ... . 1 Pice.
2¾ Pice or 11 shelles or cash=1 Puṭṭan
5½ Puṭṭans....................1 Vīrarāyan Paṇam.
3½ Vīrarāyan Paṇams=1 Rupee.

Gold Mohurs, Surat Rupees, Gold and Silver Dollars are current in Cochin: their value in the market is subject to great fluctuations, being raised or depressed by the arts of the native shroffs (Konkaṇis), who are numerous, clever and unprincipled, and subject to no check. The Sirkar, however, have an established standard, at which they are received and paid. The public accounts are kept in gold Vīrarāyan Paṇams and Surat Rupees, which are valued as Company's rupees, though generally six *per cent* less.[1]

---

1. *Memoirs of Travancore*, p. 53—(See also Ward and Conners *Survey Report*). For a shetch of the various denomination of Malabar coins, see Lawson's *Cochin*, p. 142.

LETTER XIII.

1. **Secular Authority of Nambutiris.** The Nampūṭiri Brahmans as such are not entitled to exert any secular authority. The tradition in Malabar is that Paraśurāma had made a gift of the land to the Nampūṭiris, who, it is said, ruled over the country for some time. But, since the introduction of the monarchical system, the Brahmans exercised no secular authority except within the limits of territories over which a few of them happened to possess sovereign rights also. None the less, their influence in the country was very great. They were the proprietors in freehold of the land, the spiritual preceptors of the Rajas, as well as their advisers in temporal matters. Some of them had taken to the profession of arms, and, as such, were military commanders. There were, however, a few sovereign rulers among them; the Rajas of Eṭappaḷḷi, Poṙakāḍ and Paṙūr belong to this class. These, in the words of our author, were, "the possessors of certain domains, with Nāyars or soldiers in their service, and the power of capital punishment over their subjects." The analogy of the German Prince Bishop seems not to be very apt. In fact, there is no territorial ecclesiastical hierarchy in Malabar. Neither is the Malayāḷi under the spiritual guidance of any particular person by virtue of the latter holding any ecclesiastical office. All offences against caste are dealt with by the Raja, who acts on the advice of the Vaiḍīkans. He alone can outcaste a man or restore him to caste. The Nampūṭiri communities of Paṅṅiyūr and Chōvaram had Vāḍhyans (spiritual preceptors) known as Ṭiruṅāvāye Vāḍhyān and Ṭṙśśivapērūr (Trichur) Vāḍhyān. Under these were six Vaiḍīkans (Vedic judges), a set of Mīmāmsakans (expounders of spiritual laws, and Smāṙṭṭans (professors of spiritual laws). These, by virtue of their spiritual position, have

no independent jurisdiction even in religious matters, except through the authority of the Raja.

2. **The Four principal Namboories.** Here our author is evidently mistaking Nampaṭīs for Nampūṭirīs. The description he gives of them and the names of four of their chiefs mentioned by him, unmistakably point to Nampaṭīs and not to Nampūṭirīs. The names of the first three chiefs are correctly given. Ella Enganare stands for Eḷiangāṭṭil. These Nampaṭi chiefs exercised no spiritual authority, while, as temporal rulers, they were subject to the Zamorin and the Raja of Cochin, whoever was in the ascendant for the time being.

3. **The Nampadies.** There are other versions of the tradition accounting for the origin of the Nampaṭīs. But all agree in saying that they are representatives of those Brahmans who effected the assassination of one of the earlier kings of Malabar. Buchanan gathered the following versions from the Brahmans themselves : "For many ages, the *Brahmans* retained possession of *Kerala*, and lived under a number of petty chiefs of their own caste, who were called *Poties* (Pōṯṯīs). Dissensions, petty wars, assassinations, and every other sort of disorder, became so common under this kind of government, that the *Brahmans* of *Malayala*, who are called *Namburis*, were forced to apply for a viceroy to govern them under the *Sholun Rajas*, who were at that time the most powerful princes in the south. Each of these viceroys was continued in power for twelve years, and a successor was then appointed by the sovereign. This continued until about a thousand years ago; when *Cheruman Permal*, having acquired great popularity during his viceroyalty, retained his Government for twenty years. The *Sholun Raja*, called also *Permal*, enraged at this disloyalty, marched with an army into *Malayala*, and, having forced *Cheruman Permal* to retire into the forests, established his court at

Teruvanji Callum, a place now belonging to the *Cochi* Raja. There he reigned for some time; but, at length the *Nambudiris*, who were extremely attached to *Cheruman Permal*, persuaded some of their own caste to undertake the assassination of the king. The chief of these murderers, having, from his rank and sacred character, gained admission to *Sholun Permal*, soon ingratiated himself so far into the prince's favour, that he and his companions were admitted into the inner apartments of the palace, while none of the guards nor servants were present. They embraced their opportunity, and, having cut the king's throat, made their escape to *Cheruman Permal*; who, taking advantage of the confusion occasioned by their crime, re-established his authority all over *Malayala*".' Pursuing the story further, Buchanan observes: "Before he (the Nampūṭiri who undertook to murder the Sholun Perumal) departed on this enterprise, the *Namburis* promised, that, in consideration of the laudable intention with which the deed was undertaken, the law[2] should not be enforced against men who were acting for the good of a caste so favoured by the gods. After *Putter* and his companions, however, had murdered the unsuspecting prince, and had made their escape to the tank where the Brahmans were performing their devotions, they became struck with horror and, sitting down on the steps, exclaimed, 'How can we with our bloody hands approach such pure beings!' The Brahmans replied that, in consequence of the promises which had been made, if they had come down, they must have been received; but, as they had chosen to sit at a distance, conscious of their impurity, they must ever afterwards be considered as inferior to the *Namburis*. The descendants of these persons are to this day called *Nambuddy* or *sitting on steps*, and are considered by the *Namburis* as not much higher in

1. Vol. II, p. 51.

2. The law referred to here is that every *Nambudiri* who stains his hands with blood ought to become an outcaste.

rank than *Rajas*, or other princes."[1] This account receives support from native authorities, such as the Kēraḷōtpaṭṭi and Kēraḷaviśēshamāhāṭmyam the latter of which says that the Prince who was assassinated was a Brahman known as Bhūṭarāyā Perumāl, who came to Malabar, and managed to subdue certain evil spirits, and that the murderers, on being asked to sit amongst the assembled Brahmans, said, "Nām Paṭimēl", i. e., "we (sit) on the steps." Henceforward they were known as Nampaṭies[2]. The version of the Kēraḷōtpaṭṭi is that Bhūṭarāya was a Brahman, thoroughly versed in the black art, and that he had under his control a couple of evil spirits ready to do anything at his bidding. He proved himself to be oppressive and exacting, and the Brahmans disliked his rule so much that they determined on getting rid of him by fair or foul means. Finding that witchcraft was of no avail against one who was himself a past-master of it, they determined on assassinating him. But the spirits always stood guard over him, and some means had to be devised to get them out of the way. A Bhaṭṭaṭiri (superior order of Nampūṭiri Brahman) inveigled the Perumāl into a game of chess with him and found means to defeat the king at every game with the result that the Raja lost heavily. The crafty Brahman then bargained that, if he succeeded in the next game, the king should transfer to him the services of his guardian angels. This was agreed to. The king lost the game, and the spirits were placed under the orders of the Brahman, who at once commanded them to proceed to the sea-shore, and bring him an account of the number of waves—an errand which would occupy them till eternity. Having thus got rid of the king's guards, the Brahmans had no difficulty in murdering the Perumāl. The perpetrators of this dastardly deed, conscious of the enormity of

1. Vol. II, p. 106.

2. Pp. 85—6.

the crime they had committed, preferred to sit apart from the other Brahmans in their assembly, and were henceforward known as Nampaṭīs, or "those who sat on the steps."[1] Dr. Day says that the murdered Prince was Kṛṣhṇa Row, king of Chēra, whose deputy the Perumāl or Governor of Malabar was. He also observes that a Native Prince in laying his claims before the British Commissioners, in 1793, to a small tract of land, pleaded that it had been presented to his ancestors by Chēramān Perumāl as a reward for murdering Kṛṣhṇa Row.[2]

Telepele. Ṭalappaḷḷi, now a taluk in the Cochin State.

Amkoor. Āññūr, a town not far away from Talappaḷḷi but now in British Malabar.

4. **Tellepale.** In 1743, according to the Dutch Government records of Cochin, Ṭalappaḷḷi was divided amongst four chiefs, termed Aynikkūṟṟil, Punnaṭṭūr, Maṇakkuḷam, and Kakkāṭṭu—the same mentioned by our author. Of these, the last died, and the territory passed into the hands of the other three. The Aynikkūṟṟi Nampiṭi was driven from his country in 1690 by Hendrick Adrian Van Rheede who made a present of it to the Zamorin, who privately resold it to its former ruler for 40,000 gold fanams. In 1743, it was under the Raja of Cochin, but the people were said to be very fickle in their allegiance, and to be one day in favour of the Cochin Raja and the next of the Zamorin.

The Punnaṭṭūr chief owed allegiance to the Zamorin, but was considered equally inimical to him and to the Raja of Cochin : he carried on an intrigue with the French at Mahe for three years, in hopes that they would enable him to shake off the Zamorin's yoke,

1. P. 21.
2. Pp. 43—4.

Maṇakkuḷam too was divided in its allegiance between the Zamorin and the Raja of Cochin, and caused considerable trouble. [1]

The eldest male member of the Nampiṭi families was entitled to the dignity of Kakkāṭṭu Kāraṇavappād who, by virtue of that dignity, was the generalissimo of the Cochin Raja's northern forces.

5. **Caimals.** Barbosa speaks of these as " certain counts, whom they call Caimal. " Purchas refers to them as the " Principal Nobles. " Some of the minor ruling chiefs were also known as Kaimals and Kāṛṭāvus, such as Mangāṭṭu Kaimal, Kōṭaśśēri Kaṙṭṭāvu, &c.

It is not possible at this distant date to trace all these 50 names and find out their modern representatives. Fra Bartolomeo, however, gives the names of some of these minor lords: " Alangatta, Angamale, the Karthavu of Panamucatta, Nandielette, Cingarangotta, Puducatta, Mapranam, Muriata, Cunateri, Codaceri, Cettatten, Puthenpedia, Curimpelaga."[2]

6. **Olas or leaves of cocoanut trees.** This is a mistake, for it is the palmyra leaf that is used for writing, and not the leaves of the cocoanut tree, which are not suitable for such use. The mistake is due probably to the fact that, in Malayālam, the term ōla is used to mean the leaves of the cocoanut tree also, but then they are called Ṭengōla, i.e., cocoanut leaves, while the 'ōlās' used for writing purposes are known as Pana ōla, i.e., Palmyra leaves.

Ola literally means a palm-leaf ; but especially the leaf of the palmyra (*Borassus flabelliformis*), as prepared for writing on. The preparation is by immersing the leaf in muddy water, and keeping it there for some

1. Day, p. 15.

2. Gollenesse also names some of them.

time so that it becomes well-seasoned and the grains hardened and properly adjusted.

The term is also used to mean generally a native letter in the older books. It denotes also a document, often an order.

Barbosa gives us a very interesting account of the royal scribes at Calicut and their mode of writing:

"The King of Calicut keeps many clerks constantly in his palace; they are all in one room, separate and far from the King, sitting on benches, and there they write all the affairs of the King's revenue and his alms, and that which is given at all, and the complaints which are presented to the King, and, at the same time, the accounts of the collectors of taxes. All this is on broad stiff leaves of the palm tree, without ink, with pens of iron; they write their letters in lines drawn like ours and write in the same direction as we do. Each of these clerks has great bundles of these written leaves, and wherever they go, they carry them under their arms, and the iron pen in their hands: in this way they are known to all people as scribes of the Palace. And among these are 7 or 8 who are great confidents of the King, and men held in great honour, who always stand before him with their pens in their hand and a bundle of papers (cadjan) under their arm; and each of them has always several of these leaves in blank but signed at the top by the King, and when he commands them to despatch any business, they write on these leaves."[1] Any one visiting any public office in Travancore or in Cochin some three or four decades ago, then under the enlightened administration of those great Indian statesmen, Raja Sir. T. Mādhava Rao, K. C. S. I., and Mr. T. Sankuṇṇi Mēnōn, C. S. I., respectively, would have realised the picture drawn by the Portuguese annalist well-nigh four centuries ago—only that the blank ōlas did not bear any signature before they were written

1. P. 110.

on. Barbosa further refers to a custom observed by the Malayālees of his time in regard to writing for the first time on any day which is still in full force among the orthodox in Malabar. He says : "When they get up in the morning and want to write anything, the first time that they take the pen and the leaf in the hand, they cut a small piece off it with the knife which is at the end of the pen, and they write the names of their gods upon it and worship them towards the Sun with uplifted hands ; and, having finished their prayer, they tear the writing and throw it away and after that begin writing whatever they require."[1] It is not exactly the names of the gods that are written. It is an invocation of the gods. " I make my prostrations to Vişhņu (Hari) the preserver, Śrī,—the goddess of prosperity and Gaņapaţi, the god of learning."

D'Barros says : "All the gentiles of India * * when they wish to commit anything to written records, do it on certain palm leaves, which they call Olla of the breadth of two fingers."[2] So also Correa: "All this was written by the King's writer whose business it is to prepare his *ollas*, which are palm-leaves, which they use for writing-paper, scratching it with an iron point."[3] Correa uses the word in the sense of a letter also. It will be found that Bartolomeo, two centuries later, uses the word to mean a document, e.g., "Padiola", i.e., tariff.[4] It is still used in that sense, e.g., 'Variōla', a list, Pāţţaōlakkaraņam, a kāņam deed or document.

John Nieuhoff, in his *Remarkable Voyages and Travels*, says : "They write on the leaves of wild cocoa trees (perhaps the palmyra is meant), cut off the breadth of two inches, and two hands long : of these they lay together as many as they think fit and put a small stick through them on the top, which done, they fasten the stick or both ends to the leaves with pack thread ;—

1. P. 111.
2. 1, IX, 3, (1553).
3. 1—212—213.
4. P. 184.

each of these leaves is called an *Ola*." This description gives a fair idea of how the records inscribed on *olas* were preserved in book form (Mal: Granṭha).

Olas were mainly used for writing purposes till but recently, when the goosequill, ink and paper were substituted. Even now, in country parts and, to a certain extent, in Sirkar offices of the lowest grade, the ōla has not altogether disappeared. In the Cochin State, all documents used to be ẹngrossed on stamped *olas*, till stamp papers were introduced in 1896. So also in Travancore till the year 1884. [1]

The royal scribes, that is, those who had the exclusive right of engrossing Ṭīṭṭūrams Royal writs), which bear the Sign Manual of the Raja, were hereditary dignitaries possessing peculiar rights and privileges with emoluments attached to their office. The Rajas and chiefs had, from early days, conferred this dignity on certain Nāyar families from among whom alone could the Royal scribes be selected. There were three families who possessed the dignity in Cochin, viz., the Paḷḷiyil, Pouvaṭṭil and Panṭiyil houses. The Royal scribes were known as Paṭṭōla Mēnons or Ṭīṭṭūram Eḷuṭṭu Mēnons. The iconoclastic policy of modern days has not spared even such innocent relics of ancient days, and the previous Raja of Cochin, pensioned off the last holder of the office who belonged to the Pouvaṭṭil house, and appointed in his stead a paid outsider, thus cutting asunder all ties with the hoary past.

7. **Menon mare.** This is no higher dignity, being simply the plural form of the singular Mēnon, meaning scribe. The title of Mēnon is conferred by the Raja on Nāyars. The applicant presents himself before the Raja and pays a small sum of money, not exceeding Rs. 6, and the Raja, if the application is accepted, calls him by his name with the term Mēnon

1. Now *ola* has practically disappeared and goosequill has been displaced by steelpens and fountain-pens. Ed.

added three times over, and he is thenceforward styled Mēnon by all.

8. **The Georyps (who are fencing-masters).** This word stands for the Malayālam Kurup. The fencing masters were also known as Paṇikkars. They kept schools and gymnasiums for teaching fencing, feats of agility, the use of weapons, etc.

9. **Georyp of Travankore.** There were, indeed, Kurups who held independent rule over certain circumscribed limits. Our author had, in a previous letter, referred to this 'Georyp of Travancore,' and observed that he held sway over one of the divisions of the Signaty or Quilon Raja's territory.

10. **Shakes of head.** In Malabar, it is the nodding of the head that signifies affirmation and satisfaction, while a shake of the head horizontally signifies refusal or denial.

11. **Stalk.** If, by this, the author means the broom-stick generally used for sweeping the floor, then the remark that no greater affront can be shown to "a Malabar" than by striking him with it is correct. The stalk on which the cocoanut grows is not unusually employed for sweeping purposes.

12. **Salutations.** (a) *Lowering the sword.* This form of salutation is referred to by Della Vella in 1623, he having noticed it on a visit to the Zamorin. The description that he gives is interesting: "I will not omit the manner how those that entered saluted the king; for I saw more than one do it, and particularly a youth who entered a good while after the king, by one of those little gates; to whom in particular the King spoke much, and of whom he seemed to make great account. In his salutation, he advanced his joined hands over his head, then parting them a little so extended and exalted, he smote them lightly together twice or thrice, to wit, the palm of one hand with the four longest fingers of the other joined together which

whole action he repeated twice or thrice. Such as had weapons lifted up their joined hands above their heads with their swords, poniards, bucklers, or other arms in them, and instead of striking with their fingers, as by reason of their arms they could not, they bowed down their hands so conjoined, and made the points of their swords touch the ground."[1] Bartolomeo gives almost the same description of this form of salutation a century later: "When they address themselves to a prince, Brahman, magistrate, or superior, they salute him by folding the hands together, raising them above their head, letting them then fall down, turning the fingers of both hands three times outwards, and raising up their folded hands again. They then place the left hand on their breast, the right on the mouth and in that position wait for permission to speak. This ceremony is called *Tolunnu*."[2]

(b) *Uncoveriug heads*. The younger members of the Raja's family have to salute the Raja in the same form as strangers adopt. A common form of showing respect to seniors as well as to those who are of high rank is to remove the cloth off one's shoulders, and stand bare with only the cloth tied round the waist, and covering the lower limbs. In the presence of royalty, one has to stand a little bent inwards with hands crossed on the breast covering the mouth with the right palm. No one except a Brahman or a prince of equal rank is permitted to sit in the presence of the Raja.

(c) *Obeisances by women*. Even the women of all classes have to drop their upper garment, i. e., the one covering the shoulders, in the presence of elders and superiors. Strange as this may appear, the practice is insisted on by those who ought to know better. Even now, Nāyar women have to drop their upper

1. Pp. 184—5.
2. P. 161.

garment on entering the presence of the members of the ruling families.

Of late, there are signs of a faint revolt among the younger generation who have begun to wear half jackets, but some of those in authority, regardless of all shame, insist on the old world observance. Our author's description of the mode of making obeisance by the Raja to the queen-mother or eldest Princess, senior to him in age, still holds good.

(d) *Falling on Knees*. Kneeling has never been known in Malabar as forming part of a salutation. But Christians kneel before their Metropolitans, and kiss the rings worn by these.

13. **Raja's rewards.** To receive a present from the hands of the king, however small its value, is still considered a high honour; and Rajas used to make their appreciation of services to them by making presents of gold bracelets worked in chain pattern, called *Veerachangala* (Vīra-ṣṛnkhala) and other personal ornaments. Fra Bartolomeo gives the following account of a present made to him by King Rāma Varma of Travancore in April 1784: "On this occasion, the king presented me with a gold bracelet, a gold style for writing on palm-leaves, and a small knife for cutting these leaves to the proper size. I received from him also a letter to the civil officer at Parūr in consequence of which he was to announce publicly that the king had done me the honour to appoint me one of the gentlemen of his court. The intrinsic value of the above presents was, indeed, not very considerable, for it was equal only to about twelve sequins; but, in other respects, they were of the highest importance, as the king gives such articles to those only who have merited his favour. No person in Malabar dare use any of them without the king's express permission. They were marks of honour, which he distributes in the same manner as our European princes do ribbons of different

orders. Those also who receive them enjoy certain privileges and advantages; such, for example, as that they cannot be carried before any magistrate till the king is previously informed, that they can travel everywhere along the highways; that they are not obliged to wait in the minister's ante-chamber, and that they are not required to give place to any person whatever; with other things of the like kind."[1]

14. **Cochin Raja ranks higher.** It is said that, in olden times, the Cochin Raja had the token of unlimited power carried before him: consisting of the branch of a cocoanut tree, the lower end of which was bound with a bandage leaving the top quite free. Petty princes, if subject to any higher authority, were obliged to have the branch bound at each end[2]. The peculiar privilege which, according to our author, the Cochin Rajas possessed, of first entering the house of a Pulaya is, to say the least, curious. It is not known to any in Cochin, and it would never be taken as a privilege. On the other hand, it would be considered derogatory for any Raja to enter the house of a Pulaya, who belongs to the slave caste, the lowest of the low and, according to our author himself, may never be seen in the place where the Raja is. The very idea would be scouted with indignation, and it is not possible to learn where our author gathered his information from.

Guide stands for kiṇṭi (Mal:), a brass vessel with a spout.

15. **Keeping at distances.** It is the result of the system of caste in Malabar which recognises what is called pollution by touch and pollution by approach, each lower caste being prevented from touching or approaching the higher ones.[3]

1. Pp. 190—1.
2. Day, p. 59, *Note*.
3. A mistaken impression is growing abroad that Kerala (by the words Kerala and Malabar in this are meant British Malabar

16. **Manner of eating.** There is a quaint description "concerning the manner of eating of the king

and the States of Cochin and Travancore) is the seat of untouchability and of distant pollution; and Cochin and Travancore are alleged to be the worst sinners in this respect. After all, is the state of things so bad as all that? Are the condition of affairs so dark in Malabar as is painted by certain young enthusiasts? Are there no palliative circumstances to mitigate the gravity, if any, of the situation, even so far as that is founded on facts?

"In the early ages of society, the system of caste prevailed extensively throughout the world". (Page 1 of a pamphlet on *Caste*—by Rev. J. Murcoch, S. P. C. K. Press, Madras.) Mr. Stanley Rice, in one of the issues of the *Asiatic Review*, has the following: "We need not go to Malabar for example of pariah disabilities, nor overstate the case by relying on extremes. Are they in substance worse than many European examples of ancient and modern history? The life of the Spartan helot was not one unalloyed bliss, the ergastule of Rome could doubtless tell many a tale to rival Mrs. Beecher Stowe's. Who knows with what tears and blood and sweat, with what grinding of the poor and the oppression of the helpless the Pyramids were raised to the glory of the departed king. The peasantry of France were not treated like human beings. You shake hands with your guest in a club. But you will create a scene if the waiter at your table offered to shake hands with you". (Quoted on p. 534 of the *Modern Review*, (Calcutta), of November 1925.)

The Theodosian Code in Rome, the College of Operatives in Britain and the Military Associations of Germany prove the existence of caste in those countries. At one time or other, professions in most countries were hereditary. In Peru and in Mexico, the division of castes was as precise as that which existed in Egypt and India. *Zend Avesta* shows that in Persia too there was the four-fold division of the inhabitants. What gave rise to the war between the north and south in America, and the assasination of one of its most illustrious Presidents? What fuss did the free and the civilised States make when President Col. Roosevelt invited Mr. Booker Washington, the President of the Tuskigee Institute, to the White House? What do we find in Kenya to-day? Mr. Begbie says, in his *Life of General Booth*, (Vol. 1, p. 71.) "General Booth was told that his recruits could be brought in only by the back door behind the pulpit and seated

of Calicut" given by Varthema in the early part of the 16th century, and as there is not much difference in

on obscure benches reserved for them. One might be tempted to be indignant about the decision; but to sit among a company of unwashed, maladorous, and possibly diseased humanity is not an experience healthful for the body nor conducive to religious concentration." Precisely so, Malabar will echo.

Even in India what do we find? The question of caste, it cannot be denied, has something to do with the Hindu-Muslim riots. The new Christian converts, who are generally from the low strata of society, are not in certain churches permitted, even during service, to sit with the rest of the congregation. The bickerings between Nestorians and Syrians, between Catholics and Protestants are matters of history. They are not out of date either. "Just as the fiercest caste disputes are among Pariahs and shoe-makers, so some of the native Christians who are most tenacious about caste were originally of what are called the lower castes. The excuse is made that caste is observed among Christians simply as a distinction of rank; but its features and results are the same as in the Hindu system. It is not proposed that all classes of Christians should eat together or intermarry. Their tastes and circumstances differ greatly, and as it has already been remarked with reference to Hindus, dissimilarity in these respects is a bar to happiness in the married life. But in church there should not be any distinction." (Rev. J. Murdoch on *Caste* p. 50.). Far out of Malabar, in one place you hear of a fight among bachelors of law over the pollution of a tumbler alleged to be used by caste-Hindus; in another place of a quarrel between two parties for touching the water drawn by one casteman by a person of another caste, though both can take water from the same well; and in a third place, of high caste people ostracising people of a so-called depressed class for their attempt to celebrate a marriage in a decent way. What disquieting rumours were set afloat over this innocent resolution passed by the Hindu Maha Sabha—"That the Hindu Maha Sabha appeals to the Hindus in general to remove all restraints which are at present imposed on the so-called untouchables in the way of their use of public schools, public wells and public roads and in their attendance at public meetings. This conference appeals to the authorities of Hindu temples to provide facilities for Devadarsanam"—because of the omission of the words "as far as possible according to Sastraic injunctions"?

the daily life of the Rajas all over Malabar, it may be taken as applying to all of them, of course, with slight differences consequent on local requirements.

These facts are set forth not to shield Malabar from its guilt, if and so far it is guilty, but to show that the proposition, now so seriously put forth even by some thinking people, that caste disabilities exist there alone is entirely wrong. Perhaps, they might say that in Kerala these had persisted in a degree more marked than in other parts of India. For this, the cleanliness and the conservatism of the Malayalees are responsible. But, whatever may have been the reasons for this persistence, it must be said to the credit of Kerala that this social and economic phenomenon has not been attended with any violent disturbances there as elsewhere, and this is being generally removed in a peaceful and rational way.

It is also not the purpose of the present paper to discuss the utilities of caste: its moral restraint; the respect for authority and the habits of cleanliness which it engenders; the measure of protection it gives as a consequence of caste free-masonry; and above all, the degree of excellence, of which it is a potent cause, which it gives to arts and professions. That will take us further away from the main issue, and so we shall pass on to the consideration of our theme.

A cleaner race than the Malayalees, one will never find anywhere. They keep their houses and gardens scrupulously neat. Unless—and some even when—they are ill, they bathe once, and many twice a day. Their dress is spotlessly white. All threaded Malayalees and most of the members of aristocratic and middle class Nayar families are total abstainers and strict vegetarians. That will explain the reason for their objection to freely mix with people who are dirty in person or in their habits, or who carry on, from their point of view, dirty trades, or who eat meat or use intoxicants; while their isolation, caused by the sea and the mountains, is responsible for their conservative tendencies.

An inquiring observer may very well question as to why the Malayalees do not observe distant pollution in the case of the Christians and the Mussalmans. There is good reason for this. The early converts to Christianity and Islam were, more or less from the high stratum of Malayali society. The position of those that thus change their faith was, in ancient times,—why, even now—not an enviable one; and their old relations, out of pity for the new proselytes, never wanted to make the lives of these more intolerable by the observance of distant pollution as well, especially

"When the king of Calicut wishes to eat, he uses the following customs : you must know that four of the

as these, even after their conversion, maintained their clean manners.

No civilised, reasonable person will for a moment advocate the perpetuation of untouchability and distant pollution. But he will certainly stand for a reform on lines of evolution and not of revolution. Hysterical sensibility may cry out that these are the outcome of sentiment and so must forthwith disappear from the land. These and their varied obstructions and restrictions may be due to the social customs or the prevailing sentiments in the country of which "the backward classes are, sometimes, victims and, sometimes, alas ! enthusiastic adherents." But these difficulties in the path of progress cannot be removed by legislation or by an administrative order. Sentiment rules the world and we have to reckon with that powerful factor. Social reform, in order that it may be lasting and beneficient, must be gradual and spontaneous. The mentality of the masses must be attuned to it. Any sudden and violent alteration of an existing custom will, without doubt, cause irritation, and this would occasion trouble, and, at times, bloodshed, and, in all cases, would retard progress.

Thus, there is no justification whatever to spot out Malabar and Malayalees for any special condemnation for the sins of pollution or of untouchability. Everywhere, every higher class practises these with reference to every class lower than itself. Reasons may differ. Wealth, status, caste, custom or colour may have occasioned these. Whatever may be the cause, the evil is here, there, everywhere. In Malabar, fortunately, it is the usages of caste that gave rise to it. And its removal cannot be effected by making inflamatory speeches or by indieting diatribes against individuals or even by impeaching a country or community. Education and sanitation alone will blot out this condition of social affairs ; and, even of these, one would be tempted to put sanitation first; for cleanliness, it has been rightly said, is next only to godliness. Let those who are divinely discontented with the surroundings work systematically to spread the light of education among the backward classes and to introduce habits of cleanliness among them. Let them also try to bring about by calm, peaceful talk a change in the angle of vision among the orthodox people. These are not responsible for the present state of society. It is the work of ages. So, why should they be abused? It is like punishing Popes for Caesar's wrongs. The golden dream

principal Brahmans take the food which the king is to eat and carry it to the devil (the idol in the temple) and first they worship him in this manner: they raise their clasped hands over his head and draw their hands towards them, still clasped together, and the thumb raised upwards, and then they present to him the food which is to be given to the king, and stand in this manner

' Of knowledge fusing class with class
Of civic hate no more to be,
Of love to leaven all the mass
Till every soul be free. "

will come true only with tolerance and goodwill.

Whatever the extreme wing of the reformers might say, the State of Cochin, will serve as an object lesson to those who work in the field of social reform. There, of the 500 miles of public road, only less than a mile comes within the prohibited area; and this is where the princesses live, and is on temple land. It is a common sight in Ernakulam to see Pulayas and Ulladans walking in the streets for alms and work. Every subject of the State has free access to every public school, hospital and office. Where there is any objection for the same tank or well being used by people of different classes, provision is made for separate tanks and wells. Even the well-to-do, literate persons among the backward classes do not object to this; nor do they waste their time and wind over the question of temple-entry. Every educated man and, for the matter of that, every educated woman in Cochin, to whatever caste or creed they belong, realise that it is only a question of time when these problems will be solved ; and to its easy and speedy solution, they one and all silently work. This good result is not the outcome of the work of any social propaganda, but the silent work of time, the good sense of the people and the unadvertised efforts of a few patriotic Cochinites. If any spoil the game, it is a handful of men who always

" Criticise and grumble
And sneer at every stumble."

They constantly fly into a fury over little things, cry hoarse against all usuage and custom and abuse all those who do not side with them. May their devotion to their cause spiritualise their life and work, so that they may have the grace to be tolerant to those who disagree with them, so that they may realise the error of their ways and the harm they do to the people, and thus may their tribe be absorbed itself into the class that stand for reasoned progress and the great day to be. *Ed.*

as long as a person would require to eat it; and then the said Brahmans carry the food to the king: you must know that this is done only for the purpose of paying honor to that idol ; in order that it may appear that the King will not eat unless the food is presented to Deumo. This is in a wooden vessel in which there is a very large leaf of a tree (the plantain tree) and upon this leaf is placed the said food, which consists of rice and other things. The King eats on the ground without any other things. And when he eats, the Brahmans stand round, three or four paces distant from him, with great reverence, and remain bowed down with their hands before their mouths and their backs bent. No one is allowed to speak while the King is speaking, and they stand listening to his words with great reverence. When the King has finished his meal, the said Brahmans take that food which the King did not require, and carry it into a court-yard and place it on the ground. And the said Brahmans clap their hands three times, and at this clapping, a very great number of black crows come to this said food and eat it. These crows are used for this purpose, and are free and go wherever they please, and no injury is done to them."[1]

Purchas also gives a similar account, evidently obtained from Varthema. Even now, only the Brahmans can prepare the Raja's food, and they alone can serve it to him. They are his preceptors, personal attendants, ministers and advisers, and their influence so far permeates the administration of the country that the Malabar States are in effect a theocracy wherein the power of the priestly class predominates, and where all the other classes have to submit to their authority. It is not necessary that the food should be presented to the idol before it is served to the prince, nor is it now the practice to give that which remains to crows. Of course, there are local variations in practice.

1. Pp. 139—40.

17. **Forms of letters.** Communications to a king are generally addressed to his Kāriyakkār, that is, his Secretary of State, to be communicated to His Majesty. The following is a specimen of the form in which Rajas communicate with each other on State matters:—

" Direction written by Pandel Hicomen (Panṭiyil Ikkōṅṅen), Mootseddy (Secretary) of Cochin (Raja) and addressed to Puduchery, Mootseddy (Secretary) of Travancore (Raja), dated 12th day of Dhanu of the Malabar year 937, 22nd December 1761, viz:— * * * " All the contents herein written you may read and impart to the Raja of Travancore entitled Kulasekhara Perumal." This is taken from the translation of a treaty between the Rajas of Cochin and Travancore. The translation was made by the Malabar Joint Commissioners. The Malayālam copy extant runs thus :— " Addressed—To our Pudusery" and concludes with the closing sentences above quoted.

In Travancore, this form of communication still subsists and is not confined to Rajas alone. Similar forms are used in communications between officers. Fra Bartolomeo gives a translation of a letter or order addressed by the minister of Travancore to the officer at Ampalappuḻa, in September 1783, and it is interesting to note that, though more than a century has passed since, the same form is still in use in the official communications of Travancore. " The business respecting which I write is this. * * * * ". "This rescript shall be transmitted by the clerk and Secretary of the Criminal Court to the Sarvadhiakariakkarer (Governor) at Ambalapuzha, and be registered among the royal rescripts. This was written, in consequence of His Majesty's orders, by Cumaran Cembaga Raman Pulla Raman."

" Naicoviti."—stands for Nāykkaruvīṭṭil Achchen, formerly a State dignitary in Cochin, who, at one

1. Pp. 187—8.

time, was hereditary Commander-in-chief of the Raja's forces.

" Mangatatja "—stands for Mangāṭṭ Achchen, the hereditary Prime Minister of the Zamorin, who occupied the same position in Calicut as the Pāliyaṭṭ Achchen did in Cochin.

18. **No talk when praying.** The Malabar Rajas were, and some of them still are, very strict in their religious observances. Archbishop Meneses notices this so early as the latter part of the 16th century. Hough, in giving an account of a visit paid by the Raja of Poṙakād to Meneses remarks : " He (the Raja) is said to have been very zealous in his devotions, having 900 idols (probably *Salagramams* and *Sivalingams*) in one temple, to each of which he presented daily an offering and a short prayer. While thus engaged, he was loaded with ornaments, and these superstitions employed him from 6 in the morning till noon. During this time he gave audience to no one, and attended to no secular business whatever. Not that he was peculiar in these exercises, as it was customary for all Rajas of Malabar to devote their mornings in a similar way to the worship of the idols, and assuming that they attributed their prosperity and safety to those images, we cannot but admire their zeal and think it worthy of the Christian's imitation in his daily supplications to the only true God." [1] More than two centuries after Meneses, another Catholic Missionary, Fra Bartolomeo, in his zeal for his own religion, observes of King Rāma Vaṙma of Travancore : " He is an affable man, polite, contented, prudent, and friendly. On account of the integrity of his character, and his many good moral qualities it is the more to be lamented that he is so zealously attached to idolatry, and so much blinded as not to perceive they value of the Christian religion. It cannot, however, be denied that nothing tends so much to rivet the

1 Vol. I, pp. 376—7.

affection of subjects, as when the sovereign adheres to the established religion, and worships the deity in the same manner as his people. Rāma Varma never omits being present at ceremonies and devotional exercises as will be seen in the following chapter".[1]

19. **Presents.** To give some idea of the nature of the presents given to the Rajas generally, the following references may be made.

Vasco da Gama's presents to the Zamorin at his first interview consisted of four scarlet cloths, six hats, four branches of coral, and twelve boxes each containing seven brass vessels, a chest of sugar, two barrels of oil, and a cask of honey. The Zamorin's officers, the Koṭwāl, who inspected the articles before presentation, inquired of Gama, on being shown them, whether da Gama intended to insult the Zamorin by such trivial offerings, almost the whole of which could easily be purchased in the bazaar. He further informed Gama that nothing but gold could be presented, and that all strangers admitted to the houour of an interview gave gifts proportioned to their rank and importance.

Cabral's present to the Raja of Cochin consisted of a silver basin for washing hands, full of saffron, a large silver ewer, filled with rosewater, and some branches of coral. The king received them with pleasure, returning the general thanks.

Fra Bartolomeo, on being introduced to the king of Travancore, on the 20th of June 1780, appears to have made a present of the following articles:—Two European paintings, a large mirror, fifteen pounds of red sandalwood, and twelve bottles of Persian rosewater; articles, which, says he, according to the established etiquette, must be presented to the king by those who wish to obtain an audience.

1. Pp. 175—6.

On the 30th of September, 1793, the Dutch Governor, Mr. Von Angelbeck, appears to have forwarded the following presents to the king of Travancore, "as a proof of the Company's friendship": Two flasks of cinnamon oil, two flasks of clove oil, one case of cloves, one piece of red velvet, four pieces of satin, one carboy of rosewater, two reams of gilt edged paper, one pound of red sealing wax, and four bundles of quills.

The presents that Tippu Sultan's envoys, Goolam Moidheen and Dada Row, brought for the king of Travancore consisted of a rich dress, some jewels and a horse. This was in 1789.

Now no presents are exchanged between the Rajas and British officers, excepting the ceremonial nosegay, jasmine garland, and a sprinkling of rosewater and attar. On the visit to India of the late Emperor, King Edward VII, when Prince of Wales, the Maharaja of Travancore made presents of oil paintings by Ravi Vurma, the Travancore artist, ivory work and indigenous articles of manufacture and, in return; presents of photos, etc., were made. But all presents were strictly prohibited at the visit of the present King-Emperor when Prince of Wales.

The Dutch Captain, Nieuhoff, tells us that, on a formal visit paid by him in 1662 to the Queen of Quilon, at parting, the Queen took a golden bracelet from her arm and presented it to him. At present, the British political officers are prevented from receiving presents of any kind from the Rajas.

LETTER XV.

1. **The Topasses.** Yule and Burnell say that this is a name used in the 17th and 18th centuries for dark-skinned or half-caste claimants of Portuguese descent and Christian profession. Albuquerque, during his viceroyalty, had, as a matter of policy, obliged many of the Portuguese to marry native women with a view to form a colony of European descent. The issue of these unions, at any rate, on the Malabar Coast, passed into what was known as the class of Topasses. Its application is generally, though not universally, limited to soldiers of this class. There is considerable divergence of opinion with regard to the derivation of the term. Yule and Burnell are inclined to think that it is possible that it was originally a corruption of the Persian (from Turkish) *top-che*, a gunner. Orme derives it from *topi* (ṭoppi) 'a hat'—'a hat-wearer'. Wilson also puts forward this derivation though with some hesitation. Fra Bartolomeo derives it from the Sanskrit ḍvibhāṣhi, a man who speaks two languages. This name, he says, "may indeed be given with propriety to the Topasi, because, besides their mother-tongue, they speak some of the European languages." He adds that "at Cochin they are called *Gens-de-chapean*, because they wear a *Topi* or small hat, whereas the other Indians, not descended from the Europeans make use of the *Romali*, i. e., a white turban of the purest muslin". Though Yule and Burnell scout this derivation, it is significant that, in Cochin, it is used to denote those Christians who wear hats to distinguish them from the *Munducar* or people who wear *Mundu* (Mal: muṇṭu,) a white cloth, round the loins falling to the knee. Day says that "the native Christians of Cochin were divided into two parties, the *Munducars*, or persons who wore white cloths and puggeries, and the

Topasser who were dressed in hats and drawers, each division being under a Captain or Commandant, who was accountable to the Governor of Cochin for their conduct."[1]

Von Moens, Dutch Governor of Cochin (from 1771 to 1781), observes in his *Memorial* that, "On the taking of Cochin, there were many Topasses here and along the coast, who were the descendants of the Portuguese. Some were slaves who had been given their freedom, others were the offspring of native women, with whom their masters had formed temporary alliances. After the Portuguese left the place, they assumed the surnames of their masters. Prior to 1663, they had a Bishop of their own, and a Cathedral within the town of Cochin. When the Company took the place, they came under their protection and were allowed the exercise of their religion. They were placed under a Captain and four Ensigns, as well as other subordinates: 450 of them were drilled once a month to learn the use of arms."

The Topasses are evidently those who are now known in Cochin as Parankies or Ferenghies, of whom there are about 2,539 persons in the Cochin State. This, of course, does not include the Eurasians who were originally classed with Topasses, but who, by their rise in the social scale, have been now brought under a distinct head. The Ferenghies are Catholics of the Latin rite. *The Cochin Census Report* gives the following description of them: "The males have their hair closely cropped but wear a fringe which is allowed to fall well on their forehead, and the females wear a coloured flowing garment hanging down to the knee. Those in affluent circumstances still go out in European costume."

Sir W. Hunter has described the Ferenghies thus:—

1. P. 170.

" Portuguese of mixed descent are known by the name Ferenghees, and, excepting that they retain the Roman Catholic faith and European surnames, they are scarcely to be distinguished by colour or by habits of life from the natives amongst whom they live. "

LETTER XVI.

1. **Classes of Malabar Christians.** Our author's classification of the Christians of Malabar, at the time he wrote, may be compared with the classes of Christians existing there at present.

Christians of Malabar:
- Europeans
  - Portuguese
  - English
  - Dutch
- Topasses
- Native Christians
  - New Christians
  - Old or St. Thomas Christians

(1) Protestants
- (a) Anglican Communion.
- (b) Baptist.
- (c) Congregationalist.
- (d) Lutheran and other denominations.
- (e) Presbyterian.
- (f) Minor denominations.

(2) Roman Catholics
- (a) Of the Latin rite
- (b) Of the Syrian rite.

(3) Chaldean Syrians
(4) Protestant Syrians
(5) Jacobite Syrians

Syrians.

- (a) Jacobite Syrians properly so called.
- (b) Reformed or St. Thomas Syrians.

2. **New Christians and Old**. The new Christians were converts to Christianity, mostly from the lower classes, such as the Mukkuvas or Paravas, fishermen living on the sea-coast, amongst whom the early Roman Catholic Missionaries were successful in their proselytising operations. These

were known generally as Māṙgakkār, or those who had been converted, or those who conformed to the law, i.e, those who accepted and followed the teaching of Christ. At present, these Latin Catholics (so called because they observe the Latin rite) are known by different names, such as, (a) Eḷuṅṅūṫṫikkār, (b) Aññūṫṫikkār, (c) Muṅṅūṫṫikkār, i e., communities of 700, 500, and 300 respectively. The origin of these terms has been matter of great controversy. It may probably be, as *The Cochin Census Report* remarks, that these names refer simply to the number of families that had allowed themselves to be converted originally.

The old Christians were known as St. Thomas Christians and Syrian Christians; St. Thomas Christians, because of the belief that St. Thomas preached the Gospel for the first time in Malabar, and succeeded in establishing Christianity there,—and Syrian Christians, because of the observance of the Syrian ritual and language. It is also believed that a colony of Syrians had settled in Malabar in the early years of the Christian era, and that the present Syrian Christians are the descendants of that colony by intermarriage with the native population. These are also locally known as Nasṙāṇi, because of their original home, or because of their being the first followers of Jesus of Nazareth.

3. **The Tradition of St. Thomas.** The Christians of Malabar have a strong belief in the time-honoured tradition that attributes the origin of their ancient church to the Apostle St. Thomas. It was a matter of accepted faith for a long time, and no shadow of suspicion was cast on it till the first note of dissent was struck by La Croze in his great work, *Christanismoe aux Inde's*, which was published in 1723 A. D. Since then, there have been authorities of more or less repute who have joined the chorus of dissent.

The tradition so dearly cherished by the Malabar Christians says that the Apostle Thomas landed at

To face page 444]

A CHRISTIAN MARRIAGE PARTY.

Malankara near Cranganur, founded seven churches or Christian communities in different stations in Malabar, and converted among others several families of Nampūṭiri Brahmans, notably the *Kalli*, *Kaliankara*, *Sankarapuri* and *Pakalomattom* families, on the last two of which the Apostle conferred the peculiar privilege of supplying members for the priesthood. Of the seven churches, one was at Pālayūr near Chāvakād in British Malabar, another at Malankara itself near Cranganūr in the Cochin State, a third at Kōṭṭakāyal near north Parūr, a fourth at Kokkamangalam or south Pallippuram, a fifth at Quilon or Kollam, a sixth at Niraṇam in Ṭiruvella, and a seventh at Nellakkal near Chāyel, Sabarimalai, the last five being now in Travancore. The churches now found at Pālayūr and Kōṭṭakāyal are said to be two out of these seven. After the establishment of these churches and the propagation of Christianity in Malabar, the tradition says that the Apostle crossed the Peninsula to the Coromandel Coast, laboured amongst the people there, and finally suffered martyrdom at Mylapore near Madras.

The tradition is mentioned by almost every writer on the History of the Malabar Church[1].

Among those who doubt the truth of the tradition may be mentioned Hough.[2]

Those who reject the tradition as being not founded on fact point to the following considerations, viz.—

(1) It was not possible for St. Thomas to have come to Peninsular India.

(2) St. Thomas was the Apostle of Parthia, and the sphere of his work was confined to the North West, and not to Southern India.

1. See Gibbon's *Decline and Fall of the Roman Empire*, Chap. 47: Asseman: *Bibiliothica Orientalis, De Syrio Nestorians* p. 435. *Geddes*, and *La Croze*.

2. *History of Christianity*, Vol. I, p. 40. Sir W. Hunter, *The Indian Empire*, 3rd Edn, p. 285 and Dr. Milne Rae. *The Syrian Church in India*.

(3) There were no Brahmans in South India in the early years of the Christian era, whom the Apostle could have converted, as he is said to have done.

(4) The India of the early records meant much more than the India of the present day and, therefore, references to India have to be understood in a distinctly wider sense.

(5) There is no historic evidence to support the tradition.

The existence of the St. Thomas tradition is accounted for by the theory that it has its foundation in mistaking Thomas the Apostle with St. Bartolomeo, Thomas the Manichean, and Thomas of Cana, who, it is asserted, were the early introducers of the Christian religion into Malabar. Thus the argument of the dissentients is not simply destructive, but is also constructive. They do not rest themselves content by showing that St. Thomas the Apostle was not the founder of the Malabar church, but they also try to show that it had its origin in St. Bartolomeo, Thomas the Manichean, or Thomas of Cana.

Thomas the Manichean, a follower of Manes, who, according to the historian Moshiem, was a Persian, is supposed to have visited India, and introduced Christianity there. Manes, who, before he professed Christianity, had been educated among the Magi, asserted that Christ had left his system incomplete, and that his own mission was to lead Christians into the full truth. Thomas is said to have visited Malabar in 277 A. D., and propagated the Christian religion. Dr. Burnell thinks that "the earliest Christian settlements in India were Persian, and probably therefore Manichean or *Gnostic*," and that these were not supplanted by more orthodox Nestorians "earlier than the 11th or 12th century A. D."[1] In evidence of this, the Phalvi characters of the inscriptions in the churches at Kōṭṭayam and St. Thomas Mount, and the designation of a

1. *Ind. Ant.* Vol. III, p. 311.

certain class of people in Travancore as *Mani-Gramakkar* are pointed out. The inscriptions are assigned to the Nestorian period,[1] when Phalvi was nearly extinct even in Persia, and the argument is that there was in Malabar a large Persian population presumably belonging to the Manichean church, to whom the Nestorians had come to preach. The characters adopted in the inscriptions afford but little help to sustain the theory, for it is enough to state "that a living language is not necessarily that in which inscriptions are written, or religious literature, ritualistic or hymnal, is prepared, and that it is not always correct to fix the date of an inscription at a period when its language or character was in greatest use. The Syriac, for instance, which was substituted for Latin in the Syro-Roman churches so late as A. D. 1806, was not at that time the spoken language of either the laity or of the clergy belonging to that sect and Zoroastrian priests have continued the old character Phalvi long 'after the victory of a new empire, a new religion, a new form of language (new Persian) and a new character.' "[2] The use of the Sanskrit and the Nāgari character at a certain period do not necessarily show that that language and characters were in popular use at the time. Sanskrit, it is well known, is still the language of Hindu rituals, hymns and prayers. It is in Sanskrit slōkās that Hindus still record their acts of pious charity and the characters used are either Nāgari or Grantha. And yet Sanskrit is a dead language, one for study only, and not in popular use. The Nāgari and the Grantha characters are also not used by the people.

The etymological evidence sought for from the term Maṇigrāmam is not of much more value. *Manigramam*, according to Dr. Burnell, is the village of Manes. The first part of the word, *Mani*, need not

1. 9th century.
2. *Travancore Census Report*, 1901—part I. p. 108.

necessarily refer to Manes or his followers. Its derivative meaning is 'jewel', and it indicates rather the splendour of the village or 'grāmam', than its inhabitants being the followers of Manes. "Maṇigrāmapaṭṭam", as the term is used in the Syrian Copper plate, may well be a distinction conferred on Syrian Christians by the Perumāl or king,[1] perhaps creating a Christian Principality.[2] Another strong circumstance that may be urged against the Manichean origin of Christianity in India is that Ormas, the Nestorian Monk, refers to the Christians of Maḷabar as 'believers', which he would not certainly have said about the Manicheans, whose name was an epithet of ridicule in the mouths of contemporary writers.[3] In fact, to establish the story of the labours of Thomas the Manichean in Malabar, there is no evidence of a historical nature. The story of the sending of Thomas, the disciple of Manes, before his master's death to India rests on the authority of a passage in Theodoret (died A.D. 457—458). But the *Acta disputationis* and Epiphanius, both older authorities than Theodoret, agree perfectly on the missions assigned to the three disciples of Manes. The *Acta* says that "Adda was destined to the East, Thomas went to the land of Syria, and Hermes to Egypt." According to Epiphanius, Thomas' mission was to Judea. Bishop Medlycott who has investigated the question of the Apostleship of St. Thomas to India in his learned work, *St. Thomas and India*, observes that Theodoret's statement must give way to those of Epiphanius and the *Acta* and that "there are no grounds for the supposition that the said Thomas (the disciple of Manes) ever went to India, and consequently less for the allegation" that the one Thomas is mistaken for the other.[4]

1. *History of Travancore*, p. 46.

2. *Madras Jou. of L. and S.* No. 30, p. 146.

3. *Ind. Ant.*, Vols. 4 and 5, contributions by Dr. A. C. Burnell and the Reverend Richard Collins.

4. See pp. 202, *et seq*; also Augar's *Church History of Travancore*, p. 12.

The second Thomas with whom the Apostle is said to be confounded is 'Thomas of Cana', an Armenian merchant, who is supposed to have brought a colony of Syrians to Malabar in A. D. 745. On his return, the narration of his adventures and of the state of the Church in Malabar is alleged to have induced the Patriarch of Babylon to depute him to visit Malabar once more, and he is said to have established the Syrian community on a firm footing, obtaining for it from the native princes privileges still cherished by them. His memory was so much venerated that he is alleged to have been canonised, and St. Thomas, the Armenian merchant, came to be confounded with St. Thomas, the Apostle. According to this theory, the establishment of Christianity in Malabar is later by some centuries, a fact belied by the indubitable evidence of Cosmas Indekopleustus who says that he saw Christians in South India in A. D. 522.

Again, as pointed out by the Rev. Richard Collins, "Were Mar Thomas of the eighth century converted by the Syrians into the Apostle Thomas we should surely hear of but *one* Thomas in their accounts, whereas they tell us in the most circumstantial manner possible of the advent of Mar Thomas in A. D. 745, and *also* of that of the Apostle Thomas in A. D. 52. Kaye admits, in a note, that 'it seems little likely that, if the legend of the death and burial of St. Thomas in the neighbourhood of Madras really arose out of the fact of the death and burial of Mar Thomas (the merchant)—an event which took place only about half a century before Alfred's embassage— there should have been at that time, either in Egypt or Great Britain, any confusion of an incident which occurred fifty years before, with one that was at least eight centuries old.'" [1]

We next come to the Indian Apostleship of St. Bartolomeo. This rests on the statement of Eusebius

1. *Miss* : *Ente* : p. 65.

who wrote his *Ecclesiastical History* more than two centuries after the events narrated by him had happened. Eusebius relates that St. Bartolomeo preached the Gospel in India, on the authority of Pantænus (180—190 A. D.) who is said "to have found in the hands of certain Christians the Gospel of St. Mathew in the original Hebrew supposed to have been left by St. Bartolomeo when he preached in those parts".[1] Early in the third century, St. Hippolytus, Bishop of Portus (220 A. D.) also assigns the conversion of India to the Apostle St. Bartolomeo.[2] The testimony of Eusebius is confirmed by Jerome (A. D. 390)[3]. In the 5th century, Socrates, referring to the division of the gentile world among the Apostles mentioned by Eusebius, says that India was assigned to St. Bartolomeo, and Hough observes that Rufinus, Tillimont Baronias, and others after them, have followed in the wake of this assertion, without an investigation as to its probability.[4]

But which is the India that formed the goal of Pantænus' Mission? Assemani offers strong grounds to show that it was to the Homeritœ. It must certainly have been there that the Apostle Bartolomeo found the Gospels left behind by Pantænus. Bishop Medlycott quotes the following passage from Tillimont,[5] summing up the result of his researches regarding the preaching of the Apostle Bartolomeo. "We have most certain evidence that he preached in the country which the ancients called the Indies, and which can be no other than Arabia Felix. * * He took to those Indies the Gospel of St. Mathew written in Hebrew, and Pantænus after a hundred years found it there." The same learned writer quotes the statement of Rufinus,

1. *Ecclis. History*, p. 94, translated by Mr. Parkar, 3rd Edition.
2. Hunter's, *Ind: Emp*: 3rd Ed. p.285.
3. See passage quoted by Dr. Rae in his *Syrian Church.*
4. Hough, *History of Christianity in India*, Vol. I, p. 31, Note 11.
5. *Memoires Hist. Eccl.* tom 1, p. 387.

the priest of Aquilia, that, in the drawing of lots, "while different provinces fell to different Apostles, Parthia fell to Thomas, to Mathew Ethiopia, and the adjacent India on this side (*citorior*) is said to have been assigned to Bartolomeo" and remarks: "In the above quotation he tells us that, while Mathew went to Ethiopia, 'the adjacent India on this side' was assigned to Bartolomeo. This clearly designates the lower extremity of Arabia, on the opposite shore of the Red Sea, and so in a manner adjacent to Ethiopia. This further implies that, according to Rufinus, the Apostle's Mission was to the Sabaci, who inhabited the lower extremity of Arabia." "Should there be any doubt," he continues, "as to the correctness of this inference, it ought to be completely removed by what Socrates says dealing with the same subject.[1], * * * 'When the Apostles about to disperse among the nations to preach (the faith), divided these among themselves by lot, Thomas obtained the Apostolate to Parthia, Mathew to Ethiopia, to Bartolomeo fell that India which is near to (bordering on) Ethiopia'. The mission field of St. Pantænus, then, was not to 'the India of the Brahmans' as St. Jerome, deceived by appearances, has stated."[2]

Hough who appears to have investigated the question with his usual thoroughness remarks: "That St. Bartolomeo was ever in India is very problematical indeed. The description of the country said to have been assigned to St. Bartolomeo makes it uncertain what precise locality was meant, and if it was, as observed by Cave, 'the Asian Œthiopia,' it will be the country beyond Ethiopia and not India."[3] At any rate, it is worthy of remark that there are no local traditions associating the name of St. Bartolomeo, and if the Apostle did really labour on the coast, there is no

1. *Hist. Eccl. lib.* 1, *Chap.* 19, col. 126, *migne*, *P.Gr.L*, tom, lxvii.

2. *St. Thomas and India*, pp. 175 *et. seq.*

3. Vol. 1, p. 31.

reason why the Malabar Christians should have preferred the one Apostle to the other. "After an attentive investigation of the subject, I do not hesitate," says Hough, "to affirm that the whole story is built upon a foundation too slender to sustain it."[1]

Now turning to the tradition of St. Thomas, the first question would be—was it possible for St. Thomas to have found an easy passage to come to Peninsular India? We shall briefly examine this subject.

We have a permanent record of Phœnician influence in South India in the Vaṭṭeḻuttu alphabet which, according to Dr. Burnell, is "the most ancient Tamil and almost the present Malayalam character." Earlier still, Moses specifies the appropriation to religious uses, and in large quantities too, of cinnamon and cassia which were peculiarly the productions of Ceylon and Malabar. A well-known passage in the Bible attests to the fact that these valuable aromatics figured prominently in the temple services of the Jews.[2] The traditions of the Malabar Jews carry back the date of their settlement on the Malabar coast to their escape from servitude under Cyrus in the sixth century B. C. If there be any truth in this, it was not at all difficult for them to have maintained their connection with their mother-land, for we have it from Herodotus that the Red Sea trade in myrrh and frankincense, cinnamon and cassia was in the hands of the Egyptians and Phœnicians. Now cinnamon and cassia were specially Malabar products, and Ktesias, the Knidian (B. C. 400) makes mention of cinnamon under the name *Karpian*, identified by Dr. Caldwell with the Tamil-Malayāḻam word *Karupu*. As Ktesias had not himself visited Malabar or even India, he must have gathered his information from those Indians "who in those days were occasionally to be seen at the Persian Court, whither they resorted, either as merchants or as envoys

1. P. 32.
2 *Exodus*, XXX, 23—24.

bringing presents and tribute from the princes of Northern India which was then subject to Persian rule."[1] This points to some sort of connection between the Northern and Southern India; for, unless we premise this, the Northern Indians could not have obtained the word from Southern India. There can be no doubt that there was at that time more than one overland trade-route between India, Central Asia, and Europe.[2] Apart from this, there was the sea-route between the mouths of the Red Sea and Peninsular India.[3] In the word *Oryza* and *Zingiber*, philologists have found indisputable evidence to prove the connection of the Greeks with Malabar; for, as Dr. Oppert points out, *Oryza* is but another form of the Tamil word *arisi* or Malayālam *Ari*, which denotes rice deprived of the husk, which was exactly the state in which rice was exported. The Greek word *Zingiber* (ginger) is considered by Dr. Burnell to have a distinctly Malayālam origin. According to him, the word is derived from the Malayālam terms *Inchi* and *Inchiver*, and the Greeks probably took it direct from the Province of Malabar[4]. Under the Ptolomies, the eastern trade had developed itself considerably, and Ptolemy Philadelphus gave it a further impetus by founding the city of Bernice on the west coast of the Red Sea, from whence, according to Dr. Robertson, ships destined for India took their departure. The Greek trade with the East continued flourishing till it was taken up by the Romans on the reduction of Egypt by Augustus. It received a marked impulse with the beginning of Roman rule in Egypt, B. C. 30. The precise information of the geography of the Indian coasts and marts to be found in the *Periplus Maris Erythraei* and other works of the kind make it certain that, in the first century A. D., a very extensive trade

1. Mc. Crindle, *Ancient India*, *Ktesias*, pp. 3—4.
2. *Anc. Com. of Ind.*, Dr. Gustave Opperts, pp. 16—17.
3. Robertson's *Ancient India*, p. 48. Hunter's *British India*, p. 41.
4. *Ind. Anti.*, Vol. I, p.352.

connection had existed directly between South India and the Western world. This circumstance is further attested by the find of Roman coins within localities in South India. The intercourse that existed between the East and the West and the trade routes followed by land and sea by early merchants, will furnish an answer to the question.

It is significant that it was shortly before the period attributed by tradition to the arrival of the Apostle on the Malabar Coast, that Hippalos discovered the monsoons which facilitated and shortened the voyage between the Red Sea and India, and it is further significant that the Apostle is said to have landed exactly at the port to which the Greek mariner himself was driven by the Western monsoons, viz., Muziris, identified through its Malayālam name *Muyirikkodu* and its Tamil form *Muchiri*, with the modern Crānganūr or Koṭungallūr by orientalists of all shades of views. There can thus be no inherent improbability in the tradition that the Apostle St. Thomas visited Malabar; for, if he was so minded, it was not impossible for him to find a passage from the mouths of the Red Sea to the island of Malankara, close by Muziris or Crānganūr.

Next, it is contended that India did not lie within the sphere allotted to St. Thomas, whose mission, it is said, was to Parthia. "Pretty early tradition associates Thomas with Parthia, Philip with Phrygia, Andrew with Syria, and Bartolomeo with India, but later traditions make the Apostles divide the various countries between them by lot."[1] Even if we accept the contention, there was nothing to prevent Thomas from extending his labours to India after his work in Parthia was over. "In the *Paschal Chronicle* is a fragment of a work of Bishop Dorotheus (born 254 A. D.) in which we read that 'the Apostle St. Thomas, after having

1 *Encyclopaedia Britannica*, Vol. II, p. 194.

preached the Gospel to the Parthians * * suffered martyrdom at Calaminia, a town of India.' "[1]

If, however, lots were drawn, for aught we know, India might have fallen to the lot of St. Thomas. It is then argued that, even if there be any truth in the tradition of Thomas' visit to India, he must have confined his labours to the northwest rather than cross to the Peninsula, and, in support of this theory, reference is made to the earliest record of the tradition, *The Acts of Thomas*. In recording in detail the acts and movements of the Apostle in India, it mentions the name of a king whom the Apostle is alleged to have converted. This king is said to be satisfactorily identified with king Gondophares mentioned in Indo-Scythian coins, of whose reign a stone inscription dated A. D. 46, has recently been deciphered. He reigned in North-western India, and therefore, it is urged, that the India visited by St. Thomas was North-western and not Southern India. To M. Reinaud falls the credit of first calling the attention of scholars to the connection between the coins of Gondophares and the *Acts of Thomas*. He put it forward in 1848, in his *Memoire Geographique Historique et Scientifique Sur l' Inde*[2]. He therein says that "of the number of Indo-Scythian kings who reigned in the valley of the Indus shortly after Kanarkes, coins recently discovered offer the name of a prince called Gondophares. Specimen coins of this series are to be seen at Paris in the *Bibliothique Nationale*. A tradition, according to the first centuries of the Christian era, asserts that the Apostle Thomas went to preach the Gospel in India, and that he suffered martyrdom on the Coromandel Coast. Now the *Acts of Thomas*, which have come down to us both in Greek and Latin, mention the name of a king of the interior of the Peninsula called Gondophares. * * But the

1. Cave's *Historic Literaria*, pp. 107—8, quoted by Rev. Kennet.

2 *Memoire de l' Institut National de France, tom* XVIII, II *partictirage a part*, 1849, p. 94 f.

name of Gondophares is only to be found in a certain class of coins, and the *Acts of Thomas* are the sole written documents which reproduces it. Are we then not authorised to believe that here we are really dealing with the Apostle Thomas, and with an Indo-Scythian prince, his contemporary?" The *Acts of Thomas* have been denounced as apocryphal by some, and we shall have to say something of it later on.

The Apostle's visit to Northern India gains support from another work, *Historia Certaminis Apostolici* by Abdias professed to be contemporary with the Apostles, and first Bishop of Babylon, of whom Bale says: "He deserves a place among the boldest legend writers." He is supposed to have flourished about the 10th century, and hence his traditions cannot have much weight. His work has been condemned by Pope Pius IV as spurious. [1]

The history of the Apostles by Abdias has, however, been accepted by certain writers, who think that it has undoubtedly been interpolated. They point out that, whether spurious altogether or corrupted by interpolations, "the legend of St. Thomas contained in it has been so remarkably confirmed by recent researches that it acquires a value which otherwise might not have been accorded to it." [2] In this work, Abdias says: "Now I myself recollect having seen a certain book in which the voyage of St. Thomas to India and the things he did in that country are described." He then narrates in detail the labours of the Apostle and his martyrdom, and what lends peculiar interest to the story is that he gives the name of the Indian king whom the Apostle visited as Gondophares.

M. Sylvian Levi has in the *Journal Asiatique* ably set forth all that can be said in support of the northern theory.[3] But we have not as yet been able to find any

1. Whitehouse, *Lingerings of Light in a Dark Land*, p. 15, *Note*.

2. Kellet.

3. See translation of the article entitled *St. Thomas, Gondophares and Mazdeo* by Mr. W. R. Philips in *The India Anti.*

considerations urged to prove that the Apostle had confined his labours to the north and that he did not extend, or that it was not possible for him to have extended, his evangelical operations to Southern India.

It is interesting to note that, in a Tamil version of the *Acts of Thomas* to be found in the *Mackenzie Mss.*[1], the King of Mailapur, where the Apostle is said to have suffered martyrdom, is called Kandapa Raja, most probably Gondophares, a distortion of Kandapa.[2]

Thirdly.—The contention that there were no Brahmans in Southern India in the early centuries of the Christian era, so that neither St. Thomas in the first century nor Pantaenus in the second century, could have converted them or met them is not of much avail. For there is abundant evidence of the Brahman colonisation of Southern India, and the establishment of Brahmanism at the southern end of Peninsular India long before the commencement of the Christian era. It is enough to point to the existence of a temple for the Brahman goddess, Ḍurga, at Cape Comorin, mention of which is made in the *Periplus*, to make it clear that Hinduism in the Purāṇic form had come into vogue in Southern India, at any rate, years before the arrival of St. Thomas.

Fourthly.—True, the India of the early records meant much more than the India of to-day, but it is impossible to see how that would go to disprove the tradition of the Indian Apostleship of St. Thomas. The early records mention that the Apostle had visited India and, if it appears that it was not impossible for him to have penetrated towards the south by land, or to have visited the coast by sea, the application of the name India to a wider area than at present can in no way

1. Described in Vol. I of the *South Indian Christian Repositary* for 1837, pp. 263—266.

2. Cf. Chandra Gupta and Sandercotus.

militate against the Apostle's founding churches in the south. Both the inland and sea routes were open to him. If Paraśu Rāma at the head of his Aryan colonists, or if Rāma, the hero of the Rāmāyaṇa, leading another colony of Aryans, could have, in pre-historic days, penetrated the forest-clad regions of the Dekhan, the evangelical spirit of the Apostle, caught fresh from the founder of the church himself, would have carried him through the same regions in much later days. To the objection raised by Hough that, "until about the middle of the first century, the voyage to India was long and tedious" and that "it is not probable that any but traders would venture far eastward before the second century", the Rev. Mr. Whitehouse pertinently answers: "Surely, where *traders* ventured, zeal for Christ and love for souls were powerful enough to carry divinely inspired *Apostles*."

Fifthly.—Coming to the historical testimony regarding the Indian Apostleship of St. Thomas, the following references may be found useful:—

(1) *The Acts of Thomas.*

The *Acts of Thomas* exist in Syriac, Greek, Latin, Armenian, Ethiopic and in Arabic and, in a fragmentary form, in Coptic. Professor F. C. Burkitt considers the Syriac to be beyond doubt the original text, and Dr. Wright has edited it with an English translation. According to Dr. Wright, it dates back to not later than the fourth century, while Professor Burkitt would place it before the middle of the third century and Lipsius in or about A. D. 232. As already observed, it has been described as apocryphal. Its authorship is uncertain, but it is suggested that it may have been written by one Bardesanes, a Syrian gnostic and a native of Edessa. "The object of the author of this apocryphal Gospel," says Logan, "seems to have been to promote the doctrine of celibacy, and he possibly took, as his ground-work, the current traditionary story about St. Thomas, and, possibly, in entire ignorance of what he was writing about, hauled in the name of a king, who could not possibly have had anything to do with the part of India, where St. Thomas was said to have preached and died."[1] The discovery of the name of Gondophares on coins recently unearthed as well as in the *Takht-i-Bahi* stone inscription is certainly calculated to give colour to the truth of some at least of the facts recorded in the *Acts*. But the fact that the text has undergone "ample enlargements" calls for great discrimination in sifting the wheat from the chaff[2].

The substance of the tradition as recorded in the Syriac version of the *Acts* is as follows.— "On the occasion when the 12 Apostles divided the countries of the world among themselves by lot, 'India' fell to St. Thomas. He did not wish to go there. But a merchant named Hābbān had been sent into 'the southern country' by Guduaphar, 'King of India,' to procure for him a skilful carpenter. Our Lord appeared to Hābbān, and sold St. Thomas to him for 20 pieces of silver. St Thomas and Hābbān started next day. Travelling by ship, they came to a place named Sandaruk. There they landed and attended the marriage feast of the king's daughter. Thence they proceeded into 'India,' and preached before King Guduaphar. And there St. Thomas preached in the cities and villages, and converted the King himself and his brother and many other people. After that, while St. Thomas was preaching 'throughout all India,' he went to the city of king Mazdai. There, as the result of his courting Mazdai's wife, Tertia, and a noble lady named Mygdoniā, he was condemned to death. He was slain with spears by four soldiers on a mountain outside the city. And he was buried in the sepulchre in which the kings were buried. But,

1. *Malabar*, p. 200.

2 See *St. Thomas and India, Appendix. A Critical Analysis of the Acts of Thomas the Apostle.*

subsequently, while Mazdai was still living, the bones of the Apostle were secretly removed by one of the brethren, and were taken away to 'the west.'" Dealing with this tradition, Dr. Fleet observes:[1] "The important point for us is that a Christian tradition, current in Syria, Palestine, Egypt, Asia Minor, and all other parts as far as Italy, and connecting St. Thomas with Parthia and 'India.' and with two 'Indian' kings whom it specially names, is traceable back to, at any rate, the third or fourth century of the Christian era, and perhaps to the second quarter of the third century."

As already observed, the 'Indian' king named in the *Acts* as 'Guduaphar.' has been satisfactorily identified with the 'Gondophares' of the coins and the 'Guduphia' of the *Takht-i-Bahi* inscription. Dr. Fleet observes that "the numismatists have decided on evidently quite satisfactory grounds that the Paleography of the Greek legends on the coins of both the types, Indian and Parthian, justify our placing the coins between about A. D. 8 and 50." The same learned authority, after a careful and critical examination of the inscription, places it in A. D. 46, "definitely and without any provisional treatment." It determines the commencement of the reign of the king Guduphara in A. D. 20 or 21. "This result," he continues, "placing the commencement of the reign of Gudaphra—Gondopheris in A. D. 20 or 21, and establishing the fact that, in A. D. 46, his dominions included, in India itself, at any rate the territory round about Peshawar, is reached from the *Takht-i-Bahi* inscription and the coins, without the Christian tradition. As regards the tradition, the position now is this: The above result gives us, in just the period of the death of St. Thomas, a king, Guduphara—Gondopherenes, whose name can be satisfactorily identified with that of the Guduaphar, Gundaphar, Goundapharos, and Gundaforus of the tradition, and who would be

1. *The Royal Asiatic Society's Journal* for April 1905.

quite properly mentioned as a king of India or of the Indiana." With regard to the name of the other 'Indian' king mentioned in the *Acts*—Mazdai—M. Sylvian Levi [1] makes a "not unreasonable proposal" that it stands for king Vāsuḍēva of Maṭhura, a successor of king Kanishka. Mazdai is said to be "a transformation of a Hindu name on Iranian soil and Mazdean influences, and arrived at through the forms Bazadeo, Bazdēo or Bāzadēo, Bāz dēo, which occur in Greek legends on coins." The inscriptional dates of king Vāsuḍēva, taken in the same way with the date in the *Takht-i-Bahi* inscription as dates in the Mālavia or Vikrama era, are equivalent to A. D. 22 and 40 which show that he was a contemporary of Guduphara—Gondopheruēs. In concluding his enquiry into the question, Dr. Fleet observes: "From the wide range of the localities from which his coins have been freely obtained, it is manifest that Guduphara—Gondopheruēs was the powerful ruler of an extensive territory, which included as a part of it, much more of India than simply a portion of the Pēshawār district. Yet his memory perished in India, so that he has become known there in simply recent times, and only from the inscriptions and the coins. Outside India any such name as his seems to have survived only in the tradition about St. Thomas. And the very fact that such a name has been put forward in the tradition, which in respect of synchronistic requirements it exactly suits, is at least strongly suggestive that there is an actual basis for the tradition in historical reality, and that St. Thomas did proceed to the east and visited the courts of two kings reigning there, of whom one was the Guduphara—Gondopheruēs of the *Takht-i-Bahi* inscription and the coins, and the other was very possibly Vāsuḍēva of Maṭhura."

Bishop Medlycott has instituted a critical analysis of the *Acts* and he finds sufficient clue in its contents to fix the country where the scenes narrated were

1. J. A. 1897, i 37 ff., *In. Ant*. 1904, 14f.

transacted. The *Acts* themselves mention "the realm of India" as the place to which the Apostle had gone. The learned Bishop has no doubt that it was the India 'of pearls and gems' and 'of Brahmans' of the ancients. A number of incidents disclosed by the *Acts* are 'adverted to in support of the Apostle's martyrdom in the India of the Hindus." These may be referred to here:

(a) The mention of the *Palki* or *palanquin* as a means of conveyance.[1] "In Southern India", says the learned Bishop, "to some extent, more so in the Native States of Malabar, the palki among natives is considered a more honourable means of personal conveyance than a carriage drawn by horses. It is used invariably at marriage ceremonies—indicating the older customs of the country; and in the States of Malabar the writer is aware that, after the elephant, palki was considered the conveyance next in dignity." [2]

(b) The mention of 'ceremonial bath' before meals—Regarding this the Bishop says: "It is not a casual bath, but the religious bath prescribed by Hindu usage before the day's meal. We would ask the reader if he knows of any country outside of India, where it is the custom to bathe before partaking of the evening meal or of any principal meal. He may perhaps know that this is a religious rite enjoined upon all Hindus in India that they should purify themselves by such an ablution before a meal. Another circumstance, which will escape the notice of such as are unacquainted with Indian native habits is implied in the words, 'he went and bathed and came back whilst it was still light'; this implies the bathing was outside the house and before the evening meal. Every Hindu of a respectable position—especially in Native States (of Travancore and Cochin and of the British district of Malabar)—has

1. Act VIII.

2. C.F. the observation of our author in Letter XIII that in Malabar the Raja rewards a grande or general who has done any special service, by the gift of a *Somercal*, palanquin.

generally a tank in his compound to which he resorts for this ceremonial bath."

(c) Adverting to the mention of king Mazdai's kinsman Karish's early morning visit to salute the king and his putting on 'sorry garments as an indication of misfortune', the Bishop observes: "The reader acquainted with India will realise that the customs described are purely Hindu, the Court is Hindu, and Karish is a Hindu." Regarding Karish's morning visit, he says: "The reader has here placed before him the custom of a Hindu court of Southern India—ministers, courtiers, attendants are all waiting upon the Raja at early dawn in Court. Suitors and petitioners are waiting outside the court premises even from 4 o'clock in the morning to place their petitions and plaints before the Raja. Court business in fact, in Hindu Courts, is transacted from early morning until noon. The reason why Hindu Rajas hold court so early in the day throughout the year is this—that they may have time to purify themselves with a bath before the mid-day meal. The above custom prevails to this day in the Hindu Courts of Malabar and must, more or less, be the same in other parts of India, where native Rajas yet hold Court." The learned Bishop was Vicar Apostolic of Trichur in the Malabar Native State of Cochin for some time.

(d) Referring to the mention of Mygdonia falling down on the ground before the feet of the Apostle when first she went to see him in her palki, the Bishop says: "Nothing but the Hindu custom will offer a full explanation. Any Hindu, man or woman, who approaches a Brahman priest, when not influenced by the presence of Europeans, before addressing him, performs the same act of prostration on the bare ground as Mygdonia had done, with hands joined forward over the head, prostrate on the ground, in an act not only of supplication but of semi-worship, imploring a blessing and showing the deepest veneration for the person.

The writer is informed that, in Malabar, even the Hindu Raja performs this religious act to the chief Brahman priest in the temple at his religious installation on the Guddee (coronation ceremony) and when he attends any great religious ceremony at the temple. But the act is now so performed as not to be visible to the public." We may add that the Bishop's information is to a large extent correct. [1]

(2) Pantaenus in A. D. 190 refers to the Apostolic origin of the Indian Church, but says, that it was founded by St. Bartolomeo which, however, is a mistake for St. Thomas.

(3) Dorotheus, Bishop of Tyre (254—313 A. D.), referring to the acts and journeyings of the Apostles, relates that the Apostle St. Thomas, after having preached the Gospel to the Parthians * * * * * suffered martyrdom at Calamina in India.

(4) At the Council of Nice, A. D. 325, a Bishop appears to have attended and subscribed his name as Johannes "Metropolition of Persia and the great India", a fact which seems to indicate that there was at that time a Christian church of some bulk and significance planted on the Indian Coast.[2]

(5) Thirty years later, St. Athanasius (330 A. D.) who presided over the see of Alexandria, deputed Frumentius as Bishop to India. He is said to have preached "to the people of India and received the reward of his zealous labours in the Crown of Martyrdom".[3]

(6) St. Chrysostom (347—407) writes that, from the earliest time of Christianity, the tomb of St. Thomas was, in the East, as much venerated as that of St. Peter at Rome.[4]

1. *St. Thomas and India*, pp. 277 — 281.

This sort of prostration is now made more especially before *Sanyasis*, e.g., Sankaracharyar.

2. *Kaye*, p. 7.

3. *De. Orsey*, p. 66.

4. *Ibid.*, p. 61.

(7) St. Gregory Nazianzen (A. D 370—390), in answering the reproach of his being a stranger, exclaimed:—" What? Were not the Apostles strangers? Granting that Judae was the country of Peter, what had Paul in common with the Gentiles, Luke with Achaia, Andrew with Epirus, John with Ephesus, *Thomas with India*?"

(8) Rufinus, who went to Edessa in A. D. 371 and lived there for 25 years, says that the Apostle's remains were removed from India to Edessa. The chronicles assign A. D. 394 for this event.

(9) St. Jerome (A. D. 300) speaks of the mission of St. Thomas to India as a fact universally known and believed in his time, and mentions Calamina as a town in India as the place of his death. In Epist. LIX *ad marcellam* he writes:" * * * * He (the son of God) was present in all places, *with Thomas in India*, with Peter in Rome, with Paul in Illyria etc."

(10) Theodoret, the Church Historian, (430—458 A. D.) indicates the belief handed down regarding St. Thomas and the Indians. Baronias points out that Theodoret could have maent only St. Thomas, and he is followed in this respect by later church historians, such as Nicephorus, who declares St. Thomas to be the Apostle to the Indians, and Gaudentius, who like Sophronius mentions Calaminia as the place of his death.

(11) St. Gregory of Tours (544—595) speaks o the existence of a "Monastery and temple of great size and excellent structure and ornament in that place in India where the body of Thomas lay long before it was transported to Edessa." " This," says St. Gregory, " Theodore who had been to the place narrated to us."

(12) Two Arabian Travellers of the ninth century, referrrd to by Renandot, also say that St. Thomas died in India. It is on record that the English King Alfred

the Great despatched an embassy (A. D. 883) under Sighelin, Bishop of Shireburn, to the Shrine of St. Thomas at Madras. [1]

Florintin says: "Nothing with more certainty, I find in the works of holy fathers than that St. Thomas preached the Gospel in India."

Then there are the Kōṭṭayam Syrian Christian copper plates granting various highly prized privileges to the Christian community of Malabar. Various dates have been assigned to these. Burnell and Kielhorn assign to the grant given by the Perumāl to Iravi Cortten of Crānganūr the year 774 A. D., The grant by Sṭhāṇu Ravi Gupṭa is said to have been given in 824 A. D. to a colony of Christians who landed at Quilon under the leadership of Mar Sapor and Mar Peroz.

European travellers of a later date also mention the traditionary belief among whom may be noticed:—

Marco Polo, the celebrated Venetian traveller, who visited the Apostle's tomb 1293 A. D. says: "The body of Messer St. Thomas lies in this province of Malabar (Coromandal) at a certain little town having no great population." [2]

About the same time (A. D. 1292—1293), John of Monte Corvino, who visited the Coromandal Coast and stayed there for about a year, speaks of the church of St. Thomas at Mylapore. [3]

The church of St. Thomas at Mylapore is noticed by Friar Odoric in 1318 A. D.[4]; also by John Marignolli who, as the Pope's Legate, stayed at Quilon for 14 months in A. D. 1349. He visited the church of St. Thomas at Mylapore. He gives an account of the legend of St. Thomas as usually related. [5]

1. Lingard *Hist. of Engl.*, Vol. I, p. 112.
2. Yule's *Marco Polo*, Vol. II, p. 358.
3. Do do p. 356.
4. Yule's *Cathay*, Vol. I.
5. *Cathay*, Vol. II.

Nicolo Conti, in the next century, (A. D. 1425—1430) speaks of the church in which St. Thomas lay buried, as large and beautiful.[1]

Am'r, son of Mathew, a Nestorian writer, (about 1340) hands down the Nestorian tradition regarding St. Thomas and India: "His tomb stands on the peninsular Mehan in India to the right of the altar in the Monastery bearing his name". "The position is fixed on the sea-board," says Bishop Medlycott, "and a corrupt form of the name of Mylapore is given."[2]

Joseph of Crānganūr, the Malabar Christian who went with the Portuguese to Europe in 1501, refers to the worship paid to St. Thomas.

Barbosa and Diogo Fernandez give the same version of the Apostle's martyrdom as related by native tradition.

With the assistance of Mr. Justice Hunt's judgment in the Kōṭṭayam Cheṙia Paḷḷi case, we may try to trace the probable route adopted by St. Thomas in his travels in Asia including India.

After the drawing of the lots already referred to, it would seem that St. Thomas spent his earliest labour in the city of Edessa in Syria. Probably the earliest record of his travels is a document discovered by Eusebius[3] among the public records of the city of Edessa. The contents of the document have been further corroborated by the manuscripts acquired from the Nitrian ministry in Lower Egypt by the British Museum in 1841—1843—1847 A. D. These documents have borne out the traditional stories of the journeys of St. Thomas and they have been strengthened by recent discoveries both of coins, inscriptions, and manuscripts. Dr. Cureton found a considerable portion of the Aramaic

1. *India in the Fifteenth Century*, p. 7.
2. I bid p. 96.
3. *Eccl. Hist.*, 1—13.

documents which Eusebius has preserved in the archives of Edessa.[1]

After leaving Edessa, there is ample historical evidence to show that St. Thomas preached to the Parthians, Medians, Persians and Hyrcanians.

Layard in his *Nineveh and its Remains*[2] says * * * * * "that though the Chaldeans professed Nestorius as the father of their church, yet they say that they received their faith from the Apostle Thomas."

According to the documents already referred to, St. Thomas appointed Thaddeus first Bishop of the Chaldean church at Ctessiphon, the capital of the Parthian Kings. The history of the Bishopric is chronicled by Bar Habracus, Elias of Damascus and others, and is also to be found in the *Patriarchate of Antioch* by the Rev. J. M. Neale, D.D.[3] Thus we have the head and founder of the ecclesiastical orders of Seleucia-Ctessiphon, as well as Edessa in St. Thomas.

The Apostle eventually visited the kingdom of Gondophares. Dr. Germann alludes to the ancient manuscripts, and these corroborate the narratives which were, for a long time, regarded as being purely traditional. King Gondophares ruled over an extensive kingdom, comprising territories in Afghanistan and India. The extent of these territories may be gathered from the recent discoveries of coins, dated 44 A. D., bearing the name of Gondophares, and found in Cabul, Kandahar, Seistan, and in Western and Southern Punjab.[4] These coins have also been discovered in Archamia or

1. *Anti. Nicen. Chn: Lili.*, Vol. XX, *Syri, do: Edyli. T. and T*, *Clerk* 1871, p. 1.

2. I bid p. 149.

3. London Rimington 1873.

4. Genl. Cunningham, *Coins of Indian Bhuddist Satraps with Greek Inscriptions*; *Prnisep*, p. 63. Germann, p, 25. Wilson and others.

Aricia in Driangiana Arachosia, in Beghrain and Kalmlistan.[1]

These coins prove from their dates that St. Thomas was a contemporary of King Gondophares. They further show, by the language inscribed upon them, that there must have been a considerable amount of intercourse between Europe and these parts, as is also evidenced by recent discoveries of a number of Roman coins of a similar period along the western coast of India: and, moreover, that European culture was making headway in the kingdom of Gondophares.[2]

Laymond Abbeloose[3], quoting from a Syriac manuscript in the British Museum, says that "the Apostle Thomas has preached in the inner India, taught and baptized, and has given the imposition of hands of the priesthood." From which we may assume that he had founded churches.

Having come thus far, Mr. Justice Hunt observes: "I am obliged to admit my difficulty in tracing the journey of St. Thomas from the kingdom of Gondophares to Calaminia in the kingdom of Misdoes, an Indian Satrap.[4] All the Historians seem to agree (Hough, Whitehouse and others) that St. Thomas visited *Male* (Malabar), Crānganūr (where he is said to have founded a Bishopric and to have built seven churches), Quilon, and Mylapore, although few seem to agree as to the order in which he visited these places. I take it that it would be in the order of the trade-route of those days."

Hough, of course, expresses strong doubts as to St. Thomas' visit to Malabar. The direction from which St. Thomas came to Malabar, according to tradition, was not from the land side. It says that, after

1 Germann, p. 23, *et seq.* The latter quotes from Lassen *Indesch* II, pp. 39—397. See also Dr. Fleets article in the R. A S. J., April 1905.

2. See also *Archeolo. Sur. In. Rep.* 1872—73, Vol. V, pp. 25—29 as to the inscription on the *Thati-Bahi* stone.

3. Vol. II, p. 10. note.

4. Germann, p. 18.

having established Christianity in Arabia Felix, and in the island of Dioscorides (now called Socotra), the Apostle landed at Crānganūr,[1] where the principal king of Malabar then resided.[2] Arabia Felix is the second of the three divisions into which the ancient geographers, following Ptolemy of Egypt, divided the Peninsula of Arabia. This was the country of the Sabians, whose queen is reported in the Bible to have visited King Solomon "with a very great train of camels that bore spices and very much gold and precious stones". Throughout the Bible and in many of the ancient writings, there are many references to the spices and perfumes of Sabea or Arabia. Agathercides, who wrote about 146 years after Alexander the Great, states that "the mariners of Sabea sailed in very large vessels to India, to the country where the odoriferous products grew, and planted colonies there, believed by some to be the progenitors of the Mopilas of Malabar."[3] It is not improbable that the people of the West Coast of India did themselves throw out colonies, and introduced the valuable material productions for which their country was famous into their new homes. There is abundant reason to believe that the early Dravidians of the coast were not altogether disinclined to a sea-faring life, and the aversion that they now evince is only a later development fostered and encouraged by the blasting influence of Brahmanism. Judging from traces of colonies in Arabia and elsewhere, and especially in the island of Socotra, at the mouth of the Gulf of Aden, we are constrained to conclude that the Dravidians, and amongst them not improbably the Malayālīs themselves, had, at an early period, sailed out of India and formed settlements at distant places.[4] Thus it becomes clear that the Apostle Thomas could

1. *De. Orsey*, p. 63.

2. See *La Croze's account* of the tradition given by Hough, p. 34.

3. Wilke's *Mysore*, Vol. II, p. 129.

4. See *C. C. Magazine*, Vol. V, p. 278. Reference may here be made to the colonies in Java, Bali, Sumatra, &c.

not have found any difficulty in crossing over to Malabar after his labours in Socotra or Arabia Felix.

Similarly, even if the supporters of the northern theory be correct, it was not impossible for St. Thomas to have come down to the southernmost extremity of India from the north or north-west by inland route. We have shown from the testimony of the *Periplus* that, by the early years of the Christian era, Brahmanism had been established at Cape Comorin, the southernmost point of India. The Aryan invasion and colonisation of Southern India must have taken place long before. Whether it was led by Paraśurāma, the hero of the Malabar legend, or by Rama, the hero of Rāmāyaṇa, or whether Raghu, the ancestor of the latter, did, as asserted in the Raghuvamśa, actually levy tribute from the Pāṇḍyan Kings, "Of their glory the collected excellence of the pearls of the ocean into which the Ṭāmraparṇi flows", it is evident that Hinduism had established itself on the Malabar Coast long anterior to the Christian era. We have the high authority of Professor Wilson for this position.[1] As Mr. R. C. Dutt observes, by 1000 B. C., Hindu settlers had come as far southwards as south Behar, Malwa, Southern India and Gujarat. And Bishop Caldwell, on the authority of the Ḍīpavamśa and Mahāvamśa, refers to circumstances which "carry up the era of the first introduction of Aryan civilisation into the Pāṇḍya country probably at Korkai, to a very early period; shall we say about 700 B. C?"[2] To be more specific and to come nearer home, by the 4th century B. C., the whole of Southern India had been Hinduised, and the three great kingdoms of Chēra (Kērala), Chōla and Pāṇḍya had been established, stretching as far south as Cape Comorin.[3]

Both the great Hindu Epics, the Rāmāyaṇa and the Mahābhāraṭa, show considerable knowledge of the

1. *Descriptive Catalogue of the Mackenzie* MSS.
2. *Hist. of Tinnevelly*, p. 15.
3. Dutt *Ancient India*, Vol. II, p. 25.

geography of the northern, central and southern India. Mr. Pargiter, in his article on the geography of 'Rāma's Exile',[1] has, after an examination of three versions of the story as contained in Vālmīki's Rāmāyaṇa, and in the Vana parva and Ḍrōṇa parva of the Mahā bhāraṭa, followed Rāma's route step by step till he reached Ceylon or Lanka, and attempted to identify the localities through which the hero passed. Mr. Pargiter thinks that "the *main features* of central and southern India and Ceylon portrayed in the poems are undoubtedly correct". He points out that Rāma, according to the poem, travelled in a chariot till he reached Sṛngivīrapura, where he dismissed his charioteer, which shows that, so far, his course lay along good roads. The forests that Rāma had to cross were not altogether impenetrable for "there were paths or tracks through these", and "it is often stated in the poem that Rāma received directions how to go from one place to another, and followed the road (paṭham and mārgam) in his travels". He is said to have crossed the Ganges at Sṛngivīrapura by boat, and the Yamuna at Bharadvāja's hermitage by a raft. After following Rāma's course southwards, as detailed in the poem, and attempting to identify the places mentioned therein with their modern sites, Mr. Pargiter concludes: "If the identifications now offered are reasonable and satisfactory, we must conclude that the author of the Rāmāyaṇa had a real knowledge of Centr al and Southern India. Vālmīki is said to have composed the poem while Rāma was still alive,[2] and whatever historical truth may be contained in the story of Rāma's exile and invasion of Ceylon, the geographical knowledge could hardly have been obtained except from an actual visit to those regions by some person."[3] Thus it

1. *Royal Asiatic Society's Journal* for April 1894.
2. *Adi K*. III.
3. P. 264.

becomes evident that there was a clear and defined route, whether by means of good roads or forest tracks, the rivers along the line being crossed by boats or rafts, which could be used by those who wanted to travel from the north to the southern-most extremity of India, centuries before the date of the alleged visit of St Thomas to northern or north-western India.

According to tradition, St. Thomas visited not only India, but he also preached and founded a ministry on the island of Taproleane or Ceylon.[1] This again could not have been an impossible task for the Apostle. Neither was it improbable. Having come as far as Malabar and the Coromandel Coasts, his evangelical zeal could and certainly would have impelled him to cross over to the island and spread the tenets of Christ there.

Besides the external and circumstantial evidence already adverted to in support of the tradition, there is strong internal evidence too which require consideration. The existence of the Syrian Church of Malabar from early days; of the Church of St. Thomas at Mylapore till at least the days of Marco Polo claiming St. Thomas as its founder; the fact that Christians flock to the Church of Mylapore from Malabar, Ceylon and distant parts of India and even from Arabia to deposit their offerings at the shrine of the Apostle; the circumstance that the communion office, the liturgy, and all the services of the Church are even now celebrated in the Syriac language; the fact that in the Beet Gaza or Breviary of the Syrian Church there occurs the following passage: "By St. Thomas the error of Idolatry has been confounded in the Indies"; [2] the existence of a Christian colony from very early days claiming a Syrian origin; the designation of "Christians of St. Thomas" transmitted from age to age; their steadfast allegiance to Antioch; the

1. See *Nikephoros Lib. II His. cap.* 40, *Neander Church His.* Vol. III, p. 165.
2. Hough, Vol. I, p. 37.

holy Chrism ; the institution of pontifical succession and other usages of the Church, such as the celebration of the festivals of good-will and love, usages representing those ordained by the Apostles and insisted upon in churches and among communions which they founded, and finally the very existence, long and continued, its origin being lost in antiquity, of the tradition itself so tenaciously clung to by a supremely conservative people—all these may be referred to as unmistakeably going to probablize, if not to prove, the truth of the tradition.

Even in matters for decision before judicial tribunals, where the highest possible perfection in the nature of the evidence offered in support of a position is insisted upon, the Judicial Committee of the Privy Council has thought it right to base its decision on "a body of strong persistent tradition preserved" in certain records, and called to its aid " a story still current which may possibly serve to throw some light on the transaction." How much more then in a matter, the origin of which goes back to the early years of the Christian Era, where the vision of any direct and satisfactory evidence has become almost completely obscured and darkened by the mist of ages, will the accumulated record of persistent tradition, supported by the story of the Apostle's martyrdom so circumstantially related, the existence of a church bearing his name, the belief in the miracles alleged to be worked at his shrine, the record of the removal of the martyr's remains to Edessa so far back as 349 A. D., spoken to by Rufinus, assist us in arriving at a correct conclusion regarding the truth of the legend and deserve our close and considerate attention ?

Basnage was among the first to deny the Indian Apostolate and martyrdom of St. Thomas. He was followed by La Croze, who, as we have already observed, has rejected the tradition summarily. He is of opinion that it is not entitled to credit. After giving an account of the tradition he, says: " I shall not lose time rejecting this narration of the death of the holy Apostle which is not apparently less fabulous than the coming of St. Thomas into India".[1] The legend is not universally accepted by Romish writers themselves, though most of the evidence adduced on its behalf rests on their authority. There are among them many who regard much of the account as apocryphal and express grave doubts of the truth of the legend.

The learned Tillemont, in his *Ecclesiastical History* of the first six ages, treats the whole story as worthy of little credit. Renadot, in his Translation of *The Travels of Two Mahomedans into India and China* in the 9th century, says: "It is true indeed, the common tradition of the Malabar Churches has it, that St. Thomas preached in the Indies, and the same has been admitted into the Roman Martyrology, where it is said he suffered Martyrdom at Calaminia : but there is no memorial left of any city so called in those parts, and the conjectures which some of the learned have advanced concerning this name are quite intolerable."[2] The Abbe Fleury treats it as involved in great uncertainty.

Amongst Protestant Church Historians also there are those who doubt the truth of the tradition. Fabricius classes it amongst other *questionable* traditions. Moshiem and Milner take no notice of the subject. Mr. F. Wrede declares that "the story is supported by no historical proof whatever." Hough advances some powerful arguments and refers to quotations to show that the legend derives little support from history. He remarks: "However desirous we may be to establish so interesting a fact as the visit of St. Thomas to India, yet historic truth is too important to admit an assumption, unsupported as this is by the faintest vestige of authentic history, and in itself I must continue to think it most improbable."[3] Chaplain Trevor holds that

1. Pp. 39—40.
2. P. 38.
3. P. 40.

there is better evidence that the light of Christianity extended from Egypt where it was kindled by St. Mark, through Persia towards the northern confines of India, and accounts for the tradition by the theory of confounding the Apostle for another Thomas who was a monk. The Rev. Mr. Mateer thinks that the Syrians reached Malabar only about the middle of the 4th century. And Mr. Campbell argues, for reasons set forth by him, in favour of this view. Dr. Burnell is not inclined to favour the tradition, and Mr. Logan holds that though " there is no inherent improbability in the tradition that the Apostle Thomas was one of the earliest immigrants from the west, of direct contemporary proof that he did come to Mowziris and founded the Christian Churches in the neighbourhood there is absolutely none so far as researches have yet gone." Sir John Kaye says, " It would be pleasant to accord the fullest faith to the legend of the Apostolic origin of Christianity in India, but there is really no authority in its favour to divest it of all the attributes of fable."[1] Mr. Rae, a high authority on the subject, has in his work entitled *The Syrian Church in India*, advanced some elaborate arguments to show that St. Thomas could never have visited Malabar, and that there is no historical basis whatever to credit the story. Dr. W. W. Hunter, while rejecting some of the strongest arguments advanced by Mr. Rae, accepts his conclusion regarding the untenability of the truth of the tradition. Dr. George Smith[2] ignores the subject altogether, dating the first conversion of India from A. D. 193.

Dr. Fleet, while affirming the truth of the Indian Apostleship of St. Thomas, is not prepared to accept the Malabar tradition of the Apostle's martyrdom. He says, " Certain statements, which, however, cannot be carried back to before the 7th century, if indeed to even so early a period as that, assert that the place at

1. *Christianity in India*, p. 3.
2 *The Conversion of India*, 1903.

which St. Thomas was martyred was named Kalamaic, Karamena, Kalamina or Kalamita. And the Christians of the Malabar Coast place the scene of the martyrdom at Mylapore near Madras, and in addition to following the accepted date of the 21st December, are represented as placing the event in the year A. D. 68 by some means the nature of which cannot just now be ascertained. With these matters, however, we are not here concerned beyond noting the point that there is no evidence at all that the place where St. Thomas was martyred was anywhere in Southern India. Any statement to that effect cannot be traced back beyond the middle ages. And all the real indications point in quite another direction."[1]

The Roman Catholic Bishop, Medlycott affirms the martydom of the Apostle in India and produces strong evidence to show that it must have taken place at Mylapore and that the remains lay buried there till their removal to Edessa. The shrine of the Apostle at Mylapore is still venerated and visited as a place of pilgrimage by Malabar Christians. The learned Bishop is, however, inclined to treat the name Calamina or Kalamina as fictitious.

Among those who favour the tradition may be marshalled several eminent authorities whose opinion on the subject is entitled to great weight. The *Letters Edifiantes* give much importance to the tradition. Romanist writers in general, and more especially Jesuit writers, give great prominence to it, for instance, Emmanuel Martino Martinize (A. D. 1615) believes the story. The chief Roman Catholic authorities, besides those already named, are:—Gothard Artus (1660), Gouzales d'Avila (1649) and Urbano Cerri (1716). It is a common complaint among some Protestant writers that the Portuguese have accepted it and embellished it by the invention of a number of fantastic miracles. Sir

1 Journal of the Royal Asiatic Society for April 1905.

John Kaye observes that "Maffius relates with apparent good faith the miracles that Thomas wrought in India; how he converted certain Magi; how he built a temple at Meliapore; how he brought the dead to life; how he delivered himself of certain wonderful prophecies, and finally, how he became a martyr for the faith".[1] Asseman says, "That St. Thomas was the Apostle of the Indies is attested by all Ecclessiastical Records, Greek, Latin, and Syriac."[2] Dr. Claudius Buchanan observes: "I am satisfied that we have as good authority for believing that the Apostle Thomas died in India as that the Apostle Peter died at Rome."[3] Professor Wilson, while identifying Mihilaropya of the *Hitopadesa* with Mylapore or St. Thome near Madras, accords its value to the tradition. He says "We need not be much at a loss for its identification, as the name approaches sufficiently to Mihilapoor, Meliapur, or S. Thome, where our own records indicate a city of some consequence in the beginning of the Christian Era, as the scene of the labours and martyrdom of St. Thomas, occurrences very far from invalidated by any arguments yet adduced against the truth of the tradition."[4] Bishop Heber is inclined to favour the claim of the Syro-Malabaric Church to this Appostolic origin.[5] So is Archdeacon Robinson [6] who, in his account of the Syrian Christians, says: "The fact that he preached the Gospel on these shores where we are now assembled, and that this was the scene of his martyrdom is attested by ecclesiastical records of high antiquity both in the Latin, the Greek and Syrian churches".[7] Dr. Kerr is of the same opinion. Col: Yule thinks it "so old that it is probably in its simple

1. *Christianity in India*, pp. 3—4.
2. *Dissert : de Syris Nestorianis Tom.*, Vol. IV, p. 439.
3. *Christian Researches*, p. 113.
4. *Trans. of the R. As. Soc.*, Vol. I, p. 161.
5. *Journal*, Vol. II, p. 278.
6. See *Last days of Heber*, p. 317.
7. *Mad. Jou. of L. and S.*, Vol. I, p. 8.

form true."[1] Professor Kennet has summarised almost all the evidence in favour of the tradition, and expresses his decided opinion in favour of it. With regard to the Apostle's martyrdom at Mylapore, Bishop Heber says, "That it is really the place, I see no good reason for doubting. There is as fair historical evidence as the case requires that St. Thomas preached the Gospel in India and was martyred at a place called Mylapore".[2] The Rev. Richard Collins is inclined "to accept the tradition of the Syrians themselves, that the Gospel was brought to the coast in the first instance by the Apostle St. Thomas, as at least as worthy as anything that can be said against it".[3] So also Messrs. Howard and Whitehouse, the latter of whom urges reasonable and proper grounds for accepting the tradition as in the main credible and trustworthy, and thinks that there may be some foundation stones of truth buried beneath the accumulated rubbish of centuries.[4] Dr. Perron observes that "those who know the east would find it by no means impossible, or even extraordinary, that St. Thomas should thus visit India." The Rev. Alex J. D. D'Orsay, after an examination of the Portuguese and other authorities on the question and referring to the evidence available, observes that "all these united proofs strongly confirmed the general opinion that St. Thomas was the first Apostle of India."[5]

Here we have made an attempt to present a catena of most of the available authorities for and against the tradition so dearly cherished by the Indian, and more specially by the Malabar Christians; and, where there is such divergence of opinion among the learned, one can only say with our author that it is "a tale, in my opinion, not to be scoffed at."

1. *Marco Polo*, Vol. II, p. 356.
2. *Journal*, Vol. III, p. 212, 4th *Edition*.
3. *Missionary Enterprise in the East*, p. 63.
4. *Lingerings of Light*, p. 12.
5. *Portuguese discoveries. depende Missions* p. 66.

4. **Their dress.** In a note to Fra Bartolomeo's *Voyage to the East Indies* is the following description of their dress: "The people have the upper part of their bodies quite naked; but bind round their loins a piece of white linen, which is called *Bastra* (Vasṭṛa). As long as this cloth is new, it is named *Codi* (Kōṭi). If it has interwoven in it red stripes, it is called *Somen* (Sōmen), *Zomen* and *Pudava* (Puṭava). If such stripes are painted on this linen, it is called *Tuvaden* or *Toven*. If it consists of yellow or red silk, it is named *Pattu Pudava* (Paṭṭu Puṭava). *Citta* or *Pencuppayam* (Peṉkuppāyam) is the name of a jacket lying close to the body, worn by Malabar female Christians when they appear in public. It reaches no lower than the girdle to which the *Pudava* is fastened, and which they wear as well as the men. On the head they have no ornament whatever, but turn up their hair smooth behind, and fasten it in a roll on the crown."

5. **History of Churches in Malabar.** The history of the Christian church in Malabar is a complicated one, and no two authorities seem to agree as to its origin and government. We have already discussed the question of its origin and we have found that there is no inherent improbability in recognising the Apostle Thomas as the founder of the independent body of Christians who bore his name and who maintained their church for several centuries in all its pristine purity.

Our author has incorporated in this letter an account of the origin and spread of Christianity in Malabar supplied him by the Nestorian Bishop, Mar Gabriel, and it, indeed, embodies some early tradition and later facts viewed from the Nestorian standpoint. Of the early infusion of Nestorianism in the Malabar church, there can be little or no doubt, for one of the earliest sources of information as to the history of the church of Malabar, the *Topographia Indica Christiania* Cosmos Indidicopleustes (523 A. D.) distinctly refers to the "bishops being usually ordained in Persia."

To face page 480]

A CHRISTIAN CHURCH

Whatever be the true origin of the church, it appears to have been strengthened and brought into more direct communication with the Nestorians in the eighth or nineth century by the arrival of "several priests, students, and Christian women and children from Bagdad, Nineveh and Jerusalem by the order of the Catholic Archpriest at Oerghai in company with the merchant Thomas," known generally as Thomas of Cana. The two copper-plate deeds already mentioned, specially the grant to the Christians at Quilon, are sufficiently indicative of the existence of Nestorians in Malabar at their dates.

The Nestorian period of the church of Malabar or Malankara appears to have commenced about the year 500 A. D. and to have lasted until 1599 when the latter church fell under the sway of Rome. It is useless to enter into the controversy whether the church was all along subject to Babylon or Antioch till the Portuguese appeared on the scene. One can only say that historians have differed, and that judges have also differed on the point, and we need simply refer to facts here.

Even before the arrival of the Portuguese on the Coast, Latin Missionaries had made attempts to convert the Christians of Malabar into Roman Catholicism. Early in the fourteenth century, three Latin Missionaries, John of Monte Corvino, Friar Jordanus and John de Marignolli, visited Malabar and made some converts. The second of these, Friar Jordanus, was actually appointed Bishop of the See of *Columbum* by Pope John XXII; but it is doubted if the Friar ever succeeded in reaching his See and taking charge of it. It would not, however, be incorrect to say that, until the arrival of the Portuguese, the Malabar Christians, practically all, belonged to the Nestorian church.

The Portuguese, at first, welcomed the Syrians as brother Christians and left them to their own doctrines; but, ere long, they set upon a course of violent persecution to which the Malabar Christians had hitherto been strangers. Once the Portuguese had established their head-quarters at Goa and had consolidated their power on the Coast, they proceeded to take steps to cut off the Syrian Christians from communication with the Eastern Patriarch. Various measures were adopted to bring the Malabar Christians into the Catholic fold. Franciscan and Dominican Friars and Jesuits all worked to win the Malabar church over to Rome. The first attempt to bring the Syrians of Malabar into communion with Rome, was made in 1564, by the Cordeliers or Friars of the order of St. Francis. But "seeing the inutility of all attempts hitherto made to turn them from their faith and from allegiance to their own Patriarch and attributing failure to the presence of the Syrian Bishop, they determined to remove him."[1] Mar Joseph, the Syrian Meṭrān, was accordingly sent to Portugal. Bishop after Bishop succumbed to the intrigues and violence of the Portuguese. The inquisition was established in Goa in 1560, a Jesuit church and seminary were founded at Vaipucōṭṭah near Crānganūr in 1584 and, in 1599, it was resolved finally to bring the Syrian church under subjection to Rome.

Aleixo de Meneses, Archbishop of Goa, was appointed by Pope Clement VIII "to make inquisition into the crimes and errors of Mar Abraham (the native Syrian Bishop), and, in case he found him guilty of such things as he had been accused of, to have him apprehended and secured in Goa; as also to appoint a Governor or Vicar Apostolic of the Roman Communion over his Bishopric; and upon Mar Abraham's death, to take care that no Bishop coming from Babylon should be suffered to succeed."[2] This Bull is dated the 27th of January 1595. Mar Abraham died in 1597, and Archdeacon George succeeded him. In 1599, Archbishop Meneses called the Synod of Diamper which met at Uḍayampērūr, not far from

1. Hough, I—250.
2. Geddes, p. 61.

Ṭṛppūṇiṭṭura, the seat of the Cochin Raja, on the 20th of June, and it lasted for some days. At this Synod, the Archbishop, backed by the terrors of the Inquisition and the support of the Native Rajas whom he had adroitly won over to his side, succeeded in inducing practically the whole of the Syrian church to acknowledge the supremacy of Rome, subscribe to the Latin doctrines and rituals, and disown the Patriarch of Babylon and his Nestorian heresies. They were incorporated with the Roman Catholic converts of the Jesuits in one community under the government of the Archbishop of Goa.

Pope Clement VIII, by a Brief, dated 20th December 1599, reduced the Syrian See of Angamale (Aṃkamāli) from an Archbishopric to a bishopric and gave the patronage to the King of Portugal who appointed Father Francis Roz, S. J., a Spaniard. The See was afterwards removed to Crāngaṇūr and was restored to the grade of an Archbishopric.

Thus was the Syrian church subjugated to the Portuguese. But the subjection was only for a time, and their success was short-lived. The Syrians were watching for an opportunity to throw off the irksome yoke.

In 1604, the Syrian Archdeacon, Gevurgese died appointing Archdeacon Thoma as his successor. The earnest desire of the Syrians then was to get a metrapolitan from one of the Eastern Patriarchs to consecrate their Archdeacon and make him Meṭrān. The Syrians and the Roman Catholic clergy could never agree. Every day the tension between the two became more and more pronounced. The Syrian Christians were at last in a state of smouldering revolt against the Archbishop, Garcia, S. J. The Syrian Archdeacon now worte secretly to the Nestorian Patriarch of Babylon, to the Jacobite Patriarch of Antioch at Diarbekar and to the Patriarch of the Copts in Egypt. At last, in response to repeated requests, a Bishop named Ahatalla (also called Attila or Theodore) was sent by the Jacobite

Patriarch at Diarbekar. Some say that he was the Patriarch himself, and that his name was Mar Ignatius, while others assert that he was a Nestorian and not a Jacobite. However that be, he was seized by the Portuguese on his arrival in Madras in 1653 and brought in chains to Cochin. While in Madras, he had already opened communication with the Malabar Christians.

When Ahatalla or Mar Ignatius, whoever he be, was brought to Cochin, the people became incensed at the violent conduct of the Portuguese. They at once assembled at Ālengād and in a body went to the Portuguese Governor and solicited the release of the Prelate whom they believed to be their Patriarch. The Governor declined to grant their prayer; whereupon the Syrians to the number of 25,000 men with arms resolved to forcibly effect the release of the Prelate and boldly marched to the fort where he was confined. The Portuguese in some mysterious way disposed of Ahatalla. Some believed that he was drowned in the harbour with a stone tied to his neck; some say that he was burnt to death; and others that he was shipped off to Rome. Anyhow, he was not heard of afterwards.

The rage of the Syrian Christians could no longer be restrained. None could control them. They met at Maṭṭānchēry in the suburbs of the town of Cochin and solemely resolved to reduce the church of Rome and to return to their "ancient faith." A Paṭiyōla [1] (resolutions) was drawn up, and "all unanimously, and casting themselves on the refuge of God, attached a large cable to the Roman Cross at Maṭṭānchēry and extended it both ways in the market place; and the people assembled held by this rope and unanimously and with one voice swore as stated above and separated themselves from the followers of the Roman faith.' This was in the January of 1654.

1. A Paṭiyōla is the short form of Naṭapaṭiyōla which means a cadjan in which the form of future procedure to be observed is drawn up.—Ed.

To face page 485]

ROMC-SYRIAN BISHOP & MONKS.

Of course, there were those who did not participate in this defection. Those who adhered to Rome were distinguished from those who reverted to their "ancient faith" by the name of Romo-Syrians, *Pazhayacoor* (Paḷayakūr) or old party, while the others came to be known as the *Puthencoor* (Puṭṭenkūr) Syrians or new party.

The Romo-Syrians continued to be governed by the Archbishop of Crānganūr. Attempts were made to bring back the revolted Syrians with varying success; but the capture of Cochin by the Dutch in January 1663 entirely changed the situation. Bishop Joseph Sebastioni, the Portuguese clergy, as well as the Italian Carmelites were ordered by the Dutch to quit this coast.[1] Bishop Joseph sailed to Goa after

1. " The first Carmelite Missionaries who, in 1657, came to Malabar, were sent by Pope Alexander VII with orders to reconcile the St. Thomas Christians or Syrians, with their Archbishop, Francis Jarcia, S. J., whose authority they had forsaken, and to unite them again with the Catholic Church. Having failed in the first object of their mission, they succeeded at least in the second. Rome, being informed of the partial success, decided to charge the Carmelites with the spiritual care of the Syrians. When the Dutch, after 1663, had conquered Cochin and expelled the Portuguese Missionaries, the Carmelites were entrusted with the spiritual care of the Latin Christians living in Dutch territory, the others remaining under the government of Portuguese Bishops. Since 1701, a great part of the Syrian Catholics were under the jurisdiction of the Archbishop of Cranganur ; in the absence of most of them, they were governed by the Archbishop of Goa. As long as the Goan jurisdiction lasted, the government of the Syrians was in perpetual fluctuation, the Churches freely psssing from one jurisdiction to the other." (P. 219 of the *The Catholic Directory* for 1925 published by the Madras Catholic Supply Society.)

" Of the many institutions under Carmelite management in Catholic Malabar, one of the oldest is the present Apostolic Seminary of Puthenpalli. The traditions are very old ; they are almost as old as the Carmelite Mission of Verapoly itself. The Carmelites definitely settled in Malabar in 1673 * *

" In 1674, the Cardinal Prefect of the Sacred Congregation of Propaganda Fide addressed a letter to the Procurator of the

consecrating Parambil Chānṭy *alias* Alexander a Campe, a native of Malabar and appointing him Vicar-Apostolic. In course of time, the Dutch seem to have permitted the Carmelite Fathers to return and, as Bishop Chānṭy was growing old, Governor Van Rheede permitted the appointment of a co-adjutor. On the appointment of Father Peter Paul, who was a close relative of Pope Innocent XII, as Vicar Apostolic of Malabar, in 1696, he was able, through the good officers of the Emperor Leopold I, to obtain from the Senate at Amsterdam a decree, dated April 1st, 1698, by which one bishop and twelve priests of the Carmelite order, being Italians, Germans or Belgians were allowed to reside in the territory but not in the town of Cochin. Successive Vicars Apostolic ruled over the Latin and Romo-Syrian Christians, the former being converts following the Latin rite, till 1846 when, on the 12th of May, the District of Quilon was formed into a separate charge and Father Bernardin of St. Theresa was appointed first Vicar Apostolic of Quilon. In the meanwhile, several changes of jurisdictions took

Verapoly Mission, asking him to erect a Seminary at Verapoly for training the indigenous clergy of both the Syrian and the Latin rites. For that end, the Propaganda sent 1,700 scudi (Scudo, an Italian silver coin equivalent to about 4 sh. now) in the same year. The correspondence of the period shows the deep sympathy the Holy See and the Sacred Congregation have ever entertained for their Indian children. These preliminaries took about three years, and the Seminary was opened in 1767." (Pp. 1 and 2 of *A Short Outline of the Apostolic Seminary at Puthenpalli*, Industrial School Press, Ernakulam). The Seminary was transferred to Puttenpalli in 1866.

"At present, the Seminary follows a syllabus drawn up much on the model of that of the Propaganda College in Rome with, of course, a few necessary alterations. Under the existing regulations, the course extends over a period of seven years". (P. 17 of *A Short Outline of the Apostolic Seminary of Puthenpalli.*)

"From 1890, the Rector would admit only candidates who had passed the Matriculation examination and learned as much Latin as to begin with Rhetoric and Philosophy in the Seminary." (P. 16 of *The Catholic Directory.*)—Ed.

place which need not be noticed here. Father Bernardin was subsequently, in 1852, transferred to Varāppuḷa. It is said that the rigidity of his rule induced a section of the Romo-Syrians to send a deputation to the Catholic Chaldean Patriarch of Babylon, asking him to send them an oriental bishop.

In 1868, the care of the Latin Christians was separated from that of the Romo-Syrians, a co-adjutor being placed in separate charge of the latter. In 1886, all disputes regarding patronage were settled by a concordat between the Pope and the King of Portugal under which, with the consent of the King, Rome abolished the missionary Vicars Apostolic and, in their place, established bishops of dioceses. The Bishop of Cochin is a suffragan of the Archbishop of Goa, who has the title of the Patriarch of the East Indies. Then there is the Archbishop of Varāppuḷay and the Bishop of Quilon. These now rule the Latin Churches. The historical diocese of Crānganūr has disappeared.

The care of the Romo-Syrians was divided between two Vicars-Apostolic stationed one at Trichur and the other at Kōṭṭayam. This arrangement lasted till 1896 when, at the oft-repeated request of the Romo-Syrians to have bishops of their own race, three Syrian Priests were consecrated as Vicars-Apostolics of Trichur, Eṛṇākuḷam and Changanāchēri. These have the rule over the Romo-Syrian community in Malabar.[1]

The attempt of a section of the Romo-Syrians to cut themselves away from the Vicar Apostolic of Varāpuḷay and to obtain an oriental bishop consecrated by

1. " By the decree of July 28th, 1896, these Vicariates were placed under the government of Indian Bishops of the Syrian rite". (P. 220. *The Catholic Directory* for 1925, published by the Catholic Supply Society, Madras.) " The Archdiocese of Ernakulam was erected as Vicariate Apostolic by the decree of 28th July 1896. On the erection of the Syroi-Malabar Hierarchy, it was raised to a Metrapolitan See by the Bull, dated 21st December 1923, and the Most Rev. Mar Augustine Kandathil was nominated as the first Archbishop", (Pp. 247—8. *The Catholic Directory* for 1925)—Ed.

the Chaldean Patriarch was not without success. Bishops Roccos *alias* Mar Thomas and Mellus came to Malabar successively and created considerable commotion. On Bishop Mellus leaving India in 1877, he placed Mar Ahedjesus, a native priest who had been consecrated bishop by the Nestorian Patriarch of Babylon and a Chorspiscopus, in charge of the people who adhered to him. Mar Abedjesus died at Trichur in 1900. The Church is known as the 'Independent Syro-Chaldean Church of Malabar.'

The Puṭṭenkūr Syrians, who renounced the Roman Catholic Communion at the Coonen Cross (Kūnan Kuriśu) in 1654, chose as their Bishop Mar Thomas of the Pakalōmaṯṯam family, which was, according to tradition, one of the original Brahman converts of St. Thomas. He was consecrated in 1665 by Mar Gregory, who was sent out by the Patriarch of Antioch. This section of the community continued to acknowledge the Patriarch of Antioch, and a succession of Meṭrāns or Bishops deriving authority from that quarter continued to govern them. The history of this church was comparatively uneventful till the beginning of the nineteenth century when, on the advice of Dr. Claudius Buchanan and Col. Munro, the British Resident of Travancore, the Church Missionary Society entered into friendly relations with it and began to make attempts to win it over to the Anglican Church. The Mission established a College at Kōṭṭayam for the instruction of Syrian priests and the conservative party, taught by the bitter experience of their past, took timely warning. In 1825, they appealed to the Patriarch of Antioch, and Mar Athanasius was sent to replace Mar Dionysius, who was supposed to be too much inclined to Protestantism. The dispute was settled finally in 1840 by the withdrawal of the Church Missionary Society from all connection with the Syrian Church. But, under the influence of the Society, a reform party had already risen, and it succeeded in

To face page 489)

JACOBITE SYRIAN CHRISTIAN PRIESTS.

getting a new bishop, Mathew Athanasius, consecrated by the Patriarch of Antioch. Mar Dionysius refused to give way and reported that Mathew Athanasius was the friend of Protestantism; whereupon the Patriarch sent out another bishop to supercede him. The dispute was brought finally to the High Court of Travancore, the main point at issue being whether consecration by the Patriarch of Antioch was essential to constitute a valid title to a bishopric over the Syrian Christians. The decision was ultimately given in 1899 in favour of the anti-reform party.

From this date begins the separation of the Puṭṭenkūr Syrians into the Jacobite Syrians or those who owe allegiance to the Patriarch of Antioch and the St. Thomas Syrians or those who form the Reformed Syrians. The latter consider their own Meṭrān or bishop as their spiritual head, and claim that the Church of St. Thomas is apostolic and independent.

The Latin Christians and the Romo-Syrians follow the doctrines and ritual of the Roman Catholics, the only difference between them being that the Romo-Syrians use a Syriac version of the Latin liturgy.

Both Jacobites and St. Thomas Christians use the Syriac liturgy. The Reformed Syrian Churches have now begun to adopt a Malayālam translation of the Syriac liturgy. The Jacobites say masses for the dead, but do not believe in purgatory; they invoke the Virgin Mary, venerate the Cross and relics of Saints; they recognise only three sacraments, baptism, marriage (which they always celebrate on Sundays) and the mass; they prescribe auricular confession before mass, and at mass administer the bread dipped in wine; they recite the eastern form of the Nicene creed and discourage laymen from studying the Bible. The Reformed Syrians differ from them in most of these points. These still use a Syriac liturgy, but from that liturgy they have expunged all passages that involve invocation of Saints, prayer for the dead and Transubstantiation.

Besides the Jacobites and St. Thomas Syrians, there is a section of the Syrian community which approximates more to the latter than to the former with a church and a Bishop at Anjūr or Ṭoliyūr, a small see founded in the middle of the 18th century by Mar Cyril or Kuriolos who, quarralling with the Jacobite Bishop, Mar Thomas, got himself consecrated by one of the three Bishops sent by the Patriarch of Antioch. The Bishops of Anjūr do not, however, recognise the necessity of ordination by the Patriarch of Antioch, they ordaining their own successors.

The Syrian Christian Churches are rectangular buildings with flat or arched wooden roofs and white washed facades ; they have no spire, but the chancel which is at the east end is usually somewhat higher than the nave. Between the chancel and the body of the church is a curtain which is drawn while the priest consecrates the elements at the mass. Right and left of the church are two rooms, the vestry and the sacristy. At the west end is a gallery in which the unmarried priests sometimes live. Most churches contain three altars; one in the chancel and the other two at its western ends on each side. There are no images in Jacobite or Reformed churches, but there are, sometimes, pictures; crucifixes are placed on the altars and in other parts of the churches. The clergy and men of influence are buried in the nave just outside the chancel.

The Syrian Bishops are called Meṭrāns. They are celibates and live on the contributions of their churches. They wear purple robes and black silk cowls figured with golden crosses, a big gold cross round the neck and a ring on the fourth finger of the right hand. Bishops are nominated by their predecessors from the body of Rambans, who are men selected by the priests and elders in advance to fill the episcopate. Meṭrāns are buried in their robes in a sitting posture with a quantity of frankincense filling up the grave. Their priests are called Kaṭṭanārs. They should strictly pass through the seven offices of ostiary, reader, exorcist, acolyte, sub-deacon and deacon before becoming priests; but the first three offices practically no longer exist. The priestly office is often hereditary, descending by the Marumakkaṭṭāyam system. Jacobite and St. Thomas Syrian priests are paid by contributions from their parishioners, fees at wedding and the like. Their ordinary dress consists of white trousers and a kind of long white shirt with short sleeves and a flap hanging down behind, supposed to be in the form of a cross. Over this, the Jacobites now wear a black coat. Priests are allowed to marry except in the Romo-Syrian community; but among the Jacobites, a priest may not marry after he has been once ordained, nor may he re-marry or marry a widow. Jacobites also now shave clean, while other Syrian priests wear the tonsure. Malpans or teachers are the heads of the religious colleges, where priests are trained.

Every church has not more than four Kaikkārs or church wardens, who are elected from the body of parishioners who are known as Yōgam; they are the trustees of the church property, and with the priest constitute a disciplinary body which exercises considerable powers in religious and social matters over the members of the congregation. [1]

1. *Malabar Gazetteer*, Chap. III.

Before this part of the subject is closed, it will be appropriate here to give a few extracts from a judgment of the District Court of Trichur and from one of the Chief Court of Cochin on the History of Christianity in Malabar.

"The Roman Pontiff was only one of the four Patriarchs during the first four centuries and it was only subsequently that he got absolute monarchical powers. Now he is regarded as the Head of a Sovereign state and as *jure divino* the Head of the entire Catholic Church, the centre of its unity, the successor of St. Peter,

6. **Twaukerda** stands for Sanskrit.

7. **The two so-called Syrian Copper-plate deeds.** These are reckoned by distinguished orientalists to be not less than a thousand years old.

the Vicar of Christ, and the Father and Teacher of all the Faithful. He has the primacy both of honour and jurisdiction, and from this supremacy over the entire Church, flows immediately his supreme legislative and administrative authority. He is infallible when he speaks *ex cathedra* and this he owes to a resolution of the Vatican Council of 1870. None but vain theorists will affirm that the Patriarch of Antioch occupies the above or any analogous position in relation to the Malankara Church. No instance is pointed of the exercise by him of any power of legislation over this Church." (Para 37 of the judgment in O. S. 94 of 1088 in the District Court of Trichur.)

"It is a historical fact that, in the early period of the Christian Era, the Bishops were the highest dignitories in the hierarchy of the Church. Each Bishop was in charge of a separate district called his Diocese in which he was the administrator and judge in matters ecclesiastical. But after the spread of Christianity in the Provinces within the Roman Empire and in the adjoining countries, a desire for the expression of outward unity among the Bishops manifested itself. The first step in this direction was the convening of synods in order that the Bishops might deliberate together in difficult matters. These synods were naturally held in the political capital of the province wherein the dioceses of the Bishops were situated. It thus followed as a matter of course that the metrapolitan or the Bishop of the chief city or metrapolis came to be regarded as the unifying force of the Episcopacy of the Province. Of the capitals some had peculiar importance in the eyes of the Christians. Rome was not only the capital of the world, but it held the bones of Peter and Paul, the apostolic Princes. Alexandria, the second city of the Empire, was renowned as the seat of Christian learning. Antioch, the third city of the Empire, had long had the Apostle Paul as its teacher. Ephesus numbered a specially large Christian community, and Paul as well as John had long been at its head. From this began the Patriarchal system which was a symbol of the unity of several Provinces". (Para 70 do).

"To the same effect as the above is the opinion of Sir Robert Phillimore. He says : The Church, says Giannone, even during the three first centuries, knew no other hierarchy, no other orders than those of Bishops, Priests and Deacons. But this assertion

The following are copies of the two Syrian Copper-plates as translated by Dr. Gundhert, with the notes of Mr. Logan.

though generally true, requires qualification; for the language of the council of Nice (A. D. 385) renders it quite clear that certain Bishops had pre-eminence and dignity above the rest. Let these customs, said this council, remain in force which have been as old as the customs of Egypt and Lybia and Pentapolis; by which custom the Bishop of Alexandria had authority over all these, and rather that this hath also been the use of the Bishops of Rome, and the same hath been observed in Antioch and in other Provinces (*Ecclesiastical*, p. 20). The first council of Constantinople held 30 years after the Nicene Synod, added the Bishop of Constantinople to the number of primates or metrapolitans of Alexandria, Antioch and Rome, assigning him a place second in dignity to the latter" (para 71). "Smith says in his *Elements* (Vol. I, p. 322) that though Patriarchal dignity dates back to the Apostles, the name came into general use only from the time of the council of Chalcedon (A. D. 451)" (p. 72).

"The judgment in No. 3 of 1061 M. E. of the Court of Royal Appeal upholds the independence of the See of Malankara in temporal matters, and gives the Patriarch of Antioch only a general power of supervision over the spiritual government of the Church". (para 121).

"Till 1052 M. E., there was only one Metrapolitan for the whole of Malankara and he ruled the whole of the Diocese, and was called the Malankara Metrapolitan. Malankara was divided into 7 Dioceses by Patriarch Peter III in 1052. The above judgment of the court of Royal Appeal confirms the position of the Malankara Metrapolitan. He is treated as the spiritual and the temporal Head of the Malankara Church." (para 268).

Next we shall go to the judgment of the Chief Court.

"The leading events in the History of Christianity in Malabar may be summed up in the following short paragraph: 'The foundation of the Syrian church in Malabar by the glorious apostle Thomas; the subsequent advent of a Syrian colony headed by Thomas of Cana and their favourable reception and respectful treatment by the Rajas of Malabar; the grant by Cheraman Perumal of certain political and civil privileges to them; their persecution by the Portuguese, directed by the Romish Archbishop, Alexis de Menzes, for the purpose of bringing them under the Roman sway; the ecclesiastical and social revolution which followed it, resulting in an unfortunate split in the community, a portion of whom nevertheless remained and do still remain faithful to their allegiance to the Apostolic See of the East;

"Hari Śrī. Adoration of Gaṇapaṭi. The blessed rule having devolved from the earth-ruler, Man-lord,

these few important glimpses cover almost the whole field of our history."

"The early form of Christianity in Malabar was Nestorian and all historians agree that the Malabari Syrians continued to be Nestorian in creed and discipline till the advent of the Portuguese about 1500 A. D. There are certain landmarks that stand out prominently in the period after 1500 A. D., and they may be conveniently referred to as: (1) the Synod of Diamper in 1599; (2) the revolt at the Coonen Cross in 1653; (3) the conversion of the Syrian Christians to Jacobite faith on the arrival of Mar Gegory in 1665; and (4) the grant to the Syrian Christians in 1787 of a Teetturam by H. H. the Maharaja of Cochin.

"The events which preceded the Synod of Diamper held on the 20th of June 1599 may be shortly referred to. Before the arrival of the Portuguese in the beginning of the 16th century, only Nestorian Bishops sent by the Patriarch of Babylon were seen in Malabar and one of these was Mar Jacob who died in 1549. All the Syrian Christians were then Nestorians in faith and were so for a long number of years. After Mar Jacob, three more Nestorian Bishops came to Malabar, Mar Joseph, Mar Abraham and Mar Simon. The Portuguese were not for tolerating the Nestorian faith, and they ill-treated these Bishops. All the three Bishops were arrested, and the two former were sent to Rome. The Portuguese king and the Pope who were bent on converting Malabar Christians to Roman Catholicism decided that drastic measures had to be adopted and, accordingly, Menezes, Archbishop of Goa, came to Cochin armed with the necessary authority to convert all the Syrian Christians to the Roman Catholic religion * * Menezes fully succeeded in his attempt and all the Syrian Christians who were, till the Synod of Diamper, following the Nestorian faith, were forced to submit to the Church of Rome.

"Being a forced submission, the Syrian Christians were not inwardly reconciled to the altered situation and were only waiting for an opportunity to show themselves out. The rule of the Portuguese jesuits was soon found to be oppressive, and the Syrian Christians wanted Syrian Bishops again. Though one such Bishop (Ahatala) was sent to Cochin, he did not land in Cochin. Different versions being given as to the cause of his disappearance. The Syrian Christians believed that he was done to death, and they rose in open arms against the Roman prelates. The result was the revolt at Coonen Cross in 1653 * * On account of this revolt, the Portuguese prelates lost their hold, and in 1656, the Pope

Chakṙavarṭṭi, Vīra Kēraḷa[1] (the first of the line), through regular succession, upon Śṙī Vīra Rāghava Chakṙavaṙṭṭi, now wielding the sceptre for many 100,000 years, (in the year) Jupiter[2] in Capricornus, the 21st of the Mīna month, Saturday, Rōhaṇi asterism, the following grant was made in the royal palace (of the Perumāḷ). We have given to Iravi Corttan of Mahādēveṙpaṭṭṇam [henceforth to be called Grand Merchant of the Chēramān world (Kēraḷa)], the lordship of Maṇigrāmam. We also have given to him (the right of) the feast-cloth (?), house-pillars (or pictured rooms?), all the revenue, the curved[3] sword (or dagger), and in (or with) the sword the sovereign merchantship, the right of proclamation, the privilege of having forerunners, the five musical instruments, the conch, the light (or torch burning) by day, the spreading

found it expedient to send down a Carmelite Bishop to restore order. There was no improvement in the situation. When matters stood thus, a Jacobite Bishop, named Mar Gregory, was sent by the Patriarch of Antioch, and he arrived in Malabar in 1660. On his arrival, a good number of Christians who remained defiant to Rome went over to him and adopted the Jacobite faith.

"These disputes between the Native clergy and the parishners on the one hand and the European Prelates on the other, so far as the Syrian Churches in this State (Cochin) are concerned, continued until 1787 A. D. (962 M. E.) when His Highness the Maharaja of Cochin settled the disputes between the contending parties and issued a Teetturam or Royal Proclamation to the parishioners of Amkamali and other Syrian churches situated within His Highness' territory laying down certain rules for their guidance." The Carmelite Metran of Verapoly and the Portuguese clergy willingly submitted to this Royal Decree. (Extracts from the judgment reported on pp. 69 to 236 of Vol. XIV of the *Cochin Law Reports*).—Ed.

1. This is, so far as known, the earliest instance of the use *within Malabar itself*, of this dialectic (Canarese) form of the ancient name, *Chera*, of the country.

2. "A. D. 774 is the only possible year"—Dr. Burnell in *Indian Antiquery*, I, p. 229.

3. The knife variously styled the war knife, Nayar knife, Mappilla knife, etc., is probably referred to. The possession of this weapon is now illegal.

cloth, litter, royal umbrella, Vaduca drum (drum of the Telugu's or of Bhairava ?), the gateway with seats and ornamental arches, and the sovereign merchantship, over the four classes[1] (or streets), also the oilmakers of the five kinds of artificers[2] we have subjected to him (or given as slaves to him.) We have given as eternal (literally "water"[3]) possession to Iravi Corttan, the lord of the town, the brokerage and due customs of all that may be measured[4] by the para, weighed by the balance, stretched by the line, of all that may be counted or carried, contained within salt, sugar, musk, and lamp-oil, or whatever it be, viz., within the rivermouth of Coḍungalūr and the tower, or between the four Ṭalīs (temples of the deputy Brahmans) and the grāmams belonging to them. We have given it by an unreserved[5] tenure to Iravi Corttan, Grand Merchant of the Chēramān world, and to his sons and sons' sons in proper succession.

Witnesses are :—

With the knowledge of the two Brahman[6] divisions Panniyūr and Chowaram village have we given it; with the knowledge of the Vēṇāḍu and Oḍunāḍu (rulers) have we given it; with the knowledge of the Eranāḍu and Valluvanāḍu (rulers) have we given it; given for the time that sun and moon shall last; with the knowledge of the above, written by Nambi Chadayan, grand goldsmith of the Chēramān world.

1. *Cheri*—probably foreign settlers—as corporate bodies.

2. 1. Goldsmith; 2. Carpenter; 3. Founder; 4. Ironsmith; 5. Coppersmith.

3. In the case of the Jews' grant there was no transfer by 'water." Did this part of the ceremony come into the country with the Vedic Brahmans ? See Deed No. 38.

4. "*Quæ pondere, numero, mensurave constant.*" Is there here a relic of the Roman trade with Muziris, i. e., the Codungallur of this grant ?

5. This grant is chiefly of privileges and dignities of sorts, though made with "water".

6. See pages 272-76 of the text.

No. II.

a. Hail! In the time (literally, year) of Perumāl (Cō, King, or Gō) Sṭhāṇu Ravi Gupṭa, who now rules gloriously for many 100,000 years, treading under foot hostile heads, in his fifth [1] year, this year under the concurrence of His Excellency the Ayyan Aḍigal, governing the Vēṇāḍu (the Travancore king is still called Vēṇād Aḍigal, "the adorable feet of Vēṇāḍu") of Anjuwaṇṇam (the Jewish principality of Deed No. I) and of Punnaṭṭala's Lord [2] (the next neighbour, *vide, d*), the following grant of a freehold [3] has been given by His Excellency the Ayyan Aḍigal to the Tarisā [4] church (and community), established (or built) by Īsodāta Virāi of Curakkeni Collam (the name Tarisā is perhaps to be recognized in the Dariaygal of the Syrian tradition).

b. (This sentence is the most difficult of the whole, first, on account of the many antiquated terms of country customs; secondly, on account of the construction, pērār being the negative verb which gives no plausible translation. I prefer to read pērār, and take it as the nominative for the genitive). And I also (one of the above lords or Maruwān Sapīr Īsō of the church, (*vide, n*), which formerly had the possession of the share-staff [5] (feudal tenure?) of the four families of Īlawar ("Simhalese, also Ṭīyar, Ḍwīpar, Islanders", now palm-tree cultivators), and of the eight families of Īlakeyar (Sīhala, low castes or slaves?) belonging to them, and one family of washermen coming from the

1. Probably fifty years later than deed No. II "Ninth Century" (Hang).—Burnell in *Ind. Ant*, III, 315.

2. pati.

3. peru.

4 Dr. Burnell thinks *Tarisa* is of Sēmitic origin, signifying study. In modern Persian *Tarsa* means prayer—*Ind. Ant.*, III 310. Other scholars have found in this word the Biblical "Tarshish".—*Madras Journal of Literature and Science*, XIII, Part I.

5. The shares of produce, &c., due to the Ko (King) and to the *Pati* (over-lord) were styled *varam* (see *i*,). The possession of the *varakkol* probably gave the holder authority to collect those dues. BK.

same stock as these—all these being entitled to the fetter-right [1] (the foot-rope for mounting cocoanut-trees ?) and ladder-right (for reaping pepper ?), to the tax for the elephant feeder, or to the wash gold ("*eri*", perhaps "*ari*"), which the Chāndān ("great person ? sun ?") is wont to get (māttu, "hook in" T., "get by ruse" M.), as well as to the harvest gold ("*polipon*", gold of interest ? shining gold ?), to the nightly meal of rice and to the pot measure—I, possessed of this share-staff, and of the Cavvān (or cappam? "tribute"), and of those five Kandis (pieces of ground or shares ?), have given them by a free and unrestricted transfer.

c. Maruwān Sapīr Īsō (Maruwān, the Syrian lord ?), who has received the water (hereditary possession) of this town, having arranged that these four families of Īlawar (with their servants and washermen), to families of [2],—one family of carpenters, and four families of Vellāler (Tamil agriculturists)—the latter being Carālar (Tamil, ploughmen, Malayalam, temple servants, used, *Clause m*, for trustees, hence *Clause i*, the noun Cārānmei, "trusteeship") of the Alavē (or Aladeiya) land—that all these may do their duty [3] to the God, the planter by planting (rice, etc.), the setter by setting (trees, or by building, offering?), so that the required ceremonies, such as the oil for the church, suffer no diminution, has enacted and given to the Tarisā church the land now to be described.

d. Decreed with the sanction of the Palace-Major (Kōyiladhikārikal) Vyarāka Dēvar (probably Commissioner of the Perumāl, since he is repeatedly mentioned before the Travancore vassal), and power

1. Kanam.

2. *Sic.*

3. The various members of the community were evidently told off to perform various functions; those customary functions were hereditary: hence caste. See pages 109—113 of the text. The community was evidently organized on the model of a well-ordered household.

given with (the ceremony of) water [1] drops for seizing and possessing, under the concurrence of His Excellency the Ayyan Aḍigal, His Excellency the second Rāja Rāma (brother of the former and next heir), his officers and ministers, and of the 600 [2] (a local authority, *vide, f.*); also of the (neighbouring) lords of Punnaṭṭala ("place of Calophyllum trees"), and Pūlacudi ("dwelling of silk cotton trees"), the land bounded so that the east border be Vayalcādu (open waste plain) and the backwater included; the south-east border be the wall near the little door-gate (Chiru wātil cāl matil): the west border the sea; the north border the Tōrana garden; the north-east border the garden of the unapproachable (andilan) of Punnaṭtala; the land enclosed within these four borders I have empowered to take, and by executing this copper-deed have given, for the days that earth, moon and sun exist.

e. And it has farther been settled with the concurrence of His Excellency the Ayyan Aḍigal, His Excellency Rāma, and the Palace-Major, that the church people (Palliyār, probably heads of the Tarisā citizens) alone have power to punish the (heathen) families of this land for any offence [3] whatsoever, and receive

1. See note to Deed No. 2. In this case the transfer was of land and other things; the things transferred by Deed No. II, with "water," were privileges of sorts.

2. Compare the notice of the "Six hundred" in Deed No. IV. It is almost certain that the *Karanavar* of all the *Taras* (Nayar villages) in the *Nad* constituted the "Six-Hundred;" but Dr. Gundhert in the translation of Deed No. IV says, though with some doubt, "Body-guard." See pp. 87—90 and 132—33 of the text and the word "*Kuttam*" in the Glossary, *App.* XIII.

3. Among the privileges recited in a "Malabar Jenm" deed granted by the Kolattiri Raja to the Honourable Company's linguist at Tellicherry in October 1768 are the following: "Penalties or condemnations and customs, beginning with one principal and ending with all other things," which was explained to the Joint Commissioners (Diary 16th February 1793) as meaning "the power of administering justice, both civil and criminal, even to the cutting off the hands of a thief."

the fines expenses, head-price and breast-price (probably the right of selling males and females for serious caste offences).

Mine own relations, whoever they be, whatever the charges be, shall never have the right there to speak as heads of the land dealing with subjects. Let the 600 [1] (see, *d*), the Anjuwaṇṇam and Maṇigrāmam (Jewish and Christian principalities) be the protectors.

g. Let them, even Anjuwaṇṇam and Maṇigrāmam, act both with the church and the land according to the manner detailed in this copper-deed for the times that earth, moon and sun exist.

h. Ordered with the sanction of the Palace-Major Vyarāka Dēvar, and with the sanction of His Excellency the Ayyan Aḍigal, and His Excellency Rāma, and free [2] tenure granted to these (Palliyār) as follows.—

i. (Again a difficult sentence. I take *Ulaka*, i.e, lōka for the official name of the citizens, Christian freemen formed into a corporation [3] and distinguished both from the Palliyār, who are their headmen, and from the Cudi or Heathen families, who live on their grounds as farmers or slaves). There being 61 citizens, the number

1. The deed, it will be observed, makes no allusion here to the headmen of the Jewish and Christian communities, although it is known from Deeds Nos. I and II that such headmen had been appointed. The conclusion is, therefore, that the power of protection here assumed resided not in the headmen, but in the communities *as corporate bodies*. This strengthens the view in the note to para (*d*) that the "Six Hundred" were really the *Kuttam* (see Appendix XIII) of the *Karanavar* of the *Nad*.

2. *Viduper*.

3. This and the succeeding para (*k*) prove conclusively that Dr. Gundhert's position here is correct. The Jews and Syrians were organized in guilds or corporations precisely similar to the Nayars, the *Palliyar* corresponding to the *Taravad* (*Tara-pad*) *Karanavar*, and *Anjuwannam* and *Manigramam* to the "600" of the *Nad*.

not to be increased nor to be diminished, no personal tax to be received ' if you read pērār); for admitting any conveyances or letting them out they are to receive 8 coins (Kāchu—wāyinam is vāhanam, understood horses, waggons); in the case of (female) elephants and of boats, whether for letting in or letting out, they are to receive 4 coins; merchandise belonging to the citizens to be disposed of (or removed) by them with the cognizance of the above (the Palliyār ? or the protecting lords ?); and that they (the Palliyār) do all the business (rights and duties) of a lord (Swāmi) on the place of packing the wares (or on spots where poles with leaves are set up as signs of prohibition) and elsewhere, only after deliberation with the above mentioned (Anjuvaṇṇam and Maṇigrāmam?); that Anjuvaṇṇam and Maṇigrāmam protect the citizens in every coming generation; [1] that in the space within the four gates (or in the four public offices?) and on the spot where land for sale (or "under prohibition" is given in trust, the palace (or Supreme Government) having received the King's tithe [2] (Kō-patawāram), Anjuwaṇṇam and Maṇigrāmam receive the Lord's tithe (Paṭi-ppaṭa-wāram).

k. With the sanction of the Palace-Major Vyarāka Dēvar, who has given of these (the Palliyār) the 72 Janmi[3] rights (*viduperu*), such as for marriages (or processions), the elephant's back, the earth, the water, &c. (or "earth and water on the elephant," at all events, marks of nobility), and with the concurrence of His Excellency the Ayyan Aḍigal, His Excellency Rāma, the minister and officers, the 600, and the lords of Punnaṭṭala and Pūlacudi, let Anjuwaṇṇam and Maṇigrāmam carry out this unrestricted possession right in

1. (? vilakkum=for cultivation).

2. There is here the earliest intimation of what "Pattam" was originally. See the Glossary. The King (Ko-pad) and the over-lord (Pati-pad) had each a share (varam) of the produce, not necessarily of the land alone. Is it too farfetched to derive *pattam* from *patta-varam* ?

3. See note to Deed No. I.

the manner described by this copper-deed for the time that earth, moon and sun exist.

l. If any injustice be done to these (the Palliyār? or Anjuwaṇṇam and Maṇigrāmam), they may withhold the tribute ("world-bearing hire") and remedy themselves the injury done to them. Should they themselves commit a crime, they are themselves [1] to have the investigation of it.

m. And let whatever the two chieftains [2] in Anjuwaṇṇam and Maṇigrāmam, who have taken the water (possession) as trustees for this town (*Caralar*, see, *c*), may do in unison be counted for one act.

n. And let Maruwān Sāpir Īsō, who took the water for this town, since he acquired (or transferred ? *peruttu*) the share-staff (*Varakol* of *b*), and those 5 pieces (or *Anjacandi*) which formerly were the property of the Palliyār, pay for it the full price to the church. This also I have given over by unrestricted transfer.

o. I have ceded to the Tarisā church people, by full and unrestricted tenure, every kind of revenue by this copper-deed for the time that earth, moon and sun do last.

p. Those Īlawar [3] are permitted to follow out their occupations (?) in the bazaar and on the wall. The washerman may come and do his work in the bazaar [4] and on the wall.

1. The Mahomedan community in Malabar does not seem to have possessed this privilege. *Tohofut-ul-Mujahideen* by Rowlandson, pp. 72—73.

2. The allusion here to the headmen (see Deeds I and II) shows that their respective corporate bodies or guilds *acted* through them, though the real power (see note to paragraph *f*) rested with the community. So too must it have been in the Nayar organization by *Nads*.

3. Presumably these were some of the families of the land conveyed along with it in paragraph *c*.

4. Presumably outside the limits of the land conveyed by paragraph *d*.

q. Nor havè the Island [1] ruler (or Ṭīyar head-man) and the Wall officer, or whoever it be, any power to stop them on any charges whatsoever. Though they should commit a trespass, the Palliyār alone have to try them.

r. I have given this in the manner detailed in the copper-deed, for the time that the earth, moon, and sun do last, by full, free and unrestricted tenure.

s. The person who made this full, free and unrestricted transfer to the Tarisāpalli through His Excellency the Ayyan Aḍigal, is Maruwān Sapīr Īsō.

t. To those who keep this and care to see it observed let God himself be gracious (what is *anugramam* or *anucramam*?) The writing of Ayyan; and may this benefit (*vel*, or it is a compound word?) be equal to Cula Sundara's (Vishnu?) Rule victoriously!

1. See Glossary under *Tiyan*, etc.

Note. The above is one of the deeds belonging to the Syrian Christians of the Cochin and Travancore States. This translation, by Dr. Gundhert, appeared in the *Madras Journal of Literature* etc, Vol. XIII, Part I, p. 130. (P. P. CXVII to CXXII, Nos. 2 and 3.).

LETTER XVIII

1. The Jews: tradition about arrival and settlement in Malabar. The colony of Jews domiciled in the Native State of Cochin, and living contentedly amongst the native population under a Hindu Raja for close upon 16 or 17 centuries, and preserving intact their nationality, religion and habits of life speaks volumes in favour of the tolerance and the catholicity of views of the people and of the rulers of Malabar. When and how they arrived in Malabar is still shrouded in obscurity like many facts of interest connected with that interesting land. Mr. Logan observes that "the Jews have traditions which carry back their arrival on the Coast to the time of their escape from servitude under Cyrus in the 6th century B. C."[1] This tradition is also referred to by Dr. W. W. Hunter.[2] Dr. Hunter refers to Jewish settlements in Malabar long before the second century A. D. A Roman merchantship that steered regularly from Myos Hormes on the Red Sea to Arabia, Ceylon and Malabar is reported to have found a Jewish colony in Malabar in the second century A. D. Mr. C. M. Wish observes that "the Jews themselves say that Mar Thomas the Apostle arrived in India in the year of our Lord, 52, and themselves, the Jews, in the year 69."[3] Looking to the commercial relations between the East and West already noticed, it was not impossible, and it was indeed most probable that the Jews settled on the coast in the first century of the Christian Era. One of their own traditions says that the colony came originally from Jerusalem after the destruction of the second Temple in the 3828th year of the creation and 68th year of the Christian

1. *Malabar*, Vol. I, p. 247.
2. *Hist. of British India*, Vol. 1, p. 99.
3. *The Asiatic Journal*, Vol. VI.

Era. Some ten thousand Jews and Jewesses are said to have come to Malabar and settled at Crānganōre, Pālayūr, Māla and Pullūtt, of whom three-fourths remained at Crānganōre, then called Mahādēvar-paṭṭaṇam and subsequently Sinkhali or Chingly, a corrupted form of Ṭiruvanchikkuḷam [1] under the Government of Chēramān Perumāl. Whatever truth there may be in this tradition, the earliest authentic record we have of the Hebrew nation coming in contact with the Dravidians is in the Bible. We have already referred, in another connection, to Solomon's fleet visiting Malabar and taking from there articles, the Hebrew names of which, as contained in the Bible, have been traced by philologists to their Dravidian originals. It is probable that such visits were frequent in the years that followed.

The white Jews of Cochin gave to Dr. Claudius Buchanan a narrative of the events relating to their first arrival in the country, the original of which is said to be in Hebrew handed down to them by their ancestors. It says: "After the second temple was destroyed, (which may God speedily rebuild!), our fathers, dreading the conqueror's wrath, departed from Jerusalem, a numerous body of men, women, priests and Levites and came into this land. There were among them men of repute for learning and wisdom, and God gave the people favour in the sight of the King, who at that time reigned here, and he granted them a place to dwell in, called Crānganōre. He allowed them a patriarchal jurisdiction within the district with certain privileges of Nobility; and the royal grant was engraved, according to the custom of those days, on a plate of brass. This was done in the year from the creation of the World, 4250 (A. D. 490), and this plate of brass we still have in possession. Our forefathers continued at Crānganōre for about a thousand years, and the number of heads who governed were 72." [2] Mr. Milne Rae

1. Hobson Jobson.
2. *Christian Researches*, 3rd Ed, pp. 207 etc.

argues that the three main facts mentioned in the above narration, viz., (1) that the Jews came and settled in Malabar soon after the destruction of the second Temple, (2) that they were given a charter by a certain king conferring upon them certain privileges in the year 490 A. D., and (3) that they remained a thousand years at Cranganore before they migrated to Cochin, are mutually inconsistent with, and destructive of, each other.[1] No two authorities agree on the chronology of each of these facts, and it is not, therefore, difficult to argue that they are inconsistent and mutually destructive.

In the dearth of any direct or contemporary evidence, it is rather difficult to ascertain and fix the exact date of the advent of the Jews to Malabar. The sack of Jerusalem by Nebuchadnezzar, the attack of Pompey, 64 years before the Christian Era and the bloody retribution of Hadrian in Judea in 136 A. D, were causes sufficient to induce the Jewish nation to expatriate themselves, and seek fresh fields and pastures new.

2. **Their Prosperity and grant of Charter.**— It would seem from this that, before Chēramān Perumāl granted the valued privileges set forth in the copper-plate grant and raised the community in its political status, some centuries had elasped since their original settlement. And this is not unlikely. It may be supposed that the Jews had prospered and attained considerable importance in the land: in fact it was in the heyday of their glory that Chēramān Perumāl granted them this charter. The very circumstance that the Malabar King thought it fit to raise their headman, Joseph Rabban, to the rank of nobility, and that he was allowed to exercise plenary jurisdiction in the community, points to their attainment to prosperity and power. This could only have been a work of time, and several centuries must have elapsed between their original settlement and the Royal grant.

1. *The Christian College Mag.*, Vol. VI., p 364.

3. **The Jewish Copper-plate.** The Jewish charter consists of two copper-plates with three pages of writing, and is now in the possession of one of the elders of the White Jews of Cochin. It is inscribed in the *Vatteluthu* (Vaṭṭeḻuṭṭu) character, the original Tamil alphabet which was once used in all that part of the peninsula south of Tanjore, and also in South Malabar and Travancore. Several attempts have been made to decipher it, which were all more or less unsuccessful, till Dr. Gundhert, the eminent Malayāḷam scholar, managed to unravel the secret. The Jews themselves have made an attempt, and the Hebrew version of it was perhaps the earliest rendering. But, as observed by Dr. Gundhert, "the Hebrew translator seems neither to have understood much of the original Tamil, nor to have cared about rendering it faithfully."

There is a *fac-simile* of it in the *Madras Journal of Literature and Science*;[1] also in the *Indian Antiquary*[2].

Translation of the Grant.

a. Hail! Śṛi—The King who has taken the supreme rule, King (Perumāl) Śṛi Bhāskara Ravi Vaṛman, wielding the sceptre and ruling for many 100,000 years, in his time, in the thirty-sixth year against[3] the second cycle (literally, year), on the day when he was pleased to sit in Muyirikōḍu, he was pleased to grant this favour.

[N. B.—The Jewish translation, particularly incorrect in the rendering of this sentence, deserves, perhaps, to be listened to in its translation of Muyirikōḍu "residing in Kṛānganūr or Koḍungallūr" Perhaps

1. Vol. XIII, part 2 between pages 10 and 11.

2. Vol. III between pages 334 and 335.

3. Compare a similar use of the word "*Etir*" in deed No. 4. "The date of this deed cannot be later than the eighth century A. D." Nor can the deed be "older than the beginning of the eighth century." (Burnell in *Ind. Ant* III, 334). "Probably not later than the ninth century A. D., nor earlier than the seventh." (Caldwell, *Grammar of Dravidian Languages, Introdu*, 89, *Edn.* 1875); "About 750." (Burnell, *South Indian Paleography* 2nd *Edn* 140).

the Musiris of the ancients is to be sought so far south. The calculation of the thirty-sixth year against the second cycle, which Mr. Whish has attempted, guided by the authority of other documents of considerable age, I am not prepared to criticise, as I am dobtful of the signification of "*Etir*" against (before?)].

b. We have given to Joseph Rabban (the principality) Anjuvaṇṇam, along with the 72 Janmi [1] rights, such as (going) with elephants and (other) conveyances, tribute from subordinate landholders, and the possession (or revenue) of Anjuvaṇṇam, the light by day, the spreading cloth, the litter, the umbrella, the Vaḍuca drum (Jews' transl : "drum beaten with two sticks"), the trumpet, the gateway with seats, ornamental arches, and similar awnings and garlands (charawu, i. e., T) and the rest.

[N. B.—Here the name of Anjuvaṇṇam has been mistaken by the Jewish and other translators. The Jews translate it "five colours," and the revenue of Anjuvaṇṇam is converted by them into a right to convert from the five-castes. But the language of the document forbids to take "*anju*" for the numeral 5; it would have been "*aintu*" as in the later document, II *a*[2]. The present translation of *viduperu* generally mistaken for a gift of houses, or even for a gift to 72 families is fully secured by Document II in several places; *vidu* (cf. II, *k*) is the verbal noun of *vidu*, "to leave"; signifies "remittance, freedom;" hence in ancient T. synonymous with *S. mocsha*, the derived meaning is "freehold, Janmam;" hence the modern signification "gardens, house." Some of the privileges are not quite determined; *pacudam* (T-tribute) is, in the Jewish Translation, the right of calling from the corners of the street that low castes may retire. After

1. See the note which follows : the word used is *Viduper*.
2. No. 3 in this collection.

"umbrella," the Jews have inserted a word of which they do not know the meaning.]

c. We have remitted to him the tribute to the Supreme Government (literally, the world-bearing-hire of II[1]*l*.)

[N. B.—The Jews translate literally, but ungrammatically, "and the revenue of the land and balances their hires he remitted."]

And we have enacted with this copper-deed that when the other town inhabitants pay taxes to the (Perumāl's) palace, he shall not have to pay ; when they receive, he shall also receive.

[N. B.—Nothing of the Jewish version can here be of any use; they are quite misled by the word *Coyil* which they take for synagogues, and hence conclude the sense be this: "and he shall be chief to the rest of the cities in which there are synagogues and Jewish inhabitants," without any attention to the structure of the sentence. But the sentence is difficult on account of the (antiquated) double *aru*, which I take for "time, term"; of Beschi's "tax paid at fixed times;" and the derivative *aru* used in Malayālam and Canarese for "when." From a comparison of this and the first[2] document, it appears that the residence of the Jewish and Christian chieftains was not in the little principality given to them, but that they remained in the metrapolis as the seat of commerce. The Jewish translation may give confirmation to the tradition that there were Jews and synagogues in many cities, and that naturally enough their naturalized Emir had jurisdiction over the whole nation, which he represented in the system of Government then established.]

d. (Given) to Joseph Rabban, the owner of Anjuvaṉṉam, and to his posterity, sons and daughters, nephews and sons-in-law, a hereditary appendage for

1. Deed No. 3, clause *l*.
2. No. 2 in this collection.

the time that earth and moon exist—Anjuvaṇṇam, a hereditary appendage. Śri.

[N. B.—*Pracriti*, "what is natural, essential to." I take it for synonymous with *Janmam*, which also first signifies "birth;" then in Malayālam "hereditary property." Different in the use of *pracriti* in II *a*.[1] The Jews translate it here with "standing."]

e. Thus do I know Gōvarḍhana Mārṭṭāṇḍan, owner of Vēṇāḍu (or Travancore). Thus do I know Kōṭei Śri Caṇḍan, owner of the Vēnavāli province (perhaps Bembali, wherein now Cōṭṭayam. May it not be the older name of Oḍunāḍu?)

[N. B.—These are the two Southern vassals.]

f. Thus do I know Māna Vēpala Māna Vīyan, owner of Erāla province (the name of the Ṭāmūṭiri, changed by the Jewish version, according to the current tradition, into Māna Vicrama, *vulgo* Māna Vikkiran); thus do I know Rāyaran Chāṭṭan, owner of Valluwa province.

[N. B.—These are the two northern vassals, as I.]

g. Thus do I know, Cōṭei Ravi, owner of Neḍumpureiyur district (Jewish version corrupted by the writers, but the tradition that this is the Pālacāḍu Raja seems correct. Nedumpureiyūr is an old temple on the Palghatcheri road, from which Mr. Whish obtained some inscriptions.

Thus do I know Mūrkhan Chāṭṭan commanding the Eastern Army. (The Jews take Kilpadei for a proper name. It seems these two are the great easterr vassals on the road which leads through the Coiambator gap to the old fields of battle between the Pāndi, Chōla and Chēra Princes. I conclude from Document[2] I, that in a later period the Chēra country, properly speaking, had been taken from the Chēramāns.)

1. No. 3 in this collection.

2. No. 2 in this collection

[According to Ellis, it was divided among the great vassals as early as A. D. 389, and finally, though at what period is uncertain, was reduced to a province of the Pāṇḍyan Government.][1]

h. Canḍan of Great Taleicheri Kil-way ("under-mouth," eastern Commander or Viceroy, i.e., Dhalawa 'army-mouth' or general), the mountain-splitter. The writing of Kēḷappa.

[N. B.—It is open to question whether these persons are two or three. The Jewish version has only the first and the last, leaving out the middle altogether. If Kil-way be the name of a place, we must render "the writing of Kil-way Kēḷappan, the mountain-splitter," and the latter appellation may be taken for a title given to the writer, because he deals in metals. (Compare the grand-goldsmith of I[2] document. But as Buchanan says the Jews find in the names of the subscribing Rajas the Cōlaṭṭiri and the Cuṙumbenāḍu rulers, we may find it possible to recognise in the Canḍan of Ṭaleichēri a family member or vassal of of Kōlaṭṭiri, who with this sea-town recognised the rule of the Perumāl, and in the mountain-splitter the chieftain of the Cuṙumbar or jungle-dwellers, so called either from his mines at Ṭāmarachēri or from a pass he opened through the ghats. It does not seem that in the time of these three documents, the northern Malabar or Cōlaṭṭiri did belong to the Perumāls; for if it did, its Rajas would certainly have obtained as high and conspicuous a place in the line of witnesses as their relations of Vēṇāḍu, to whom in old times, they appear certainly superior. They recognised[3] perhaps a Tulu or Maisur dynasty as supreme lords].

[" Perimpaḍappu, who is now the Raja of Cochin, is here not mentioned, because (the Perumāl) made

1. *Trans. Madras Lit. Society*, p. 19.

2. No. 2. in this collection.

3. It is suggested in the text that *Keralam* was at this time more or less under the Western Chalukya Kings and that the Northern Kolattiri family had not at this time been founded.

him his heir and successor." There is certainly some truth in this remark, from what is said about the name Vīra Kērala, now the standing appellation which the Perumpaḍappu assumes on his accession to the throne.][1]

The translation of the Deed by Mr. Kanakasabhai Pillay may be compared with the above as made by a Tamil Scholar[2].

There has been considerable controversy and difference of opinion regarding the date of this document, specially with reference to the obscure terms in which the date is given in the deed itself. Dr. Burnell endeavours to fix its date with reference to the two other deeds in the possession of the Syrian Christians. He attempts to do this in the following manner.—Dr. Haug had assigned the Syrian grant of Sṭhāṇu Ravi Gupṭa to the early part of the 9th century A. D. on paleographical grounds. This presupposes the Jewish and the other Syrian deeds, as it mentions the Jewish and Christian principalities of Anjuvaṇṇam and Maṇigrāmam, which had been established by those grants. Dr. Burnell accordingly assigned those two grants to the 8th century A. D. He then attributes the first Syrian deed to A. D. 774 as the *only* year in which the astronomical details of the date furnished by the grant are possible. This latter position is scarcely tenable as pointed out by Dr. Keilhorn who says that A. D. 774—775 is not the only possible year: "For I can myself point out two days either of which would suit the astronomical requirements of the date,—Saturday the 10th March A. D. 680 and Saturday, the 11th March A. D. 775."[3] Thus the basis on which Dr. Burnell seems to have worked, cannot

1. *Note.*—This translation of the Cochin Jews' deed was published by Dr. Gundhert in the *Madras Journal Lit. Sc., XIII, Part I.* p. 137. Other translations by Ellis and Burnell are to be found in *Madras J. L. S. XIII, II*, and *Ind. Ant. III*, 34 ; also by K. Kelu Nayar in *M. J., L. S., N. S., V.* 42.

2. See p. 6 of *The Tamils, 1,800 Years Ago.*

3. *Ind. Anti.*, Vol. XXII, pp. 138-9.

afford us any support in arriving at a definite conclusion. Dr. Day refers to three translations obtained by the Dutch Governor Moens, in one of which the *Kali* year 3481 (379 A. D.) is given as the date of the grant. But this date does not appear on the face of the deed as translated by Dr. Gundhert, and Burnell and Mr. Ellis. Mr. Logan and Professor Rae are inclined to agree with Dr. Burnell. The clue given in the deed itself is rather obscure. The grant is said to have been made in " *the 36th year opposite to the 2nd year,* " during the reign of Bhāskara Ravi Varma. This expression has been variously interpreted. Mr. Whish interprets it to mean "the 36th year of the second cycle (of Paraśu Rāma) = 139 B. C." Sir Walter Elliot renders it as "the 36th year opposed to or in contradistinction to the second which would be third cycle (of Paraśu Rāma) = 861 A. D." Dr. Burnell suggested that the first " Āṇṭu " or year might refer to the year of the reign and the second to that of the King's age, while Dr. Caldwell takes the second Āṇṭu for the year of the reign, and the first for the 60 years cycle of Brahaspaṭi. Dr. Hultzsch thinks that the first year indicated the date of the King's appointment of the *Yuva Raja* or heir-apparent, and the second the year of his reign. Mr. Kanakasabhai Pillay observes that " neither of these cycles are however applicable to all the deeds whose dates are given in double years. From the researches made by the Portuguese Missionary, Beschi, who resided in Madura for forty years, it appears that the cycle then used in Southern India was the Grahaparivirṭṭi cycle of 90 years. The epoch of this cycle occurs on the expiration of the 3078th year of the Kaliyuga, in 24 B. C. The years follow the ordinary solar or siderial reckoning. The concurrent Christian year for any year reckoned by the cycle may readily be found by multiplying the number of the cycle by 90 and adding the year and subtracting 24. Thus the 36th year of the second cycle is equal to $2\times90+36-24$ or 192 A. D."[1] Dr. Day observes: "For this event (the death of the Perumāl and the date of the grant) various authors have indulged in dates of their own, without advancing any argument whatever tending to prove them correct ; for instance, Moens gives A. D. 426, Dr. C. Buchanan, 490, Bishop Middleton, 508, Mr. Lawson, 750, the Rev. T. Whitehouse, 825, Paolino, 10th century, and the Jews themselves, A. D. 379, making a trifling difference of 446 years between the date given by them and that by Mr. Whitehouse". In this bewildering array of conflicting views, it is indeed difficult to arrive at a definite conclusion as to its date. The deed itself affords but little help towards its elucidation.

4. **Nature of the Privileges.** To our author, the privileges looked frivolous. But there are more modern European writers who think otherwise. Sir Charles Lawson refers to the deed as "a most valuable grant from the ruling sovereign". [3] The Rev. Richard Collins observes :" Many of the privileges sound strange to European ears ; but it must be remembered that they were granted in a country where to this day a low-caste man must wear a cloth of a certain cut, and must not carry an umbrella, or ride in a palanquin; where a low-caste-woman must not cover the upper portion of her person, or wear but the prescribed cloth round her loins. " [4] The privileges granted by the Rajas of Cochin already noticed will show that those mentioned in the Jewish grant are still highly prized.

The genuineness of the deed itself has been suspected. Paṇḍit Naṭēśa Śāsṭri, while dealing with the Ṭirunelli copper-plate alleged to be a grant from the same Bhāskara Ravi Varma, says: " If I am not mistaken, the Jewish grant has been suspected to be a forgery by the antiquarians, and I think its fate is sealed by the the appearance of the Ṭirunelli grant."

1. P. 60.
2. P. 350, *Note.*
3. *British and Native Cochin*, p. 117.
4. *Miss. Ent.*, p. 47.

He comes to this conclusion in view of the fact that, though both grants are said to belong to the same period, the Jewish grant contains several Grantha Characters, while the Tirunelli grant contains none at all, excepting the opening *Svasti Sri*. He adds that even these words in the Tirunelli grant are, from paleographical indications, older by a century or two than the grantha characters in the Jewish grant.[1] Except for the learned Pandit's remarks, no whisper of suspicion has hitherto been heard regarding the genuineness of the Jewish deed.

"Cheramand" stands for Cheraman Nad, i. e., the land of Cheraman.

"Mappella" is an honorific term still in use among the Black Jews of Cochin.

5. **Their subsequent History**. The Jews lived at Cranganore a prosperous community for more than a thousand years after Bhaskara Ravi Varma granted the charter referred to above. Their own account says that "soon after our settlement, other Jews followed us from Judea; and among these came that man of great wisdom, Rabbi Samuel, a Levite of Jerusalem, with his son, Rabbi Jehuda Levite. They brought with them the silver Trumpets, made use of at the time of the Jubilee, which were saved when the second Temple was destroyed; and we have heard from our fathers that there were engraven upon those trumpets the letters of the ineffable Name. There joined us also from Spain and other places, from time to time, certain tribes of jews, who had heard of our prosperity."[2] Rabbi Benjamin of Tudela in 1167 notices the Jews of Malabar. "All the cities and countries inhabited by this people," says the Jewish Rabbi, "contain about 100 Jews, who are of black colour, as well as the other inhabitants. The Jews are good men, observers of the law and possess the

1. *C. C. Magazine*, Vol IX p. 198.
2. *Hough*, Vol. I, p. 465.

Pentateuch and some little knowledge of the Thalmud and its decisions."[1] The next notice available is that by Ibn Batuta in 1324. Proceeding from Calicut towards Quilon by the backwater route, the traveller arrived after five days' journey at a place which he names as "Kanjerkara, which stands on the top of a hill, is inhabited by the Jews, and governed by an Emir, who pays tribute to the King of Kwalam" (Quilon). The situation described points dimly to the Jewish settlement of Chēṅṅamangalam, but the identification of the name is somewhat difficult. It is, however, significant that the river that flows by the hill on the top of which the Synagogue stands at Chēṅṅamangalam is still known as Kāṅṅirappuḷa, i. e., the Kāṅṅira river and Kāṅṅirakkara similarly means the land bordering on the Kāṅṅira. Another stumbling block is the subordination of the Jewish Emir to the Raja of Kwalam (Quilon) Can it be that the Raja of Quilon had extended his territory northwards so as to take in Chēṅṅamangalam and Cṙāṅganōre under his jurisdiction by the 14th century?—a not unlikely thing—for Jayasimha, King of Quilon, had conquered all Kēraḷa and ruled over it with Quilon as his capital until M. E. 441 (1296 A. D.) and was followed by his son Ravi Vaṙma Kulaśēkhara;[2] or is it likely that Ibn Batuta is referring to a colony situated further south and nearer Quilon? But we have no information of any such colony of Jews south of Cṙāṅganōre at that time. Coupling Ibn's notice with that of Rabbi Benjamin, one is inclined to think that nearer Quilon there might have been a colony of black Jews, the colour being expressly mentioned by the latter.

The Cṙāṅganōre Jews lived prosperously for several centuries till harassed and oppressed by Christians and Moslems they had to quit their earlier home and migṙate southwards to Cochin. Some time about a

1. Translation by Mr. Asher of Berlin.
2. See *Archaeological Report* for 1900 & 1906.

thousand years after their arrival at Cr̄angan̄ore, dissensions arose amongst them, the black Jews claiming equal privileges with the white Jews, a demand which was resented by the latter. The interference of a neighbouring chief was invited, and he seems to have thoroughly destroyed the settlement. An element of discord now arose which brought about internecine quarrels. About this time, two brothers of a noble family quarrelled for the chieftainship of the principality of Anjuvaṇṇam which had fallen vacant on the extinction of the line of Joseph Rabban. The younger brother who was backed by his converted slaves slaughtered the white Jews who enlisted themselves under the banner of the elder brother. The Native powers intervened and dispossessed the Jews of Anjuvaṇṇam, and the younger brother fled to Cochin with his dependants, followed soon after by the elder brother. It might be after this that a party of white Jews came to a place called by the Portuguese *Senhora Soude*, about half a league from the town of Cochin as our author says. They seem to have lived there for 50 years before moving on to Cochin. Writing in the year 1723,[1] our author says that the Cochin Jews had dwelt there then for 202 years. The *Senhora Soude* colony must have therefore left Cr̄angan̄ore 252 years before 1723, i. e., in the year 1471. About this time, the Mahomedans were in high favour with the Zamorin of Calicut, then the most powerful ruler on the coast, and they bore no goodwill to the Jews who were successfully competing with them in the spice trade. In the year 1524, the Mahomedans with the approval of the Zamorin, made an onslaught on the Jews of Cr̄angan̄ore on the pretext that the Jews were tampering with the pepper and other articles they were bringing into the market on the allegation that the Mahomedans had resorted to various tricks for adulterating them. Zeen-ud-deen, the Mahomedan historian, says with reference to this attack: "A disagreement also had

1. See para 2 of his letter.

occurred between the Mahomedans at Cranganore and the Jews inhabiting that place, and a Musalman, having in consequence fallen a victim, a general battle took place between them; and the Mahomedans sent messengers to all their brethren in the neighbouring towns begging their assistance, in order that they might make retaliation upon the Jews. On this appeal, the Mahomedan population of Calicut and Fundreeah (with the natives of that place themselves) and of their dependent villages, and of Kalikat, Turkoz, and Shaleeat (with the natives of Shaleeat) and Purpoorangore, and Travancore, and Tanur and Parinoor and Tunan and Balunghat (which is in the collectorate of Shaleeat) having all leagued together, prepared to attack the Jews of Cranganore; designing at the same time to extirpate the Franks (i. e. the Portuguese), and resolved to make no terms with them. And they entered into this combination with the permission of the Zamorin and his entire approbation. This happened in the year 931 (1524 A. D.); and the people of the towns above-named embarked in their fleet of grabs (which consisted of a hundred sail), commenced hostilities against Cranganore, where they put to death a great number of the Jews, and drove out the rest to a village in the neighbourhood of Cranganore, that lies to the eastward of it (probably Pulluṭṭ). The Mahomedans burnt their houses and Synagogues, and proceeded to destroy the houses and Churches of the Christians of that place; upon which a misunderstanding took place between the Mahomedans and the Nāyars residing there, and several of the latter were slain; in consequence of which the Mahomedans who dwelt in Cranganore were compelled to seek safety elsewhere and to remove to other towns."[1]

This sealed the doom of the Jewish settlement at Cranganore. The Jews themselves likened the desolation of Cranganore to a miniature destruction of Jerusalem.

1. *Tohfut-ul-Mujahideen*, pp. 118—20.

face page 519)

JEWS' TOWN, MATTANCHERY.

The Portuguese, on their arrival in Cochin, found no Jews there, but at Crānganōre there were a few in destitute circumstances. Those continued there to eke out a miserable existance for forty years more, when the Zamorin, assisted by his Moorish allies, invaded Cochin and slew four of its Rajas in battle. The Zamorin's hordes devastated the country with fire and sword, and the Jews finally deserted their ancient settlement of Anjuvaṇṇam, and fled to Cochin and placed themselves under the immediate protection of the Raja of Cochin, who, in the words of Sir Charles Lawson, "with a liberality that can hardly be understood" granted them a site for a town for them to live in by the side of his own palace. This was in A. D. 1565, and it is said that the ground allotted was given in the names of Samuel Castil, David Belilia, Ephraim Salah and Joseph Levy. The buildings were completed in 1567, and the community settled itself in the present Jews' Town at Maṭṭāncheri. The Portuguese, however, continued, in spite of the protection afforded by the Raja, to persecute and rob them. The Jews had their revenge when the Dutch appeared on the scene. They actively assisted the new-comers, and had to pay the penalty for doing so soon after. When the Dutch retired after their first attack on Cochin, the Portuguese sacked Jews' Town on the plea that the Jews had by stratagem allowed the Dutch to slip unobserved by the Portuguese. Their copy of the Pentateuch was lost on this occasion. The Dutch returned next year, resumed the attack on the Fort and captured Cochin. The new masters, in recognition of the services rendered by the Jews, granted them many privileges, and traded with them. Henceforward they enjoyed peace and happiness, but "they have never yet recovered from their misfortunes at Crānganōre, but seem to bewail the loss of their former wealth and power, without feeling any energy to strive to recover somewhat of either."[1]

1. Lawson, p. 119.

In the words of the *Cochin Census Report*, "While in England, in France, in Italy, in Germany, in Spain, and in Portugal, the Jew enjoyed for the sake of his wealth a fitful toleration with intervals of furious persecution, in Cochin he found the advantages of a kindly toleration. Here the Jews enjoyed full privileges of citizenship, and every path to distinction lay open to them. Even the temporal government of the community became by royal charter vested in their chiefs. Thus the down-trodden and oppressed sons of Israel were able to preserve the best part of their civil and religious liberty, and to remain here for centuries unseen, unknown and unsearched for by their persecutors." The Cochin Raja as well as the other Native powers within whose dominions the Jews have made settlements have continued to protect them and afford them full liberty of conscience. The intolerant spirit of civilized Europe that still persecutes and massacres this unfortunate nation, as in Christian Russia, has not marred the policy of the Hindu Rajas as yet. Dr. Claudius Buchanan, in January 1807, sitting on an eminence above the town of Aṃḱamāli, contemplated the "interesting spectacle; a Jewish synagogue and a Christian church standing over against each other, exhibiting, as it were, many revolving ages, the Law and the Gospel to the view of the heathen people—" certainly detached from that element of discord and persecution which he must have noticed and deplored as their invariable companion in the civilised west. At Chēṅṅamangalam, or, as Buchanan calls it, Chennoth, he "was surprised to meet Jews and Christians in the same Street." He, however, has failed to notice the Hindu temple standing in close proximity to the Jewish settlement at Maṭṭāñchēri. Here a Jewish synagogue, a royal palace, a Hindu temple and a Christan church may be seen not far removed from one another, the first three being as close as they possibly could be, being contiguous to one another. After the viŏlent persecution meted out to the "Elect of God', 'God's chosen nation' by Christian Europe for centuries on centuries continuously, the Reverend gentleman must certainly have been strongly impressed with the surprising sight of "heathens", Jews and Christians jostling one another in the street, cheek by jowl, and resorting for worship to temples, synagogues and churches standing in close proximity of one another. And all this, be it noted, not in civilised Christian Europe but in the territories of a "heathen" prince who could not as yet be brought to believe in Christ, the Redeemer!

6. **The Mudaliars.** On the settlement of the Jews in Jews' Town at Maṭṭānchēri, the Raja of Cochin appears to have appointed a chieftain among them with the title of " Mudaliar ", apparently a revival of the privilege granted to Joseph Rabban by Bhāskara Ravi Varma. The *Mudaliar* was given a rod of office with silver knobs. It is said that the *Mudaliars* exercised civil and criminal jurisdiction over the members of their community in days of their glory, the Raja reserving to himself the right of trying great and capital causes. They were also given power to impose and remit fines. On the taking of Cochin by the Dutch, the Jews came under their protection. Their leading man then was a Shem Thob Castiel, a lineal descendant of one of the four elders already named. To him, in addition to the rod of office given by the Raja, the Dutch Governor gave an official staff with its top mounted in gold, bearing the motto of the Dutch East India Company. In the year 1683, a Ṭīṭṭūram or Royal writ was given to Chenna Mudaliar (Shem Thob), granting him the power of punishment within the walls of the synagogue of the white Jews who are called ' Paradēśies, ' foreigners, probably in contradistinction to the native Jews or converts to Judaism. Thirty years later, another Ṭīṭṭūram was granted to the successor of Shem Thob giving him the same rights and privileges as were enjoyed by his predecessor. The title of *Mudaliar*,

conferred on the chieftain, was a personal distinction, and the power of punishment could not be exercised by his successor unless renewed on the death of the grantee. Five Ṭīṭṭūrams of the kind are now in the possession of the descendants of the early chieftains. There were evidently some others which were lost or destroyed. The oldest of these Ṭīṭṭūrams refers to the year 1683. The Mudaliars continued to exercise plenary powers until the State passed into the hands of the English. It was in the time of Col. Macaulay (A. D. 1800—1810), British Resident in Travancore and Cochin, that the *Mudaliars* ceased to exercise the power of punishment, and that the Jews sank to the level of the other classes of the Raja's subjects. The Jews made strenuous efforts to retain the power of punishment in their own hands, but they were borne down by the advancing tide of reform, which sought centralisation and unification of all authority and power in the Raja under the protection of the *Pax Britannica*. Although, with the advent of the English, the Jews ceased to be a political body, they still retain the free-hold of the land granted to them by the earlier Rajas of Cochin. The descendants of the old chieftains are still called *Mudaliars* by courtesy. They have fallen from their greatness, but still possess some wealthy men amongst them.[1]

A writer in the *Jewish Chronicle* of the 5th October 1906 traces the succession of the hereditary title of '*Mudaliars*'. According to him, Baruch Joseph Levi, from Crănganōre, was the first *Mudaliar* in Cochin. His son, Joseph Levi, followed him. On his death, his family became extinct, and Samuel Castiel who was the then next prominent man was dubbed *Mudaliar*, which title continued in his family for four or five generations. The last *Mudaliar*, Shentholi Castiel, and his brother, Elias Castiel, dying childless, the Hallegua family came to acquire the title, and the

1. *Mal. Qu. Rev.* P Vol. I, p. 130.

members of this family are still titular *Mudaliars* shorn of all power.

7. **Three classes of Jews.** There are really three classes amongst the present Jews of Malabar, namely, (1) The White Jews, (2) The Brown Jews and (3) The Black Jews. The earliest exponent of this threefold division, which no doubt is scientific, was the Rev: T. Whitehouse in the *Evening Hours.* But European writers generally speak only of two classes, the "White" and the "Black" Jews. There is a world of dispute as to which of these represent the early settlers in Malabar. So also with regard to their origin. Mr. Whitehouse followed by Drs. Burnell and Day, Professor Milne Rae and others would account for the Brown Jews as "the offspring of White Jews by native mothers," and for the Black Jews as "the offspring of proselytes from among the low caste natives of India." The White Jews are granted by them the honour of being the original settlers on the Coast. These positions have, however, been vigorously combated by the Rev. Henry Lord, who has taken up the cudgels on behalf of the Black Jews, the Brown Jews being, according to him, only a section of the Black.[1] Mr. Lord endeavours to establish that it is amongst the Black Jews of Cochin that the lineal descendants of the earliest Jewish settlers on the Malabar Coast are to be sought. He is not prepared to accept any theory based on colour. He observes that, as a rule, the description of the Jews of Malabar as 'White' and 'Black' emanated from European travellers accustomed to see one colour alone in all Jews in Europe and other countries, and were therefore surprised to meet with Jews of colour on the Malabar Coast. The different shades of colour do not indeed carry any individious suggestions with them.

The Rabbi Benjamin of Tudela, in A. D. 1167,

1. See *Malabar Quarterly Review*, Vol. I, p 168 *et seq.* and other publications by him.

speaks of there being "only about one hundred Jews *who are of black colour*" in Quilon. Menasseh Ben Israel, in A. D. 1655, when addressing Cromwell with the hope of inducing the Lord High Protector to permit the return of the Jews to England, points to their affluence and high political standing in Cochin and remarks: "These in India, in Cochin, have four synagogues, one part of these Jews being there of a white colour, and three of a tawny; these being most favoured of the King". Jacob Saphir, a Jewish traveller, who visited his co-religionists in Cochin in recent years, having described some of the Jews resident there as black, hastens to tone down his words and adds: "They are not black like the raven, or as the Nubians but only as the appearance of copper." But Hayim Jacob Ha Cohen, another modern Jewish traveller, chastising the latter for calling them "black" at all, declares that he will write of this class everywhere as the "non-white", and never anywhere (God forbid!) as the "black". It is very wrong, he says, to exaggerate in this manner, for their colour is like that of the Yemen or Arabian Jews, whereas some writers erroneously confuse them with the M'Shuhararim, the section of the converted Slaves, by calling them "Black Jews."[1]

Mr. Lord refers to certain European writers who agree with him in thinking that among coloured Jews may be found the descendants of the original settlers. Dr. Claudius Buchanan, speaking of the Jews in Cochin, says: "The resident Jews are divided into two classes, called Jerusalem or White Jews; and the *ancient* or Black Jews"[2] and goes on to record his deliberate opinion that "it is only necessary to look at the countenance of the Black Jews to be satisfied that their ancestors must have arrived in India many ages before the White Jews.[3]" Dr. Wilson writes: "The accounts

1. *Ibid* p. 168—169.
2. *Christ. Res:* 11th Ed., p. 221.
3. P. 221.

given of themselves by the White Jews of Cochin are, to a great extent, fabulous. These Jews profess to be descendants of Jews who came to India immediately after the destruction of Jerusalem; but their family names, such as David Castil (David the Castelian) go to prove that they are descended of the Jews of Spain, probably of those driven from the country in the reign of Ferdinand and Isabella, and of German and Egyptian Jews— a fact which has been long ago noticed. The real ancient Jews of Cochin are the Black Jews."[1] Drs. Buchanan and Wilson are indeed high authorities on the question. The writer of the article on Cochin in the *Encyclopaedia Britannica* says that "the Black Jews have been supposed by some to be Hindu converts, but it is probable that they were an earlier race of Jews from Palestine." Among Jewish writers themselves, this view is held by many. The Rabbi David D'Beth Hillel of Jerusalem writes: "The Black Jews believe themselves to be the descendants of the first captivity who were brought to India, and did not return with the Israelites who built the Second Temple. This account I am inclined to believe is correct; though called Black Jews, they are of somewhat darker complexion than the White Jews, yet they are not the colour of the natives of the country or of persons descended from Indian slaves." Concerning the White Jews he writes: "I * * * * have reason to suppose that the White Jews arrived there some little time before the Portuguese, for I have met in parts of Europe with persons of the same family names with those in Cochin, e.g., the Rotenboorgs, Tserfates, Ashkenazim and Sargons etc. They have no MSS. more than two or three centuries old". Again Mr. Asher, who has edited the *Itinerary* of Benjamin of Tudela, remarks: "We hope to have proved that Benjamin of Tudela is no mean authority, and it certainly remains difficult to explain why *he* should not

1. *The Beni Israel of Bombay; an Appeal for Their Christian Education etc.*, quoted in the *Malabar Quarterly*, p. 172.

have mentioned the White Jews also, had they been established in his time; he who so diligently collected all information respecting his brethren would certainly not have omitted to give an account of this remarkable colony. * * *." The only draw-back in this apparently strong argument is that it has been shrewdly suspected that Benjamin had not visited Malabar at all and that his account of the Malabar Jews is all hearsay. [1] However, in the *Noticias dos Judocos de Cochin*, published in Amsterdam in 1686, it is stated that the Spanish Jews arrived at Cochin in A. D. 1511. It is further added that "the Black Jews are from early times; the white ones from the preceding century."

The pros and cons of the controversy will be found ably stated by the Editor of the *Malabar Quarterly* and by Mr. Lord in the first volume of that *Review*, and it would be profitless to repeat them here. Suffice it to say that the early disputes as to superiority of race, etc., are still warmly kept up and there is no near prospect of the two classes burying the hatchet and settling themselves quietly as brethren and followers of the same law.

As to the number of Jews in Malabar, grossly exaggerated accounts are given by various writers. The original settlement is said to have consisted of 10,000 men. Dr. Buchanan, in the beginning of the last century, computed their number at 16,000. Captain Alexander Hamilton, who travelled in Malabar in the closing years of the 17th century, speaks of there having been 80,000 families reduced in his own days to 4,000. In the *Madras Manual of Administration*, the Jews of Malabar are said to amount to about 30,000. Dr. Burnell says that "the Jews in South Western India have been in past ages most successful missionaries; the number of Black Jews or proselytes amounts to several thousands even now." In 1839, the White Jews of Cochin are said to have

1. *The Jewish Chronicle.*

numbered only 183 souls. The total number of White, Black and emancipated Jews in Malabar, in the year 1839, is said to have been 1,039. In 1891, there were in all 1,142 Jews in the Cochin State, and the last Census shows the number to be 1,137, of whom 180 are classed as 'Fair or White' Jews and 957 as Black. The chief places where they reside are Jew-Town in Maṭṭānchēri and Chēṅṅamangalam in the Cochin Taluk, Ernakulam in the Kaṇayaṇnūr Taluk and Māla in the Mukundapuram Taluk. "From an account given by Van Rheede, dated 1677, it would appear," says Mr. Whitehouse, "that the Jew-town (Maṭṭānchēri) then was much what it is now (1859.)" He says: "At the place where they reside, they have houses built of stone, in two rows, which form a street like that of a small village." This description is as true to-day as it was when it was written: so little change has centuries affected them.

8. **Subsequent Arrivals.** From time to time, the stock in Cochin was replenished from Europe by occasional importations, so that it is scarcely correct to say that the White Jews of Jew-Town, Maṭṭānchēri, are all descendants of those who came originally. In 1685, some Jewish merchants came from Amsterdam and were kindly received by the Dutch Governor, Commodore Vosbury. Some Spanish Jews also lived in Cochin during the time of the Dutch.[1] Mr. Asher observes "that all the family names of the White Jews *now* living on the spot viz., Mizri, Alegua, Koder, Sarphatz, Rottenburg, etc., at once prove their origin to have been either Egyptian, Spanish or German."

9. **Synagogues.** There are in Cochin three chief synagogues, one at the northern end of the Jew-Town close to the Raja's place used exclusively by the White Jews. Another at its southern extremity used by the Black Jews. There is a third smaller one also used by the latter. The synagogues of the Black Jews

1. *Historical Sketches of Cochin*, p. 35.

bear dates anterior to those of the White. Thus the date on the Mural slab of the now disused and dilapidated "Cochin Angāḍi" synagogue is A. D. 1639. That of the Kaṭavumbhāgam synagogue is A. D. 1639. That of the Ṭekumbhāgam synagogue is A. D. 1586. The date of the synagogue of the White Jews is A. D. 1666.[1]

Dr. Day gives the following description of the synagogue of the White Jews: "The chief or northern synagogue is about 40 feet long and 30 wide, and by no means a fine building. Tawdry brass chandeliers hold numerous tumblers of oil for lights. The reading desk is in the centre facing the Books of the Laws to the west where they are kept in a cupboard behind a curtain, and consist of five copies of the Pentateuch, most beautifully written in Hebrew characters on vellum. Having no altar, they have no sacrifices, and the yearly oblation of a cock, said to take place in Europe, does not take place in Cochin, where no bloody sacrifices are made. The flooring of the synagogue is of blue and white China tiles. The women's gallery is screened from the body of the church, around which are benches for the men. On passing inside the gateway, through the first court-yard, where four ostrich eggs are suspended, the porch of the synagogue is arrived at: here the Jew leaves his shoes, before he enters the house of prayer. There is an iron safe for the reception of alms for the poor fixed against the outer wall of the building."[2]

Dr. Day adds that the synagogues belonging to the Black Jews have nothing remarkable about them.[3]

10. **Their Dress, Customs, etc.** Of the White Jews, Sir Charles Lawson observes: "Their complexion is not exactly European, but it is the pale olive freshness most nearly allied to it, and the delicate carnation

1. *Malabar Quarterly Review*, p. 174.
2. *Land of the Perumals*, p. 338.
3. P. 344.

To face page 528]

WHITE JEWS AND JEWESSES.

To face page 528]

THE SYNAGOGUE OF THE WHITE JEWS, MATTANCHERY.

To face page 530]

THE BLACK JEWS OF COCHIN

(Kurava) of women. Divorce is not effected through a civil tribunal, marriages being dissolved by returning the amount mentioned in the Keṭṭuba or the marriage document. Though polygamy is not prohibited, monogamy is the rule.

The Cochin Jews observe the Sabbath strictly. The great feasts of the Passover, Pentecost and Tabernacles are celebrated with the most exact attention to ritual. The feast of Trumpets is also observed. So also the day of atonement and the anniversary of the Destruction of Jerusalem.

10. **Disputes between the Black and the White Jews.** Such disputes have been known from early times. They existed even during the Portuguese period and before. Mr. Moens, Dutch Governor of Cochin in 1773, observes that "previous to the coming of the Portuguese, there had been a considerable commotion among the Jews at Crānganūr, *in consequence of the Black Jews revolting from the White.*"

LETTER XIX.

1. **Malabar Mahomedans—Moors.** The Mahomedans of Malabar are divisible into two portions, viz., those who live in small communities and do not mingle themselves with the other class termed Māppilās, and those who, though followers of the same creed, are, to a great extent, distinct from them. While the Māppilās are of indigenous growth, the others are emigrants from foreign parts. Portuguese writers of the 15th and 16th centuries used the term *Moors* to denote all Malabar Mahomedans, and this practice has been followed by the Dutch and the English. The word, as used by the Portuguese, referred to religion only and implied no nationality. In the 18th century, the term *Moor* was also used to denote the Hindustani language, just as the term *Malabar* was used to denote *Tamil*.

2. **Race for Malabar Trade.** The arrival of the Portuguese in Calicut aroused the greatest jealousy of the Mahomedans, who held the Red Sea and Persian Gulf trade with Europe entirely in their own hands. They also distributed the merchandise thus brought to the consumer on lands. These immediately began to intrigue with the Zamorin's ministers for the destruction of the expedition. Two of the chief ministers were liberally bribed, and all sorts of obstacles were thrown in the way of Vasco da Gama, the leader of the expedition, to prevent him from having an audience with the King. Da Gama had, however, been warned by a Castilian Mahomedan, Monsayde by name, whom the Portuguese had found at Calicut, and he, therefore, bided his time and declined to deliver his message to any but the King personally. Arrangements were made to supply the newcomers with pepper and other spices, but the Mahomedans managed to thwart their endeavours to obtain good articles. At ast, da Gama determined to have one more interview

with the Zamorin, and, fearing to place himself in the hands of his enemies, demanded hostages before landing. The nephew and heir of the King's Chief Justice was sent as a pledge. Da Gama came on shore and was admitted to the Zamorin's presence, when he pressed for freedom to trade in the produce of the kingdom, explaining what he would give in return; but to no practical effect, for the Mahomedans had bribed heavily the chief officer of the palace guard, a personage of considerable influence. This officer is said to have inveigled da Gama and his party under pretext of the King desiring to have a second interview with him, into a house situated in the interior, where the party was shut up for a whole day and night. The same tactics were pursued further, till da Gama left the shores of Calicut disgusted and discomfited. The Castilian Monsayde had already warned the Portuguese of their position. He told them: "You must know, gentlemen, that from the moment you put into port here (Calicut), you caused disturbance of mind to the Moors of this city who are numerous, and very powerful in the country."[1] How the Portuguese were detested by the Moors will appear from the following extract from the *Roteiro de Vasco da Gama.*

"The Moors never came to the house; when this trading went on and we became aware that they wished us ill, in so much that, when any of us went ashore, in order to annoy us, they would spit on the ground and say Portugal, Portugal."[2]

The above is the Portuguese account, but there are others which give a different colour to the transaction.

3. **Mappilas.** This shows that our author is in this letter dealing with the indigenous Mahomedans of Malabar, i. e. the Māppilas. The references to Moors by the writers of the 16th century make it clear that the Moors of Calicut and Cochin were, in the beginning

1. *Correa*, p. 166.

2. P. 75.

of the century, people of a mixed race just as the Māppilas are now. "These were middle-men who had adopted a profession of Islam for their own convenience, and in order to minister to their own profits to the constant traffic of merchants from Ormuz and the Arabian ports."[1]

Of these Māppilas, we have the following description given by Day: "They no doubt are descended from Arab fathers who traded to this coast, and formed fugitive alliances, with Ṭeear or Chōgan women, for ideas regarding the marriage tie are rather peculiar in Malabar. The children never appear to have been claimed by the fathers, in fact the very word 'Māppila' is said to have been derived from mother, *ma* and child, *pilla*, showing to whose care the offspring fell. These *mother's children*, now known as Māppilas, could not be considered Hindus, neither were they pure Mahomedans, by whom those with a bar sinister are regarded as a disgrace. Thus the Māppilas, rejected both by the Hindus and Mahomedans, formed communities and churches of their own, combining the superstitions of the former race with the intolerance of the latter. Looked down upon and despised by others, they became morose and bigotted, and as their wealth and importance augmented, so did their jealousy of all interference with them. The old Māppilas assert that, being of Arabic extraction, they consider themselves of better birth than the Tartar races of Northern India."[2]

These 'Mōpilas' are also known in Cochin as *Jonaka Mappilas*, a term seldom used in British Malabar. Various derivations have been suggested for the term *Mappila*, of which one has been already given in the extract from Day. Mr. C. P. Brown[3] derives it from *Muabar* or Malabar and says that "the Tamils in those lands could not pronounce the *ua* or the letter *b*,

1. *Hobson Jobson*, p. 445.
2. P .366.
3. *Jour. R. A. S.*, Vol. III

and *Muabar* was softened into Māppiḷa, the name borne by the descendants of Africans who are now called Māppiḷas." This derivation is indeed curious. How the word underwent the last change, it is difficult to conceive. No slight change, either by way of mispronunciation or verbal transformation, can possibly distort *Muabar* or Malabar into *Mapilla*. The term Māppiḷa has an independent derivation of its own, quite unconnected with the word Malabar. It is indifferently used to denote both Christians and Mahomedans, and it is also applied to Jews as an honorofic. But its application is more strictly limited to Mahomedans in the northern parts of Malabar. Some think that the word Māppiḷa is a contracted form of *Maha* (great) and *pilla* (child), an honorary title, as among Nāyars in Travancore. That the term *pilla* or *pillay*, as an honorary title, is not confined to Nāyars or Śūḍras is evident from the Kannadian copper-plate wherein a Brahman is styled *pillay*—"Nārāyaṇa Piḷḷay, son of Gōpāla Piḷḷay, *Brahman* of Śrivaṭsagōṭram (line) professing the Yajur Vēḍa and residing in the old villages or Brahman hamlet built by Chēramān Perumāl Raja."[1] Mr. Logan surmises that it (*maha-pilla*) was probably a title of honour conferred on early Mahomedans or possibly on the still earlier Christian immigrants, who are also down to the present day called Māppiḷas. The Mahomedans generally go by the name of Jōnaka Māppiḷas, while the Christians are designated Nazrāṇi Māppiḷas. It will have been noticed that our author in his 18th letter, has said that Chēramān Perumāl had conferred on the Jewish chief, Joseph Rabban, and his successors "the title of Chēramanāḍ Māppiḷa", i. e., "the merchant whose office it is to furnish the Emperor's lamps with wicks, which must be regarded as a tribute to the monarch in acknowledgment of his dignity." He adds that the word Māppiḷa does not express any supreme or independent authority. Jōnaka is believed to stand for *Yavanaka*, i. e., Greek. Dr. Caldwell says that

1. *His. of Trav.* p. 36.

a class akin to these on the Eastern coast are styled by the Tamil people Ṭulukkar (Turks) or *Jonagan* (Yavanan). It is, indeed, remarkable that in the *Payyan-nur-pat*,(Payyannūr-pāṭ) perhaps the earliest Malayāḷam poem extant, some of the sailors mentioned in it are called *Chonavars*. As already observed, the Māppiḷas, Mahomedans of the Malabar coast, are said to be descendants of the early Arab traders who formed temporary alliances with low-class women. It will be remembered that, according to Agarthicedes (A. D. 177), the mariners of Sabea had sailed to the Indian Coast, where the odoriferous products grew, and had planted colonies there. Wilks observes that it is believed that the Māppiḷas of Malabar are descended from those colonists.[1]

Dr. Day's derivation of the word, indicating to whose care the offspring of the temporary connections of the early Arab traders fell, is not accepted by the Māppiḷas of the Coast. Mahomedan purists of Malabar disown altogether the application of the term in this sense to those who belong to the religion of the Koran. Duncan says that a Kazi derived the name from *ma* =mother, and *pilla*= a "puppy," as a term of reproach. Maclean, in the *Asiatic Researches*, considers that the word came from *maha* or *mohai* "Mocha" and *pilla*"= '*a child*,' and, therefore, translated into children or native of Mohai or Mocha. A more likely, and perhaps a more correct, derivation of the word is that given by Mr. Percy Badger in a note to his edition of *Varthema*[2]. "I am inclined to think," says Mr. Badger, "that the name is either a corruption of the Arabic *Muflih* (from the root *falah*= to till the soil), meaning prosperous or victorious, in which sense it would apply to the successful establishment of those foreign Mussalmans on the Western coast of India, or that it is a similar corruption of *Muflih* (the active participial form of the same verb) an agriculturist, a

1. Vol. II, p. 129.
2. P. 123.

To face page 536] A MUSLIM LADY STUDENT.

[To face page 537]

A JONAKA MAPPILA MOSQUE.

still more appropriate designation of the Māppilas who, according to Buchanan, are both traders and farmers. In the latter sense, the term, though not usually so applied among the Arabs, would be identical with Fella'h, which is also a derivative from the tri-literal root falaha."

4. **The ancient position of Mappilas.** We have already referred to the tradition of the building of the town of Calicut by a Mahomedan merchant. The traditional policy of equity and justice characterised the rule of the Zamorin, and the complete security of person and property that the Zamorin vouchsafed to all those who frequented his dominions had attracted many trading settlers to Calicut. Among these, the Arab and Mahomedan element predominated and, according to the Kēraḷōṭpaṭṭi, it was through the aid rendered by these Mahomedans that the Zamorin was enabled to conquer the surrounding countries and to obtain a paramount position in Malabar. It was the Koya of Calicut, perhaps the ancestor of the chief merchant, who, in our author's time, "walked about attended by armed retainers," who installed the Zamorin as the President of the Great National festival of Mahāmakham at Ṭiruṅāvāya. We learn from Zien-ud-deen that "from the Mahomedans of Malabar, having no Emir amongst them who was possessed of sufficient power and authority to govern them and to watch over their interests, they, in consequence, paid allegiance to the pagans. Notwithstanding this, however, engaging in hostilities against (Christian) infidels, and freely expending the substance in warring against them, each according to the extent of his means, being assisted in this warfare by that friend of the Mahomedans, the Zamorin, and being enabled to carry on hostilities against them by his distribution to them of money and of warlike equipments generally".[1] Ibn Batuta tells us that "the greatest part of the Mahomedan merchants of

1. *Tahfat*, pp. 21-2.

this place (Calicut) are so wealthy that one of them can purchase freightage of such vessels as put in here and fit out others like them." Such was the opulence of the Mahomedan merchants of Calicut in the 14th century. In the 15th century, Abdur-Razak found Calicut "to contain a considerable number of Mussalmans, who are constant residents and have built two mosques, in which they meet every Friday to offer up prayer. They have one Kadi, a priest and, for the most part, they belong to the set of schafie." Again, the same writer observes that the Zamorin, in sending an embassy to Sha Rokh, "charged the ambassador with a despatch in which he said; 'In this port, on every Friday and on every solemn feast day, the Kotabah is celebrated, according to the prescribed rule of Islamism. With your Majesty's permission, these prayers shall be adorned and honoured by the addition of your name and of your illustrious titles.' " The Mahomedan historian, Zien-ud-deen, assures us that the Mahomedans of Malabar "formerly lived in great comfort and tranquility in consequence of their abstaining from exercising any oppression towards the people of the country as well as from the consideration which they invariably evinced for the ancient usages of the population of Malabar and from the unrestricted intercourse of kindness which they preserved with them." They stood in such esteem with the Zamorin that, as Barbosa says, "the king gave each one (Moorish merchant) a Nāyar to guard and serve him, a Chetty scribe for his accountant and to take care of his property and a broker for his trade. To each of these three persons, a merchant would pay something for their maintenance, and all of them served very well."

5. **Ali Rajas of Cannanore.** In Malabar, the Mahomedans never attempted to acquire political independence save where such independence was essential to the conservation of their community. On the South Indian Coast, they found a settled polity

and they accepted it. They never did found a State on the Malabar Coast. The Māppiḷa chieftain known as the Āli Raja is the only Mahomedan chief on the Malabar Coast who had or has any semblance of ruling authority. As regards the origin of his family, there are various accounts extant. One of them is noticed by our author. It is said that one of the Kōlaṭṭiri princesses, having had a mis-alliance with a Mahomedan, the Kōlaṭṭiri Raja allotted the territory, now owned by the Āli Raja, as a provision for the issue of the princess. These, in memory of their origin, are said to conform to the Marumakkaṭṭāyam system of inheritance, in spite of their religion. One version of the Keralōṭpaṭṭi would have it that Chēramān Perumāl invited a Mahomedan and his wife from his native land of Aryapuram and installed them at Cannanore. This Mahomedan was called Āli Raja (Āli=deep), i. e., 'the lord of the deep' or the sea.[1] According to Mr. Logan, "tradition is tolerably unanimous that the first chieftain of the family was a Nāyar by name Āryankuḷangara Nāyar, one of the ministers of Kōlaṭṭiri, who is said to have lived about the end of the 11th or the beginning of the 12th century A. D., and who embraced Islam and adopted the name of Mahomed or Mammad Ali. Owing to his skill and ability, it is said, the Kōlaṭṭiri retained him as his minister after his conversion, and his successors were known as *Mammali Kitavus*, who were hereditary ministers of the Kōlaṭṭiris. Tradition says that Mahomed Ali and his successors were admitted to all the important counsels of the Kōlaṭṭiri, and that they used to stand on such occasions with the sword's point resting on a box, implying by that, whatever decision was come to, they would find the money to carry it out. Hamilton gives an interesting account of these chieftains after they had become independent of the Kōlaṭṭiris. He describes Cannanore as "a pretty large town built in

1. Logan's *Malabar*, p. 236.

the bottom of the bay," and independent of the Dutch stationed in Fort Angelo. It was under "Adda Raja, a Mahomedan Malabar prince, who upon occasion can bring near 20,000 men into the field." His Government is not absolute nor is it hereditary; and instead of giving him the trust of the treasury which comes by taxes and merchandise, they have chests made on purpose with holes made in their lids, and, their coin being all gold, whatever is received from the treasurer is put into these chests through these holes and each chest has four locks, and their keys are put in the hands of the Raja, the Commissioner of Trade, the Chief Judge, and the Treasurer, and, when there is occasion for money, none can be taken out without all these four being present or their deputies."[1] It is surprising that, Zien-ud-deen has very little to say about the only Mahomedan ruling chief in Malabar. It is probable that in his time, the family had not come into that prominence which it attained not long after. We have indications in his work of a powerful Mahomedan who is styled "that great warrior Alee Azraja the Chief of Cannanore" fighting the Portuguese in defence of the Mahomedans. Referring to a quarrel that took place between the Franks and the Mahomedans residing at Cannanore and Durmfatan in A. D. 1555, the Mahomedan historian says: "And during the warfare against the infidel Franks, Alee Azraja, a Mahomedan leader of great consideration (upon whom may God shower down his best blessings!) greatly distinguished himself having exerted himself with superior zeal and bravery and lavished his wealth without sparing the cause." 'The Islands of Malabar' (the Laccadives) are said to have belonged to him, and we may, therefore, conclude with some degree of confidence that the person referred to was the Āli Raja of Cannanore. In the name Alee Azraja, there is no difficulty in detecting

1. Logan's *Malabar*, pp. 360 1.

the designation Alee (Az) Raja by which term the Mahomedan Chiefs of Cannanore have always been known. For a long time, these chiefs were subordinate to, and dependent on, the Chiṙakkal or Kōlaṭṭiri Rajas. But, after the Portuguese reprisals on the Moorish commerce and the part that the Kōlaṭṭiris played in the wars consequent upon the conduct of the European nations that visited the Coast, the relations between the Āli Raja and the Kōlaṭṭiris had become strained. The Āli Rajas were more or less backed up by the Dutch, from whom they are said to have purchased the fort of Cannanore.[1]

Not long after our author wrote this letter, the Dutch had set up the Āli Raja to seize Coḍuliy, which had belonged to the Kōlaṭṭiri, with a view to gain for themselves the pepper of 'the Randattaṙa' country. This enabled them to thwart the English who seem to have exercised considerable influence in that quarter. The Tellichery factory diary records, on the 6th of June 1727, that Āli Raja "did last night treacherously seize the said hill and fort (namely Codalla), which the Prince Regent in Kōlaṭṭuṅāḍ had erected 'purely as a barrier to a large country which produce a great quantity of pepper.' "[2] A detachment sent to Agarr, in June 1727, to protect the English warehouse there, was stopped at Ḍharmapaṭṭaṇam Island by Āli Raja's people and turned back with insults. The Chief (English) appealed to the Prince Regent (of Kōlaṭṭiri) to "unite with those of the Royal line" and maintain peace. But the Prince quaintly replied that "as there are so many of the Royal line, 'tis extreme difficult to effect the necessary union." The Kōṭṭayam Raja, however, came to his assistance, and, between them, they, in February 1728, took one of Āli Raja's forts on Ḍharmapaṭṭaṇam Island. The Prince Regent soon joined the war and succeeded in destroying the Mahomedan settlement

1. Logan's *Malabar*, p. 361.

2. *Ibid*, p. 359.

at Vaḷaṙpaṭṭaṇam. The Prince, being in want of funds to carry on the war, applied to the English factors for money and supplies, but these were refused. He then negotiated with the Dutch, to hand over Ḍharmapaṭṭaṇam Island, the possession of which was essential to the English trade of Tellicherry. Thereupon, the factors resolved to advance funds, taking care, in the meanwhile, to exact from the prince the grant of a monopoly of trade in Iruvaḷināḍ, Ḍharmapaṭṭaṇam and Randattara with permission to hoist the English flag, if the French or the Dutch threatened to take possession of these places. The quarrel between the Prince and the Mahomedan chief was kept up for some time, till, on the 9th June 1713, peace was arranged through the mediation of the Kalliāḍ Nambiār, the Māppiḷas agreeing to pay an indemnity of 1,00,000 fanams at once and a similar sum in four months' time. Hearing this, the English Chief, Mr. Braddyl, promptly applied for repayment of the loans, forgetting for the moment that the loans were advanced mainly to enable the Raja to render the necessary assistance to the English factors themselves. The Prince replied: "The present treaty is only to give me a breathing for four months." Before the laspe of these four months, greater difficulties arose for the Prince on the Canarese side.

The Āli Raja made common cause with Hyder Ali on his invasion of Malabar, and was invested by the Nabob with extensive powers. But after Hyder's death, Tippu's excesses in Malabar exasperated even his co-religionists themselves so much so that even they fought against the Sultan. In 1785, a powerful Māppiḷa of Manchēry rose in rebellion against the Sultan's Government, and the Āli Raja himself, in 1789, sought refuge in the English fort of Tellicherry. Next year, however, they arranged matters, and the Āli Raja returned to Tippu. In the final settlement of Malabar, after the defeat of Tippu, the Āli Raja was left only with a mere semblance of authority.

At present, the Āli Rajas hold only a small portion of territory on the mainland, comprising 31 Ḍēśams (villages), about 2,364 acres in extent, in and about the town and cantonment of Cannanore in the Ṭālūk of Chīrakkal known as the *Kirar* (Karār—contract?) territory. They pay for their mainland territory a lump sum of Rs. 3,801 to the British Government.

The Laccadive Islands now subject to the family are:—

	Islands	Area	Population	Dependent Islands
1	Agatti	1⅜ miles	302	with four dependent Islets
2	Kavarathi	1¾ ,,	2,129	,, 2 ,, ,,
3	Andoroth	1 2/3 ,,	2,884	,, ,, ,, ,
4	Kalpeni	1 ,,	1,222	,, 3 ,, ,,
5	Mincoy(Menkajah)	1¾ ,,	3,191	,, 1 ,, ,,
	Total	7⅛ ,,	10,801	

The Islets are all uninhabited.

The Peishcush due by Sultan Āli Raja of Cannanore, according to the engagement, dated 28th October 1796, is Rs. 15,000 *per annum.* An abatement of 1,500 star pagodas, equivalent to 5,280 rupees, was allowed by the Court of Directors in 1822 as compensation for the loss of the Amin Ḍēvi Islands attached to the South Canara District.

The judicial administration of the *Kirar* territory is conducted by the British Government. The Raja is merely permitted to collect rents on the lands comprised within the *Kirar* limits, and has no power to interfere with the collection of special rates chargeable under Municipal or fiscal laws. Over the Islands, the Raja retains the right of exercising full authority. The patriarchal method of administration, originally constituted in these islands, seldom controlled by the Raja or his ministers, soon degenerated into a corrupt and effete engine of oppression, which goaded the islanders into open rebellion against and resistance to, the Cannanore authority. The Peishcush payable by the Raja fell into arrears, till at last, in 1877, the islands were placed under attachment for arrears of revenue, and the administration taken over by the British Government.

Mr. Logan has given the traditionary list of the Āli Rajas who have reigned since the foundation of the family in his *Manual of the Malabar District.* [1]

The Āli Raja lived at a house called the Arakkal in the town of Cannanore almost under the guns of the Dutch fort Angelo, which they had taken from the Portuguese. The Raja was completely under the Dutch influence, having already broken with his Suzerain, the Kōlaṭṭiri Raja, who was suspected to have a leaning towards the English. The town and bazaar, as Hamilton says, was built at "the bottom of the bay" and had considerable trading facilities. The Raja carried on a large maritime trade with the outside world and had formed an offensive and defensive alliance with the Dutch.

6. **Quarrels among the Coast Rajas.** This gives us an insight into the petty quarrels between the Coast Rajas which led to open warfare, fomented, more or less, by European nations who took advantage of such opportunities to better their own position by taking sides with the belligerents and finally wrecking both parties. Notwithstanding the assurance of our author, we may be pardoned for suspecting that the Āli Raja had the active support of the Dutch, to balance the weight of the other side, which had the support of the English. The incident referred to by our author finds no mention in Mr. Logan's *Manual.*

7. **Jealousy between the Mahomedans and the Portuguese.** Zien-ud-deen, after referring to the

1. P. 360

arrival of first and second Portuguese expeditions on the Malabar Coast, observes: "But no long time elapsed before they endeavoured to persuade the agents of the Zamorin to prohibit the Mahomedans from engaging in the trade of the country and from making voyages to the ports of Arabia, saying to them, 'the advantage that you will derive from a commercial intercourse with us will greatly exceed any that they can afford you.' In the same spirit, these Franks proceeded also to trespass on the property of the Mahomedans and to put down their commerce. Now, in consequence of this conduct on the part of the Franks, the Zamorin having resolved upon their destruction, he attacked them and put to death 50 or 70 of their party, the rest escaping to their vessels, from which they opened fire upon the people on the shore, who, in return, cannonaded them. Shortly after this event, they sailed into the harbour of Cochin, and imposing themselves upon its inhabitants as an inoffensive and honest race, they succeeded in building a mud fort at that place which was the first piece of fortification that was constructed by them in India and, after taking up their dwelling in this building, they proceeded to demolish the mosque which stood on the seashore at Cochin erecting in its place a Christian church, whilst they imposed the labour of building this edifice upon the inhabitants of Cochin." The good Sheik goes on in this strain. In his first chapter, he had already told us that "that friend of the Mahomedans,' the Zamorin," used to supply them with the sinews of war, and that warfare having been early commenced by the Mahomedans, they had kept on fighting until their own condition in Malabar had become greatly reduced, in consequence of the interruption to their trade, and the sacrifice of life and devastation of property, to which they had, in consequence of such course, subjected themselves. Indeed, by their resolute adherence to it, their necessities became every day more urgent; so that shortly they had arrived at the last stage of poverty and decay and wretchedness.[1] Let us leave the Sheik here and have a peep at the other side of the shield. The Portuguese accounts, of course, differ materially from that of the Mahomedan historian. After mentioning the hospitable reception of the Zamorin of Vasco da Gama and his companions, Maffeius says: "His rebuo, ut fit, extemplo vulgatis "cum caeteri "mercatores tum Saraceni praecipue atque Arabes "magnopere commoventur, ac praeter capitale in "Christianos "odium, rati etiam, quod res erat, quan- "tum ad Lusitanorum commercia accederet, tantum de "suis lucris imminui, et si praevalidus manceps in eam "negotiationem se interponeret, nihil sibi ad quaestum "et navigationem loci relictum iri; institutam et coa- "lescentem novam societatem omni conatu dirimere "instituunt."[2]

"Having these things, as it happens, got quickly divulged, the rest of the merchants as well as the Saracens, especially the Arabs, were exceedingly moved, and besides the deadly hatred against the Christians, deeming as a matter, of course, that by how much the commerce of the Portuguese increased by so much their profit would be diminished, and that, if a very powerful merchant would interfere with this commerce, no business and navigation of the place would be left to themselves, so they determined to destroy by every effort the newly established and growing Society."

The sudden attack of the Portuguese by the Zamorin mentioned by the Sheik is thus described by Maffeius:—"Neque ita multo post, assiduis Mahomet- "anorum stimulis, et Nairum aliquot ac principum "auctoritate compulsa; et quod caput est, praesentis "praedae illecta dulcedine, vel inscio, vel consentiente, "certe non prohibente Rege, subito arreptis armis, "Lusitanorum diversorium aggredittur; ibi ingenti

1. Pp. 22—
2. Lib., i. p. 8.

" clamore ac tumultu ex citato, claustra convellere,
" fores effringere, per vim conatur irrumpere. Nostri,
" quamquam improviso malo perterriti, e fenestris
" tamen tectisque fortiter primos barbarorum impetus
" repulere : sed perfosso demum, dirutoque pariete,
" vis ac numerus ultra sustineri non potuit, hos-
" tium ad quattuor millia telis ac sagittis instructa
" convenerant. Lusitani, septuaginta non amplius,
" in hospitio versabantur ; ex iis ad quinquaginta
" partim capti, partim interfecti, reliqui male multati,
" in iis, Henricus antistes cumsodalibus quattuor,
" multis acceptis vulneribus, ad classem vix evaseri."[1]

"Not long after, by the constant incitements of the Mahomedans and pushed forward by the authority of some Nairs and leading men, and, above all, enticed by the charm of the ready booty, the king, either not knowing or consenting, certainly not prohibiting, they all on a sudden seizing arms attacked the lodging of the Portuguese; having raised immense clamour and tumult, they began to destroy the locks, to break open the doors and tried to rush in by force. Our people, although terrified by the unexpected evil, yet began to repel bravely the first attacks of the barbarians from the windows and roofs; but at last the wall being dug and undermined, their force and numbers could no longer be sustained ; four thousand enemies furnished with spears and arrows had come. The Portuguese not more than seventy were lodging in a hotel, of whom some fifty were captured, some were killed and the rest were badly treated. Of these, the Bishop, Henry by name, with his four companions, severely wounded and with the greatest difficulty escaped to the fleet."

Again, of the reception of the Portuguese in Cochin, Maffeius observes that they were received by the Raja with much hospitality, he desiring to conciliate them as valuable allies against the Zamorin of whose power he was greatly jealous. Osorius mentions

1. Lib., ii, p. 35.

that a strong house in Cochin was alloted by the Raja as a factory for the Portuguese, and a treaty of commerce solemnly concluded.

As Lieut. Rowlandson observes: "That an early and mutual jealousy should have been entertained by the Mahomedans and Portuguese of one another was natural; for when was it ever known that one body of intruders could patiently endure the presence of another or consent to a division of those spoils, which they had before viewed as exclusively as their own? D'Sousa and Osorius also, like Maffeius, make the first aggression to have been on the part of the Mahomedans of Mecca, who, they say, not only did all in their power to depress the trade of the Portuguese, but, from the time of da Gama's arrival, held secret conferences resolving upon their destruction, it being their anxious desire that not one man might return, so that European nations, from their fate, might be deterred from any further attempts at an intercourse with India."[1]

8. **Islam in Malabar.** The following extract taken from Dr. Subrahmanya Ayyar's *Report on the Census of Travancore* (1901) gives us a succinct account of the introduction, rise and growth of Islam in Mababar.—

"When the religion of the Koran was first brought in from Arabia is an undecided question. That commercial relations laid the foundation for the spread of Islam may, however, be taken as established. The conquest by the Arabs of Egypt and Persia, two important trading centres of the old world, about A. D. 640, converted them from a fighting into a commercial nation. The sights that Alexandria could then show fired them with an ambition for commerce which is even now the sustaining feature of all Mussalman communities in the world. Friar Bartolomeo says that the first batch of Mussalmans came to Malabar during the reign of Caliph Valid in the 90th year of the Hegira[2]

1. Note, p. 80.
2. *Voyage to the East Indies*, p. 106.

(710 A. D.) which accords with the date given in the Mackenzi MSS.[1] If the story about the conversion of the last of the Perumāls be true, there is nothing hypothetical in supposing that Moslem tradesmen entered this coast as early as the eighth century after Christ.

" But individual followers of the Prophet had already settled themselvès in Malabar. A Mahomedan inscription at Panṭalāyani Kollam in North Malabar records the death of one Abbu Ibn Udthorman in Hegira 166.[2] Masudi of Bagdad (890—956 A. D.)[3] writes that, although the Arabs made no permanent settlement, there were, in the seventh and eighth centuries, Arab merchants in Malabar and that the Arab name was held in high respect. Arabian travellers, such as Ibn Kurdad Bah (869—885 A. D.)[4] and Abu Zaid of Ziraf (916 A. D.)[5] refer in flattering terms to the nature of the commercial dealings between Arabia and Malabar. Ibn Hankal, writing sometime after Masudi, agrees with him in saying that the Mussalmans had publicly celebrated the five prayers and built mosques. In the twelveth century, the inviting ports of Malabar seem to have received high praise from Al Idrisi, the Mahomedan geographer at the court of Sicily and one of the recognised authorities in matters of history relating to that period. In the famous voyages of *Sindbad the Sailor*, there are numerous allusions to the country of Kērala. His fourth voyage must have been to Malabar where he "found men carrying pepper." In his fifth voyage again, he crosses the Maladives and then returns to the pepper country. Passing on to the Peninsula of Comorin, he found the aloes-wood called *Santy* (Sandal-wood). In his sixth voyage, he visited the country where grew purple aloes of the kinds, *Santy*

1. *Madras Journal of Literature and Science*, Vol. VII, p. 339.
2. *Malabar*, Vol. I, p. 195.
3. *India in the Fifteenth Century*, Intro., p. XIV.
4. *Old Records of the India Office*, p. 109.
5. Kerr's *Collection of Voyages and Travels*, Vol. I, p. 79.

and *Comari*. The Arab merchants, to adopt the words of Jonathan Duncan, "bringing annually sums of money to the Malabar Coast for pepper and other spices that they carried from it for the supply of all the rest of the world, received every encouragement and the fullest protection for their property and religion from the successive Samoories or Zamorins."[1]

The spicy shore of "Araby the blest" to which the author of *The Paradise Lost* refers with such characteristic effect evidently owes its "Sabean odours" to the fair land of the Perumāls. Ibn Batuta, writing in the early years of the fourteenth century, notes the rich Mussalman merchants by whom every town of Malabar was crowded, the respect and affection in which they were held by the reigning sovereigns and the public, and the wayside pandals all over the country of Malabar started for passers-by to quench their thirst, pouring water in these places into the hands of the followers of Islam. He also refers to the five mosques which stood as an ornament to the noble emporium of Quilon, and bestows high praise on the generosity and power of its Hindu Sovereigns. Abdur-Razak, writing in 1442 A. D., informs us that, on every Friday and on every solemn feast day, the Khotba was celebrated according to the prescribed rules of Islam. Historians and travellers of the 16th century refer in high terms to the commercial prosperity of the Mahomedans in Malabar. Barbosa notices the Māppilas of Calicut, who wore a small round cap on their head, and Ludovico Varthema writes:—"It must be known that the Pagans do not navigate much, but it is the Moors who carry the merchandise, for in Calicut there are at least 15,000 Moors, who are for the most part natives of the country. The time of their navigation is this. From Persia to the Cape Comorin, which is distant from Calicut by eight days' journey by sea towards the south; you can navigate

1. Part I, pp. 104—5.

through six months in the year, that is to say September to all April; then from the middle of May to the middle of August, it is necessary to avoid this coast, because the sea is very stormy and tempestuous. At the end of April, they depart from the coast of Calicut and pass the Cape Comorin and enter into another course of navigation, which is safe for these four months and go for small spices." The Mussalmans monopolised the trade of Malabar then. They occupied every habitable sea-port, and were, in fact, the constructors of the towns on the Malabar coast. In the many wars that ensued between the Zamorin and the Portuguese, the Mussalmans assisted their Hindu sovereign against the foreigner. The Jew's Town at Cochin was burnt by the Moors; but the Portuguese, increasing in power and prosperity, resolved to wreak their vengeance. Zien-ud-deen gives an unsavoury description of the persecutions and cruelties committed by the Portuguese. To whatever credence this account may be entitled, it is evident that they dispersed the flourishing Mahomedans of the Malabar Coast to the nooks and corners of the country.

"After a comparatively uneventful period of two centuries, Hyder Ali and Tippu Sultan appeared on the scene, carrying fire and sword into the peaceful dominions of the Malabar kings. The former never reached Travancore, but Tippu entered the country by the north, and formed settlements at convenient centres. In connection with the opening of the sea-port of Alleppey by Maha Raja Rāma Varma with a view to destroy the commercial monopoly of the Dutch at Purakad, 12 miles to the south, a number of Mussalmans from Sindh, Kutch and Gujarat were invited to settle and carry on commerce in Travancore. Successive immigrations have followed and have resulted in the conversion of this port into the largest Mahomedan centre in the State. The share of proselytism has also to be remembered in connection with the present strength of the Mussalman population. The followers of Mahomedanism form 6·5 per cent of the total population."

In Cochin, the percentage is almost the same. Not so however in Malabar, where it is very high, numbering almost 30 per cent of the whole population. In every 10,000 of population, Travancore contains 645·5, Cochin, 671·06 and Malabar, 2,985·25 Mahomedans.

Of the Mussalmans of Cochin, the Census Reporter observes: " Though among the followers of Islam in Cochin are found persons of high character and social position, enjoying important privileges granted by the native rulers, they consist mainly of converts from the lower orders of the Hindu community, mostly Dravidians in race, who eagerly took advantage of the opportunity to shake off the humiliating disabilities they groaned under, and tried by one bound to raise themselves considerably in the social scale. The proselytes still point back to their origin by retaining some of their original customs, such as the bridegroom tying a Ṭāli (a thin plate of gold shaped like the leaf of the pipal) round the neck of the bride at the wedding, the distribution of *pan supari*, *Kurava* (joyful shouts of women), muisc and tom-tom on the occasion and the observance of caste distinctions in the matter of marriage. Once in a way, an itinerant preacher crosses the Ghats to preach to the local followers of the prophet the adoption of the principles of their faith in their entirety, but such occasional attempts at reform produce very little effect upon deep-rooted customs and long-standing usages.

" The Mussalman section of the population of the State numbering 54,492, consists chiefly of Jōnaka Māppilas, Rāvuṭṭans or Lubbays and Pathans with a slight sprinkling of Sheiks, Sayyids, Moghuls, Kactchhi Memons, Hussains and Boras. Divided according to sect, all the Moslems in the State, except the Boras and Sunnis, or those who

To face page 552)

A MUSLIM HOSTEL DAY GATHERING.

acknowledge the first four Caliphs as the lawful successors of Mahomed, accept the *sunnets* or traditions as of equal authority with the Koran. The Boras, numbering but 7, are Shiahs, who regard Ali, the nephew and son-in-law of Mahomed, as the rightful successor of the prophet. While they reject the *sunnets* as of no authority whatever, they have for themselves a separate set of traditions. Regarded again as the followers of the founders of the four schools of Moslem jurisprudence, Malik, Hanifa, Shafii and Hanbal, who divide among them the whole orthodox Moslem world, the Jōnaka Māppiḷas, who form 80 per cent of the Mahomedans in the State, are Shafiites, while the rest of the Sunni sect are Hanfiites. Malik and Hanbal have no followers in Cochin."

9. **The Mappillas. Their Appearance, Dress, Ornaments, etc.** We have the following description of the Māppiḷas by Burton: "They are a light-coloured and good-looking race (this description applies only to the higher orders; the labouring classes are dark and ill-favoured), of men with high features, the proud expression and the wiry forms of the descendants of Ishmael; their delicate hands and feet, and their long and bushy beards show that a little Hindu blood flows in their veins. They shave the hair and trim the moustaches according to the *sunnet* and, instead of a turban, wear a small silk or cloth cap of peculiar shape upon their heads. The chest and shoulders are left exposed, and a white or dyed piece of linen, resembling in cut and colour the "lung" or bathing cloth of Central Asia, is tied round the loins. The garment, if we may so call it, worn by the males does not reach below the calves of the legs, whereas the fair sex prolong it to the ankles. The upper portion of the female figure is modestly concealed by a shirt round the neck with large sleeves, and the opening in the front. According to the custom of the faithful, a veil is always thrown over the head."

The ordinary dress of the men is a *mundu* or cloth, generally white with a purple border, but sometimes orange or green or plain white. It is tied on the left (Hindus tie them on the right) and kept in position by a *nul* or waist string, to which are attached one or more *elassus* (small cylinders) of gold or silver or baser metal, containing texts from the Koran or magic *yantrams*. A small knife is usally worn in the waist. Persons of importance wear, in addition, a long flowing white garment of fine cotton; and over this again may be worn a short waist-coat-like jacket.[1] Day says that girls have holes bored in their ears, as a mark of affection; consequently, the more they are bored, the greater their parent's love for them. At an early age, the lobe of the ear is pierced and a bit of lead inserted, and the flap distended. But this is common with women of other castes also in Malabar. Adult women among Māppilas indulge in gold and silver ornaments like their sisters among other classes, gold chains, necklaces, bracelets, etc. adorn their person; but they are seldom partial to ornaments set with precious stones or gems. Among the generality, the necks are often covered with strings of beads, their arms with bangles as are also their ankles, while their ears are weighed down with ornaments. The countenance of the Māppila, especially when it assumes the expression with which he usually regards infidels and heretics, is strongly indicative of his ferocious and fanatic disposition. They used to arm themselves from an early age with a long knife that usually hangs from the waist; when entering battle, they generally carried two, one in the hand and the other between the teeth and these did great havoc. Their knives have however been now interdicted by Government. As a class, they have steadily begun to engage themselves in the more peaceful walks of life, such as agriculture and commerce. Educational facilities are also afforded them, of which the community has begun to take advantage, and capable members of the class have also been

1. *Malabar Gazetteer*, p. 192.

entertained in the public service on terms more favourable than those allowed to other classes. As a rule, they are frugal, industrious and enterprising. They are traders to a large extent and have amassed considerable wealth which they have invested on land. They engaged themselves in clearing and planting waste-land on the margin of the jungle. The lower classes are fishermen, labourers and petty cultivators.

Their fanaticism—The Māppilas of British Malabar have always been a troublesome class requiring the special attention of the authorities. Even Tippu Sultan, their co-religionist, failed in 1774 to quell a rising, his troops, a thousand in number, being defeated, and the Hindu temple at Manjēri burnt down. Their fanatic acts seem to be always directed against this shrine. In August 1849, after desecrating the rebuilt temple, thirty of them repulsed two Companies of sepoys, and, being joined by others, pursued their career of violence, until they were destroyed by a detachment of H. M's 94th Regiment. Further raids followed, costing many lives, in 1851 and 1852. Mr. Conolly, Collector of Malabar, who had reported on the recent disturbances, expressed his feeling of despair and inability to devise any method of preventing a recurrence of such scenes or of capturing any of those who had taken part in them. "The Moplah," he wrote, "is a fanatic madman, whose sole object is to throw away his life after doing all the damage possible to his adversary. They will receive no quarter; they fight like madmen." A high priest, whom the Collector suspected of inciting them, was banished from the country in 1853. In October 1854, Act XXIII of 1854, known as the 'Mopla Act' was passed for the suppression of Māppila outrages, under which forfeiture of property, confinement of persons suspected of an intention to commit such offences, and the cremation of bodies of those killed in attacks or sentenced to suffer capital punishment, might be inflicted. The result was that, before one year was out after the passing of the Māppila Act, in September 1855, Mr. Conolly was murdered by a party of Māppilas who had escaped from the Calicut Jail. Notwithstanding the severe measures adopted by successive Governments, the fanatical savagery of the Māppilas has not abated. In March 1896, a rising took place, in this instance also, at Manjēri, when twenty men of H. M.'s South Stafford Regiment were attacked by nearly a hundred Māppilas, of whom eighty-four were killed or wounded. Several of them were mere youths under fifteen years of age.[1]

It has been suspected by some that the causes that contribute towards these outbreaks lie deeper than mere religious fanaticism, that the disturbances are more agrarian than religious, and that the spread of education and a better treatment of them by the higher classes would tend to bring about favourable results. The experiment is being made, and let us hope that the desired for-result will follow.

The Māppilas of the Cochin State form a peaceful community and have never been troublesome like their brethren of Malabar. Not so those of Travancore. Forbes tells us that "the Moplas of Travancore were constantly at variance with the Nāyars, and that the king of Travancore, jealous of their ambitious and revengeful temper, keeps them in great subjection, and levies frequent contributions on their property to which they reluctantly submit from knowing that they would experience the same treatment from other Governments. At one period, the Māppilas created a great commotion in Travancore and, towards the end of the 17th century, massacrred the chief of Anjengo and all the English gentlemen belonging to the settlement when on a public visit to

1. The recent out-break covered a wider area and asssumed very serious proportions. It took some time to quell it, and it was put down only after the loss of several lives, and a good deal of damage was done to property, private and public.—Ed.

To face page 557] A MUSLIM LANDLORD—HAJIAR

the Queen of Attinga."[1]

The Māppilas are Sunnees and Hanafites and are strict followers of the Koran. Their chief priest, whose office is hereditary, is called a *Tangal* who usually resides at Ponnāni. They acknowledge the spiritual supremacy of the Sultan of Constantinople. The principal authority on religious subjects is the Makhdum Tangal of Ponnāni. The chief priest of a mosque is also called a Tangal. Their prayers are repeated five times daily, and on Friday this is done at the Musjid. They strictly observe the five essentials of the Mahomedan religion, viz., the recital of the *kalinia* or creed, the five daily prayers (*niskaram*), the Ramzan fast, the duty of alms (*Zakkath*, *tithe*), and the Haj pilgrimage to Mecca. Their mosques (*palli*) are rectangular buildings with sloping roofs, tiled or thatched, and ornamental gables in front like those of the Hindu temples; some of them have gate-houses. They are built with the main entrance to the west so that the congregation faces east towards Mecca. There is often a tank close by. A mulla versed in Arabic is attached to every mosque to lead the services. He is appointed by the congregation, though the *Kazi*, as a rule, nominates him. The *Kazi* is the head of the *Jamat* (lit. assembly) or Friday mosque. His functions include the reading of the Friday sermon (*Kutba*), the registration of marriages and general arbitration in civil and religious matters.

They observe the Ramzan or thirty days fast which begins as soon as the Ramzan new moon is seen and ends with the appearance of the next new moon. The fast is strictly observed, a good Māppila refraining even from swallowing his spittle from sunrise till sunset; after which he may take food.

1. The Cochinite Mussalmans have as a rule been always loyal and law-abilding. Some of them belong to ancient and respectable families. Among them, there is a healthy activity to improve the social, literary and economic conditions of their community.—Ed.

All those who can afford it performs the Haj or pilgrimage to Mecca. It may be done even by proxy after a man's death.

Of festivals, the Māppilas celebrate the Bakrid, or *Valiya perunnal* in the third month after the Ramzan. They only observe the ninth and tenth days of Muharam; they do not make *taboots*.

Birth and ceremonies after.—As soon as a child is born, it is bathed in cold water. The Mulla or priest then takes it in hand and, raising it up to the breast, recites in the child's ears the two formulæ of prayer-call which are repeated five times daily. The mother undergoes the "15th day's bath," "28th day's bath" and "40th day's bath." The last day's ceremony is performed with much pomp and circumstance, and much money is squandered on it.

The sventh day after birth is the prescribed day for naming the child, but the time varies in different places and extends up to six months. When the child receives its name, its head also ought to be shaved. Male children may be circumcised at any age, but generally are before ten. This rite is performed with great ceremony and is called Mārga Kalyāṇam to which invitations are sent out all round. Those who can afford it spend large sums on these occasions. The ceremony corresponding to this for females, celebrated with great *eclat*, is the *ear-boring*.

Marriage.—It is essential for Māppilas to marry. The marriage rite is considered as a species of foretaste of their paradise. Consequently, they are particular about the feasts and ceremonies connected with it. Mahomed advised those of his followers, who were too poor to marry, to retire from the world and pass their days in devotion. The bride's family people seek a husband for her; thus a father sends some persons to the friends of a youth whom he considers suitable, and the bride-groom requires a present, in return for marrying the daughter, as well as her dowry. Early marriage is never the rule; but, of course, there are exceptions. Hanafites sometimes espouse brides under ten years of age, but the Shafiis do this more rarely. All preliminaries being settled and a day for celebration of the betrothal fixed, the bridegroom, attended by his friends, proceeds to the bride's house, where her father meets him and sprinkles him with rose-water, while some matrons, anoxious to avert the evil eye, advance with a basin containing water, turmeric and *Kusa* grass. The party then proceeds to a pandal, under which they sit on carpets or mats spread on the ground. Here they amuse themselves by chewing betel, and some elder introduces the subject. Numerous questions are asked by both sides, at the termination of which betrothal takes place in the form of a contract in which the amount to be paid is stipulated. Trays containing part of the money, are then brought in, together with some presents and a gold ring, which is touched successively by each person present. The priest then places the ring on the bride-groom's finger, and the bride's father gives the contract to the kazi, to file amongst the records of the mosque. Betel is then distributed, and, after the bride's father has rubbed sandal-wood paste on the breasts of his guests, they withdraw.

It is needless to give details of the whole ceremony, the most important and concluding part of which is, when the Tangal goes into the inner room with the bridegroom and unites his little finger to that of the bride and pronounces the benediction. A gold chain or a string, sometimes of beads, in the form of a *tali* is usually hung around the bride's neck at some convenient time, subsequent to the ceremony. The chief religious ceremony in marriage is called *Nikkale*. The Kazi makes the two repeat the necessary formulæ in the presence of two competent witnesses. The Mahomedan law and religion allows polygamy and the full complement of wives permitted is four. Mr. Kunjayan, from personal knowledge of the Ernād and Walluvanād Ṭālūks of south Malabar, says that "it can be stated without fear of contradiction that more than 80 per cent are polygamists of whom not less than 20 have more than two." He also says that the practice of marrying a deceased brother's wife is very common among the Māppilas of South Malabar, but rarely among those of North Malabar.

Divorce.—Under the Mahomedan law, divorce is an easy matter for the husband. He need assign no reason whatever. Not so in the case of a wife wishing to have a divorce from her husband. She can have it only on specified grounds such as the following.—(1) inability of the husband to maintain the wife with the least amount of comfort she can put up with. This includes the provision of a house, the payment of of the *Mahur* (dower), if demanded, before intercourse etc; (2) incurable and loathsome diseases of the husband, such as leprosy, insanity, etc. ; (3) permanent impairment of powers. Practically, instances of divorce by a wife are so rare that they can be counted on one's fingers. In North Malabar, divorce by the husband is, says Mr. Kunjayan in the *Malabar Quartely Review*, "is the exception, and is looked upon with much concern, and society does not view the man with particular favour, but in South Malabar, divorce is almost the rule. Divorce, even on the very next day after marriage, is not of unfrequent occurrence."[1] Generally, the husband recites the formula of divorce in the presence of the near relations of the wife, or, in their absence, he intimates to the Kazi, having jurisdiction over the woman, the fact of his having divorced her. Utterance of the formula is, however, indispensable. In the Cochin State, the Kazi receives his appointment from the Raja.

1. Vol. II, p. 91.

Here is a specimen of the deed of appointment: "Be it known to our Abdur Rahiman, son of Moosa Kutty Kadiar, residing at Kurinchira in Ṭaṭṭamangalam. As we have appointed you Kadiar of the followers of Islam living in the four villages of Chittūr, Ṭaṭṭamangalam, Nallēppilly and Paṭṭanchēri, you are to perform for them the ceremonies of Kaveneluṭṭu, Moulōṭṭu and such other ceremonies as have to be performed in the mosque, and receive emoluments due for the same. You are to govern them in their religious matters according to old custom. To this effect we have given you this Royal writing in the month of Ḍhanu (January) 1061 M. E. (1886 A. D.). Issued from our palace at Kaṇayannūr in the handwriting of Pavvaṭṭil Ammuṇṇy."

Māppila woman do not generally seclude themselves and are not held to be *ghosha* like other Mahomedan women. They walk about and do their work like their Hindu sisters. However, women of the higher classes are kept secluded, and hide their faces when they go abroad holding an umbrella so low as to hide their faces from the vulgar eye.

Death and ceremonies after.—As soon as life is ascertained to be extinct, the pillow on which the head rested is removed and the clothes worn at death are removed, and replaced, and the body is shifted so as to bring the face towards the *Kebla* (Mecca). The big toes are tied together with a piece of cloth, and the hands are crossed on the chest, the right over the left and the jaws are also secured with a piece of cloth. Before the body is taken for burial, it is bathed in hot water, after which it is placed on a mat over which a clean cloth on which rose-water is sprinkled and grains of camphor strewn, is spread. The ears, nostrils, the space between the lips, the fingers and toes are stuffed and covered with cotton. Three pieces, in the case of males and five pieces, in the case of females, of white cloth of the length of the body are tightly wrapped round the corpse, and the ends of the cloth are tied with two narrow strips of cloth, and one narrow strip is tied about the middle of the body about the abdomen. From the moment of death till the body is taken for burial, Mullas are employed to read the Koran by the side of the corpse. The body is carried to the mosque on a bier which is placed near the western wall of the outer room and the assembled people pray over it. It is then removed to the grave and lowered into the inner pit. The three knots are untied, and the body is so turned as to make it lie on the right side facing towards the *Kebla*, the position of the grave being from north to south. A handful of earth is placed below the right cheek as an emblem of humility. The grave is covered with cut laterite stones, and each of the assembled throws a handful of earth all reciting prayers. Prayers are continuously repeated over the grave by priests according as the family of the deceased can afford to have it kept up, for three days, a week and 40 days. Mullas read the Koran in the house of the deceased also continuously for three days. On the third day, a grand and costly ceremony takes place, when a *Maulud* (history of the birth &c. of the Prophet) is read. Alms are given away, and the Mullas recompensed for their services. This is repeated on the 15th and 40th days after death when large numbers are fed. Those who can afford it observe in a similar manner the anniversary of the death of a relative.

Law of inheritance.—As regards their law of inheritance and testamentary powers, they follow the precepts of the Koran, though there are Mahomedan Māppilas in North Malabar and in Travancore who have retained the Nāyar system of succession by nephews.

Food and drink.—Their food is principally rice, fish and meat. The animals have to be properly killed (*hal'al*) by having its throat cut. Pork is strictly prohibited by their religion; so also are intoxicating liquors in which very few indulge.

Education.—Their general education is very meagre. Boys are sent to *payal* schools, where they are taught to repeat the letters of the Arabic language from small planks on which the characters are traced. It is seldom that boys go beyond this. Burton, however, observes: "They carefully cultivate the classical and religious branch of study, such as *Sarf* or native grammar and syntax, *Mantek* or logic, *Hadis* or traditions of the Prophet, and *Karat* or the chanting of the Koran. They seldom know Persian: but as they begin the Arabic language almost as soon as they can speak, and often enjoy the advantage of instructors, their critical knowledge of it is extensive and their pronunciation good." This was perhaps a correct picture of the high class Māppiḷas when Burton wrote. But it is very doubtful if the studies described above are kept up by even the high class Māppiḷas of the present day. Burton goes on to observe that "the vernacular dialect of the Māppiḷas is the Malayāḷam, into which, for the benefit of the unlearned, many sacred books have been translated. The higher classes are instructed by private tutors and appear to be usually well-educated. The priest has charge of the lower orders, and little can be said in praise of the schoolmaster or the scholar. The mother-tongue of the Māppiḷa is, and has always been, Malayāḷam, and the infinitesimal few who acquire any sort of proficiency in Arabic regard it as the laboured acquisition of a foreign language." If Burton's description is the rule among Māppiḷas of Malabar, then, those of Cochin and Travancore are surely exceptions to that rule. Of late, schools have been started in Malabar for Māppiḷas, and they are being slowly weaned from their fanatic habits into more favourable paths of life by means of a system of almost eleemosynary education.

BIBLIOGRAPHY.

These books are in addition to those already listed in the first volume.

A.

A short outline of the Apostolic Seminary of Puttenpalli.

Almanacs issued by the Travancore Government.

B.

Begbie—Life of General Booth.

C.

Catholic Directory, 1925.

Cave—Historic Literaria.

Cochin Law Reports.

Cochin Sirkar Grandhavari.

Cunningham, General—Coins of India.

Do Sir Arthur—Coins of Ancient India from the earliest times to the 7th century A. D.

D.

Dissert—De Syris Nestorianis.

Dyer—Mordern Europe.

G.

Government Epigraphists' Collection, Madras.

Jewish Chronicle.

L.

Letter Edificantes.

M.

Malabar Joint Commissioner's Report.

Malabar Law Reports.

Mateer, Rev. S.—The Land of Charity.

Modern Review, of Calcutta.

Munro, Sir Thomas—Report on Malabar.

Murdoch, Rev. J—Caste.

N.

Neander—Church History.

Nelson—Manual of the Madura District.

Nikephoros, Lib. II His.

P.

Philips, W. R.—The Indian Anti.
Phillimore, Sir Robert—Ecclesiastical.
Primitive Folk, Contemporary Science Series.

R.

Report of the Archaeological Department, Madras.
Do on Epigraphy, Madras.
Do of the Jenmi Kudiyan Commission, Travancore.

S.

Selections from the Asiatic Journal.
Smith—Elements.
Do Dr. George—The Conversion of India.

T.

Travancore Archaeological Series.
Do Law Reports.
Thornton—Life and Sport in Southern India.
Turner, Sir Charles—Minute on the Land Bill, Madras.
Do Do Minute on the Land Tenures of Malabar.

The Transliteration Table followed in the printing of this work.

The Press has accented letters only for 12 point capitals and lower case letters ; and, even among these, the sets are not complete.

In spite of great care, a few mistakes have crept in to mar the uniformity attempted to be maintained in spelling the names of places and of persons. For this, the Editor craves the pardon of the reader.

This Press owns no letters of the Nagara alphabet, and so Malayalam characters have to be used.

അ	a	ഖ	kha	പ	pa
ആ	ā	ഗ	ga	ഫ	pha
ഇ	i	ഘ	gha	ബ	ba
ഈ	ī	ങ	nga	ഭ	bha
ഉ	u	ച	cha	മ	ma
ഊ	ū	ഛ	chha	യ	ya
ഋ	ṛ	ജ	ja	ര	ra
ൠ	ṝ	ഝ	jha	ല	la
ഌ	ḷ	ഞ	ña	വ	va
ൡ	ḹ	ട	ṭa	ശ	śa
എ	e	ഠ	ṭha	ഷ	ṣha
ഏ	ē	ഡ	ḍa	സ	sa
ഐ	ai	ഢ	ḍha	ഹ	ha
ഒ	o	ണ	ṇa	ള	ḷa
ഓ	ō	ത	ṭa	ക്ഷ	kṣha
ഔ	au	ഥ	ṭha	റ	ṙa
അം	aṃ	ദ	ḍa	ഴ	l̄a
അഃ	aḥ	ധ	ḍha	റ്റ	ṙṙạ
ക	ka	ന	ṅa	ന്റ	ṅṙa

INDEX TO THE NOTES.

A

B

B: *cont.*

C

C.—*cont.*

C—*cont.*

D

E

E—*cont.*

F

G

H

I

J

K

K—*cont.*

K.—*cont.*

L

M

M—*cont*.

N

N —*cont.*

O

P

P—*cont.*

P—*cont.*

Q

R

S

T

T—*cont.*

U

V

V—*cont.*

W

X

Y

Z